# ANNUAL REVIEW OF MICROBIOLOGY

# ANNUAL REVIEW OF MICROBIOLOGY

MORTIMER P. STARR, *Editor*
University of California

JOHN L. INGRAHAM, *Associate Editor*
University of California

SIDNEY RAFFEL, *Associate Editor*
Stanford University

*VOLUME 28*

*1974*

ANNUAL REVIEWS INC. 4139 EL CAMINO WAY PALO ALTO, CALIFORNIA 94306

ANNUAL REVIEWS INC.
Palo Alto, California, USA



*International Standard Book Number: 0-8243-1128-0*
*Library of Congress Catalog Card Number: 49-432*



## REPRINTS

The conspicuous number aligned in the margin with the title of each article in this volume is a key for use in ordering reprints. Available reprints are priced at the uniform rate of $1 each postpaid. Effective January 1, 1975 the minimum acceptable reprint order is 10 reprints and/or $10.00, prepaid. A quantity discount is available.

PRINTED AND BOUND IN THE UNITED STATES OF AMERICA

# PREFACE

About the time that the page proofs of Annual Review of Microbiology come from the compositor, the Assistant Editor gives the Editor a gentle reminder to the effect that copy for the Preface is awaited. Now that we have reached this penultimate stage in the making of Volume 28, it might be good to pause and report to our constituency on the subject of how we've been doing that which we do.

This volume was conceived by the 1972 Editorial Committee when it met about two years ago. At the Committee's meeting, the state-of-the-art in the vast domain of microbiology was scrutinized by an assemblage of knowledgeable and seemingly prescient microbiologists, our past product was reviewed, a list of "working titles" for the topics considered suitable for the future volume was compiled, and possible authors were nominated for each topic. Then came months of correspondence and telephone calls during which "possible authors" became "accepting invitees," outlines of chapters arrived, and assorted problems were ironed out. Somewhere after the first year of gestation ended, the typescripts appeared—usually peaceably, but sometimes with a bit of wrenching. Converting the typescripts into a book occupied the next seven or eight months, and was a joint enterprise of the authors, the several editors, the compositor and printer, and the staff of Annual Reviews Inc. Somewhere in the middle of this two-year period, another volume was breathed into life by a similar procedure and, as I write this note, we're getting ready for a meeting of the 1974 Editorial Committee which will plan the 1976 volume. This elaborate system is very much like an Elizabethan round or a tri-level carrousel!

To all those individuals and institutions who have contributed to this enterprise go my heart-felt thanks: to the authors and their home institutions, to the members of the Editorial Committee individually and collectively, to the Associate Editors (Sidney Raffel and John Ingraham), to the indexers, to the staff of Annual Reviews Inc., to the compositor and printer. Purposely saved for prominence of my last-but-by-no-means-least thanks is Jean McComish, our Assistant Editor. Assistant Editors, in general, are the key links in this entire operation; the quantity and quality of tender loving care dispensed on Annual Review of Microbiology by our Jean deserve a special "Well Done!". And, regrettably, also a final cheer, because this talented young person will soon be leaving us for a somewhat more spiritual enterprise. Fare well, Jean—and Peace!

MORTIMER P. STARR

ANNUAL REVIEWS INC. is a nonprofit corporation established to promote the advancement of the sciences. Beginning in 1932 with the *Annual Review of Biochemistry,* the Company has pursued as its principal function the publication of high quality, reasonably priced Annual Review volumes. The volumes are organized by Editors and Editorial Committees who invite qualified authors to contribute critical articles reviewing significant developments within each major discipline.

Annual Reviews Inc. is administered by a Board of Directors whose members serve without compensation.



Annual Reviews are published in the following sciences: Anthropology, Astronomy and Astrophysics, Biochemistry, Biophysics and Bioengineering, Earth and Planetary Sciences, Ecology and Systematics, Entomology, Fluid Mechanics, Genetics, Materials Science, Medicine, Microbiology, Nuclear Science, Pharmacology, Physical Chemistry, Physiology, Phytopathology, Plant Physiology, Psychology, and Sociology (to begin publication in 1975). In addition, two special volumes have been published by Annual Reviews Inc.: *History of Entomology* (1973) and *The Excitement and Fascination of Science* (1965).

# CONTENTS


A Microbiologist Turned Administrator—How It Happened, *Emil M. Mrak* 1
Viroids: The Smallest Known Agents of Infectious Disease, *T. O. Diener* 23
Bacterial Photosynthesis, *William W. Parson* 41
Metabolic Compartmentation: Symbiotic, Organellar, Multienzymic, and Microenvironmental, *Paul A. Srere and Klaus Mosbach* 61
Mechanisms of Inorganic Oxidation and Energy Coupling, *Isamu Suzuki* 85
Fungal Cell Wall Glycoproteins and Peptido-Polysaccharides, *J. E. Gander* 103
Space Microbiology, *Gerald R. Taylor* 121
Regulation of Enzyme Activity During Differentiation in *Dictyostelium discoideum*, *Kathleen A. Killick and Barbara E. Wright* 139
Inclusion Bodies of Prokaryotes, *J. M. Shively* 167
*Leishmania*, *R. S. Bray* 189
Bacterial Genetics Excluding *E. coli*, *Mark Levinthal* 219
Slow Virus Diseases, *David A. Fuccillo, Jerome E. Kurent, and John L. Sever* 231
Persisting Bacteriophage Infections, Lysogeny, and Phage Conversions, *Lane Barksdale and Sheldon B. Arden* 265
Mycoplasmas and Rickettsiae in Relation to Plant Diseases, *K. Maramorosch* 301
Virus-Induced Modification of Cellular Membranes Related to Viral Structure, *Daniel B. Rifkin and James P. Quigley* 325
Cyclic AMP in Prokaryotes, *H. V. Rickenberg* 353
Microscopes, Microscopy, and Microbiology, *Robert Barer* 371
Budding Bacteria, *Peter Hirsch* 391
Models of Genetic Recombination, *Rollin D. Hotchkiss* 445
Other Reviews of Microbiological Interest 469
Author Index 471
Subject Index 491
Cumulative Index of Contributing Authors, Volumes 23 to 28 507
Cumulative Index of Chapter Titles, Volumes 23 to 28 508

# ERRATUM

Volume 27 (1973): *The Role of the Host Cell Membrane in the Replication and Morphogenesis of Bacteriophages,* by Pamela J. Siegel and Moselio Schaechter. Page 272, line 11, for "RNA" read "DNA"; line 12, for "DNA polymerase" read "RNA polymerase."

Emil M. Mrak

# A MICROBIOLOGIST TURNED ADMINISTRATOR—HOW IT HAPPENED

❖1627

*Emil M. Mrak*
Chancellor Emeritus, University of California, Davis, California 95616

CONTENTS

MY EARLY YEARS ..... 1
COLLEGE—THE FIRST GREAT CHANGE IN ENVIRONMENT ..... 2
*Back in the Fall* ..... 2
*A Major—What Should it Be?* ..... 2
GRADUATION AND THEN WHAT ..... 4
*A Permanent Position* ..... 7
THE CLOUDS OF WAR ..... 8
THE END OF THE WAR ..... 9
A VISIT FROM PRESIDENT CLARK KERR ..... 11
A CALL FROM GOVERNOR NELSON ROCKEFELLER ..... 16
HEW AND PESTICIDES ..... 17
THE ENVIRONMENTAL PROTECTION AGENCY ..... 19
CONCLUSION ..... 21

## MY EARLY YEARS

My parents were both immigrants to the United States and neither of them had any formal education. This background had a great effect on their thinking and subsequently affected my motivation and desire for an education. To them, an education was godly and meant more than anything else in the world. No matter what, I had to obtain an education and continue as long as possible in an institution of higher learning. To them, education meant more than money and the material things of life; it was the source of understanding, creativeness, and a life of satisfaction. This was impressed on me over and over, and I know now that they were certainly right.

I grew up on a farm in the Santa Clara Valley of California—an environment that encouraged an interest in many sciences, particularly botany. Clarabell Boesch, my high school botany teacher, was an inspirational person and one of the best teachers I have ever had. She was able to make a person live with fungi and other plants and truly enjoy them. She was responsible, I am certain, for initiating my intense interest in botany, and especially my fascination with fungi.

While I did like chemistry, physics, and mathematics, the inspirational teaching was not there. It seemed that most of the high school teachers were so burdened with courses that they could devote little, if any, time to individual students. The botany teacher on the other hand, who was somewhat less burdened, was able to devote extra time, which made a lasting impression on me.

## COLLEGE—THE FIRST GREAT CHANGE IN ENVIRONMENT

After graduation from high school I was admitted to the University of California at Berkeley and found it to be a frightening place—even orientation was frightening. Being one of 8000 students—more than ten times the size of my home town—was a confusing and strange experience for me. Classes with a hundred or more students in them seemed large—in fact, overwhelming. The adjustment did not come easy, but then it was not for long since I came down with the flu during the first great epidemic in California. I entered the student health center, and as soon as possible, left for home.

### *Back in the Fall*

In the fall, I returned to the Berkeley campus with a higher degree of confidence. I was actually excited about some of my courses, particularly botany and chemistry. Here again, there were two great teachers—Richard Holman in botany and Joel Hildebrand in chemistry. In addition I took a course given by J. C. Whitten in horticulture, which was really a course in ecology showing relationships between various living things including insects, plants, and larger animals and their environment.

About this time, too, I was invited to join a fraternity, which I did. This was a most helpful experience. Here, I was among friends and no longer lost in the masses on the campus. It was for this reason that, when I became Chancellor, I insisted on the construction of small living group facilities that would enable small groups to coalesce into happy social units.

To support myself as an undergraduate, I held various jobs as waiter to a girls' boarding house; faculty club janitor; house manager of a fraternity; manager of the *California Countryman,* a campus publication; and certified milk inspector for the Oakland, Berkeley, and San Francisco areas. The last, though it paid well, involved getting up at 3:30 AM and working till 7 AM.

### *A Major—What Should it Be?*

As time went on, it became apparent that I must choose a major. I liked botany very much in high school and college, but I could not envision making a living with an intense education in botany. Since I did not have the benefit of an advisor, I chose agriculture, simply because I came from a farm. Since we had fruit on the farm, I narrowed the scope of my major to horticulture. Sometime, later, however, I learned that there was a new, evolving field termed food technology. While not well accepted by the academic community as a whole, it was an interesting area with great potential, so I changed to food technology.

Food technology actually came into being as a result of Prohibition. Before Prohibition there was the field of enology, which was concerned with the art and science of wine making. When the Prohibition Act was passed, people involved in this field suddenly found themselves without an area for teaching and research. W. V. Cruess, who was the junior member in the Department of Enology and Viticulture, decided that he should initiate a new field of science concerned with food. The field was not understood and few could see its potential, so criticism and even insults were many, for many academicians frowned on anything that was not pure and fundamental science. On a number of occasions distinguished professors confronted me with the greeting, "Well, how's the jelly and jam scientist today?" Many of them wanted to have me go into their respective fields, but their attitude not only hurt me, but angered me to the point where I refused to change. Had they approached me differently, it is possible that they might have convinced me to change to some other field of study in agriculture, botany, or chemistry. In any event, remaining in food technology turned out to be a fortunate decision for this was a limitless new venture. People must always eat, and today new horizons are opening up in ways that neither I nor the critical professors could imagine.

Since the department was small, Cruess and his wife were able to take a personal interest in each of us and, by having all the students to their house, they helped to develop a great esprit de corps within the department. As student enrollment increased and likewise the demand for experiment station work in the field, Cruess brought into the department a group of young people trained in basic fields such as chemistry, plant physiology, microbiology, and mycology. These included M. A. Joslyn, G. Mackinney, R. Vaughn, and G. L. Marsh.

It was not long before I realized that food technology had a definite place for a person trained in mycology. Fungi and yeasts caused spoilage, and yeasts were used in producing fermented beverages. Eventually, I saw the need in food technology for just about every field of science. In one way or another the courses I took in chemistry, biochemistry, physics, botany, bacteriology, horticulture, and even soil and plant nutrition were all important to the foods we were producing and processing. Such an interplay of sciences and the diversity of young scientists literally made the field a magnet for my interests.

In the department there were but two professors, Cruess and A. W. Christie, and an associate named Paul Nichols. They did all the teaching and research. Cruess was a good teacher, but Christie was superb. Even such areas as dehydration, which could be deadly if taught by the wrong person, were lively when he taught them.

At that time there were no PhDs in the department, although Cruess obtained one later. The absence of PhDs among professors at Berkeley was not a novelty for there were some very distinguished and internationally known professors, such as D. R. Hoagland and J. Bird in plant nutrition, E. C. Voorhies in agricultural economics, W. Mulford in forestry, and C. B. Hutchinson in genetics, who did not have the PhD degree. Hutchinson later became Vice President of the University for Agriculture. This man with great vision and advanced thinking did much for the field of food technology. His breadth of thinking and understanding had such a profound and lasting effect on me that what I learned from him was most useful when I became Chancellor.

My experience in the department and with courses that were changing and improving every year was a rewarding and stimulating one. The closeness of students and professors had a great effect on me, and gave me an understanding of the problems students so often face today, especially those of not knowing where to go for advice and a helping hand. As a result I have always exerted every effort to stay close to students, to understand their problems and their needs, and to work with them—an attitude and effort that I believe has been worthwhile.

## GRADUATION AND THEN WHAT

When the time of graduation came around, it was a period of great uncertainty for me. Jobs for students graduating from college were indeed scarce. There were only two opportunities offered to me in the food field and I was giving serious consideration to these when Cruess came to the rescue. In the department, a fellowship had been established by the California Prune and Apricot Growers Association for a graduate student to work on prune products. Cruess convinced me that I should accept this graduate fellowship, devote as much time as possible to the fellowship project, and then go on for graduate work and a PhD in my field of choice. I accepted the position and it soon became clear to me that if I wished to remain with the University in any capacity it would be necessary to obtain a PhD degree. While Cruess was as thoughtful and as helpful as he could be, he was also a hard taskmaster. He expected one to work full-time on a fellowship while graduate study must be done on one's own time. This, therefore, meant not only full days, but full evenings and weekends. I took courses in botany, mycology, plant physiology, zoology, and biochemistry, but my choice of thesis field was still uncertain and progress was slow.

After two years on the fellowship, Cruess indicated that he could obtain a position for me as a research assistant. I did not really know what this meant. The title and position were not well defined at that time, and, as a matter of fact, are not well defined today. In any event, after some discussion, I accepted the offer and embarked on several directed experiment station projects. It provided a job, experience, and the opportunity for a better education. It was, however, a full-time job, and Cruess insisted that I continue working toward the PhD.

In many ways, from the very beginning, food science had many problems which were in today's terms simple and inappropriate for university work. Yet, there was no place else where this type of experimentation might be done, as industrial research laboratories had not evolved. Accordingly, I became involved in a multiplicity of problems as they arose.

When prunes were canned the cans would often swell as a result of hydrogen formation, so we tackled the problem of preventing this. We knew little about it, but soon learned it was a matter of improving the tin plate. Another problem was related to the nutritive value and composition of prunes. A great many analyses were made and in collaboration with others, nutritional tests were conducted. My task was to make chemical analyses and prepare various fractions of the extracts of prunes to determine whether a laxative principle was present in prunes and, if so, to try to identify it. In collaboration with Chauncey Leake at the San Francisco Medical School, it was established that prunes do contain a laxative principle. The active principle, which is broken down by hydrolysis, has otherwise certain chemical and physiological properties similar to three chemicals: dihydroxyphenylisatin and caffeic and chlorogenic acids. We also did work on the blood plasma $CO_2$-combining capacity of the blood plasma and composition of urine as affected by prunes in various diets. This work was done, to a large extent, in San Quentin prison.

We were also concerned with the matter of moisture-proofness of dried fruit cartons, the composition of figs at various stages of maturity, factors affecting the sulfuring of fruits, effects of various pretreatments and dehydration on the oxidation of raisins, and so on. Fortunately, I was able to enlist the help of Charles D. Fisher, Chief Chemist of the Dried Fruit Association of California. His help was invaluable. We worked together closely and eventually published a bulletin on the sulfuring of fruit. The most important and interesting observation was that the retention of $SO_2$ by dried fruits is related directly to the rate of drying.

At that time there seemed to be problems in exporting some of our fruit to Europe. Using various preservatives, extensive tests were made with peeled and pitted peaches in large containers, which in turn were shipped to Europe for use in industrial canning. Experiments were also done with M. A. Joslyn on the treatment of peeled and cored apples with sulfurous acid for baking use.

For a time I was involved in determining the corrosion of metals by vinegar, wines, and juices and the effect of the metals on the stability of the products. From this I developed an interest in and an ever-increasing appreciation for wines.

These activities were fine but a few years of such potpourri convinced me that it was time for a change if I was to have a future in or out of a university. The question of my future was uppermost in my mind. While the work I did was worthwhile, it was not something I wished to continue to do throughout my life. Then, too, Cruess had laid the law down—I should either get a PhD degree as soon as possible or move out into industry. By this time I had taken all the needed background courses so it was a matter of choosing a thesis problem and passing the preliminary and language examinations. I began to pursue the PhD work intensively. The second great decision of this period was to marry Frances Holman and it proved to be a happy one until her death. Thus it was essential that my degree work be done in Berkeley since I now had to support a wife on the salary of my research assistantship. In deciding upon a thesis topic, my thoughts went back to botany and since it was apparent that it should be related to the field of food science, fungi, or more specifically yeast, seemed to be the answer.

Since botany was my first love and because I had taken courses in mycology, taxonomy, and the physiology of fungi from Lee Bonar and T. Barrett, I discussed with them the matter of working on fungi and yeast. The interim of Prohibition had literally brought all investigations in California relating to yeast to a standstill, and a great deal of the knowledge and information that was available on yeast prior to

Prohibition was lost or discarded. As it became apparent that Prohibition would be repealed, food scientists became more interested in yeasts, as we needed to know about pure cultures to be used in the wine industry of California.

Furthermore, I worked on the problem of film yeast occurring on the surface of cucumber-pickle holding tanks, olive-brine storage tanks, and even ham- and bacon-pickle brine tanks. Then too, while working on prunes I became curious about the white substance that frequently formed on the dried product during storage. I placed some of this material on a slide, examined it microscopically, and was surprised to find that most of what was considered to be sugar was actually made up of yeast cells. It seemed at the time to be such an unbelievably simple observation. I observed any number of sugared prunes from many areas to be certain of the presence of such large amounts of yeast. In every case, the material consisted substantially, if not entirely, of yeast. The possibility of yeast growing in both a concentrated sugar medium and saturated salt brines was fascinating.

But that was not all. Observing yeast on prunes instilled in me a curiosity about other food surface growths, especially the slime on sausages. I examined these slimes and here again yeast was present in abundance. After discussing these observations with Bonar and Cruess, it was decided that I should study these organisms to find out what they are, where they occur, under what conditions they occur, their taxonomy, and so on. It was decided that I should work with Bonar, who pointed out to me that he knew very little about yeasts, and so in the end it would be largely just yeast and me.

On any number of occasions I would talk with people on the Berkeley campus about this work and though they may have been good listeners, they were rarely able to help or advise me. In order to learn about yeast, therefore, it was necessary to resort to the German and French literature. I literally memorized a book by Guilliermond which had been translated into English. Accordingly, it was the starting point of my self-education. After a great deal of exploration, study, and observation of yeasts, it was decided that my efforts should be restricted to film-forming yeasts and particularly those that were obtained from various brines. Furthermore, after spending considerable time on the film-forming yeasts isolated from various sources in California, we concluded that emphasis should be placed on the genus *Debaryomyces.* This resulted in the clarification of confusion that existed among pre-Prohibition California workers as to what these film-formers really were. In most instances, anything that formed a film was termed *Mycoderma.*

The genus *Mycoderma* was first described by Persoon in 1822, but he had not differentiated the film-forming yeast from film-forming bacteria. As time went on, there continued to be more and more confusion with respect to the film-forming yeasts. It seemed as though most researchers concerned with yeasts and especially the film-forming yeast added to the confusion. For example, in 1896, E. Chr. Hanson, who was interested in beer and what might cause the spoilage of beer, described a new species of *Mycoderma.* Later, in 1910, D. Vuillemein transferred such genera as *Ospora, Oidium,* and *Geotrichum* into *Mycoderma.* Medical mycologists appeared on the scene and added to the confusion. This confusion was extended to the people in this country and especially in California. There were medical mycologists in this country such as A. T. Henrici and C. N. Dodge and enologists such as Cruess and F. T. Bioletti who, although they used the same terminology, were talking about entirely different organisms. It was not until N. M. Stelling-Dekker and J. Lodder and, later, H. A. Diddens and J. Lodder came out with their monographs that there was any element of clarification.

In any event, my thesis was completed in 1937 and though it was largely taxonomic, it did contribute to an understanding of some of the organisms we were working with in California.

## *A Permanent Position*

About the time I obtained my PhD, I received an appointment as an Instructor in Food Technology and as a Junior Mycologist in the Experiment Station in the College of Agriculture. Before Prohibition went into effect, Cruess and Bioletti maintained a large collection of wine yeasts used in California, but during Prohibition practically all of these had disappeared. Hence it was considered essential that a study be made of California yeasts and a collection developed. Of Cruess's original collection only two cultures were viable, a strain of *Saccharomyces cerevisiae* variety *ellipsoideus,* and a strain of French champagne yeast. There was a need for a complete study of all aspects of wine production for we had not only lost the art, but also the science during the period of nonproduction. As an Instructor and Junior Mycologist in the Experiment Station, therefore, my first task was to collect California yeast from vineyards and wineries and learn as much as possible about their characteristics. This resulted in a publication in collaboration with Leland McClung.

Later, as wine production was underway, white wines showed a tendency to cloud. At first this was considered to be related to metals, or possibly pectins—anything but microbial growth. As it turned out, however, some of the clouding was caused by yeast, so an extensive study of this phenomenon was undertaken. One of the interesting aspects of this was that in an effort to produce good sherry, some of the sherry type yeasts used in Spain were brought to this country and into the wineries. With William Sheffer it was determined that these yeasts have a greater tolerance for alcohol than do those we use in normal fermentations. Since some of the wineries were using the same hoses and pipelines to transport sherry as they were for the dry white wines, the yeast did indeed cause problems.

About this time, Herman Phaff came to Berkeley from Holland with the intention of learning about fruit juices. Because of his studies with A. J. Kluyver at Delft University, it was natural that I should ask him to work with me on yeasts. Together we became quite active in this field and eventually Phaff lost his interest in juices and concentrated on yeast. In time he obtained his PhD degree with Joslyn and subsequently became an active and productive member of the Department of Food Technology.

Phaff and I worked with a great many cultures and, in doing so, soon realized that the media used to induce sporulation, such as gypsum blocks, a variety of vegetable wedges, and the so-called Gorodkowa medium, were laborious and burdensome. One of the first things we did, in collaboration with H. C. Douglas, therefore, was to develop our own simple sporulation medium which was a vegetable agar containing carrots, beets, potatoes, and cucumbers. It turned out to be a simple and indeed effective medium. Later this medium was further simplified by merely using V8 juice, which greatly facilitated our work. We developed a large yeast collection and knew the characteristics of most of the organisms. It was not long before our interest turned to the ecology of yeasts. This field of study impressed me to such an extent that when I was inaugurated as Chancellor at Davis in 1959 the title of my address was "The University and the Ecology of Man."

About this time I was able to team up with M. A. Joslyn to start a new course on yeasts. It was the only one in the University of California and, aside from that given by C. B. van Niel at the Hopkins Marine Station of Stanford University, perhaps the only one in the West.

Later it seemed as though interest in the occurrence of yeast spoilage was spreading. Nicholas Hansen of the Department of Plant Pathology in Berkeley had done an enormous amount of work on the spoilage of the Calimyrna fig. This fig is fertilized by the so-called *Blastophaga* wasp which carries pollen from the male fig to the female fig and fertilizes it. The wasp not only carries pollen, but also microorganisms which cause spoilage. As the fig spoiled, odors evolved from the eye of the fig which attracted insects; and so, not only did spoilage result from fermentation and vinification, but also mold and insect contamination. I undertook a study, therefore, to determine the type of yeasts that might induce fermentation in the fig. My work in this area was a collaborative project with Phaff, Vaughn, and Hansen.

## THE CLOUDS OF WAR

About this time the clouds of war were looming and it was necessary to redirect our efforts to problems of importance to the war effort. Being located in California and in a Department of Food Technology, it was logical that these efforts should be concerned with the dehydration of fruits and vegetables and the quality control of these products. The combined effort with Phaff, Russell Perry, and Fisher, therefore, was directed toward improvement of the dehydrated cut fruits and the prevention of microbial spoilage after packing and during storage and shipment. There was a team effort with H. A. Barker and Earl Stadtman in the studies relating to the deterioration of these concentrated dried products by the so-called browning reaction. This was important because not only did the appeal of the product decrease as a result of discoloration, but also edibility and nutritive value.

In collaboration with Phaff, Rita Welton, and Fisher, I also conducted studies on the prevention of microbial spoilage of dried fruits containing a higher moisture content by the use of epoxide fumigation. The procedure was indeed successful and in fact we even obtained a public service patent on it.

We were encouraged by the Research and Development Office of the Quartermaster General to become involved in all phases of the dehydration of fruits and vegetables. This effort on my part went on for approximately two years. I was then invited to Washington to take a position in the Office of the Quartermaster General.

There I was asked to assume chairmanship of a newly created committee, entitled the Committee on Food Research, which was to develop external research programs relating to various foods used in rations, to hold symposia, to call on scientific personnel throughout the country for help, and so on. The work was fascinating and a diverting relief from the sadness of unexpectedly losing my wife. The committee was an excellent and interesting one with which to work. The other members were George Stewart, who is now at Davis; Samuel Lepkovsky of Berkeley; Herb Longenecker, President of Tulane University; and M. T. Anson who was a co-founder of the journal, *Advances in Protein Chemistry.* After the war it was Anson who suggested that Stewart and I start the series entitled *Advances in Food Research.*

The Committee on Food Research stimulated needed research on rations. Research was financially supported for important studies related to the acceptability, utility, stability, and nutritive value of rations. This involved studies relating to color, flavor, and texture. For the improvement of taste and texture the so-called high-moisture pack of prunes, figs, and dates was developed.

The term utility was used to describe the ease of use of rations in the field. Could they be eaten either cold or hot, was water needed, and were they of convenient weight and volume? Stability, too, was an all important problem for many rations deteriorated and became inedible when handled under adverse conditions, such as being stored on the North African desert. Problems relating to stability were numerous and could involve the rancidification of fats and oils; the browning reaction; retrogradation of starch or staling such as takes place in bread; the gelling of condensed milk, and the loss of desirable texture, flavor, and solubility.

## THE END OF THE WAR

When the war was over and my duties in Washington completed, I headed back to Berkeley. Shortly after returning, I married Vera Greaves, a nutritionist in Agricultural Extension with whom I had worked on the home preservation of foods during the war. We have had much in common, having worked together often, and, with our two children, have been very happy.

Once again Phaff and I joined forces to reestablish a research program relating to the ecology of yeast and to give a course on the biology of yeast. At this time I was asked to be chairman of the department in Berkeley. Strange as it may seem, Phaff and I were in a sausage factory collecting yeast from slimy sausage when a call came inviting me to accept chairmanship of the department.

It was a time of great growth and stress for the University and the department. The so-called battle of the oath was about to take place and I became involved in it. As a matter of fact, three of us in food technology were among the few in agriculture to join forces with those objecting to the required oath.

My first exposure to departmental administration indicated clearly that it was most important to maintain a close working relationship with the people in the University and certainly with those outside the University. It was important to use every means possible to obtain funds and to build an esprit de corps in the department. My experience in Washington and my memories of undergraduate life helped in both respects.

In spite of all these changes, I found it possible to continue to collaborate with Phaff in teaching and research. We continued our surveys and studies relating to the distribution and the ecology of yeasts. This was well underway in Berkeley when, in 1950, it was decided by the Administration that the department would be moved to the Davis campus. Some of the members of the department accepted the edict and planned to move to Davis; others decided to remain in Berkeley. Phaff, yeast, and I planned to move. It was imperative that I move since I was chairman of the department, but fortunately, Phaff, who had then become a permanent member of the department, decided he too would move. This enabled us to continue our joint efforts in teaching and research. Together we initiated another course on the biology of yeast at Davis.

I found the Davis campus to be small, friendly, and dynamic. It was barely starting to develop into a full-scale university. The department had a new modern building which, at the time, was the best and largest food technology building in the country. With its teaching and research laboratories and large pilot and freezing plant, it truly was an outstanding facility. While in Berkeley, Phaff and I were cramped in a small part of a small laboratory. At Davis, we had laboratories to ourselves and facilities that made it comfortable for us to work with yeast. We even had people to wash our dishes and prepare media and an ample supply of glassware and dishes, amenities which were not available to us in Berkeley.

During this collaborative period we wrote a review on yeast in the *Annual Review of Microbiology* in which we emphasized the importance of ecology, an area that we would pursue actively during the next several years. The review was the first one on yeast since that written by A. T. Henrici in 1941 and brought the subject up to date. Subsequently, we wrote reviews on the sporulation of yeast.

At the same time O. B. Williams of Texas asked us to collaborate with him on the occurrence of yeast in shrimp collected on the Gulf Coast. He had an extensive collection, a large number of which were red and yellow yeasts, and some of them were indeed unusual. Here again we found that the procedure that had been used for the determination of the presence of carotenoid pigments was cumbersome and difficult. With Gordon Mackinney we were able to develop a simple method for the determination of carotenoids. This indeed did facilitate our taxonomic work being done in collaboration with Williams.

About this time a number of students became interested in the taxonomy and ecology of yeast. One of these was Robert Bouthilet who came to us from Minnesota, at the suggestion of C. P. Skinner, to work on his thesis. Bouthilet had taken his preliminary examinations at Minnesota, but his research on the taxonomy of soil yeast was done in our laboratory. His work indicated the value of using the fermentation of trehalose as a taxonomic character.

El Tabey Shehata was another student who desired to work on taxonomy and distribution of yeasts. About the time he appeared on the scene, Ledyard Stebbins encouraged us to work with T. Dobzhansky on the taxonomy of yeasts used as food by Drosophila flies. Dobzhansky was studying the distribution of these flies and the factors that influence the appearance of different species at different times. He had studied various ecological factors that might influence the species cycling but not their food and, since he had become interested in this factor, we were called on to help. Because these flies lived, to a large extent, on yeast, Dobzhansky wondered if there might be some relation between the type of yeast and the occurrence of the various species of fruit flies at various times. We embarked on a very extensive study of the types of yeasts that various Drosophila would ingest, their preferences, and so on. It was a fascinating study that opened up a new world to us and involved developing new techniques so flies could be collected in the mountains of California and brought to our laboratory before they could digest the yeast in their alimentary tracks. We had to develop techniques to remove the crops from the flies and the yeast from the crops, and, equally important, a procedure involving impairment of the digestive process. Shehata was able to work out procedures whereby the digestive processes of the flies were brought to a standstill by holding them at a very low temperature in insulated containers. The flies accomplish digestion by a process involving destruction of the cytoplasmic membrane. The cell contents can then be extracted and utilized as a food. The flies seemed strongly attracted to apiculate type yeasts, namely *Hanseniaspora* and *Kloeckera.* Apparently these yeasts give off chemo-attractants to which flies respond.

One of the common feeding places of the Drosophila was the slime fluxes or exudates of various trees. These slimy exudates have yielded some interesting organisms but they had been investigated only on an occasional basis. Here, then, came the realization of an opportunity to investigate slime flux for yeast and yeast-like organisms, not only in various areas of California but throughout the world.

While all this was going on, problems relating to the spoilage of foods came to my attention. Concentrated citrus products were undergoing yeast spoilage and with Jack Recca we made a study of yeast causing this spoilage. This yielded an interesting new yeast for which a new genus, *Lodderomyces,* was subsequently established. Then there was work with Martin Miller relating to yeast attracting the dried-fruit beetle and the organisms associated with it. My participation in these extensive studies was brought to a standstill when I moved into the Chancellor's office.

## A VISIT FROM PRESIDENT CLARK KERR

While in the pilot plant one day, President Clark Kerr and Vice President Harry Wellman of the University came into the building and just started looking around. I approached them and asked if there was anything I might do for them and the answer was "no"—they were just looking around.

About a week later, however, I had another visit and it was then that Kerr asked me to become Chancellor of the Davis campus. This was truly a frightening offer, for it was something far beyond any of my aspirations. It would mean leaving an activity that I was enjoying very much and undertaking something I was not certain I could handle. I asked if I might have some time to think about it and his reply was—"how long?" I requested a couple of months, but his answer was: "I'll give you two weeks." It was two weeks of worry and soul searching—what would happen if I did accept and what would happen if I did not. I could thoroughly understand his insistence on a decision in a few weeks, for rumors arise in such a situation with every passing day. Fortunately I never heard one that applied to me—I must have been a dark horse.

A few weeks later, Kerr asked for my decision and I accepted, but with qualms, humility, and trepidation. I expressed my concerns and worries to him but he reassured me that I had nothing to worry about for my long association with the University, as a department chairman and member of the Davis Budget Committee, would make it an easy transition.

One of the most difficult tasks confronting me, one which took nearly two years, was to convince myself that I would have to forget about working in the laboratory and teaching on yeasts. In spite of this, it was a thrilling experience when K. Thimann of Harvard invited me to write a book on the life of the yeast some years later. Although it was a privilege I could not turn down, I recognized that I could not do it alone. Therefore, I contacted Phaff and Miller and the three of us prepared the book which has now been through one printing and is ready to be rewritten.

I succeeded Chancellor Stanley Freeborn, a wonderful and helpful man, who did everything possible to help me understand the complexities of the position I was assuming. Some of the complex problems were related to the development of academic and physical plans, the formulation and subsequent defense of adequate budgets, and the establishment of good relationships with students, faculty, statewide university officers, the outside world, the elected and appointed officers in Sacramento, The Regents, and the other chancellors. It was indeed a very large public relations job and required the use of every mood available and the best of dramatic resources.

Developing academic and physical plans required consideration of the educational needs of a growing campus, uniqueness and personality of the campus, interaction between students and faculty and the outside world, transportation needs, aesthetics, and so on. It was necessary to give serious consideration to the rate of growth and the creation of new schools, colleges, and research institutes. We also found it necessary to think in terms of utilities, such as water, power, and sewage; roads; and security needs, such as police and fire protection. The beauty, space, and geography of the campus, of course, were also most important.

I soon learned that there is a relationship between space and the contentment of people. This is well defined in the book *The Hidden Dimension.* After reading this, I was convinced that there is a student-space relationship, as well as aesthetic needs, which does indeed have an influence on contentment and accomplishment. I am more certain of this today than ever and believe sincerely that the physical size and careful planning of the campus has contributed to the stability of Davis.

Throughout these very intensive times of planning, statewide officers and, in particular, Kerr and Vice Presidents Wellman and Morgan were most helpful and understanding. It was from these men that I learned that the attitude of a leader should be—what can I do to help you, rather than what can I do to stop you.

The problem of planning involved more than just growth, educational plans, facilities, and so on—for if we were to accomplish anything we needed funds. It was essential that we become heavily involved in budget planning and documentation of our needs for years ahead. This involved convincing Kerr and his staff, The Regents, State officials in Sacramento, various agencies in Washington, and of course industry, that our needs and the budget plans drawn up were accurate. This once again required the use of various modes of drama, as well as sound documentation. In addition I soon learned that I had to remember I was dealing with people and that each case and need required individual study and a personal approach. With respect to the latter, I often think of what the President of the University of Tokyo once said to me when characterizing a university president. He said that a university president is a beggar with a cast iron stomach; a person that must be gentle with winning ways; a weak person; a strong person; a person with humility; or a person without humility, as may be needed. In any event he must be enthusiastic and forthright, always telling the truth—then he will not have to remember what falsehoods he may have indulged in and when. These are lessons I had to learn too.

One of the more important and enduring facets of being Chancellor was the opportunity to work with students, faculty, and staff on the campus. In arriving at the right attitude and approach to dealing with such groups I spent a great deal of time discussing the subject with Vice Chancellors Everett Carter, Vernon Cheadle, and later C. O. McCorkle. It eventually became apparent that I had to surround myself with talented people, who were capable of carrying on the day to day tasks of a chancellor, and that I must be easily accessible to all members of the university community at all times. This was indeed a burdensome undertaking but it set the tone for the evolution of a unique, friendly, and stable campus. I was indeed accessible and always willing to collaborate with groups, listen to them, and be helpful whenever possible. In pursuing this policy I found myself at times at the lonely outpost of leadership, a position which I described in the following statement which appeared in the 1963–1964 *UCD Catalog.* "The ability and willingness to take responsibility, to go to the lonely outpost of thought and action, to persuade others to follow you there—truly, this ability is the rarest of commodities in the world. We live in a world of tremendous numbers, mass pressures, of enormous voices working at the leveling out of talent and conformity of opinion. The only way to keep this world a good world, and make it better, is to assert creative and constructive individualism, which to me is another way of saying 'leadership'." It was with this philosophy that I proceeded to explore the world of men, things, and ideas.

It was also necessary to build personal relationships with those in the outside world, particularly with the legislative and administrative people in Sacramento. In doing so I struggled to understand that those in Sacramento represented a cross section of people just as we have in the University. Eventually I became well acquainted with many of the legislators and did indeed develop a high regard for them. When I finally realized this I had no hesitation whatsoever in telling them about my change in attitude and my understanding and appreciation of their approach. Out of this I believe grew a mutual respect and, indeed, an understanding and respect for the Davis campus. I also became well acquainted with The Regents and found them to be generally conscientious. Many devoted much time, effort, and thought to the University and its problems, although I cannot say I always agreed with the conclusions they drew.

Finally, it was essential to maintain a close relationship with the other chancellors with whom I worked, for together they represented a center of considerable influence in the University. It was indeed a new world to me and one that I truly started to enjoy. As I adapted to the situation it became easier to move away from the ecology of yeasts toward the ecology of people. The Chancellor's job was, to a considerable extent, a public relations job which required careful, quick thinking to decide on which mode of drama or communication to use, or when to change the mode for each particular situation. It was my policy to never ask who was calling when my phone rang, since whenever I am asked that question I always have the urge to inquire who is asking. When students came to my office I made an effort to talk with them, even though I might be involved in a meeting. Such accessibility and consideration I am certain had much to do with the stability, friendliness, and personality of the campus that eventually evolved.

The University of California is indeed a complex organism and even within a single campus it requires various individuals to help formulate policies and implement them. Many individuals of varied backgrounds helped so very much in my thought and idea processes. Mortimer P. Starr, for example, helped much in organizing our disheveled and diffuse grant and research support policies into an effective and workable system.

In ten years a small agricultural college was converted into a general university, yet one that is unique. There is, of course, a College of Letters and Sciences with its full spectrum and curricula, and with particularly strong departments in botany, chemistry, and bacteriology. There are also distinguished departments in other areas and since Davis has been primarily known in the past for its agricultural strength, I would like to mention that it has many excellent departments in the humanities and social sciences. For example, the Department of Dramatic Art is blessed with a modern theater and an authentic Shakespearean theater. As the result of a gift from Fred Wyatt, an old animal judging pavilion was converted into a theater in the round.

Because of this growth in varied areas it became necessary to develop a library to meet the needs of the people in the humanities and social sciences. Davis has always had an excellent library for agriculture and some of the sciences, but such facilities were almost nonexistent in other fields. Today a library to meet these needs has been developed.

It became apparent that it was continually necessary to plan for the needs of this expanding campus and to obtain funds year after year to fulfill these plans and hopes. Such funds made it possible to construct, in accordance with the academic plan, a College of Engineering. The surprising and continued high enrollment in engineering at Davis may be the result of the focus of the program which stresses engineering as such, rather than engineering science.

At one point, Nobel Prize winner Ernest Lawrence indicated that he would be glad to have the 60 inch cyclotron at Berkeley transferred to the Physics Department at Davis. This was a thrill until I learned that cyclotrons are expensive luxuries and just moving it from Berkeley to Davis would involve hundreds of thousands of dollars. The Atomic Energy Commission was willing to help with a substantial contribution, on the condition that we match it with $100,000. It was then that Chancellor Glenn Seaborg of the Berkeley campus came to our rescue with funds earned by the Berkeley cyclotron. This commitment was made just 70 minutes before the deadline set by the Federal government. The cyclotron has been such a successful addition to the Davis campus that the stresses and strains of securing funds are naturally forgotten. It was the result of a wonderful relationship with Seaborg and the Berkeley campus that we were able to fulfill our cyclotron hopes.

There were also professional school problems. The legislature had implied that it might be a good idea to have schools of law and medicine on the Davis campus and, accordingly, these eventually came into being, though the statewide university plan had not even considered Davis for a medical school. The law school was developed by Edward Barrett who came from Berkeley. The school of medicine was developed at a record-breaking pace under the direction of Dean John Tupper who came from the University of Michigan. The initial budget of the medical school was approximately $60,000. Starting with this and with zero space and no equipment or staff of any type, we were able to develop a school in temporary buildings (some of which were later termed Mrak Shacks) and open a medical school with 100 students within 26 months. To my knowledge this had never been accomplished before in less than five years. At the same time the School of Veterinary Medicine was expanded and new facilities were developed.

As a result of our contacts in Washington and elsewhere, we were also able to build the National Center for Primate Biology, and to develop an Institute for the Study of Criminal Justice and one for the study of governmental affairs.

As the campus grew it became my hope that its growth would be limited to 10,000 students. We were permitted to do so providing we were willing to accept another 1500 as professional students. Later the planning goals increased to a total number of 18,500 students. Even though it was highly desirable, it was difficult to hold the rate of growth down. We knew that close student-faculty relationships could not continue if we grew too fast or too large. It was for this reason that I did everything possible to put restraints on the rate of growth. Forty to sixty new faculty members in one year were extremely difficult to indoctrinate in the spirit and friendliness of the Davis campus. This was especially so in the case of those who came from large and indifferent institutions where the attitude toward students was so different. Then again large numbers of students entering each year were most difficult to assimilate.

In addition a campus that grows too rapidly and becomes too large outgrows its facilities. This was a serious problem, especially with respect to those facilities that the State would not fund, such as the Student Health Center. Once again the friendship with Berkeley came to the rescue and with the help of William Monahan, an assistant to President Kerr, we were able to obtain a grant of $750,000 from the Cowell Foundation to expand the present facility.

Among the faculty there were many members that I could count on to maintain the friendly personality of the campus in spite of the growth. However, there appeared to be an increasing change in the attitude of the younger faculty members, and this was the cause of much concern. In my early years as Chancellor, I felt that the faculty exhibited a great loyalty to their discipline, profession, departments, and to the University. This seemed to decline among some of the younger faculty members as time went on, which prompted me to comment that many of them have but one loyalty and that is to themselves. Needless to say, this stimulated severe criticism. But I believe this attitude of disinterest eventually resulted in the deterioration of the Academic Senate and the establishment of a faculty representative assembly.

There has been a tendency for some of the faculty to speak for a teachers' union and, while it appears there is some justification for one, it must be realized that this could mean the loss of academic freedom. When one is given individual responsibility and accepts it, then one deserves all that goes with academic freedom. On the other hand, if one works under a blanket contract such as exists in unionized organizations, then one may expect as time goes on to lose many things that go with what is now termed academic freedom—perhaps, though I hope not, even to the extent of punching a time clock.

The student body also changed to some extent as time went on. This may have been related to contact with other universities. At times there were many students here from other campuses and some individuals not connected with any campus. Thus Davis became a staging area for young activists moving toward Sacramento. We were fortunate, however, in not having any serious confrontations. This, without doubt, was related to the attitudes and policies that developed on the campus. Although it was not possible to involve students in all phases of activity on the campus, an attempt was made, through Project Involvement, to induce students to become active in one or more on-campus or off-campus activities. In addition we constructed snack bars, walking and bicycling paths, picnic areas, and even quiet areas of beauty for meditation. We developed intramural athletic programs so there was an opportunity to exercise, relax, and "blow off steam." We financed the athletic program, so it was not a burden on the students, and dramatic productions, so that students paid the barest minimum for this type of entertainment.

We felt strongly that the collaboration between students and faculty was important in determining the proper diet for well-nourished minds. The particular strength of students was in contributing new ideas generated by their practical concerns, while the faculty, on the other hand, offered the wisdom to evaluate traditional forms of education. The result of such intercommunication could be a better diet, balanced between wisdom and realism. This collaboration produced many new courses and curricula and even an experimental college.

## A CALL FROM GOVERNOR NELSON ROCKEFELLER

Several months prior to retirement as Chancellor, I began to wonder what I might do upon retirement, how I would occupy my time, and how I would relax and enjoy life. My wonderment changed as I received many invitations to become involved in many different activities. Though I was reluctant to accept any of these, I found myself accepting too many. One of the most intriguing was a call from Governor

Nelson Rockefeller inviting me to be a member of the Presidential Mission, led by him, to Latin American and Caribbean countries. The purpose of the trip was to listen and learn about their concerns and attitudes toward the U.S. Clifton Wharton and I were invited to represent the areas of food and agriculture.

The Mission came into being as a result of Gallo Plaza, President of the Organization of American States, who urged President Nixon not to forget Latin America. When questioned as to what he meant by this, Plaza indicated that there was a need for us to listen and learn rather than negotiate or tell. When the President asked who he should send on such a trip, Plaza's reply was that there was only one person, Rockefeller, who could do the job. The result was a Mission to listen and report back to the President. We visited all but two countries in Latin America and the Caribbean. Wharton and I listened to the Secretaries of Agriculture, government officials, and representatives of AID, FAO, and the private sector. I wrote an extensive report on each country, outlining the problems and concerns that are of interest to us. Many of these problems were related to public health, plant and animal diseases, diets, and education in the agricultural and veterinary sciences. Some material from my reports became part of a book about the Mission entitled *The Rockefeller Report on the Americas—The Official Report of the United States Presidential Mission for the Western Hemisphere* by Nelson A. Rockefeller.

The Mission involved four separate trips, after which we met with Rockefeller and for two days discussed observations and recommendations. It was concluded that the general tone of the report should relate to the quality of life in the Latin American and Caribbean countries. I felt that the Mission was worthwhile, but poorly reported—in fact, inaccurately reported by the news media. It is unfortunate that world events did not permit a follow through on these suggestions by our government.

About four years later I received another call, this time from the White House inviting me to participate in another Presidential Mission to five Latin American countries. This was under the leadership of Presidential Counselor Robert Finch and was to a large extent a goodwill mission. Once again my assignment was food and agriculture, although I did have an opportunity to meet with the leaders of these countries. Just as in the case of the first visit, it was apparent to me that there is a great need on the part of the U.S. to build better relations with our neighbors in Latin America.

## HEW AND PESTICIDES

About the time I was to leave on my first trip with the Rockefeller Mission, an exciting phone call came from Under-Secretary John Veneman of the Department of Health, Education, and Welfare. He asked me to act as chairman of a new commission to be concerned with pesticides. He was confronted with a problem relating to DDT occurring in Coho salmon in the Great Lakes area, particularly in Lake Michigan. The Food and Drug Administration had observed the occurrence of DDT in these fish in quantities in excess of the tolerance of 3 ppm. This was a serious situation for Coho salmon is an important game fish in that area. The question arose as to why there was such a low tolerance when there was no evidence to indicate DDT was harmful to the human organism in much larger amounts. Secretary Robert Finch, therefore, decided to appoint a commission to study the relationship of pesticides to environmental health. Although I was by no means an authority on pesticides or human health, I was willing to take on the task of handling the commission. I requested that William Darby, Chairman of the Department of Biochemistry at Vanderbilt University and presently President of the Nutrition Foundation, and Leon Golberg, toxicologist at the Union College of Medicine, be given membership on the Commission, and that Dale Lindsay, who was then Assistant Chancellor at the Davis campus, be made a consultant.

While I was away with the Rockefeller Mission, Lindsay acted for me and divided the commission into five subcommissions concerned with the use and benefits of pesticides, contamination of the environment, effects on nontarget organisms other than man, interaction of pesticides with other chemicals, and the effects on man. Then we set up panels concerned with carcinogenicity, mutagenicity, and teratogenicity of pesticides under the subcommission for the effects on man.

The Commission was formed about mid-summer in 1969 and the deadline for the completion of the report was December 1969. This was an unbelievable task, but with adequate help and with the great talent of the members of the Commission and panels, the report was completed in time. The report consisted of 677 pages, representing a review of over 6000 references, in some cases every piece of literature relating to a specific subject was reviewed. At that time 20,000 copies were published and subsequently an index volume has been published. The report has been well received and has had considerable impact in the broad area of pesticide use and safety throughout the world.

While I have received a great deal of credit for this report, it really belongs to the members of the Commission, for my task was really that of organizer and mediator. In some cases there was a great divergence of opinion among the other members and the only solution I saw was to insist that there be a minority and majority report and, if necessary, three divergent reports if we could not agree. As it turned out, only in one case did a divergence of opinion appear and that was in the cancer panel report on the statistical significance of the occurrence of what was termed nodules in livers of weanling mice fed enormous doses of DDT. When the data had been reported upon, a report was prepared summarizing the work and the recommendations of the Commission for presentation to the Secretary.

With respect to DDT, the report recommended the phasing out of this chemical where possible. When needed, however, the Commission's recommendation was that its use be continued until a substitute was available. The recommendation was not based on harm to human health, but rather on the possibility of its accumulation in the environment. The Commission felt that if we could find other means of controlling pests, this would be best, but that it should not be completely excluded from use when needed for human health and welfare, including food production. Unfortunately this reasoning was not followed by the Environmental Protection Agency which completely banned DDT.

As a result of the report, a Secretary's Pesticide Advisory Committee was created to advise the Secretary on handling future pesticide problems. Here again I was asked to act as chairman. This was a unique situation since it meant a higher level advisory group reporting to the Secretary on subjects that should be handled by agencies at a much lower level in HEW.

## THE ENVIRONMENTAL PROTECTION AGENCY

Soon after the Advisory Committee was appointed, however, the Environmental Protection Agency (EPA) was created by "cannibalizing" a number of existing government agencies. EPA resulted from assembling portions of existing departments in Agriculture, HEW, and Interior into a single agency. The Advisory Committee was then moved to the EPA and renamed the Hazardous Materials Advisory Committee. In this capacity it has issued a number of publications related to toxaphene, the use of chemicals in food plants, and sanitizing agents.

One of the general observations that I have been able to make as a result of this activity is that very often government agencies feel that they must respond to the pressures of advocates and misinformed, but vocal, people. The result is that so often decisions are made by the rule of emotion, rather than the rule of reason. Even judges seem to abide by the fashions of the day rather than the rule of reason.

In EPA, the strains and stresses of reorganization are still obvious and one can agree with Petronius, who lived in Caesar's time, when he commented with respect to reorganization: "We trained hard—but it seems that every time we are beginning to form into teams, we would be reorganized. I was to learn later in life that we tend to meet any new situation by reorganizing; and what a wonderful method it can be for creating the illusion of progress while producing confusion, inefficiency and demoralization." We never seem to learn, for 2000 years later this observation is so true with respect to Washington, D.C.

It is my hope that we can improve communications between divisions of the agency and within the divisions. I am certain that if the organization had not been changed so often and dramatically, communication would have been better and the agency more effective.

In any event, my association with EPA has been a stimulating one, and it appears that new problems are always on the horizon. One of the most recent relates to hexachlorobenzene (HCB), a biproduct of the manufacture of chlorinated hydrocarbons. It occurs in the waste tars that have in the past been buried in land fills as a way of disposal. These waste tars not only contain hexachlorobenzene, but also hexachlorobutadene and other chemicals. They dissolve into water or perhaps sublimate and thus contaminate the environment. They have been found in feed in a Louisiana grazing area and also in the fat of beef animals feeding in that area. This problem was first observed by scientists in the U.S. Department of Agriculture, who in turn asked the EPA to establish a tolerance. Since HCB was a waste product it appeared that the logical agency to establish a tolerance was the Food and Drug Administration (FDA). The FDA, however, pointed out that a small amount of

HCB has been used in the northwest for the treatment of wheat seeds to be planted, so the FDA insisted that the EPA should establish a tolerance. My advisory committee suggested an extensive study on the occurrence of HCB in soil, water, air, feed, wildlife, plants, and even humans, as well as toxicological studies. However, the tendency has been to think only in terms of the establishment of a tolerance level. This troublesome situation is related to deficient communication, which I have observed through the years is so often the mark of large organizations and especially the Federal government. Data on which to establish a tolerance was meager, so an interim tolerance of 0.5 ppm was established until a panel appointed by my advisory committee could follow the experimental toxicological studies underway and advise the EPA whether or not the interim tolerance should be increased, decreased, or maintained.

There were also problems related to polychlorinated biphenyls (PCB). After the Commission report was made to the Secretary, it was observed that what was thought to be DDT in the Great Lakes salmon actually was mostly PCB. Such faulty chemical analysis was also made with regard to mercury. Investigators using the wet method of analysis reported much less mercury than those using the atomic absorption procedure. Furthermore, methyl mercury, the real toxicological problem, is difficult to determine by analysis.

One of the greatest problems confronting the committee was the need to develop generally accepted protocols to use in testing for safety. As the situation now stands, there are no such procedures and the result is complete chaos. Our committee, therefore, has been heavily involved in the creation and development of the National Center for Toxicological Research which is located at Jefferson (near Pine Bluff), Arkansas. The purpose of this laboratory is to develop generally accepted protocols to use in testing for safety. The Center is now about two years old and has underway a great number of tests with animals, using a powerful chemical carcinogen as a model, to develop a protocol for testing for carcinogenesis.

Now another problem has arisen. The Occupational Safety and Health Act (OSHA), which is administered by the Department of Labor, may very well require safety regulations, which if enforced, could close the Jefferson laboratory. The suggested requirements for laboratory safety are so stringent and unrealistic that they could very well diminish or eliminate research in many laboratories. The average bench scientist is not generally aware of this impending threat to research.

Another problem which I have observed is the failure of responsible scientists to make themselves heard at all levels of government. So often the government seems to yield to the voice of irresponsible pseudoscientists and even to lawyers rather than to the voice of responsible scientists. This is true whether it be Washington or Sacramento, yet if the responsible community of scientists does not speak up, the government has no other source to consult. In some way or another, the careful and reliable scientist must find a way to make his views acceptable to and influential with the lawmakers, their assistants, and others in government involved in making decisions, judgments, and regulations. The evolution of bills to come before Congress requires about three years of study and preparation. Even though early scientific input would be highly advantageous, it is seldom done until the bill is about ready to be introduced. More often than not, if Congress calls upon scientists, it is when the proposed law has moved to the point where it is about to be presented to a congressional committee. It is too late at this point to have a substantial input or influence. Accordingly, the Commission on Natural Resources of the National Research Council, of which I am a member, has developed the view that scientists must work with the assistants to the elected legislators when the development of a law is begun, with an eye to presenting sound and reliable information but not lobbying for one bill or another.

When called upon to testify, a responsible scientist will often permit himself to be pushed to a point of uncertainty at a hearing concerning a bill. More often than not, he will speak with an element of uncertainty and indicate the need for more research. An advocate on the other hand, leaves no doubt as to whether a specific bill is desirable or undesirable. The confused legislator or his assistant may then very well accept the views of the positive advocates who impress them as being more certain.

In some way or another, those who work with the legislators must be convinced that every situation is really a matter of odds, or probabilities rather than certainties. How safe is safe when it comes to a specific chemical, or what are we willing to accept in one situation and not in another? For example, when the FDA was asked by a congressional committee to comment on the banning of diethylstilbestrol (DES) and what it really meant, the reply was as follows: "DES.—Based on findings of 5 percent of liver samples containing 2 ppb of DES, and assuming that 2 percent of the average diet is beef liver, a person would have to consume 5 million pounds of liver per year for 50 years to equal the intake from one treatment of day-after oral contraceptives." If this is the situation, then it appears that we may be unreasonably overprotective in the case of food, but when it comes to social situations and drugs, we may have minimal standards, if any. This has occurred in spite of the fact that there are well informed and responsible scientists who could help avoid such inconsistencies. My pathway into governmental problems has led to these observations and the hope that something can and will be done to put the scientist in his deserved and proper place in making governmental decisions.

## CONCLUSION

The journey from graduate student to Chairman of an EPA committee now seems a long and tortuous route. There have been a diversity of stops along the way. As I look back, each stop was an interesting and fascinating one and there was no indication of where the next path would lead.

Today, it seems impossible to think of moving from prunes to yeast, then to the war effort concerned with dried fruits, and then to the postwar collaborative work with Phaff on yeasts. My thoughts in those days were far removed from administrative concerns, yet the chairmanship of a department came along and I took it with some reluctance. This stop seemed to be a permanent one and the possibility of moving out of Berkeley did not seem probable, yet on to Davis we went, and at Davis came all the fascinations of building a department and helping to develop a campus.

Upon retirement as Chancellor, there were indeed uncertainties about moving overnight from an environment of great activity to one of inactivity, but unexpectedly this did not happen. Participation in Presidential missions to Latin America and chairing a Commission for HEW and then an Advisory Committee for EPA maintained my level of activity, but with less emotional strain.

Through it all, there was on my part an uncertainty of whether or not I should leave one stop and proceed to the next; nevertheless, in each case, I went on and it seemed to work out. There was a common denominator in all the stops; in each there was the need to deal with people, the need to communicate, the need to keep my thinking alive and expansive, and above all the need for judgment—good judgment based on reason and not on emotion.

My journey involved on exploration of the world of men, things, and ideas. It involved the ability and willingness to take responsibility and go to the lonely outpost of thought and action and to persuade others to follow me there. Truly, I have lived in many worlds, but they were happy worlds and even now, I am ready to move on to another—perhaps this time complete retirement or even a peek into the microscope now and then. In any event, so has it been with a hopeful microbiologist turned administrator.

# VIROIDS: THE SMALLEST KNOWN AGENTS OF INFECTIOUS DISEASE[1]

❖1628

*T. O. Diener*

Plant Virology Laboratory, Agricultural Research Service, U.S. Department of Agriculture, Beltsville, Maryland 20705

CONTENTS

INTRODUCTION ........ 23
EVIDENCE FOR EXISTENCE OF VIROIDS ........ 24
*Sedimentation Properties and Nuclease Sensitivity* ........ 24
*Absence of Virions* ........ 25
*Subcellular Location* ........ 26
*Molecular Weight Estimates of Native Viroids* ........ 26
PURIFICATION ........ 29
PHYSICAL AND CHEMICAL PROPERTIES ........ 29
*Molecular Weight of PSTV* ........ 29
*Thermal Denaturation of PSTV* ........ 30
*Radiation Sensitivity* ........ 30
*Electron Microscopy of PSTV* ........ 30
*Molecular Structure of Viroids* ........ 31
BIOLOGICAL PROPERTIES ........ 33
*Replication* ........ 33
*Pathogenesis* ........ 34
*Transmission* ........ 35
IMPLICATIONS ........ 35
*Question of Viroid Origin* ........ 35
*Question of Animal Viroids* ........ 37

## INTRODUCTION

The term viroid has been introduced to denote a newly recognized class of subviral pathogens (12). Presently known viroids consist solely of a short strand of RNA with a molecular weight in the neighborhood of 75–100,000 daltons. Introduction of this low molecular weight RNA into susceptible hosts leads to apparent replication of the RNA and, in some hosts, to disease.

[1]The survey of the literature pertaining to this review was concluded on December 15, 1973.

The first viroid came to light during efforts to purify and characterize the agent of the potato spindle tuber disease (PSTV), a disease which, for many years, had been assumed to be of viral etiology (22). In 1967, Diener & Raymer (20) reported that the infectious agent of this disease is a free RNA and that virus particles, apparently, are not present in infected tissue. Later, sedimentation and gel electrophoretic analyses conclusively demonstrated that the infectious RNA has a very low molecular weight (12) and that the agent, therefore, basically differs from conventional viruses.

Two additional plant diseases, chrysanthemum stunt (19) and citrus exocortis (61, 68), are now known also to be caused by low molecular weight RNAs, i.e. by viroids.

In this chapter, presently known characteristics of viroids will be reviewed. Emphasis will be placed on very recently elucidated properties; for earlier work, the reader is referred to previous reviews of the subject (13, 15, 17). PSTV and the agent of the citrus exocortis disease (CEV) are considered here as separate entities; recent evidence suggests, however, that the two agents may be closely related or identical (69).

The recognition of viroids as a novel class of pathogens raises several questions with potentially important implications for microbiology, molecular biology, plant pathology, and veterinary and human medicine. Some of these possible implications will be discussed briefly in light of present knowledge of viroids affecting higher plants.

## EVIDENCE FOR EXISTENCE OF VIROIDS

### *Sedimentation Properties and Nuclease Sensitivity*

Early work had shown that in crude extracts from potato or tomato leaves affected with the potato spindle tuber disease, most of the infectious material sediments at very low rates (ca 10S), making it unlikely that the extracted infectious agent is a conventional virus particle. As the agent was found to be insensitive to treatment with various organic solvents, lipid-containing virus particles of low density also appeared to be ruled out. Treatment of crude extracts with phenol neither affected infectivity nor the sedimentation properties of the agent. In view of these findings, it was proposed that the agent is a free nucleic acid. Incubation of crude extracts with nucleases revealed that the agent is sensitive to ribonuclease, but not to deoxyribonuclease (20). The observation that the agent could readily be concentrated by ethanol precipitation and resuspension in a small volume of buffer is compatible with the concept that the extractable agent is a free nucleic acid. Incubation of extracts with ribonuclease in media of high ionic strength disclosed that the agent partially survived this treatment. This property, as well as the elution pattern from columns of methylated serum albumin, suggested that the extractable agent may be a double-stranded RNA (20, 21).

Singh & Bagnall (71) extracted infectious nucleic acid from PSTV-infected tissue and compared some of its properties with those of PSTV in crude extracts. They found that, compared with the agent in a crude extract, the RNA had a greater infectivity dilution end point and higher thermal inactivation point, and was more sensitive to ribonuclease. Also, when infectivity of a crude extract was removed by heating or by incubation with ribonuclease, it could be restored by treatment with phenol (71). From comparative centrifugation studies, the authors concluded that no free infectious RNA was present in crude extracts, but did not specify what the RNA was bound to.

Results similar to those of Diener & Raymer (20) were reported by Semancik & Weathers (65), who worked with CEV. They found that most infectivity present in clarified extracts prepared from infected tissue remained in the supernatant solution after high-speed centrifugation; the authors came to the conclusion that the infectious entity possesses a sedimentation coefficient of about 10–15S. Because of these results and because no typical virus particles could be observed in electron micrographs of infectious aliquots, the authors suggested that "the virus might represent an infectious nucleic acid form perhaps analogous to either the unstable form of tobacco rattle virus, the nonassembling mutants of tobacco mosaic virus, or a protein-free, double-stranded RNA molecule."

A third plant pathogen, the agent of chrysanthemum stunt disease, was shown by Lawson (46) to have properties somewhat similar to those of PSTV and CEV. With this agent, however, the larger portion of the infectious entity was pelleted during high-speed centrifugation. The agent was shown to be sensitive to treatment with ribonuclease and could be concentrated by ethanol precipitation followed by resuspension. Treatment of such concentrated preparations with phenol yielded samples with infectivity comparable to that of the untreated preparations.

### *Absence of Virions*

Although there is little doubt that the slowly sedimenting infectious entities in preparations from PSTV-, CEV-, and chrysanthemum stunt-infected tissues are free RNA molecules, the question arises as to whether these infectious entities exist as such in situ or whether they are released from conventional virus particles during extraction.

So far, this question has been systematically studied only with PSTV. Diener (11) demonstrated that the sedimentation properties of the faster-sedimenting infectious material which is present in crude extracts (and which could presumably consist of virions) are not significantly altered by treatment of crude extracts with phenol or with phenol in the presence of sodium dodecyl sulfate. These results made it unlikely that the RNA is bound to protein or that it is present in the form of complete or partially degraded virions. This conclusion was strengthened by the observation that highly purified RNA preparations from PSTV-infected tissue also contain infectious material that sediments at faster rates than those expected of free RNA (11). If the faster-sedimenting infectious material were composed of viral nucleoprotein particles, these particles would, therefore, have most unusual properties. On the one hand, their protein coat would have to be loose enough to allow access to ribonuclease (since all infectivity is sensitive to treatment with ribonuclease); yet, on the other hand, these structures would have to be resistant to treatment with phenol and sodium dodecyl sulfate.

As there are apparently no known nucleoproteins with these properties, Diener (11) concluded that the faster-sedimenting infectious material is not composed of viral nucleoprotein particles.

This conclusion was further strengthened by the observation that, in situ, PSTV is sensitive to treatment with ribonuclease. Vacuum infiltration of ribonuclease solutions into PSTV-infected leaves resulted in complete or nearly complete loss of infectivity under conditions where the infectivity of conventional virus particles was not affected (13).

Zaitlin & Hariharasubramanian (79) analyzed proteins isolated from PSTV-infected leaves and compared them with proteins isolated from uninfected leaves. They found no evidence for the production in infected leaves of proteins that could be construed as coat proteins under conditions where coat protein of a defective strain of tobacco mosaic virus could readily be demonstrated.

If the RNA in the faster-sedimenting infectious material is not contained in virions, what is it bound to? In view of the strong dissociating properties of phenol, it is difficult to believe that the fast sedimentation rate of some infectious material is due to its association with protein. More likely, the RNA is bound to cellular constituents in complexes that are not degraded by phenol, or it occurs in aggregates of varying size. It was of interest, therefore, to determine the location of PSTV within infected cells.

### *Subcellular Location*

Bioassays of subcellular fractions from PSTV-infected tissue disclosed that appreciable infectivity is present only in the original tissue debris and in the fraction containing nuclei. Chloroplasts, mitochondria, ribosomes, and the soluble fraction contain no more than traces of infectivity. Furthermore, when chromatin was isolated from infected tissue, most infectivity was associated with it and could be extracted as free RNA with phosphate buffer (11). These and other experiments suggest that, in situ, PSTV is associated with the nuclei, and particularly with the chromatin, of infected cells. The significant amount of infectivity regularly present in the tissue debris most probably is a consequence of incomplete extraction of nuclei by the method chosen (43), but the possibility that some PSTV is associated with cell membranes cannot be ruled out at present.

The association of PSTV with chromatin may explain its heterogeneous sedimentation properties in crude extracts. In addition to free PSTV, PSTV associated with chromatin fragments of varying size may be present; and the latter entities may constitute the faster-sedimenting portions of infectious material.

Experiments with CEV disclosed that the infectious RNA is similarly located in the nuclei of infected cells and that it exists in close association with the chromatin (61).

### *Molecular Weight Estimates of Native Viroids*

Until very recently, attempts to determine physical and chemical properties of viroids were hampered by the fact that the RNAs could be recognized only by virtue of their biological activity, and not as physical entities. This handicap was particularly severe in efforts to determine the molecular weights of the RNAs.

Although it had been known for some time that PSTV sediments at a lower rate than single-stranded viral RNA molecules (20), no conclusions as to its molecular weight could be drawn from this observation, since the conformation of the RNA was unknown.

A principle elaborated by Loening (48), however, was thought to make it possible to obtain a molecular weight estimate based on biological activity alone. Loening reasoned that the effects of secondary structure of an RNA on its sedimentation properties are opposite to the effects of secondary structure on its electrophoretic mobility in polyacrylamide gels. Thus, a combination of the two analytical methods should be useful for distinguishing differences in structure from differences in weights of RNAs. With either method, biological activity is the only parameter necessary for evaluation of the results.

Application of this principle to PSTV led to the unexpected conclusion that the RNA has a very low molecular weight (12). An estimate of ca $5 \times 10^4$ daltons was in accord with the experimental results. Further evidence for the low molecular weight of PSTV came from the observation that the RNA is able to enter gels of high polyacrylamide concentration (i.e. small pore size), from which high molecular weight RNAs are excluded. In such gels, PSTV moves as a well defined, homogeneous band with a rate of migration that is compatible with the above molecular weight estimate (24).

Singh & Clark (72) reported some results that appear also to indicate that PSTV is an RNA of low molecular weight. They concluded from a determination of the electrophoretic mobility of PSTV in a 7.5% polyacrylamide gel that "peak infectivity corresponded to a particle size of 4–5 Svedberg units."

Partial purification of the infectious agent responsible for the chrysanthemum stunt disease by methods developed for the purification of PSTV, followed by sedimentation and electrophoretic analyses, demonstrated that the chrysanthemum stunt agent also is a low molecular weight RNA (19). The infectious RNA sediments at rates corresponding to values of 5–7.5S, and coelectrophoresis of the stunt RNA and PSTV in 20% polyacrylamide gels showed that the RNA migrates into such gels and moves through them as a well-defined, homogeneous band with a migration rate somewhat greater than that of PSTV.

With CEV, electrophoresis of infectious preparations in polyacrylamide gels indicated that the RNA has a molecular weight of $1.25 \times 10^5$ daltons, and suggested that a UV-absorbing component was correlated with infectivity distribution in the gels (68).

Sänger similarly examined CEV in polyacrylamide gels. His results, however, indicate that the RNA has a molecular weight of $5–6 \times 10^4$ daltons (61).

Although these determinations conclusively demonstrate that presently known viroids are low molecular weight RNAs, the molecular weight values arrived at must be regarded with caution for two reasons: First, all determinations are based on the electrophoretic mobility in polyacrylamide gels of native RNA molecules relative to RNA standards of known molecular weight. The electrophoretic mobilities of RNAs, however, are a function not only of their molecular weights (or, more correctly, of their molecular volumes), but also of their particular secondary and tertiary structures (9). Thus, if the examined viroids should appreciably differ in structure from the RNA standards used, the reported molecular weight values could be substantially in error. Second, results with PSTV suggest that the RNA may occur in several states of aggregation (12). Some of the values reported, therefore, may be based on aggregates, and not on the monomeric form of the RNA.

When native PSTV was analyzed in 3, 5, or 7.5% polyacrylamide gels, paucidisperse distribution of the RNA was observed with apparent molecular weight values mainly of about $5 \times 10^4$ and $1 \times 10^5$ daltons (12). Because of the 1:2 ratio of the apparent molecular weights and because of the fact that all of PSTV entered 20% polyacrylamide gels and migrated with an apparent molecular weight of $5 \times 10^4$ daltons (24), the hypothesis was advanced that native PSTV occurs in several states of aggregation, and that electrophoresis in gels of high concentration (small pore size) leads to disaggregation to the monomeric form of the RNA (12, 24).

In the case of CEV which, as mentioned above, may be identical with PSTV (69), Semancik et al reported that, at gel concentrations less than 8–10%, the RNA migrates with an apparent molecular weight of about $1 \times 10^5$ daltons, whereas at gel concentrations greater than 8–10%, it migrates with an apparent molecular weight of about $5 \times 10^4$ daltons (64). The authors accepted the $1 \times 10^5$ dalton value as correct and concluded that the migration of native CEV in high-percentage gels is aberrant, "presumably resulting from its unusual structural properties" (64).

Evidently, the discrepancy in the reported apparent molecular weights of native PSTV ($5 \times 10^4$ daltons) and native CEV ($1–1.25 \times 10^5$ daltons) is not a consequence of different experimental results, but of different interpretation of essentially identical results. If, as postulated, the greater electrophoretic mobility of CEV in gels of high concentration, as compared with that in gels of low concentration, were due to its aberrant mobility in the former gels, it is difficult to understand why this process should not gradually become more pronounced as the gel concentration is increased. This clearly is not the case. At a gel concentration of 8–10%, an abrupt change in migration rate occurs and no intermediate values are observed (64).

This sudden change in apparent molecular weight can readily be explained by the assumption that above a critical gel concentration (below a critical pore size) disaggregation of a dimer to a monomer occurs. This explanation appears plausible in view of the reported 1:2 ratio of the respective molecular weight values. Furthermore, Sänger reported an apparent molecular weight of $5–6 \times 10^4$ daltons for native CEV, irrespective of whether the RNA was analyzed in gels of 5, 10, 15, or 20% concentration (61). Evidently, aberrant migration of CEV is not an inherent property of the RNA. More likely, Sänger's method of CEV isolation (61) mostly results in the monomeric form of the RNA, whereas that of Semancik and co-workers (64) mostly results in RNA dimers which, when introduced into gels of high acrylamide concentration, disaggregate to monomers. Direct evidence for the existence of RNA aggregates in preparations of purified PSTV has been obtained by electron microscopy (see below).

## PURIFICATION

In view of these uncertainties, it became evident that further progress in the characterization of viroids required their isolation in purified form, followed by conventional biophysical and biochemical analyses.

As a first step towards purification of PSTV, nucleic acids were extracted from relatively large quantities of infected and healthy leaves. After removal of DNA, ribosomal RNAs, transfer RNA, and polysaccharides, the resulting preparations were analyzed by gel electrophoresis (14). In preparations from healthy leaves, at least three UV-absorbing components, aside from 5S RNA, were discernible; in preparations from infected leaves, the same components were present but, in addition, another prominent component was evident (14).

Bioassay of individual gel slices demonstrated that infectivity coincided with this component (14). This coincidence, the high level of infectivity, and the fact that this component does not occur in preparations from healthy leaves constitutes strong evidence that the component is PSTV.

With CEV also, a UV-absorbing component present in preparations from infected leaves, but not in preparations from healthy ones, could be detected in polyacrylamide gels (64, 68). Deviations from coincidence of the absorbance peak with infectivity distribution in the gels, however, were noticed; but these deviations were ascribed to technical difficulties involved in scanning and cutting the same gel (68).

Purification of PSTV in quantities sufficient for biophysical and biochemical analyses was achieved by subjecting preparations to electrophoresis in 20% polyacrylamide gels (with extended running time to assure complete separation of the RNA from normal host constituents), excising of the gel portion containing PSTV, and recovery of the RNA from the gel slices by a method involving hydroxyapatite chromatography and shaking with methoxyethanol (18).

Electrophoretic analysis of the final preparations revealed that only one UV-absorbing component was present, that this component had the same electrophoretic mobility as PSTV in less highly purified preparations, and that UV absorbance of the component coincided with infectivity distribution in the gel (14).

## PHYSICAL AND CHEMICAL PROPERTIES

### *Molecular Weight of PSTV*

With the availability of purified PSTV, a redetermination of its molecular weight based, not on its biological activity, but on its absorption of UV light, became possible.

For this purpose, a method described by Boedtker (9) was chosen because it permits the determination of the molecular weight of RNAs independent of their conformation (secondary or tertiary structure). With this method, RNAs are denatured with formaldehyde, and their relative electrophoretic mobilities are compared with those of similarly denatured RNA standards of known molecular weight.

Application of this principle to PSTV, using denatured tobacco ringspot satellite virus- (62), transfer-, ribosomal-, 5S-, and carnation mottle virus- (77) RNAs as molecular weight standards, indicated that the molecular weight of PSTV is in the range of 7.5–8.5 $\times 10^4$ daltons (26).

The pronounced discrepancy between this value and that obtained with native PSTV (5 $\times 10^4$ daltons) is most likely due to the compact structure of the RNA (see below) and illustrates the substantial error inherent in efforts to estimate molecular weights of viroids by gel electrophoresis of native molecules.

### *Thermal Denaturation of PSTV*

To determine whether PSTV is single- or double-stranded, the thermal denaturation of the RNA was studied. The total hyperchromicity shift of PSTV in 0.01 $\times$ SSC was found to be about 24% and the $T_M$ about 50°C (14). The thermal denaturation curve indicates that PSTV is not a regularly base-paired structure such as double-stranded RNA since, in this case, denaturation would be expected to occur over a much narrower temperature range and at higher temperatures. The curve does not, however, rule out an irregularly base-paired single-stranded RNA molecule, similar to transfer RNA, in which single-stranded regions alternate with base-paired regions.

Determination of the thermal denaturation properties of PSTV dissolved in buffer of higher ionic strength (0.1 $\times$ SSC) confirmed these conclusions since, again, denaturation occurred over a wide temperature range. Under these conditions, $T_M$ was ca 54°C (T. O. Diener, unpublished observations).

### *Radiation Sensitivity*

In view of the low molecular weight of PSTV, it was of interest to determine its sensitivity to irradiation with UV light. Although one might expect that a small molecule, such as PSTV, would be considerably more resistant to UV irradiation than a conventionally sized viral RNA or DNA, the effect of size on UV sensitivity of nucleic acids is not well understood (1).

Exposure of purified PSTV, of tobacco ringspot virus, and of its satellite to UV radiation of 254 nm showed that the inactivation dose for PSTV and satellite virus is 70 to 90 times as large as that for tobacco ringspot virus (23). Although other explanations are possible (23), this marked difference in sensitivity to UV radiation most likely is a consequence of the smaller size (smaller target volume) of PSTV and satellite RNA, as compared with tobacco ringspot virus RNA.

Semancik et al exposed preparations of CEV and tobacco mosaic virus to ionizing radiation and determined from comparative rates of biological inactivation a molecular weight of 1.1 $\times 10^5$ daltons for the target size of CEV (64).

### *Electron Microscopy of PSTV*

Sogo et al (73) processed purified preparations of PSTV for electron microscopy by the protein monolayer spreading technique of Kleinschmidt & Zahn (42).

When PSTV preparations in 4 *M* sodium acetate were spread onto a hypophase of distilled water, very short structures, mostly in compact aggregates but occasionally as separate particles, were revealed. These structures could not be detected in nucleic acid-free controls, and they were absent from preparations treated with ribonuclease (73).

Because of the association of PSTV molecules in aggregates, it was difficult to draw conclusions as to their length and structure. Consequently, methods which promised to dissociate the aggregates and to make possible the visualization of individual PSTV molecules were investigated. Indeed, large numbers of individual short strands of relatively uniform length were visible when PSTV preparations in 8 *M* urea were spread (73). No such strands were discernible in control samples or after treatment with ribonuclease. Average length of molecules was found to be ca 500 Å.

Since the mass per unit length is unknown, the lengths of PSTV molecules were compared with those of nucleic acids of known molecular weight, which were added to PSTV preparations and were thus treated identically.

Figure 1 shows an electron micrograph of a mixture of a double-stranded DNA, namely, coliphage $T_7$-DNA and PSTV. Measurements indicated that $T_7$-DNA is about 280 times longer than PSTV. It is also apparent that the width of PSTV is similar to that of $T_7$-DNA. Assuming a molecular weight of $T^7$-DNA of $25 \times 10^6$ daltons (44) and that PSTV in urea is formed by two more or less base-paired strands (either as a hairpin or a double helix), then one obtains a molecular weight estimate for PSTV of $8.9 \times 10^4$ daltons.

Electron microscopy of mixtures of PSTV and formaldehyde-denatured viral RNA [carnation mottle virus-RNA (41)] revealed that PSTV is thicker than this single-stranded RNA and that the viral RNA is about 17 times longer than denatured PSTV (73). This comparison leads to a molecular weight estimate of $7.9 \times 10^4$ daltons for PSTV.

The molecular weight estimates obtained by electron microscopy are, therefore, in excellent agreement with the values obtained from analysis of heat-denatured, formylated PSTV in polyacrylamide gels.

### *Molecular Structure of Viroids*

Although the low molecular weight of viroids has been conclusively demonstrated, a decision as to their exact structures cannot be made unambiguously in light of present knowledge. In some analytical systems, viroids display properties typical of double-stranded RNA, in others of single-stranded RNA.

Thus, the elution pattern of PSTV from columns of methylated serum albumin suggests double-strandedness (21), whereas the elution pattern from CF-11 cellulose columns (30) is consistent with both single- and double-stranded molecules (21). A possible explanation for this observation, however, may be deduced from the work of Engelhardt (28), who showed that the extent of secondary structure of an RNA has a profound influence on its elution pattern from such columns. He found that the greater the amount of secondary structure of an RNA at the time of addition to the column, the greater is the fraction that will elute in ethanol-free buffer; i.e. in the eluate that formerly was believed to consist solely of double-stranded RNA (30). Judged by this criterion, native PSTV has an extensive secondary structure.

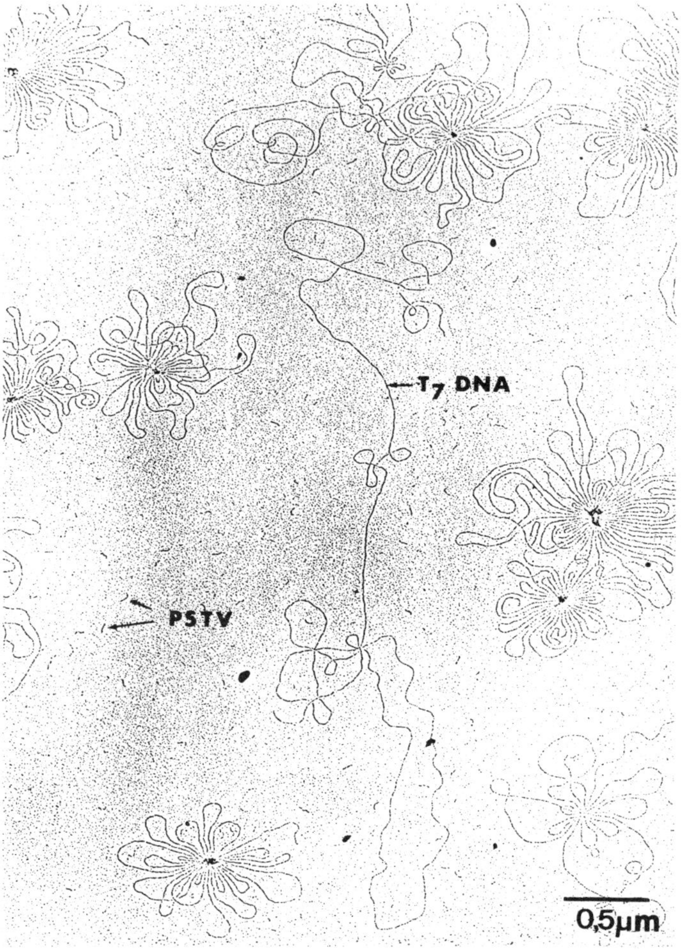


*Figure 1* Electron micrograph of PSTV mixed with a double-stranded DNA, coliphage $T_7$-DNA. (Courtesy of T. Koller and J. M. Sogo, Swiss Federal Institute of Technology, Zurich.)

From hydroxyapatite, on the other hand, PSTV elutes mostly at a phosphate buffer concentration lower than that expected of a double-stranded RNA (13, 47). Some PSTV, however, elutes at higher buffer concentration (13).

The thermal denaturation properties of PSTV clearly rule out a regularly base-paired double helix; yet, in electron micrographs, PSTV appears definitely thicker than single-stranded RNA, and of about equal thickness as double-stranded DNA (73).

Immunological tests made with antisera that react specifically with double-stranded RNA (63) gave no evidence for the presence of double-stranded RNA in highly infectious PSTV preparations (75). Heat-denatured, formylated PSTV, however, was shown to consist of two components with somewhat different electrophoretic mobilities (26).

With CEV, Semancik & Weathers (66) reported that the infectious RNA occurs in two forms, one sedimenting in the range of 10–15S, the other above 25S. Like PSTV, CEV elutes from columns of methylated serum albumin in the range of host DNA, but unlike PSTV, CEV elutes from cellulose columns almost exclusively in ethanol-free buffer (66). Although these properties are compatible with a double-stranded structure, attempts to melt the suspected double-stranded RNA or to observe any resistance to ribonuclease in a high ionic strength medium were unsuccessful. Later, however, the authors did achieve a suggestion of strand separation by heating and rapid cooling (67). They furthermore determined that the RNA is partially resistant to incubation with diethylpyrophosphate, a result that parallels those of Singh & Clark (72) with PSTV and suggests a structure that is at least partially double-stranded (53). Contrary to expectations, however, CEV is readily inactivated by formaldehyde (67).

As compared with single-stranded viral RNAs, CEV is remarkably resistant to inactivation by heating and by exonucleases (66, 67). The latter property exocortis RNA shares with PSTV (13, 72). Although resistance to inactivation by exonucleases may suggest a circular structure of the RNA (13, 66), the degree of resistance was later considered insufficient to postulate this (67, 72).

On the basis of its low buoyant density in cesium sulfate equilibrium density gradients, Semancik & Weathers suggested that CEV is either a low molecular weight, transfer RNA-like RNA or a RNA-DNA hybrid molecule (67), but showed later (68) that the duration of sedimentation had been insufficient to achieve equilibrium of low molecular weight RNAs.

In summary, two models are compatible with these properties of viroids: 1. The RNAs may be single-stranded molecules with some sort of hairpin structure, involving extensive base-pairing, or 2. the RNAs may be double-stranded, but incompletely base-paired, molecules.

## BIOLOGICAL PROPERTIES

### *Replication*

The low molecular weight of viroids raises the question as to how such RNAs can contain sufficient genetic information to induce their replication in susceptible hosts. The molecular weight of PSTV is sufficient only to code for 70 to 80 amino acids, i.e. it is barely sufficient to code for a very small protein, but not for a subunit of a specific RNA-dependent RNA polymerase (replicase) of a size comparable to those of known replicase subunits (38).

It is conceivable, however, that PSTV is not a single molecular species, but rather a population of several RNA molecules of similar length, with different nucleotide sequences, which together may comprise a viral genome of more or less conventional size. As discussed previously (15, 17), existing knowledge does not support this model, and the high resistance of PSTV to UV (23) and of CEV to ionizing radiation

(64) may be interpreted as further evidence for the smallness of the PSTV and CEV genomes.

Possibly, synthesis of viroids is a normal capacity of the host genome which, however, is completely repressed in normal plants. If so, viroids act as derepressors of this latent capacity, either directly or via a polypeptide translated from the RNA. Such a scheme invites the question as to why a completely repressed DNA segment which contains genetic information detrimental to the organism should be maintained during evolution. Also, one would expect that spontaneous derepression of the DNA segment occasionally would occur. Large-scale commercial cultivation of tomato plants without reported outbreaks of the disease incited by PSTV indicates that this is not the case.

More plausible, at first glance, is the assumption that PSTV is similar to a satellite RNA that requires a helper virus for its own replication. Efforts to demonstrate the presence of such a helper virus in uninoculated tomato plants gave negative results (12). They revealed, however, that if such a virus exists, it must be vertically transmitted through the seed to every single progeny plant. As discussed previously (12), high rates of seed transmission of plant viruses are relatively rare. Since PSTV is able to replicate in a number of solanaceous plant species, aside from potato and tomato (54), hypothetical helper viruses would have to be involved in PSTV replication in these species also. In O'Brien and Raymer's tests, such viruses could have been introduced into the plants concurrently with PSTV during inoculation with crude sap from infected plants. Diener et al (25), however, showed that solanaceous plant species that can be infected with PSTV-containing crude extracts can also be infected with low molecular weight RNA eluted from polyacrylamide gels. Thus, if helper viruses are involved in the replication of PSTV, such viruses must be universally present in apparently normal plants of a number of solanaceous plant species.

In view of these and other results (12, 15, 17), it appears unlikely that helper viruses are involved. Hence, PSTV, in spite of its small size, appears to be able to replicate autonomously in susceptible plants. So far, nothing is known about the biochemical mechanisms of this process; theoretically possible schemes have been discussed elsewhere (15, 17).

### *Pathogenesis*

In view of the small amount of genetic information which viroids introduce into their host cells, it is surprising that in certain hosts they are able to incite severe diseases with a variety of symptoms resembling those of typical virus infections. Since only very small amounts of the known viroids are present in infected tissues, it is unlikely that a shortage of nucleotides available for host nucleic acid synthesis is responsible for these derangements. This contention is supported by the fact that in many hosts viroids are replicated efficiently without obvious damage to the host (54, 61).

A more specific interference with host metabolic functions, therefore, appears to occur. Viroids might, for example, act as abnormal transfer RNAs, with the result that faulty proteins are synthesized; or they might interfere with host genome transcription, either by repressing normally expressed cistrons, or by derepressing normally repressed cistrons. Alternatively, interference may be via a polypeptide translated from the viroid RNA. Because of their limited information content, viroids should be useful model systems in efforts to elucidate the biochemical mechanisms of pathogenesis on the molecular level.

### *Transmission*

The presently known viroids are transmissible by mechanical means, either readily (PSTV and chrysanthemum stunt viroid) or with some difficulty (CEV). With PSTV, mechanical transmission is mainly responsible for the spread of the disease in nature (22). In view of the absence of protective protein coats, survival of the RNA during this process was difficult to understand until it became clear that PSTV and CEV are located within the nuclei of infected cells, where they are well protected from enzymatic attack (61). Presumably, during natural transmission pieces of nuclei containing PSTV or fragments of PSTV-containing chromatin rather than free RNA are transferred from infected into normal cells.

PSTV is transmitted vertically either through the pollen or the ovules of infected potato or tomato plants (29, 35, 70). Vertical transmission rates vary from 0 to 100%, depending on the individual collection tested (29).

## IMPLICATIONS

In light of present knowledge, there is little doubt that PSTV, CEV, and the chrysanthemum stunt viroid are the first known representatives of a novel class of subviral pathogens consisting solely of a monocistronic genome. They are the smallest known agents of infectious disease.

### *Question of Viroid Origin*

The question arises as to whether viroids are related to viruses or to cellular RNAs. Analogies may be drawn with certain RNAs occurring in virus-infected cells or, alternatively, with certain normal cellular RNAs.

In recent years, low molecular weight RNAs have been found in association with a number of virus infections. Reich et al (59) showed that a new low molecular weight RNA appears in the soluble fraction of the cytoplasm at the late stage of the replicative cycle of adenoviruses in KB cells. This RNA is found only in infected cells. Its nucleotide sequence has been determined (56), and the authors concluded that it is a unique species of RNA with large regions of intramolecular base-pairs (57). Ohe (55) showed that the RNA is coded for by the viral DNA. Its function is unknown, but Ohe (55) suggested a specific participation of this low molecular weight RNA in the process of adenovirus multiplication.

Low molecular weight RNA has also been identified in *Escherichia coli* infected with $Q\beta$ bacteriophage (6) and after induction of prophage $\lambda$ (49). Similarly, infection of tobacco leaves with tobacco mosaic virus (5, 37), and of broadbean leaves with broadbean mottle virus (60), lead to the appearance of low molecular weight RNAs that are not present in uninfected leaves.

In purified virions of Rous sarcoma virus (8) and of other oncogenic RNA viruses (34), low molecular weight RNAs have been shown to occur.

The function of none of these RNAs is known, and it is not clear whether they are related to one another. If, however, the synthesis of unique species of low molecular weight RNAs is a common consequence of virus infection, one might speculate that viroids developed from low molecular weight RNAs which were originally virus-induced, but which have become autonomous. They would thus represent degenerate viral entities.

RNAs with some properties of double-stranded RNA have been identified in a variety of apparently uninfected animal cells (27, 51, 74, 76), as well as in tomato leaves (47). Significantly, synthesis of some of these RNAs is less sensitive to treatment with actinomycin D than is that of the major cellular RNA species (51, 74).

Although other interpretations are possible, Montagnier (52) suggested that "some self-replicating RNAs may have become part of cell genetic information"; and Stern & Friedman (74) concluded that "the assumption that the synthesis of all informational RNA in normal mammalian cells is directed by DNA templates must be held in abeyance until the origin of the present RNA has been determined."

Some of these RNAs share certain properties with viroids. Stern & Friedman (74) pointed out that although the RNA studied by them has many properties of double-stranded RNA, it is not a simple base-paired structure. Its sedimentation coefficient, its sensitivity to ribonuclease in media of low and high ionic strength, its elution from Sephadex G-100 columns, its properties after heating to 100°C followed by quick-cooling, and its properties after treatment with dimethyl sulfoxide all resemble properties of PSTV.

In view of these results, it is tempting to speculate that, as discussed previously (12), RNAs which are synthesized on RNA templates may occur in most, if not all, seemingly healthy cells. If so, viroids may have originated from these cellular RNAs. They might thus be regarded as primitive viral entities which have neither achieved the genetic sophistication to induce in susceptible hosts novel biosynthetic machinery for their own replication, nor to code for specific coat proteins.

Low molecular weight RNAs, aside from transfer RNA and 5 S ribosomal RNA, occur in normal cells, particularly in nuclei and nucleoli (58, 78), and are associated with chromatin (7). Although the function of these RNAs is unknown, it has been suggested that certain nuclear RNAs may have a role in regulating some nuclear functions, and that they may be involved in the regulation of RNA transcription from the genome (31). Kanehisa et al (39, 40) added credence to such concepts by demonstrating that RNA synthesis in a cell-free system of *E. coli* polymerase with chromatin as template was stimulated by the addition of a low molecular weight chromatin RNA whereas, with DNA as template, RNA synthesis was inhibited by addition of this RNA.

Conceivably PSTV, which is associated with chromatin, and which is in the same molecular weight range, may be related to certain normal nuclear or nucleolar RNAs. One might speculate that PSTV, and presumably other viroids, originated from nuclear RNAs which are normal constituents of the organism and which are essential for its development. The change from a normal constituent to a pathogenic RNA might have occurred either by mutation or by chance introduction into a foreign species, in which the RNA is replicated. In either case, the disease would be a consequence of interference with the functions of normally occurring nuclear RNAs.

### *Question of Animal Viroids*

Although the viroids so far identified cause diseases of higher plants, similar agents may exist in other forms of life. It appears reasonable to search for viroids in the many instances where viral etiology of an infectious disease has been assumed, but where no causative agent has ever been identified.

One case in point is the agent of the scrapie disease of sheep. Based on comparisons of known properties of PSTV with those of the scrapie agent, the hypothesis has been advanced that the latter may also be a viroid (16).

From the dose of ionizing radiation required to give an average of one inactivating event per infective unit of scrapie, Alper et al (3) calculated a target volume corresponding to a molecular weight of $1.5 \times 10^5$ daltons and concluded that this target size "is implausibly small as a nucleic acid code." This value, however, is compatible with the proposition that the agent is a viroid.

The scrapie agent is known to be highly resistant to UV irradiation (33, 45) and this high resistance has led some investigators to suggest that scrapie does not depend on a nucleic acid replicating system (4). Other investigators believe, however, that the high resistance of the scrapie agent to UV irradiation does not necessarily rule out nucleic acid as the genetic material (1).

Since the scrapie agent so far has not been separated from cellular constituents (36), all experiments with scrapie have been made with relatively crude extracts from infected tissue. Hence, energy-transfer processes, interactions between parts of a complex (45), or shielding from UV radiation by surrounding structures (1) may all contribute to the apparent high resistance of the scrapie agent to UV irradiation.

Although purified PSTV does not appear to be as resistant to UV irradiation as the scrapie agent, definitive comparisons await purification of the scrapie agent. Recent results (23) suggest, however, that low molecular weight nucleic acids are far more resistant to UV irradiation than high molecular weight nucleic acids.

Trace amounts of a small, single-stranded DNA have been identified in extracts from scrapie-infected brains, but not in extracts from healthy brains (2). No evidence exists, however, as to whether or not this DNA is specific scrapie agent DNA (2).

Other infectious animal diseases where a viroid etiology may be suspected include transmissible mink encephalopathy (50), Kuru (32), and Creutzfeldt-Jakob disease (10). Recently, Zuckerman (80) advanced the hypothesis that hepatitis may be caused by viroids.

Evidently, only future work will determine whether some of these, and possibly other infectious diseases of obscure etiology, are caused by agents resembling presently known viroids affecting higher plants.

*Literature Cited*


1. Adams, D. H. 1970. *Pathol. Biol.* 18:559–77
2. Adams, D. H. 1972. *J. Neurochem.* 19:1869–82
3. Alper, T., Haig, D. A., Clarke, M. C. 1966. *Biochem. Biophys. Res. Commun.* 22:278–84
4. Alper, T., Cramp, W. A., Haig, D. A., Clarke, M. C. 1967. *Nature* 214: 764–66
5. Babos, P., Shearer, G. B. 1969. *Virology* 39:286–95
6. Banerjee, A. K., Rensing, U., August, J. T. 1969. *J. Mol. Biol.* 45:181–93
7. Benjamin, W., Levander, O. A., Gellhorn, A., DeBellis, R. H. 1966. *Proc. Nat. Acad. Sci. USA* 55:858–65
8. Bishop, J. M. et al 1970. *Virology* 42:927–37
9. Boedtker, H. 1971. *Biochim. Biophys. Acta* 240:448–53
10. Cathala, F., Brown, P. 1973. *Pathol. Biol.* 21:299–308
11. Diener, T. O. 1971. *Virology* 43:75–89
12. Ibid 45:411–28
13. Diener, T. O. 1971. *Comparative Virology,* ed. K. Maramorosch, E. Kurstak, 433–78. New York: Academic. 584 pp.
14. Diener, T. O. 1972. *Virology* 50:606–9
15. Diener, T. O. 1972. *Advan. Virus Res.* 17:295–313
16. Diener, T. O. 1972. *Nature New Biol.* 235:218–19
17. Diener, T. O. 1973. *Perspect. Virol.* 8:7–30
18. Diener, T. O. 1973. *Anal. Biochem.* 55:317–20
19. Diener, T. O., Lawson, R. H. 1973. *Virology* 51:94–101
20. Diener, T. O., Raymer, W. B. 1967. *Science* 158:378–81
21. Diener, T. O., Raymer, W. B. 1969. *Virology* 37:351–66
22. Diener, T. O., Raymer, W. B. 1971. *Descriptions of Plant Viruses,* No. 66. Kew, Surrey, England: Commonw. Mycol. Inst. Assoc. Appl. Biol. 4 pp.
23. Diener, T. O., Schneider, I. R., Smith, D. R. 1974. *Virology* 57:577–81
24. Diener, T. O., Smith, D. R. 1971. *Virology* 46:498–99
25. Diener, T. O., Smith, D. R., O'Brien, M. J. 1972. *Virology* 48:844–46
26. Diener, T. O., Smith, D. R. 1973. *Virology* 53:359–65
27. Duesberg, P. H., Colby, C. 1969. *Proc. Nat. Acad. Sci. USA* 64:396–403
28. Engelhardt, D. L. 1972. *J. Virol.* 9:903–8
29. Fernow, K. H., Peterson, L. C., Plaisted, R. L. 1970. *Am. Potato J.* 47:75–80
30. Franklin, R. M. 1966. *Proc. Nat. Acad. Sci. USA* 55:1504–11
31. Frenster, J. H. 1965. *Nature* 206: 680–83
32. Gajdusek, D. C., Gibbs, C. J., Alpers, M. 1966. *Nature* 209:794–96
33. Haig, D. A., Clarke, M. C., Blum, E., Alper, T. 1969. *J Gen. Virol.* 5:455–57
34. Harter, D. H., Schlom, J., Spiegelman, H. 1971. *Biochim. Biophys. Acta* 240:435–41
35. Hunter, D. E., Darling, H. M., Beale, W. L. 1969. *Am. Potato J.* 46:247–50
36. Hunter, G. D., Millson, G. C. 1967. *J. Comp. Pathol.* 77:301–7
37. Jackson, A. O., Zaitlin, M., Siegel, A., Francki, R. I. B. 1972. *Virology* 48: 655–65
38. Kamen, R. 1970. *Nature* 228:527–33
39. Kanehisa, T., Fujitani, H., Sano, M., Tanaka, T. 1971. *Biochim. Biophys. Acta* 240:46–55
40. Kanehisa, T., Tanaka, T., Kano, Y. 1972. *Biochim. Biophys. Acta* 277:584–89
41. Kaper, J. M., Waterworth, H. E. 1973. *Virology* 51:183–90
42. Kleinschmidt, A. K., Zahn, R. K. 1959. *Z. Naturforsch. B* 14:770–79
43. Kühl, L. 1964. *Z. Naturforsch. B* 19:525–32
44. Lang, D. 1970. *J. Mol. Biol.* 54:557–65
45. Latarjet, R., Muel, B., Haig, D. A., Clarke, M. C., Alper, T. 1970. *Nature* 227:1341–43
46. Lawson, R. H. 1968. *Phytopathology* 58:885 (Abstr.)
47. Lewandowski, L. J., Kimball, P. C., Knight, C. A. 1971. *J. Virol.* 8:809–12
48. Loening, U. E. 1967. *Biochem. J.* 102:251–57
49. Marcaud, L., Portier, M. M., Kourilsky, P., Barrell, B. G., Gros, F. 1971. *J. Mol. Biol.* 57:247–61
50. Marsh, R. F., Hanson, R. P. 1969. *J. Virol.* 3:176–80
51. Montagnier, L. 1968. *C. R. Acad. Sci. Ser. D.* 267:1417–20
52. Montagnier, L. 1968. *Symp. Soc. Gen. Microbiol.* 18:125–48
53. Öberg, B. 1970. *Biochim. Biophys. Acta* 204:430–40
54. O'Brien, M. J., Raymer, W. B. 1964. *Phytopathology* 54:1045–47
55. Ohe, K. 1972. *Virology* 47:726–33
56. Ohe, K., Weissman, S. M. 1970. *Science* 167:879–80

57. Ohe, K., Weissman, S. M. 1971. *J. Biol. Chem.* 246:6991–7009
58. Prestayko, A. W., Tonato, M., Busch, H. 1970. *J. Mol. Biol.* 47:505–15
59. Reich, P. R., Forget, B. G., Weissman, S. M., Rose, J. A. 1966. *J. Mol. Biol.* 17:428–39
60. Romero, J. 1972. *Virology* 48:591–94
61. Sänger, H. L. 1972. *Advan. Biosci.* 8:103–16
62. Schneider, I. R. 1971. *Virology* 45:108–22
63. Schwartz, E. F., Stollar, B. D. 1969. *Biochem. Biophys. Res. Commun.* 35:115–20
64. Semancik, J. S., Morris, T. J., Weathers, L. G. 1973. *Virology* 53:448–56
65. Semancik, J. S., Weathers, L. G. 1968. *Virology* 36:326–28
66. Semancik, J. S., Weathers, L. G. 1970. *Phytopathology* 60:732–36
67. Semancik, J. S., Weathers, L. G. 1972. *Virology* 47:456–66
68. Semancik, J. S., Weathers, L. G. 1972. *Nature New Biol.* 237:242–44
69. Semancik, J. S., Weathers, L. G. 1972. *Virology* 49:622–25
70. Singh, R. P. 1970. *Am. Potato J.* 47:225–27
71. Singh, R. P., Bagnall, R. H. 1968. *Phytopathology* 58:696–99
72. Singh, R. P., Clark, M. C. 1971. *Biochem. Biophys. Res. Commun.* 44:1077–83
73. Sogo, J. M., Koller, T., Diener, T. O. 1973. *Virology* 55:70–80
74. Stern, R., Friedman, R. M. 1970. *Nature* 226:612–16
75. Stollar, B. D., Diener, T. O. 1971. *Virology* 46:168–70
76. Stollar, V., Stollar, B. D. 1970. *Proc. Nat. Acad. Sci. USA* 65:993–1000
77. Waterworth, H. E., Kaper, J. M. 1972. *Phytopathology* 62:959–64
78. Weinberg, R. A., Penman, S. 1968. *J. Mol. Biol.* 38:289–304
79. Zaitlin, M., Hariharasubramanian, V. 1972. *Virology* 47:296–305
80. Zuckerman, A. J. 1973. *Lancet* i:1486–87

# BACTERIAL PHOTOSYNTHESIS ❖1629

*William W. Parson*
Department of Biochemistry, University of Washington, Seattle, Washington 98195

CONTENTS

INTRODUCTION .......... 41
ANTENNA BACTERIOCHLOROPHYLL-PROTEIN COMPLEXES .......... 41
$P_{870}$ .......... 43
CYTOCHROMES .......... 45
PRIMARY AND SECONDARY ELECTRON ACCEPTORS .......... 50
OVERVIEW AND UNANSWERED QUESTIONS .......... 53

## I. INTRODUCTION

Bacterial photosynthesis begins with the absorption of light by an array of light-harvesting, or antenna, bacteriochlorophyll (BChl)[1]. Energy migrates rapidly across the antenna until it reaches a specialized site, where an electron-transfer reaction occurs. This review will consider the structure of the light-harvesting antenna and then will examine the electron carriers that participate in the photochemical reaction and the secondary reactions that follow. It will touch only briefly on how the electron-transfer reactions drive the phosphorylation of ADP. Because controversy and mystery continue to enshroud the study of bacterial photosynthesis, the discussion represents the author's personal view more than it does a consensus of workers in the field.

## II. ANTENNA BACTERIOCHLOROPHYLL-PROTEIN COMPLEXES

Most, if not all, of the antenna pigments probably occur noncovalently bound to proteins. The best known of the BChl-protein complexes is one which Olson and his colleagues (126, 131, 178) have isolated from the green bacterium *Chlorobium limicola* (*Chloropseudomonas ethylica*) and *Chl. thiosulfatophilum.* This is a water-soluble protein with a molecular weight of 152,000, which can be crystallized after

[1]Abbreviations: BChl, bacteriochlorophyll; BPh, bacteriopheophytin; CD, circular dichroism; $E_{m7}$, midpoint redox potential at pH 7; EPR, electron paramagnetic resonance; SDS, sodium dodecylsufate; UQ, ubiquinone.

purification without the use of detergents. It contains four subunits, each with five BChl molecules (178). The multibanded CD and absorption spectra of the complex indicate that all five of the BChl molecules within a subunit interact strongly, so as to delocalize excitons extensively over the assembly (131, 139). The hopping of energy from one subunit to another or between different complexes may entail a slower process, better described in terms of weaker resonance interaction or localized exciton migration.

Much larger BChl-protein complexes also have been obtained from the *Chlorobacteriaceae* (59, 60, 131). These contain a photochemical reaction center in addition to light-harvesting BChl. The spectral properties of their light-harvesting pigments differ somewhat from those of the pigments in the purified light-harvesting protein, but no information is available on the structural changes that underlie this difference.

Extraction of pigment-protein complexes from the purple photosynthetic bacteria requires the aid of detergents or organic solvents. These more drastic techniques naturally raise technical problems, including perturbation of the protein structure and degradation of the BChl to BPh. (In BPh, two protons replace the Mg of BChl).

On disruption of *Rhodopseudomonas spheroides* chromatophores with detergents, the antenna BChl emerges in association with a polypeptide with a molecular weight of about 10,000. Fraker & Kaplan (62, 63) have isolated this hydrophobic protein by solubilization of chromatophores with 2-chloroethanol, followed by SDS-gel electrophoresis. The product contains phospholipid and about 1.4 equivalents of BPh per mole of protein. It gives no immunological cross-reaction with the BChl-protein of the green bacteria. Clayton & Clayton (22) have described gentler isolation procedures employing the detergent lauryldimethylamine oxide, and have shown that at least 60% of the BChl in the chromatophores is associated with the small protein. Their procedures appear to provide the BChl-protein initially in the form of large aggregates with molecular weights exceeding 100,000. These dissociate into the small units upon boiling with 1.5% SDS.

From *Chromatium vinosum,* Thornber (177) has isolated a large light-harvesting pigment-protein assembly, with a molecular weight of approximately 100,000. The complete complex contains about 10 BChl molecules, along with several carotenoid molecules (177). SDS-gel electrophoresis under dissociating conditions indicates that most of the BChl in *C. vinosum* is associated with polypeptides with molecular weights on the order of 10,000 (Y. Halsey, personal communication).

Treatment of chromatophores from *Rps. spheroides* or *Rhodospirillum rubrum* with urea and Triton at high pH affords a preparation which appears to have a molecular weight near 100,000 and which contains both a photochemical reaction center and many molecules of light-harvesting BChl (108, 110). Loach et al (108, 110) have interpreted this to mean that the reaction center and the antenna assembly occur together in the membrane, in complete photoreceptor subunits. Electrophoresis in the presence of SDS reveals that their preparation contains the 10,000 molecular weight pigment-protein complexes, along with the reaction center polypeptides (see below) and other materials (23). The light-harvesting BChl in the preparation is able to transfer energy efficiently to the reaction center, indicating that the two components must somehow associate closely (108).

A carotenoid-protein complex has been obtained from *Rds. rubrum,* after solubilization of chromatophores with SDS (154). It appears to contain one equivalent of spirilloxanthin on a polypeptide with a molecular weight of about 12,000. The absorption spectrum of the isolated complex is quite different from that of the carotenoids in the intact membrane. How energy can transfer efficiently from carotenoids to the BChl-protein complexes is a special problem. Excited states of carotenoids generally undergo radiationless internal conversion to the ground state so rapidly that they are essentially nonfluorescent.

In summary, the antenna pigments in the *Thiorhodaceae* and *Athiorhodaceae* seem to occur on hydrophobic polypeptides with molecular weights on the order of 10,000, with each polypeptide holding a small number of pigment molecules. These complexes associate to form larger assemblies, bringing many molecules of pigment into interaction in a manner that remains to be elucidated.

## III. $P_{870}$

The electron donor in the primary electron-transfer reaction is a complex called $P_{870}$, with P standing for pigment, and 870 for a wavelength at which bleaching of a major absorption band occurs when the complex loses an electron (1, 20, 52). The oxidation of $P_{870}$ also results in other absorbance changes throughout the UV, visible, and IR regions of the spectrum. Although the positions of the maxima and minima in the absorption spectrum vary among different species of photosynthetic bacteria (especially if one turns to species that contain BChl b) (70, 103), the basic properties of the reactive complex probably are much the same (140), and the name $P_{870}$ is useful in a general sense.

The proposal that $P_{870}$ oxidation was the primary electron-transfer reaction of bacterial photosynthesis reached firm ground with the demonstration that the reaction occurred with high speed and with a quantum yield of approximately 1.0, following the illumination of chromatophores with a brief flash from a Q-switched laser (134). Cytochrome oxidation, which also occurred with high quantum yield, proved to be a secondary reaction in which an electron moved from the cytochrome to $P_{870}^+$. This was shown by measurements of the absorbance changes that accompany the reduction of $P_{870}^+$ and the oxidation of the cytochrome, following the flash; the kinetics of the two processes were identical (134). (For a review of this work, see reference 137.)

Studies of $P_{870}$ entered the realm of biochemistry in 1968, when Reed & Clayton (144) succeeded in purifying a protein-pigment complex that contained $P_{870}$ but was free of antenna BChl. Subsequent work done by Clayton, Reed, Feher, and others (27, 55, 125, 143) has refined the purification procedure, leading to purer and simpler preparations. A typical recent protocol (27) for preparation of reaction center particles from *Rps. spheroides* strain R-26 (a carotenoidless mutant) includes treatment of chromatophores with lauryldimethylamine oxide, centrifugation in a sucrose gradient, fractionation with ammonium sulfate, and Agarose column chromatography. The product exhibits all of the spectral properties that characterize $P_{870}$ in chromatophores and intact cells. The $P_{870}$ in the preparation responds to illumination by undergoing photooxidation with a quantum yield of 1.02 ± 0.04 (186).

On polyacrylamide gel electrophoresis with 1% SDS, the reaction center particle dissociates into three proteins, with molecular weights of approximately 21,000, 24,000, and 28,000 (23, 125, 164). All of the pigments dissociate from the proteins under these conditions. Under gentler conditions, the largest protein can be split from the two smaller members of the trio, leaving them holding all of the pigment (125). The complex of the two lighter proteins still is photochemically active. Like those of many membrane proteins, the amino acid compositions of all three of the reaction center proteins are strongly hydrophobic: approximately 70% of the amino acids are nonpolar (164).

Reaction center preparations also have been obtained from wild-type *Rhodopseudomonas spheroides,* from *Rps. viridis,* and from *Rhodospirillum rubrum* (79, 121, 148, 159, 160, 162, 164, 179), but each species has demanded its own special preparative procedures. *Chromatium vinosum* and the green bacteria *Chlorobium limicola* and *Chl. thiosulphatophilum* have yielded preparations which are enriched in $P_{870}$, but which also contain some antenna BChl (59, 60, 131, 177). The three distinguishing polypeptides have been detected in *Rsp. rubrum,* and in *Rps. capsulata* and *palustris,* though not in *Rps. gelatinosa* or *viridis* (23). The amino acid composition of the *Rds. rubrum* preparation is similar to that from *Rps. spheroides,* but it differs somewhat in detail, and the two preparations surprisingly give no immunological cross-reaction (164).

In addition to protein, reaction center preparations generally contain BChl, BPh, nonheme Fe, and UQ. In this case, the BPh appears to be a true component of the reaction center, rather than a degradation product or a contaminant (146, 165). To determine the number of each of the pigments that make up one functional unit, reaction center preparations from *Rps. spheroides* R-26 were illuminated with short flashes in the presence of mitochondrial cytochrome *c* (86, 165). $P_{870}^+$, generated during the flash, was reduced again rapidly by the cytochrome. Because molar extinction coefficients were known for the cytochrome, a comparison of the absorbance changes due to the reduction of $P_{870}^+$ with those due to the oxidation of the cytochrome provided extinction coefficients for $P_{870}$. Taken with analytical data, this information allowed the conclusion that each functional reaction center contains four molecules of BChl and two of BPh (146, 165).

The CD spectrum of reaction center particles shows that at least three of the four BChl molecules interact strongly (139, 145, 152). Fluorescence polarization measurements (54) agree with the CD measurements in showing that the BChl planes cannot all be parallel, but little else is certain of the geometry of the complex. The two BPh molecules appear to interact less strongly with the BChl, judging from the CD spectrum (139), although they do sensitize photochemistry effectively (187). On loss of an electron from the complex, the CD spectrum changes profoundly, revealing a disruption of the interaction that occurs among the BChl molecules in the reduced complex. EPR and electron nuclear double resonance (ENDOR) measurements (56, 113, 122, 123) show that the oxidized complex contains a radical cation in which two of the four BChl molecules share the unpaired electron. Model studies with simpler porphyrin cations and $^{25}$Mg EPR measurements on the reaction center complex indicate that the unpaired electron delocalizes over the porphyrin rings of the BChl molecules, rather than confining itself to the Mg atoms (42, 43).

In a model which Katz & Norris (85) have proposed, two of the BChl molecules link through a water molecule, and it is these two that lose an electron on photooxidation and share the remaining unpaired electron. The CD spectra suggest that the two additional BChl molecules interact through the central pair from roughly opposite sides; the oxidation of the central pair would disrupt this interaction (145, 152).

The question has arisen frequently whether photosynthetic bacteria contain other photochemical reaction centers in addition to $P_{870}$ (37, 39, 61, 64, 66, 67, 69, 117, 153, 168, 170). In the author's opinion, there is no convincing evidence that they do. One impetus for postulating additional reaction centers has been the observation that illumination can cause IR absorbance changes other than those due to $P_{870}$. In *Chr. vinosum,* for example, illumination can lead to absorbance increases at 905 and 850 nm and decreases at 800 and 836 nm, even under conditions that do not reveal photooxidation of $P_{870}$ (14, 37, 153, 183, 184). But these absorbance changes almost certainly are due to shifts in the absorption spectrum of the antenna BChl, rather than to the oxidation or reduction of a second reaction-center BChl (14). The absorption band shifts appear to reflect electrical fields that are set up in the membrane as a result of electron transfer in the $P_{870}$ reaction center (see section VI). In *Chr. vinosum,* the band shifts do not occur when $P_{870}$ itself becomes oxidized, but rather when $P_{870}^+$ in turn oxidizes a particular cytochrome (cytochrome $c_{555}$) (14). This means that under steady illumination the band shifts can be most pronounced when $P_{870}$ remains predominantly in the reduced form. A similar association of the band shifts with a particular cytochrome could explain the anomalous absorbance changes that have been observed (5a, 61, 101, 168, 170) in *Rds. rubrum.*

## IV. CYTOCHROMES

Shortly after its appearance, $P_{870}^+$ extracts an electron from a *c*-type cytochrome. At this point, the photosynthetic bacteria reveal their diversity, displaying a bewildering array of cytochromes (6, 71, 83). But there are several common themes. All species that have been examined contain at least two pools of different types of cytochromes. One of these invariably is a *c*-type cytochrome with a midpoint potential ($E_m$) on the order of 0.3 V (somewhat lower in the *Chlorobacteriaceae*), and this cytochrome appears to react directly with $P_{870}^+$ in all cases. Many species also contain a *c*-type cytochrome with an $E_m$ near 0 V. In some cases, the low-potential cytochrome also has been shown to react directly with $P_{870}^+$; in other cases, this point has not yet been settled. Finally, some species contain *b*-type cytochromes. These evidently do not transfer electrons directly to $P_{870}^+$, but react instead with the high-potential *c*-type cytochrome. This section will describe some of the cytochrome systems that have been studied most extensively.

The finding that illumination can result in the oxidation of several different cytochromes has provided an additional reason for asking whether the photosynthetic bacteria contain several different types of photochemical reaction centers. If all of the light-harvesting pigments funnel energy to a single type of reaction center, one might expect to find the same action spectrum for all of the reactions that occur there. In other words, the quantum yield for oxidation of one of the cytochromes, relative to that for another, should not depend on the wavelength of the actinic illumination. Contrary to this expectation, different action spectra have been described for the photooxidation of the low- and high-potential *c*-type cytochromes in both *Chromatium vinosum* and *Rhodospirillum rubrum* (117, 169). In the case of *Chr. vinosum,* these observations were not readily confirmed (138). But even if the action spectra do differ, one need not conclude that a reaction center other than $P_{870}$ oxidizes one of the cytochromes. Action spectra can be misleading for several reasons. First, measurements that are made with continuous illumination may conceal a cycling of some of the components. Further, one almost invariably must provide different conditions for the determination of the two action spectra. The net oxidation of one cytochrome may, for example, demand a higher light intensity or a longer period of illumination than does that of the other. As a result of the difference of conditions, the efficiency of energy transfer from the light-harvesting complexes to $P_{870}$ may not be the same. Changes in the efficiency of energy transfer are well documented in chloroplasts (118). Evidence that they may occur in *Rds. spheroides* comes from the observation that the yield of fluorescence from the antenna BChl can decrease dramatically during illumination, in concert with the appearance of a pH gradient across the chromatophore membrane (158).

In *Chr. vinosum,* each photosynthetic unit contains two copies of the high-potential cytochrome ($C_{555}$) and two (or possibly three) of a low-potential cytochrome, $C_{552}$ (12, 14, 15, 37, 44, 92, 93, 117, 127, 128, 136, 138, 155). (The nomenclature identifies maxima in the $\alpha$-bands of the reduced-minus-oxidized difference spectra.) Both types of cytochrome are bound tightly to the chromatophore membrane. On disruption of the membrane with SDS, the two emerge together as part of a reaction-center particle that contains $P_{870}$ and some antenna BChl (177). Further dissolution with deoxycholate solubilizes the cytochromes, but still does not afford a separation of the two types (92, 93). This observation leaves unsettled the question of whether all of the hemes reside on a single protein (which might contain several different subunits), or whether they occupy separate, but very similar proteins.

At redox potentials below the $E_m$ of cytochrome $C_{555}$ (+0.34 V) but sufficiently above that of $C_{552}$ (+0.01 V), only cytochrome $C_{555}$ can supply electrons to $P_{870}^+$, and a flash of light causes photooxidation of this cytochrome with high quantum yield (134, 138, 155). At redox potentials low enough so that cytochrome $C_{552}$ also is reduced, the photooxidation of this cytochrome replaces that of $C_{555}$ (14, 15, 37, 138, 155). $P_{870}^+$ clearly is the oxidant for both cytochromes, because the absorbance changes that characterize its reduction to $P_{870}$ occur with appropriate kinetics in both cases (15, 48, 138, 156). The same primary electron acceptor also appears to remove electrons from $P_{870}$ in both cases, judging from the kinetics of the reaction in which electrons continue on to a secondary acceptor (138) (see section V).

Because cytochrome $C_{555}$ photooxidation can occur at redox potentials so high that cytochrome $C_{552}$ is fully oxidized, electrons must be able to proceed from $C_{555}$ to $P_{870}$ directly, rather than through $C_{552}$. But cytochrome $C_{552}$ also must communicate directly with $P_{870}$, because its photooxidation can occur at very low temperatures, when the photooxidation of $C_{555}$ fails (19, 40, 44, 48, 96). The preference for the photooxidation of $C_{552}$ when both types of cytochrome are available stems partly from the different kinetics of the two reactions. The reaction of $P_{870}^+$ with $C_{552}$ has a rate constant of $8.6 \times 10^5$ $sec^{-1}$ at 298°K, about twice that of the reaction with $C_{555}$ (138, 155). The greater speed of the $C_{552}$ oxidation provides additional evidence that this reaction must proceed directly, rather than via cytochrome $C_{555}$. Following the initial reaction, electrons probably equilibrate rapidly between the two cytochrome pools, so that the large thermodynamic preference for oxidizing the low-potential cytochrome prevails heavily (14).

Because a photosynthetic unit contains two or more hemes of each of the two cytochromes, the geometry of the assembly becomes a complex problem. The difficulty of imagining direct paths from all of the hemes to $P_{870}^+$ suggests that only one heme of each type has access to such a path. Distal hemes then would communicate with $P_{870}$ through the proximal ones. This communication probably does not limit the rate of the reaction with $P_{870}^+$, because the kinetics of the cytochrome $C_{555}$ oxidation are the same whether one or both hemes are initially reduced (136).

In addition to the membrane-bound cytochromes $C_{555}$ and $C_{552}$, *Chr. vinosum* also contains relatively large amounts of two soluble, low-potential cytochromes—flavocytochrome $C_{552}$ and cytochrome *c'* (formerly called *cc'*), and small amounts of a soluble, high-potential cytochrome with a split $\alpha$-band (8, 36, 92, 94). Cytochrome *c'* may bind to the chromatophore membrane (49), but whether or not any of these cytochromes is directly involved in photosynthesis remains unclear.

Two pools of *c*-type cytochromes undergo photooxidation in cell suspensions of *Chlorobium limicola* (167). One of the two, a high-potential cytochrome, is membrane-bound. Its photooxidation also occurs in membrane vesicles and reaction-center preparations from this species and from *Chl. thiosulfatophilum* (60, 100). The other cytochrome dissociates from the membrane readily and its identity has been elusive. Of three soluble, *c*-type cytochromes that have been isolated from *Chl. thiosulfatophilum* (114), two appear to participate in the oxidation of thiosulfate (104, 105).

Like *Chr. vinosum, Rps. viridis* contains two membrane-bound *c*-type cytochromes which can be isolated together as part of a common reaction-center particle (130, 179). Again, the assembly contains several hemes of each type. Again, the low-potential cytochrome reacts the more rapidly with $P_{870}^+$, but photooxidation of the high-potential cytochrome occurs readily if the low-potential one is unavailable (15). *Rps. viridis* lacks cytochrome *c'*, but it does contain several other soluble, *c*-type cytochromes (163).

*Rhodopseudomonas gelatinosa* (44, 47, 97) and *Ectothiorhodospira shaposhnikovii* (102, 149, 150) also contain both high- and low-potential *c*-type cytochromes, both of which appear to feed electrons directly to $P_{870}^+$ by parallel paths. *Thiocapsa pfennigii* contains very similar membrane-bound cytochromes (115, 129). These respond to continuous illumination just as do the cytochromes of *Chr. vinosum*, but they have not yet been studied with short-flash techniques.

The similarity of the cytochrome assemblies of all of these bacteria is striking, in view of the physiological and morphological differences that distinguish the species. In most of these species, and in many others, the cytochrome oxidations proceed at enormous speed, with half-times of 10 μsec or less. In most cases, the cytochromes communicate so intimately with $P_{870}$ that the oxidation even occurs at cryogenic temperatures (19, 40, 41, 95, 96). On examining 15 species of *Thio-* and *Athiorhodaceae*, Kihara & Chance (95) observed cytochrome oxidation at 77°K in 12. In addition to several of the species that are mentioned above and other species of *Chromatium*, *Rhodopseudomonas*, and *Thiocapsa*, the 12 included *Rhodospirillum fulvum* and *Rhodomicrobium vannielii*, but not *Rds. rubrum* or *Rps. spheroides*. Some of these species resemble *Chr. vinosum* in restricting low-temperature activity to the low-potential cytochromes, but the high-potential cytochromes may also participate in several cases. None of these membrane-bound cytochromes has been purified sufficiently for structural studies.

The *c*-type cytochromes of *Rds. rubrum* and *Rps. spheroides* are not so tightly bound. Of the two *c*-type cytochromes that undergo photooxidation in *Rds. rubrum*, the high-potential one ($E_m \approx +0.30$ V) appears to be identical with the well-known soluble cytochrome $c_2$ (46, 82, 163). Most of the cytochrome $c_2$ in the cells is liberated during the preparation of chromatophores, but reaction-center preparations made with SDS still contain approximately one equivalent of the cytochrome per $P_{870}$ (162). In whole cells the cytochrome undergoes photooxidation after a flash, with a half-time of approximately 1 msec (88).

Studies of cytochrome $c_2$ in its soluble and crystalline forms have culminated in the description of the crystal structure at 2 Å resolution (151). The structure is basically similar to that of mitochondrial cytochrome *c* (176). In both cases, the heme occupies a hydrophobic cleft in the protein, with a cluster of lysyl residues conferring a strong positive charge to the perimeter of the cleft. Histidyl and methionyl residues supply the fifth and sixth ligands of the Fe atom, keeping the Fe low-spin in both the ferrous and ferric forms. Salemme et al (151) suggest that the methionyl S bears a partial positive charge in the ferricytochrome, causing the S to interact electrostatically with the phenolic oxygen of an adjacent tyrosyl residue. They propose that an extended bridge of H-bonds connects the tyrosyl –OH to a seryl –OH on the exterior of the protein, near the edge of the heme cleft. If the reduction of the heme eliminates the positive charge on the S, the H-bond bridge would relay this information to the serine, promoting the uptake of a proton from the solution. The $E_m$ of the cytochrome decreases by about 25 mV/pH between pH 5 and 8, in agreement with this suggestion (84). This is not a common theme in bacterial photosynthesis, however, for the $E_m$s of the membrane-bound cytochromes of *Chr. vinosum* do not depend on pH (12), nor do those of the purified cytochromes $c_2$ of *Rps. capsulatus* and *Rps. palustris* (84), nor that of cytochrome $c_2$ in situ in *Rps. spheroides* chromatophores (53). Nonetheless, the rates of oxidation and reduction of several different cytochromes (including $C_{552}$ of *Chr. vinosum*) all show a $^2H_2O$ isotope effect of 1.41, suggesting that a reorganization of H-bonds may generally control the rate of electron transfer (97).

The positive charge of the lysine cluster seems likely to dominate the interaction of the cytochrome with $P_{870}$, because polylysine strongly inhibits the oxidation of mitochondrial cytochrome *c* by *Rps. spheroides* reaction centers (86). The rate of the cytochrome oxidation in this case depends on the pH and ionic strength, as it should if it hinges on electrostatic interactions (86).

The second cytochrome that undergoes photooxidation in *Rds. rubrum* has an $E_m$ of approximately 0 V, like those of the low-potential cytochromes that are discussed above; but it has an atypical reduced-minus-oxidized difference spectrum, with maxima at 428 and 562 nm (61, 169). These properties suggest the soluble cytochrome *c'*. *Rds. rubrum* cells do contain cytochrome *c'* (7, 82), and both chromatophores and reaction-center preparations can photooxidize it if it is added to them (163). Smith et al (163), therefore, have suggested that the low-potential cytochrome is bound cytochrome *c'* and that $P_{870}^+$ oxidizes this cytochrome as well as cytochrome $c_2$. [The latter suggestion departs from the earlier proposal from the same laboratory (61, 169) that different photochemical reaction centers mediate the photooxidation of the two cytochromes.] The similarities between purified cytochrome *c'* and the low-potential cytochrome that is photooxidized in vivo could be misleading, however, because the properties of cytochrome *c'* may change when the cytochrome is solubilized. The $E_m$ of cytochrome *c'* in *Chr. vinosum* chromatophores appears to be approximately +0.25 V (49), quite unlike the $E_{m7}$ of +0.01 V that characterizes purified cytochrome *c'*. The purification of the protein also changes its CO-binding properties markedly (17, 38).

Another cytochrome with a *b*-type absorption spectrum and a substantially lower $E_m$ [–0.11 V (46); –0.16 V (82)] also occurs in *Rds. rubrum* chromatophores. This may be identical with a cytochrome that Bartsch et al (7) have purified under the name $b_{557.5}$. Illumination of cells or chromatophores in the presence of antimycin A leads to the reduction of a cytochrome with these spectral properties (119, 132). The reduction presumably involves electrons from the primary and secondary electron-acceptors which are discussed in the following section. The *b*-type cytochrome evidently does not communicate directly with $P_{870}$, but passes electrons instead to cytochrome $c_2$. Antimycin A (which inhibits electron flow between cytochromes *b* and *c* in mitochondria) must block this step, forcing cytochrome $c_2$ to accumulate in the oxidized form and the *b*-type cytochrome in the reduced.

Electron flow from *b*- to *c*-type cytochromes also occurs in *Rps. spheroides.* Chromatophores of this species contain appreciable quantities of only one *c*-type cytochrome (32, 46). This is a readily-soluble, high-potential cytochrome $c_2$ that probably is essentially identical with the $c_2$ of *Rds. rubrum.* (163). It undergoes photooxidation with a half-time of approximately 150 $\mu$sec, following illumination of the chromatophores with a short flash (46, 78), or 8 $\mu$sec in whole cells (95). In place of the membrane-bound, low-potential *c*-type cytochromes that other species contain, *Rps. spheroides* features three *b*-type cytochromes, with $E_m$s of approximately –0.10, +0.05, and +0.17 (32, 46, 80). To unravel the interconnections among these cytochromes has been a formidable task, because their kinetics overlap and the absorption spectra do not differ helpfully. Adding to the confusion, all of the cytochromes, including $c_2$, also occur in the membranes of cells that are grown nonphotosynthetically (aerobically), though their relative contributions do change (32). In spite of these difficulties, a kinetic analysis indicates that the *b*-cytochrome with $E_{m7} = +0.17$ is photooxidized by way of cytochrome $c_2$ (46). Electron transfer between the two cytochromes has a half-time about 1 msec and is sensitive to antimycin A.

The *b*-cytochrome with $E_m \approx +0.05$ V does not undergo immediate photooxidation after a flash, but rather first becomes reduced, also with a half-time of about 1 msec (46). The fate of the reduced cytochrome is unclear. The third *b*-cytochrome ($E_m \approx -0.10$ V) seems not to participate in the events that follow flash excitation, and its relevance to photosynthesis remains obscure. Cells of *Rps. spheroides* also contain cytochrome *c*' and another atypical, soluble cytochrome (163).

## V. PRIMARY AND SECONDARY ELECTRON ACCEPTORS

The identity of the component X that accepts an electron from $P_{870}$ in the primary photochemical reaction continues to enjoy spirited debate. The ranks of contestants for this position have thinned, however, leaving two principal contenders—nonheme iron and ubiquinone (UQ). Chromatophores contain both of these components and various reaction-center preparations contain one or the other, or both. One might hope to decide between the two by examining the composition of increasingly refined preparations of reaction centers. Thus, the finding that the UQ can be removed from reaction centers or chromatophores without destroying their capacity for performing $P_{870}$ photooxidation would argue that UQ is not X (28, 68, 87, 175). But one can make the same statement of nonheme Fe: reaction-center preparations that are depleted of Fe also exhibit $P_{870}$ photooxidation (57, 109). Rather than showing that neither UQ nor Fe is X, these disconcerting observations may mean that $P_{870}$ is flexible enough to tolerate a variety of reaction partners. If the native electron acceptor is incapacitated, a substitute may take its place.

A parallel approach is to seek optical or EPR signals that correlate with the reduction of X. Again, various reaction-center preparations exhibit light-induced absorbance changes and EPR signals that appear to reflect the reduction of nonheme Fe in some cases (50, 51, 55), and the reduction of UQ in others (9, 24, 25, 57, 109, 160).

The puzzling behavior of reaction-center preparations encourages one to return temporarily to chromatophores in the search for the real X. Here, Dutton & Leigh (49) have made a strong case for a nonheme Fe complex, which they call photoredoxin and which they measure by the $g = 1.82$ EPR signal (where $g$ is the gyromagnetic ratio) that its reduced form displays. To develop the case, we must digress into the reactions that allow X to return to the oxidized state after its photoreduction. There are two routes for this return: a back-reaction with $P_{870}^+$ and a forward-reaction with a secondary electron acceptor.

If chromatophores are illuminated with a single, short flash, $P_{870}$ passes an electron to X and then generally returns to the reduced state within several $\mu$sec, as a cytochrome becomes oxidized. Even though $P_{870}$ should be prepared to react again at this point, a short flash may cause essentially no photochemistry (135). This most likely means that X is still in the reduced state, and that the reaction center cannot function again until the electron has continued on to a secondary acceptor, Y. Judging from the rate at which the system recovers the capacity for photochemistry, the electron-transfer reaction between $X^-$ and Y at pH 7 has a half-time of 60 μsec in *Chromatium vinosum* chromatophores (135) and 6 μsec in *Rhodopseudomonas viridis* (R. Carithers and W. Parson, in preparation). The reaction is sensitive to pH and to several inhibitors (see below), but it does not depend on which cytochrome supplies electrons to $P_{870}^+$ (138). Of particular importance for what will follow is that the reaction has an activation energy of about 8 kcal/mole (135). This means that the reaction cannot occur at a significant rate at cryogenic temperatures.

As section IV indicates, one can prevent the rapid reduction of $P_{870}^+$ by cytochromes in several ways—by raising the redox potential so as to oxidize the cytochromes, by turning to preparations that lack cytochromes, or in some cases by lowering the temperature. The rate at which $P_{870}^+$ is reduced after a flash under any of these conditions apparently depends primarily on whether or not the secondary electron-transfer reaction between $X^-$ and Y occurs. If the electron cannot escape from $X^-$ to Y, it can return to $P_{870}$ in a back-reaction. The back-reaction probably involves quantum mechanical electron tunneling, because to a first approximation its rate is independent of temperature (26, 28, 112, 132). The half-time is 20 to 50 msec in many species. If the $X^-$ to Y reaction can occur, the return of the electron from Y to $P_{870}$ must follow a more tortuous path, for it is slower and more sensitive to temperature. As the double-flash experiments would suggest, one can encourage the back-reaction by lowering the temperature or by adding an appropriate inhibitor of the forward-reaction. If, for example, one examines *Chr. vinosum* chromatophores at 77°K or below and at a redox potential that is high enough to hold cytochrome $C_{552}$ fully oxidized, a single laser flash causes a reversible photooxidation of $P_{870}$ (48). The reversal has a half-time of about 25 msec. If the potential is lower, so as to provide cytochrome $C_{552}$ initially in the reduced form, the flash results in oxidation of the cytochrome by $P_{870}$. The cytochrome oxidation is irreversible at these temperatures and the passage of the electron from $X^-$ to Y cannot occur, so X remains reduced indefinitely.

The critical point here is that the photosynthetic apparatus can transfer only a single electron at low temperatures, because the $X^-$ to Y reaction fails. An EPR signal due to a photoreduced product must therefore be due to the primary electron acceptor, rather than to a secondary acceptor. The $g = 1.82$ EPR signal of reduced nonheme Fe in fact appears on illumination under these conditions, and its decay kinetics are exactly as one would predict (49). If the redox potential is low enough to allow cytochrome $C_{552}$ to function, the Fe is reduced irreversibly. If the cytochrome cannot function, the Fe is reduced reversibly, and its decay matches that of $P_{870}^+$.

The nonheme Fe also can be reduced chemically in the dark, with the appearance of the same EPR spectrum. Redox titrations of this effect yield $E_{m7.4}$ values of –0.13 V in *Chr. vinosum* and –0.05 V in *Rps. spheroides* (49–51). These titrations run closely parallel to titrations (12, 29, 33, 37, 44, 72, 107, 147, 157) of the loss of the ability of the photosynthetic apparatus to perform photochemistry. The agreement supports the identification of the Fe with X, but it would not be conclusive evidence by itself because the loss of photochemistry could be due to the reduction of a secondary electron-acceptor.

The evidence identifying Fe as the primary electron-acceptor does have several weak links. First, it is possible that the reactions that occur at very low temperatures differ from those that occur at physiological temperatures. Because the EPR spectrum of the nonheme Fe can be measured only at temperatures below 20°K, kinetic studies at higher temperatures will require techniques for rapid quenching and cooling. Second, no quantum yields have been reported. Until the quantum yield is shown to be as high as that of $P_{870}$ photooxidation, it will remain possible that the Fe EPR signal reflects a side reaction. But this possibility seems remote, in view of the finding that the decay kinetics match those expected for $X^-$.

Essentially nothing is known of the structure of the nonheme Fe center that provides the $g = 1.82$ EPR signal. *Rps. spheroides* reaction-center preparations that contain the Fe do not contain inorganic S, and none of their three polypeptides (section III) has more than three cysteines (164). The lightest and the heaviest of the polypeptides each contain either two or three half-cystines; the one of intermediate size, none (164). This means that the Fe-binding site cannot closely resemble that of rubredoxin (which involves four cysteines) or those of the ferredoxins or *Chromatium* high-potential iron protein (which involve both cysteines and one inorganic S atom per Fe). Conceivably, the Fe could call upon both the light and the heavy polypeptides for sulfhydryl groups, but such an arrangement would lack precedent. The EPR spectrum of the reduced Fe also differs significantly from those of other known nonheme Fe proteins (49, 50). The three $g$ values ($g_x = 1.68$, $g_y = 1.82$, $g_z \approx 1.91$) indicate that the Fe is in a very asymmetric environment, which might result from its having several different types of ligands.

The details of the primary photochemical reaction between $P_{870}$ and X are currently under active study. Because the topic has been reviewed recently elsewhere (21, 137), the present discussion will not develop it further, except to point out some of the major questions that remain at issue. These include the speed of the reaction, the changes in enthalpy and entropy that accompany it, the probability of back-reactions, the role of triplet states of $P_{870}$ as intermediates or side-products, and the manner in which the photochemistry competes with fluorescence from the antenna BChl.

If lyophilized chromatophores from *Chr. vinosum* are extracted with petroleum ether so as to deplete them of UQ, they lose their capacity to perform photochemistry on a second flash, even though the two flashes are many milliseconds apart (68). They also display the $X^-$ to $P_{870}^+$ back-reaction (at redox potentials high enough to decouple cytochrome $C_{555}$), with kinetics similar to those that prevail in the presence of inhibitors of the $X^-$ to Y reaction. Reaction center preparations from *Rps. spheroides* that are depleted of UQ behave similarly (26). These effects probably result from the removal (or destruction) of the secondary electron-acceptor Y, because the extraction has no significant effect on the photooxidation of $P_{870}$ or cytochrome on the first flash. The effects of the extraction can be reversed completely by reconstitution of the extracted chromatophores with the lipid extract (68). Pure UQ will replace the extract in restoring the secondary electron-transfer reaction, and analysis of the extract from *Chr. vinosum* shows that UQ is the only active material that it contains in detectable quantity. The simplest conclusion from these observations is that UQ is Y. This conclusion fits well with earlier evidence that illumination of chromatophores causes the reduction of endogenous UQ (2, 173, 174). It would be imprudent, however, to ignore the possibility that the presence of UQ is merely a requirement for the activity of an unidentified component. It also is possible that menaquinone replaces UQ as the secondary electron acceptor in some species. Menaquinone is widely distributed among the photosynthetic bacteria (64, 106, 111, 141, 171, 172).

The amount of UQ that chromatophores contain is quite large, on the order of 5 to 10 moles per mole of $P_{870}$ (38, 65, 68, 172); but whether or not all of the UQ forms a single pool is unclear. External electron donors such as succinate must feed into at least part of the UQ pool, for they cause extensive reduction of the UQ in the dark (98, 133, 166, 174). During illumination, electrons also can be withdrawn from the pool (133, 142, 173, 174), probably by energy-linked, reverse electron transport to pyridine nucleotides. The reduction by succinate implies that the $E_{m7}$ of the bulk of the UQ pool is on the order of +0.03 V (the $E_{m7}$ of succinate/fumarate) or more positive, similar to the value of +0.05 V that has been assigned (180) to UQ in mitochondria. Operational titrations of the apparent $E_{m7}$ of Y in *Chr. vinosum* chromatophores have given numbers that either agree roughly with this value (+0.07 V) or disagree (–0.09 V), depending on the conditions of the measurements (12). The reasons for this discrepancy are not clear. If the negative value is correct, the UQ which acts as the secondary electron acceptor may not be part of the bulk pool of UQ.

The conclusion that the primary and secondary electron-acceptors of the photosynthetic apparatus are nonheme Fe and UQ suggests an analogy with the respiratory dehydrogenases of mitochondria and aerobic microorganisms. In support of the analogy, piericidin A, which inhibits respiratory electron flow between nonheme Fe and UQ also inhibits the $X^-$ to Y reaction (68). Certain 6-alkyl-5,8-quinolinequinones and *o*-phenanthroline block both systems (26, 68, 138). The most potent inhibitor of the $X^-$ to Y reaction known, 5-*n*-pentadecyl-6-hydroxy-4,7-dioxobenzothiazole (68), also inhibits the mitochondrial dehydrogenases (K. Folkers, personal communication).

## VI. OVERVIEW AND UNANSWERED QUESTIONS

The picture that emerges from the preceding sections is that light pumps electrons from two or more types of cytochromes, through $P_{870}$ and nonheme Fe, to UQ. The cytochrome pools supply $P_{870}$ with a large reservoir of electrons, and UQ may provide a reservoir for the storage of electrons at the opposite pole of the system. The $E_{m7}$ of the high-potential cytochrome is near +0.3 V; so if we take the $E_{m7}$ of UQ as +0.05 V, the standard free energy change for the promotion of one mole of electrons from the high-potential cytochromes would be about 5.8 kcal. But electron transfer from the low-potential cytochromes to UQ would appear to be futile as a mechanism for energy storage. As we have seen, there is little support for the notion that the low-potential cytochromes might supply electrons to a different acceptor with a much lower $E_m$. Photosynthetic bacteria evidently meet their need for reduced pyridine nucleotides by energy-linked reverse electron flow, rather than by the direct photoreduction of an acceptor with a very low $E_m$. The evidence for this is that ATP or pyrophosphate can replace light in driving the reduction of $NAD^+$ by succinate, and that uncouplers prevent the reduction whether it is energized by light or by ATP or pyrophosphate (73, 81, 89, 90, 99). (For dissenting opinions, see references 10, 66, 67, 124.)

What, then, is the physiological meaning of the different types of cytochromes? We do not know. The answer must lie somewhere in the pathways that return electrons to the cytochromes, either by a cyclic course from UQ, or by tributaries draining external electron donors. Is the reduction path cyclic for one type of cytochrome and noncyclic for the other? These paths are virtually uncharted with the exception of the step that links *b*- and *c*-type cytochromes in some *Athiorhodaceae.* In *Chromatium vinosum,* there is circumstantial evidence (49, 91) that cytochrome $C_{555}$ draws electrons from the high-potential iron protein, a soluble, nonheme Fe protein with an $E_m$ of +0.35 V. This possibility awaits a critical kinetic study.

The uptake of protons from the solution outside the chromatophore accompanies the reduction of X or Y. The proton uptake has been measured with a glass electrode during continuous illumination (76, 181, 182), and with pH indicator dyes after flash excitation (16, 18, 30, 31, 34, 74). It also reveals itself in the dependence of the $E_m$ values of X and Y on pH and ionic strength (12, 13, 29, 72). The $H^+$-uptake that follows excitation with a short flash lags slightly behind $X^-$ to Y reaction (11, 16, 18, 68). In *Chr. vinosum,* the extent of the flash-induced H+ uptake (about 1 gm-atom $H^+$ per mole of $P_{870}$) is independent of whether the high- or the low-potential cytochrome supplies electrons to $P_{870}$ (35), as one might anticipate if Y is the same in either case. Whether the electron-carriers themselves actually bind protons is not clear: their reduction could provoke secondary responses of other components of the system, much as the binding of $O_2$ does in hemoglobin (16, 18). Evidence that this may be the case comes from the observation that the $E_m$ of the primary electron-acceptor loses its sensitivity to pH in the course of the purification of reaction centers (51).

Does the flow of electrons through other stretches of the chain release protons on the inside of the chromatophore? Although this is a central postulate of the chemosmotic theory of photophosphorylation (116, 185), there is as yet little direct evidence for internal $H^+$-release. Uncouplers (which increase the $H^+$-conductivity of the membrane) facilitate the decay of the flash-induced pH rise, as measured on the outside of the vesicle (30). This is what one would expect if the uncouplers allow the efflux of protons that the electron-transport system releases on the inside. But it could also mean only that they make the internal buffering capacity accessible to the solution outside. [This criticism is less forceful in experiments with continuous illumination, when the total $H^+$-uptake can be quite large (77).] Direct measurements of pH changes on the inside of the chromatophore are needed, and they should be feasible with appropriate indicators. If internal $H^+$-release does occur, it probably accompanies the steps that reduce the *c*-type cytochromes, rather than the oxidation of these cytochromes or of $P_{870}$. As section IV points out, the $E_m$ values of the *c*-type cytochromes generally are independent of pH. The $E_m$ values of the *b*-type cytochromes of *Rps. spheroides* do depend on pH, changing by approximately –60 mV/pH unit (53). This means that $H^+$-release should accompany electron flow from the *b*-type cytochromes to cytochrome $c_2$. Whether these protons appear first on the inside of the chromatophore, as the chemosmotic theory requires, remains to be proven. Electron flow between the *b*- and *c*-type cytochromes must be linked somehow to phosphorylation, because the addition of ATP or pyrophosphate to *Rhodospirillum rubrum* chromatophores reverses the electron flow, causing an oxidation of cytochrome $c_2$ and a reduction of cytochrome *b* (4, 45). Uncouplers prevent this effect.

Shifts in the absorption bands of carotenoids and the antenna BChl accompany the electron-transfer reactions in many different species (5, 5a, 14, 58, 76, 78, 120, 161, 183, 184). Jackson & Crofts (75, 76) have proposed that the band shifts are electrochromic effects that reflect the formation of electrical fields across the membrane. They and others (56, 76, 120) have demonstrated that uncouplers and ionophores which specifically increase the electrical conductivity of the membrane cause decay of the band shifts that result from illumination. In an elegant set of experiments Jackson & Crofts (75) also showed that similar band shifts resulted from the construction of a membrane potential in the dark, which they did by adding KCl to chromatophores in the presence of valinomycin, or by adding acids or bases in the presence of uncouplers. In agreement with the notion that the band shifts reflect a high energy state that is fundamental to the mechanism of phosphorylation, the addition of ATP or pyrophosphate causes similar shifts (3). On the other hand, a volume decrease that develops and decays in concert with the band shifts is not simply explained by a membrane potential (11).

In several species, the band shifts have been shown to accompany specific electron-transfer reactions (14, 44, 46, 78). In *Chr. vinosum,* for example, they accompany the oxidation of cytochrome $C_{555}$ by $P_{870}{}^+$, but not the oxidation of cytochrome $C_{552}$, nor that of $P_{870}$ itself (14). The shifts cannot simply reflect local electrical fields due to cytochrome $C_{555}$ itself, for they persist after the cytochrome has returned to the reduced state. Repeated cycling of the cytochrome through its oxidized form causes a cumulative buildup of the band shifts. One could explain these observations on the assumption that an electrogenic translocation of ions across the membrane accompanies the cytochrome oxidation. The oxidation of either $P_{870}$ or the cytochromes clearly results in the uptake of protons on the outside of the chromatophore, but evidence is sorely lacking for the uptake or release of any ions at all on the inside. B ecause the $E_m$s of $P_{870}$ and cytochrome $C_{555}$ depend almost identically on the ionic strength of the solution, the oxidations of the two carriers probably result in very similar changes in the net electrical charge on the membrane—a decrease in the net negative charge (13). Why then does only the cytochrome oxidation cause the band shift?

The mechanism of energy transduction thus remains entangled in the puzzle of the complex pools of cytochromes. We still have much to unravel, before we shall truly understand bacterial photosynthesis.

*Literature Cited*


1. Arnold, W., Clayton, R. K. 1960. *Proc. Nat. Acad. Sci. USA* 46:769–76
2. Bales, H., Vernon, L. P. 1963. *Bacterial Photosynthesis,* ed. H. Gest, A. San Pietro, L. P. Vernon, 269–74. Yellow Springs, Ohio: Antioch Press
3. Baltscheffsky, M. 1969. *Arch. Biochem. Biophys.* 130:646–52
4. Ibid 133:46–53
5. Barsky, E. L., Samuilov, V. D. 1973. *J. Bioenerg.* 4:391–95

5a. Barsky, E. L., Samuilov, V. D. 1973. *Biochim. Biophys. Acta* 325:454–62

6. Bartsch, R. G. 1968. *Ann. Rev. Microbiol.* 22:181–200
7. Bartsch, R. G., Kakuno, T., Horio, T., Kamen, M. D. 1971. *J. Biol. Chem.* 246:4489–96
8. Bartsch, R. G., Kamen, M. D. 1960. *J. Biol. Chem.* 235:825–31
9. Bolton, J. R., Cost, K. 1973. *Photochem. Photobiol.* 18:417–21
10. Buchanan, B. B., Evans, M. C. W. 1969. *Biochim. Biophys. Acta* 180:123–29
11. Callis, J. B., Parson, W. W., Gouterman, M. 1972. *Biochim. Biophys. Acta* 267:348–62
12. Case, G. D., Parson, W. W. 1971. *Biochim. Biophys. Acta* 253:187–202
13. Ibid 1973. 292:677–84
14. Ibid 325:441–53
15. Case, G. D., Parson, W. W., Thornber, J. P. 1970. *Biochim. Biophys. Acta* 223:122–28
16. Chance, B., Crofts, A. R., Nishimura, M., Price, B. 1970. *Eur. J. Biochem.* 13:364–74
17. Chance, B., Horio, T., Kamen, M. D., Taniguchi, S. 1966. *Biochim. Biophys. Acta* 112:1–7
18. Chance, B., McCray, J. A., Bunkenburg, J. 1970. *Nature* 225:705–8
19. Chance, B., Nishimura, M. 1960. *Proc. Nat. Acad. Sci. USA* 46:19–25
20. Clayton, R. K. 1962. *Photochem. Photobiol.* 1:201–10
21. Clayton, R. K. 1973. *Ann. Rev. Biophys. Bioeng.* 2:131–56
22. Clayton, R. K., Clayton, B. J. 1972. *Biochim. Biophys. Acta* 283:492–504
23. Clayton, R. K., Haselkorn, R. 1972. *J. Mol. Biol.* 68:97–105
24. Clayton, R. K., Straley, S. C. 1970. *Biochem. Biophys. Res. Commun.* 39:1114–19
25. Clayton, R. K., Straley, S. C. 1972. *Biophys. J.* 12:1221–34
26. Clayton, R. K., Szuts, E. Z., Fleming, H. 1972. *Biophys. J.* 12:64–79
27. Clayton, R. K., Wang, R. T. 1971. *Methods Enzymol.* 23:696–704
28. Clayton, R. K., Yau, H. F. 1972. Biophys. *J.* 12:867–81
29. Cogdell, R. J., Crofts, A. R. 1972. *FEBS Lett.* 27:176–78
30. Cogdell, R. J., Jackson, J. B., Crofts, A. R. 1972. *J. Bioenerg.* 4:413–29
31. Cogdell, R. J., Prince, R. C., Crofts, A. R. 1973. *FEBS Lett.* 35:204–8
32. Connelly, J. L., Jones, O. T. G., Saunders, V. A., Yates, D. W. 1973. *Biochim. Biophys. Acta* 292:644–53
33. Cramer, W. A. 1969. *Biochim. Biophys. Acta* 189:54–59
34. Crofts, A. R., Cogdell, R. J., Jackson, J. B. 1971. *Energy Transduction in Respiration and Photosynthesis,* ed. E. Quagliariello, S. Papa, C. S. Rosi, 883–901. Bari: Adriatica Editrice
35. Crofts, A. R., Cogdell, R. J., Jackson, J. B. *Proc. Conf. Mechanisms in Bioenergetics,* Bari, Italy, 1972. In press
36. Cusanovich, M. A., Bartsch, R. G. 1969. *Biochim. Biophys. Acta* 189:245–55
37. Cusanovich, M. A., Bartsch, R. G., Kamen, M. D. 1968. *Biochim. Biophys. Acta* 153:397–417
38. Cusanovich, M. A., Kamen, M. D. 1968. *Biochim. Biophys. Acta* 153:376–96
39. de Klerk, H., Govindjee, Kamen, M. D., Lavorel, J. 1969. *Proc. Nat. Acad. Sci. USA* 62:972–78
40. De Vault, D., Chance, B. 1966. *Biophys. J.* 6:825–47
41. De Vault, D., Parkes, J. H., Chance, B. 1967. *Nature* 215:642–44
42. Dolphin, D., Felton, R. 1974. *Accounts Chem. Res.* 7:26–32

43. Druyan, M. E., Norris, J. R., Katz, J. J. 1973. *J. Am. Chem. Soc.* 95:1682–83
44. Dutton, P. L. 1971. *Biochim. Biophys. Acta* 226:63–80
45. Dutton, P. L., Baltscheffsky, M. 1972. *Biochim. Biophys. Acta* 267:172–78
46. Dutton, P. L., Jackson, J. B. 1972. *Eur. J. Biochem.* 30:495–510
47. Dutton, P. L., Kihara, T., Chance, B. 1970. *Arch. Biochem. Biophys.* 139: 236–40
48. Dutton, P. L., Kihara, T., McCray, J. A., Thornber, J. P. 1971. *Biochim. Biophys. Acta* 226:81–87
49. Dutton, P. L., Leigh, J. S. 1973. *Biochim. Biophys. Acta* 314:178–90
50. Dutton, P. L., Leigh, J. S., Reed, D. W. 1973. *Biochim. Biophys. Acta* 292: 654–64
51. Dutton, P. L., Leigh, J. S., Wraight, C. A. 1973. *FEBS Lett.* 36:169–73
52. Duysens, L. N. M., Huiskamp, W. J., Vos, J. J., van der Hart, J. M. 1956. *Biochim. Biophys. Acta* 19:188–90
53. Dutton, P. L., Morse, D. S., Wong, A. M. 1974. *Britton Chance Festschrift*, ed. L. Ernster. New York: Academic. In press
54. Ebrey, T. G., Clayton, R. K. 1969. *Photochem. Photobiol.* 10:109–17
55. Feher, G. 1971. *Photochem. Photobiol.* 14:373–87
56. Feher, G., Hoff, A. J., Isaacson, R. A., McElroy, J. D. 1973. *Abstr. Biophys. Soc. 17th Ann. Meet.*, Columbus, Ohio, p. 61a
57. Feher, G., Okamura, M. Y., McElroy, J. D. 1972. *Biochim. Biophys. Acta* 267:222–26
58. Fleischman, D. E., Clayton, R. K. 1968. *Photochem. Photobiol.* 8:287–98
59. Fowler, C. F., Gray, B. H., Nugent, N. A., Fuller, R. C. 1973. *Biochim. Biophys. Acta* 292:692–99
60. Fowler, C. F., Nugent, N. A., Fuller, R. C. 1971. *Proc. Nat. Acad. Sci. USA* 68:2278–82
61. Fowler, C. F., Sybesma, C. 1970. *Biochim. Biophys. Acta* 197:276–83
62. Fraker, P. J., Kaplan, S. 1971. *J. Bacteriol.* 108:465–73
63. Fraker, P. J., Kaplan, S. 1972. *J. Biol. Chem.* 247:2732–37
64. Frenkel, A. W. 1970. *Biol. Rev.* 45: 569–616
65. Fuller, R. C., Smillie, R. M., Rigopoulos, N., Yount, V. 1961. *Arch. Biochem. Biophys.* 95:197–202
66. Govindjee, R., Sybesma, C. 1970. *Biochim. Biophys. Acta* 223:251–60
67. Govindjee, R., Sybesma, C. 1972. *Biophys. J.* 12:897–908
68. Halsey, Y., Parson, W. W. 1974. *Biochim. Biophys. Acta* In press
69. Hind, G., Olson, J. M. 1968. *Ann. Rev. Plant Physiol.* 19:249–82
70. Holt, A. S., Clayton, R. K. 1965. *Photochem. Photobiol.* 4:829–31
71. Horio, T., Kamen, M. D. 1970. *Ann. Rev. Microbiol.* 24:399–428
72. Jackson, J. B., Cogdell, R. J., Crofts, A. R. 1973. *Biochim. Biophys. Acta* 292: 218–25
73. Jackson, J. B., Crofts, A. R. 1968. *Biochem. Biophys. Res. Commun.* 32: 908–15
74. Jackson, J. B., Crofts, A. R. 1969. *Eur. J. Biochem.* 10:226–37
75. Jackson, J. B., Crofts, A. R. 1969. *FEBS Lett.* 4:185–89
76. Jackson, J. B., Crofts, A. R. 1971. *Eur. J. Biochem.* 18:120–30
77. Jackson, J. B., Crofts, A. R., von Stedingk, L.-V. 1968. *Eur. J. Biochem.* 6:41–54
78. Jackson, J. B., Dutton, P. L. 1973. *Biochim. Biophys. Acta* 325:102–13
79. Jolchine, G., Reiss-Husson, F. 1972. *Biochem. Biophys. Res. Commun.* 48: 333–40
80. Jones, O. T. G. 1969. *Biochem. J.* 114:793–99
81. Jones, O. T. G., Saunders, V. A. 1972. *Biochim. Biophys. Acta* 275:427–36
82. Kakuno, T., Bartsch, R. G., Nishikawa, K., Horio, T. 1971. *J. Biochem. (Tokyo)* 70:79–94
83. Kamen, M. D., Horio, T. 1970. *Ann. Rev. Biochem.* 39:673–700
84. Kamen, M. D., Vernon, L. P. 1955. *Biochim. Biophys. Acta* 17:10–22
85. Katz, J. J., Norris, J. 1973. *Curr. Top. Bioenerg.* 5:41–75
86. Ke, B., Chaney, T. H., Reed, D. W. 1970. *Biochim. Biophys. Acta* 216: 373–83
87. Ke, B., Garcia, A. F., Vernon, L. P. 1973. *Biochim. Biophys. Acta* 292: 226–36
88. Ke, B., Ngo, E. 1967. *Biochim. Biophys. Acta* 143:319–31
89. Keister, D. L., Minton, N. J. 1969. *Biochemistry* 8:167–73
90. Keister, D. L., Yike, N. J. 1967. *Arch. Biochem. Biophys.* 121:415–22
91. Kennel, S. J., Bartsch, R. G., Kamen, M. D. 1972. *Biophys. J.* 12:882–96
92. Kennel, S. J., Kamen, M. D. 1971. *Biochim. Biophys. Acta* 253:153–66
93. Ibid 234:458–67
94. Kennel, S. J., Meyer, T. E., Kamen, M. D., Bartsch, R. G. 1972. *Proc. Nat. Acad. Sci. USA* 69:3432–35

95. Kihara, T., Chance, B. 1969. *Biochim. Biophys. Acta* 189:116–24
96. Kihara, T., Dutton, P. L. 1970. *Biochim. Biophys. Acta* 205:196–204
97. Kihara, T., McCray, J. A. 1973. *Biochim. Biophys. Acta* 292:297–309
98. King, M. T., Drews, G. 1973. *Biochim. Biophys. Acta* 305:230–48
99. Klemme, J. -H. 1969. *Z. Naturforsch. B* 24:67–76
100. Knaff, D. B., Buchanan, B. B., Malkin, R. 1973. *Biochim. Biophys. Acta* 325: 94–101
101. Kononenko, A. A. et al 1973. *FEBS Lett.* 30:239–42
102. Kononenko, A. A., Venediktov, P. S., Lukasev, E. P., Matorin, D. N., Rubin, A. B. 1971. *Stud. Biophys. DDR* 28: 15–22
103. Kuntz, I. D., Loach, P. A., Calvin, M. 1964. *Biophys. J.* 4:227–49
104. Kusai, A., Yamanaka, T. 1973. *Biochem. Biophys. Res. Commun.* 51: 107–12
105. Kusai, A., Yamanaka, T. 1973. *FEBS Lett.* 34:235–37
106. Lester, R. L., Crane, F. L. 1959. *J. Biol. Chem.* 234:2169–75
107. Loach, P. A. 1966. *Biochemistry* 5: 592–600
108. Loach, P. A., Hadsell, R. M., Sekura, D. L., Stemer, A. 1970. *Biochemistry* 9:3127–35
109. Loach, P. A., Hall, R. L. 1972. *Proc. Nat. Acad. Sci. USA* 69:786–90
110. Loach, P. A., Sekura, D. L., Hadsell, R. M., Stemer, A. 1970. *Biochemistry* 9:724–33
111. Maroc, J., de Klerk, H., Kamen, M. D. 1968. *Biochim. Biophys. Acta* 162: 621–23
112. McElroy, J. D., Feher, G., Mauzerall, D. C. 1969. *Biochim. Biophys. Acta* 172:180–83
113. Ibid 1972. 267:363–74
114. Meyer, T. E., Bartsch, R. G., Cusanovich, M. A., Mathewson, J. H. 1968. *Biochim. Biophys. Acta* 153:854–61
115. Meyer, T. E., Kennel, S. J., Tedro, S. M., Kamen, M. D. 1973. *Biochim. Biophys. Acta* 292:634–43
116. Mitchell, P. 1966. *Biol. Rev.* 41: 445–502
117. Morita, S. 1968. *Biochim. Biophys. Acta* 153:241–47
118. Murata, N. 1971. *Biochim. Biophys. Acta* 245:365–72
119. Nishimura, M. 1963. *Biochim. Biophys. Acta* 66:17–21
120. Ibid 1970. 197:69–77
121. Noël, H., von der Rest, M., Gingras, G. 1972. *Biochim. Biophys. Acta* 275: 219–30
122. Norris, J. R., Druyan, M. E., Katz, J. J. 1973. *J. Am. Chem. Soc.* 95:1680–82
123. Norris, J. R., Uphaus, R. A., Crespi, H. L., Katz, J. J. 1971. *Proc. Nat. Acad. Sci. USA* 68:625–28
124. Nozaki, M., Tagawa, K., Arnon, D. I. 1963. *Bacterial Photosynthesis,* ed. H. Gest, A. San Pietro, L. P. Vernon 175–94. Yellow Springs, Ohio: Antioch Press
125. Okamura, M. Y., Steiner, L. A., Feher, G. 1974. *Biochemistry* 13:In press
126. Olson, J. M. 1971. *Methods Enzymol.* 23:636–44
127. Olson, J. M., Chance, B. 1960. *Arch. Biochem. Biophys.* 88:26–39
128. Ibid 40–53
129. Olson, J. M. et al 1969. *Biochim. Biophys. Acta* 172:338–39
130. Olson, J. M., Nadler, K. D. 1965. *Photochem. Photobiol.* 4:783–91
131. Olson, J. M., Philipson, K. D., Sauer, K. 1973. *Biochim. Biophys. Acta* 292: 206–17
132. Parson, W. W. 1967. *Biochim. Biophys. Acta* 131:154–72
133. Ibid 143:263–65
134. Ibid 1968. 153:248–59
135. Ibid 1969. 189:384–96
136. Ibid 397–403
137. Parson, W. W. 1974. *Chemical and Biological Applications of Lasers,* ed. C. B. Moore. New York: Academic. In press
138. Parson, W. W., Case, G. D. 1970. *Biochim. Biophys. Acta* 205:232–45
139. Philipson, K. D., Sauer, K. 1972. *Biochemistry* 11:1880–85
140. Ibid 1973. 12:535–39
141. Powls, R., Redfearn, E. R. 1969. *Biochim. Biophys. Acta* 172:429–37
142. Redfearn, E. 1967. *Biochim. Biophys. Acta* 131:218–20
143. Reed, D. W. 1969. *J. Biol. Chem.* 244:4936–41
144. Reed, D. W., Clayton, R. K. 1968. *Biochem. Biophys. Res. Commun.* 30: 471–75
145. Reed, D. W., Ke, B. 1973. *J. Biol. Chem.* 248:3041–45
146. Reed, D. W., Peters, G. A. 1972. *J. Biol. Chem.* 247:7148–52
147. Reed, D. W., Zankel, K. L., Clayton R. K. 1969. *Proc. Nat. Acad. Sci. USA* 63:42–46
148. Reiss-Husson, F., Jolchine, G. 1972. *Biochim. Biophys. Acta* 256:440–51
149. Rubin, L. B., Dubrovin, V. N., Adamova, N. P., Shvinka, Y. E. 1970. *Microbiology USSR* 39:264–68

150. Rubin, L. B., Rubin, A. B., Dubrovin, V. N., Shvinka, Y. E. 1969. *Mol. Biol. USSR* 3:700–8
151. Salemme, F. R., Freer, S. T., Xuong, N. H., Alden, R. A., Kraut, J. 1973. *J. Biol. Chem.* 248:3910–21
152. Sauer, K., Dratz, E. A., Coyne, L. 1968. *Proc. Nat. Acad. Sci. USA* 61:17–24
153. Schmidt, G. L., Kamen, M. D. 1971. *Biochim. Biophys. Acta* 234:70–72
154. Schwenker, V., Gingras, G. 1973. *Biochem. Biophys. Res. Commun.* 51:94–99
155. Seibert, M., DeVault, D. 1970. *Biochim. Biophys. Acta* 205:220–31
156. Ibid 1971. 253:396–411
157. Seibert, M., Dutton, P. L., DeVault, D. 1971. *Biochim. Biophys. Acta* 226: 189–92
158. Sherman, L. A., Cohen, W. S. 1972. *Biochim. Biophys. Acta* 283:54–66
159. Slooten, L. 1972. *Biochim. Biophys. Acta* 256:452–66
160. Ibid 275:208–18
161. Smith, L., Ramirez, J. 1959. *Arch. Biochem. Biophys.* 79:233–44
162. Smith, W. R., Sybesma, C., Dus, K. 1972. *Biochim. Biophys. Acta* 267: 609–15
163. Smith, W. R., Sybesma, C., Litchfield, W. J., Dus, K. 1973. *Biochemistry* 12: 2665–71
164. Steiner, L. A., Okamura, M. Y., Lopes, D. A., Moskowitz, E., Feher, G. 1974. *Biochemistry* 13:In press
165. Straley, S. C., Parson, W. W., Mauzerall, D. C., Clayton, R. K. 1973. *Biochim. Biophys. Acta* 305:597–609
166. Sugimura, T., Okabe, K. 1962. *J. Biochem. Tokyo* 52:235–36
167. Sybesma, C. 1967. *Photochem. Photobiol.* 6:261–67
168. Sybesma, C. 1969. *Biochim. Biophys. Acta* 172:177–79
169. Sybesma, C., Fowler, C. F. 1968. *Proc. Nat. Acad. Sci. USA* 61:1343–48
170. Sybesma, C., Kok, B. 1969. *Biochim. Biophys. Acta* 180:410–13
171. Takamiya, K.-I. 1971. *Biochim. Biophys. Acta* 234:390–98
172. Takamiya, K.-I., Nishimura, M., Takamiya, A. 1967. *Plant Cell Physiol.* 8: 79–86
173. Takamiya, K.-I., Takamiya, A. 1967. *Plant Cell Physiol.* 8:719–30
174. Ibid 1969. 10:113–27
175. Takamiya, K.-I., Takamiya, A. 1970. *Biochim. Biophys. Acta* 205:72–85
176. Takano, T., Kallai, O. B., Swanson, R., Dickerson, R. E. 1973. *J. Biol. Chem.* 248:5234–55
177. Thornber, J. P. 1970. *Biochemistry* 9: 2688–98
178. Thornber, J. P., Olson, J. M. 1968. *Biochemistry* 7:2242–49
179. Thornber, J. P., Olson, J. M., Williams, D. M., Clayton, M. L. 1969. *Biochim. Biophys. Acta* 172:351–54
180. Urban, P. F., Klingenberg, M. 1969. *Eur. J. Biochem.* 9:519–25
181. von Stedingk, L.-V. 1967. *Arch. Biochem. Biophys.* 120:537–41
182. von Stedingk, L.-V., Baltscheffsky, H. 1966. *Arch. Biochem. Biophys.* 117: 400–4
183. Vredenberg, W. J., Amesz, J. 1966. *Biochim. Biophys. Acta* 126:244–53
184. Vredenberg, W. J., Amesz, J., Duysens, L. N. M. 1965. *Biochem. Biophys. Res. Commun.* 18:435–39
185. Walker, D. A., Crofts, A. R. 1970. *Ann. Rev. Biochem.* 39:389–428
186. Wraight, C. A., Clayton, R. K. 1974. *Biochim. Biophys. Acta* In press
187. Yau, H. F. 1971. *Photochem. Photobiol.* 14:475–82

# METABOLIC COMPARTMENTATION: SYMBIOTIC, ORGANELLAR, MULTIENZYMIC, AND MICROENVIRONMENTAL

❖1630

*Paul A. Srere and Klaus Mosbach*

Pre-Clinical Science Unit, Veterans Administration Hospital and Department of Biochemistry, The University of Texas Health Science Center, Dallas, Texas 75216 and Chemical Center, Biochemistry 2, The University of Lund, Lund, Sweden

CONTENTS

INTRODUCTION .... 61
SYMBIOTIC COMPARTMENTALIZATION .... 62
ORGANELLE COMPARTMENTALIZATION .... 66
*Prokaryotes* .... 66
*Eukaryotes* .... 67
MULTIENZYME COMPLEXES .... 70
*General Features* .... 70
*Isolatable Complexes* .... 71
*Metabolic Pools-Putative Complexes* .... 74
MICROENVIRONMENTAL EFFECTS .... 75
*Microenvironmental Matrix-Effects* .... 76
*Microenvironmental Effects Due to Enzymic Activity* .... 77
*Multi-Step Enzyme Systems* .... 77
OVERVIEW .... 80

## I. INTRODUCTION

Compartmentalization has been recognized as a necessary structural feature of all living cells and cell systems. In his excellent review of this subject Moses (97) indicated that it is likely that compartmentation is involved in cellular regulation and differentiation. In another recent review concerning compartmentation in plants, Oaks & Bidwell (100) expressed the belief that not only does all metabolic regulation depend on this phenomenon but perhaps enzyme induction occurs as a result of separation of metabolites. Cori (20) indicated almost 20 years ago that compartmentation offered a convenient means of regulating metabolism. Weiss

(135) has discussed the uniqueness inherent in the properties of a living cell due to its hierarchical order and organization of its components. Certainly the structural complexity of cells—even of the simplest microorganisms—has been made clearly visible by electron microscopy. In spite of the apparent need for, usefulness of, and physical existence of compartments in cells, a major problem has existed in terms of the difficulty of obtaining experimental evidence showing the metabolic functioning of compartments in vivo. Further, what about the existence and function of unseen compartments—the microenvironments? Do they exist and what is their role?

There are many easily recognized forms of biological compartmentation. 1. In the biosphere each life form is a separate compartment (composed of a set of complex biological compartments) and the interaction between them is referred to as the study of ecology. 2. In each multicellular species the carrying out of special functions by differentiated cells is another example of compartmentation. 3. Within the individual cells compartmentation is achieved with organelles (nuclei, mitochondria, chloroplasts, lysosomes, peroxisomes, vacuoles) separated from each other by enclosing membranes. Even prokaryotic cells, at one time thought to be devoid of organelles, have minimally the separate regions of cytosol and periplasmic space. 4. In the absence of membrane-limited organelle compartmentation, functional separation exists by means of isolatable, stable complexes of enzymes. 5. Finally, it seems probable that compartmentation exists even in the absence of membranes and stable enzyme complexes. In the latter case the compartment may be the microenvironment in a region of weakly interacting proteins, or the microenvironment near a surface due to unstirred water layers (29, 30, 145) or due to a proposed water structure (36, 37, 142) in the cell. Indeed, certain nonbiological catalytic systems in homogeneous solution have been shown to become an oscillating structure as a result of cyclical changing microenvironments (146, 149).

In this review we shall consider only the following subjects: 1. The function of compartmentalization in the case of cells of different species which live in symbiotic relation; 2. compartmentalization due to the existence of organelles and spaces separated by membrane; 3. compartmentalization due to multienzyme complexes; and 4. microenvironmental effects due to loose enzyme association or unstirred layer effects.

Below the level of stable multienzyme complexes direct evidence for microenvironmental effects in cells is unavailable. If separate microenvironments exist within the same physical compartment of a cell, all the present experimental attempts to evaluate which metabolites are regulatory in the various pathways are far from the mark. This experimental problem is at present so formidable that only the evaluation of microenvironmental effects in the regulatory behavior of model systems is possible.

## II. SYMBIOTIC COMPARTMENTALIZATION

Of various symbiotic forms known, lichens appear unique in that both symbionts, alga and fungus, participate with their entire organism to form a new functional entity, the lichen (1). The two symbionts, alga (phycobiont) and fungus (mycobiont), can be looked upon as two separate cellular compartments. Although only limited information is available on the role of each symbiont in a lichen's metabolism, which may be referred to in broader terms as the biochemistry of symbiosis, this symbiotic relationship has been the most studied. Both symbionts are in close contact, the fungal cell often enveloping the algal cell or penetrating it with special sucking organs (haustoria) to ensure rapid exchange of metabolites (Figure 1). The degree of penetration of the phycobiont's cell by fungal haustoria varies (1). Although the algal cell wall is always penetrated, it is difficult to determine whether the algal protoplast membrane is also penetrated. On the other hand, the fungal haustorial cell wall is generally thinner than normal walls of hyphae, probably to allow transport of organic material.

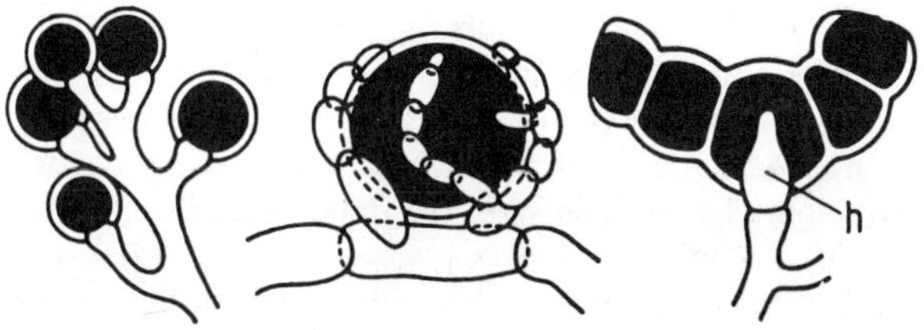


*Figure 1* Several forms of coupling between lichen alga (●) and lichen fungus (h = haustoria).

Carbon for the lichen is furnished primarily by the photosynthetic activity of the algal partner. About 35 lichen species with 12 different types of algal partners have been studied to determine the nature of the substances which pass from the alga to the fungus as well as the rate of movement between the symbionts. Smith and associates (33, 34, 107–109), succeeded in identifying the carbon compounds that participate in the transport of the fixed carbon from the alga to the fungus. In some representative investigations (33, 34) pieces from the thallus of *Peltigera polydactyla,* a lichen with a blue-green *Nostoc* alga, were taken and introduced into a medium containing $NaH^{14}CO_3$. Individual thallus pieces were collected at intervals, and the algal layer was separated from the medulla layer, the latter consisting only of fungal hyphae. As expected, the activity initially appeared in the algal layer, the $^{14}C$-glucose formed then migrated to the fungal part. After a 45-min incubation period in light, 60% of the fixed carbon was present in the fungal part in the form of mannitol. In most lichens the soluble carbohydrates of the fungus are different from those of the algae. Mannitol in particular is exclusively a fungal product in the great majority of lichens. This fact facilitated the studies mentioned. By contrast, in the *Xanthoria aureola* lichen, containing the green alga *Trebouxia* as phycobiont, the first labeled product found was ribitol which was subsequently converted into mannitol and arabitol in the mycobiont (108). A comparative study with four different *Lobaria* lichens containing *Trebouxia* and *Nostoc* algae led to the establishment of the two following principal patterns of carbohydrate movement (109).

Alga Fungus
(blue-green) ⟶ glucose ⟶ (⟶ glucose ⟶ mannitol)
(green) ⟶ sugar alcohol ⟶ (⟶ mannitol)

Accordingly, the algal partner participating in the symbiosis appears to influence the type of carbohydrate moving from algal to fungal compartment. In studies on the rate of transport between algal and fungal component it was shown that [$^{14}$C]-labeled mannitol appeared after 2 min of photosynthesis by the thallus sample (34).

In another study (40) the appearance of $^{14}$C-activities from $^{14}CO_2$ in the tridepside gyrophoric acid (Figure 2), following incubation of the lichen *Umbilicaria papulosa* in light was investigated. Labeling of the depside occurred within 1 min. Since at least the monocyclic units of these compounds must be synthesized in the fungal part, the entire sequence takes place during this short time, i.e. photosynthesis in the alga, transport of the sugar alcohols to the fungus, and biosynthesis of the depside from acetate and malonate units formed from the sugar alcohol.

Mobile sugar alcohols other than ribitol that have been identified include erythritol and sorbitol. A summary of the characteristics of carbohydrate movement between the symbionts based mainly on the data found in references 33, 34, 61, 107–109 is given by Richardson (106).

Nitrogen is supplied to the organism by absorption of both organic and inorganic nitrogen compounds by the lichen thallus, i.e. mainly by the fungal partner. Henriksson (58) and Scott (114) were able to show with $^{15}$N that lichens with blue-green algae can also fix atmospheric nitrogen.

Little is known about the vitamin balance of intact lichens, but thiamine and biotin are known to be essential to the isolated mycobiont. It appears that in the intact lichen at least part of the vitamins required is provided by the phycobiont.

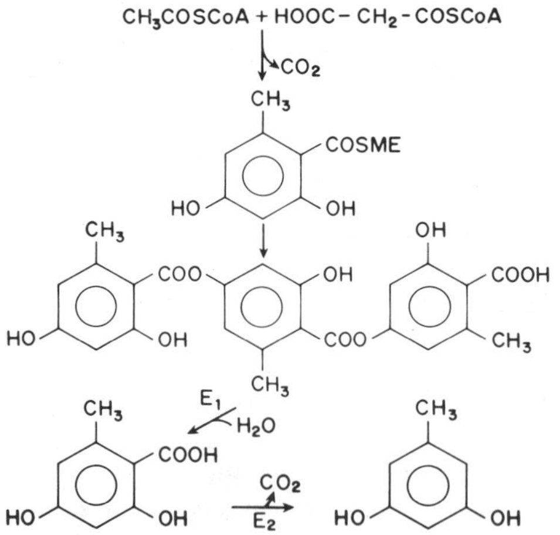


*Figure 2* Biosynthesis and enzymic breakdown of the lichen depside gyrophoric acid. ME = multienzyme complex, $E_1$ = orsellinate depside hydrolase, $E_2$ = orsellinate decarboxylase.

The important question as to the mechanism of exchange between the symbionts is the subject of much study. It is still not clear what makes the alga release nutrients to the fungus, or whether the role of the fungus is active or passive (106). In the nonsymbiotic condition, the general direction of membrane transport of neutral or weakly ionized molecules is inwards. In symbiosis physical contact results in either the elimination of this tendency to inward movement for certain nutrients or even a positive reversal of direction to produce an outflow from the cell. In most lichens the transferred carbohydrate is rapidly converted to mannitol. This presumably maintains a concentration gradient facilitating the outflow of the mobile carbohydrate. However, flow reversal at times would also be necessary for the algal component to obtain vitamins or growth factors from the fungus. Such fluctuation would not need to be a disadvantage for the fungus if the alga cannot utilize the polyol.

Although the adaptation of both symbionts to their symbiotic metabolic relationship is highly developed, both can be grown separately on special media. Their morphological appearance, however, differs sharply from the natural lichen. The fact that lichens do represent a new functional entity and not merely the sum of both components is illustrated by the number of typical lichen compounds found. Thus the structural classes such as depsides, depsidones, depsones, dibenzofurans, and pulvic acid derivatives are almost exclusively confined to lichens. Whether both symbionts participate directly with their enzyme systems in their biosynthesis and catabolism is still an open question. It could very well be that again a division of labor takes place as indicated from studies on the enzymic catabolism of the typical lichen metabolite, the depside, gyrophoric acid (96, 113). The first step, hydrolysis of the depside catalyzed by the enzyme orsellinate depside hydrolase, possibly present in the algal component, is followed by a decarboxylation step catalyzed by orsellinate decarboxylase, likely to be present in the fungal part (Figure 2). In analogy both symbionts may participate in their biosynthesis. Whether or not the algal component contains enzymes which participate directly in the synthesis of lichen compounds, it should be stressed that it is the metabolic activity of the algal component and in particular photosynthesis, that provides the prerequisites for the synthesis of lichen substances.

Other symbiotic forms also show metabolic compartmentation. During the symbiosis of the nitrogen-fixing nodular bacteria with legumes, the nitrogen fixed in the nodules is given up to the plant partner which, in turn, furnishes carbon compounds. In mycorrhiza, the symbiotic association of fungi with higher plants, the fungal partner supplies the water and mineral salts required and takes carbon compounds from its plant partner.

The high degree of integration in symbiotic associations is demonstrated very clearly by the appearance of substances and structures that the individual components could not produce. Examples are a special hemoglobin, leghemoglobin, that participates in the fixation of nitrogen in the nodules of legumes (3, 132), the development of rhizotamines (root nodules) in *Actinomycetes* symbioses, and the morphogenetic effect of the intestinal flora in mammals on the development of the lymphatic system. It is tempting to draw a parallel between the intact lichen thallus and the individual cell (38, 92, 93). The latter also represents a symbiotic form of life, although in a smaller scale, being made up of genetically semiautonomous, closely integrated small organelles such as chloroplasts and mitochondria.

## III. ORGANELLE COMPARTMENTALIZATION

### *Prokaryotes*

Electron microscopy has revealed a rich, fine structure present within the cell membrane of most protists. Most of the inclusions (granules, vacuoles, mesosomes, nuclear body) are condensed materials without a membrane separating the inclusion from the rest of the cell. The mesosomes seem to be structured invaginations of the cell membrane. Some vacuoles are believed to be formed when material evaporates in the electron beam. It is not clear whether such formations serve the purpose of allowing the accumulation of material (extra membrane, substrates) or whether they represent a primitive attempt of separating functional microenvironments.

Many protists do have at least two separate compartments: the space within the cell membrane and the space between the cell membrane and the cell wall (periplasmic space). It is clear that the periplasmic space contains a specific set of enzymes and thus must represent a functional separation. Heppel (59) has reviewed the work reported on periplasmic enzymes and what he refers to as surface enzymes in general. The periplasmic enzymes have been compared to the lysosomal enzymes whose function is proposed as a digestive one operating in cells for autolysis after cell death. It has also been proposed that periplasmic enzymes may serve as protective agents against environmental injurious agents. Glaser et al (47) have postulated that this compartment is concerned with control of intracellular concentration of nucleotides.

A number of oxidative enzymes in bacteria can be isolated in a membrane bound form (for review see 35). Some of these membrane bound enzymes in *Bacillus cereus* may not be active in situ (77). It had been assumed for many years that these enzymes were associated with mesosomes where they exist. Thus *Azotobacter* with its enormous oxidative capacity has highly structured and invaginated mesosomes. Reusch & Burger (105) have reviewed this problem and conclude, however, that no good evidence exists for supposing that the oxidative enzymes are associated with mesosomes, nor do they serve a transport function in *Bacillus licheniformis* (83). The mesosome is constructed so that the interiors are extracytoplasmic but the folding of the membrane is such that the cytoplasm has access to the inner regions of the overall structure. Among the proposed functions of the mesosome are cell division, cell envelope synthesis, and exoenzyme synthesis and excretion. Reusch & Burger (105) suggested that the mesosome represents a primitive form of compartmentation serving a function similar to lysosomes.

A recent report by Shively et al (117) showed that the polyhedral inclusion bodies of *Thiobacillus neapolitanus* contained ribulose diphosphate carboxylase. This may be the first metabolically functional organelle shown to exist in a prokaryotic cell. Not every photosynthetic parokaryote contains this organelle nor is the surrounding membrane a typical trilamellar membrane.

An interesting report of Burger & Pavlasová (13) showed that a mutant of *E. coli* apparently lost its amylomaltase activity by its being bound to a membrane in the cell. Treatment of intact cells of the mutant by ribonuclease or histone, to release the membrane bound enzyme, led to utilization of maltose.

Coleman (17) reviewed the area of membrane bound enzymes and indicates that this represents a method of achieving compartmentation of metabolic sequences. A cell devoid of structure, therefore, still contains at least two compartments: the membrane region and the inside region.

### *Eukaryotes*

Several interesting examples of metabolite separation in separate cellular organelles have been reported recently. In *Neurospora* there are two pathways which utilize carbamyl phosphate; one is concerned with arginine production and the other is involved in pyrimidine biosynthesis. Davis and his co-workers showed by nutritional studies of *Neurospora* mutants that each pathway had its own carbamyl phosphate synthetase (see 25 for review; also 143).

While under certain conditions overflow from one synthetase could be used for the other pathway, analysis of a number of pyrimidine mutants suggested that the carbamyl phosphate synthetase of the pyrimidine pathway and the next enzyme of that pathway, aspartate transcarbamylase, were at adjacent genetic sites. The hypothesis that these two enzymes formed an aggregate was tested with positive results. Lue & Kaplan (82) showed that these two enzymes were similarly genetically related in yeast and that carbamyl phosphate produced in the yeast aggregate did not mix with an external pool of carbamyl phosphate.

There is no similar genetic connection or aggregation with the carbamyl phosphate synthetase of the arginine pathway and the next enzyme of that pathway ornithine transcarbamylase. However, it had been shown by histochemical means in the rat hepatocyte that the ornithine transcarbamylase was a mitochondrial enzyme (89, 91) and the aspartate transcarbamylase was associated with the endoplasmic reticulum (122) which is consistent with centrifugation data of Jones (66). When Bernhardt & Davis (7) applied the histochemical techniques to *Neurospora* cells it was found that ornithine transcarbamylase was a mitochondrial enzyme and that the aspartate transcarbamylase was a nuclear enzyme. Davis (25), however, points out that separation of the two pathways into the separate organelles does not demonstrate the separateness of the two carbamyl phosphate pools since data exist indicating mixing of these two carbamyl phosphate pools despite different locations of the two enzymes in the cell.

Further studies by Davis and his co-workers (136, 137) have indicated that ornithine and arginine occur in two separate locations in the cell. The bulk of these two compounds appear to be sequestered in large vacuoles. Exogenous sources of ornithine and arginine do not mix with these storage pools of the compounds. Subramanian et al (127) have postulated that as a result of the arginine being sequestered in vesicles the arginine concentration is low in the cytoplasm and urea formation takes place only at a low rate. No explanation is given for the necessity of having available a large amount of ornithine and arginine.

Evidence for the existence of multiple pools of amino acids in microorganisms has accumulated for a number of years (23, 85, 120, 150). Wiemken & Nurse (141) in a recent paper were able to extend the earlier studies to indicate that one of the separate pools was located in vacuoles of the cell. In their experiments they treated cells of *Candida utilis* with cytochrome *c* which made the cell membrane permeable but did not affect the membrane surrounding the vacuoles. In this way they could release the amino acids of the cytosol compartment and measure their radioactivity. Additional treatment with osmotic shock and basic proteins released the vacuolar amino acids. They showed that specific activities of several amino acids after pulse labeling were always higher in the cytoplasm than in the vacuolar fractions. It is probable, they point out, that further separation of amino acids into separate pools occurs in the cytoplasm.

There are several structural compartments in eukaryotes involved in the different aspects of carbohydrate metabolism. Glycolytic enzymes are cytosolic; Krebs cycle enzymes are mitochondrial; glyoxylate shunt enzymes are preoxisomal (glyoxysomal); pentose phosphate shunt enzymes may be microsomal, while it seems that several enzymes of glycogen metabolism may be bound to glycogen particles.

Another case of organelle compartmentation that has been well studied concerns multiple pools of acetyl CoA in certain organisms (27). A number of bacteria, some plants, and protozoa contain the metabolic pathway known as the glyoxalate shunt. In this pathway two acetyl CoA molecules are converted to a succinate molecule, thereby allowing for a mechanism for the conversion of fat to carbohydrate. The enzymes of the eukaryotes which contain this pathway are located in a separate organelle known as glyoxisomes. A recent report by Bieglmayer et al (9) has indicated that in glyoxisomes of castor-bean endosperm citrate synthase and malate synthase, two enzymes of the pathway, were bound to the glyoxysomal membranes. It is obvious, on the basis of enzyme location and known biosynthetic pathways in such cells, that we can now account for at least three different acetyl CoA pools: 1. mitochondrial, 2. glyoxisomal, and 3. cytosolic. Blum and his co-workers (18, 19, 79, 103) have analyzed the metabolism of *Tetrahymena pyriformis,* a protozoan which contains the glyoxalate shunt pathway. They have utilized specifically labeled compounds which can generate labeled acetyl CoA (1-$^{14}$C acetate, 1-$^{14}$C octanoate, 2-$^{14}$C pyruvate) and analyzed the distribution of isotope into products for which acetyl CoA is utilized in the organism (glycogen, lipid, $CO_2$). If the acetyl CoA pools which are the precursors of these products are in rapid equilibrium (i.e. functionally a single pool), one would expect similar labeling patterns and dilution patterns from the differently labeled acetyl CoA precursors. The experimental results showed quite different labeling and dilution patterns. Thus cold octanoate reduced incorporation of labeled acetate into lipid but did not reduce its conversion to $CO_2$, whereas cold acetate reduced conversion of labeled octanoate into $CO_2$ but not its incorporation into lipid. The final model proposed by Blum and his co-workers (102) contains three separate acetyl CoA pools, one would be glyoxysomal and two would be mitochondrial. Blum considers the possibility of other models but has been unable to construct a one pool model to fit the data. Since the mitochondrion is a two membrane structure it is possible to visualize the two pools as being membrane separated.

Blum and his co-workers' studies are all based on steady state measurement of isotope distribution and as such their interpretations cannot be criticized on the same basis as some of the kinetic isotope data. Their findings do not pose any conceptual difficulties. Enzyme distribution studies in relation to the structure present in the cell easily allow for the existence of three (and possibly even more) pools of acetyl CoA. In metazoan eukaryotes then there is no difficulty in accepting isotopic evidence for the existence of multiple pools of one metabolite since there are many different cell types and organelles. The same kind of data indicating multiple pools of metabolites also exists with unicellular prokaryotic organisms, but the structural opportunities are often much limited.

A subject that is not reviewed here is the metabolic compartmentation due to the nucleus in cells and due to the endoplasmic reticulum. Generally speaking it is believed that the nuclear membrane is quite permeable to many substrates and to some enzymes; this has made studies difficult. In the area of protein synthesis on the endoplasmic reticulum, there exist the two compartments of bound and free polysomes in cells. This subject has been recently reviewed by Campbell (14).

Even within an individual compartment there may be separate organization of enzymes. Thus Rothstein et al (111) studying extracts of lyophilized yeast concluded that the glycolytic enzymes existed in two structures; one was concerned only with fermentation while the other was associated with respiratory enzymes. Shaw & Stadie (116) had indicated that rat diaphragm behaved as if two glycolytic pools existed within the cytosol. In one pathway glucose was converted to glycogen, in a second it was converted to lactic acid. Identical intermediate sugar phosphates in the two pools did not mix. Recent work by Landau & Sims (76) gave support for the idea of two glucose-6-phosphate pools and proposed that one compartment might be the sarcotubular system of muscle.

Another kind of glycolytic organization concerns the binding of glycolytic enzymes to mitochondria. Crane & Sols (24) had shown that hexokinase binds to mitochondria and other workers had extended this observation. Bessman and his co-workers (8, 53, 54) presented evidence that this binding has functional significance in that ADP and Pi lead to higher rates of glucose-6-phosphate formation for the mitochondrial bound hexokinase than does ATP. This would seem to indicate that the active site of hexokinase was oriented toward the mitochondrion to receive the ATP made within. Blum and his co-workers have shown that in *Tetrahymena* both the kinases of glycolysis, hexokinase and phosphofructokinase, are bound to the mitochondria (39, 110).

In any case what has been shown in recent years by Krebs (144), Veech (55), and their colleagues is that vast differences exist between cytosol and mitochondria in eukaryotic cells in the redox potential (NAD/NADH), the phosphorylation potential (ATP/(ADP) (Pi), and the acylation potential (acyl CoA/CoA). These differences, calculated from near equilibrium assumptions, illustrate dramatically the need for compartmentalization. Thus the NAD/NADH value for cytosol is 1000 whereas that for a mitochondrion is 7. If such differences are important for efficient energy production and utilization, then in the absence of similar ability to separate metabolic systems in prokaryotes either these differences are achieved by membrane localization or microenvironmental effects, or there exist different metabolic requirements.

## IV. MULTIENZYME COMPLEXES

### *General Features*

Pollard (101) applied elementary collision kinetics to several metabolic processes occurring in cells. He concluded for cells of 1 $\mu$ or less diffusion times are sufficiently fast that at average concentrations of intermediates, metabolic processes could occur at rates equal to those observed. Cells with dimensions greater than 1 $\mu$ "must therefore have a submicroscopic order to secure the closeness of reacting elements which are in low concentrations." He also adds that "the presence of an activation energy will require that successive reactions be produced in an organized system."

Several experiments indicate that most enzymes within cells do exist in a bound (organized?) state. Thus Lloyd-Davies et al (81) showed that 60% of the enzyme of rat liver cells was bound.

An interesting experiment was carried out by Kempner & Miller (68, 69) who centrifuged *Euglena* cells and then looked for enzymes in the various strata within the cell. They concluded that there was no free or unbound enzyme in the cell.

There are situations where diffusion times can be sufficiently fast so that organization of enzymes would not be necessary, even in cells greater in size than 1 $\mu$.

Srere (123) has pointed out that many enzymes exist at rather high concentrations within cells. Hess & Boiteux (60) have extended this calculation to determine the average distance between glycolytic enzymes within yeast cells. Thus the total concentration of monomers of the glycolytic enzymes in yeast is 1.3 mM. It is possible to calculate that the average distance between monomers is 40–50 Å. Using Einstein's law and a diffusion coefficient of $10^{-5}$ cm$^2$/sec they computed a transit time in the microsecond range. Since turnover times are in the 100/sec range they concluded that diffusion is not limiting in this case. Thus even in a cell larger than 1 $\mu$ sufficiently high enzyme concentrations would nullify the need of organization if diffusion times were the only consideration.

Hübscher et al (62) had made similar calculations for the glycolytic enzymes of rat liver cells. In this case the enzymes are much less concentrated. They used a diffusion coefficient of $8 \times 10^{-7}$ cm$^2$/sec so that their calculations indicated that transit times would be too long (2.3 sec for phosphofructokinase, 18 msec for aldolase) to sustain the observed rate of glycolysis. They therefore postulate an organization of these enzymes within the cytosol.

A situation similar to the glycolytic enzymes of yeast must exist within mitochondria where high concentrations of Krebs cycle enzymes exist ($10^{-6}$–$10^{-5}$ M). In spite of these high concentrations Srere (124) has postulated that these enzymes exist as a multienzyme system bound to the inside of the inner membrane. He bases this on structural and metabolic considerations. No evidence exists for this postulate—

indeed like the evidence presented by Hess & Boiteux (60) for glycolytic enzymes, no direct interactions of Krebs cycle enzymes have been observed. However, a model which illustrates the kinetic advantages of such an organization will be discussed in a later section.

It is clear that many cells contain organized enzyme systems even though diffusion is not a rate-limiting process. The possible advantages of such multienzyme systems other than decreased diffusion time are: 1. Competition with other pathways is minimized by keeping an intermediate in a limited microenvironment; 2. the restriction to a microenvironment of a few molecules of intermediate could present an effectively high concentration to the next active site (this is especially true for systems where intermediates are covalently bound and are delivered to the next enzyme); 3. the protein-protein interactions of a complex may be necessary for control features of the system (42); 4. protection of unstable intermediates; and 5. specific environments of varying nature (hydrophobicity) can be created to enhance specific reactions.

There is no apparent single type or mechanism to characterize multienzyme complexes. Some are simply two partial reactions (acetyl CoA carboxylase), others consist of an enzymatic and a regulatory subunit (ATCase). Fatty acid synthetase consists of seven enzymes which are inactive when separated, while $\alpha$-keto acid dehydrogenases can be dissociated into their separate activities (128). In fatty acid synthetase and the related 6-methyl salicylic acid synthetase (32) the intermediates are covalently bound, but this may not be the case in tryptophan synthetase.

All of the multienzyme complexes mentioned above have protein components which are tightly bound to each other. There are other multienzyme systems in which the components are apparently linked to or embedded in membranes and those not linked to each other. The entire field of bound enzymes has been thoroughly reviewed in recent years and no attempt will be made to repeat these data (17, 46, 82a). Only a few of the more recent advances and examples of multienzyme complexes will be cited.

## *Isolatable Complexes*

Recent biochemical and genetic experiments (see 70) have indicated that DNA replication takes place in a large macromolecular complex. Gentle lysis of cells on cellophane membranes keep these large complexes intact and rates of DNA replication can be observed which are much higher than seen in extracts from conventionally broken cells (56).

In Chinese hamster ovary cells grown in cell culture there is a differential distribution of aminoacyl-tRNA synthetases. In ribosomal, nuclear, postribosomal, and supernatant fractions they must exist as high molecular weight particles (4).

Shoaf & Jones (118) have recently shown that three of the six enzymes involved in the biosynthesis of uridylic acid can be isolated as a multienzyme complex from Ehrlich ascites cells.

A large number of studies continue to present additional evidence for the existence of multienzyme complexes for a wide variety of biosynthetic pathways. Two recent additions to this group are systems which involve pantetheine. Pantetheine has already been shown to be involved in the multienzyme system for fatty acid synthesis as part of a protein called acyl carrier protein. It was first detected in *E. coli* where the enzymes are not bound in a tight complex. Lipmann and his co-workers (78, 80) have studied the mechanism of biosynthesis of gramicidin S and tyrocidin, both polypeptide antibiotics. They have reported that pantetheine is involved with thioesterification of the amino acids which are bound to a polyenzyme. The mechanism is apparently similar to fatty acid biosynthesis in its elongation aspects with pantetheine and to some extent it is similar to conventional peptide bond formation.

Still another example of pantetheine in the role of a carrier is the mechanism of citrate lyase from *E. coli* and *Klebsiella aerogenes.* Srere and his colleagues (121, 125) have shown that an acetyl pantetheine is involved in this mechanism. Eggerer and his co-workers (31) have identified and isolated an acetyl ACP as part of the enzyme. Formation of acetyl ACP in *E. coli* and *K. aerogenes* takes place via an activating enzyme and acetyl phosphopantetheine. The enzyme from this source has two different subunits and an ACP. The purified enzyme from *Streptococcus diacetilactis* can be acetylated in the absence of an activating enzyme. SDS polyacrylamide analyses of this protein show one band more than the protein from *K. aerogenes* (M. Singh and P. A. Srere, unpublished observations). They feel that the extra band is the activating enzyme. In any case this multienzyme system can catalyze its own activation as well as the cleavage of citrate.

Progress continues to be made in understanding the mechanism and control of pyruvate dehydrogenase complex. Reed and his co-workers (104) have shown that control of this enzyme complex takes place by a phosphorylation and dephosphorylation of one of the enzyme units. There is no clear evidence as yet whether the kinase and phosphatase responsible for these modifications constitute part of the multienzyme complex. This control has not been reported for bacterial $\alpha$-keto acid dehydrogenase complex.

Henning and his co-workers (57) have studied this enzyme from the viewpoint of genetically assembling this complex from *E. coli.* Their conclusions are that the enzyme complex does not have a unique subunit structure nor does cooperativity exist during its assembly. They also believe that the pyruvate dehydrogenase component of the complex regulates (by repression) the overall synthesis of the complex.

It seems clear that the biosynthetic pathway of many amino acids includes multienzyme complexes. The best studied of these is the tryptophan synthetase complex from *E. coli.* There are also many studies on the complex involved in biosynthesis of aromatic amino acids in *Neurospora.* Jacobson et al (63) have shown that the multienzyme complex encoded in the arom gene cluster in *Neurospora* is an aggregate containing five separate enzyme activities of approximate molecular weight of 230,000. It is believed this is composed of two identical 115,000 mol wt clusters. Gaertner, Ericson & DeMoss (43) had shown that the system uses precursors in the pathway in preference to externally supplied intermediates. Matchett & DeMoss (85) have provided evidence that at least two pools of tryptophan existed in growing *Neurospora.*

*Saccharomyces cerevisiae* can use urea as a sole source of nitrogen. Whitney & Cooper (140) have presented evidence that the conversion of urea to $NH_3$ is a two-step process involving urea carboxylase and allophanate hydrolase which can be isolated as a multienzyme complex.

Moses (97) has reported on a multienzyme complex from *E. coli* which catalyzes the conversion of glutamate to glutamic semialdehyde through glutamyl phosphate. This is part of the path of proline biosynthesis. Earlier Vogel & Kopac (134) had reported channeling of glutamic semialdehyde pools of arginine and proline biosynthesis in *Neurospora.*

Bearden & Moses (6) looked for evidence of compartmentation of histidine biosynthesis both in *Salmonella typhimurium* and *Saccharomyces cerevisiae.* They measured the dilution of the incorporation of labeled glucose into the histidine of cell proteins by adding exogenous cold histidinol. In the case of *S. typhimurium* the added histidinol caused a dilution of the labeled glucose incorporated into histidine in proteins. This indicated that separate functional compartments did not exist in this bacterium. Quite different results were obtained in the yeast cell.

In yeast cells exogenous histidinol, which was able to penetrate the cell, was incapable of diluting the incorporation of label from $^{14}C$ glucose into histidine. It had been shown earlier that three enzymes of the his-4 region formed an aggregate. Bearden & Moses (6) postulated that even a larger aggregate may exist for the whole pathway in yeast. It is interesting to note that the ten histidine genes are contiguous in *Salmonella,* where no evidence for a complex was obtained, while this is not so in the yeast, in which aggregation occurs. Vogel & Bacon (133) presented evidence that the not closely linked genes of the arginine system in *E. coli* could occur as gene aggregates by folding of the DNA. A similar consideration might explain the yeast data on histidine biosynthesis. It is interesting to note that Kühn et al (75) have shown that the genes of FA synthetase in yeast are contiguous.

There exists another type of multienzyme system known as multifunctional enzymes. In these cases a single protein molecule contains more than one enzyme activity. Cohen and his co-workers (16) have described a protein from *E. coli* that catalyzes both the aspartokinase and homoserine dehydrogenase reactions. Oddly enough these two activities are the first and third steps of a sequence, from aspartate to homoserine, where the second step is a separate enzyme. A trifunctional enzyme has been isolated from *Neurospora* by Minson & Creaser (90). The three activities are 1-N-(5'-phosphoribosyl)-ATP pyrophosphohydrolase, 1-N-(5'-phosphoribosyl)-AMP allohydrolase, and histidinol dehydrogenase, all nonsequential steps in histidine biosynthesis. Two more bifunctional enzymes from *Aerobacter aerogenes, E. coli, S. typhimurium,* and *Pseudomonas aeruginosa,* concerned with the biosynthesis of tyrosine and phenylalanine, have been studied (2, 21, 26, 73). These two enzymes are chorismate mutase-prephenate dehydratase and chorismate mutase-prephenate dehydrogenase, specific for phenylalanine and tyrosine, respectively. These are sequential reactions in each pathway.

DNA polymerase is an example of a multifunctional enzyme somewhat different from the others cited here. This enzyme has a number of different activities all associated with DNA synthesis or repair: 1. It can polymerize the nucleotide triphosphates; 2. it can act as a 3' ⟶ 5' nuclease, 3. it can act as a 5' ⟶ 3' nuclease, and 4. it can act as a pyrophosphatase (74). It is possible that these unusual systems represent residual evidence of the genetic pressure to form multienzyme systems and thus metabolic compartmentation.

### *Metabolic Pools-Putative Complexes*

A rather substantial body of evidence exists testifying to the possible existence of multiple metabolite pools in prokaryotes. MacNab et al (84) reported tracer experiments which provided evidence for metabolic compartmentation of glycolysis in *E. coli* during aerobic growth. In these experiments the substrates glycerol and maltose were presented singly and in pairs to *E. coli* with just one substrate being labeled. Incorporation into the amino acids alanine, aspartate, glutamate, glycine, histidine, proline, and valine was measured. More maltose carbon than glycerol carbon was found in alanine, valine, histidine, and proline. They postulate that two different glycolytic compartments must exist to explain the difference in the labeling patterns. Similar results were obtained with the substrate pair of galactose and lactose. If two pools exist, they postulate that either they exist as separate stable multienzyme complexes or perhaps are separated by the bacterial cell membrane. An earlier paper by Moses & Sharp (98) reported that glycolytic intermediates could be detected in the extracellular growth medium which they interpret as evidence favoring the latter distribution of enzymes (87).

Sercarz & Gorini (115) showed that the efficiency of repression of the arginine enzyme of a strain of *E. coli* varied depending on the source of arginine. Exogenous arginine seemed to be a source of arginine for repression while endogenous arginine was linked to the protein compartment. Later Tabor & Tabor (129) showed that in auxotrophic strains of *E. coli* polyamines were formed preferentially from exogenous arginine. No such difference was found in prototrophic strains of *E. coli.* These results are consistent with those of Sercarz and Gorini and suggest that exogenous arginine is metabolized at some site other than where endogenous arginine is metabolized. Recently Bollon & Vogel (12) obtained results in double mutants of *E. coli* which suggest channeling of arginine and citrulline. Their results indicate that citrulline has either a repressive or derepressive effect on the synthesis of the arginine enzymes depending on the source of arginine. In addition they have shown that it is possible independently to alter the growth rate of *E. coli* arginine auxotroph and the repression of the arginine enzymes by varying exogenous arginine concentration, indicating separate biosynthetic and regulatory arginine pools. It is possible that one of the arginine pools is in the periplasmic space since Heppel (59) notes that arginine binding proteins are found there.

A number of experiments indicate that multiple pools of nucleic acid precursors exist in *E. coli* (22). Mueller & Bremer (99) proposed that in *E. coli* there was an inhomogeneous spatial distribution of RNA precursors. The proposal included peripheral pools for UMP, UDP, UTP, and CTP and internal pools for UTP and CTP. This proposal was based on data which showed that labeled uracil was incorporated into uracil residues of RNA more rapidly than into UTP and into cytosine residues of RNA more slowly than into CTP.

Werner (138, 139) has studied the incorporation of labeled thymine into *E. coli* DNA. He concluded that DNA replication and repair synthesis drew their precursors from separate pools. He was unable to distinguish between the possibility of chemically different precursors or the same precursor from physically separated pools. His later work showed that under steady-state conditions, TDP and TTP were more immediate precursors of DNA than was TMP. In the presence of deoxyadenosine only TMP was on the direct pathway to DNA. Rather than postulate two different triphosphate pools Werner proposed the existence of an unknown activated deoxyribonucleoside-5'-monophosphate. A mathematical analysis of Werner's data by Rubinow & Yen (112) indicated that dTDP was a more likely precursor of DNA than was dTTP.

Billen and his co-workers (10) suggest that in *Bacillus subtilis* "two DNA synthesizing systems exist in separate, non-mixing cellular compartments. . . ." They showed that in freeze-treated *B. subtilis,* TTP incorporation into DNA was enhanced and that this synthesis was of the repair type. Incorporation of Tdr into DNA was reduced but this synthesis was of the semiconservative type. They suggest that these two types of DNA synthesis are either functionally or physically compartmentalized.

Jacobson & Lark (64) present evidence consistent with the existence of two types of DNA short chains (okazaki pieces). One type is labeled with thymine or thymidine located at the replication fork and is the immediate precursor of DNA. The majority of short chains do not behave as immediate precursors for DNA.

Baumunk & Friedman (5) postulated the existence of two pools of TTP in HeLa cells. One was said to be large with a minimal role in DNA synthesis. Recent evidence of Wittes & Kidwell (148) in mouse L cells, however, shows that the observed incorporation of $^{3}H$ thymidine could be explained on the basis of a single pool of dTTP.

In human lymphoblast cells $^{3}H$-dUrD and $^{3}H$-dThd into DNA reached a maximum while dTTP specific activity was still increasing. Fridland (41) concluded that different TTP pools existed in the cell to account for these results.

Till et al (131) report experiments using $^{32}Pi$ for labeling human red cell nucleotides and phosphorylated intermediates. The pattern of labeling suggested the existence of several compartments. They rule out the membrane as a possible compartment on the basis that the size of this compartment is too small.

These studies on pools have been considered separately because no evidence exists to define the mode of compartmentation. It is possible that some of the effects are due to the existence of separate organelles, as has been found for certain amino acids (see above), and some due to microenvironmental effects.

## V. MICROENVIRONMENTAL EFFECTS

It is generally accepted that few enzymes in vivo exist as free protein molecules in an aqueous environment. They are either membrane bound or solid-state assemblies like those found in the mitochondria, or are present in gel-like surroundings. Under these circumstances it is likely that individual microenvironments (microcompartments) will exist. In principle, two major factors are responsible for such microenvironments: (*a*) the effect on enzyme action attributable to the chemical nature of the surrounding membrane or matrix on which, or within which, the enzyme is located and (*b*) the enzymic activity itself leading to changes in local concentration of materials which effect enzyme activity. It is not possible experimentally to assess the nature of or the importance of microenvironments in situ. Most of what we will discuss below, therefore, will concern model systems in which enzymes are immobilized to or within artificial polymer particles or membranes. With such systems one microenvironmental effect at a time can be studied. Such data obtained will then assist in evaluating the possible roles of microenvironmental parameters in metabolism. These studies may also uncover unrecognized effects on enzyme activity which may be relevant for the in situ situation.

### *Microenvironmental Matrix-Effects*

The current concept of membrane structure is that of a lipid bilayer with embedded and partially embedded protein and glycoprotein molecules. Thus the exterior of the membrane will be polar due to the negative charges of the phospholipid continuum, the negative charges of sialic acid residues, and the charges of the proteins. The net charge on all natural membrane surfaces is negative. In model studies on the effects arising from the chemical and physical nature of the supporting matrix two areas have been investigated: the effect of charge and the effect of hydrophobicity.

As an example of studies on the charge effect, Goldstein et al have shown that the pH-activity profiles of polyanionic derivatives of several proteolytic enzymes, such as the ethylene maleic acid copolymer derivative of trypsin (51, 52), are displaced by 1 to 2.5 pH units towards the alkaline side as compared to the native enzyme. Polycationic derivatives of the same enzyme exhibited the reverse behavior displacing the pH optimum to more acidic pH values (50). Also, the apparent Michaelis constant of the positively charged substrate benzoyl L-arginine amide decreased by more than one order of magnitude using the polyanionic derivative of trypsin (51). The $K_m$ of an uncharged substrate was unchanged.

These effects are probably due to an unequal distribution of protons or charged substrates between the polyelectrolyte phase or compartment, within which or to which the enzyme is immobilized, and the outer solution.

Since lipids are abundant in all biological membranes, effects of lipids on enzymic activities have been studied extensively. It is outside the scope of this review to discuss all the reports showing evidence for lipid requirement for enzyme action. These requirements may be due to either specific enzyme-lipid interaction or due to the need for the establishment of a lipophilic or hydrophobic medium as a suitable nonaqueous phase. It suffices to point out that the later steps in the biosynthesis of cholesterol, triglycerides, and phospholipids take place in a lipid-rich environment. To investigate the effect of hydrophobicity on enzyme action a model study was carried out in which alcohol dehydrogenase was immobilized within matrices of varying degree of hydrophobicity (using acrylamide/methylmethacrylate copolymers). With the substrate n-butanol, the apparent $K_m$ values shifted to lower values as the enzyme was bound to the more hydrophobic copolymer preparations (65).

It should be pointed out that besides the specific effects exerted by a matrix and discussed above, the general chemical and physical nature of the medium surrounding the matrix may also be affected—leading to changed solvation of reactants and intermediates. This would be the case for a medium containing polar and nonpolar solutes. Although we do not know of studies on this effect, it suffices to point out that a hydrophobic matrix will attract a more lipophilic medium with its low dielectric constant.

### *Microenvironmental Effects Due to Enzymic Activity*

The catalytic activity of an enzyme or its neighboring enzymes may also alter the microenvironment of an enzyme by leading to different local concentrations of substrate, product, protons, effectors, etc. With neutral substrates which give rise to ionized products Thomas et al, using urease crosslinked into an albumin matrix (130), observed a substantial increase in pH in the interior of the membrane. When a reaction producing protons in a collodion membrane containing papain was studied, the reverse effect was observed in the extensive studies carried out by Katchalski and his colleagues (49, 67). The changed pH dependence of membrane-bound acetyl choline esterase compared to soluble esterase can be explained by such effects, that is, local pH changes in the vicinity of the membrane-bound enzyme as a consequence of hydrolysis of substrate (119).

The above experiments measure effects on an enzyme by changing proton concentration produced by the enzyme itself. Since many enzymes produce or utilize protons it is possible that such action could modify other enzyme activities and thus regulate metabolic pathways. A model system (45) containing entrapped hexokinase, glucose oxidase, and trypsin was studied. At an assay pH of 8.6 (the optimum of hexokinase) 15% of added glucose converted was phosphorylated and the remainder oxidized by glucose oxidase (pH optimum 6.6). A trypsin substrate was then added. Its cleavage produced protons in the microenvironment of the two glucose-utilizing enzymes (the external pH was kept constant at 8.6). This acidification of the microenvironment caused a decrease in the hexokinase activity and a simultaneous increase in glucose oxidase activity so that all of the glucose was now oxidized.

Nothing definite, however, can be said at this time about proton concentration as a regulator of enzyme activity since not much is known about actual buffer capacities present within the cell. But as pointed out by McLaren & Packer (88) because of probable point to point variations, the meaning of the gross-intracellular pH even of a moderate-size cell is unclear.

### *Multi-Step Enzyme Systems*

Microenvironmental effects in immobilized multi-step enzyme systems have been recently studied. In the first study of this kind (94), the following two-enzyme system was investigated.

$$\text{ATP} + \text{glucose} \xrightarrow{\text{hexokinase}} \text{glucose-6-P} + \text{ADP}$$

$$\text{glucose-6-P} + \text{NADP}^+ \xrightarrow{\text{glucose-6-P dehydrogenase}} \text{6-P gluconolactone} + \text{NADPH} + \text{H}^+$$

It was shown that the immobilized system with both enzymes bound to the same polymer beads, reached a steady-state rate much faster than the corresponding soluble system (or when the enzymes were bound to separate beads), although the latter eventually reached the same steady-state rate. These results were interpreted in the following way: In the immobilized system the product from the first enzyme-catalyzed reaction is available at a higher concentration around the second enzyme than is the case in the corresponding free system and thus the steady-state rate is achieved earlier. This is in part due to the close proximity of the enzymes in the immobilized state. Also, impeded out-diffusion of the intermediate caused by the Nernst diffusion layer may contribute. Theoretical calculations on the behavior of an immobilized two-step enzyme system are in good agreement with the above data (48). In a subsequent study the above system was extended to the three-step enzyme system (86).

$$\text{lactose} \xrightarrow{\beta\text{-galactosidase}} \text{glucose} + \text{galactose}$$

$$\text{glucose} + \text{ATP} \xrightarrow{\text{hexokinase}} \text{glucose-6-P} + \text{ADP}$$

$$\text{NADP}^+ + \text{glucose-6-P} \xrightarrow{\text{glucose-6-P dehydrogenase}} \text{6-P-gluconolactone} + \text{NADPH} + \text{H}^+$$

In this case the lag phase for the soluble system was increased and again a shorter lag time was observed with the corresponding immobilized system. With the three-enzyme system the relative shortening of the lag period was greater than with the two-enzyme system. The significance of the results obtained as to their possible role in regulation is not obvious since the soluble systems eventually reached the same rate as the immobilized system. However, in the living cell the rates of metabolic events are continuously being increased and decreased and it would be advantageous to attain steady-state rates quickly.

In recent reports (95, 126), an immobilized three-enzyme system has been studied where the kinetic advantage of such a system over the corresponding soluble system is permanent, i.e. the soluble system never attained the rate of the immobilized system. The three-enzyme system studied was:

$$\text{malate} + \text{NAD}^+ \xrightarrow{\text{malate dehydrogenase}} \text{oxalacetate} + \text{NADH} + \text{H}^+$$

$$\text{oxalacetate} + \text{acetyl SCoA} + H_2O \xrightarrow{\text{citrate synthase}} \text{citrate} + \text{CoASH} + \text{H}^+$$

$$\text{pyruvate} + \text{NADH} + \text{H}^+ \xrightarrow{\text{lactate dehydrogenase}} \text{lactate} + \text{NAD}^+$$

Here the malate dehydrogenase-catalyzed step is thermodynamically unfavorable in the direction of oxalacetate and hence high concentrations of the intermediate cannot be obtained. Catalysis by malate dehydrogenase creates a constant concentration of oxalacetate in the microenvironment of the enzyme and a decreasing concentration gradient of oxalacetate away from its site of production. Therefore the immobilized system, where the statistical mean distance between molecules of malate dehydrogenase and citrate synthase is shorter when the enzymes are matrix-bound than when they are free in solution, operates at a higher rate than the corresponding free system. Up to 100% rate enhancements were observed with the immobilized system over the corresponding free and an even more pronounced increase in rate of up to 400% was measured after addition of pyruvate (to reoxidize formed NADH).

This model study had been initiated as an attempt to resolve the apparent discrepancy between the known high rate of the citric acid cycle in mitochondria and the rate possible if citrate synthase had to operate at the low apparent concentration of free oxalacetate present in the mitochondrial matrix. Assuming an organization of Krebs cycle enzymes within the matrix, segregated metabolic compartments in which locally high substrate concentrations could be maintained in the region of each enzyme's active site would be possible to obtain.

In a somewhat similar study the apparent $K_m$ of ribulose diphosphate carboxylase for $CO_2$ was changed by binding urease in proximity to this enzyme. In this coupled two-enzyme system the apparent $K_m$ of the carboxylase decreased [reported $K_m$ of ribulose-1,5-diphosphate carboxylase for $H_2CO_3 = 22$ mM, $K_m$ of the intact chloroplast for $H_2CO_3 = 0.6$ mM]. It was suggested that in the chloroplast carboxylase is associated in some manner with a $CO_2$ generating enzyme such as malic dehydrogenase in the case of $C_4$ (Hatch-Slack pathway) plants, with the two enzymes sharing the same microenvironment. Thus no special transcarboxylase would be required to provide the carboxylase with high concentrations of $CO_2$ (L. E. Anderson, personal communication).

Another study (44) points to the fact that care should be taken on applying over-all pH optima obtained for soluble sequential enzymic reactions to the natural membrane-bound situation. In this study amylo-α-1,4-α-1,6-glucosidase (pH optimum 4.8), glucose oxidase (pH optimum 6.4), were covalently bound to Sepharose®. A difference between the pH optima of the coupled reaction of the immobilized and the soluble system of 0.3 pH units was determined. On variation of the ratios of enzyme activities a ΔpH of up to 0.75 was obtained. These results have been interpreted in the following way. In the immobilized system, local enrichment of intermediate substrate concentration takes place which will lead to a different pH optimum of the system as the next enzyme in the sequence obtains more favorable substrate conditions resulting in a new pH optimum for the whole system.

While it appears rather evident that a matrix or membrane will create and form its specific microenvironment, establishment of invisible compartments due to enzymic action appears less obvious. The degree of such compartmentation will vary depending on various parameters, in particular the chemical and physical nature of the surrounding matrix and of course on the enzymic activity itself.

With the enzyme entrapped within membranes, diffusional resistance will be higher than encountered with free enzymes, thus leading to compartmentation of intermediates. Even if enzymes within a cell are not bound, but the enzymes are in a region of increased viscosity and containing high concentration of macromolecules, both diffusional resistance and exclusion effects (77a) will also create microenvironments. But, assuming the enzyme to be truly surface-bound and assuming that there are no diffusional limitations due to viscosity or other factors affecting the system, the existence of an unstirred layer (Nernst diffusion layer), assumed to be present at solid-solution interfaces when stirring occurs (110a), will affect the kinetic behavior. Movements taking place within the interior of a cell may cause such unstirred layers, although this can at present only remain an assumption. However, even assuming that such layers are not found in situ, the arrangement of enzymes in a cluster or as organized system will lead to microenvironmental compartments. Some recent papers treat the effects of diffusional resistance on the kinetic behavior of a great number of immobilized enzymes (11, 28, 147).

## VI. OVERVIEW

We have not attempted to document the entire area of compartmentation. Rather we have chosen to emphasize the ubiquitous nature of the division of metabolites and enzymes into isolated regions and the variety of methods that living cells have used in order to achieve such microenvironments. The difficulty for unique interpretation of data (especially kinetics of isotope incorporation), as well as the nature of this series, has curtailed our reference to research on compartmentation in animal systems. To a lesser degree the same difficulties of interpretations apply to similar data in microorganisms. Koch (71, 72) shows that quite unusual kinetic behavior of isotope incorporation can still be explained using single pool models. Clark, Rognstad & Katz (15) also decry the postulate of multiple pools before all other alternate explanations are exhausted, i.e. nonsynchronous cell population, multiple cell types, etc. In microorganisms with organelles there is the possibility of separation of pools within cells at the structural level.

Nonetheless the metabolic advantages of microenvironments and compartmentation are so manifold that in spite of the weakness of some data in this area it seems to warrant acceptance.

It is our contention that regulation does occur at the microenvironmental and compartmental level. This bias is derived from teleological considerations, as well as consideration of the structural complexities of cells, and the obvious functional relation seen between organelles in various specialized cells, i.e. mitochondria in spermatozoa helically arranged around the contractile protein or the linear array of mitochondria in heart muscle.

### Acknowledgments

We are indebted to a number of our colleagues for preprints and/or discussions of this area: Vivian Moses who supplied us with a preprint of his most recent review on compartmentalization; J. J. Blum who sent preprints of his compartment studies in *Tetrahymena;* and Drs. R. H. Davies, J. DeMoss, A. Koch, H. Bremer, S. Bessman, and B. Mattiasson. This research was supported by grants from the USPHS and the Swedish National Science Foundation.

*Literature Cited*


1. Ahmadjian, V. 1967. *Symbiosis,* ed. S. M. Henry, 7:35–92. New York: Academic
2. Ahmed, S. I., Campbell, J. J. R. 1973. *J. Bacteriol.* 115:205–12
3. Appley, C. A. 1962. *Biochim. Biophys. Acta* 60:226–35
4. Bandyopadhyay, A. K., Deutscher, M. P. 1973. *J. Mol. Biol.* 74:257–61
5. Baumunk, C. N., Friedman, D. L. 1971. *Cancer Res.* 31:1930–35
6. Bearden, L., Moses, V. 1972. *Biochim. Biophys. Acta* 279:513–26
7. Bernhardt, S. A., Davis, R. H. 1972. *Proc. Nat. Acad. Sci. USA* 69:1868–72
8. Bessman, S. P., Gots, R. E. 1973. *Intra Sci. Chem. Rep.* 8:In press
9. Bieglmayer, C., Graf, J., Ruis, H. 1973. *Eur. J. Biochem.* 37:553–62
10. Billen, D., Carreira, L. B., Hadden, C. T., Silverstein, S. J. 1971. *J. Bacteriol.* 108:1250–56
11. Blaedel, W. J., Kissel, T. R., Boguslaski, R. C. 1972. *Anal. Chem.* 44: 2030–37
12. Bollon, A. P., Vogel, H. J. 1973. *J. Bacteriol.* 114:632–40
13. Burger, M., Pavlasová, E. 1964. *Biochem. J.* 93:601–6
14. Campbell, P. N. 1970. *FEBS Lett.* 7:1–7
15. Clark, D. G., Rognstad, R., Katz, J. 1973. *Biochem. Biophys. Res. Commun.* 54:1141–48
16. Cohen, G. N. 1969. *Curr. Top. Cell. Regul.* 1:183
17. Coleman, R. 1973. *Biochim. Biophys. Acta* 300:1–30
18. Connett, R. J., Blum, J. J. 1972. *J. Biol. Chem.* 247:5199–5209
19. Connett, R. J., Wittels, B., Blum, J. J. 1972. *J. Biol. Chem.* 247:2657–61
20. Cori, C. F. 1956. *Currents in Biochemical Research,* ed. D. E. Green, 198–214. New York: Interscience
21. Cotton, R. G. H., Gibson, F. 1965. *Biochim. Biophys. Acta* 100:76–88
22. Cowie, D. B., Bolton, E. T. 1957. *Biochim. Biophys. Acta* 25:292–98
23. Cowie, D. B., McClure, F. T. 1959. *Biochim. Biophys. Acta* 31:236–45
24. Crane, R. K., Sols, A. 1953. *J. Biol. Chem.* 203:273
25. Davis, R. H. 1972. *Science* 178:835–40
26. Dayan, J., Spranson, D. B. 1971. *J. Bacteriol.* 108:1174–80
27. Delisle, G., Fritz, I. B. 1967. *Proc. Nat. Acad. Sci. USA* 58:790–97
28. DeSimone, J. A., Caplan, S. R. 1973. *Biochemistry* 12:3032–39
29. Diamond, J. M., Wright, E. M. 1969. *Ann. Rev. Physiol.* 31:581–646
30. Dietschy, J. M., Sallee, V. L., Wilson, F. A. 1971. *Gastroenterology* 61:932–34
31. Dimroth, P., Dittmar, W., Walther, G., Eggerer, H. 1973. *Eur. J. Biochem.* 37:305–15
32. Dimroth, P., Walter, H., Lynen, F. 1970. *Eur. J. Biochem.* 13:98–110
33. Drew, E. A., Smith, D. C. 1966. *Lichenologist* 3:197–206
34. Drew, E. A., Smith, D. C. 1967. *New Phytol.* 66:389–400
35. Drews, G., Giesbrecht, P. 1971. *Die Zelle,* ed. H. Metzner, 407–67. Stuttgart: Wissenschaftliche MBH
36. Drost-Hansen, W. 1969. *Ind. Eng. Chem.* 61:10–47
37. Drost-Hansen, W. 1970. *Physical Principles of Biological Membranes,* ed. F. Snell, 243–58. New York: Gordon & Breech
38. Dubos, R. 1963. *Symbiotic Associations. Symp. Soc. Gen. Microbiol., 13th*
39. Eldan, M., Blum, J. J. 1973. *J. Biol. Chem.* 248:7445–48
40. Fox, C. H., Mosbach, K. 1967. *Acta Chem. Scand.* 21:2327–30
41. Fridland, A. 1973. *Nature New Biol.* 243:105–7
42. Frieden, C. 1971. *Ann. Rev. Biochem.* 40:653–96
43. Gaertner, F. H., Ericson, M. C., DeMoss, J. A. 1970. *J. Biol. Chem.* 245:595–600
44. Gestrelius, S., Mattiasson, B., Mosbach, K. 1972. *Biochim. Biophys. Acta* 276: 339–43
45. Gestrelius, S., Mattiasson, B., Mosbach, K. 1973. *Eur. J. Biochem.* 36:89–96
46. Ginsburg, A., Stadtman, E. R. 1970. *Ann. Rev. Biochem.* 429–72
47. Glaser, L., Melo, A., Paul, R. J. 1967. *J. Biol. Chem.* 242:1944–54
48. Goldman, R., Katchalski, E. 1971. *J. Theor. Biol.* 32:243–57
49. Goldman, R., Kedem, O., Silman, I. H., Caplan, S. R., Katchalski, E. 1968. *Biochemistry* 7:486–500
50. Goldstein, L., Katchalski, E. 1968. *Z. Anal. Chem.* 243:375–96
51. Goldstein, L., Levin, Y., Katchalski, E. 1964. *Biochemistry* 3:1905–13
52. Goldstein, L., Pecht, M., Blumberg, S., Atlas, D., Levin, Y. 1970. *Biochemistry* 9:2322–34
53. Gots, R. E., Bessman, S. P. *J. Biol. Chem.* In press
54. Gots, R. E., Gorin, F. A., Bessman, S.

P. 1972. *Biochem. Biophys. Res. Commun.* 49:1249–55
55. Guynn, R. W., Gelberg, A. B., Veech, R. L. 1973. *J. Biol. Chem.* 248:6957–65
56. Hampel, A., Enger, M. D. 1973. *J. Mol. Biol.* 79:285–93
57. Henning, U., Vogel, O., Busch, W., Flatgaard, J. E. 1972. *Protein-Protein Interactions,* ed. R. Jaenicke, E. Helmreich, 343–64. New York: Springer
58. Henriksson, E. 1957. *Physiol. Plant.* 10:943–48
59. Heppel, L. A. 1971. *Structure and Function of Biological Membranes,* ed. L. I. Rothfield, 223–47. New York: Academic
60. Hess, B., Boiteux, A. 1972. *Protein-Protein Interactions,* ed. R. Jaenicke, E. Helmreich, 271–97. New York: Springer
61. Hill, D. J. 1970. *The carbohydrate movement between the symbionts of lichens.* PhD thesis. Univ. Oxford, England
62. Hübscher, G., Mayer, R. J., Hansen, H. J. M. 1971. *Bioenergetics* 2:115–18
63. Jacobson, J. W., Hart, B. A., Doy, C. H., Giles, N. H. 1972. *Biochim. Biophys. Acta* 289:1–12
64. Jacobson, M. K., Lark, K. B. 1973. *J. Mol. Biol.* 73:371–96
65. Johansson, A. C., Mosbach, K. Unpublished observations
66. Jones, M. E. 1971. *Advan. Enzyme Regul.* 9:19
67. Katchalski, E., Silman, I., Goldman, R. 1971. *Advan. Enzymol.* 34:445–536
68. Kempner, E. S., Miller, J. H. 1968. *Exp. Cell Res.* 51:141–49
69. Ibid 150–56
70. Klein, A., Bonhoeffer, F. 1973. *Ann. Rev. Biochem.* 41:301–32
71. Koch, A. L. 1971. *J. Theor. Biol.* 32: 429–50
72. Ibid 451–69
73. Koch, G. L. E., Shaw, D. C., Gibson, F. 1971. *Biochim. Biophys. Acta* 229:794–804
74. Kornberg, A. 1969. *Science* 163: 1419
75. Kühn, L., Castorph, H., Schweizer, E. 1972. *Eur. J. Biochem.* 24:492–97
76. Landau, B. R., Sims, E. A. H. 1967. *J. Biol. Chem.* 242:163–72
77. Lang, D. R., Felix, J., Lundgren, D. G. 1972. *J. Bacteriol.* 110:968–77
77a. Laurent, T. C. 1971. *Eur. J. Biochem.* 21:498–506
78. Lee, S. G., Roskoski, R. Jr., Bauer, K., Lipmann, F. 1973. *Biochemistry* 12: 398–405
79. Liang, T., Raugi, G. J., Blum, J. J. 1973. *J. Biol. Chem.* 248:8073–78
80. Lipmann, F. 1971. *Science* 173:875–84
81. Lloyd-Davies, K. A., Michell, R. H., Coleman, R. 1972. *Biochem. J.* 127: 357–68
82. Lue, P. F., Kaplan, J. G. 1970. *Biochim. Biophys. Acta* 220:365–72
82a. Lynen, F. 1972. *Structure and Function of Multienzyme Complexes,* 29: 177–200. FEBS, North Holland: American Elsevier
83. MacLeod, R. A., Thurman, P., Rogers, H. J. 1973. *J. Bacteriol.* 113:329–40
84. Macnab, R., Moses, V., Mowbray, J. 1973. *Eur. J. Biochem.* 34:15–19
85. Matchett, W. H., DeMoss, J. A. 1964. *Biochim. Biophys. Acta* 86:91–99
86. Mattiasson, B., Mosbach, K. 1971. *Biochim. Biophys. Acta* 235:253–57
87. McBrien, D. C. H., Moses, V. 1968. *J. Gen. Microbiol.* 51:159–72
88. McLaren, A. D., Packer, L. 1970. *Advan. Enzymol.* 33:245–308
89. Merker, H.-J., Spors, S. 1969. *Histochemie* 17:83–88
90. Minson, A. C., Creaser, E. H. 1969. *Biochem. J.* 114:49–56
91. Mizutani, A. 1968. *J. Histochem. Cytochem.* 16:172–80
92. Mosbach, K. 1969. *Angew. Chemie Int. Ed. Engl.* 8:240–50
93. Mosbach, K. 1973. *Lichens,* ed. V. Ahmadjian, M. E. Hale, 523–46. New York: Academic
94. Mosbach, K., Mattiasson, B. 1970. *Acta Chem. Scand.* 24:2093–2100
95. Mosbach, K., Mattiasson, B., Gestrelius, S., Srere, P. A. 1974. *International Symposium on Insolubilized Enzymes,* ed. S. Garratini. New York: Raven Press. In press
96. Mosbach, K., Schultz, J. 1971. *Eur. J. Biochem.* 22:485–88
97. Moses, V. 1971. *Die Zelle,* ed. H. Metzner, 260–75. Stuttgart: Wissenschaftliche MBH
98. Moses, V., Sharp, P. B. 1972. *J. Gen. Microbiol.* 71:181–90
99. Mueller, K., Bremer, H. 1968. *J. Mol. Biol.* 38:329–53
100. Oaks, A., Bidwell, R. G. S. 1970. *Ann. Rev. Plant Physiol.* 21:43–66
101. Pollard, E. 1963. *J. Theor. Biol.* 4:98–112
102. Raugi, G. J., Liang, T., Blum, J. J. 1973. *J. Biol. Chem.* 248:8064–72
103. Ibid
104. Reed, L. J. 1969. *Curr. Top. Cell. Regul.* 1:233–52
105. Reusch, V. M. Jr., Burger, M. M. 1973. *Biochim. Biophys. Acta* 300:79–104

106. Richardson, D. H. S. 1973. *Lichens,* ed. V. Ahmadjian, M. E. Hale, 249–88. New York: Academic
107. Richardson, D. H. S., Hill, D. J., Smith, D. C. 1968. *New Phytol.* 67: 469–86
108. Richardson, D. H. S., Smith, D. C. 1966. *Lichenologist* 3:202–6
109. Richardson, D. H. S., Smith, D. C., Lewis, D. H. 1967. *Nature* 214:879–82
110. Risse, H. J., Blum, J. J. 1972. *Arch. Biochem. Biophys.* 149:329–35
110a. Rosenberg, M. D. 1966. *Intracellular Transport Fluxes—Can They be Accurately Determined,* ed. K. B. Warren, 45–69. New York: Academic
111. Rothstein, A., Jennings, D. H., Demis, C., Bruce, M. 1959. *Biochem. J.* 71: 99–106
112. Rubinow, S. I., Yen, A. 1972. *Nature New Biol.* 239:73–74
113. Schultz, J., Mosbach, K. 1971. *Eur. J. Biochem.* 22:153–57
114. Scott, G. D. 1956. *New Phytol.* 55: 111–18
115. Sercarz, E. E., Gorini, L. 1964. *J. Mol. Biol.* 8:254–62
116. Shaw, W. N., Stadie, W. C. 1959. *J. Biol. Chem.* 234:2491–96
117. Shively, J. M., Ball, F., Brown, D. H., Saunders, R. E. 1973. *Science* 182: 584–86
118. Shoaf, W. G., Jones, M. E. 1973. *Biochemistry* 12:4039–51
119. Silman, I. H., Karlin, A. 1967. *Proc. Nat. Acad. Sci. USA* 58:1664–68
120. Sims, A. P., Folkes, B. F. 1964. *Proc. Roy. Soc. Ser. B.* 159:479–502
121. Singh, M., Böttger, B., Stewart, C., Brooks, G. C., Srere, P. A. 1973. *Biochem. Biophys. Res. Commun.* 53:1–9
122. Spors, S., Merker, H. J. 1969. *Histochemie* 17:78–82
123. Srere, P. A. 1967. *Science* 158:936–37
124. Srere, P. A. 1972. *Energy Metabolism and the Regulation of Metabolic Processes in Mitochondria,* ed. M. A. Mehlman, R. W. Hanson, 79–91. New York: Academic
125. Srere, P. A., Böttger, B., Brooks, G. C. 1972. *Proc. Nat. Acad. Sci. USA* 69: 1201–2
126. Srere, P. A., Mattiasson, B., Mosbach, K. 1973. *Proc. Nat. Acad. Sci. USA* 70: 2534–38
127. Subramanian, K. N., Weiss, R. L., Davis, R. H. 1973. *J. Bacteriol.* 115: 284–90
128. Sumper, M., Lynen, F. 1972. *Protein-Protein Interactions,* ed. R. Jaenicke, E. Helmreich, 365–94. New York: Springer
129. Tabor, H., Tabor, C. W. 1969. *J. Biol. Chem.* 244:6383–87
130. Thomas, D., Broun, G., Sélégny, E. 1972. *Biochimie* 54:229–44
131. Till, U., Köhler, W., Ruschke, I., Köhler, A., Lösche, W. 1973. *Eur. J. Biochem.* 35:167–78
132. Virtanen, A. J. 1945 *Nature* 155:747–48
133. Vogel, H. J., Bacon, D. F. 1966. *Proc. Nat. Acad. Sci. USA* 55:1456–59
134. Vogel, R. H., Kopac, M. J. 1959. *Biochim. Biophys. Acta* 36:505–10
135. Weiss, P. 1963. *J. Theor. Biol.* 5: 389–97
136. Weiss, R. L. 1973. *J. Biol. Chem.* 248:5409–13
137. Weiss, R. L., Davis, R. H. 1973. *J. Biol. Chem.* 248:5403–6
138. Werner, R. 1971. *Nature* 230:570–72
139. Werner, R. 1971. *Nature New Biol.* 233:99–103
140. Whitney, P. A., Cooper, T. G. 1972. *Biochem. Biophys. Res. Commun.* 49: 45–51
141. Wiemken, A., Nurse, P. 1973 *Planta* 109:293–306
142. Wiggins, P. M. 1971. *J. Theor. Biol.* 32:131–46
143. Williams, L. G., Bernhardt, S. A., Davis, R. H. 1971. *J. Biol. Chem.* 246: 973–78
144. Williamson, D. H., Lund, P., Krebs, H. A. 1967. *Biochem. J.* 103:514–27
145. Wilson, F. A., Dietschy, J. M. 1972. *J. Clin. Invest.* 51:3015–25
146. Winfree, A. T. 1972. *Science* 175: 634–36
147. Wingard, L. B. Jr. 1972. *Advan. Biochem. Eng.* 2:1–48
148. Wittes, R. E., Kidwell, W. R. 1973. *J. Mol. Biol.* 78:473–86
149. Zaikin, A. M., Zhabotinsky, A. M. 1970. *Nature* 225:535–37
150. Zalokar, M. 1961. *Biochim. Biophys. Acta* 46:423–32

# MECHANISMS OF INORGANIC OXIDATION AND ENERGY COUPLING

❖1631

*Isamu Suzuki*

Department of Microbiology, University of Manitoba, Winnipeg 19, Manitoba, Canada

CONTENTS

INTRODUCTION .......... 85
AMMONIA OXIDATION .......... 86
NITRITE OXIDATION .......... 89
IRON OXIDATION .......... 90
SULFUR OXIDATION .......... 91
ENERGY COUPLING .......... 96

## INTRODUCTION

Inorganic compounds are oxidized by many living organisms, but intensive studies on the mechanisms of their biological oxidation have been done mainly with the so-called chemoautotrophic or chemolithotrophic bacteria. These bacteria depend on the oxidation of inorganic compounds for a source of energy for growth and this unique mode of life has captured the imagination of many scientists. The simplicity of the system seems to offer clear advantages to research scientists interested in energy metabolism. In fact these bacteria could compete effectively with mitochondria as model systems of energy transformation if only a large quantity of cells were easily obtainable.

In this review the discussion will be limited mainly to ammonia oxidation by *Nitrosomonas,* nitrite oxidation by *Nitrobacter,* iron oxidation by ferrobacilli, inorganic sulfur oxidation by thiobacilli, and hydrogen oxidation by *Hydrogenomonas.* Recent reviews of this and related areas are by Peck (90) on energy-coupling mechanisms, Kelly (52) on autotrophy, Trudinger (132) and Roy & Trudinger (102) on sulfur metabolism, Aleem (5) and Wallace & Nicholas (139) on nitrogen metabolism, Lemberg & Barrett (71) on cytochromes, and Zajic (145) on microbial biogeochemistry.

## AMMONIA OXIDATION

*Nitrosomonas* oxidizes ammonia to nitrite: $NH_4^+ + 1\frac{1}{2} O_2 \longrightarrow NO_2^- + 2 H^+ + H_2O$. Hydroxylamine was shown to be an intermediate by Lees (65) and Hofman & Lees (41); it was oxidized by cell-free extracts (6, 11, 35, 85) only in the presence of an electron acceptor and air. Anaerobically nitrous oxide ($N_2O$) rather than nitrite was produced. Lees (67, 68) suggested that nitroxyl (NOH) is the first unstable intermediate after hydroxylamine which is further oxidized to nitrite or decomposed to $N_2O$: $NH_4^+ \longrightarrow NH_2\,OH \longrightarrow (NOH) \longrightarrow NO_2^-$ or $2(NOH) \longrightarrow N_2O + H_2O$.

Hydroxylamine-cytochrome *c* reductase (6, 45) or hydroxylamine oxidase (35) seems to be involved only in the oxidation of $NH_2OH$ to the (NOH) level. Although inhibitor studies suggested the involvement of flavin (11, 35, 45), it could not be detected; only cytochromes *b* and *c* were present in the enzyme (45). Rees (94, 95) purified the enzyme to a homogeneous preparation with a molecular weight of 200,000. The purified enzyme contained both *b*- and *c*-type cytochromes, but no flavin. Using a mammalian cytochrome *c* as electron acceptor only 5–10% of the hydroxylamine that disappeared was converted to nitrite (45); while with an artificial electron acceptor, such as phenazine methosulfate or pyocyanine, the value reached 70% (85, 94), suggesting a possible aerobic oxidation of (NOH) in the presence of such a dye.

Hooper (42) partially purified an enzyme complex which reduced nitrite with hydroxylamine or leuco-pyocyanine as electron donor. Since the product was $N_2O$ along with some NO (nitric oxide), the reaction catalyzed was possibly: $NH_2OH + H\,NO_2 \longrightarrow N_2O + 2\,H_2O$, involving the combined action of hydroxylamine oxidase and nitrite reductase. The nitrite reductase was sensitive to inhibition by copper-binding agents as is the case with ammonia oxidation by *Nitrosomonas* cells (66).

The formation of nitrous oxide by *Nitrosomonas* was reinvestigated by Yoshida & Alexander (143, 144) and by Ritchie & Nicholas (99). At high concentrations of substrate, cells produced nitrous oxide from hydroxylamine and also from ammonia, thus reducing the yield of nitrite. $N_2O$ was also formed from nitrite during ammonia oxidation or under anaerobic conditions (99). An interesting finding was that a 75-fold purified hydroxylamine oxidase not only formed $N_2O$ and NO from hydroxylamine in the presence of phenazine methosulfate, but also from nitrite—suggesting a close association of hydroxylamine oxidase and nitrite reductase activities (99). The inhibition of nitrite formation from hydroxylamine by chloride ion in intact cell experiments (96) may also be due to $N_2O$ production, although this has not been determined.

In addition to cytochromes of the *a, b,* and *c* types which are readily reduced by hydroxylamine (6, 35, 45), *Nitrosomonas* contains cytochrome *o* (97) and cytochrome P-450 (97) or P-460 (33), both of which combine with carbon monoxide with characteristic spectra. P-460 was recently purified and its properties were found to be similar to those of P-450, from mammalian microsomes or *Pseudomonas* (33), suggesting its possible involvement in hydroxylation. The *a*-type cytochrome oxidase was also purified by Hooper (34) from a membrane fraction (44). The activity was inhibited by cyanide, azide, and hydroxylamine, normal inhibitors of *a*-type cytochrome oxidase. Diethyldithiocarbamate was also a strong inhibitor. Carbon monoxide, although capable of combining with the reduced pigment, did not inhibit the activity. The *c*-type cytochrome was shown to exist in multiple forms in *Nitrosomonas* (94, 95), one of these having an unusually high $E'_0$ value and reacting with CO (125). Peroxidase was purified from *Nitrosomonas* (12), but no evidence was obtained in support of its possible involvement in ammonia oxidation.

The mechanism of ammonia oxidation was not studied intensively until recently because of difficulties encountered in obtaining active cell-free systems. Rees & Nason (98) found a small incorporation of $^{18}O$ from $^{18}O_2$ into nitrite during ammonia oxidation by *Nitrosomonas* cells. Hooper (43) reported the elimination of an initial lag phase of ammonia oxidation by resting cells by the addition of a small quantity of hydroxylamine. Spheroplasts of the organism oxidized ammonia only when primed with hydroxylamine or when preincubated with $Mg^{2+}$ (117). It was suggested that oxidation of ammonia to hydroxylamine was catalyzed by a mixed-function oxygenase coupled to the oxidation of hydroxylamine to nitrite and that a structural requirement of cell membranes was important in the ammonia oxidation (117).

The ammonia-oxidizing cell-free extracts were independently and simultaneously obtained from a halophilic marine bacterium, *Nitrosocystis oceanus* (140) and *Nitrosomonas europaea* (118), both by use of a French Pressure Cell. For the marine organism, seawater, $Mg^{2+}$, and occasionally ATP were required for the preparation of active extracts (140). Most of the activity was found in the membrane fraction consisting of vesicles covered with 80–100 Å particles (140). The *Nitrosomonas* system, on the other hand, required either protection or activation by bovine serum albumin, $Mg^{2+}$, or spermine when prepared in 0.1 M phosphate buffer (118). In both extracts the ammonia-oxidizing activity was 10–20% that of intact cells. In the *Nitrosomonas* system both the membrane and soluble fractions were required for activity and ATP had no effect. Stoichiometry of oxygen consumed and nitrite formed was established, showing that the complete ammonium oxidizing system was present in the extracts. Both extracts oxidized hydroxylamine as well as ammonia to nitrite, but only the latter oxidation was inhibited by dipyridyl or allylthiourea (118).

The *Nitrosomonas* cell-free system was further studied in our laboratory (62; I. Suzuki, S. C. Kwok, and U. Dular, unpublished observations). The ammonia-oxidizing activity was optimal around pH 7.7 and 25°C. The $K_m$ for ammonia was 0.4 mM agreeing with the values for whole cells. The system was resolved into three fractions by anaerobic Sephadex or Sepharose chromatography: a membrane fraction, a hydroxylamine-cytochrome *c* reductase, and a fraction which was sometimes replaced with NADH. In the cell-free oxidation of ammonia there was always a lag period of 0.5–1.0 min following ammonia addition before the initiation of oxygen uptake. Small amounts of NADH or hydroxylamine not only eliminated the lag, but stimulated the ammonia oxidation. It should be recalled that oxidation of NADH and hydroxylamine may share the same electron transport components (35). A kinetic study of *c*- and *a*-type cytochromes during ammonia oxidation showed that the oxygen consumption started only after near complete reduction of these cytochromes. There was an initial lag of 5–10 sec before the initiation of cytochrome *c* reduction. After depletion of oxygen there was some reoxidation of cytochromes, possibly by nitrite reductase (42, 99).

Based on current knowledge of ammonia oxidation, the following scheme is proposed:

$$NH_3 + O_2 + AH_2 \longrightarrow NH_2OH + A + H_2O \qquad 1.$$

$$NH_2OH + 2 \text{ cytochrome } c\ (Fe^{3+}) \longrightarrow (NOH) + 2H^+ + 2 \text{ cytochrome } c\ (Fe^{2+}) \qquad 2.$$

$$2 \text{ cytochrome } c\ (Fe^{2+}) + \tfrac{1}{2}\, O_2 + 2\, H^+ \longrightarrow 2 \text{ cytochrome } c\ (Fe^{3+}) + H_2O \qquad 3.$$

$$(NOH) + A + H_2O \longrightarrow NO_2^- + AH_2 + H^+ \qquad 4.$$

$$\text{Sum: } NH_3 + 1\tfrac{1}{2}\, O_2 \longrightarrow NO_2^- + H_2O + H^+$$

Reaction 1 is catalyzed by hypothetical ammonia hydroxylase and A may be cytochrome P-460. Reaction 1 is coupled to reaction 4. Reaction 2 is catalyzed by hydroxylamine-cytochrome *c* reductase and reaction 3 by cytochrome oxidase of *a* or *o* type. NADH can possibly replace the substrate in reaction 4. Possibly nitroxyl oxidation is mediated by flavin before the electron transfer to P-460, since there are conflicting reports on the involvement of flavin in hydroxylamine oxidation (11, 35, 45, 94, 95), depending on the purity of hydroxylamine oxidase.

In order to explain the oxidation of hydroxylamine in the absence of ammonia it is necessary to assume the oxidation of nitroxyl without coupling to reaction 1. Possibly it is oxidized through cytochrome *c* and cytochrome oxidase. Obviously, however, this pathway is not as efficient, and leads to the accumulation of (NOH) which decomposes to $N_2O$. Oxygen is required for cytochrome oxidase or for autooxidation, in the presence of an artificial electron acceptor. The oxygen requirement for nitrite production with substrate quantities of such acceptors (6, 11, 35, 85) may be due to the action of nitrite reductase (42, 99) which could prevent the accumulation of nitrite in the presence of reduced electron acceptors. It is not yet known whether the hypothetical nitroxyl oxidase (reaction 4) is identical to nitrite reductase, but interestingly nitrite reductase is strongly inhibited by inhibitors of ammonia oxidation (42).

During steady-state oxidation of ammonia by active cells or cell-free extracts, reactions 1 to 4 must all proceed at the same rate. The initial lag may be the period when $AH_2$ accumulates. Elimination of the lag by $NH_2OH$ or NADH is easily understandable by this scheme. In the cell-free system (62) artificial electron acceptors such as phenazine methosulfate and methylene blue at 0.1 mM completely inhibited the ammonia oxidation if added before ammonia, but only partially inhibited it if added during the oxidation. Hooper & Terry (46) recently reported an extensive study on inhibitors of ammonia oxidation in *Nitrosomonas* cells. These dyes were among the potent inhibitors including metal- and heme protein-binding agents. These dyes probably oxidized $AH_2$, preventing the initiation of ammonia oxidation, but once the oxidation reached a steady-state level their effects were reduced because of a tight coupling of all four reactions.

Although the mechanism of ammonia oxidation by nitrifying bacteria is still far from being completely understood, the availability of cell-free ammonia-oxidizing systems (118, 140), purified cytochromes (33, 34, 125), and hydroxylamine oxidase (94) should lead to a better understanding of the mechanism.

## NITRITE OXIDATION

*Nitrobacter* oxidizes nitrite to nitrate with molecular oxygen as terminal electron acceptor: $NO_2^- + \frac{1}{2} O_2 \longrightarrow NO_3^-$. Lees & Simpson (70) first observed the reduction of cytochromes *c* and $a_1$ by nitrite in *Nitrobacter* cells. Aleem & Nason (8) isolated a particulate fraction designated nitrite oxidase which contained these cytochromes. The electron flow was believed to be: $NO_2^- \longrightarrow$ cytochrome $c \longrightarrow$ cytochrome $a_1 \longrightarrow O_2$. Kiesow (54) and Aleem, Lees & Nicholas (7) showed the reduction of NAD by an energy-requiring reversed electron flow. The studies by Kiesow and Aleem led to the conclusion that cytochrome $a_1$ rather than cytochrome *c* is first reduced by nitrite and the latter is reduced only at the expense of ATP (5, 56, 57). Thus NAD reduction is visualized as: $NO_2^- \longrightarrow$ cytochrome $a_1 \longrightarrow$ cytochrome $c \longrightarrow$ flavoproteins $\longrightarrow$ NAD, requiring 3 moles of ATP. Kiesow believes that the electron flow to oxygen branches off from cytochrome *c*, but Aleem proposes a pathway: $NO_2^- \longrightarrow$ cytochrome $a_1 \longrightarrow$ cytochrome $a_3 \longrightarrow O_2$ to account for a net production of 1 ATP/$NO_2^-$ (3).

O'Kelley, Becker & Nason (86) reinvestigated the particulate nitrite oxidase and confirmed the presence of energy-independent nitrite-cytochrome *c* reductase. Interestingly, nitrite showed a higher affinity for the enzyme at a lower pH, suggesting $HNO_2$ rather than $NO_2^-$ as the substrate for nitrite oxidase system. In *Nitrosomonas,* ammonia shows a higher affinity at a higher pH, suggesting $NH_3$ rather than $NH_4^+$ as the substrate for oxidation (U. Dular and I. Suzuki, unpublished observation). If it is assumed that *Nitrobacter* membranes are more permeable to uncharged $HNO_2$ than to $NO_2^-$ ion, then it is quite possible that the product of oxidation, $NO_3^-$, may only be removed efficiently by a transport system. The role of energy in the cytochrome *c* reduction may be related to the removal of nitrate, preventing reoxidation of the cytochrome by nitrate reductase activity present (86). The reduction of *Nitrobacter* cytochrome *c* by nitrite seems more complete with intact cells than with cell-free systems (86, 134), a possible indication of more efficient operation of nitrate transport system in intact cells.

Cytochrome *c* purified from *Nitrobacter* had a standard redox potential ($E'_0$) of +0.28 V, as compared to the value of +0.43 V for the nitrite/nitrate couple (53). The possibility of an intermediate with an oxidation number of +4 was suggested in order to overcome the thermodynamic difficulty in the reduction of cytochrome *c* by nitrite (53, 86). The importance of cytochrome $a_1$ in nitrite oxidation was confirmed by the photochemical action spectrum for the relief of carbon monoxide-inhibited respiration of *Nitrobacter* cells (40). Redox potentials of five cytochromes were determined in *Nitrobacter* extracts (110). Cytochrome $a_1$ was shown to have two components with $E'_0$ values of +0.35 V and +0.1 V, but curiously neither component bound carbon monoxide and only cytochrome $a_3$ ($E'_0$=+0.4 V) did bind carbon monoxide.

Although the standard redox potential is an important criterion in determining the entry point of electrons from nitrite, it should be remembered that the actual redox potential operating has a concentration term for ($NO_2^-$), ($NO_3^-$), (cytochrome-$Fe^{3+}$), and (cytochrome-$Fe^{2+}$). Thus an effective removal of nitrate could possibly facilitate the reduction of cytochromes by nitrite.

Although cytochrome $a_1$ is believed to be the initial acceptor of electrons from nitrite by Aleem (5) and Kiesow (56), evidence is still not conclusive enough to eliminate the possibility of direct reduction of cytochrome *c* by nitrite. Some of the experiments (3, 109) in support of the former theory were criticized on the basis of interpretation and lack of sufficient control experiments (86). There is also the curious observation that the steady-state reduction levels of cytochrome $a_1$ and cytochrome *c* during nitrite oxidation depend on the temperature, favoring cytochrome *c* reduction at higher temperatures (134). It is interesting that Kiesow's kinetic experiments for the reduction of two cytochromes were carried out at 5°C (56).

In addition to nitrite oxidase activity, the nitrite oxidase particles contain formate oxidase (87, 133), NADH oxidase (3, 86), and succinoxidase (86) activities, as well as nitrate reductase (86, 114). They all seem to use basically the same electron transport system, although the entry sites may not be the same. The oxidation of nitrite, formate, or NADH has been coupled to oxidative phosphorylation (3, 87). There is a strong possibility that nitrate reductase purified by Straat & Nason (114) may in fact be a component of nitrite oxidase system as suggested by Peck (90). A similar situation is found with nitrite reductase in *Nitrosomonas.*

## IRON OXIDATION

Iron-oxidizing bacteria, *Ferrobacillus ferrooxidans* and *Thiobacillus ferrooxidans,* oxidize ferrous to ferric iron: $4\,Fe^{2+} + O_2 + 4\,H^+ \longrightarrow 4\,Fe^{3+} + 2H_2O$. The oxidation is believed to be initiated by $Fe^{2+}$-cytochrome *c* reductase followed by electron transfer to the cytochrome system: $Fe^{2+} \longrightarrow$ cytochrome *c* $\longrightarrow$ cytochrome *a* $\longrightarrow$ $O_2$ (13, 14, 29, 30, 135, 141). Although the oxidation of iron looks quite simple, its study was made difficult by the instability of the substrate especially when chelated and nonacidic.

Blaylock & Nason (14) were first to purify a heat-stable $Fe^{2+}$-cytochrome *c* reductase from *F. ferrooxidans,* but Yates & Nason (142) attributed the activity to its DNA content because of the enhancement of cytochrome *c* reduction by nucleic acids. A heat-labile enzyme was isolated by sonicating the cells in protamine sulfate and its activity was destroyed by pronase (141). The heat-stable enzyme was reinvestigated and found to contain protein and RNA rather than DNA. Separation of RNA from the protein did, indeed, inactivate the enzyme irreversibly (30).

It is quite possible that the heat-labile and heat-stable enzymes are identical with respect to their protein portion and differ only in their nucleic acid content. The nucleic acid might simply substitute for the natural polyanionic environment of the cell membrane where the enzyme might be located and where iron might be chelated to facilitate oxidation. The sulfate requirement for iron oxidation by *Ferrobacillus* cells, originally observed by Lazaroff (64) and further studied by Dugan & Lundgren (32), may also be related to the formation of such iron-chelating sites. It is a well-known fact that the redox potential of $Fe^{2+}/Fe^{3+}$ couple is considerably lowered by chelation. Apparently sulfate can be replaced by phosphate and its effect is to increase the $V_{max}$ of iron oxidation without affecting the $K_m$ for $Fe^{2+}$ (108).

Removal of the oxidation product facilitates the oxidation as discussed for *Nitrobacter*, and in *Ferrobacillus* the insolubility of ferric hydroxide becomes a driving force in iron oxidation by increasing the free-energy change (69).

## SULFUR OXIDATION

*Thiobacillus thiooxidans* isolated by Waksman & Joffe in 1922 (137) oxidizes sulfur to sulfuric acid: $S^o + 1\frac{1}{2}\ O_2 + H_2O \longrightarrow SO_4^{2-} + 2H^+$.

The first cell-free system from *T. thiooxidans* capable of oxidation of elemental sulfur required reduced glutathione (GSH) and produced thiosulfate (120). The sulfur-oxidizing enzyme was partially purified and a possible mechanism of sulfur oxidation involving glutathione polysulfide as intermediate was proposed (115). The initial product of sulfur oxidation was identified as sulfite, rather than thiosulfate, which was subsequently formed through a nonenzymatic condensation of sulfur and sulfite (119). The mechanism of sulfur-oxidizing enzyme seems to be expressed by the following equations, where $S_n$ is elemental sulfur in its normally polymerized molecular state ($S_8$ ring structure): $S_n + GSH \longrightarrow GSS_nH$ and $GSS_nH + O_2 + H_2O \xrightarrow{Enzyme} GSS_{n-1}H + SO_3^{2-} + 2H^+$. Thus sulfur atoms can be oxidized one by one to sulfite until GSH is produced and reacts with $S_n$ again. Whenever GSH itself is oxidized to GSSG (oxidized glutathione) the glutathione reductase present (121) is capable of regenerating GSH at the expense of NADPH oxidation. The sulfur-oxidizing enzyme was tentatively identified as oxygenase on the basis of an $^{18}O_2$ experiment (116), but a more definite identification is still required before excluding other possibilities.

The sulfur-oxidizing enzyme has now been demonstrated in *T. thiooxidans* (115), *Thiobacillus thioparus* (119), *Thiobacillus novellus* (26), and *Ferrobacillus ferrooxidans* (111). In these organisms sulfite is further oxidized to sulfate either through sulfite: cytochrome *c* oxidoreductase (25), or through adenosine phosphosulfate (APS) reductase (88, 89).

In the past several years a number of workers were successful in obtaining cell-free membrane or particulate systems which oxidized elemental sulfur to sulfate. In many respects the relationship of these systems to whole bacterial cells is analogous to that of submitochondrial particles to mitochondria. The study of such systems is obviously very important in bridging a gap between the study of whole cells and that of isolated enzymes, such as sulfur-oxidizing enzyme, sulfite:cytochrome *c* oxidoreductase, and APS reductase.

Adair was the first to report such a system from *T. thiooxidans* (1). His membrane system prepared by a French Pressure Cell was similar to whole cells in achieving the oxidation of elemental sulfur to sulfate; he did not further fractionate the system. Kodama & Mori (60) prepared an extract of a strain of *T. thiooxidans* by sonication under a nitrogen atmosphere. Both the soluble and particulate (membrane) fractions were required for the oxidation of sulfur (to sulfate?), while only the particulate fraction was required for sulfite oxidation. Kodama (59) fractionated the soluble fraction further into the collodion membrane permeable and impermeable fractions and identified the former as NADP plus NAD. Either the oxidized or reduced form of NADP or NAD was effective in the reconstitution of the sulfur-oxidizing system. Taylor (124) obtained a cell-free extract of *Thiobacillus neapolitanus* by a French Pressure Cell which oxidized sulfur to sulfate. This extract, although called soluble, was prepared by centrifugation at 30,000 X *g* and could contain membrane or particulate materials. In all three systems sulfur was oxidized to sulfate in the absence of glutathione and in one case glutathione was inhibitory (124). It is possible that the sulfur-oxidizing enzyme is bound in a complex in these systems not accessible to externally added glutathione. The nucleophilic scission of the $S_8$ ring may be carried out by sulfhydryl groups or by polysulfides present in the complex. Supporting this possibility is the observation that anaerobic incubation of *T. neapolitanus* extracts (124) with sulfur produces hydrogen sulfide. The inhibition by glutathione therefore may be a consequence of its binding to the reactive sulfhydryl groups or polysulfides through its sulfur atom, thus preventing the access of elemental sulfur to the complex. Glutathione had no inhibitory effect once the sulfur oxidation started (124). The effect of NADP in Kodama's system (59) is difficult to explain, but it may participate in the generation of reactive sulfhydryl groups by a reaction similar to glutathione reductase.

Tano & Imai (123) used colloidal sulfur as substrate with a sonicated extract of *T. thiooxidans.* A soluble fraction oxidized colloidal sulfur to thiosulfate. Since the fraction contained glutathione reductase and since sulfide was also produced from collodial sulfur, the sulfur-oxidizing enzyme was probably responsible for the oxidation in this system. Moriarty & Nicholas (82, 83) studied the oxidation of sulfide by a membrane fraction of *Thiobacillus concretivorous* prepared by a French Pressure Cell. Sulfide was oxidized to elemental sulfur through the cytochrome system. Sulfur remained bound on the membrane as polysulfide which was slowly oxidized further to sulfate upon addition of a dialyzed crude extract. In this system, therefore, the sulfur-oxidizing enzyme was probably present in the soluble fraction, although this possibility was not tested by the authors.

It would be interesting if these membrane systems were further fractionated and the specific enzymes involved were identified. It might be possible then to reconstitute a sulfur-oxidizing system capable of oxidizing sulfur to sulfate with purified enzymes and membranes.

Sulfite, a key intermediate in the oxidation of inorganic sulfur compounds, is further oxidized to sulfate in thiobacilli either by sulfite oxidase (sulfite:cytochrome *c* oxidoreductase) or APS reductase (adenosine-phosphosulfate reductase): $SO_3^{2-} + H_2O \longrightarrow SO_4^{2-} + 2H^+ + 2e^-$ or $SO_3^{2-} + AMP \longrightarrow APS + 2e^-$.

The pathway involving APS reductase and ADP sulfurylase was proposed by Peck in 1960 (88). The pathway achieves substrate level phosphorylation when APS is converted to ADP and sulfate. APS reductase was purified from *Thiobacillus denitrificans* (21) and was shown to be similar to that from *Desulfovibrio desulfuricans* (91). The enzyme was recently purified from *Thiobacillus thioparus* (73), the organism used by Peck in his original work. The properties were again similar to those of the *Desulfovibrio* enzyme containing FAD, iron, and, in addition, labile sulfide. Surprisingly the enzyme could use a yeast cytochrome *c* as well as ferricyanide as the electron acceptor. The $K_m$ values for substrates were nearly a hundredfold lower with the cytochrome (2.5 mM $\longrightarrow$ 17 $\mu$M $SO_3^{2-}$, 100 $\mu$M $\longrightarrow$ 2.5 $\mu$M AMP). The pH optimum also shifted from 7.4 (ferricyanide) to 9.5 (cytochrome). A possible reaction mechanism was proposed from a kinetic study of the enzyme (74). APS reductase with a cytochrome *c* as physiological electron acceptor should be able to conserve energy through oxidative phosphorylation as well as substrate level phosphorylation. The low $K_m$ values for substrates would ensure the efficiency of the system. Since APS reductase comprises 3–4% of the cell protein in *T. thioparus* (73) and 4–5% in *T. denitrificans* (21), the APS pathway must play an important role in the energy metabolism of these organisms.

Sulfite oxidase (25) oxidizes sulfite to sulfate with cytochrome *c* as electron acceptor and has now been purified from *T. novellus* (25), *T. thioparus* (75), and *F. ferrooxidans* (136). The enzyme is similar to liver sulfite oxidase (48). Sulfite oxidase is strongly inhibited by sulfhydryl-binding agents (25, 75) and also by anions such as chloride and phosphate (25, 75, 136). There was a marked shift in the $K_m$ value for sulfite from 40–90 $\mu$M to 2 $\mu$M when the pH was lowered from 8 to 6 (25, 75), indicating an extremely high affinity of the enzyme protein toward sulfite on the acid side of neutrality. The *T. thioparus* enzyme contained a nonheme iron and was inhibited by metal chelators (75). From a kinetic study of the enzyme reaction a mechanism was proposed where the transfer of two electrons from sulfite to cytochrome *c* is accomplished one at a time with a possible mediation of nonheme iron (74).

The sulfite oxidase system isolated from *T. neapolitanus* (39) differs markedly from sulfite:cytochrome *c* oxidoreductase in that cytochromes are not involved and oxygen directly participates in the oxidation of sulfite. The system is reminiscent of sulfite oxidation initiated by free radicals (38, 77) in that a very high sulfite concentration is required and cysteine and glutathione inhibit it possibly by acting as chain breakers. The system requires a reinvestigation at a sulfite concentration sufficiently low to prevent the chain reaction before any physiological role is assigned.

Many thiobacilli grow on thiosulfate as an energy source, oxidizing both sulfur atoms to sulfate: $S_2O_3^{2-} + 2\ O_2 + H_2O \longrightarrow 2\ SO_4^{2-} + 2H^+$.

Under certain growth conditions tetrathionate accumulates in the medium. A thiosulfate-oxidizing enzyme catalyzing the following reaction: $2\ S_2O_3^{2-} \longrightarrow$

$^{-}O_3SSSSO_3^{-} + 2\ e^{-}$ was first isolated by Trudinger (126, 127). Although ferricyanide was used as electron acceptor in his study, native cytochrome was shown to be a natural electron acceptor. The enzyme was purified from *T. thioparus* (76) and *F. ferrooxidans* (112). The *T. thioparus* enzyme (76) was shown to reduce mammalian cytochrome *c*, although slower than ferricyanide with a marked increase in affinity for thiosulfate ($K_m$, 0.1 mM with ferricyanide $\longrightarrow$ 5 $\mu$M with cytochrome *c*). The enzyme was inhibited by sulfhydryl inhibitors and, most surprisingly, was strongly inhibited by sulfite. The sulfite inhibition was time-dependent and irreversible with 5 $\mu$M sulfite destroying 50% of the enzyme activity in 5 min. The *Ferrobacillus* enzyme (112) catalyzed the reaction only with ferricyanide, but not with native or mammalian cytochrome *c* as electron acceptor. It is interesting that the thiosulfate-oxidizing enzyme is found in a sulfur-grown organism, but its role in sulfur oxidation is unknown.

Thiosulfate can be metabolized to sulfate without tetrathionate formation. Peck (88) and Peck & Fisher (92) proposed a reductive cleavage of $SSO_3^{2-}$ with glutathione by thiosulfate reductase as the initial reaction followed by the oxidation of resulting $SO_3^{2-}$ through the APS pathway to sulfate. In *Thiobacillus novellus*, however, thiosulfate oxidation to sulfate required no GSH and since rhodanese was present as well as sulfur-oxidizing enzyme and sulfite oxidase the following scheme of thiosulfate oxidation was proposed (26):

$$SSO_3^{2-} \longrightarrow S + SO_3^{2} \quad \text{[thiosulfate-cleaving enzyme (rhodanese)]}$$

$$S + O_2 + H_2O \longrightarrow SO_3^{2-} + 2\ H^+ \quad \text{[sulfur-oxidizing enzyme]}$$

$$2\ SO_3^{2-} + O_2 \longrightarrow 2\ SO_4^{2-} \quad \text{[sulfite oxidase, cytochrome oxidase]}$$

Rhodanese was purified from *T. denitrificans* (20), *F. ferrooxidans* (122), and *Chromatium* (113). Bovine rhodanese accepts the cleaved sulfur in the form of persulfide groups (RSSH) in the protein (37). The enzyme can catalyze the transfer of sulfur from thiosulfate to glutathione, although much more slowly than to cyanide (61), and to apoferredoxin in the formation of labile sulfur (sulfide) of a nonheme iron protein, ferredoxin (36). Thus rhodanese may be considered as sulfur transferase capable of transferring sulfur from polysulfides, as well as from thiosulfate, to various acceptors (61). Although a separate thiosulfate reductase may exist (22, 61), the ability of rhodanese to catalyze the reductive cleavage of thiosulfate (22, 61) supports the proposed mechanism of thiosulfate cleavage for both *Thiobacillus thioparus* (119) and *T. novellus.*

The presence of both APS reductase and sulfite oxidase in *T. thioparus* (75) poses an interesting question about the respective roles of these two enzymes in sulfite oxidation. APS reductase may have an evolutionary priority originating from ancient sulfate-reducing bacteria (90). *T. novellus* (24), *Thiobacillus intermedius* (23), and *Ferrobacillus ferrooxidans* (136) with only sulfite oxidase present may be evolutionary newcomers adapted to strictly aerobic environment. In this regard, it is interesting that both *T. denitrificans* and some strains of *T. thioparus* are capable of growing anaerobically in the presence of nitrate (131).

Metabolism of tetrathionate and polythionates has been discussed in detail by Trudinger (131) and Roy & Trudinger (102), based largely on whole cell studies. Tetrathionate is produced from thiosulfate by thiosulfate-oxidizing enzyme in many thiobacilli and often accumulates in the medium. Further oxidation of tetrathionate requires low oxygen concentration or catalytic sparking by thiosulfate (128). It also requires a high cell concentration (128) and a high protein concentration in the case of crude extracts (72). These results (72, 128, 129) may be explained by a reductive cleavage of tetrathionate ($^-O_3SSSSO_3^- + 2\ e^- \longrightarrow SO_3^{2-} + S + SSO_3^{2-}$) coupled to oxidation of sulfite to sulfate ($SO_3^{2-} + H_2O \longrightarrow SO_4^{2-} + 2\ H^+ + 2\ e^-$). Anaerobically $SO_4^{2-}$, S, and $SSO_3^{2-}$ are the products (129). Aerobically there would be a shortage of electrons required for the initial cleavage. Thiosulfate or endogenous substrates could supply the necessary electrons to spark the oxidation of tetrathionate. Shortage of oxygen should favor such a process.

Trithionate can be formed chemically from tetrathionate and sulfite (129) and therefore is expected to accumulate when the rate of sulfite formation is faster than that of sulfite oxidation. The oxidation of trithionate probably also starts with a reductive cleavage, ($^-O_3SSSO_3^- + 2\ e^- \longrightarrow SO_3^{2-} + S_2O_3^{2-}$) since anaerobically $SO_4^{2-}$ and $S_2O_3^{2-}$ are the products (130). Thus the situation is analogous to that with tetrathionate. Such a reductive cleavage of trithionate was proposed by Imai et al (49).

The following scheme of inorganic sulfur oxidation explains most of the experimental results in the past and, significantly, all the enzymes involved have been isolated and characterized with the exception of tetrathionate reductase which may be similar to thiosulfate reductase or rhodanese. Although sulfide oxidase was not isolated, there is some evidence for its existence (82, 83).

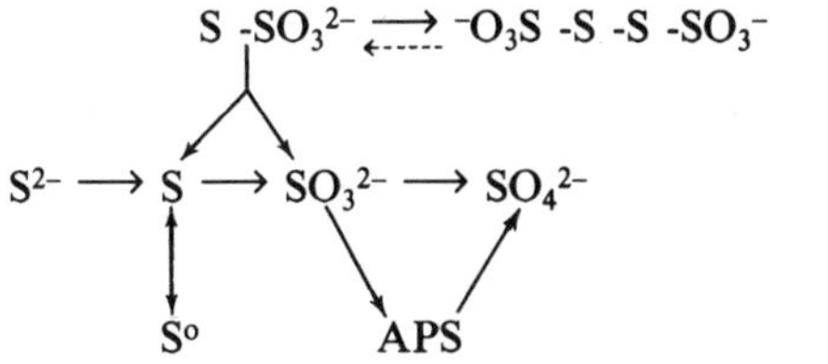


*Scheme 1* Inorganic sulfur oxidation.

When sulfide or sulfur is the substrate for oxidation it enters the main pathway ($S \longrightarrow SO_3^{2-} \longrightarrow SO_4^{2-}$). Thiosulfate oxidation starts with its cleavage to S and $SO_3^{2-}$. Sulfite is oxidized to sulfate by one of the two pathways. Sulfur is oxidized to sulfite, but when the oxidation rate is slower than the rate of thiosulfate cleavage it is excreted outside of cells as elemental sulfur. When thiosulfate cleavage is hindered cells obtain energy by its oxidation to tetrathionate. Once thiosulfate is cleaved, sulfite inhibits the thiosulfate-oxidizing enzyme (76). Tetrathionate accumulated is possibly oxidized further after a reductive cleavage to thiosulfate, sulfur, and sulfite.

*Thiobacillus denitrificans* is a facultative anaerobe capable of utilizing $NO_3^-$ instead of $O_2$ as a terminal electron acceptor. Sulfide, thiosulfate, tetrathionate, and sulfite were oxidized by the organism with $NO_3^-$ (2, 93). A particulate, sulfite-linked nitrate reductase was isolated (2). In a recent paper Aminuddin & Nicholas (10) reported on the oxidation of sulfide and proposed a mechanism where sulfide is first oxidized by nitrite reductase to a membrane-bound polysulfide which is in turn oxidized to sulfite by a soluble fraction. Sulfite is oxidized by APS reductase present in the soluble fraction or by sulfite-linked nitrate reductase present in the membrane fraction. It would be interesting to see whether the membrane-bound polymeric sulfur is oxidized by an enzyme similar to the sulfur-oxidizing enzyme found in aerobic thiobacilli but using an intermediate of denitrification as an oxygen donor rather than molecular oxygen. Nitrite or nitroxyl (NOH) might be such an intermediate. The organism produces nitrous oxide ($N_2O$), a possible decomposition product of (NOH), in addition to NO and $N_2$, from nitrite (10).

## ENERGY COUPLING

Energy coupling in chemoautotrophic bacteria has been extensively discussed by Peck (90), Kelly (52), Wallace & Nicholas (139), and Aleem (5). In this review only more recent aspects will be discussed.

Oxidative phosphorylation coupled to the oxidation of an inorganic compound was first demonstrated in *Nitrobacter* extracts (9). Aleem recently reported improved P/O ratios approaching 1.0 with nitrite and 2.0 with NADH (3). O'Kelley & Nason (87) observed phosphorylations with nitrite, NADH, and formate using similar nitrite oxidase particles. Apparently the organism can utilize the energy from formate oxidation for growth (133). The energy generated from nitrite oxidation can be used for the reduction of NAD by reversed electron flow (5, 56, 109). According to Wallace & Nicholas (138) *Nitrobacter* is capable of reducing nitrate to nitrite, then to ammonia, but the nitrate reduction with NADH did not lead to phosphorylation in contrast with Kiesow's report (55). They found, however, an active adenylate kinase and ATPase which might interfere in the phosphorylation studies.

Bock developed a technique of measuring oxidative phosphorylation directly by a pH change caused by the uptake of phosphate when *Nitrobacter* cells were exposed to air after anaerobic incubation (15, 16). Phosphate was mainly incorporated into polyphosphates (16). Photooxidation of cytochrome *c* inhibited nitrite oxidation and oxidative phosphorylation with nitrite, suggesting its importance in its mechanism of oxidation (17). Interestingly nitrite inhibited endogenous oxidative phosphorylation (16), presumably because the two phosphorylating systems are closely linked (17).

Calorimetric measurement of free energy utilization by *Nitrobacter* and *Nitrosomonas* cells (63) during nitrite and ammonia oxidations provided the efficiency values of 15–51% and 11–27%, respectively. 2,4-Dinitrophenol, an inhibitor of these oxidations at higher concentrations, unexpectedly increased the energy efficiency. The result might be explained if it is assumed that 2,4-dinitrophenol affects the membrane permeability of these cells facilitating either substrate entry or product exit. Energy normally required for such a purpose and dissipated as heat might then be stored in the cells as energy storage compounds such as polyphosphates. Free energy efficiency in *Nitrobacter* is a function of initial nitrite concentration (28) and $CO_2$ partial pressure (58).

*Hydrogenomonas* obtains energy for growth by the oxidation of $H_2$ in the presence of $O_2$. The production of biomass from $H_2$ and $CO_2$ by the organism was reviewed by Schlegel & Lafferty (107). Its metabolism and energy coupling were reviewed by Schlegel & Eberhardt (106) and by Peck (90). Bongers (18) originally proposed an abbreviated electron transport chain from $H_2$ to cytochrome *b* to oxygen using cell-free extracts of *Hydrogenomonas* H-20. He also demonstrated oxidative phosphorylation. NAD was not an obligatory intermediate as previously believed. Ishaque & Aleem (50) reinvestigated the problem with extracts of *Hydrogenomonas eutropha* and concluded that $H_2$ oxidation was mediated by NAD using a standard mitochondrial type electron transport chain. A P/O ratio of 2.0 reported with $H_2$ or NADH was considerably higher than 0.2–0.7 reported by Bongers. There was also a succinate- or ascorbate-linked, ATP-dependent reversal of electron transfer to NAD. A further study of the problem by Ishaque, Donawa & Aleem (31, 51) with $H_2$-grown *Pseudomonas saccharophila* confirmed the entry of electrons from $H_2$ at cytochrome *b,* the noninvolvement of NAD, and the low P/O ratio reported by Bongers. Since the organism has hydrogen dehydrogenase which can directly reduce NAD with $H_2$ without electron carriers (90), the electron transport-coupled oxidation of $H_2$ may be used only for the generation of energy. It is quite possible, then, that the soluble hydrogen dehydrogenase, when associated with the electron transport complex in membranes, might form an NAD-mediated hydrogen oxidation system. In the intact cells hydrogen probably enters the electron transport system at NAD in order to account for its high energy efficiency for growth with proper $H_2$:$O_2$:$CO_2$ ratio (19, 146).

Oxidative phosphorylations coupled to the oxidation of thiosulfate; and of thiosulfate, succinate, or ascorbate were demonstrated in cell-free extracts of *Thiobacillus neapolitanus* (100) and *Thiobacillus novellus* (27), respectively. The former extract required bovine serum albumin for the phosphorylation, but not for the oxidation. The latter extract was a 144,000 X *g* supernatant, but a possibility of its containing small membrane fragments with high content of lipid still exists. They could possibly reassociate into larger particles during incubation with substrates and cofactors. Oxidative phosphorylations by these extracts were effectively uncoupled by 2,4-dinitrophenol and other uncouplers (27, 100), although there was no mitochondrial type respiratory control. P/O ratios approached 1.0 and 2.0 with thiosulfate and succinate. These extracts presumably oxidize thiosulfate to tetrathionate (105). Sulfide was oxidized by *T. neapolitanus* by a mechanism similar to that proposed by Moriarty & Nicholas (82, 83) and the oxidation was coupled to a low level of phosphorylation (105). The oxidation of sulfide and sulfite by *T. concretivorous* extracts is also coupled to ATP generation (84). Although a proton gradient and chemiosmotic coupling (80, 81) might eventually explain the mechanism of energy generation and substrate entry or product exit in chemoautotrophic bacteria, experimental evidence is insufficient to formulate a theory at this stage. Saxena &

Aleem (105) reported briefly an acid-induced ATP synthesis sensitive to uncouplers of oxidative phosphorylation in *T. neapolitanus* cells, but the result is not compatible with a nonparticulate nature of the *T. novellus* phosphorylation system by Cole & Aleem (27).

Adenylate kinase, the last enzyme in the APS pathway of sulfite oxidation that generates ATP (90), was purified from *T. neapolitanus* (79). The optimal pH for 2ADP $\longrightarrow$ ATP + AMP was found to be around 10 and the enzyme was closely associated with and protected by cytochrome *c*, suggesting its possibly intimate involvement in the action of APS reductase with a similar optimal pH when coupled with cytochrome *c* (73). Discovery of a sulfite-dependent particulate ATPase from *T. thiooxidans* by Marunouchi & Mori (78) is interesting because of its suggested involvement in ion transport. Inorganic pyrophosphatase is present in *T. thiooxidans* (78) and *Ferrobacillus ferrooxidans* (47), but its role has not been studied.

Mechanism of pyridine nucleotide reduction by *T. neapolitanus* was studied by Aleem (4) and Saxena & Aleem (104). It was concluded that thiosulfate oxidation could be coupled to the reduction of pyridine nucleotide by the energy-dependent reversed electron flow. Roth et al (101) carried out a detailed study of concentration changes in adenine and pyridine nucleotides as well as intermediates of gluconeogenesis in *T. neapolitanus* cells during thiosulfate oxidation. Within a few seconds of thiosulfate addition ATP was formed and pyridine nucleotides were reduced. Although NAD was reduced 4.5-fold faster than NADP, NADH was rapidly reoxidized for the reduction of phosphoglyceric acid for carbohydrate synthesis. All these processes were inhibited by an uncoupler of oxidative phosphorylation. Amytal did not affect ATP synthesis but inhibited pyridine nucleotide reduction. Interestingly, when sulfide was used as oxidizable substrate NAD and NADP reduction was still inhibited by both amytal and an uncoupler, suggesting an inability of sulfide to reduce these pyridine nucleotides directly, in spite of the presence of low potential *c*-type cytochromes in the organism (103). The rate of pyridine nucleotide reduction was much faster than that in the cell-free systems (4, 104). These experiments with intact cells substantiate the results of cell-free studies (4, 104) and support the original hypothesis of Aleem, Lees & Nicholas (7) and Kiesow (54) that pyridine nucleotide reduction in chemoautotrophic bacteria could occur by the energy-dependent reversal of electron transport system.

## Acknowledgments

Work from our laboratory was supported by grants from the National Research Council of Canada. Assistance by Odean Lukow in the literature survey is acknowledged.

*Literature Cited*


1. Adair, F. W. 1966. *J. Bacteriol.* 92: 899–904
2. Adams, C. A., Warnes, G. M., Nicholas, D. J. D. 1971. *Biochim. Biophys. Acta* 235:398–406
3. Aleem, M. I. H. 1968. *Biochim. Biophys. Acta* 162:338–47
4. Aleem, M. I. H. 1969. *Antonie van Leeuwenhoek J. Microbiol. Serol.* 35:379–91
5. Aleem, M. I. H. 1970. *Ann. Rev. Plant Physiol.* 21:67–90
6. Aleem, M. I. H., Lees, H. 1963. *Can. J. Biochem. Physiol.* 41:763–78
7. Aleem, M. I. H., Lees, H., Nicholas, D. J. D. 1963. *Nature* 200:759–61
8. Aleem, M.I.H., Nason, A. 1959. *Biochem. Biophys. Res. Commun.* 1: 323–27
9. Aleem, M. I. H., Nason, A. 1960. *Proc. Nat. Acad. Sci. USA* 46:763–69
10. Aminuddin, M., Nicholas, D. J. D. 1973. *Biochim. Biophys. Acta* 325:81–93
11. Anderson, J. H. 1964. *Biochem. J.* 91:8–17
12. Anderson, J. R., Stumeyer, D. H., Pramer, D. 1968. *J. Bacteriol.* 96:93–97
13. Beck, J. V. 1960. *J. Bacteriol.* 79:502–9
14. Blaylock, B. A., Nason, A. 1963. *J. Biol. Chem.* 238:3453–62
15. Bock, E. 1967. *Arch. Mikrobiol.* 58: 169–80
16. Ibid 1968. 63:70–84
17. Ibid 1970. 70:217–39
18. Bongers, L. 1967. *J. Bacteriol.* 93: 1615–23
19. Ibid 1970. 104:145–51
20. Bowen, T. J., Butler, P. J., Happold, F. C. 1965. *Biochem. J.* 97:651–57
21. Bowen, T. J., Happold, F. C., Taylor, B. F. 1966. *Biochim. Biophys. Acta* 118:566–76
22. Burtner, C., Akagi, J. M. 1971. *J. Bacteriol.* 107:375–76
23. Charles, A. M. 1969. *Arch. Biochem. Biophys.* 129:124–30
24. Charles, A. M., Suzuki, I. 1965. *Biochem. Biophys. Res. Commun.* 19: 686–90
25. Ibid 522–34
26. Charles, A. M., Suzuki, I. 1966. *Biochim. Biophys. Acta* 128:510–21
27. Cole, J. S., Aleem, M. I. H. 1970. *Biochem. Biophys. Res. Commun.* 38: 736–43
28. Dessers, A., Chaing, C., Laudelout, H. 1970. *J. Gen. Microbiol.* 64:71–76
29. Din, G. A., Suzuki, I. 1967. *Can. J. Biochem.* 45:1547–56
30. Din, G. A., Suzuki, I., Lees, H. 1967. *Can. J. Biochem.* 45:1523–46
31. Donawa, A. L., Ishaque, M., Aleem, M. I. H. 1971. *Eur. J. Biochem.* 21:292–300
32. Dugan, P. R., Lundgren, D. G. 1965. *J. Bacteriol.* 89:825–34
33. Erickson, R. H., Hooper, A. B. 1972. *Biochim. Biophys. Acta.* 275:231–44
34. Erickson, R. H., Hooper, A. B., Terry, K. R. 1972. *Biochim. Biophys. Acta* 283:155–66
35. Falcone, A. B., Shug, A. L., Nicholas, D. J. D. 1963. *Biochim. Biophys. Acta* 77:199–208
36. Finazzi Agrò, A., Cannela, C., Graziani, M. T., Cavallini, D. 1971. *FEBS Lett.* 16:172–74
37. Finazzi Agrò, A., Federici, G., Giovagnoli, C., Cannela, C., Cavallini, D. 1972. *Eur. J. Biochem.* 28:89–93
38. Fridovich, I., Handler, P. 1961. *J. Biol. Chem.* 236:1836–40
39. Hempfling, W. P., Trudinger, P. A. 1967. *Arch. Mikrobiol.* 59:149–57
40. Hill, J. E., Taylor, C. P. S. 1969. *Can. J. Biochem.* 47:507–9
41. Hofman, T., Lees, H. 1953. *Biochem. J.* 54:579–83
42. Hooper, A. B. 1968. *Biochim. Biophys. Acta* 162:49–65
43. Hooper, A. B. 1969. *J. Bacteriol.* 97: 968–69
44. Hooper, A. B., Erickson, R. H., Terry, K. R. 1972. *J. Bacteriol.* 110:430–38
45. Hooper, A. B., Nason, A. 1965. *J. Biol. Chem.* 240:4044–57
46. Hooper, A. B., Terry, K. R. 1973. *J. Bacteriol.* 115:480–85
47. Howard, A., Lundgren, D. G. 1970. *Can. J. Biochem.* 48:1302–7
48. Howell, L. G., Fridovich, I. 1968. *J. Biol. Chem.* 243:5941–47
49. Imai, K., Okuzumi, M., Katagiri, H. 1962. *Koso Kagaku Shimpojiumu* 17: 132
50. Ishaque, M., Aleem, M. I. H. 1970. *Biochim. Biophys. Acta* 223:388–97
51. Ishaque, M., Donawa, A., Aleem, M. I. H. 1971. *Biochem. Biophys. Res. Commun.* 44:245–51
52. Kelly, D. P. 1971. *Ann. Rev. Microbiol.* 25:177–210
53. Ketchum, P. A., Sanders, H. K., Gryder, J. W., Nason, A. 1969. *Biochim. Biophys. Acta* 189:360–65
54. Kiesow, L. 1963. *Biochem. Z.* 338: 400–6
55. Kiesow, L. 1964. *Proc. Nat. Acad. Sci. USA* 52:980–88

56. Kiesow, L. 1967. *Curr. Top. Bioenerg.* 2:195–233
57. Kiesow, L. A. 1972. *Aldrichim. Acta* 5:33–37
58. Kiesow, L. A., Shelton, J. B., Bless, J. W. 1972. *Arch. Biochem. Biophys.* 151:414–19
59. Kodama, A. 1969. *Plant Cell Physiol.* 10:645–55
60. Kodama, A., Mori, T. 1968. *Plant Cell Physiol.* 9:725–34
61. Koj, A. 1968. *Acta Biochim. Pol.* 15: 161–69
62. Kwok, S. C. 1972. *Cell-free ammonia oxidation by Nitrosomonas europaea extracts.* M.Sc. Thesis. Univ. Manitoba, Winnipeg. 55 pp.
63. Laudelout, H., Simonart, P. C., Van Droogenbroeck, R. 1968. *Arch. Mikrobiol.* 63:256–77
64. Lazaroff, N. 1963. *J. Bacteriol.* 85: 78–83
65. Lees, H. 1952. *Nature* 169:156
66. Lees, H. 1952. *Biochem. J.* 52:134
67. Lees, H. 1955. *Biochemistry of Autotrophic Bacteria.* London: Butterworth. 112 pp.
68. Lees, H. 1960. *Ann. Rev. Microbiol.* 14:83–98
69. Lees, H., Kwok, S. C., Suzuki, I. 1969. *Can. J. Microbiol.* 15:43–46
70. Lees, H., Simpson, J. R. 1957. *Biochem. J.* 65:297–305
71. Lemberg, R., Barrett, J. 1973. *Cytochromes.* London: Academic. 580 pp.
72. London, J., Rittenberg, S. C. 1964. *Proc. Nat. Acad. Sci. USA* 52:1183–90
73. Lyric, R. M., Suzuki, I. 1970. *Can. J. Biochem.* 48:344–54
74. Ibid 594–603
75. Ibid 334–43
76. Ibid 355–63
77. MacLeod, R. M., Farkas, W., Fridovich, I., Handler, P. 1961. *J. Biol. Chem.* 236:1841–46
78. Marunouchi, T., Mori, T. 1967. *J. Biochem.* 62:401–7
79. Mazzotta, M. Y., Johnson, E. J. 1973. *Biochim. Biophys. Acta* 321:512–25
80. Mitchell, P. 1966. *Biol. Rev.* 41: 445–505
81. Mitchell, P. 1972. *Bioenergetics* 3:5–24
82. Moriarty, D. J. W., Nicholas, D. J. D. 1969. *Biochim. Biophys. Acta* 184: 114–32
83. Ibid 1970. 197:143–51
84. Ibid 216:130–38
85. Nicholas, D. J. D., Jones, O. T. G. 1960. *Nature* 185:512–14
86. O'Kelley, J. C., Becker, G. E., Nason, A. 1970. *Biochim. Biophys. Acta* 205: 409–25
87. O'Kelley, J. C., Nason, A. 1970. *Biochim. Biophys. Acta* 205:426–36
88. Peck, H. D. Jr. 1960. *Proc. Nat. Acad. Sci. USA* 46:1053–57
89. Peck, H. D. Jr. 1962. *Bacteriol. Rev.* 26:67–94
90. Peck, H. D. Jr. 1968. *Ann. Rev. Microbiol.* 22:489–518
91. Peck, H. D. Jr., Deacon, T. E., Davidson, J. T. 1965. *Biochim. Biophys. Acta* 96:429–46
92. Peck, H. D. Jr., Fisher, E. 1962. *J. Biol. Chem.* 237:190–97
93. Peeters, T., Aleem, M. I. H. 1970. *Arch. Mikrobiol.* 71:319–30
94. Rees, M. K. 1968. *Biochemistry* 7: 353–66
95. Ibid 366–72
96. Rees, M. K. 1968. *J. Bacteriol.* 95: 243–44
97. Rees, M. K., Nason, A. 1965. *Biochem. Biophys. Res. Commun.* 21:248–56
98. Rees, M. K., Nason, A. 1966. *Biochim. Biophys. Acta* 113:398–402
99. Ritchie, G. A. F., Nicholas, D. J. D. 1972. *Biochem. J.* 126:1181–91
100. Ross, A. J., Schoenhoff, R. L., Aleem, M. I. H. 1968. *Biochem. Biophys. Res. Commun.* 32:301–6
101. Roth, C. W., Hempfling, W. P., Conners, J. N., Vishniac, W. V. 1973. *J. Bacteriol.* 114:592–99
102. Roy, A. B., Trudinger, P. A. 1970. *The Biochemistry of Inorganic Compounds of Sulfur.* London: Cambridge Univ. Press. 400 pp.
103. Sadler, M. H., Johnson, E. J. 1972. *Biochim. Biophys. Acta* 283:167–79
104. Saxena, J., Aleem, M. I. H. 1972. *Arch. Mikrobiol.* 84:317–26
105. Saxena, J., Aleem, M. I. H. 1973. *Can. J. Biochem.* 51:560–68
106. Schlegel, H. G., Eberhardt, U. 1972. *Advan. Microbial Physiol.* 7:205–42
107. Schlegel, H. G., Lafferty, R. M. 1971. *Advan. Biochem. Eng.* 1:143–68
108. Schnaitman, C. A., Korczynski, M. S., Lundgren, D. G. 1969. *J. Bacteriol.* 99:552–57
109. Sewell, D. L., Aleem, M. I. H. 1969. *Biochim. Biophys. Acta* 172:467–75
110. Sewell, D. L., Aleem, M. I. H., Wilson, D. F. 1972. *Arch. Biochem. Biophys.* 153:312–19
111. Silver, M., Lundgren, D. G. 1968. *Can. J. Biochem.* 46:457–61
112. Ibid 1215–20
113. Smith, A. J., Lascelles, J. 1966. *J. Gen. Microbiol.* 42:357–70
114. Straat, P. A., Nason, A. 1965. *J. Biol. Chem.* 240:1412–26

115. Suzuki, I. 1965. *Biochim. Biophys. Acta* 104:359–71
116. Ibid 1965. 110:97–101
117. Suzuki, I., Kwok, S. C. 1969. *J. Bacteriol.* 99:897–98
118. Suzuki, I., Kwok, S. C. 1970. *Biochem. Biophys. Res. Commun.* 39:950–55
119. Suzuki, I., Silver, M. 1966. *Biochim. Biophys. Acta* 122:22–33
120. Suzuki, I., Werkman, C. H. 1959. *Proc. Nat. Acad. Sci. USA* 45:239–44
121. Suzuki, I., Werkman, C. H. 1960. *Biochem. J.* 74:359–62
122. Tabita, R., Silver, M., Lundgren, D. G. 1969. *Can. J. Biochem.* 47:1141–45
123. Tano, T., Imai, K. 1968. *Agr. Biol. Chem.* 32:51–54
124. Taylor, B. F. 1968. *Biochim. Biophys. Acta* 170:112–22
125. Tronson, D. A., Ritchie, G. A. F., Nicholas, D. J. D. 1973. *Biochim. Biophys. Acta* 310:331–43
126. Trudinger, P. A. 1961. *Biochem. J.* 78:673–80
127. Ibid 680–86
128. Ibid 1964. 90:640–46
129. Trudinger, P. A. 1964. *Aust. J. Biol. Sci.* 17:446–58
130. Ibid 459–68
131. Trudinger, P. A. 1967. *Rev. Pure Appl. Chem.* 17:1–24
132. Trudinger, P. A. 1969. *Advan. Microbial Physiol.* 3:111–58
133. Van Gool, A., Laudelout, H. 1966. *Biochim. Biophys. Acta* 127:295–301
134. Van Gool, A., Laudelout, H. 1967. *J. Bacteriol.* 93:215–20
135. Vernon, L. P., Mangum, J. H., Beck, J. V., Shafia, F. M. 1960. *Arch. Biochem. Biophys.* 88:227–31
136. Vestal, J. R., Lundgren, D. G. 1971. *Can. J. Biochem.* 49:1125–30
137. Waksman, S. A., Joffe, J. S. 1922. *J. Bacteriol.* 7:239–56
138. Wallace, W., Nicholas, D. J. D. 1968. *Biochem. J.* 109:763–73
139. Wallace, W., Nicholas, D. J. D. 1969. *Biol. Rev.* 44:359–91
140. Watson, S. W., Asbell, M. A., Valois, F. W. 1970. *Biochem. Biophys. Res. Commun.* 38:1113–19
141. Yates, M. G., Nason, A. 1966. *J. Biol. Chem.* 241:4872–80
142. Ibid 4861–71
143. Yoshida, T., Alexander, M. 1970. *Soil Sci. Soc. Am. Proc.* 34:880–82
144. Yoshida, T., Alexander, M. 1971. *Soil Sci.* 111:307–12
145. Zajic, J. E. 1969. *Microbial Biogeochemistry.* New York: Academic. 345 pp.
146. Zolotukhin, N. V. 1972. *Biofizika* 17:642–46

# FUNGAL CELL WALL GLYCOPROTEINS AND PEPTIDO-POLYSACCHARIDES

❖1632

*J. E. Gander*

Department of Biochemistry, College of Biological Sciences, University of Minnesota, St. Paul, Minnesota 55101

CONTENTS

INTRODUCTION .......... 103
CELL WALL MORPHOLOGY .......... 104
EXTRACELLULAR AND MURAL GLYCOPROTEINS AND GLYCOPEPTIDES .......... 105
*Yeasts* .......... 105
*Saccharomyces spp.* .......... 105
*Other yeasts* .......... 106
*Dermatophytes* .......... 107
*Neurospora* .......... 109
*Aspergillus* .......... 109
*Penicillium* .......... 110
EXTRACELLULAR AND MURAL GLYCO-ENZYMES .......... 111
*Invertase* .......... 111
*Galactofuranosidase* .......... 112
*Other Glycohydrolases* .......... 113
*Acid Phosphatases* .......... 113
*Proteases* .......... 113
BIOSYNTHESIS OF GLYCOPROTEINS AND PEPTIDO-POLYSACCHARIDES .......... 113
BIOLOGICAL PROPERTIES AND FUNCTIONS .......... 115
CONCLUDING REMARKS .......... 116

## INTRODUCTION

The renewed interest in the structure and function of glycoproteins and peptido-polysaccharides on the surface of eukaryotic cells has carried over to yeasts and other fungi. This review is restricted to considerations of structure, biosynthesis, and function of glycoproteins, glycopeptides, and so-called peptido-polysaccharides which are found outside of the plasma membrane of fungi. Some consideration is given to glycoproteins which are bound to specific organelles (vacuole and Golgi apparatus) that may fuse with the plasma membrane. Substances located outside of the plasma membrane are divided into two categories. Mural glycoproteins are those associated with or entrapped in the cell wall. Extracellular glycoproteins are those which are located in the medium outside of the cell wall. In this chapter a selective rather than a comprehensive coverage of the topic is presented.

Reviews by Gorin & Spencer (53) on fungal polysaccharides, Phaff (114) and Bartnicki-Garcia (11) on fungal cell walls and morphogenesis, and Pazur & Aronson (110) on glyco-enzymes should be consulted for a more comprehensive coverage of topics peripheral to this chapter.

## CELL WALL MORPHOLOGY

The cell wall of fungi and yeasts is a dynamic, complex, multilayered structure composed of at least two major polysaccharides (11), proteins, lipids, and lesser quantities of other substances. Bartnicki-Garcia (11) divided 13 taxonomic groups of fungi and yeasts into 8 different categories on the basis of the major polysaccharides found in the cell wall. This review considers primarily those organisms containing chitin-glucan (Ascomycetes, Basidiomycetes, Chytridiomycetes, and Deuteromycetes), and those containing glucan-mannan (Saccharomycetaceae and Cryptococcacea) as the major polysaccharides. Cell walls of fungi and yeasts are unlike the bacterial cell wall in that there is no evidence for muramic acid-containing peptidoglycan, teichoic acid, or lipopolysaccharide in the wall.

The location and/or orientation of various polymers within the wall has been investigated by 1. degradative techniques, 2. electron microscopy, and 3. fluorescent-antibody binding to cell walls. Mahadevan & Tatum (85, 86) chemically degraded *Neurospora crassa* walls and found that 2 N alkali released a peptido-glucogalactosamine complex. They proposed that this complex is on the outside of the wall and that inner layers of $\beta$-1,3-glucan and chitin occur. In contrast, Hunsley & Burnett (63) selectively degraded *N. crassa* walls with enzymes and sequentially removed the layers. Following each treatment the preparation was examined in the electron microscope. They proposed that the layers consisted of $\beta$-glucan, protein or glycoprotein, and chitin, progressing from the outermost to innermost layer, respectively. Treatment with mild reagents (2-mercaptoethanol, 1 *M* KCl, ethylenediamine) often releases glycoproteins from the cell wall (32, 73, 79, 149, 159). The effectiveness of these reagents in releasing glycoproteins is variable when treatment is applied to differing species. The data suggest species cell wall diversity.

Some, but not all fungi exhibit dimorphism, that is they grow in either a yeast-like or mycelial form. The form is determined by nutritional (39, 115) and environmental conditions (70, 125). The biochemical phenomenon dictating the morphological form is poorly understood. The occurrence of an active protein disulfide reductase in the yeast form, and its low activity in the mycelial form (104), is consistent with the conclusion that protein disulfide reductase is necessary to provide sufficient plasticity for bud formation (105). The composition of the cell wall of a species may be dependent on the morphological form (28, 69, 71). *Paracoccidioides brasiliensis* shows thermal dimorphism. It is yeast-like and mycelial at 37 and 20°C, respectively. Both forms contain chitin and glucan(s) as the major polysaccharides (68,

69). Only the mycelial form contains appreciable quantities of galactomannan (69), possibly a peptidogalactomannan. Chattaway et al (34) suggested that control over chitin and mannan synthesis may be provided by regulating phosphofructokinase activity, and that NADPH generation allows cell division to occur; a conclusion consistent with that of Nickerson (105, 106).

Cell walls of *Saccharomyces cerevisiae* in log phase are removed by lytic enzymes in snail gut (42). In contrast, a similar treatment of *S. cerevisiae* in stationary growth phase does not effectively remove the cell wall. Thus, the cell wall architecture changes as nutrient and culture conditions change. However, glucose and glucosamine are metabolically inert once they are incorporated into the cell wall polymers (36). This suggests that little turnover of hexosyl residues in the cell wall occurs. In starved *Penicillum chrysogenum,* lysis of protein, DNA, and RNA occurs before appreciable lysis of cell wall becomes apparent (153).

## EXTRACELLULAR AND MURAL GLYCOPROTEINS AND GLYCOPEPTIDES

### *Yeasts*

SACCHAROMYCES SPP. Electron microscopy shows that the wall is composed of two or more layers (107). Chemical analyses shows that the wall contains about 29% glucan, 31% mannan, 13% protein, 8.5% lipid, and 3% ash. Protein associated with mannan in cell walls is extracted into hot water. Nickerson et al (44, 75) showed that yeast walls contain three protein complexes: glucan-protein, mannan-protein I, and glucomannan-protein II. Cell walls also contain a peptido-polysaccharide (peptidophosphomannan) in which low molecular weight mannose-containing oligosaccharides are attached by O-glycosidic linkage to seryl and threonyl residues, and a high molecular weight phosphomannan is attached by N-glycosidic linkage to a glucosaminyl residue to the amide group of an asparaginyl residue in the peptide (72). Mannose 6-phosphate was found in the hydrolysate following treatment of the glycopeptide with 2 N HCl. Cawley et al (30) have shown that phosphorus occurs as an $\alpha$-1,6'phosphodiester bridged between a nonreducing terminal mannosyl residue and a second mannosyl residue which is in turn attached to the mannan backbone. It is unclear whether the structure of the phosphomannan region of yeast peptidophosphomannan is the same as the mannan and phosphomannans so extensively investigated in many laboratories (29, 52, 68, 75, 80, 113, 132, 133). Ballou and colleagues (29, 141, 142) have shown that the mannan backbone is composed of (1⟶6) linked mannopyranosyl residues and that mannopyranosyl, mannobiosyl, and mannotriosyl residues are attached by (1⟶2) linkages to the backbone. The mannopyranosyl:mannobiosyl:mannotriosyl ratio is not constant from *Saccharomyces* species to species. The ratio also varies with the age of the culture (141). The molar ratio mannose:P is dependent on both species and age of culture.

Ballou and colleagues have developed the acetolysis procedure sufficiently that different yeast mannans provide unique "fingerprints" (ratio of oligosaccharides released) (74, 80). Gorin & Spencer (54) determined the ratio of $\alpha$-O- to $\beta$-O-glycosidic linkages in mannans from nearly 500 species of yeasts with proton magnetic resonance spectroscopy, and they obtained 180 different spectra (139). The proton magnetic resonance spectra show the occurrence of α-(1⟶2) and α-(1⟶6) linkages as predominant. Jones & Ballou (66) and Gorin et al (55) used an *exo*-α-D-mannopyranosidase to degrade yeast mannans. The crude enzyme, used by Gorin, degraded α-D-(1⟶6)-linked mannan main chain as well as the side chain until β-D-linked residues were adjacent to a nonreducing terminal α-D-linkage. Jones & Ballou (67) observed that purified *exo*-α-D-mannopyranosidase released less mannose as the phosphorus content of the mannan increased.

Rabbit antisera against one of three yeasts (*S. cerevisiae, Saccharomyces lactis,* and *Kloeckera brevis*) cross react with the mannans from the other two species (5). Ballou proposed that the immunodominant group was the tetrasaccharide side chain [O-α-D-mannopyranosyl-(1⟶3)-O-D-mannopyranosyl-(1⟶2)-O-D-mannopyranosyl-(1⟶3)-O-D-mannopyranosyl-] because it was the most effective inhibitor of the homologous precipitin reaction. The phosphomannans from the three yeasts give similar, but not identical, "fingerprints" following acetolysis (74) or proton magnetic resonance spectroscopy (139).

It appears that yeast cell walls contain at least two types of phosphomannans; one which is attached to protein (peptido-phosphomannan), and the other which is part of the outer cell wall layer (79). Treatment of intact yeast cells with a phosphomannanase (PR-factor) results in the release of a phosphomannan (92), and when combined with a small amount of snail gut enzyme preparation (a β-1,3-glucanase source) the yeast cell is converted to a protoplast (91). The phosphomannanase cleaves a mannopyranosyl residue adjacent to a mannopyranosyl linked through a phosphodiester group. The forces holding the various glycoproteins to the wall can be surmised only. The phosphomannan outer layer may form a sufficiently tight mesh that glycoproteins and peptido-polysaccharides do not escape until the mesh is loosened, or alternatively, the phosphomannan region of the glycoprotein may be complexed through divalent ions to structural phosphomannan comprising the outer layer. Removal of divalent metal ions would promote the release of glycoproteins without a major structural change in the outer phosphomannan matrix.

OTHER YEASTS Similar, although not nearly as extensive, investigations have been conducted on the cell walls of other yeasts, including *K. brevis,* various *Hansenula* species (65, 135), *Cladosporium werneckii* (82, 83), *Candida albicans,* and *Sporobolomyces* species (65, 135, 136). Each species produces a phosphomannan, phosphogalactan, or peptidophosphogalactomannan. In each the phosphorus is bridged as a phosphodiester between two hexosyl residues. Limiting the phosphate in the culture results in production of altered phosphohexosans or neutral extracellular mannans by yeasts that secrete phosphogalactans or phosphomannans (137). *C. werneckii* cells release a peptidophosphogalactomannan when extracted at 100°C with pH 7 phosphate buffer. The polymer is in the 150,000–200,000 daltons range. Peptidophosphogalactomannan from *C. werneckii* contains 11% protein, mannose-containing oligosaccharides, and a phosphogalactomannan attached to the peptide. The phosphogalactomannan is composed of D-mannopyranosyl residues that are predominantly 1⟶2 linked, and smaller amounts of 1⟶6 and 1⟶3 substituted mannopyranosyl residues. Methylation and analysis of the products showed that galactose occurred primarily as nonreducing terminal D-galactofuranosyl and D-galactopyranosyl residues (82). The phosphogalactomannan contains phosphodiester groups bridging a side chain containing 7 mannosyl and 1 galactosyl residues to the main polysaccharide core. The main core also contains phosphodiester groups bridging 33 hexosyl (27 mannosyl and 6 galactosyl) residues (83). Lloyd proposes that the phosphogalactomannan is comprised of approximately 7 phosphodiester groups in the main chain each bridging a 33 hexosyl-containing galactomannan. However, the relatively large number of nonreducing terminal mannopyranosyl and galactosyl residues found (82) is inconsistent with the proposed model (83). The low molecular weight saccharides attached to the peptide contain only mannose.

The peptide contains relatively large quantities of seryl and threonyl residues and only traces of, or minimal quantities of, tyrosine, phenylalanine, methionine, and cysteine. The saccharides and phosphogalactomannan are attached to seryl and threonyl residues. The peptide's composition resembles that of glycopeptides from *S. cerevisiae* (72), *Trichophyton mentagrophytes* (38), and *Penicillium charlesii* (122). Lloyd (82) suggests that the peptide region is heterogeneous.

### *Dermatophytes*

Patients infected with a species of fungus in the dermatophyte class usually develop hypersensitivity to extracts from the mycelium of that species. The allergenic agents which cause these hypersensitive reactions have been investigated. *Trichophyton* or *Microsporum* species are found frequently as the infective agent. Trichophytin (a peptido-polysaccharide), isolated from *T. mentagrophytes,* gives immediate and delayed hypersensitive skin reactions in man and guinea pigs (8). Trichophytin must be located sufficiently near the outer cell wall surface to serve as an immunogenic substance. The immediate and delayed reactions are caused by the glycan and peptide, respectively. Related glycopeptides are obtained from the following *Trichophyton* and *Microsporum* species: *T. granulosum, T. interdigitale, T. rubrum, T. schoenleinii, T. ferrugineum, T. sabouraudii, M. quinckeanum,* and *M. praecox* (7, 17). Dermatophytes contain chitin and glucan as major cell wall polysaccharides. Allergenic glycopeptides are derived from glycoproteins or peptido-polysaccharides.

Barker et al (6) isolated a peptidogalactomannan from *T. mentagrophytes* mycelium. The polymer contained 73% D-mannose, 9% D-galactose, 9% protein, and an estimated molecular weight of 40,000 daltons. The phosphorus content was not measured. Galactose occurred only in nonreducing termini and in the furanosyl configuration. The galactomannan was estimated to have an equal number of termini and branch points. The predominant mannosyl linkages were 1⟶2 and 1⟶4 to mannopyranosyl residues. The occurrence of 1⟶4 and lack of 1⟶6 linkages is unique among peptidogalactomannans from dermatophytes. They (6) resolved, on DEAE-Sephadex, the peptidogalactomannan into galactomannan peptide 1 and 2. The amino acid composition of the two species was dissimilar. However, both species contained mannopyranosyl and galactofuranosyl residues.

Galactomannan peptides 1 and 2 contained 16.2% and 7.4% galactofuranosyl residues, respectively. N-terminal amino acid analysis suggest peptidogalactomannan (unresolved) contained at least three chains. All galactomannan peptides tested gave immediate and delayed hypersensitive skin reactions in guinea pigs sensitized with whole *T. mentagrophytes* mycelia. Removal of galactosyl residues did not alter reactivity.

Galactomannan was isolated from extracts of *T. granulosum* mycelium that were incubated with trypsin at pH 8.1 for 2 weeks. This procedure effectively releases galactomannans from peptidogalactomannans when the insoluble residue is extracted with hot 3% NaOH. Galactomannan contained 16% galactose and 84% mannose with 1⟶2 and 1⟶6 linked residues (17). Di-substituted mannosyl species accounted for one fifth of all mannosyl residues, and they represent residues at which branching occurred. Galactose occurred exclusively as nonreducing galactofuranosyl residues.

The chemical composition of galactomannan obtained from *T. interdigitale* mycelium was determined by a similar procedure and methylation analysis performed (21); D-galactose occurred exclusively as nonreducing terminal galactofuranosyl residues, and they comprised about 12% of the polymer.

Bishop et al (19) fractionated polysaccharides from *T. schonleinii, T. rubrum, T. granulosum, T. interdigitale,* and *M. quinckeanum* into galactomannans I and II, and glucan. The composition and hexosyl linkages in galactomannan I were determined (18). Galactomannan I from all these species was similar with some variations in the extent of branching; D-galactose occurred only as nonreducing galactofuranosyl termini—its quantity was variable from species to species. The polymer (mannan I) from *T. rubrum* contained no galactose. Galactomannan I from the other species contained 12% or less of galactose. The data suggest each mannan contained about 1% mannofuranosyl residues but this observation needs verification.

Galactomannan II was investigated in a similar manner. The percentage galactose (23–33%) was species dependent. Galactomannon II from *T. rubrum* contained 23% galactose. Galactose occurred only in nonreducing terminal positions. Thus one of every three mannosyl residues in the mannan is substituted. The occurrence of 10% of the hexosyl residues as mannofuranosyl residues is inconsistent with the observations of Grappel et al (56, 58) who prepared mannan I and II by treatment of galactomannan I and II from *M. quinckeanum, T. Rubrum, T. interdigitale,* and *T. schoenleinii* with 0.025 N oxalic acid at 97°C. They showed that the resulting mannans cross react with rabbit anti-*M. quinckeanum* serum. Acid hydrolysis should cleave mannofuranosyl and galactofuranosyl residues resulting in degradation of the mannan to oligosaccharides. They (57, 59) found that terminal galactofuranosyl residues contributed greatly to the antigenic specificity and to cross-reactivity of galactomannan II from various species. Galactofuranosyl residues are less significant antigenic determinants in galactomannan I species than in galactomannan II species.

The glucans, which comprise only 3–7% of the total soluble polysaccharide extracted from the mycelium, contained 1⟶3 and 1⟶6 linked glucopyranosyl residues (1, 20). How et al (61) extracted the mycelia of *T. rubrum, T. mentagrophytes, T. schoenleinii,* and *Microsporum canis* with ethylene glycol, and obtained a mixture of glycopeptides which contained glucosyl, galactosyl, mannosyl, and small amounts of xylosyl residues. An $\alpha$-1,4-glucan was obtained also.

### *Neurospora*

Little is known concerning glycoprotein or peptido-polysaccharides in *Neurospora* species cell wall. Five peptides were solubilized by treating *Neurospora crassa* walls with 0.5 N NaOH (160). However, this treatment generates dehydroaminoacyl residues by $\beta$-elimination of saccharides attached to seryl and threonyl residues. These peptides are subject to side reactions. Therefore, the estimate (3800 daltons) of the peptides molecular weight is of doubtful validity. They (160) also observed a polygalactosamine-containing polymer which precipitated from 67% alcohol.

Preliminary investigations (J. E. Gander and V. Woodward, unpublished observations) of an extracellular peptido-polysaccharide from *N. crassa* shows it contains glucosyl, mannosyl, and galactosyl residues. The galactosyl residues are not released by either dilute acid or *exo*-$\beta$-D-galactofuranosidase.

### *Aspergillus*

*Aspergillus fumigatus* is responsible for human aspergillosis, and *Aspergillus* species are important sources of allergens which enhance bronchial asthma symptoms (2). *A. fumigatus* produces a peptidogalactomannan containing galactofuranosyl residues (2, 128). This substance gives a hypersensitive skin reaction, and a positive precipitin reaction in rabbits or guinea pigs immunized with *A. fumigatus* and in patients with aspergillosis (3). Galactomannan was obtained from *A. fumigatus* growth medium and mycelium (127, 145). Both preparations of galactomannan were homogeneous by ultracentrifugal and electrophoretic analysis. A molecular weight of 20,000–30,000 daltons was estimated. Both galactomannans have similar chemical and physical properties, and galactose:mannose molar ratio is 1:1. Galactofuranosyl residues are presumed on the basis of lability to dilute acid. Removal of galactofuranosyl residues resulted in a polymer which was no longer reactive in the precipitin assay. Azuma et al (2, 3) extracted a peptidogalactomannan and a glucan from *A. fumigatus.* Large quantities of threonine, serine, and alanine, and only traces of tyrosine, cysteine or methionine occurred in the peptide. A relatively large quantity of glucosamine was found along with $\alpha$-(1$\longrightarrow$2) and (1$\longrightarrow$6) linked mannopyranosyl residues, and D-galactofuranosyl residues branching through (1$\longrightarrow$6) linkages from the mannan backbone. It is not clear whether more than one galactofuranosyl residue per side chain was found.

Azuma et al (3) also purified and investigated the chemical and serological properties of galactomannans from *A. flavus, Aspergillus effsus, Penicillium charlesii, Penicillium notatum, Penicillium frequentans,* and *Penicillium expansum.* They conclude that galactomannan is a common antigen of *Aspergillus* and *Penicillium* species.

It is of interest to determine if the galactomannans and peptidogalactomannans from dermatophytes, *Neurospora* and *Aspergillus* spp., contain phosphorus. If they do contain phosphodiester groups a structural relationship between the peptidophosphogalactomannans of *Cladosporium werneckii* and *P. charlesii* with those in dermatophytes, *Neurospora* and *Aspergillus* species, is established.

## *Penicillium*

Clutterbuck et al (35) first reported that *P. charlesii* produces during a 28-day culture period two extracellular homopolymers, galactocarolose and mannocarolose. Galactocarolose contains ten 5-O-β-D-galactofuranosyl residues, and mannocarolose eight or nine D-mannopyranosyl residues. Preston et al (116, 117, 119) demonstrated that cultures of *P. charlesii* grown under conditions similar to those described by Clutterbuck et al (35), produced heteropolysaccharides ranging in molecular weight from 20,000–60,000 daltons. They contained mannosyl, galactosyl, and small quantities of glucosyl and phosphoryl residues. Following fractionation on Sephadex G-100 the molar ratio of glucose:galactose:mannose:P showed that the polymers were heterogeneous (116).

Extracellular peptido-polysaccharides were isolated from *P. charlesii* cultures aerated for varying intervals. The polymer was characterized as a peptidophosphogalactomannan (48). The percentage galactose decreases from 65% to 12–15% in polymers isolated from 6-day and 20-day cultures, respectively (124). This decrease in percentage galactose results from an extracellular *exo*-β-D-galactofuranosidase that accumulates in the media between the sixth and fifteenth day. It degrades peptidophosphogalactomannan to peptidophosphomannan (123). Peptidophosphogalactomannan containing 70% or 12% galactose have molecular weights of 65,000 or 25,000 daltons, respectively.

Treatment of peptidophosphogalactomannan with 0.4 N NaOH results in formation of phosphogalactomannan, mono-, di-, and trisaccharides (48), which are composed of mannose. No amino sugars were found.

The phosphogalactomannan was characterized by acetolysis and methylation, followed by analysis of the products (48). Galactosyl residues all occur in the furanosyl configuration, and they are located in 8–10 chains in which each residue is attached by β-(1⟶5) linkage to the adjoining galactofuranosyl residue. Each polygalactofuranosyl chain is attached through a (1⟶3) glycosidic linkage to the mannan. The length of the chain varies between 1–15 residues depending on the percentage galactose in the polymer.

The mannan is composed of approximately 90 mannopyranosyl residues linked α-(1⟶2) and α-(1⟶6). Acetolysis, a procedure that cleaves (1⟶6) linkages, degraded the mannan. Mannopentaose, mannotetraose, mannotriose, mannobiose, and mannose in the molar ratio of 2:11:4:5:13 were formed, respectively (48).

The mannan contains 9–10 phosphodiester groups per mole. They are not attached to the same mannopyranosyl residues to which the polygalactofuranosyl chains are linked. Preliminary evidence suggests that a mixture of ethanolamine (122) and N-methyl ethanolamine derivatives are attached to the P atoms (J. E. Gander, unpublished observations). Radioactivity from [$^{14}CH_3$-]-L-methionine and [$^{3}H$]-ethanolamine were incorporated into the peptidophosphogalactomannan. Degradation of the phosphogalactomannan with periodate suggested that phosphorus was bridged between an ethanolamine derivative and either C-6 or C-2 atom of a mannopyranosyl residue.

The peptide contains approximately 30 amino acyl residues (122). The peptide is similar to those obtained from other fungi and yeasts in that it contains large quantities of threonyl, seryl, and alanyl residues and negligible quantities of the aromatic and sulfur-containing amino acids. Following treatment with alkali, 7 of 9 seryl residues and 7 of 7 threonyl residues were destroyed. Approximately one half of the amino acyl residues are attached through O-glycosidic linkage to mannose-containing saccharides. The peptidophosphogalactomannan is resistant to degradation by phosphodiesterases and proteases.

Cell walls from *P. charlesii* grown in [$^3$H]-ethanolamine were fractionated according to the procedure of Mahadevan & Tatum (85). The 2 N NaOH soluble, 67% ethanol insoluble substances (Fraction I) contained galactofuranosyl, glucosyl, and mannosyl residues. Approximately 15% of the total $^3$H incorporated into the cell wall was isolated in Fraction I (J. E. Gander, unpublished observations). The supernatant solution contained an additional 50% of the $^3$H. The remainder of the $^3$H was released from the insoluble residue with 1 N sulfuric acid at 90°C for 16 hr. The position of attachment of ethanolamine is unknown.

Galactomannan from *P. chrysogenum* mycelia and culture filtrates contains galactofuranosyl residues, 0.85% phosphorus and 1.4% N but no sulfur (100, 129).

Extracellular peptidophosphogalactomannan from *P. charlesii* reacts with rabbit and guinea pig anti-*P. charlesii* serum (49, 118). Peptido-polysaccharides from other *Penicillium* species (*P. chrysogenum, P. claviforme, P. raistrickii,* and *P. patulum*) all cross react with anti-*P. charlesii* sera, and galactose is released from each polysaccharide treated with galactofuranosidase (J. E. Gander and F. Fang, unpublished observations). In contrast, the polysaccharide from *Penicillium varians* contains no galactofuranosyl residues and it does not cross react with anti-*P. charlesii* serum. This polymer contains galactopyranosyl and glucopyranosyl residues (60).

## EXTRACELLULAR AND MURAL GLYCO-ENZYMES

### *Invertase*

Many mural and extracellular enzymes from yeasts and fungi have carbohydrate covalently attached to the peptide. These glyco-enzymes (112) modify constituents in the media which makes the nutrients more available to the organism. Invertase ($\beta$-D-fructofuranoside fructohydrolase, E.C. 2.3.1.26) has received the most attention. It is widely distributed among the fungi and yeasts. *Saccharomyces* species produces two proteins with invertase activity (51). The minor species (invertase), located within the plasma membrane, has a molecular weight of 135,000 daltons and it is composed of amino acyl residues only (50). The major species (glyco-invertase) is located outside of the plasma membrane and it is a glycoprotein containing 50% mannosyl and 3% glucosaminyl residues (103). The two proteins have the same antigenic determinants, and their synthesis appears to be controlled by a common gene.

Beteta & Gascon (14) suggested that the vacuolar membrane serves as the site of glyco-invertase glycosylation. Both invertases were located in *Saccharomyces* protoplast vacuoles. They proposed that invertase and glyco-invertase are located on the outside and within the vacuole, respectively. Presumably invertase is glycosylated on or within the vacuolar membrane, the vacuole fuses with the plasma membrane, and glyco-invertase is released into the periplasmic space. Most of the newly formed glyco-invertase at the surface of a *Saccharomyces* cell surrounds the developing bud (147, 148). The process may be directed by the location of vesicles produced by endoplasmic reticulum which fuse in the bud region with the plasma membrane (101).

The exact location of glyco-invertase and the forces holding it to the wall are not completely understood (95). Phosphomannanase releases glyco-invertase and phosphomannan from the yeast cell wall (79). Covalent linkage between glyco-invertase and phosphomannan was suggested. Kidby & Davies (73) proposed that glyco-invertase is trapped behind rigid S-S-containing structures.

Metzenberg (95–97, 152) purified and investigated glyco-invertase from *Neurospora crassa* walls. His findings show that the enzyme contained only a small quantity of hexosamine (96). Meachum & Colvin (94) later demonstrated that purified glyco-invertase contained 11% mannose and 3% glucosamine. The enzyme is released from the cell wall by chitinase (93). Chang & Trevithick (32) confirmed this observation and also showed that $\beta$-1,3-glucanase and cellulase did not release glyco-invertase from the cell wall. The enzyme was not released by dithiothreitol, high concentration of salt, or EDTA. Apparently the glyco-invertase is covalently bound to a cell wall component. The enzyme is located between the plasma membrane and outer cell wall (95). *N. crassa* protoplasts produce glyco-invertase at a nearly linear rate for 18 hr (151). Mutants of *N. crassa* secrete 95% of the glyco-invertase produced into the growth medium (16). The enzyme appears to be identical to glyco-invertase found in the wild-type organism. Further, wall *N. crassa* glyco-invertase is destroyed by 0.1 N HCl. However, the organism synthesizes new enzyme (88, 89) after treatment with 0.1 N HCl.

*N. crassa* glyco-invertase distribution on the cell wall surface changes during germination and hyphal growth. Conidial glyco-invertase is uniformly distributed along the cell periphery (31, 33). Glyco-invertase concentrates in the apical tip of hypha and the enzyme disappears from conidial wall following germination. Glyco-invertase is also found associated at sites of new hyphal branches. Its location may facilitate rapid glucose transport (79).

### *Galactofuranosidase*

The rapid decrease in percentage galactose in *P. charlesii* peptidophosphogalactomannan is coincident with the appearance of extracellular galactofuranosidase (123, 124). The purified enzyme contains approximately 60% carbohydrate. Glucosyl, mannosyl, and galactosyl residues were found. The enzyme activity increases as the length of the polygalactofuranosyl chain in the substrate increases, a phenomenon which is common with other *exo*-glycohydrolases (62). The enzyme catalyzes the removal of galactofuranosyl residues from polymers of *P. chrysogenum, P. clavi-*

*forme, P. raistrickii, P. patulum,* and *P. charlesii,* and it hydrolyzes 1-O-$\beta$-methyl-D-galactofuranoside but not the other three 1-O-methyl-D-galactoside anomers (123).

### *Other Glycohydrolases*

Pazur et al (111) isolated glucoamylase A and B, and $\alpha$-amylase from *Aspergillus niger.* All three enzymes were purified and shown to be glycoproteins. Their location is presumed to be outside of the plasma membrane.

Reese & Mandels (120) isolated mycodextranase which splits only $\alpha$-(1$\longrightarrow$4) linkages in mycodextran which is composed of alternating $\alpha$-(1$\longrightarrow$3) and $\alpha$-(1$\longrightarrow$4) linked glucopyranosyl residues. Mycodextran is found in *Aspergillus* and *Penicillium* species but not in other genera tested. Mycodextran is buried in *A. niger* cell walls, but the polymer is released by extracting the mycelia with hot water (154). Tung & Nordin purified mycodextranase to homogeneity and showed that the enzyme contains about 15% carbohydrate, and exists as two similar but not identical species. Both peptides are rich in seryl, threonyl, glutamyl, and aspartyl residues, and are low in cysteinyl and tryptophanyl residues (155).

### *Acid Phosphatases*

Acid phosphatases are released from *Saccharomyces mellis* or *Saccharomyces fragilis* by a combination of high concentration of salt and reductive cleavage of S-S-linkage (158). Acid glyco-phosphatase from *Candida albicans* was purified to homogeneity and the enzyme shown to contain a mannose:protein ratio of 7:1 on a weight basis (108). Acid glyco-phosphatase from *Saccharomyces cerevisiae* has a mannose:protein ration of about 1:1 (22). Baker's yeast protoplasts from actively dividing cells grown in low phosphate medium secrete about 50 molecules of glyco-phosphatase/sec per protoplast. The enzyme contains approximately 50% mannan and 4% glucosamine (156). However, phosphatase enrichment in the yeast vacuole fraction, as occurs with glyco-invertase, was not observed (14).

### *Proteases*

Four glyco-proteases were isolated from autolyzing *Saccharomyces carlsbergensis* (84). Three of the proteases contained mannose and glucose; however, the glucose: mannose molar ratio was unique to the enzyme. Mannose is the only carbohydrate in protease D. Lysed protoplasts from the yeast also released four proteases, but the enzymes were not glycoproteins. However, when the yeast protoplasts were placed in a medium containing N-acetyl-L-tyrosine ethyl ester as the N source, four glyco-proteases were secreted into the growth medium.

## BIOSYNTHESIS OF GLYCOPROTEINS AND PEPTIDO-POLYSACCHARIDES

Glycoprotein and peptido-polysaccharide biosynthesis have been studied in vivo and in vitro. *Saccharomyces* protoplasts synthesize both invertase and glyco-invertase (64, 77). Only glyco-invertase is secreted and 95% of the enzyme synthesized is secreted (138). Cycloheximide or 2-deoxy-D-glucose inhibit both synthesis and secretion of glyco-invertase (78, 81). The relative quantities of invertase and glyco-invertase in the protoplasts remained constant. A glucose:2-deoxy-D-glucose molar ratio of 4:1 in the medium is required to inhibit *S. cerevisiae* wall glucan synthesis, and a 20:1 ratio inhibits cell wall mannan-protein formation (46). They claim that 2-deoxy-D-glucose has little influence on protein synthesis (45). 2-Deoxy-D-glucose is converted to GDP-2-deoxy-D-glucose, an analogue of GDP-D-mannose. Presumably the analogue inhibits mannosyl transferase (15). Sentandreu & Lampen (131) suggest that following peptide synthesis on polyribosomes, the carbohydrate is attached to the peptide during its transport to its site of incorporation in the wall.

Cycloheximide has little or no effect on glucan synthesis (43), although it does inhibit glycoprotein synthesis. Cycloheximide may prove to be a useful tool in studying cell wall glycan synthesis independent of peptido-glycan synthesis. Cycloheximide causes the walls of *Aspergillus nidulans* to thicken around the cell, and it inhibits elongation. They suggest that elongation of hyphae occurs by inserting new wall at the apex, and that cycloheximide alters the site of chitin incorporation (140). Polyoxin D is a competitive inhibitor of chitin synthetase in *N. crassa* (12). Both glucan and mannan biosynthesis in *S. cerevisiae* occur continuously through the cell cycle (134). The half-life of mRNA for glyco-invertase and glyco-phosphatase may be relatively long.

In vivo studies of peptidophosphogalactomannan biosynthesis in *Penicillium charlesii* show that approximately 80% of the residues in phosphogalactomannan are derived from glucose and phosphate in the growth medium at the time that it became depleted of $NH_4^+$ (41). We concluded that peptidophosphogalactomannan is not derived by autolysis of cell walls. Further, 2-deoxy-D-glucose causes minimal inhibition of peptidophosphogalactomannan synthesis but it blocks galactofuranosidase synthesis (J. E. Gander and F. Fang, unpublished observations).

UDP-N-acetyl-D-glucosamine and GDP-D-mannose were first isolated from yeast and suggested as glycosyl donors in chitin and mannan synthesis, respectively (25). GDP-Mannose and other nucleotide diphosphosugars serve as glycosyl-containing intermediates in glycoprotein biosynthesis in animals, higher plants, and fungi (9, 10, 13, 27, 126, 130, 146, 157). The protein glycosylating agent may be mannopyranosyl phosphoryl polyisoprenol rather than GDP-mannose (4, 9, 10, 27, 130, 146, 157). Yeast extracts catalyze mannosyl transfer from GDP-D-mannose into dolichol monophosphate resulting in formation of GDP and mannosyl phosphoryl dolichol (4). Dolichol occurs naturally in yeasts. A membrane fraction from *S. cerevisiae* catalyzes mannosyl transfer from GDP-mannose partly via the dolichol intermediate into a heterogeneous glycoprotein (4). Only mannosyl residues linked directly to protein were derived from mannosyl phosphoryl dolichol. Mannosyl residues in the oligosaccharides other than those linked to the polypeptide were derived directly from GDP-D-mannose. Ficaprenyl phosphoryl glycosides may be the glycosyl donor in lipid-linked sugar biosynthesis in *S. cerevisiae* (109).

Barr & Hemming isolated a polyprenyl phosphate (*exo*-methylene-hexahydropolyprenol phosphate) from *A. niger,* and showed that it accepted mannosyl residues from GDP-D-mannose and transferred mannosyl residues from the polyprenol to mannolipid and mannan (9, 10).

The enzymatic synthesis of phosphomannan using particulate preparations from *Hansenula holstii* and *Hansenula capsulata* has been investigated (23, 76 90). The phosphomannopyranosyl residue of GDP-D-mannose is transferred to form 1-O-D-mannopyranosyl 6'-phosphoryl mannan and GMP as the products. This may represent a general scheme by which phosphoryl groups are incorporated into phosphomannans and peptidophosphomannans.

Studies of peptidophosphogalactomannan biosynthesis are limited. Uridine 5'-(α-D-galactofuranosyl pyrophosphate) (UDP-D-galactofuranoside) has been isolated and characterized from *P. charlesii* extracts (150). Although in vitro galactocarolose biosynthesis is claimed, it is likely that the preparation contained unbroken cells. The product was not characterized. Fobes & Gander (47) isolated an enzyme that oxidizes UDP-D-galactopyranoside to a 2-keto galactose derivative. The role, if any, of this enzyme in the conversion of UDP-D-galactose from the pyranosyl to the furanosyl form has not been established.

Chitin is the main component of the primary septum formed during division of budding yeast (24). Yeast chitin synthetase has been isolated in a particulate, inactive (zymogen) form (26). Yeast vacuoles contain a factor that converts the zymogen to active chitin synthetase. These studies, like those on glyco-invertase (14), suggest an active role for the vacuole in cell wall glycoprotein and polysaccharide biosynthesis. McMurrough & Bartnicki-Garcia (98) suggested that chitin synthetase in *Mucor rouxii* is produced in a zymogen state and fully activated via proteolytic action. A soluble inhibitor of zymogen activation occurs in the cytoplasm and it blocks the protease (98).

## BIOLOGICAL PROPERTIES AND FUNCTIONS

A mural or extracellular enzyme's function is apparent from the reaction it catalyzes. The role(s) of the glycan region of these glyco-enzymes is likely only partially understood. Glyco-enzymes frequently are relatively stable to proteolytic enzymes, elevated temperatures, and a wide range of pH. This property is assumed to result from the glycan(s).

Mural glycoproteins without known enzymatic activities may serve as recognition sites for cells of opposite mating type (37), and in flocculation of cells (99).

Growth of *Neurospora crassa* is inhibited by a partially N-acetylated galactosaminyl-containing mucopolysaccharide obtained from *Neurospora.* The polymer causes vacuolation and agglutination of *N. crassa* cells (121). Complete N-acetylation abolishes the polymer's biological activity. A glycoprotein from *Candida albicans* is toxic to mice (87). The polymer contains glucosyl and mannosyl residues. The phosphomannans from four strains of *Hansenula* induce interferon in rabbit cell cultures (143). The effect appears more related to the percentage of phosphorus in the polymer than to the polymer's composition and structure (40, 144).

The function of mural or extracellular peptidophosphopolysaccharides is unknown currently. These may be derived from cytoplasmic glycoproteins, and they may represent the proteolytic resistant material remaining after proteolysis of cytoplasmic glycoproteins. Alternatively, these substances may have a role in ion transport into the cell.

## CONCLUDING REMARKS

Many excellent structural studies on cell wall glycoproteins and peptidopolysaccharides have been conducted. However, it appears that some constituents may have been overlooked because they occur in only minor quantities. Their location and structure may provide important clues to the function of the polymer. Knowledge of the details of biosynthesis of these polymers will undoubtedly progress more rapidly once the complete structures are known.

### ACKNOWLEDGMENTS

Research from the author's laboratory was supported by National Science Foundation Research Grant GB-21261, University of Minnesota Graduate School, and the University of Minnesota Agricultural Experiment Station (Scientific Journal Series No. 8534, Agricultural Experiment Station, University of Minnesota, St. Paul Minnesota). The work from this laboratory is largely the result of the efforts of former students: Dr. L. R. Drewes, Dr. John Jordan, Dr. K. P. Klatt, Dr. J. F. Preston, Dr. P. D. Rick, Dr. M. Rietschel-Berst, Mr. W. S. Fobes, and Mr. N. H. Jentoft. I am grateful for their assistance.

*Literature Cited*

1. Alfes, H., Bishop, C. T., Blank, F. 1963. *Can. J. Chem.* 41:2621–27
2. Azuma, I., Kimura, H., Hirao, F., Tsubura, E., Yamamura, Y., 1968. *Jap. J. Med. Mycol.* 9:289–303
3. Azuma, I. et al 1971. *Jap. J. Microbiol.* 15:237–46
4. Babczinski, P., Tanner, W. 1973. *Biochem. Biophys. Res. Commun.* 54:1119–24
5. Ballou, C. E. 1970. *J. Biol. Chem.* 245:1197–1203
6. Barker, S. A., Basarab, O., Cruickshank, C. N. D. 1967. *Carbohyd. Res.* 3:325–32
7. Barker, S. A., Cruickshank, C. N. D., Holden, J. H. 1963. *Biochim. Biophys. Acta* 74:239–46
8. Barker, S. A., Cruickshank, C. N. D., Morris, J. H., Wood, S. R. 1962. *Immunology* 5:627–32
9. Barr, R. M., Hemming, F. W. 1972. *Biochem. J.* 126:1193–1202
10. Ibid 1203–8
11. Bartnicki-Garcia, S. 1968. *Ann. Rev. Microbiol.* 22:87–108
12. Bartnicki-Garcia, S., Lippman, E. 1972. *J. Gen. Microbiol.* 71:301–9
13. Behrens, N. H., Leloir, L. F. 1970. *Proc. Nat. Acad. Sci. USA* 66:153–59
14. Beteta, P., Gascon, S. 1971. *FEBS Lett.* 13:297–300
15. Biely, P., Bauer, Š. 1968. *Biochim. Biophys. Acta* 156:432–34
16. Bigger, C. H., White, M. R., Braymer, H. D. 1972. *J. Gen. Microbiol.* 71:159–66
17. Bishop, C. T., Blank, F., Hranisavljevic-Jakovljevic, M. 1962. *Can. J. Chem.* 40:1816–25
18. Bishop, C. T., Perry, M. B., Blank, F. 1966. *Can. J. Chem.* 44:2291–97
19. Bishop, C. T., Perry, M. B., Blank, F., Cooper, F. P. 1965. *Can. J. Chem.* 43:30–39
20. Bishop, C. T., Perry, M. B., Hulyalkar, R. K., Blank, F. 1966. *Can. J. Chem.* 44:2299–2303
21. Blank, F., Perry, M. B. 1964. *Can. J. Chem.* 42:2862–71
22. Boer, P., Steyn-Parve, E. P. 1966. *Biochim. Biophys. Acta* 128:400–2
23. Bretthauer, R. K., Kozak, L. P., Irwin, W. E. 1969. *Biochem. Biophys. Res. Commun.* 37:820–27
24. Cabib, E., Farkas, V. 1971. *Proc. Nat. Acad. Sci. USA* 68:2052–56
25. Cabib, E., Leloir, L. F. 1954. *J. Biol. Chem.* 206:779–90
26. Cabib, E., Ulane, R., Bowers, E. 1973. *J. Biol. Chem.* 248:1451–58
27. Caccam, J. F., Jackson, J. J., Eylar, E. H. 1969. *Biochem. Biophys. Res. Commun.* 35:505–11

28. Carbonell, L. M. 1969. *J. Bacteriol.* 100:1076–82
29. Cawley, T. N., Ballou, C. E. 1972. *J. Bacteriol.* 111:690–95
30. Cawley, T. N., Harrington, M. G., Letters, R. 1972. *Biochem. J.* 129:711–20
31. Chang, P. L. Y., Trevithick, J. R. 1970. *J. Bacteriol.* 102:423–29
32. Chang, P. L. Y., Trevithick, J. R. 1972. *J. Gen. Microbiol.* 70:13–22
33. Ibid 23–29
34. Chattaway, F. W., Bishop, R., Holmes, M. R., Odds, F. C., Barlow, A. J. E. 1973. *J. Gen. Microbiol.* 75:97–109
35. Clutterbuck, P. W., Haworth, W. N., Raistrick, H., Smith, G., Stacey, M. 1934. *Biochem. J.* 28:94–110
36. Corina, D. L., Munday, K. A. 1971. *J. Gen. Microbiol.* 65:253–57
37. Crandall, M. A., Brock, T. D. 1968. *Science* 161:473–75
38. Cruickshank, C. N. D., Trotter, M. D., Wood, S. R. 1960. *J. Invest. Dermatol.* 35:219–23
39. Detroy, R. W., Ciegler, A. 1971. *J. Gen. Microbiol.* 65:259–64
40. Dorner, F., Scriba, M., Weil, R. 1973. *Proc. Nat. Acad. Sci. USA* 70:1981–85
41. Drewes, L. R. 1970. *Fungal polysaccharides: structure and biosynthesis of an exocellular phosphopolysaccharide of Penicillium charlesii.* PhD thesis. Univ. Minnesota, Minneapolis. 136 pp.
42. Eddy, A. A., Williamson, D. H. 1957. *Nature* 179:1252–53
43. Elorza, M. V., Sentandreau, R. 1969. *Biochem. Biophys. Res. Commun.* 36:741–47
44. Falcone, G., Nickerson, W. J. 1956. *Science* 124:272–73
45. Farkas, V., Svoboda, A., Bauer, S. 1970. *Biochem. J.* 118:755–58
46. Farkas, V., Svoboda, A., Bauer, S. 1969. *J. Bacteriol.* 98:744–48
47. Fobes, W. S., Gander, J. E. *Biochem. Biophys. Res. Commun.* 49:76–83
48. Gander, J. E., Jentoft, N. H., Drewes, L. R., Rick, P. D. 1974. *J. Biol. Chem.* 249: In press
49. Gander, J. E., Rudbach, J. A. 1973. *Immunochemistry* 10:81–92
50. Gasćon, S., Lampen, J. O. 1967. *J. Biol. Chem.* 243:1567–72
51. Gasćon, S., Neumann, N. P., Lampen, J. O. 1967. *J. Biol. Chem.* 243:1573–77
52. Gorin, P. A. J., Perlin, A. S. 1956. *Can. J. Chem.* 34:1796–1803
53. Gorin, P. A. J., Spencer, J. F. T. 1968. *Advan. Carbohyd. Chem.* 23:367–417
54. Gorin, P. A. J., Spencer, J. F. T., Bhattacharjee, S. S. 1969. *Can. J. Chem.* 47:1499–1505
55. Gorin, P. A. J., Spencer, J. F. T., Eveleigh, D. E. 1969. *Carbohyd. Res.* 11:387–98
56. Grappel, S. F., Blank, F., Bishop, C. T. 1967. *J. Bacteriol.* 93:1001–8
57. Ibid 1968. 96:70–75
58. Ibid 95:1238–42
59. Ibid 1969. 97:23–26
60. Haworth, W. N., Raistrick, H. K., Stacey, M. 1935. *Biochem. J.* 29: 2668–78
61. How, M. J., Withnall, M. T., Cruickshank, C. N. D. 1972. *Carbohyd. Res.* 25:341–53
62. Huotari, F. I., Nelson, T. E., Smith, F., Kirkwood, S. 1968. *J. Biol. Chem.* 243:952–56
63. Hunsley, D., Burnett, J. H. 1970. *J. Gen. Microbiol.* 62:203–18
64. Islam, M. F., Lampen, J. O. 1962. *Biochim. Biophys. Acta* 58:294–302
65. Jeanes, A., Pittsley, J. E., Watson, P. R., Dimler, R. J. 1961. *Arch. Biochem. Biophys.* 92:343–50
66. Jones, G. H., Ballou, C. E. 1968. *J. Biol. Chem.* 243:2442–46
67. Ibid 1969. 244:1052–59
68. Kanetsuna, F., Carbonell, L. M. 1970. *J. Bacteriol.* 101:675–80
69. Ibid 1971. 106:946–48
70. Kanetsuna, F., Carbonell, L. M., Azuma, I., Yamamura, Y. 1972. *J. Bacteriol.* 110:208–18
71. Kanetsuna, F., Carbonell, L. M., Moreno, R. E., Rodriguez, J. 1969. *J. Bacteriol.* 97:1036–41
72. Kessler, G., Nickerson, W. J. 1959. *J. Biol. Chem.* 234:2281–85
73. Kidby, D. K., Davies, R. 1970. *J. Gen. Microbiol.* 61:327–33
74. Kocourek, J., Ballou, C. E. 1969. *J. Bacteriol.* 100:1175–81
75. Korn, E. D., Northcote, D. H. 1960. *Biochem. J.* 75:12–17
76. Kozak, L. P., Bretthauer, R. K. 1970. *Biochemistry* 9:1115–22
77. Kuo, S. -C., Lampen, J. O. 1971. *J. Bacteriol.* 106:183–91
78. Ibid 1972. 111:419–29
79. Lampen, J. O. 1968. *Antonie van Leuwenhoek J. Microbiol. Serol.* 34:1–18
80. Lee, Y. C., Ballou, C. E. 1965. *Biochemistry* 4:257–64
81. Liras, P., Gascon, S. 1971. *Eur. J. Biochem.* 23:160–65
82. Lloyd, K. O. 1970. *Biochemistry* 9:3446–53
83. Ibid 1972. 11:3884–90
84. Maddox, I. S., Hough, J. S. 1970. *Biochem. J.* 117:843–52
85. Mahadevan, P. R., Tatum, E. L. 1965. *J. Bacteriol.* 90:1073–81

86. Mahadevan, P. R., Tatum, E. L. 1967. *J. Cell. Biol.* 35:295–302
87. Mankowski, Z. T. 1968. *Mycopathol. Mycol. Appl.* 34:113–18
88. Marzluf, G. A. 1973. *J. Bacteriol.* 115:146–52
89. Marzluf, G. A., Metzenberg, R. L. 1967. *Arch. Biochem. Biophys.* 120: 487–96
90. Mayer, R. M. 1971. *Biochim. Biophys. Acta* 252:39–47
91. McLellan, W. L., McDaniel, L. E., Lampen, J. O. 1970. *J. Bacteriol.* 102: 261–70
92. McLellan, W. L., Lampen, J. O. 1968. *J. Bacteriol.* 95:967–74
93. Meachum, Z. D., Braymer, H. D. 1969. *Proc. Am. Chem. Soc., 158th.* Abstr. 195
94. Meachum, Z. D., Colvin, H. J., Braymer, H. D. 1971. *Biochemistry* 10:326–32
95. Metzenberg, R. L. 1963. *Biochim. Biophys. Acta* 77:455–65
96. Metzenberg, R. L. 1963. *Arch. Biochem. Biophys.* 100:503–11
97. Metzenberg, R. L. 1964. *Biochim. Biophys. Acta* 89:291–302
98. McMurrough, I., Bartnicki-Garcia, S. 1973. *Arch. Biochem. Biophys.* 158: 812–16
99. Mill, P. J. 1966. *J. Gen. Microbiol.* 44:329–41
100. Miyazaki, T., Yadomae, T. 1968. *Chem. Pharm. Bull.* 16:1721–25
101. Moor, H. 1967. *Arch. Mikrobiol.* 57: 135–46
102. Mosser, J. L., Tomasz, A. 1970. *J. Biol. Chem.* 245:287–98
103. Neumann, N. P., Lampen, J. O. 1967. *Biochemistry* 6:468–75
104. Nickerson, W. J., Falcone, G. 1956. *Science* 124:318–19
105. Nickerson, W. J. 1963. *Bacteriol. Rev.* 27:305–24
106. Nickerson, W. J., Edwards, G. A. 1949. *J. Gen. Physiol.* 33:41–55
107. Northcote, D. H., Horne, R. W. 1952. *Biochem. J.* 51:232–36
108. Odds, F. C., Hierholzer, J. C. 1973. *J. Bacteriol.* 114:257–66
109. Palamarczyk, G., Chojnacki, T. 1973. *FEBS Lett.* 34:201–3
110. Pazur, J. H., Aronson, N. N. 1972. *Advan. Carbohyd. Chem.* 27:301–41
111. Pazur, J. H., Kleppe, K., Ball, E. M. 1963. *Arch. Biochem. Biophys.* 103: 515–16
112. Pazur, J. H., Simpson, D. L., Knull, H. R. 1969. *Biochem. Biophys. Res. Commun.* 36:394–400
113. Peat, S., Turvey, J. R., Doyle, D. 1961. *J. Chem. Soc.* pp. 3918–23
114. Phaff, H. J. 1963. *Ann. Rev. Microbiol.* 17:15–30
115. Mardon, D., Balish, E., Phillips, A. W. 1969. *J. Bacteriol.* 100:701–7
116. Preston, J. F., Gander, J. E. 1968. *Arch. Biochem. Biophys.* 124:504–12
117. Preston, J. F., Lapis, E., Gander, J. E. 1969. *Arch. Biochem. Biophys.* 134: 324–34
118. Preston, J. F., Lapis, E., Gander, J. E. 1970. *Can. J. Microbiol.* 16:687–94
119. Preston, J. F., Lapis, E., Westerhouse, S., Gander, J. E. 1969. *Arch. Biochem. Biophys.* 134:316–23
120. Reese, E. T., Mandels, M. 1964. *Can. J. Microbiol.* 10:103–14
121. Reissig, J. L., Glasgow, J. E. 1971. *J. Bacteriol.* 106:882–89
122. Rick, P. D., Drewes, L. R., Gander, J. E. 1974. *J. Biol. Chem.* 249: In press
123. Rietschel-Berst, M., Gander, J. E. 1973. *Fed. Proc.* 32:528
124. Rietschel-Berst, M., Rick, P. D., Jentoft, N. H., Gander, J. E. 1975. *J. Biol. Chem* 250:In press
125. Romano, A. H. 1966. *The Fungi,* ed. G. C. Ainsworth, A. S. Sussman, 2:181–209. New York: Academic
126. Roseman, S. 1970. *Chem. Phys. Lipids* 5:270–97
127. Sakaguchi, O., Suzuki, M., Yokota, K. 1968. *Jap. J. Microbiol.* 12:123–24
128. Sakaguchi, O., Yokota, K., Suzuki, M. 1967. *Yakugaku Zasshi* 87:1268–72
129. Sakaguchi, O., Yokota, K., Suzuki, M. 1969. *Jap. J. Microbiol.* 13:1–7
130. Scher, M., Lennarz, W. J. 1969. *J. Biol. Chem.* 244:2777–89
131. Sentandreu, R., Lampen, J. O. 1970. *FEBS Lett.* 11:95–99
132. Sentandreu, R., Northcote, D. H. 1969. *Carbohyd. Res.* 10:584–85
133. Sentandreu, R., Northcote, D. H. 1968. *Biochem. J.* 109:419–32
134. Sierra, J. M., Sentandreau, R., Villanueva, J. R. 1973. *FEBS Lett.* 34: 285–90
135. Slodki, M. E. 1963. *Biochim. Biophys. Acta.* 69:96–102
136. Slodki, M. E. 1966. *J. Biol. Chem.* 241:2700–6
137. Slodki, M. E., Safranski, M. J., Hensley, D. E., Babcock, G. E. 1970. *Appl. Microbiol.* 19:1019–20
138. Sommer, A., Lewis, M. J. 1971. *J. Gen. Microbiol.* 68:327–35
139. Spencer, J. F. T., Gorin, P. A. J. 1973. *Biotechnol. Bioeng.* 15:1–12
140. Sternlicht, E., Katz, D., Rosenberger, R. F. 1973. *J. Bacteriol.* 114:819–23

141. Stewart, T. S., Ballou, C. E. 1968. *Biochemistry* 7:1855–63
142. Stewart, T. S., Mendershausen, P. B., Ballou, C. E. 1968. *Biochemistry* 7: 1843–54
143. Suzuki, S., Suzuki, M., Imaya, M. 1971. *Jap. J. Microbiol.* 15:485–92
144. Suzuki, S., Suzuki, M., Imaya, M., Chaki, F. 1972. *Jap. J. Microbiol.* 16:1–5
145. Suzuki, S., Suzuki, M., Yokota, K., Sunayama, H., Sakaguchi, O. 1967. *Jap. J. Microbiol.* 11:269–73
146. Tanner, W., Jung, P., Behrens, N. H. 1971. *FEBS Lett.* 16:245–48
147. Tkacz, J. S., Lampen, J. O. 1972. *J. Gen. Microbiol.* 72:243–47
148. Tkacz, J. S., Lampen, J. O. 1973. *J. Bacteriol.* 113:1073–75
149. Tonomura, K. Tanabe, O. 1964. *J. Bacteriol.* 87:226–27
150. Trejo, G., Haddock, J. W., Chittenden, G. J. F., Baddiley, J. 1971. *Biochem. J.* 122:49–57
151. Trevithick, J. R., Metzenberg, R. L. 1964. *Biochem. Biophys. Res. Commun.* 16:319–25
152. Trevithick, J. R., Metzenberg, R. L. 1966. *J. Bacteriol.* 92:1010–15
153. Trinci, A. P. J., Righelato, R. C. 1970. *J. Gen. Microbiol.* 60:239–49
154. Tung, K. K., Nordin, J. H. 1967. *Biochem. Biophys. Res. Commun.* 28: 519–24
155. Tung, K. K., Rosenthal, A., Nordin, J. H. 1971. *J. Biol. Chem.* 246:6722–36
156. Van Rijn, H. J. M., Boer, P., Steyn-Parve, E. P. 1972. *Biochim. Biophys. Acta* 268:431–41
157. Waechter, C. J., Lucas, J. J., Lennarz, W. J. 1973. *J. Biol. Chem.* 248:7570–79
158. Weimberg, R., Orton, W. L. 1965. *J. Bacteriol.* 90:82–94
159. Ibid 1966. 91:1–13
160. Wrathall, C. R., Tatum, E. L. 1973. *J. Gen. Microbiol.* 78:139–53

# SPACE MICROBIOLOGY

❖1633

*Gerald R. Taylor*
Life Sciences Directorate, L. B. Johnson Space Center, Houston, Texas 77058

CONTENTS

INTRODUCTION ........ 121
EXTRATERRESTRIAL LIFE DETECTION STUDIES ........ 121
EVALUATION OF TERRESTRIAL MICROORGANISMS IN SPACE ........ 122
*Balloon and Sounding Rocket Studies* ........ 122
*Studies on Earth-Orbital and Lunar Exploration Missions* ........ 123
*Studies conducted to help qualify man for Earth orbital flight* ........ 123
*The use of bacteriophage induction as a model system for visualizing genetic effects* ........ 124
*Studies conducted to determine the need for spacecraft sterilization* ........ 126
*Genetic effects of inflight ionizing radiation* ........ 128
*Effect of solar UV and space vacuum on microbial systems* ........ 128
MONITORING OF ASTRONAUT MICROBIAL FLORA ........ 130
*Alterations in the Load of Medically Important Microorganisms* ........ 130
*Changes in the Mycological Autoflora* ........ 132
*Changes in the Bacterial Autoflora* ........ 134
SUMMARY ........ 125

## INTRODUCTION

Space microbiology studies may be divided into three major categories, each of which will be discussed in light of the current state of knowledge in that field. The first involves analysis of samples collected outside the Earth's biosphere. The second includes the many studies in which pure cultures of terrestrial microorganisms were evaluated either during or after exposure to components of the spaceflight environment. The third category contains studies of the autoflora of crew members and the microbial load of recoverable spacecraft components which were performed to evaluate changes in populations of microorganisms. Although some spaceflight studies were performed in a manner which produced equivocal results, the composite picture allows for definitive conclusions in each of the three major categories.

## EXTRATERRESTRIAL LIFE DETECTION STUDIES

Extraterrestrial materials have been collected during several American spaceflight missions and returned to Earth for microbiological analyses. In the first of these, micrometeorite collection devices were successfully opened and exposed to space for 16.75 hr and 6.5 hr, respectively, during the Gemini 9A and the Gemini 12 spaceflights (43). These devices were designed to eliminate the possibility of internal microbial contamination before opening and after closing in space. As anticipated, no viable forms could be detected from the samples collected among the micrometeorite population in the near-Earth space environment (33). Additional devices were flown which contained deposits of *Penicillium roqueforti*, Coliphage T-1, *Bacillus subtilis,* and Tobacco Mosaic Virus (TMV) as viability controls. These species were recovered in high numbers, verifying the assumption that trapped viable cells would likely have survived the return to Earth. The survival characteristics of these species will be more completely discussed in a later section.

In another series of tests, samples of lunar material returned from each of the six American lunar exploration missions were subjected to a variety of autotrophic and heterotrophic growth media (53, 74) in an effort to detect the largest variety of different organisms practicable. Neither viable microbes nor identifiable biological formed elements were recovered from the many samples evaluated (52, 53, 77). Although extracts from one of the lunar samples were reported to be toxic to terrestrial microorganisms, this event was not considered to be representative of the other samples tested and therefore would not contribute significantly to the apparent sterility of lunar samples (73). These studies were useful because the absence of viable microbes or toxic agents in the lunar material permitted release of the astronauts from postflight quarantine and release of lunar samples to other investigators throughout the world (36). It is also important to note that the process of lunar exploration did not contaminate the surface of the moon in a manner which could subsequently be detected in returned samples, although the lunar landing vehicles and the extravehicular activity space suits were contaminated with a variety of microorganisms before flight (55, 70). Various components of the American Surveyor III spacecraft, which had resided on the moon for 2.5 yr, were returned during the Apollo 12 mission and analyzed for the presence of viable microorganisms (37, 49). Except for the presence of *Streptococcus mitis,* which was considered by the investigators to have been deeply embedded within the camera body before it left the Earth, no viable microbes were recovered from any of the tested components.

The near-Earth micrometeorite population, lunar material, and returned spacecraft components have all been evaluated for the presence of viable microorganisms. However, only a single isolate, easily recognizable as being of terrestrial origin, has been recovered. These data attest not only to the sterility of the tested environments but to the low level of contamination affected by these spaceflights.

## EVALUATION OF TERRESTRIAL MICROORGANISMS IN SPACE

### *Balloon and Sounding Rocket Studies*

Investigations of the effects of the environments of space and spaceflight on microbiological specimens were initiated in 1935 with the stratospheric flight of the American high altitude balloon, Explorer 2 (69). During this flight seven species of fungi were exposed to space at 25 km for 4 hr. Other early studies were conducted in manned and unmanned high altitude balloons which permitted exposure of biological materials to the low temperatures, decreased atmosphere, and direct solar irradiation available at altitudes up to 150 km. These early studies have been chronicled by Beischer & Fregly (8) who indicated that, in the six years from 1954 to 1960, various species of *Neurospora* were carried on no less than 30 high altitude balloon and sounding rocket flights. Other microbiological systems were evaluated in four additional flights. These early tests, reviewed by Jenkins (35) and Parfenov & Lukin (54), were conducted with the expressed objective of determining if certain species could survive high altitude flight. Although rudimentary, these studies permitted the investigators to observe that a large percentage of fungal spores and dormant vegetative cells could survive direct exposure to the space environment at these modest altitudes.

## *Studies on Earth-Orbital and Lunar Exploration Missions*

Investigations of microbiological specimens in Earth-orbital flight were initiated with the launch of the Russian craft, Sputnik 2, in 1958 (4). The first generation of American and Russian studies was conducted to identify any gross biological effects of galactic radiation, weightlessness, and other space flight factors on biological systems; and to test prototype life support systems and determine if surrogate astronauts (such as dogs and monkeys) could survive the rigors of launch, orbital flight, and reentry (35). The approaches taken in the two space programs were somewhat different, although the results were generally similar.

The early philosophy adopted by Russian investigators was to fly a large number of different species on as many orbiting vehicles as possible in an effort to determine the total effect of spaceflight on biological systems in general. In all cases dogs were used as the prime surrogate cosmonaut test system. In contrast, the early American philosophy called for analysis of fewer species on fewer flights using primates, rather than dogs, to test biomedical and life support parameters. This difference is reflected in the review by Jenkins (35) which shows that in the first decade of orbital flight, Russian scientists evaluated 56 different species and preparations of biological materials including viruses, bacteria, yeasts, fungi, plants, animals, and tissue cultures. During the same period the United States evaluated 35 different species and cellular preparations. Several of the Russian satellites were flown primarily to obtain biological information considered necessary to qualify man for spaceflight but no dedicated satellites were flown by the United States until the launch of Biosatellite II in September 1967. In fact, the early American biology studies were conducted as small, piggyback, payloads which were operated on a noninterference basis (35).

STUDIES CONDUCTED TO HELP QUALIFY MAN FOR EARTH ORBITAL FLIGHT Three Russian unmanned orbital satellites (Sputnik 5, 9, 10) were successfully returned to Earth for evaluation before the launch of Vostok 1, the first manned flight (63). Data gathered from the Sputnik series of flights were important because they provided the basis upon which the permit for the first manned flights was granted (5). Inflight microbial growth was monitored during the flights of Sputnik 5 (88) and other nonrecovered satellites (4) with the aid of an automated device known as "Bioelements". This device was designed to measure the rate of gas production in actively growing *Clostridium butyricum* cultures, and to relay these data to Earth. Major differences were not obtained between flight samples and the ground control group. Likewise no postflight differences could be detected in returned cultures. These findings are supportive of the results reported by Bulban (19) for *Clostridium sporogenes* flown aboard the American Discoverer 17 satellite. These cells remained viable, although there was some degree of labilization which could be correlated with the measured irradiation from an intense solar flare which occurred during the flight (35). *Aerobacter aerogenes* 1321 bacteriophage and T-2 coliphage were also carried aboard the 24-hr flight of the Sputnik 5 satellite. Postflight analyses revealed that the number of viable phage particles, plaque morphology, and reproduction rate were essentially the same in the flight and ground control samples (88). Actinomycetes (*Streptomyces* spp.) were first tested as part of the Sputnik 5 mission. The growth of returned inflight colonies was accelerated sixfold when compared with analogous laboratory controls (4). Since this was the only event, of all the systems tested, which demonstrated a spaceflight correlated response, Russian scientists concluded that spaceflight did not affect microbes in a manner which would make it unsafe to initiate short manned spaceflights (5).

*A. aerogenes* 1321, *Escherichia coli* B, *Staphylococcus aureus* 0.15, and *C. butyricum* spores were included in the early Russian manned orbital flights in an attempt to monitor inflight growth and to evaluate postflight survival and/or genetic changes on actual manned missions. No postflight differences were noted for any of these species either for the 108 min flight of Vostok 1 or the 1518 min flight of Vostok 2 (88). A modification of the Bioelements device was used to determine the inflight growth rate of *C. butyricum* during the Vostok 1 and 2 missions. No statistical difference between the volume of gas produced in flight, as compared with ground controls, could be determined. The authors assumed that these data demonstrated the primary invulnerability of microbial cells to the tested spaceflight conditions and that it was microbiologically safe to proceed with longer-duration manned flights (88).

THE USE OF BACTERIOPHAGE INDUCTION AS A MODEL SYSTEM FOR VISUALIZING GENETIC EFFECTS The team headed by Zhukov-Verezhnikov reported studies employing *E. coli* K-12 (λ) phage on many Russian flights starting with the second Earth-orbiting satellite. This test system has been carried aboard most of the flights of the Sputnik series, all six of the manned flights of the Vostok series, Voskhod 1 and 2, the unmanned biosatellite Cosmos 110, and Zond 5 and 7 which carried these organisms around the Moon and returned them to Earth (88–96). This system was used as a radiation dosimeter because increases in phage production could be stimulated by as little as 0.3 rad of gamma (γ) radiation as well as by comparatively small doses of protons and rapid neutrons (90, 94). Because the method of phage induction consists of injury to the genetic apparatus, the lysogenic bacteria system could also provide information about the potential mutagenic activity of cosmic radiation. The Sputnik flights demonstrated that the test system could remain intact and viable during spaceflight and thus was suitable for use as an inflight experimental model (89). Accordingly, this sensitive system became a component of a complex of biological indicators of the space factors which could affect genetic changes (88). This complex included microbiological, cytological, and multicellular objects which varied in their sensitivity to the potential mutagenic factors of spaceflight (92).

Results from the first two Vostok flights appeared to support the earlier view that orbital flight had no detectable effect on the elementary and poorly compensated genetic process, as reflected in the production of phage by lysogenic bacteria (88). However, these were very short flights of 2 and 25 hr duration. Continuation of studies throughout the remainder of the Vostok series demonstrated that the number of resulting phage in the spaceflight samples exceeded that in the ground controls. This was interpreted as indicative that spaceflight factors had an inducing effect on the lysogenic bacteria (90). Further, it was reported that the spaceflight effect, measured in terms of increased phage production as compared with the magnitude of spontaneous phage production in the ground controls, increased with mission duration throughout the Vostok series (54, 93). This effect was not considered to be entirely due to the galactic radiation received because there was not a linear relationship between excessive phage production and length of time in orbit and the resultant effect was much greater than would be expected from measurements of incoming radiation (94). Laboratory studies conducted in conjunction with the Vostok 1 through 4 missions have shown that simulated launch vibration followed by exposure to $^{60}Co$, $\gamma$-radiation results in an increase in mutation rate, as measured by phage production, which is somewhat higher than that obtained by the same level of $\gamma$-radiation alone (91, 93). Simulated launch vibration alone, or following radiation had no effect on the measured parameter (94). These results engendered the speculation that the launch vibrations produced by the Vostok rocket increased the sensitivity of the lysogenic bacteria to subsequent galactic radiation (94), thus accounting for the excessive phage production. The flights of Zond 5 and Zond 7 afforded an opportunity to measure the effect of long-duration missions into deeper space, on the lysogenic system. However, the number of phage induced on these flights was essentially the same as that obtained on the six-day missions of Vostok 4 and 6 (96). The authors observe that this situation may be attributed to a change in the physiological state of the bacterial cell, with extended storage, which resulted in the production of inhibitors of the induced phage.

Tests were conducted on Voskhod 1 and 2 to determine the effectiveness of radiation protecting substances while at the same time evaluating the contribution space radiation actually plays in genetic disturbances in the *E. coli* K-12 ($\lambda$) bacteriophage system (6). Two substances, $\beta$-mercaptopropylamine and 5-methoxytryptamine were used to treat the test systems. Although phage production was reduced as expected, there also was a reduction in the incidence of spontaneous phage production. This indicated that some mechanism in addition to, or in place of, radiation protection was influencing the test. The investigators concluded that the radiation protectors were effective in space but they were unable to separately evaluate the effect of galactic radiation on the microbial genetic apparatus (90).

Two different bacteriophage induction systems were tested as part of the 45 hr Earth-orbital flight of the American Biosatellite II (46, 47, 58). *Salmonella ty-*

*phimurium* BS-5 (P-22)/P-22, and *E. coli* C-60 (λ)/λ were tested for alterations in bacterial cell growth and bacterial prophage induction following spaceflight. During the flight, different aliquots of cells were exposed to a total dose of from 265 to 1648 rad of $^{85}Sr$ γ-radiation with the resulting radiation response curves being compared with appropriate ground control curves. Neither ultrastructural nor viability differences were noted between flight and ground-control *E. coli* systems (47). However, with the *S. typhimurium* system the authors reported an increased cell density in the space-flown culture fluid indicating increased growth activity. This same result was later duplicated in clinostat studies which supplied a continually shifting gravitation vector, did not allow settling of cells, and kept the growth medium continually agitated (47). Even though the resultant increase in growth could be simulated on the ground the mechanism was probably different. In any event this finding supports other observations that suspended, growing microbial cells may propagate at a different rate in space than they do on Earth.

Testable numbers of phage were not produced with the *E. coli* system because the flight was shorter than had been planned. In the *S. typhimurium* system there was no difference between free P-22 density in flown cultures, although the space-flown cells were more resistant to γ-radiation, as indicated by a decrease in phage production (46, 47). Efforts to reproduce these results with acceleration, vibration, and clinostat tests were unsuccessful. This decrease in phage induction supports the results reported for the *E. coli* system flown on Cosmos 110 (95) but is counter to the results reported for all of the other Russian coliphage studies (94, 96).

This apparent contradiction is not surprising in view of the greatly different test conditions involved. The fact remains that the total spaceflight environment has been shown to exert an influence on the bacteriophage induction system, and that the degree of the effect is dependent upon the combination of environmental factors which have yet to be studied in detail.

STUDIES CONDUCTED TO DETERMINE THE NEED FOR SPACECRAFT STERILIZATION In 1963 a concerted effort was made by American scientists to evaluate the need for sterilization of vehicles probing deep space or landing on extraterrestrial bodies. In this series of tests *Penicillium roqueforti,* T-1 coliphage, *Bacillus subtilis* spores, and Tobacco Mosaic Virus (TMV) were seeded on plastic-coated devices carried aboard the Agena 8 orbitor and the Gemini 9A and 12 manned spacecraft (32, 43). Viable representatives of all species were recovered following nearly 17 hr of direct exposure to space conditions on the Gemini craft. Similarly, viable representatives of all systems shielded from direct solar irradiation were recovered from the Agena 8 rocket following 4 months of exposure to space conditions. Unprotected samples were lost from the surfaces of the Agena rocket, presumably because they were exposed to propellant blasts and friction heating during launch (43). Although perturbations in the control cultures made statistical analyses of space-mediated lethality impossible, survival of some individuals of each type of biological object in the harsh environment of space outside the spacecraft was reported. These data lend supportive evidence to a previous study conducted by the same group of investigators aboard an Aerobee sounding rocket, described as the first successful direct exposure and recovery of unprotected terrestrial microorganisms to the environment of space (33, 43). In this test, dry spores of *B. subtilis,* type III poliovirus, and *E. coli* bacteriophage T-1, were exposed to space for a total of 500 sec at a maximum altitude of 155 km. They reported no loss of viability for T-1 phage when shielded, although viability of both viruses was reduced when exposed directly to space conditions. *B. subtilis* spores were lost due to mechanical problems.

Many other spaceflight experiments support the conclusion that microorganisms survive in space for short periods of time. Vaccinia Virus, Infectious Bovine Rhinotracheitis (IBR) Virus, Canine Hepatitis (CN) Virus, and Influenza PR8 Virus survived the 94.5 hr Earth-orbital flight of Gemini 12 (32). *Streptococcus mitis* was recovered from internal components of a Surveyor III television camera which had resided on the surface of the Moon for 2.5 yr (49). No measurable losses of viability or changes in radiosensitivity to $^{60}Co$ were noted with *Hydrogenomonas eutropha* Z-1, diploid cells of *Saccharomyces ellipsoides* negri strain 139-B, haploid cells of *Zygosaccharomyces baili,* and dormant cells of *E. coli* K-12 flown aboard the Russian satellite Cosmos 368 (1) or with *H. eutropha* Z-1 aboard the automatic lunar station Zond 8 (57). These types of studies have been used to support the view that there is a distinct possibility that microorganisms in and on interplanetary spacecraft may be capable of surviving to contaminate extraterrestrial bodies (9, 29, 32, 45, 49, 57).

More recently, the Biostack experiment was conducted by a consortium of European investigators under the direction of Bücker (14, 17). This experiment, flown aboard the American Apollo 16 and 17 spacecraft, contained *B. subtilis* 168 spores and other nonmicrobiological species. Spores were imbedded in thin sheets of polyvinyl-alcohol (PVA) between layers of dosimeters capable of recording tracks made by the passage of high-energy, multicharged (HZE) particles. Using the resulting tracks as guides, single cells were evaluated for the response to exposure to these components of cosmic radiation (31). Individual cells in the path of HZE particles were evaluated for germination, outgrowth, and rate of cellular elongation, and compared to other cells in the same PVA layer as well as to suitable ground controls. No differences could be detected between cells on HZE tracks, cells not on HZE tracks, or ground controls, implying that exposure of resting bacterial spores to HZE particles in space has no effect on subsequent germination and outgrowth (31). As genetic studies were not conducted in this experiment, the possibility of genetic alterations in HZE-exposed cells remains an open question. However, this study was important in that it provided the first direct evidence that spores which are in the path of HZE particles in space do not lose the ability to germinate.

In an attempt to better understand the individual lethal factors of spaceflight, Lorenz et al (42) compiled data on survival of T-1 coliphage, *P. roqueforti,* and Tobacco Mosiac Virus from six sounding rocket, six balloon, and three satellite studies. After relating biological inactivation to the length of exposure to direct solar rays in space they concluded that solar ultraviolet irradiation with wavelengths between 200 and 300 nm is the main cause of inactivation of both suspended phage and TMV. Further, they have reported that *Penicillium* spores and T-1 phage in saline were affected by irradiation in this range but were resistant to irradiation at wavelengths below 200 nm and that there was no significant biological activity between 300 and 5000 nm (42). These data do not differ from the results of the many laboratory UV-response experiments, suggesting that ground-based studies may be used as model systems for preparation of inflight experiments. The authors concluded that sterilization of interplanetary spacecraft is necessary since contaminating microbes may survive space travel if shielded against lethal solar irradiation (40, 41, 42).

GENETIC EFFECTS OF INFLIGHT IONIZING RADIATION With the advent of the manned Gemini series and the Biosatellite II program, American investigators became more interested in determining the possible separate effects of weightlessness, vibration, acceleration, and radiation as individual components of the space environment (34, 35). Accordingly, genetic studies were conducted on Gemini XI and Biosatellite II to measure the effect of ionizing radiation, in combination with reduced gravity, on *Neurospora crassa* conidia. In the former test, conidia which were either layered on the surface of Millipore® membrane filters, or suspended in agar, were exposed to a $^{32}P$ beta-source during the flight. In the Biosatellite II test, conidia were prepared on Millipore membrane filters only and were exposed to a $^{85}Sr$ $\gamma$-ray source for 41 hr (59, 60). For both experiments the assayed system was a genetically marked two-component heterokaryon which was heterozygous for two different genes that control sequential steps in purine biosynthesis. The exposure of ground control and inflight cells to a range of radiation in both tests allowed for comparative analyses of dose response curves (60).

Analyses of the Gemini XI samples indicate that neither the survival nor the mutation frequency of conidia deposited on Millipore membrane filters was altered by 71 hr of orbital flight. However, the flight cells suspended in agar demonstrated higher levels of survival and lower frequencies of mutation induction, indicating that the spaceflight affected a protective influence (61). The authors point out that these data must be considered equivocal since they could have been the result of anoxia caused by high temperatures in the spacecraft. However, when the experiment was repeated 12 months later in the Biosatellite II unmanned orbitor (where there was even less control over internal temperatures), agar suspensions were not used and this portion of the test was never repeated. As in the Gemini XI test, there was no difference between the flight and ground control radiation survival curves and there was no difference in overall induction of the tested mutations for conidia of *N. crassa* deposited on Millipore membrane filters (62). On the basis of these two experiments, and reports of alterations among space-flown plant and animal systems, the authors concluded that positive effects are simply due to the temporary influence of weightlessness on fundamental metabolic processes, with induction and recovery phenomena being more drastically altered in rapidly metabolizing systems than in relatively inert systems such as resting spores.

EFFECT OF SOLAR UV AND SPACE VACUUM ON MICROBIAL SYSTEMS An experiment system, designed to establish dose-response relationships to ambient inflight solar UV irradiation and space vacuum, was conducted by a group of

American and European investigators under the direction of Taylor (78, 79). Ten microbial strains were placed outside the command module so that they could be exposed to solar ultraviolet light and space vacuum during the return of Apollo 16 from the Moon. The use of various combinations of optical filters to provide exposure of different test aliquots to varying amounts of solar irradiation at peak wavelengths of 254, 280, and 300 nm, allowed for a different dose-response curve at each of these three wavelengths (21).

The T-7 bacteriophage preparations of *E. coli* which were exposed to inflight irradiation were found to be more sensitive to UV light than were irradiated ground-based controls (68). Although the lethal effect of inflight irradiation, measured in terms of resulting plaque forming units, was considerably higher than ground-based controls, the characteristic shape of the dose response curves was similar in both cases. Nonirradiated flight phage experienced no greater loss of viability than did nonirradiated ground controls. The mechanism responsible for this apparent sensitization of space-flown microorganisms to a known lethal factor is currently under study (J. Spizizen, personal communication).

Spores from three strains of *Bacillus subtilis* and one strain of *Bacillus thuringiensis* were exposed to solar UV as well as the vacuum of space during this same Apollo 16 experiment. There was no significant difference between the mean of inflight survivors and any of the appropriate ground-based controls (78). These data affirm previous spaceflight studies which indicated the resistance of inactive spores to spaceflight factors, including moderate amounts of UV irradiation. With *B. thuringiensis* var. *thuringiensis* there was a measurable difference in the survival rate of those groups exposed to full sunlight in space when compared with the nonirradiated flight group. As was expected from the results of ground-based studies (20), this indicates that the space-flown spores of this species are resistant to the tested levels of solar UV but were sensitive to the full light of the sun (85). This species was also evaluated in terms of the production rate of a lipolytic $\alpha$-exotoxin, a deforming $\beta$-exotoxin, and a crystalline $\delta$-endotoxin, all of which have well established biological behavior (30). Statistically significant differences in the capability of the postflight isolates to produce toxins were not found among the treatment groups (85). The manner in which spores of *B. subtilis* strain 168 survived when exposed to one or more factors of the spaceflight environment was studied by two different groups within this same experiment system (71, 78). One group reported that the combined action of space vacuum and solar UV irradiation at a peak wavelength of 254 nm resulted in greater loss of viability than was observed in irradiated ground-based controls. This was interpreted as a synergistic effect in which the spores were sensitized to solar UV by the space vacuum. Space vacuum alone did not alter the survival of predried spores, indicating that air dried spores may survive exposure to space vacuum if shielded against solar UV irradiation (15, 16). The other investigative group reported the results of inflight exposure of strain HA 101 and Strain HA 101 [59] F, both of which contain multiple genetic markers. In addition, strain HA 101 [59] F is defective in the ability to repair radiation damage and is therefore highly susceptible to the damaging effects of ultraviolet irradiation. Survival rates for these space-flown spores did not differ significantly from analogous ground controls (68). Detailed genetic analyses of the mutational effects of spaceflight on these strains are in progress (J. Spizizen, personal communication).

*Aeromonas proteolytica* was incorporated into this Apollo 16 microbial experiment system as a model system to evaluate the effect of spaceflight and solar UV on the production of an endopeptidase which can cause intracutaneous hemorrhage and a hemolysin which is active against human erythrocytes (25, 78). Postflight analyses of retrieved cells indicated that there was no difference between survival rates, enzyme production, or UV sensitivity of space-flown cells when compared with appropriate ground-based controls (25, 78). The yeasts *Rhodotorula rubra* and *Saccharomyces cerevisiae* and the filamentous fungi *Trichophyton terrestre* and *Chaetomium globosum* were likewise incorporated in the Apollo 16 study (78, 81). In no case was there a significant difference between postflight survival rates of nonirradiated cells when compared with appropriate ground-based controls, although the survival of flown *C. globosum, R. rubra,* and *S. cerevisiae* was slightly depressed. In addition, samples of *T. terrestre* and *S. cerevisiae* demonstrated some sensitivity to inflight solar UV irradiation when measured in terms of a loss of cell viability. Corresponding ground-based control irradiations have not been reported.

## MONITORING OF ASTRONAUT MICROBIAL FLORA

Preflight and postflight microbiological analyses designed to detect potential pathogens, with some additional emphasis on selected species, have been conducted on crew members of the Russian Vostok, Voskhod, and Soyuz space exploration missions (S. N. Zaloguyev, personal communication). On the longer duration missions, such as the 425-hr flight of Soyuz 9 and the 570.5-hr flight of Soyuz 11, detailed analyses of the fungal and bacterial autoflora were performed (86). In the American space program, crew microbial evaluations were initiated at the beginning of the Apollo series. Initially these studies were designed to characterize the microbial load of astronauts preparing for lunar surface exploration. This procedure was considered necessary to facilitate the identification of any possible terrestrial contaminants in the returned lunar material (84). Studies conducted during the final missions of the Apollo series were designed to identify and prepare for possible microbial problems associated with the lengthy Skylab missions. Although only a portion of the data recovered from the Russian and American flights has yet been reported, the patterns discussed below have been established.

### *Alterations in the Load of Medically Important Microorganisms*

Detailed medical microbiological evaluations of American astronauts were initiated with the Apollo series of spaceflights. Illness events of microbial origin were not uncommon in the first three missions with crew members experiencing upper respiratory problems, influenza, viral gastroenteritis, rhinitis, pharyngitis, or mild dermatologic problems (7, 11, 12, 84). In addition to these clinical problems, postflight alterations in the recovery of potentially pathogenic species from the Apollo 7 through Apollo 11 astronauts have been reported (13, 26). Following each of these missions the number of crew members from whom a particular pathogen could be recovered was generally higher than before launch, indicating transfer of pathogenic species between individuals during spaceflight. Also, postflight increases in the number of body sites from which these species were isolated were observed, with *Staphylococcus aureus* and the $\beta$-hemolytic streptococci most consistently displaying postflight increases (11, 13, 26). Similar increases in staphylococci, accompanied by increases in antibiotic resistance, have been reported to occur following Russian flights (2, 86). These data agree with the results of several ground-based chamber studies in which numerical increases were reported and were often associated with enhanced pathogenic potential as measured by such factors as proteolytic activity and increased virulence (38, 51, 65).

Several authors have warned that returning space travelers may experience a microbial shock and may respond negatively to renewed contact with potentially pathogenic microorganisms which are absent in the spaceflight environment (13, 44, 48, 65, 67, 83). This warning is based on the assumption that contact with potential pathogens during spaceflight would be very limited, resulting in a reduction of immunocompetence (10, 26, 38, 44, 51, 65, 83). However, data from actual spaceflights show that there is usually an increase in the distribution of pathogens (11, 24, 26, 48, 70, 72, 86). Therefore, if a reduction in immunocompetence were to occur it is not likely that it would be in response to decreased contact with pathogenic components of the autoflora. There is no clinical or microbiological evidence which suggests microbial shock following any of the spaceflight missions yet reported.

The results of chamber studies and the early Apollo missions prompted several investigators to propose the continuation of pre- and postflight microbial monitoring (13, 22, 56, 64, 65, 67). Also preflight and postflight quarantine periods have been proposed to reduce the probability of inflight (65, 67, 80) and postflight (38, 51, 67) disease events. Accordingly, extensive quarantine preventive measures were initiated with the Apollo 14 mission and have continued through the remainder of the American spaceflights (84). This quarantine procedure was designed to allow the autoflora to equilibrate at a level consistent with confinement and to allow contracted infectious agents to demonstrate themselves before flight. It is likely that this contributed to the complete lack of microbial problems during, or immediately following any of these flights (11, 26, 48, 72). However, this quarantine procedure had no apparent effect on the incidence and dispersion of *S. aureus.* The postflight incidence of this species was always higher the day of recovery whether or not a pre- or postflight quarantine had been employed. Use of phage-typing analyses definitely established that intercrew transfer of this pathogenic species was a common occurrence during the lunar landing missions (72). In most cases the transferred strain was again isolated from subsequent samples, indicating that it had established more than a transitory relationship with the new host (72). These data closely approximate similar results demonstrated in ground-based spaceflight simulators (50, 64), indicating that this cross-contamination and increased incidence of *S. aureus* is not peculiar to spaceflight but is typical of habitation of small chambers for several days. Although not unique to spaceflight, monitoring of the *S. aureus* population is of considerable importance, especially in view of ground-based spaceflight-simulation studies which have reported increases in toxigenic activity, virulence, $\beta$-hemolysin production, and fibrinolysin production (51).

An inflight malfunction of the Apollo 13 service module provided an opportunity to evaluate the effect of a crippled life support system on the infectious disease process. Following several days in a cold, damp, habitat associated with an extremely stressful situation, one of the astronauts developed a severe urinary tract infection from which *Pseudomonas aeruginosa* was eventually isolated in high numbers. This situation required inflight antibiotic therapy, which was ineffective until the crew member could be returned to Earth where bacterial isolation and antibiotic sensitivity tests could be performed (72). Several investigators have demonstrated a reduction in body resistance and increases in microbial toxigenic activity, virulence, or pathogenicity following stressful confinement of the human host in space-simulation studies (22, 51, 56, 64, 87). Combined evaluation of these reports illustrates the requirement for an inflight clinical sample analysis capability to be included on future spaceflight missions. This is especially important for long-duration missions in which it would be either inconvenient or impossible for crew members to quickly return to Earth for diagnosis and treatment.

In addition to the more obvious exogenous diseases which may afflict crew members, the importance of endogenous infections has been identified by several authors (18, 22, 23, 27, 28, 44, 83, 87). Concern for infections involving endogenous microorganisms is based upon the recognition that the unusual environment offered by the space ship may so influence the indigenous microflora that previously innocuous microorganisms may become noxious. An example of this potential problem may be found with the potentially pathogenic yeast *Candida albicans* which has been recovered from the oral cavity of a large number of astronauts throughout the Apollo series (24, 70, 72). Although it is not uncommon to find this species in the mouth of healthy adults, its subsequent behavior during spaceflight is of medical importance. Russian investigators have reported a 30-fold increase in incidence of *C. albicans* in the pharynx of subjects who had been confined to a closed test chamber for one month. These investigators concluded that the confinement normalized the bacterial flora, resulting in reduced microbial competition, with subsequent overgrowth of this potentially pathogenic yeast (87). Such a normalization of bacterial species has not been demonstrated in samples collected from Apollo crew members, although *C. albicans* is often the only fungal species recoverable from Apollo crew member samples collected immediately after termination of a mission (70, 76). It has been observed that this resistance of *C. albicans* populations to spaceflight could become quite important if long-term inflight antibiotic therapy was required, providing the opportunity for a loss of competing species and eventual overgrowth of this organism (28). The above observations tend to support the view, proposed by several authors (10–13, 22, 26, 27, 44, 64, 70, 76), that microflora changes may occur in the spacecraft environment and that these changes may not be compatible with man's health and welfare on extended duration missions.

### *Changes in the Mycological Autoflora*

Extensive mycological analyses of spaceflight crew members have been reported only for the Apollo 14 and 15 and Soyuz 9 missions (70, 76, 86). Because little work has been done on the fungal load of healthy male adults, all of the fungi isolated from 12 body sites of each Apollo crew member were identified in an attempt to evaluate which were common to a particular individual and which were transitory. Of the 57 genera isolated from the 6 crew members throughout the Apollo 14 and 15 missions, only 10 species from 5 different genera were isolated from at least 44% of the sample sets. These were identified by the authors as frequently isolated species (70, 76). The transient nature of most recovered species was further demonstrated by their response to changing mission environments. The number of different genera and species was significantly reduced during a preflight isolation period with the lowest preflight count occurring from samples collected the morning of launch (76). This decrease in mycological load reflects a stabilization of the normal flora with a loss of transients and a reduction in the presence of unstable contaminants. Such a stabilizing reduction would serve to decrease the probability of future exogenous infections since the number of potential agents was greatly reduced. However, because there was no change in the incidence of potentially pathogenic microorganisms such as *C. albicans,* the probability of endogenous infection remained about the same.

A similar analysis, conducted for 38 days prior to entry of aquanauts into the Tektite I chamber, demonstrated that when no attempt was made to isolate crew members from recontaminating sources the fungal load remained essentially stable (39). In studies with environmental restrictions, conditions of poor hygiene have generally resulted in increased microbial load (87). In cases where adequate hygienic conditions have been maintained, a stabilization of the microbial population is often observed (10, 44, 64–66, 83). Unfortunately, the environmental conditions for these studies vary so much from each other that the results are not comparable except in the broadest terms.

Analysis of the immediate postflight samples obtained from the Apollo 14 and 15 crew members showed that the observable mycological flora were reduced to less than one third of the immediate preflight value (76). At the beginning of the flight the internal hardware components were quite clean (70), and the astronauts exercised a vigorous hygiene regimen throughout the mission which was conducted in an environment of nearly pure oxygen at a pressure of one third atmosphere. Under these conditions the equilibrium was shifted to favor a loss of fungi from the body without a compensating recontamination from the environment within the spacecraft. No changes were detected in the quantitative composition of fungi recovered from cosmonaut samples following the Soyuz 9 mission (86).

Few other confinement studies have been conducted in which the fungal load of healthy adults has been evaluated. Zaloguyev et al (87) reported changes in the incidence of *C. albicans* recovered from the skin and upper respiratory tract of subjects confined to a test chamber for 12 months. They report a 30-fold increase in the incidence of *C. albicans* in the pharynx the first months with a similar increase in the incidence of *Candida tropicalis* starting the sixth month of confinement. They suggest that such confinement normalizes the bacterial flora and is invariably accompanied by the predominant growth of *Candida* fungi. They are referring here to an increase in the numbers of viable colony-forming units recovered from a particular sample. Comparable quantitations were not performed on samples obtained from Apollo crew members, although it was reported that the number of times this species was recovered, relative to all other fungi, was significantly elevated following the flights of Apollo 14 and 15 (70, 76). In fact *Candida albicans* was frequently the only fungal species recovered from Apollo astronauts postflight. This postflight decrease in the number of recoverable fungal species is the only significant evidence of spaceflight-associated microbial simplification. This phenomenon has been reported following human confinement in small closed chambers (38, 44, 51, 75), but has not been otherwise demonstrated following spaceflight.

### *Changes in the Bacterial Autoflora*

Russian scientists have long been concerned with crew microbiological profiles and natural bactericidal activity. A decade ago Alekseyeva reported that the composition and properties of the autoflora of cosmonauts remained within normal limits during preflight evaluations but that there were occasional postflight changes (2, 3). A postflight increase in oral autoflora was accompanied by dysbacteriosis in which the normal throat flora were almost entirely crowded out by Gram-negative, nonhemolytic diplococci. Similarly, increase of hemolytic micrococci were detected in the deep layers of the skin (2, 3). More recently, interchange of microbes between subjects has been observed following several Russian flights (51). Extensive microbial evaluations were performed on the crew of the 18-day Soyuz 9 spaceflight, the longest Russian flight to date for which data are available. Tests performed 1.5 hr after launching and on the second day in the postflight recovery environment revealed a large quantity of Gram-positive, nonsporogenous bacteria on the skin which was not there preflight (86). These same organisms were recovered from the nasal cavity postflight and contributed to an increase in the postflight microbial load in this location. It was also reported that this dysbacteriotic change in the skin and nasal automicroflora was accompanied by variations of some characteristics of natural immunity (86). Russian interest in autoflora has not been restricted to human cosmonauts. Studies with dogs flown since 1960 show that whereas acceleration and vibration on the ground had no effect on the microflora, the flown dogs demonstrated intestinal bacilli in their oral cavity after two days of flight. This was interpreted to be the result of a spaceflight-mediated decrease in the immunological activity of the subjects (3).

Microbiological monitoring of American spaceflight crews began with comparisons between pre- and postflight specimens collected on one of the Gemini flights. A decrease in types, an increase in the total numbers of recoverable microorganisms, and microbial transfer between the crew members was reported (82). The most complete analysis to be reported for American astronauts involved the crew of Apollo 14 (70). In this evaluation, throat, urine, fecal, nasal, and seven body surface swab samples were examined for the quantitative presence of aerobic and anaerobic bacterial species. These specimens were collected five different times throughout the pre- and postflight monitoring period so that alterative patterns could be established. The following comparisons between preflight and postflight results were reported (70). There was a reduction in the incidence of $\beta$-hemolytic streptococci, an intercrew transfer of *Staphylococcus aureus,* a slight increase in the number of aerobic bacterial genera and species, and no change in the number of anaerobic bacterial genera and species postflight. These data do not confirm the bacterial simplification postulated by several authors on the basis of ground-based spaceflight simulation studies (38, 44, 51). The total aerobic bacterial quantitation was 8.3 times higher than the preflight norm, largely due to an increase in the quantitation of the genus *Escherichia* in the stool. A postflight reduction in the incidence of *Propionibacterium acnes* from the skin and fusobacteria in the oral cavity contributed to a lowered anaerobic bacterial quantitation. In general the microbial load returned to the preflight norm during the postflight quarantine period (70).

## SUMMARY

The results of many space microbiology studies have demonstrated that bacteria, fungi, and viral agents are capable of surviving direct exposure to the space environment, although viable microbes have never been recovered from material of extraterrestrial origin. This indicates either that these samples were in fact sterile or that viable forms may have been present but were not responsive to the culture media used. Most of the space microbiology studies conducted over the last forty years have failed to establish any demonstrable changes in microbes returned to Earth, although there were some positive findings. Increased growth rates of actinomycetes and *Salmonella typhimurium* were reported. Also, repeated studies revealed an elevated induction rate in *E. coli* K-12 (λ), although a decrease in phage induction was reported for a *S. typhimurium* system. There is evidence that these changes may have resulted from the action of launch vibrations or other mechanical factors which altered the radiation sensitivity of the cells. Similarly, T-7 coliphage and *Bacillus subtilis* 168 spores were shown to be more sensitive to the lethal effects of UV irradiation in the space environment. These data indicate that additional critical analyses of the response of microbes to space is required. Such studies could only be conducted in a functioning space laboratory, where well controlled and repetitive experiments could be conducted to explain these reported anomalies.

Autofloral analyses of Apollo and Soyuz crew members have shown that the microbial load of a particular crew member is generally stable during a flight, although certain postflight anomalies were commonly found. There often was an intercrew transfer, and an increase in incidence, of potentially pathogenic microorganisms. Except for the near loss of fungi, microbial simplification has not occurred following spaceflight. Likewise there has been no incidence of microbial shock among crew members returning from any of the reported flights. Future studies should be conducted to establish the relationship between the noted increase in the incidence of pathogens and alterations, if any, in the immunocompetence of astronauts.

### ACKNOWLEDGMENTS

My special thanks are given to Dr. John Spizizen, Mr. Walter Ellis, and Dr. Jerry Mayeux for their critical analyses of this manuscript.

*Literature Cited*


1. Abramova, V. M., Benevolenskiy, V. N., Druzhinin, Yu. P. 1971. *Kosm. Biol. Med.* 5:18–21
2. Alekseyeva, O. G. 1965. *Probl. Space Biol.* 4:278–89
3. Alekseyeva, O. G., Volkova, A. P. 1962. *Probl. Space Biol.* 1:201–209
4. Antipov, V. V. et al, See Ref. 3, 295–313
5. Antipov, V. V. 1967. *Probl. Space Biol.* 6:67–83
6. Antipov, V. V., Kozlov, V. A., Parfenov, G. P., Saksonov, P. P. 1967. *Life Sci. Space Res.* 5:119–21
7. Apollo 12 Mission Report. 1970. *National Aeronautics and Space Administration Document MSC-01855*
8. Beischer, D. E., Fregly, A. R. 1962. *USNSAM,* Monograph 5
9. Benevolenskiy, V. N., Kapul'tsevich, Yu. G., Korogodin, V. I., Chepelev, S. A., See Ref. 1, 14–18
10. Bengson, M. H., Thomae, F. W. 1965. *Contam. Contr.* 4:9–12
11. Berry, C. A. 1969. *National Aeronautics and Space Administration Document TMX-58027*
12. Berry, C. A. 1969. *National Aeronautics and Space Administration Document TMX-58034*
13. Berry, C. A. 1970. *Aerosp. Med.* 41: 500–19
14. Bücker, H. 1973. *The Biostack Experiment I and II Aboard Apollo 16 and 17.* Presented XVI COSPAR Conference, Konstanz FRG
15. Bücker, H., Horneck, G., Wollenhaupt, H. 1973. Proceedings of the Microbial Response to Space Environment Symposium, ed. G. Taylor, *National Aeronautics and Space Administration Publication TMX-58103,* pp. 87–103
16. Bücker, H., Horneck, G., Wollenhaupt, H., Schwager, M., Taylor, G. R. 1973. *Viability of Bacillus subtilis spores exposed to space environment in the M-191 experiment system aboard Apollo 16.* Presented XVI COSPAR Conference, Konstanz FRG
17. Bücker, H. et al 1972. Apollo 16 Preliminary Science Report. *National Aeronautics and Space Administration Document Sp-315,* pp. 27–1 to 27–10
18. Bücker, H. et al 1972. *Life Sci. Space Res.* 10:191–95
19. Balban, E. J. 1961. *Aviat. Res.* 74:40–41
20. Cantwell, G. E., Franklin, B. A. 1966. *J. Invertebr. Pathol.* 8:256–58
21. Chassay, C. E., Taylor, G. R., See Ref. 15, 21–39
22. Chukhlovin, B. A., Ostroumov, P. B., Ivanova, S. P., See Ref. 1, 61–65
23. Drozdova, V. I., Petrov, R. V., Shilov, V. M. 1970. *Kosm. Biol. Med.* 4:51–55
24. Ferguson, J. K. 1974. Apollo Experience Report. *National Aeronautics and Space Administration Document.* In press
25. Foster, B. G., See Ref. 15, 137–51
26. Fox, L. 1971. *Life Sci. Space Res.* 9:69–74
27. Gall, L. S., Riely, P. E. 1967. *National Aeronautics and Space Administration Contractor Report CR-661*
28. Ginsberg, H. S., See Ref. 26, 1–9
29. Grigoryev, Yu. G. et al, See Ref. 18, 113–18
30. Heimpel, A. M. 1967. *Ann. Rev. Entomol.* 12:287–332
31. Horneck, G., Facius, R., Enge, W., Beaujean, R., Bartholomä, K. P. 1973. *Microbial studies in the Biostack experiment of the Apollo 16 mission: Germination and outgrowth of single Bacillus subtilis spores hit by cosmic HZE particles.* Presented XVI COSPAR Conference, Konstanz FRG
32. Hotchin, J., Baker, F. D., Benson, C. L. 1969. *Life Sci Space Res.* 7:67–68
33. Hotchin, J., Lorenz, P., Hemenway, C. L. 1968. *Life Sci. Space Res.* 6: 108–14
34. Jenkins, D. W. 1965. *Life Sci. Space Res.* 3:230–40
35. Jenkins, D. W. 1968. *BioScience* 18: 543–49
36. Kemmerer, W. W. Jr., Mason, J. A., Wooley, B. C. 1969. *BioScience* 19: 712–15
37. Knittel, M. D., Favero, M. S., Green, R. H. 1971. *Proc. Second Lunar Sci. Conf.* 3:2715–19
38. Lebedev, K. A., Petrov, R. V. 1971. *Usp. Sovrem. Biol.* 71:235–52
39. Levine, H. B., Cobb, J. M., Cobet, A. B. 1970. *Arch. Environ. Health* 20:500–5
40. Lorenz, P. R., Hemenway, C. L., Hotchin, J., See Ref. 33, 100–7
41. Lorenz, P., Hotchin, J., Markusen, A. M., Hemenway, C. 1968. *Kosm. Biol. Med.* 2:28–37
42. Lorenz, P. R., Orlob, G. B., Hemenway, C. L. 1969. *Space Life Sci.* 1: 491–500
43. Lorenz, P. R. et al 1968. *Space Life Sci.* 1:118–30
44. Luckey, T. D. 1966. *Aerosp. Med.* 37:1223–28
45. Lukin, A. A., Parfenov, G. P., See Ref. 1, 8–10
46. Mattoni, R. H. T. 1968. *BioScience* 18:602–8
47. Mattoni, R. H. T., Keller, E. C. Jr., Ebersold, W. T., Eiserling, F. A.

Romig, W. R. 1971. The Experiments of Biosatellite II., ed. J. Saunders. *National Aeronautics and Space Administration Document SP-204,* 309–24
48. Mikhaylovskiy, G. P. et al 1967. *Kosm. Biol. Med.* 1:66–70
49. Mitchell, F. J., Ellis, W. L. 1971. *Proc. Second Lunar Sci. Conf.* 3:2721–33
50. Moyer, J. E., Farrell, D. G., Lamb, W. L., Mitchell, J. L. 1966. *Aerosp. Med.* 37:597–600
51. Nefedov, Yu. G., Shilov, V. M., Konstantinova, I. V., Zaloguyev, S. N., See Ref. 26, 11–16
52. Oyama, V. I. 1972. *Space Life Sci.* 3:377–82
53. Oyama, V. I., Merek, E. L., Silverman, M. P. 1970. *Science* 167:773–75
54. Parfenov, G. P., Lukin, A. A. 1973. *Space Life Sci.* 4:160–79
55. Puleo, J. R., Oxborrow, G. S., Fields, N. D., Hall, H. E. 1970. *Appl. Microbiol.* 20:384–89
56. Riely, P. E., Prince, A. E., Gatts, J. D., Shorenstein, D. 1967. *Significant differences in microbial levels in closed environments.* Presented, Aerosp. Med. Assoc., Ann. Sci. Meet., Washington, D.C.
57. Romanova, E. A. et al, See Ref. 1, 41–43
58. Saunders, J. F., Reynolds, O. E., Smith, G. D., See Ref. 47, 1–14
59. Serres de, F. J., See Ref. 32, 62–66
60. Serres de, F. J., See Ref. 47, 325–31
61. Serres de, F. J., Miller, I. R., Smith, D. B., Kondo, S., Bender, M. A. 1969. *Radiat. Res.* 39:436–44
62. Serres de, F. J., Webber, B. B. 1968. *BioScience* 18:590–95
63. Shelton, W. 1968. *Soviet Space Exploration: The First Decade.* New York: Washington Square
64. Shilov, V. M., Lizko, N. N., Borisova, O. K., Prokhorov, V. Ya., See Ref. 26, 43–49
65. Shilov, V. 1970. *Aerosp. Med.* 41:1353
66. Sofios, M., Swatek, F. E. 1972. *National Aeronautics and Space Administration Contractor Report CR-112018 MDC G2826*
67. Spizizen, J., See Ref. 26, 65–68
68. Spizizen, J., Isherwood, J. E., See Ref. 15, 65–85
69. Stevens, A. 1936 *Nat. Geogr. Mag.* 69:693–712
70. Taylor, G. R. 1972. *National Aeronautics and Space Administration Publication TMX-58094*
71. Taylor, G. R. See Ref. 15, 3–19
72. Taylor, G. R. 1974. Apollo Experiences Report. *National Aeronautics and Space Administration Publication.* In press
73. Taylor, G. R., Ellis, W., Johnson, P. H., Kropp, K., Groves, T. 1971. *Proc. Second Lunar Sci. Conf.* 2:1939–48
74. Taylor, G. R., Ferguson, J. K., Truby, C. P. 1970. *Appl. Microbiol.* 20:271–72
75. Taylor, G. R., Henney, M. R. 1973. *Mycological studies of SMEAT crewmembers.* Presented, Am. Soc. Microbiol. 73rd Ann. Meet., Miami Beach, Florida
76. Taylor, G. R., Henney, M. R., Ellis, W. L. 1973. *Appl. Microbiol.* 26:804–13
77. Taylor, G. R., Wooley, B. C. 1973. *Proc. Fourth Lunar Sci. Conf.* 2: 2267–74
78. Taylor, G. R. et al 1972. Apollo 16 Preliminary Science Report. *National Aeronautics and Space Administration Document SP-315,* pp. 27–11 to 27–17
79. Taylor, G. R. et al 1974. *BioScience.* In press
80. Vashkov, V. I., Nikiforova, E. N., Ramkova, N. V., Rogatina, L. N., Scheglova, G. V., See Ref. 26, 61–64
81. Volz, P. A., See Ref. 15, 121–35
82. Wheeler, H. O., Kemmerer, W. W., Dietlein, L. F., Berry, C. A. 1967. *Bacteriol. Proc.* 16
83. Wilkins, J. R. 1967. Biotechnology. *National Aeronautics and Space Administration Publication SP-205,* 133–43
84. Wooley, B. C. 1972. Apollo Experience Report: Protection of Life and Health. *National Aeronautics and Space Administration Publication MSC-04748*
85. Wrenn, R. T., Simmonds, R. C., Heimpel, A. M., See Ref. 15, 105–20
86. Zaloguyev, S. N., Shinkareva, M. M., Utkina, T. G. 1970. *Kosm. Biol. Med.* 4:54–59
87. Zaloguyev, S. N., Utkina, T. G., Shinkareva, M. M., See Ref, 26, 55–59
88. Zhukov-Verezhnikov, N. N. et al, See Ref. 3, 133–48
89. Zhukov-Verezhnikov, N. N. et al, See Ref. 3, 149–55
90. Zhukov-Verezhnikov, N. N. et al 1963. *Aviation and Space Medicine,* ed. V. V. Parin, 158–160. Moscow: *Akad. Med. Nauk.*
91. Zhukov-Verezhnikov, N. N. et al, See Ref. 90, 161–64
92. Zhukov-Verezhnikov, N. N. et al 1964. *Probl. Space Biol.* 3:198–205
93. Zhukov-Verezhnikov, N. N. et al 1966. *Probl. Kosm. Med.* 172–73
94. Zhukov-Verezhnikov, N. N. et al, See Ref. 2, 252–59
95. Zhukov-Verezhnikov, N. N. et al 1968. *Kosm. Issled.* 6:144–49
96. Zhukov-Verezhnikov, N. N. et al, See Ref. 26, 99–103

# REGULATION OF ENZYME ACTIVITY DURING DIFFERENTIATION IN *DICTYOSTELIUM DISCOIDEUM*

❖1634

*Kathleen A. Killick and Barbara E. Wright*
Department of Developmental Biology, Boston Biomedical Research Institute, Boston, Massachusetts 02114

CONTENTS

INTRODUCTION ........ 139
*Life Cycle* ........ 140
ULTRASTRUCTURAL DIFFERENTIATION ........ 140
BIOCHEMICAL DIFFERENTIATION ........ 143
*Saccharide Interconversions* ........ 143
*Essential versus critical variables* ........ 144
*Analyses at the Nucleic Acid and Genetic Level* ........ 145
*Nucleic acid characterization* ........ 145
*The use of drugs* ........ 147
*The use of mutants* ........ 148
*Analyses at the Level of Enzyme Modulation* ........ 150
*Metabolite flux* ........ 150
*Enzyme concentration* ........ 151
*Catalytic properties and compartmentation* ........ 153
FUTURE PROSPECTS ........ 162

*WELCOME TO OUR WORLD*

## INTRODUCTION

For purposes of the present analysis, biochemical differentiation may conveniently be defined as a specialization process during which a cell (or its progeny) accumulates significant amounts of materials not present at an earlier (specified) point in time. This new material may be of any chemical composition, e.g. bone tissue, a specific protein (such as silk fibroin), pigment, or carbohydrate. With respect to the cellular slime mold, *Dictyostelium discoideum,* some of the new materials which accumulate and hence characterize the differentiated state are specific saccharides. The following discussion will be concerned with the accumulation of these saccharides. The proteins involved will not be considered as endproducts of differentiation, but solely as catalysts (enzymes).

The editors of the Review encouraged the authors to present a critical discussion of the current status of the field, rather than an encyclopedic coverage of the literature. Due to space limitations, this review must be restricted in scope, and will be confined to a critical analysis of several mechanisms by which enzymatic activity may be modulated during differentiation in *Dictyostelium.*

### *Life Cycle*

The life cycle of *D. discoideum* consists of two mutually exclusive phases: growth and differentiation (8). The eukaryotic amoeboid cells are usually grown in the laboratory either in a defined axenic medium or with bacteria (*Escherichia coli* or *Aerobacter aerogenes*) as the food source (8, 106). Under conditions of starvation, induced by depletion or removal of nutrients, mitosis ceases and differentiation is initiated. In the presence of a chemotactic substance(s), one of which may be cyclic adenosine 3',5'-monophosphate (cyclic AMP) (5, 7–9, 81), the unicellular amoebae stream together to form multicellular aggregates. Each aggregate, as a result of an orderly and precise series of cell movements, is transformed into a mature fruiting body or sorocarp, consisting of a slender, cellulose-ensheathed stalk, and a sorus or spore mass which is supported by the stalk. This entire morphogenetic sequence is completed within 24 hr at 22°C.

## ULTRASTRUCTURAL DIFFERENTIATION

The gross morphological changes which accompany differentiation in the cellular slime molds (*Acrasiales*) have been described numerous times since *D. discoideum* was first isolated in 1935 by Raper (120). It is only within the past decade, however, that electron microscopy has been used extensively as a probe for those structural changes which serve as the organizational framework of intracellular biochemical differentiation (3, 23, 30, 35, 48–50, 53, 55, 61, 62, 69, 71–73, 76, 95, 96, 133). Many observations at the biochemical level already suggest the involvement of compartmentation in the regulation in vivo of enzyme activity (32, 54, 59, 79, 111, 112, 125, 130, 132, 134, 156). The isolation and analysis of various organelles during development should soon permit direct correlations between ultrastructural and biochemical differentiation.

During development, the cytoplasm of the myxamoebae of *D. discoideum* is partitioned into three distinct areas: peripheral, vacuolar, and nonvacuolar (50). Each of these cytoplasmic segments, together with the plasma membrane, undergoes a characteristic morphological transformation during the life cycle (see Figure 1).

The well-defined nucleus and nucleolus of the predominantly haploid myxamoebae have been described (3, 50, 104) and the apparent lack of nuclear deterioration during morphogenesis has been noted (72). In contrast to the nuclear apparatus, mitochondria undergo striking ultrastructural transformations during development. The first signs of mitochondrial degeneration occur at the pseudoplasmodial stage of development (3, 50), characterized by an increased frequency of inclusions (50). During later stages of development, the outer membrane of this organelle vanishes

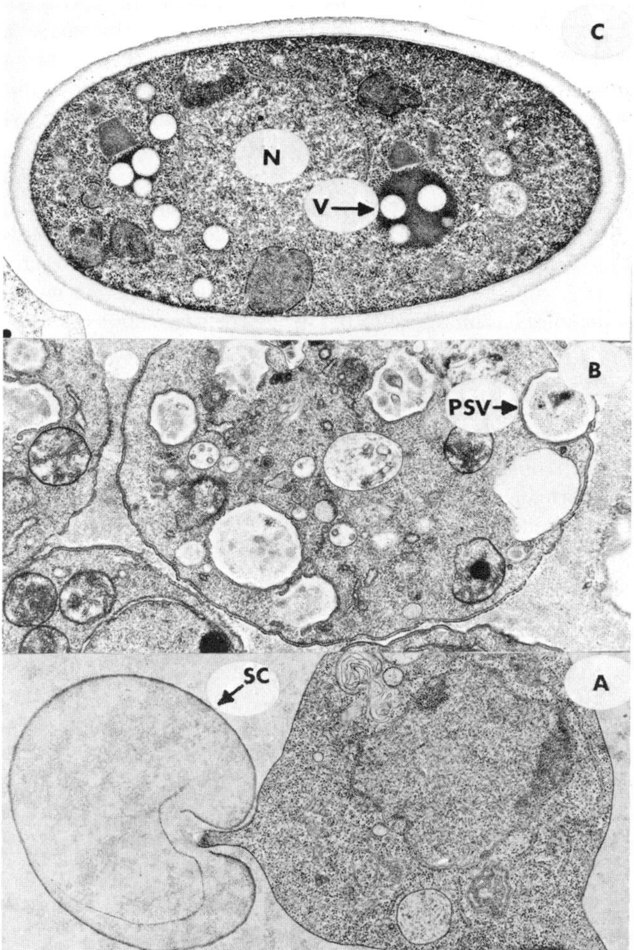


*Figure 1* Ultrastructural differentiation in *Dictyostelium discoideum.* (A) Myxamoeba emerging from a spore case (SC) 3.5 hr. after heat activation (23) X 17,400; (B) fusion of prespore vacuole (PSV) with plasma membrane during the beginning of spore coat formation (72) X 19,000; (C) dormant spore with nucleus (N) and electron transparent vacuoles (V) (72) X 17,300.

and the dense mitochondria become crenated (23, 72). Coincident with mitochondrial deterioration is the greatly diminished respiratory capacity of the differentiating cells (84).

The cell membrane properties of the myxamoebae of *D. discoideum* exhibit several distinct alterations during differentiation. For example, as a result of starvation, the motile phagocytic vegetative cells are transformed into nonphagocytic, multicellular aggregates under the chemotactic influence of cyclic AMP. Within each aggregate, cells maintain continuous adhesion during movement. This cellular interaction appears to be mediated at least in part by the extracellular polysaccharide slime coat which is secreted by the cells (48, 73, 93) and also by the numerous architectural and biochemical modifications of the plasma membrane which appear to be occurring at this time (6, 60, 62, 83, 124, 173).

With the onset of starvation, the slime mold assumes the metabolic characteristics of a closed system (65). By the pseudoplasmodial stage of the life cycle, the vacuolar system of the amoebae has responded to the challenge elicited by starvation. The number of food vacuoles (71) within the amoebae has dropped, presumably caused (at least in part) by their expulsion from the cells, while the number of autophagocytic vacuoles has increased (50). During the later stages of development, the ultrastructure of the vacuolar system is further modified to accommodate the changing functions of the two differentiated cell types. Exhaustive vacuolization and generalized necrosis characterize the adaptation of the stalk cells to their supportive role in the mature sorocarp (50). This is in sharp contrast to the sequential and orderly vacuolar transformations that occur in prespore cells as a prelude to their final state of dormancy (72).

The prespore vacuole (PSV), is an organelle which is unique to those cells destined to become spores (72). As the size and number of the PSVs increase early in the culmination process, they move to the cell periphery where they fuse with the plasma membrane. Three important consequences follow this event: (*a*) the contents of the PSV are released to the outside, (*b*) the plasma membrane of the prespore cell is replaced by that of the PSV, and (*c*) the coat of the PSV becomes the initial layer of the spore wall. Fusion of the PSV with the plasma membrane may as a consequence also constitute a unique mechanism for modifying cell membrane properties during spore maturation. Although the exact origin of the PSV is unknown, Hohl & Hamamoto (72) have suggested that the apparent functions of the PSV point strongly, though indirectly, to a dictyosomal origin. An alternative explanation has been offered by Maeda & Takeuchi (96) who have concluded that the PSVs may originate from the mitochondria.

An additional vacuole specific for prespore and spore cells is the spore vacuole (SV), which is often lined with endoplasmic reticulum and may be associated with lipoid bodies (23, 61, 72). These electron transparent spherical inclusions disappear during spore germination (23) and reappear again during the aggregation stage of development (61, 72). It has been proposed (61) that compartmentation of trehalose within the SV may be a means of maintaining the in vivo latency of spore trehalase (79, 134).

Upon fusion of the PSV with the plasma membrane of the prespore cell, the inner layer of the PSV forms the initial layers of the spore wall (72). The innermost wall layer (approximately 30 nm thick) has an amorphous or slightly fibrillar structure which is easily solubilized with cellulase and pronase (69). The two middle layers (both sensitive to cellulase) are fibrillar, differing only in the orientation of their fibers, while the outermost wall layer is amorphous and appears to consist of the acid mucopolysaccharide lining, which was once the inner coat of the PSV. Numerous filamentous aggregates have been observed associated with the surface of the PSV membrane (76). Although biochemically unsubstantiated at present, it is tempting to speculate that spore wall cellulose may have its origin in these aggregates.

## BIOCHEMICAL DIFFERENTIATION

### *Saccharide Interconversions*

In this laboratory, the analysis of differentiation is usually begun at aggregation (about 10 hr after the initiation of starvation) to insure that the residual growth has ceased and that the metabolic reorganization involved in shifting from exogenous to endogenous energy sources has occurred. The major endogenous energy source is protein. This material, together with RNA, lipid (87), dry weight, and cell volume, decreases by about 40% during differentiation (for a recent review, see 65). In contrast, total carbohydrate remains constant, at about 10% of the dry weight of aggregated cells. The change in composition of various carbohydrate fractions is summarized in Table 1. A number of lines of evidence suggest that gluconeogenesis is not significant during differentiation in the wild-type strain under the usual condition of culture (21, 65, 84), and that cellular glycogen is the ultimate source of glucose residues for the synthesis of new saccharides (mainly cellulose and

**Table 1** Approximate saccharide composition during differentiation[a]

| Carbohydrate | Stages of Differentiation | |
|---|---|---|
| | *Aggregation* | *Sorocarp* |
| Soluble glycogen[b] | 50 | 23 |
| Trehalose | 0.2 | 11 |
| α-Cellulose | 0 | 16 |
| β-Cellulose | 0 | 16 |
| Cell wall glycogen | 0 | 6 |
| Mucopolysaccharide (154) | 0 | 5 |
| Glycoprotein (52)[c] | 14 | — |
| Glucose | 0.2 | 0 |
| Unknown[d] | 35.6 | 23.0 |

[a]Expressed as μmole glucose equivalents/ml packed cell volume (pcv) at aggregation or as percentage of total carbohydrate [1 ml pcv is equivalent to 35 x $10^8$ cells (102, 154)].
[b]Determined after KOH extraction of whole cells.
[c]Determined in amoebae (52).
[d]Total carbohydrate remains constant during differentiation and in glucose equivalents, is 100 ± 5 μmoles/ml pcv at aggregation (P. Rosness and B. E. Wright, unpublished data). The unknown is largely ethanol-soluble material.

trehalose). By manipulating nutritional conditions during the growth phase of axenic mutants, Ashworth and co-workers have been able to alter subsequent metabolism during differentiation [e.g. glycogen content and the occurrence of gluconeogenesis (1, 2, 47, 62, 68)]. Therefore, the above description of metabolism in the wild-type strain does not apply to this interesting axenic system, which must also utilize control mechanisms unique to the particular metabolism involved.

ESSENTIAL VERSUS CRITICAL VARIABLES In order to analyze the biochemical basis of differentiation, it is necessary to know: (*a*) which cellular constituents are *essential* to saccharide interconversion, and (*b*) which are also *critical*, i.e. limit the rates of specific reactions required for saccharide interconversion at particular points in time during differentiation (164, 170). Specification of the time element is very important, in order to avoid confusion concerning so-called triggers of differentiation and to provide a rational basis for the identification of critical variables. For example, assume that the messenger RNA (mRNA) for the essential enzyme, glycogen phosphorylase, is not limiting for enzyme synthesis during differentiation (i.e. between aggregation and sorocarp). Furthermore, assume that this mRNA is absent in the dormant spore, first appears at germination, and is then synthesized continuously during vegetative growth and differentiation. Thus, at germination, gene activation is necessary for the formation of glycogen phosphorylase, but is not a critical variable over the time period chosen for analysis (i.e. between aggregation and sorocarp). As a second example, assume that the level of cellulose synthetase present at the beginning of differentiation (aggregation) is limiting for cellulose synthesis, i.e. that this enzyme is a critical variable. If the enzyme level increases during differentiation due to an increased rate of mRNA synthesis, then gene activation is an earlier critical variable. Thus, in order to determine whether a variable is critical, the period of analysis must be specified precisely.

At least 30 metabolites and 40 enzymes are known to change in concentration or specific activity, respectively, during the saccharide interconversions. Available evidence indicates that they are essential as substrates, effectors, inhibitors, or catalysts in the specific degradative and synthetic pathways involved. Which variables are critical in controlling the rates of specific reactions between aggregation and sorocarp formation? The orientation of this review will be to analyze the current approaches which are being used in an attempt to elucidate the role of enzymes as variables during differentiation in *Dictyostelium*. For the discussion that follows, it should be pointed out that the primitive form of multicellular differentiation exhibited by the cellular slime molds occurs in the absence of mitosis. Hence development in this system need not involve those control mechanisms associated with transcription and translation characteristic of higher organisms or of those specific cases in which protein is the endproduct of differentiation [e.g. hemoglobin (86) and silk fibroin (146, 147)]. In the latter cases, alterations in the expression of mRNA and the utilization of accessory metabolic machinery must be involved directly in time as critical variables controlling the rate of protein accumulation. However, in systems where protein is not the endproduct of differentiation, components at the nucleic acid level are implicated as critical variables only when the rate of enzyme synthesis limits the rate of accumulation of the endproducts of differentiation.

Genetic analyses of biochemical differentiation in *Dictyostelium* are based upon the widespread assumption that differential gene activation is the primary critical variable controlling differentiation. In other words, it is assumed that qualitative and/or quantitative changes in the rate of enzyme synthesis are the major variables which limit differentiation, and that the rate of enzyme synthesis is limited by the rate of synthesis of mRNA. The latter must be synthesized as a result of gene activation and not, for example, accumulate because of the stabilization or activation of existing (potential) mRNA. In a number of systems, gene activation has been excluded as a critical variable, since differentiation can proceed in the absence of concurrent control at the genetic level, i.e. the requisite mRNA population is already present (for a review, see 170). Aside from regulation at the genetic level, there are many mechanisms which do not involve qualitative or quantitive changes in the rate of enzyme synthesis, i.e. the modulation of the activity and/or concentration of existing enzymes by substrate availability, allosteric control, enzyme stabilization, activation, and compartmentation. The latter mechanisms *must* in part deal with critical variables as they operate concurrently with endproduct accumulation. The most important variable is the rate of availability of precursors which are actually consumed as the product is made. The importance of changes in metabolite level and flux, as critical variables during differentiation in *Dictyostelium,* was clearly recognized in 1960 (158, 160), and analyses of biochemical differentiation at these levels are now becoming more frequent (1, 2, 127, 153).

## *Analyses at the Nucleic Acid and Genetic Level*

NUCLEIC ACID CHARACTERIZATION In an extensive series of excellent papers, Firtel, in collaboration with Bonner (39) and Lodish & Jacobson (37, 40, 41), has analyzed various classes of DNA and RNA in *D. discoideum.* The DNA fractions were characterized by their behavior during CsCl buoyant density-gradient centrifugation and by renaturation and hybridization experiments. Of whole-cell DNA, 28% is mitochondrial. Of the nuclear DNA, 70% is composed of nonreiterated (single copy) sequences and 30% of reiterated sequences. Of the latter fraction, 2.2% represents ribosomal RNA (rRNA) cistrons. Messenger RNA was purified, characterized, and found to contain equimolar amounts of two classes of polyadenylic acid [poly (A)]: 100 adenylic acid residues at the 3' end (40), and a shorter poly (A) sequence about 25 nucleotides long (77). Messenger RNA synthesized by isolated nuclei contains only the latter sequence; the longer poly (A) sequences are added post-transcriptionally (41, 77). In hybridization studies with excess *Dictyostelium* DNA, at least 90% of the mRNA reassociates with single copy DNA. A nuclear poly (A)-containing RNA, the presumptive precursor of cytoplasmic mRNA, was also isolated and characterized (41).

In an analysis of changes during development in mRNA transcripts of the genome, Firtel (36) extracted RNA from cells at the amoebae through the culmination stages of development and hybridized it with purified single-copy nuclear DNA. The amount of DNA which hybridizes to such RNA at high RNA/DNA ratios is thought to reflect the fraction of the genome represented as RNA transcripts at that particular stage of differentiation. From the amoebae through the culmination stage of development, 56% of the genome was represented by transcripts as judged by this criterion. The data suggests that an increasing fraction of the genome is transcribed as differentiation progresses. However, the hybridization data suggesting stage-specific qualitative differences in RNA-transcripts do not appear to be statistically significant.

If a change in the pattern of transcription does occur during development in *Dictyostelium,* it may be mediated by changes in the relative proportions of DNA-dependent RNA polymerases I and II or by a modification of the template specificity of either one of them. A thorough examination of the characteristics of this enzyme, isolated from nuclei of the slime mold during exponential growth and during differentiation into fruiting bodies has been made (117). In the absence of any detectable differences in either enzymatic or physical properties of this enzyme during development, Pong & Loomis (117) have suggested that changes in transcriptive pattern may depend upon factors other than an alteration of DNA-dependent RNA polymerase. This suggestion is intriguing in view of the recent observations of Farrell & DeToma (33), who have demonstrated that exposure of aggregating cells to cyclic AMP stimulates the capacity of their nuclei for the synthesis of RNA. Although the mechanisms responsible for this effect have not yet been investigated in *Dictyostelium,* they may be analogous to those proposed by Korinek et al (82) to explain the cyclic AMP-mediated increase in RNA polymerase II activity in rat sarcoma cells.

The only definitive evidence for the functional identification of a species of mRNA is, of course, its translational capacity in directing the synthesis of a specific protein. This has been achieved for structural proteins in highly specialized differentiating tissue (86, 146). Until a single species of mRNA can be isolated, the mechanism(s) responsible for changes in its concentration must remain unknown. Thus, if stage-specific alterations in the mRNA population (as determined by the hybridization technique) do occur in *D. discoideum,* a change in the rate of transcription is not necessarily implicated. A particular species of mRNA [or nuclear precursor thereof (41)], could accumulate through alterations in the rate of its degradation rather than synthesis. Such a mechanism has been demonstrated for the accumulation of UDP-glucose pyrophosphorylase (see section on enzyme concentration). In order to examine this possibility, a specific species of mRNA must be isolated following isotope incorporation studies designed to examine its rate of turnover. Changing mRNA populations might also result from cytoplasmic modifications of existing species of mRNA. The developmental significance of a change in concentration of a specific mRNA depends upon establishing the relationship of this transcript to a particular structural or enzymic protein which must be a critical variable limiting differentiation. The rate of synthesis of this protein must be limited and regulated by the availability of mRNA during differentiation. If such changes in the concentration of a species of mRNA are found in *Dictyostelium,* they are as likely to be concerned with the synthesis of structural proteins [e.g. actin (157)] as with enzymic proteins. As seen from ultrastructural analyses during differentiation, various vacuoles, vesicles, and membranes undergo striking morphological changes. Evidence documenting a change in composition of the structural proteins involved is, however, presently unavailable. Since unit membranes may be formed from amorphous pools of precursor material through template action of pre-existing membranes (71), it is possible that formation of these organelles may be primarily regulated at the level of subunit assembly. Alterations in the morphology of these organelles may then arise from modification(s) of the pre-existing subunits as opposed to their de novo synthesis. The great majority of enzymes are present throughout the life cycle, and evidence documenting a change in the rate of synthesis of any one of them is so far lacking. However, the ease of assaying enzymic (as opposed to structural) proteins assures their more thorough investigation as products of gene expression (40). Until changes in the rate of enzyme synthesis can be demonstrated in this differentiating system, it is perhaps premature to seek associated changes at the mRNA level. Alterations at the genetic or any other level which can be correlated with successive stages of differentiation may or may not be mechanistically relevant. For example, new species of mRNA may be synthesized during differentiation but not be translated until germination. In this connection, a mutant of *D. discoideum* apparently defective in an enzyme(s) essential to DNA repair was $\gamma$-irradiated to an extent preventing cell proliferation. However, the cells proceeded through normal differentiation, although the spores of the sorocarp were incapable of germination (26).

THE USE OF DRUGS In recent years, numerous studies have been carried out concerning the effect of drugs such as actinomycin D, cycloheximide, and daunomycin on changes in enzyme specific activity during differentiation, in an attempt to determine the level of involvement of transcription and translation in controlling these changes (4, 88, 92, 116, 129, 131, 141, 144, 145, 148). Based upon experiments using actinomycin D and cycloheximide, "maps" of specific periods of genetic transcription and mRNA translation for specific enzymes have been constructed. These inhibitor studies have recently been extended to situations in which differentiation is perturbed by manipulation of the environment, also resulting in deviations from the normal enzyme activity profile (29, 107, 108, 110). The latter again are interpreted to originate at the level of genetic transcription ("quantal control"). The assumptions upon which such deductions are based should be clearly stated and critically examined, as the interpretations offered by proponents of such inhibitor studies in the cellular slime mold are being widely accepted (10, 38, 44, 103, 136, 138). This uncritical acceptance may have suppressed the orientation of investigators towards other mechanisms which are perhaps more fundamental to the regulation of enzyme activity during differentiation in *Dictyostelium.*

Actinomycin D is a general metabolic poison (for references, see 74, 137, and 163) which, in order to inhibit changes in enzyme specific activity, must be used at levels preventing subsequent differentiation. The primary effects of this drug may be the inhibition of differentiation by a variety of mechanisms, with only secondary consequences to those changes in enzyme specific activity which accompany normal differentiation. Thus, interference with the synthesis of an enzyme essential to energy metabolism will undoubtedly prevent differentiation. However, it does not follow that this enzyme is unique to the differentiation process—only that it is one of many prerequisites. There is little basis for singling out the inhibition of transcription by actinomycin D as primarily responsible for affecting enzyme activities, especially in view of the evidence that mRNA synthesis is *less* sensitive to inhibition than are protein and rRNA synthesis (37). In *D. discoideum* overall cellular protein synthesis is inhibited by actinomycin D and daunomycin individually or in combination, in a manner comparable to their effects on changes in enzyme specific activity (37). Regardless of the mechanism, the former inhibition may suffice to explain the latter, especially if enzymes constitute a class of proteins the synthesis of which is particularly sensitive to inhibition.

If there is a specific effect of actinomycin D on RNA synthesis in *D. discoideum,* it appears to occur at low levels and to be directed at rRNA synthesis (37). This observation suggests an interpretation of earlier studies on the effects of low levels of actinomycin D (10 μg/ml) on differentiation (70, 115). When amoebae were exposed to the drug, subsequent development was completely blocked. Sensitivity of the cells to inhibition progressively decreased as development proceeded, i.e. by late aggregation, no inhibition of subsequent development was observed. The progressive decrease in sensitivity to the drug paralleled the period of net RNA degradation (164). One could conclude that rRNA turnover during the early phases of starvation is required for subsequent multicellular differentiation.

Another assumption on which the interpretations of the inhibitor studies depend is that an increase in enzyme specific activity results from an increase in the amount of enzyme protein, due solely to an increase in the rate of enzyme synthesis. This is not true in many cases, for example, trehalose-6-phosphate (T6P) synthetase and uridine diphosphoglucose (UDP-glucose) pyrophosphorylase (see subsequent discussions). There is as yet no evidence for an increase in the rate of synthesis of any enzyme during multicellular differentiation. [For further discussion of the use of drugs in this system, see Wright (163) and Gustafson & Wright (65).]

THE USE OF MUTANTS Erdos et al (31) and Clark et al (19) have recently reported evidence indicating the existence of a sexual phase in the life cycle of a cellular slime mold. Appropriate mating types can form macrocysts, which represent the diploid phase of the life cycle. This discovery will undoubtedly stimulate extensive investigations using the available developmental mutants (145) in recombination experiments.

Another approach using mutants is based upon the observation that synergism can occur between two morphogenetically deficient mutants (140). Using this technique in *D. purpureum,* three classes of mutants blocked in the early stages of development were recently analyzed (174). Only mutants paired from different classes responded synergistically to form normal sorocarps. The interpretation of these interesting observations must await a detailed knowledge of the underlying biochemical events.

Loomis (89) has described temperature-sensitive mutants which are presumably characterized by specific thermolabile proteins. One class cannot grow but does differentiate at 27°C; many genes could be required only for growth, such as one responsible for an enzyme involved in DNA replication. The more intriguing strains do not differentiate but do grow at 27°C; these are deficient only in functions required during aggregation. Very few mutants showed gross abnormalities during development, suggesting relatively few species of mRNA unique to morphogenesis. This possibility has been discussed previously on other grounds (160, 161, 163, 164). A similar investigation, in which cells were very heavily mutagenized (killing 99.9%) also revealed surprisingly few mutations specifically affecting differentiation (27). The expression of a gene during development need not imply that mRNA synthesis occurs only at that time. Such a mRNA may normally be present during growth and may only be translated during development.

Are developmental mutants useful to the elucidation of biochemical mechanisms limiting differentiation? They are minimally so in our present state of ignorance about these mechanisms. A developmental mutant presumably results from a deficiency in, or alteration of, a structural protein or an enzyme catalyzing a reaction essential to differentiation. A lesion could be qualitative but is more likely quantitative, as the mutant is viable and the great majority of enzymes required for development are also present and essential to the growth phase of the life cycle. First, consider a mutation which diminishes the catalytic turnover number of an enzyme essential at low levels during vegetative growth, but required at full capacity during differentiation. Glycogen phosphorylase is an excellent example. This enzyme becomes more active in vitro and in vivo during development (78). A mutation reducing its activity to 10% may therefore result in a morphogenetic mutant, yet not impair vegetative growth. Analysis of this mutant alone would demonstrate the obvious—that the enzyme is essential—but add little to an understanding of its role during differentiation. Only through our present knowledge of its role based on analyses in vivo and simulation studies (170) could the significance of this mutation be appreciated.

Now consider a qualitative mutation affecting an enzyme presumably active only at the later stages of differentiation. Such an enzyme would catalyze the synthesis of a material unique to the differentiated state—such as trehalose or cellulose. Assume that trehalose synthesis at culmination is essential for sorocarp construction, and that a morphogenetic mutant lacks T6P synthetase. Although this enzyme is normally present (at maximum concentration) from the beginning of differentiation (see section on enzyme modulation), the mutation would be expressed only at culmination, when the enzyme is unmasked in vivo. The mutant would be arrested in development at culmination. What would have been learned? Only that trehalose accumulation is essential to sorocarp construction. It has not been possible to distinguish between the synthesis of an enzyme at culmination and an enzyme which is always present (overt or latent) but only active at culmination. Nor has information been obtained about the mechanism by which the enzyme normally becomes active in vivo. Even if an enzyme is found to be both essential and unique to differentiation, it may not be rate limiting to the accumulation of the endproducts of differentiation. That is, a change in enzyme activity may not occur; if it does, the change may not affect development. Whether or not an enzyme is a critical variable within the metabolic network under analysis may be assessed through the construction and exploration of kinetic models (see section on metabolite flux). At present, mutants are not very effective tools in this search; an indepth analysis of the many parameters controlling metabolism in vivo during normal differentiation is the most fruitful approach, difficult as that may be. When a great deal more is known about the details, dynamics, and control of metabolism during normal differentiation, and when lesions of the developmental mutants have been identified, only then may the latter serve an important supporting role in a more sophisticated understanding of the control mechanisms involved.

### *Analyses at the Level of Enzyme Modulation*

METABOLITE FLUX For many years H. A. Krebs and others (for a review, see 164) have repeatedly emphasized the fact that substrate availability usually limits the rates of reactions in vivo. During differentiation, changes in metabolite flux and level may also control reaction rates by allosteric modulation, product inhibition, and by affecting the rate of synthesis or degradation of enzymes. Since the importance of metabolite flux as a critical variable in *D. discoideum* has recently been the subject of a number of reviews and a book (65, 159, 164, 172), it will not be discussed here in any detail. Suffice it to say that, with rare exceptions such as the reaction catalyzed by glycogen phosphorylase, the rate of substrate availability must be a critical variable controlling the rate of most reactions essential to differentiation. In general, the role of metabolite flux as a critical variable in differentiating systems is rarely considered, apparently due to a widespread need for a simple solution to a complex problem. Thus, triggers are sought, and the obvious candidate is differential gene activation. The major emphasis has therefore been to correlate changes at the nucleic acid and enzyme level with differentiation. Hopefully, the concept of triggers will eventually be abandoned, and emphasis placed on the *interaction* of the many types of variables operative in the intact cell. In the differentiation of *D. discoideum* other laboratories, notably that of Ashworth, have recently stressed the role of metabolites as critical variables in differentiation (1, 2, 127, 153).

When sufficient information (e.g. metabolite levels, reaction rates in vivo, etc) is available for a differentiating system, kinetic models may serve as a powerful tool in determining the critical variables involved (65, 164). Such models simulate the steady-state conditions which prevail during differentiation, and allow the investigator to perform exploratory experiments in vivo, so to speak, by changing various parameters and observing the effects on the metabolic network under analysis. Such an approach has allowed specific enzymes and metabolites to be identified in their role as critical variables in limiting the rates of reactions essential to differentiation (65, 162, 164). A kinetic model can serve as a framework in which to judge the relevance of in vitro data to the intact cell. Perhaps the most interesting example is the comparison of the activity of an enzyme in extracts ($V_{max}$) to its activity in the intact cell (this is called $V_v$). In the model, the value of $V_v$ for any enzyme is taken as the unknown and is calculated, using the appropriate enzyme kinetic expression to integrate information, as to the rate of the reaction in vivo (V), the kinetic constants ($K_m$ and $K_i$), and the cellular levels of substrates and effectors. When the estimated value, $V_v$, corresponds to the in vitro value of $V_{max}$, it is very probable that those parameters operative in vivo have been correctly assumed or measured in vitro. A lack of correspondence may suggest the participation in vivo of an unsuspected activator, inhibitor, compartment, etc. Relatively few enzymes have been studied in sufficient detail to realistically consider a comparison of $V_v$ and $V_{max}$. It is therefore exciting to note the similarity of these values in two cases: UDP-glucose pyrophosphorylase and T6P synthetase. The details of comparing $V_v$ and $V_{max}$ for the latter enzyme are discussed below.

ENZYME CONCENTRATION It is widely assumed that an increase in enzyme activity during differentiation in a variety of systems is due to an increase in the concentration of enzyme protein, which in turn is due to an increase in the rate of enzyme synthesis. In *D. discoideum* these important assumptions have been examined in only one case: UDP-glucose pyrophosphorylase. During differentiation this enzyme increases approximately eightfold in specific activity or about fourfold in total enzyme units per cell (63). Immunological studies by Franke & Sussman (45, 46) and Gustafson & Wright (63, 64, 66, 67) have shown that this increase in enzyme activity can be correlated with a proportionate increase in the amount of antigen, precipitable from crude extracts with pyrophosphorylase-specific antisera.

An increase in the rate of enzyme synthesis could be responsible for enzyme accumulation. However, if the rate of enzyme synthesis during growth [about 20%/hr (166)] were maintained during differentiation, enzyme accumulation could result from a decrease in the degradative phase of enzyme turnover. Such a mechanism has been demonstrated for rat liver tryptophan pyrrolase (135). In order to examine these two alternatives, isotope studies coupled with immunological and electrophoretic techniques were used by Gustafson & Wright (63, 66) to label and isolate enzyme during successive stages of morphogenesis.

An examination of enzyme turnover during differentiation in *Dictyostelium* is technically much more complicated than, for example, a study of enzyme turnover in rat liver (135). In the cellular slime mold as a function of time, permeability increases about tenfold, total cellular protein decreases significantly, and overall protein turnover decreases about threefold (Table 2). Because of these simultaneous changes, all of which affect the labeling of proteins, isotope data were expressed as specific (rather than total) radioactivity, in order to clarify interpretation of the results (63). The rate of enzyme protein synthesis was compared to the rate of

**Table 2** Protein turnover in *D. discoideum*[a]

| Stage | No. Experiments | % Incorporation $[^{35}S]$ methionine/hr |
|---|---|---|
| Amoebae | 4 | 17.9 ± 3.4 |
| Aggregation-pseudoplasmodium | 5 | 12.9 ± 2.4 |
| Preculmination | 3 | 7.0 ± 1.2 |

[a]Taken from Wright & Anderson (165, 166).

synthesis of other soluble cellular proteins, as turnover of the latter acid-precipitable proteins had already been determined in a careful study which had taken the permeability changes into account. During the first 10 hr of differentiation, protein turnover is both heterogeneous and extensive, involving about 90% of the protein present in the amoebae. Over this time period, when the concentration of enzyme protein is low and constant, enzyme was labeled at a rate 2–3 times more rapidly than acid-insoluble protein. Following an initial lag in the case of enzyme specific radioactivity, both rates of incorporation are linear, even over a period of 11 hr (63, 66). This is apparently due to the fact that endogenous [$^{35}$S] methionine precursor specific radioactivity is continuously increasing due to a comparable increase in cellular permeability as a function of time (165, 166). Only during the period of maximum enzyme accumulation (culmination) was acid-insoluble protein labeled more rapidly than enzyme protein. All the data are consistent with the conclusion that, on the initiation of starvation, enzyme turnover is very rapid, possibly as high as 50%/hour. Thereafter, during the course of differentiation, the rate of enzyme synthesis is relatively constant while the rate of enzyme degradation decreases, allowing enzyme to accumulate.

The mechanism underlying this decreased rate of degradation of enzyme protein is unknown. The apparent dissimilarity in size of enzyme subunits prepared from amoebae as opposed to culminating cells may be related to differences in their rates of degradation. In addition to post-translational modification of subunit structure, epigenetic regulation of subunit assembly may also play a role in regulating the effective in vivo concentration of this enzyme. Earlier studies have indicated that both UTP and UDPG stabilize the enzyme in crude extracts (168). Since an increase in the intracellular level of UDPG coincides with the time of maximal in vitro and in vivo activity of this enzyme, it is possible that this nucleotide sugar as well as other low molecular weight metabolites (109) may be involved in the stabilization and/or assembly of UDP-glucose pyrophosphorylase.

In parallel studies Franke and Sussman (46, 142, 143) have arrived at opposite conclusions to those of Gustafson and Wright. They find insignificant labeling of the enzyme in amoebae and conclude that enzyme turnover is negligible. The discrepancies between the conclusions of the two series of investigations are due to important differences in experimental technique and to several erroneous assumptions made by Franke and Sussman. With respect to experimental techniques, the most important appear to be the following. The enzyme used by Gustafson and Wright to obtain antisera was fourfold higher in specific activity than that of Franke and Sussman. Thus, more specific antibody was obtained by the former investigators; using an incorrect value for enzyme specific activity, the latter investigators actually precipitated one quarter as much enzyme protein as they thought. Gustafson and Wright were able to demonstrate quantitative recovery of enzyme activity in the enzyme-antibody complex. This was not demonstrated by Franke and Sussman, who measured only the disappearance of enzyme activity from the supernatant after addition of antisera. Under the conditions used, amoebae enzyme exhibits pronounced instability even in the absence of antibody (109, 167). Under the experimental conditions of Franke and Sussman, more than 90% of the protein present at the enzyme position on the gel was $\gamma$-globulin (45, 46). In contrast, Gustafson and Wright employed a technique separating enzyme from $\gamma$-globulin and measured the concentration and radioactivity of enzyme protein directly (63). In addition to the differences in methodology summarized above, at least two incorrect assumptions appear to be responsible for the interpretations and conclusions of Franke and Sussman. Their estimate of the expected recovery of enzyme protein precipitated was based on a specific enzyme activity of their purified enzyme, which is fourfold lower than the maximal value which has been obtained (63). Therefore, their calculation of enzyme recovery was also too low, i.e. instead of 60–80% recovery, the actual recovery was 240–320%. This comparison establishes the fact that at least two thirds of the material counted was not enzyme protein. If less than 100% enzyme was recovered, proportionately less material actually represents enzyme. It was therefore impossible for Franke and Sussman to accurately measure the amount of enzyme protein. Assuming 100% recovery and correcting for enzyme specific activity, Franke and Sussman were dealing with 0.3–0.6 $\mu$g of enzyme protein. By direct measurement Gustafson and Wright were dealing with 8–9 $\mu$g of enzyme protein. Finally, the major conclusions in the discussion of Franke and Sussman were based on the erroneous assumption that protein turnover is 7%/hr in amoebae (Table 2).

CATALYTIC PROPERTIES AND COMPARTMENTATION Differentiation in the cellular slime mold is characterized by the in vivo expression of new biosynthetic pathways at particular stages of morphogenesis. The specific activities of a number of the enzymes involved have been determined in crude extracts at successive stages of morphogenesis (1, 13, 22, 38, 47, 56, 78, 89–92, 94, 116–118, 125, 127, 131, 142, 148, 151). Such enzyme profiles, or stage studies, have been considered by many investigators as accurately depicting the changes in vivo in activities of these enzymes. However, a number of in vitro artifacts suggest extreme caution in the interpretation of such data.

The profiles of the majority of "developmental" enzymes follow a bell-shaped curve. The specific activity is usually low at early stages of development, peaks during the culmination process, and shortly thereafter falls to a low level. Conditions for the optimal preparation, stabilization, and assay of an enzyme are usually determined with extracts prepared at that developmental stage showing the highest specific activity. Such methodology may not, however, be applicable to other stages of development. Changes in the cellular milieu which accompany differentiation alter the composition of crude extracts prepared throughout development, and hence necessitate that optimal conditions of enzyme preparation, stabilization, and assay be determined for each developmental stage examined.

It is essential to assay the enzyme at that temperature which will be optimal (not necessarily maximal) throughout development. For example, glycogen phosphorylase activity can be detected in amoebae and culmination extracts at 25°C (78), but only in the latter extracts at 37°C (38). Moreover, to have developmental as well as physiological significance, the temperature of assay for any enzyme should not exceed 25°C, since differentiation is inhibited above this temperature. Extreme care must also be taken regarding the protein concentration employed in assays, in the event a stage-specific inhibitor is present. With crude extracts the range over which the initial velocity shows a linear relationship with enzyme concentration will vary with the stage of morphogenesis if the level of an endogenous inhibitor is also a function of the developmental stage. Preliminary evidence suggests that this is true for T6P synthetase (K. A. Killick and B. E. Wright, unpublished data).

The importance of differential enzyme instability in vitro has been stressed by Wright (158). Of 30 enzymes examined, about one fourth are subject to rapid inactivation in extracts prepared at early but not late stages of differentiation (162). In some cases, the addition of substrates prior to cell rupture stabilizes enzyme activity and allows it to be assayed (20, 158). More recently, $\beta$-N-acetylglucosaminidase has been added to the list of those enzymes apparently subject to differential inactivation (2). Although its molecular basis may vary with the enzyme in question, this phenomenon is of such a generalized nature as to warrant serious consideration.

Classical techniques such as freeze-thaw (78, 118), sonication (118, 131), and detergent-extraction (127) are routinely used in the preparation of cell-free extracts of *D. discoideum.* Because of the extensive damage that such methods impose upon the cells, it is often impossible to conclude anything decisive about the physical state (soluble or particulate) of an enzyme in vivo. Moreover, since many particulate enzymes exhibit structure-linked latency, their activity after preparation by either detergent-extraction or sonication may easily be an artifact resulting from the unmasking of a latent enzyme. Erroneous conclusions about the activity in vivo of such enzymes might then be drawn based upon their measurable (overt) activity in vitro. Freeze-thawing of cells can also unmask latent enzymes, especially when the latter fall within the category of "loosely particulate." The most definitive conclusions about enzyme localization are those obtained after cell fractionation under isotonic conditions (59, 113, 156). Such methods preserve organelle integrity and allow for an assessment of compartmentation and its potential effect on the regulation in vivo of enzyme activity (75, 111).

Of the intracellular enzymes examined, most show an increase in specific activity during development in *Dictyostelium.* In some instances this increase merely reflects a corresponding decrease in the amount of buffer-soluble protein. For the majority of enzymes, however, the increased specific activity results from a change in the amount of measurable (overt) enzyme activity. Such changes may be divided into those which result solely from net accumulation of enzyme protein (UDPG pyrophosphorylase) and those which are the result of decompartmentation and/or an alteration (either direct or indirect) of catalytic properties. To illustrate the developmental significance of the latter mechanisms, 9 enzymes (of the 40-odd studied in *Dictyostelium*), showing specific activity changes elicited via mechanisms other than alterations in enzyme level, have been selected for the following discussion.

*Trehalase* Trehalose is thought to serve as an energy and carbon source during the emergence stage of spore germination (25) and at that time in the life cycle trehalase probably achieves its maximal activity in vivo (13). Although trehalase activity is detectable at all stages of the life cycle, dramatic changes in specific activity occur during morphogenesis. Maximal in the vegetative myxamoebae, enzyme specific activity decreases by approximately tenfold during the first 12–14 hr of development (13, 79, 130) as a result of trehalase secretion by aggregating cells (13, 79). The specific activity of extracellular trehalase at this stage of development is approximately fifteenfold higher than in extracts from vegetative cells (13, 79). Based on changes in the specific activity of the extracellular enzyme, trehalase secretion appears to occur in two phases (79). Approximately one third of the total extracellular enzyme is secreted prior to the pseudoplasmodial stage of development, while the remainder is released over a fairly brief period during the culmination process (79). The mechanism(s) underlying this secretion profile is unknown.

Following the pseudoplasmodial stage of development, the specific activity of intracellular trehalase increases during the remainder of development (79, 130). Intracellular trehalase activity (units/cell) measured in extracts prepared from mature sorocarps is approximately 40–50% of that observed with vegetative myxamoebae (79). Since activity and not enzyme protein was the parameter measured in the studies on both the extracellular and intracellular enzyme, definitive conclusions concerning the basis of the modulation of trehalase activity cannot be drawn (79). Compartmentation or a decrease in level of an endogenous activator as well as alterations at the level of enzyme synthesis and/or degradation are possibilities which deserve consideration.

*Cellulase* In addition to trehalase, cellulase is thought to be maximally active in vivo during spore germination (24). During the swelling stage of germination extracellular cellulase having a high specific activity is first detectable (T. Jones and L. Leung, unpublished data). The time of appearance of this extracellular enzyme coincides with that of the dissolution of both the outermost mucopolysaccharide layer and the two middle cellulosic wall layers (23, 69). In a manner comparable to that of trehalase, cellulase activity in vitro during differentiation parallels the accumulation of its substrate in vivo (125). Unlike the former enzyme, however, cellulase activity is undetectable in extracts prepared prior to the sorocarp stage of development. Preliminary evidence suggests that this absence of overt activity may be due to the presence of a cellulase inhibitor (presumably a protein) rather than to an absence of enzyme protein. Since the extent to which cellulase is inhibited after exposure to the inhibitor is not time-dependent, it is unlikely that this protein is a protease.

The thin innermost wall layer of the spore is amorphous or slightly fibrillar and contains at least two components, cellulose and protein (69). In vitro solubilization of this portion of the wall requires consecutive treatment with cellulase and pronase (69). This layer, in contrast to the other segments of the spore wall, remains intact until the emergence stage of germination. Since the in vivo unmasking of cellulase activity occurs during swelling, prior to emergence, it cannot be a critical variable which limits the rate of protoplast emergence from the spore case. As emergence is prevented by cycloheximide, it has been suggested that dissolution of the innermost wall layer is dependent on protein synthesis (69). Efforts are now being directed towards the identification of those enzymes, apparently activated during germination, which are involved in the hydrolysis of the proteinaceous component of the innermost wall layer of the spore (69).

*Alkaline phosphatase* Alkaline phosphatase from *Dictyostelium* is a 5'-nucleotidase, which therefore differs from the nonspecific enzyme of *E. coli* (56). Although alkaline phosphatase activity is detectable throughout the life cycle of the cellular slime mold (56, 90), enzyme specific activity increases approximately fivefold over a brief period during the culmination process (56). Since vegetative enzyme (present throughout the life cycle) is electrophoretically distinct from the alkaline phosphatase apparently unique to culminating cells (139), it has been suggested (90) that accumulation of the latter enzyme during the terminal stages of development may be responsible for the observed enzyme profile. It is apparent from the observations of others (56), however, that alternative mechanisms may be operative. Thus, storage of cell-free extracts at 4°C results in a reversible loss of activity, which is most pronounced in those extracts prepared early in development (56). Immediate dilution of the extract after preparation, followed by subsequent incubation at 4°C (24–48 hr), elevates enzyme specific activity 1.5–2.0-fold over that of the undiluted control. The reversibility and sensitivity of this phenomenon to dilution suggest that an endogenous inhibitor of the phosphatase may be instrumental in promoting these events. In this respect, it is interesting to note that a heat-labile protein has been isolated from *E. coli* which inhibits the 5'-nucleotidase from the same organism (28).

Low molecular weight metabolites, either exogenous or endogenous to the cells, may also modulate phosphatase activity in vivo (56). For example, although adenosine and deoxyadenosine (5 mM) retard the rate of morphogenesis, extracts prepared from cells which have differentiated in their presence contain enzyme which has a specific activity about 1.5-fold higher than that from nonexposed controls (56). The mechanism of this stimulation is not known, but may be analogous to that observed for the enzyme from rat liver (155). In the latter system, 5'-AMP stabilizes enzyme activity by preventing the formation of insoluble and hence inactive aggregates of 5'-nucleotidase. The most critical endogenous metabolite produced during culmination which could limit phosphatase activity in vivo is inorganic orthophosphate (Pi). Phosphate concentration increases about twentyfold during development, reaching a maximal level of 65 mM in dormant spores (56). If accessible to alkaline phosphatase in vivo, Pi at this level would inhibit enzymic activity by more than 90%. Based on the intracellular Pi level as a function of developmental stage, phosphatase activity in vivo would be expected to be maximal during culmination (56).

However, compartmentation of Pi between stalk and spore cells occurs (C. Rutherford, unpublished data) and intracellular compartmentation may also occur between Pi and phosphatase during differentiation in *Dictyostelium.* Furthermore, in several systems, alkaline phosphatase is membrane-associated (15, 16, 85, 105, 149). If particulate in *Dictyostelium,* the catalytic properties of alkaline phosphatase may also be modulated by membrane alterations during development.

*Phosphodiesterase and adenylate cyclase* Cyclic AMP is a chemotactic substance thought to be responsible for the aggregation of cells of *Dictyostelium* during the early stages of morphogenesis (see 10 for a review). The concentration of cyclic AMP appears to be determined largely, if not entirely, by the relative activities of adenylate cyclase and a phosphodiesterase, specific for cyclic AMP (17, 18, 51, 114). As the cells of *Dictyostelium* approach the end of the exponential phase of growth, there is an approximate tenfold increase in the extracellular concentration of cyclic AMP (51, 99). This appears to result from the inactivation of extracellular, soluble phosphodiesterase (PD) by an inhibitor released from the cells early in the stationary phase of growth (50, 122). The inhibitor, which is specific for PD from the cellular slime mold, is a heat-stable protein having a molecular weight of about 40,000 (50, 123). The stoichiometric interaction between PD and inhibitor suggests that inactivation of PD does not result from proteolysis.

In addition to extracellular enzyme, cells of *Dictyostelium* contain both soluble and particulate forms of intracellular PD. The soluble enzyme is lysosomal, nonspecific for cyclic nucleotides, and appears to be unrelated to maintenance of the extracellular cyclic AMP gradient. Activity of the membrane-bound PD (presumably localized in the cell surface) is low during vegetative growth and increases about fifteenfold during differentiation, reaching a maximum activity at about 9 hr after the initiation of starvation (98, 100). In contrast to both the soluble intracellular and extracellular forms of the enzyme, cell-bound PD is resistant to inhibition by reduced glutathione and the extracellular PD-inhibitor (98). Recently Malchow et al (97) have shown that binding of cyclic AMP analogues to particle-bound PD is fairly well correlated with the ability of these analogues to trigger a chemotactic response in amoebae. Although the exact function of particle-bound PD is unknown, Malchow et al (97, 98) have proposed that this enzyme could be the receptor which is responsible for the increased responsiveness of the cells to cyclic AMP. Pannbacker & Bravard (114) have suggested, however, that the particulate enzyme may function to supplement or replace external PD in establishing the concentration gradients of cyclic AMP.

Cyclic AMP-binding proteins have been detected in a variety of biological systems (57). Changes in the specific activity of such a protein(s) during slime mold morphogenesis have been described by Malkinson et al (101). PD and cyclic AMP-binding proteins appear to be distinct molecular species and it has been suggested that both proteins may serve as receptors for cyclic AMP during aggregation (101).

The plant lectin, concanavalin A (CON A), binds to specific sites ($\alpha$-1-glycoside residues) on the cell surface and, at relatively low concentrations (10 $\mu$g/ml), induces agglutination of *Dictyostelium* cells (152). At higher concentrations (50–400 $\mu$g/ml) CON A delays aggregation without affecting the morphology of the resulting sorocarps (58). It has been suggested that CON A may affect aggregation by changing the activity of PD through its interaction with the surface membrane (58). Within 30 min after amoebae have been exposed to CON A, the specific activity of isolated particulate PD is 4 times greater than that of the nonexposed controls. Similar effects of this lectin on PD activity have been observed on whole cells except that a 60 min exposure time is required before an appreciable effect on enzyme specific activity is noted. As this effect of CON A on particulate PD can be prevented by actinomycin D, it has been suggested that CON A increases the rate of synthesis of PD as opposed to unmasking a latent enzyme (58). However, a fourfold increase in enzyme level in 30 min would require an extremely high rate of enzyme synthesis, and it is also difficult to interpret this observation because of the numerous non-specific effects of actinomycin D. Since interaction of CON A with the plasma membrane may stimulate diverse metabolic events, it is possible that the effects of this plant lectin on PD activity are indirect. For example, CON A might modulate PD activity through activation of membrane-bound phospholipases (e.g. lysophospholipase and phospholipase A) which are known to be present in the amoebae (34). Such a speculation may be relevant, as it has recently been found (11) that low levels of various naturally occurring lipids (e.g lecithin, lysolecithin, phosphatidylinositol, etc) stimulate PD activity.

In addition to cyclic AMP-specific phosphodiesterase, adenylate cyclase is thought to play an important role in the chemotactic process (127, 128). Adenylate cyclase activity has been identified and a preliminary characterization of this enzyme in detergent extracts of *Dictyostelium* has been described (127). Since enzyme specific activity remains fairly constant in the presence of cycloheximide, it has been suggested that enzyme turnover is negligible. However, this does not necessarily follow, since both enzyme synthesis and degradation may be inhibited by this drug (121). If cyclase is involved in the regulation of chemotaxis, it may do so via a modulation of its catalytic properties as opposed to its level (127).

A cyclic AMP-dependent ATP pyrophosphohydrolase activity has also been detected and together with adenylate cyclase has been purified approximately 50–100-fold from extracts prepared after whole-cell sonication (128). Activation of cyclase activity by 5'-AMP and the significant degree of cooperativity between pyrophosphohydrolase activity and cyclic AMP concentration suggest that both enzymes may constitute an important regulatory loop during the aggregation process (128).

In animal as well as fungal cells (42, 43), adenylate cyclase has been shown to be membrane-associated. Since detergent completely solubilizes fungal cyclase (42, 43) and the enzyme prepared from *Dictyostelium* by detergent extraction cannot be sedimented by high speed centrifugation, it is very possible that the kinetics reported for *Dictyostelium* adenylate cyclase are those which characterize the enzyme subsequent to its solubilization. The physical state (soluble or particulate) of this enzyme in *Dictyostelium* remains to be determined. If the proposed regulatory loop is to have physiological significance, the kinetics of the response of membrane-associated cyclase to 5'-AMP must be analogous to that already known to occur with the solubilized enzyme. As some particulate enzymes are known to exhibit allotopic behavior (119), it may be unjustified to assume similar kinetic properties in the two physical states. Since the proposed loop requires that cyclic AMP be available to activate ATP pyrophosphohydrolase, definitive evidence as to the in vivo location of this second participant in the proposed loop should be obtained.

*Threonine deaminase* *Dictyostelium* contains two distinct enzymes catalyzing the deamination of threonine (94). The enzyme synthesized in growing cells is sensitive to feedback inhibition by isoleucine and is most likely a biosynthetic enzyme, while the enzyme characteristic of differentiating cells is insensitive to isoleucine and may function catabolically. Both enzymes have been partially purified and thoroughly characterized. They differ in thermosensitivity, stability to freeze-thaw, and sensitivity to inhibition by potassium phosphate. Although enzyme from vegetative cells is apparently soluble, that prepared from differentiating cells appears to be associated with a particle of greater than 600,000 mol wt. After disassociation from this structure the differentiation-specific enzyme elutes from Sepharose 6B in a manner similar to the enzyme from vegetative cells. Differentiation-specific enzyme does not appear to display allotopic properties characteristic of certain particulate enzymes, as the catalytic properties are apparently not altered by the physical state of the enzyme.

*Glycogen synthetase* As summarized earlier, there is approximately a 50% decrease in glycogen content during the culmination process, coincident with the time of rapid trehalose and cellulose accumulation (Table 1). Prior to culmination and assembly of the spore wall, glycogen synthetase is completely soluble and apparently unassociated with any structural elements of the cell. During the culmination process, a fraction of the cytoplasmic enzyme undergoes a shift in primer specificity as it becomes involved in the synthesis of glycogen-containing cell wall precursors (150, 169).

Cytoplasmic glycogen synthetase has been purified 480-fold using differential adsorption and elution from amylose (167) and its properties have been described. This enzyme catalyzes the synthesis of both soluble cytoplasmic glycogen and alkali-insoluble wall glycogen (167, 169). In contrast to wall-associated enzyme, the activity of soluble glycogen synthetase is dependent upon the presence of added primer in the assay system. In analogy to higher organisms, *Dictyostelium* contains two forms of cytoplasmic glycogen synthetase: a G6P-dependent (D) form and a G6P-independent (I) form. I-activity decreases from the amoebae to the culmination stage of development, whereas D-activity increases (126). Since total activity (I+D) is constant, the data suggest that the I form is quantitatively converted to the D form during this developmental period.

Although wall-associated enzyme does not require G6P as an allosteric effector lowering the $K_m$ for UDP-glucose, an interesting correlation can be made between primer solubility and G6P-dependency of the enzyme when not associated with the wall. The more insoluble the primer used as acceptor for glycogen synthetase, the less dependent is the enzyme on G6P for activity (150). With spore wall as primer, there is no dependency on G6P for activity.

*Glycogen phosphorylase* This enzyme holds an extremely important position of control in the saccharide interconversions occurring during differentiation, as glycogen is the ultimate source of glucose units for the synthesis of trehalose and cellulose. Simulation analyses have indicated that changes in the activity of this enzyme affect both the rate of differentiation and the final ratio of cellulose to trehalose (B. E. Wright and D. Park, unpublished data). Enzyme specific activity increases by an unknown mechanism about sixfold during differentiation, peaking at culmination

(78). The enzyme was partially purified (38, 78) and kinetic constants determined. The $K_m$ for inorganic phosphate is close to the cellular level of Pi. Recent studies of Rutherford (unpublished data) have demonstrated that Pi is preferentially localized in the stalk cells as a gradient increasing tenfold from the apical tip downwards to the basal disc. An inverse gradient of even greater magnitude occurs for stalk glycogen, strongly suggesting that the Pi level is an important critical variable controlling the rate of glycogen degradation. Another variable of obvious importance is cyclic AMP, which elicits the rapid depletion of glycogen in vivo (126). Adenylic acid (5'AMP) stimulates both glycogen degradation and synthesis. No evidence for the mechanism of action of cyclic AMP is yet available, but 5'AMP appears to act at least in part by overcoming the inhibition of glycogen phosphorylase by glucose-1-phosphate.

*T6P synthetase* A major carbohydrate endproduct of differentiation in *Dictyostelium* is the nonreducing disaccharide, α-α'-trehalose. In mature sorocarps, the content of this sugar amounts to 1.5% of the cell dry weight and comprises 11% of the total anthrone-positive material. Trehalose is detectable in extracts prepared throughout the life cycle (14). Dramatic increases in the rate of trehalose accumulation, however, occur late in the culmination process, resulting in an approximate tenfold increase in trehalose content between the culmination (19 hr) and sorocarp (28 hr) stages of development (see Table 1).

T6P synthetase catalyzes the synthesis of T6P, the immediate precursor of trehalose (12), from UDP-glucose and glucose 6-phosphate. The presence of T6P synthetase activity in cell-free extracts of both the wild-type and axenic strains (47, 131, 151) of *Dictyostelium* has been established. The stoichiometry of this reaction has been confirmed and the properties of T6P synthetase activity in crude extracts have been described (130, 131). In an analysis of this enzyme during morphogenesis, Roth & Sussman (131) observed that T6P synthetase activity first became detectable in vitro after 5 hr of development. Enzyme specific activity reached its maximum value at preculmination (16 to 18 hr from the initiation of starvation) and then rapidly declined during the remainder of development (131).

Kinetic models have been constructed by Wright & Marshall (171) which simulate the observed accumulation pattern of trehalose during differentiation. These models have predicted that T6P synthetase cannot increase in activity in vivo during that time period suggested by the specific activity profile [i.e. 5 to 16 hr of development (131)]. This prediction was substantiated by Sargent & Wright (134) with in vivo studies on the rate of trehalose synthesis. The rate of trehalose synthesis was determined between the aggregation and late culmination stages of development. Although trehalose is present at all stages of differentiation, the rate of turnover is insignificant prior to late culmination [about 20 hr after initiation of development (134)]. At that time, the rate of synthesis increases about a hundredfold over a 2 hr period. Using a bimolecular initial velocity expression, cellular substrate concentrations, and $K_m$ values, the maximum rate of trehalose synthesis observed in vivo requires an enzyme specific activity ($V_v$; see section on metabolite flux) of approximately 100 μmoles/30 min/mg protein (170). This value is about 160-fold higher than the maximum specific activity initially observed in vitro (131, 170).

Based upon the striking changes in the rate of trehalose synthesis observed in these in vivo studies, it was suggested (171) that a primary critical variable in the initiation of trehalose synthesis late in culmination may be some type of activation mechanism, e.g. the release of masked T6P synthetase, the activation or synthesis of T6P phosphatase, or decompartmentation.

Since a maximal enzyme specific activity was obtained in extracts prepared approximately 4–6 hr before a significant rate of trehalose synthesis is observed in vivo, it would appear that modulation of T6P synthetase activity in vivo late in the culmination process results primarily from a change in catalytic properties or decompartmentation as opposed to a change in enzyme level.

Variations in the specific activity of any enzyme examined in crude extracts prepared during development in *Dictyostelium* may result from the presence or absence of inhibitors or activators of the enzyme being studied. In general, extracts prepared at those developmental stages showing minimal and maximal specific activity are mixed. A comparison of the theoretical with the experimental activity of this mixture is considered by most investigators to provide information on the presence or absence of potential modulators of catalysis. Demonstration of an inhibitor in a low-activity extract using this mixing procedure, however, depends upon the presence of a level of free inhibitor (not associated with enzyme) sufficiently high to inactivate enzyme in the high activity extract and upon the absence of inactivators of the inhibitor in the latter extract. Moreover, any metabolite present in the high activity extract (or assay system) which can increase the rate of dissociation of the enzyme-inhibitor complex will play a role in determining the amount of enzyme remaining in the inactive complex and hence the degree of final inhibition observed.

In analyzing the basis of the low T6P synthetase activity in 5-hr amoebae extracts relative to that observed at preculmination, Roth & Sussman (130) mixed extracts prepared at these two developmental stages and compared the activity of the mixture with the theoretical value which was to be expected if no inhibitor were present in the low activity extract. In the absence of carrier trehalose there was a 56% inhibition of the summed activity, while in the presence of trehalose, inhibition was reduced to 39%. (The values may have differed had initial velocities been measured.) It is apparent from these observations that amoebae extracts contain an inhibitor(s) of T6P synthetase at a level sufficiently high to inhibit enzyme present in a mixture of amoebae and preculmination extracts. The inhibitor(s) may be responsible for the low T6P synthetase activity in amoebae extracts. Although the level of the inhibitor in amoebae extracts is sufficiently high to titrate free enzyme in preculmination extracts, the available data do not provide information on the amount of either inhibitor or enzyme present as inactive enzyme-inhibitor complex in these extracts. Since activity can be detected at a low level in amoebae extracts, even in the presence of an apparently high concentration of inhibitor, this suggests that inhibition is reversible and that active enzyme results from dissociation of the enzyme-inhibitor complex in the extract and/or during the assay. Support of such a view comes from the observations of Killick & Wright (80) who have obtained evidence for a latent (masked) form of T6P synthetase in amoebae extracts. These studies have recently been extended using conditions of enzyme preparation, stabilization, and assay, which result in maximal specific activity at each stage of development. Overt T6P synthetase activity per cell appears to remain relatively constant throughout differentiation, and, available evidence suggests that this enzyme exists in both an overt and a latent form in extracts prepared at preculmination (K. A. Killick and B. E. Wright, unpublished data). The specific activity of T6P synthetase after unmasking latent enzyme is approximately one half that required ($V_v$) to achieve the maximum rate of trehalose synthesis observed in vivo (170). It is probable that other variables play an important role in the in vivo modulation of T6P synthetase activity in addition to the unmasking mechanism. The relationship between the in vitro masking and in vivo latency of this enzyme which is known to exist at this as well as earlier stages of morphogenesis remains to be further investigated.

## FUTURE PROSPECTS

The changes in vivo in enzyme activity which occur during development in *Dictyostelium* may be mediated by: (*a*) changes in enzyme level, (*b*) modulation of catalytic properties, and (*c*) decompartmentation phenomenon. Since the differentiating cellular slime mold is a metabolically closed system, the most energetically advantageous mechanisms may play a particularly prominent role in regulation.

The only enzyme which has been shown to increase in specific activity during development as a result of an increase in its concentration is UDP-glucose pyrophosphorylase and future studies will undoubtedly extend this observation to many other enzymes. We speculate that the majority of these enzymes will be shown to change in concentration as a result of alterations in the degradative phase of enzyme turnover, and only secondarily in response to changes in the rates of synthesis. In systems other than *Dictyostelium,* current provocative studies have suggested that regulation of the rates of degradation of specific enzymes may be exerted primarily by the unmasking of latent inactivating enzymes as well as the inactivation of their overt counterparts. Moreover, the participation of various organelles (e.g. microsomes and lysosomes) as well as the importance of the energy state of a cell in the regulation of protein degradation has been demonstrated. It is probable that similar if not identical mechanisms are involved in the regulation of enzyme degradation in *Dictyostelium.*

Evidence for modification of the catalytic properties of an enzyme by proteolytic and nonproteolytic enzymes, as well as by complex formation with regulatory proteins, has been well documented for many systems. This particular area of contemporary biochemistry should receive more attention with respect to *Dictyostelium,* as the above mechanisms are particularly suited to regulating metabolism in this system. For example, control of the catalytic properties of an enzyme by enzyme-catalyzed interconversion reactions has a significantly smaller energy requirement than that associated with regulation via an alteration in enzyme level. The increased capacity for effector binding sites and the possibility for cascade amplification are two additional characteristics which make this form of modification an attractive means of controlling enzyme activity in a starving developmental system such as the cellular slime mold. At present, preliminary evidence suggests that the activities of at least three enzymes [i.e. glycogen synthetase, glycogen phosphorylase, and glutamate dehydrogenase (F. DeToma, unpublished data)] may be modified by interconversion reactions analogous to those known to occur for these enzymes in higher organisms. Other interconvertible enzymes as well as new mechanisms for the modification of catalytic properties will probably be detected in *Dictyostelium* in the years to come.

Although *Dictyostelium* is one of the simplest and most thoroughly analyzed of differentiating systems, mechanisms underlying biochemical differentiation are just beginning to be discerned and defined. Thus far, investigators have been primarily concerned with correlating various biochemical events with successive stages of development. Criteria must now be established for deciding which of these events are critical mechanistically, that is, limiting the rate of differentiation. The information now available in *Dictyostelium* on metabolite levels and flux in vivo is of particular importance to a dynamic analysis of the many variables operative during differentiation under the steady-state conditions of the living cell. Only an integration of these complex variables essential to differentiation can reveal those which are critical at particular points in time.

## Acknowledgments

This work was supported by research grants HD05357 and HD04667 from the National Institutes of Health, and GB15055 from the National Science Foundation to Barbara E. Wright and by a Special Fellowship (1F03 6M 53117-01) from the National Institutes of General Medical Sciences to Kathleen A. Killick.

For constructive criticisms of the manuscript, we are indebted to Drs. W. Loomis, E. Bell, G. Gustafson, E. Coe, and J. Gross. We are also grateful to our many colleagues for making available unpublished material; unfortunately, only a portion of this was relevant to the orientation of this review. We appreciate the generosity of Dr. H. Hohl in providing the electron micrographs (Figure 1), which are printed with the permission of the publishers, *Journal of Bacteriology* (23) and *Journal of Ultrastructure Research* (72). Finally, we wish to thank Mrs. Carol Hoben for her patience and expertise in the preparation of this manuscript.

*Literature Cited*

1. Ashworth, J. M. 1971. *Symp. Soc. Exp. Biol.* 25:27–49
2. Ashworth, J. M. 1974. *MTP International Review of Science,* ed. J. Paul. In press
3. Ashworth, J. M., Duncan, D., Rowe, A. J. 1958. *Exp. Cell. Res.* 58:73–78
4. Ashworth, J. M., Sussman, M. 1967. *J. Biol. Chem.* 242:1696–1700
5. Barkley, D. S. 1969. *Science* 165: 1133–54
6. Beng, H., Katz, F. E., Gerisch, G. 1973. *J. Cell Biol.* 56:647–58
7. Bonner, J. T. 1947. *J. Exp. Zool.* 106: 1–26
8. Bonner, J. T. 1967. *The Cellular Slime Molds.* Princeton, NJ: Princeton Univ. Press. 205 pp.
9. Bonner, J. T. 1969. *Sci. Am* 220:78–91
10. Bonner, J. T. 1971. *Ann. Rev. Microbiol.* 25:75–92
11. Bublitz, C. 1973. *Biochem. Biophys. Res. Commun.* 52:173–80
12. Cabib, E., Leloir, L. 1958. *J. Biol. Chem.* 231:259–75
13. Ceccarini, C. 1967. *Biochim. Biophys. Acta* 148:114–24
14. Ceccarini, C., Filosa, M. 1965. *J. Cell. Comp. Physiol.* 66:135–40

15. Chang, C., Moog, F. 1972. *Biochim. Biophys. Acta* 258:154–65
16. Ibid 166–77
17. Chang, Y. Y. 1968. *Science* 161:57–59
18. Chassy, B. M. 1972. *Science* 175: 1016–18
19. Clark, M. A., Francis, D., Eisenberg, R. 1973. *Biochem. Biophys. Res. Commun.* 52:672–78
20. Cleland, S. V., Coe, E. L. 1968. *Biochim. Biophys. Acta* 156:44–50
21. Ibid 1969. *Biochim. Biophys. Acta* 192:446–54
22. Coston, M. B., Loomis, W. F. Jr. 1969. *J. Bacteriol.* 100:1208–17
23. Cotter, D. A., Miura-Santo, L. Y., Hohl, H. R. 1969. *J. Bacteriol.* 100: 1020–26
24. Cotter, D. A., Raper, K. B. 1966. *Proc. Nat. Acad. Sci. USA* 56:880–87
25. Cotter, D. A., Raper, K. B. 1970. *Develop. Biol.* 22:112–28
26. Deering, R. A., Adolf, A. C., Silver, S. M. 1972. *Int. J. Radiat. Biol.* 21:235–45
27. Dimond, R. L., Brenner, M., Loomis, W. F. Jr. 1973. *Proc. Nat. Acad. Sci. USA.* 70:3356–60
28. Dvorak, H. F., Anraku, Y., Heppel, L. A. 1966. *Biochem. Biophys. Res. Commun.* 24:628–32
29. Ellingson, J. S., Telser, A., Sussman, M. 1971. *Biochim. Biophys. Acta* 244: 380–95
30. Erdos, G. W., Nickerson, A. W., Raper, K. B. 1973. *Develop. Biol.* 32:321–30
31. Erdos, G. W., Raper, K. B., Vogen, L. K. 1973. *Proc. Nat. Acad. Sci. USA* 70:1828–30
32. Every, D., Ashworth, J. M. 1973. *Biochem. J.* 133:37–47
33. Farrell, C. A., DeToma, F. J. 1973. *Biochem. Biophys. Res. Commun.* 54: 1504–9
34. Ferber, E., Munder, P. G., Fischer, H., Gerisch, G. 1970. *Eur. J. Biochem.* 14: 253–57
35. Filosa, M. F., Dengler, K. 1972. *Develop. Biol.* 29:1–16
36. Firtel, R. A. 1972. *J. Mol. Biol.* 66: 363–77
37. Firtel, R. A., Baxter, L., Lodish, H. F. 1973. *J. Mol. Biol.* 79:315–27
38. Firtel, R. A., Bonner, J. 1972. *Develop. Biol.* 29:85–103
39. Firtel, R. A., Bonner, J. 1972. *J. Mol. Biol.* 66:339–61
40. Firtel, R. A., Jacobson, A., Lodish, H. F. 1972. *Nature New Biol.* 239:225–28
41. Firtel, R. A., Lodish, H. F. 1973. *J. Mol. Biol.* 79:295–314
42. Flawia, M. M., Torres, H. N. 1972. *J. Biol. Chem.* 247:6873–79
43. Flawia, M. M., Torres, H. N. 1972. *J. Biol. Chem.* 247:6880–83
44. Francis, D. 1969. *Quart. Rev. Biol.* 44:277–90
45. Franke, J., Sussman, M. 1971. *J. Biol. Chem.* 246:6381–88
46. Franke, J., Sussman, M. 1973. *J. Mol. Biol.* 81:173–85
47. Garrod, D., Ashworth, J. M. 1973. *Symp. Soc. Gen. Microbiol.* 23:407–35
48. George, R. P., Albrecht, R. M., Raper, K. B., Sachs, I. B., MacKenzie, A. P. 1970. *Proc. Cambridge Stereoscan Colloq.,* 159–65
49. George, R. P., Albrecht, R. M., Raper, K. B., Sachs, I. B., MacKenzie, A. P. 1972. *J. Bacteriol.* 112:1383–86
50. George, R. P., Hohl, H. R. 1972. *J. Gen. Microbiol.* 70:477–89
51. Gerisch, G., Malchow, D., Reidel, V., Müller, E., Every, M. 1972. *Nature New Biol.* 235:90–92
52. Gerisch, G., Malchow, D., Wilhelms, H., Lüderitz, O. 1969. *Eur. J. Biochem.* 9:229–36
53. Gezelius, K. 1961. *Exp. Cell Res.* 23: 300–10
54. Gezelius, K. 1972. *Arch. Mikrobiol.* 85: 51–76
55. Gezelius, K., Ranby, B. G. 1957. *Exp. Cell Res.* 12:265–89
56. Gezelius, K., Wright, B. E. 1965. *J. Gen. Microbiol.* 38:309–27
57. Gill, G. N., Garren, L. D. 1971. *Proc. Nat. Acad. Sci. USA* 68:786–89
58. Gillette, M. U., Filosa, M. F. 1973. *Biochem. Biophys. Res. Commun.* 53: 1159–66
59. Githens, S., Karnovsky, M. L. 1973. *J. Cell. Biol.* 58:522–35
60. Gregg, J. H., Aldrich, H. C. 1972. *J. Cell Biol.* 55:95a
61. Gregg, J. H., Badman, W. S. 1970. *Develop. Biol.* 22:96–111
62. Gregg, J. H., Nesom, M. G. 1973. *Proc. Nat. Acad. Sci. USA* 70:1630–33
63. Gustafson, G. L., Kong, W. Y., Wright, B. E. 1973. *J. Biol. Chem.* 248:5188–96
64. Gustafson, G. L., Wright, B. E. 1971. *Fed. Proc.* 30:1069 (Abstr.)
65. Gustafson, G. L., Wright, B. E. 1972. *CRC Crit. Rev. Microbiol.* 1:453–78
66. Gustafson, G. L., Wright, B. E. 1973. *Biochem. Biophys. Res. Commun.* 50:438–42
67. Gustafson, G. L., Wright, B. E. 1973. *Fed. Proc.* 32:652 (Abstr.)
68. Hames, B. D., Weeks, G., Ashworth, J. M. 1972. *Biochem. J.* 126:627–33
69. Hemmes, D. E., Kojima-Buddenhagen, E. S., Hohl, H. R. 1972. *J. Ultrastruct. Res.* 41:406–17

70. Hirschberg, E., Ceccarini, C., Osnos, M., Carchman, R. 1968. *Proc. Nat. Acad. Sci. USA* 61:316–23
71. Hohl, H. R. 1965. *J. Bacteriol.* 90: 755–65
72. Hohl, H. R., Hamamoto, S. T. 1969. *J. Ultrastruct. Res.* 26:442–53
73. Hohl, H. R., Jehli, J. 1973. *Arch. Mikrobiol.* 92:179–87
74. Honig, G. R., Rabinowitz, M. 1965. *Science* 149:1504–6
75. Hultin, H. O. 1972. *J. Food Sci.* 37: 524–29
76. Ikeda, T., Takeuchi, I. 1971. *Develop. Growth Differentiation* 13:221–29
77. Jacobson, A., Firtel, R. A., Lodish, H. F. *Proc. Nat. Acad. Sci. USA* In press
78. Jones, T. H., Wright, B. E. 1970. *J. Bacteriol.* 104:754–61
79. Killick, K. A., Wright, B. E. 1972. *Biochem. Biophys. Res. Commun.* 48:1476–81
80. Killick, K. A., Wright, B. E. 1972. *J. Biol. Chem* 247:2967–69
81. Konijn, T. M., Van de Meere, J. C. C., Bonner, J. T., Barkley, D. S. 1967. *Proc. Nat. Acad. Sci. USA* 58:1152–54
82. Korinek, J., Spelsberg, T. C., Mitchell, W. M. 1973. *Nature New Biol.* 246: 455–58
83. Lee, K. C. 1972. *J. Cell. Sci.* 10:229–48
84. Liddel, G. U., Wright, B. E. 1961. *Develop. Biol.* 3:265–76
85. Lieberherr, M., Vreven, J., Vaes, G. 1973. *Biochim. Biophys. Acta* 293: 160–69
86. Lockard, R. E., Lingrel, J. B. 1969. *Biochem. Biophys. Res. Commun.* 37: 204–12
87. Long, B. H., Coe, E. L. 1973. *J. Biol. Chem.* 249:521–29
88. Loomis, W. F., Jr. 1969. *J. Bacteriol.* 99:65–69
89. Ibid 97:1149–54
90. Ibid 100:417–22
91. Ibid 1208–17
92. Ibid 1970. 103:375–81
93. Loomis, W. F. Jr. 1972. *Nature New Biol.* 240:6–9
94. Loomis, W. F. Jr. 1973. *J. Biol. Chem.* 248:4867–73
95. Maeda, Y. 1971. *Develop. Growth Differentiation* 13:211–19
96. Maeda, Y., Takeuchi, I. 1969. *Develop. Growth Differentiation* 11:232–45
97. Malchow, D., Fuchila, J., Jastorff, B. 1973. *FEBS Lett.* 34:5–9
98. Malchow, D., Nagele, B., Schwarz, H., Gerisch, G. 1972. *Eur. J. Biochem.* 28:136–42
99. Malkinson, A. M., Ashworth, J. M. 1972. *Biochem. J.* 127:611–12
100. Ibid 1973. 134:311–19
101. Malkinson, A. M., Kwasniak, J., Ashworth, J. M. 1973. *Biochem. J.* 133: 601–3
102. Marshall, R., Sargent, D., Wright, B. E. 1970. *Biochemistry* 9:3087–94
103. Mandelstam, J. 1971. *Symp. Soc. Exp. Biol.* 25:27–49
104. Mercer, E. H., Shaffer, B. M. 1960. *J. Biophys. Biochem. Cytol.* 7:353–56
105. Naito, Y. 1972. *Physiol. Chem. Phys.* 4:27–36
106. Newell, P. C. 1971. *Essays Biochem.* 7:87–126
107. Newell, P. C., Franke, J., Sussman, M. 1972. *J. Mol. Biol.* 63:373–82
108. Newell, P. C., Longlands, M., Sussman, M. 1971. *J. Mol. Biol.* 58:541–54
109. Newell, P. C., Sussman, M. 1969. *J. Biol. Chem.* 244:2990–95
110. Newell, P. C., Sussman, M. 1970. *J. Mol. Biol.* 49:627–37
111. Oaks, A., Bidwell, R. G. S. 1970. *Ann. Rev. Plant Physiol.* 21:43–66
112. O'Day, D. H. 1973. *Exp. Cell. Res.* 79:186–90
113. O'Day, D. H. 1974. *Cytobios.* In press
114. Pannbacker, R. G., Bravard, L. J. 1972. *Science* 175:1014–15
115. Pannbacker, R. G., Wright, B. E. 1966. *Biochem. Biophys. Res. Commun.* 24:334–39
116. Pong, S. S., Loomis, W. F. Jr. 1971. *J. Biol. Chem.* 246:4412–16
117. Ibid 1973. 248:3933–39
118. Ibid 4867–73
119. Racker, E. 1967. *Fed. Proc.* 26:1335–40
120. Raper, K. B. 1935. *J. Agr. Res.* 50:135–47
121. Reel, J. R., Kenny, F. T. 1968. *Proc. Nat. Acad. Sci. USA* 61:200–6
122. Reidel, V., Gerisch, G. 1971. *Biochem. Biophys. Res. Commun.* 42:119–24
123. Reidel, V., Malchow, D., Gerisch, G., Nagele, B. 1972. *Biochem. Biophys. Res. Commun.* 46:279–87
124. Rosen, S. D., Kafka, J. A., Simpson, D. L., Barondes, S. H. 1973. *Proc. Nat. Acad. Sci. USA* 70:2554–57
125. Rosness, P. A. 1968. *J. Bacteriol.* 96: 639–45
126. Rosness, P. A., Gustafson, G., Wright, B. E. 1971. *J. Bacteriol.* 108:1329–37
127. Rossomando, E. F., Sussman, M. 1972. *Biochem. Biophys. Res. Commun.* 47:604–10
128. Rossomando, E. F., Sussman, M. 1973. *Proc. Nat. Acad. Sci. USA* 70:1254–57
129. Roth, R., Ashworth, J. M., Sussman, M. 1968. *Proc. Nat. Acad. Sci. USA* 59:1235–42

130. Roth, R., Sussman, M. 1966. *Biochim. Biophys. Acta* 122:225–31
131. Roth, R., Sussman, M. 1968. *J. Biol. Chem.* 243:5081–87
132. Rutherford, C. L., Wright, B. E. 1971. *J. Bacteriol.* 108:269–75
133. Sakai, Y., Takeuchi, I. 1971. *Develop. Growth Differentiation* 13:231–40
134. Sargent, D., Wright, B. E. 1971. *J. Biol. Chem.* 246:5340–44
135. Schimke, R. T. 1973. *Advan. Enzymol.* 37:135–87
136. Schjeide, O. A., de Vellis, J. 1970. *Cell Differentiation.* New York: Reinhold. 606 pp.
137. Schwartz, R. J. 1973. *J. Biol. Chem.* 248:6427–35
138. Smith, J. E., Galbraith, J. C. 1970. *Advan. Microb. Physiol.* 5:45–134
139. Solomon, E. P., Johnson, E. M., Gregg, J. H. 1964. *Develop. Biol.* 9:314–16
140. Sussman, M. 1954. *J. Gen. Microbiol.* 10:110–20
141. Sussman, M. 1967. *Fed. Proc.* 26:77–83
142. Sussman, M. 1972. In *Biochemistry of the Glycosidic Linkage,* ed. R. Piras, H. G. Pontis, 431–48. New York: Academic. 787 pp.
143. Sussman, M. 1972. *Develop. Biol.* 28:f–13–20
144. Sussman, M., Sussman, R. 1965. *Biochim. Biophys. Acta* 108:463–73
145. Sussman, M., Sussman, R. 1969. *Symp. Soc. Gen. Microbiol.* 14:403–35
146. Suzuki, Y., Brown, D. D. 1972. *J. Mol. Biol.* 63:409–29
147. Suzuki, Y., Gage, L. P., Brown, D. D. 1972. *J. Mol. Biol.* 70:637–49
148. Telser, A., Sussman, M. 1971. *J. Biol. Chem.* 246:2252–57
149. Vreven, J., Lieberherr, M., Vaes, G. 1973. *Biochim. Biophys. Acta* 293:170–77
150. Ward, C., Wright, B. E. 1965. *Biochem.* 4:2021–27
151. Washington, A. C. 1971. *Correlation of enzyme activity and trehalose accumulation during the development of the slime mold, Dictyostellum discoideum.* PhD Thesis. Illinois Inst. Technol. Chicago. 76 pp.
152. Weeks, G. 1973. *Exp. Cell Res.* 76:476–70
153. Weeks, G., Ashworth, J. M. 1972. *Biochem. J.* 126:617–26
154. White, G. J., Sussman, M. 1961. *Biochim. Biophys. Acta* 53:285–93
155. Widnell, C. C., Unkeless, J. C. 1968 *Proc. Nat. Acad. Sci. USA* 61:1050–57
156. Wiener, E., Ashworth, J. M. 1970. *Biochem. J.* 118:505–12
157. Woolley, D. 1972. *Arch. Biochem. Biophys.* 150:519–30
158. Wright, B. E. 1960. *Proc. Nat. Acad. Sci. USA* 46:798–803
159. Wright, B. E. 1963. *Ann. NY Acad. Sci.* 102:740–54
160. Wright, B. E. 1963. *Bacteriol. Rev.* 27:273–81
161. Wright, B. E. 1964. In *Biochemistry and Physiology of Protozoa,* ed. S. H. Hutner, 3:341–81. London: Academic. 616 pp.
162. Wright, B. E. 1968. *J. Cell. Physiol.* 72:Suppl. 1, 145–60
163. Wright, B. E. 1972. *Develop. Biol.* 28:f–13–20
164. Wright, B. E. 1973. *Critical Variables in Differentiation.* Englewood Cliffs, NJ: Prentice-Hall. 109 pp.
165. Wright, B. E., Anderson, M. L. 1960. *Biochim. Biophys. Acta* 43:62–66
166. Wright, B. E., Anderson, M. L. 1960. *Biochim. Biophys. Acta* 43:67–78
167. Wright, B. E., Dahlberg, D. 1967. *Biochemistry* 6:2074–79
168. Wright, B. E., Dahlberg, D. 1968. *J. Bacteriol.* 95:983–85
169. Wright, B. E., Dahlberg, D., Ward, C. 1968. *Arch. Biochem. Biophys.* 124:380–85
170. Wright, B. E., Gustafson, G. L. 1972. *J. Biol. Chem.* 247:7875–84
171. Wright, B. E., Marshall, R. 1971. *J. Biol. Chem.* 246:5335–39
172. Wright, B. E., Rosness, P., Jones, T. H., Marshall, R. 1973. *Ann. NY Acad. Sci.* 210:51–63
173. Yabuno, K. 1971. *Develop. Growth Differentiation* 13:181–90
174. Yamada, T., Yanagisawa, K. O., Ono, H., Kanagisawa, K. 1973. *Proc. Nat. Acad. Sci. USA* 70:2003–5

# INCLUSION BODIES OF PROKARYOTES

◆1635

*J. M. Shively*
Department of Biochemistry, Clemson University, Clemson, South Carolina 29631

CONTENTS

INTRODUCTION .......... 167
NONMEMBRANE-ENCLOSED INCLUSIONS .......... 168
*Polyglucoside (α, Glycogen) Granules* .......... 168
*Polyphosphate (Volutin, Metachromatic) Granules* .......... 168
*Cyanophycin (Structured) Granules* .......... 170
*Phycobilisomes* .......... 171
*Crystals and Paracrystalline Arrays* .......... 172
*Tubules, Microtubules, and Raphidosomes* .......... 176
MEMBRANE-ENCLOSED INCLUSIONS .......... 176
*Polyglucoside (Glycogen) Granules* .......... 176
*Poly-β-hydroxybutyrate Granules* .......... 178
*Sulfur Globules* .......... 179
*Gas Vacuoles* .......... 179
*Polyhedral Bodies (Carboxysomes)* .......... 180
*Chlorobium Vesicles* .......... 182
OTHER INCLUSIONS .......... 184
CONCLUDING REMARKS .......... 185

## INTRODUCTION

This review summarizes our current knowledge of prokaryotic inclusion bodies. The inclusions have been divided into two major groups based on the presence or absence of a surrounding membrane. A third group (see section: OTHER INCLUSIONS) includes those which, due to a lack of information, could not be classified.

Comparisons of the inclusion bodies of prokaryotes and eukaryotes, evaluations of experimental methodology, and a discussion of endospores (36, 42, 43, 54, 130) and ribosomes (70, 83) are not included. Only the structure of the inclusions revealed by electron microscopy is described, i.e. light microscope appearances are not presented.

The literature cited has been reduced to what this author feels is a listing of the most pertinent references. When a recent review is available it is listed following the section title, e.g. *Polyphosphate Granules* (46), and the reader is directed to this review for more details, background information, and literature citations.

## NONMEMBRANE-ENCLOSED INCLUSIONS

### *Polyglucoside (α, Glycogen) Granules*

Many prokaryotic organisms have been shown to store polymers of glucose (9, 14, 24, 72, 86, 96, 139). The polyglucoside may be dispersed throughout the cytoplasm or deposited as membrane-enclosed (see below) or nonmembrane-enclosed granules (138).

The granules consist of highly branched, high molecular weight polymers which resemble either glycogen or amylopectin (9, 24, 44, 72, 86, 96, 139). In the bacteria (Figure 1), the granules are 20–100 nm in diameter and commonly have an uneven appearance (14, 86). The granules of the blue-green algae may be crystals, spheres (Figure 2), or rods and are generally observed between the thylakoid membranes (139). The rods of *Nostoc muscorum* are 30 nm wide, 65 nm long, and consist of two equal parts (9); those of *Oscillatoria rubescens* (Figure 3) may be as long as 300 nm and are composed of 7.0 nm discs with a central pore (62). In the blue-green algae the spherical granules are generally 25–30 nm in diameter (139). The maximum size of the granule, at least those with a regular shape, may be governed by packing limitations (92). The granules are commonly very electron dense in thin sections stained with lead citrate.

Bacteria produce the polymer in response to excess carbon when nitrogen, sulfur, or phosphorous are limiting, or when the pH is low (24, 96). Granule formation in the blue-green algae is correlated with active photosynthesis (72, 139). The polymer is hypothesized to be a storage form of energy and/or carbon. Synthesis in plants and bacteria occurs by the following reactions (96):

$$\text{ATP} + \alpha\text{-glucose-1-P} \rightleftharpoons \text{ADP-glucose} + \text{P P}_i$$
$$\text{ADP-glucose} + \alpha\text{-1,4-glucan} \rightleftharpoons \text{ADP} + \alpha\text{-1,4-glucosyl-glucan}$$

### *Polyphosphate (Volutin, Metachromatic) Granules* (46)

Polyphosphates are widely distributed in prokaryotes (23, 31, 46, 57, 58, 72, 82, 110, 124, 129, 138, 139). The bulk of the polyphosphate is present as linear, high molecular weight molecules, e.g. greater than 500 residues per molecule have been reported (31, 46). Small linear molecules, as well as cyclic tri-, tetra-, penta-, and hexameta-

*Figure 1* Polyglucoside granules (arrows) in *Escherichia coli.* Except where noted marker bar in all figures equals 100 nm. All micrographs are thin sections except where indicated. Courtesy of J. W. Greenawalt, Johns Hopkins University Medical School, Baltimore, Md.

*Figure 2* Polyglucoside granules (PG), cyanophycin granules (CG), and gas vacuoles (GV) of *Aphanizomenon flos-aquae.* Courtesy of R. B. Wildman (137); with permission.

*Figure 3* Isolated polyglucoside granules of *Oscillatoria rubescens:* negative stain. Courtesy of M. Jost, AEC-Michigan State University, Plant Research Laboratory, East Lansing.

*Figure 4* Polyphosphate granules (arrows) in *Thiobacillus novellus.* J. M. Shively (113); with permission.

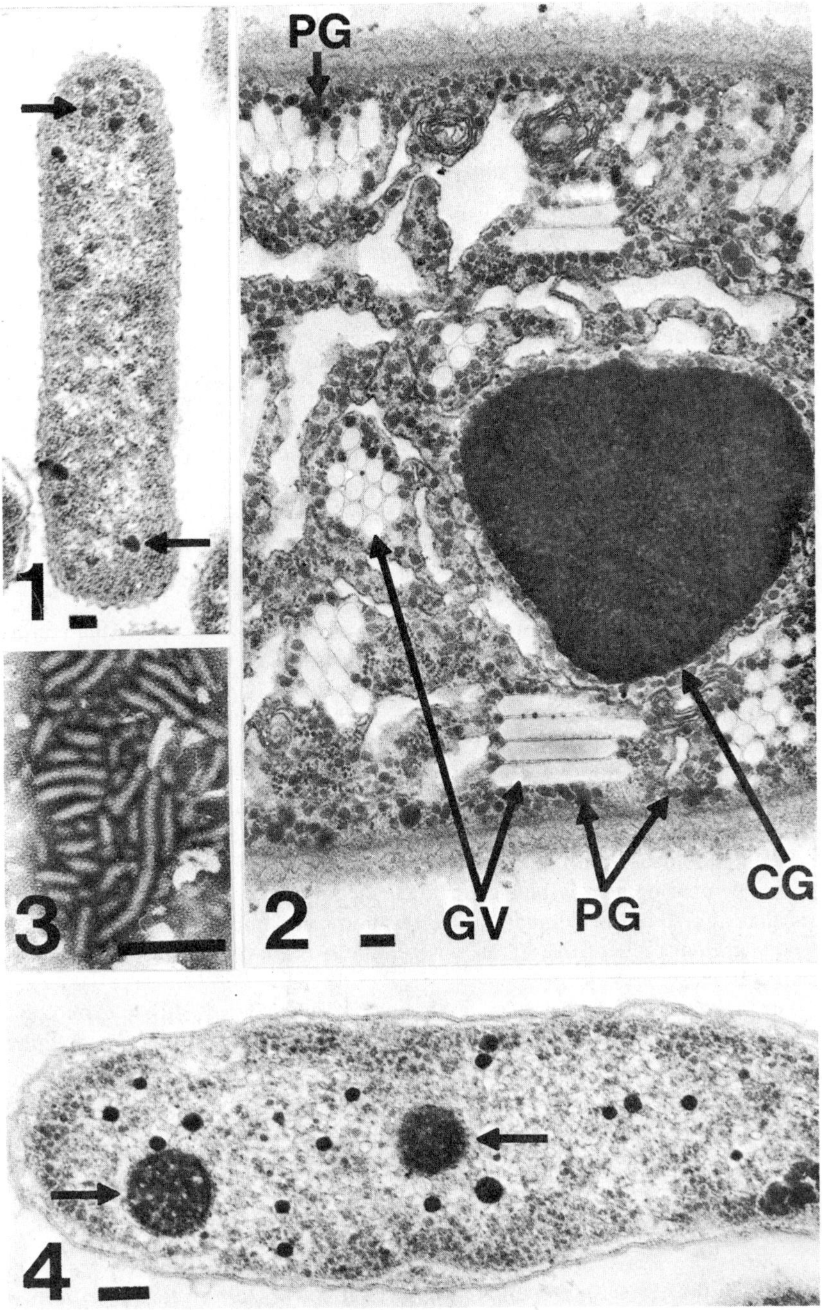
PG
1
3
2
GV
PG
CG
4

phosphates have been found in some cases (46, 82). The polyphosphate may constitute 40–50% of the total cell phosphorous (31, 72).

The polymer is commonly deposited as spherical, electron-opaque granules (Figure 4) which range in diameter from 48 nm to greater than 1 $\mu$m; size depends on the organism examined and on the state of granule development (31, 46, 56–58, 72, 114, 139). The granules are usually located in the nucleoplasmic region of the cell (56, 57, 72, 139), but have been seen in association with other cell components (46, 129). In many instances the granules reportedly evaporate in an electron-beam of high intensity and assume a "holey" or mottled appearance (46, 139). Although some researchers have observed a surrounding membrane (31, 56, 72), it is generally considered to be absent (46, 72, 114).

The presence of other constituents in the granules, e.g. RNA, DNA, protein, and lipid, is still in doubt (31, 46, 82, 139). Neimeyer & Richter (82) found that the polyphosphate of *Anacystis nidulans* was extracted with the nucleic acids but could be separated by thin-layer and column chromatography. The granules were recently isolated from *Micrococcus lysodeikticus* and found to contain 24% protein, 30% lipids, and 27% polyphosphate; some carbohydrate, nucleic acid, and polyvalent cations were also detected (31). The *M. lysodeikticus* granules do have an unusual appearance, but it appears that this preparation is grossly contaminated. Earlier reports (46) indicate that the granules are composed primarily of polyphosphate with only trace amounts of DNA, RNA, and protein.

The granules occur at a fairly constant number during the exponential phase of growth when phosphate is in excess (23, 31, 138, 139), and decrease under limiting phosphate conditions (82, 139) or during periods of cell inactivation (23, 31).

The polymer is synthesized by the enzyme, polyphosphate kinase, which catalyzes the following reaction: $ATP + (HPO_3)_n \rightleftharpoons ADP + (HPO_3)_{n+1}$ (46). How the polymer is organized into a granule is not known, but Voelz et al (129) proposed that the polymer strands are precipitated onto cytoplasmic material and become tightly coiled into granules. Harold (45) suggests that the polymer is precipitated by the high ionic strength of the cytoplasm. Jensen (57) reports a number of stages in granule development in blue-green algae including the formation of an electron translucent area in the cytoplasm, a porous body, and finally the mature, electron-opaque granule. What these stages represent must await critical isolation and characterization studies.

The polymer can be degraded by a number of enzymes (46): polyphosphate kinase, polyphosphate-adenosine monophosphate-phosphotransferase, polyphosphate glucokinase, polyphosphate fructokinase, and polyphosphatases.

The polyphosphate may function as a phosphagen, i.e. energy storage, as a phosphate reserve, or as a regulator of phosphate economy (46). Its primary function appears to be phosphate storage, but its possible role in the storage of energy should not be overlooked (8, 23, 47, 124).

### *Cyanophycin (Structured) Granules*

Cyanophycin granules are observed in most, if not all, of the blue-green algae (72). When well preserved by proper fixation, they appear in thin sections (Figure 2) as "tightly packed, undulating, flattened sacs" (72). These inclusions are without a limiting membrane and are variable in size and shape; diameters of greater than 500 nm have been reported in older cells (72, 73). Simon (115) isolated the granules from *Anabaena cylindrica* and found them to consist of 25,000–100,000 dalton molecular weight polypeptides containing arganine and aspartic acid in a 1:1 ratio.

The number of granules is lowest in cells of exponentially growing cultures and highest in cells of stationary phase cultures and akinetes. The number decreases upon germination of the akinete or upon transfer of the maximum stationary phase culture to conditions suitable for growth (72, 78, 116). Furthermore, as the cyanophycin granule polypeptide increases in the late exponential phase of growth, phycocyanin decreases.

Addition of chloramphenicol to exponentially growing cultures of *A. cylindrica* resulted in a rapid cessation of protein synthesis and growth, but an accumulation of cyanophycin granule polypeptide; the polypeptide is therefore not synthesized by a mRNA-ribosomal system (117). Upon removal of the chloramphenicol, growth resumes and the cyanophycin granule polypeptide is hydrolyzed. The cyanophycin granule polypeptide-synthesizing enzymes must be present in the cells of exponentially growing cultures; chloramphenicol rapidly inhibits protein synthesis and the polypeptide is then produced. The synthesis is an energy dependent process; (3, 4-dichlorophenyl)-1,1-dimethyl urea, a specific photophosphorylation inhibitor, blocks the synthesis of the polypeptide after the addition of chloramphenicol (117).

All of the information is consistent with the theory that the granules are cellular nitrogen reserves (117). During normal growth, amino acids are incorporated into protein, but upon cessation of growth, nitrogen fixed from the atmosphere is stored in the polypeptide.

The observation (18) that the cyanophycin granules participate in the synthesis of polyphosphate needs to be carefully evaluated.

### *Phycobilisomes* (10, 139)

Three biliproteins have been reported in the blue-green algae: C-phycocyanin (C-PC), allophycocyanin (allo-PC), and C-phycoerythrin (C-PE). C-PC and allo-PC appear to be universal constituents; C-PE may or may not be present. The chromophores, the tetrapyrrole pigments phycocyanobilin and phycoerythrobilin, are readily separated from their apoproteins (10, 139). The C-PC, allo-PC, and C-PE have maximum absorbance peaks at 615 nm, 650 nm (shoulder at 620 nm), and 565 nm, respectively. The molecular weights of the biliproteins have been a subject of some controversy. The most recent evidence indicates that the monomers of C-PC and C-PE have molecular weights of ca 30,000 and 40,000 daltons, respectively (10, 66, 125). Furthermore, the monomers, in both instances, are composed of two polypeptides of unequal size (66, 125, 139). Because the monomers aggregate to particles of varying sizes it is difficult to ascertain what the predominant in vivo species is for each biliprotein; a hexameric structure appears to be most likely (10).

The biliproteins constitute 14–28% of the cell dry weight, depending on the organism examined and growth conditions, and function in the harvest of light energy and its subsequent transfer to chlorophyl (37, 139).

Phycobilisomes, high molecular weight aggregates of C-PC, allo-PC, and frequently C-PE, were originally demonstrated in the Rhodophyta, but have subsequently been observed in many blue-green algae (22, 27, 37, 75, 136, 137). These inclusions (Figure 5) are 35–50 nm in diameter and are attached to the photosynthetic lamellae (22, 27, 37, 75, 139). It is still to be resolved whether all of the biliproteins are attached, or if a certain quantity is free in the cytoplasm (22, 27, 37, 139).

The C-PC containing phycobilisomes of *Synechococcus lividus* are described as rods, 35 nm in diameter, consisting of heptamers of smaller rods each of which is composed of a stack of dimeric discs (22). Each dimeric disc is 3.0–3.5 nm thick and 12.0–12.5 nm in diameter. It is proposed that these discs are hexamers of phycocyanin. The phycobilisomes of *Anacystis nidulans* also lack C-PE and are rod shaped (37), while those of *Nostoc* species (Figure 6), which possess all three biliproteins, are compact structures with a rounded surface and a flattened base (40 nm in diameter) which attaches the complex to the photosynthetic lamellae (37).

Isolated phycobilisomes (Figure 7) are variable in size and shape (37). This may be the result of natural heterogeneity or damage during isolation.

### *Crystals and Paracrystalline Arrays*

Several members of the genus *Bacillus* form parasporal inclusions (79, 84, 101). The best characterized, because of its toxicity to *Lepidoptera* larvae, is the parasporal crystal of *Bacillus thuringiensis* (84). The crystal (Figure 8), a bipyrimidal octahedra with a square base plane, is composed of rod-shaped subunits 4.7 nm by 11.8 nm. Norris (84) reports that the rod-shaped subunits have a molecular weight of 230,000 daltons and break down to smaller subunits upon treatment with alkali. Whether there is one or more polypeptide species is a controversial subject which has been aggravated by the use of different strains and solubilizing agents. Sayles et al (107) reported the existence of a heterogenous population of small polypeptides with molecular weights of 1,000–1,500 daltons. Herbert et al (49) found two subunits with molecular weights of 55,000 and 120,000 daltons in a ratio of 2 to 1 and Glatron et al (35) discovered only a single subunit of 80,000 dalton mol wt. The controversy is further deepened by the discovery that three antigens are associated with the spore crystal (74, 84). Norris (84) attributes these to different subunits, but Lecadet & Dedonder (74) believe that they may result from the association of an identical subunit. The crystal protein or proteins are synthesized by RNA-mediated

→

*Figure 5* Phycobilisomes (arrows) in *Microcoleus vaginatus.* Courtesy of R. B. Wildman (136); with permission.

*Figure 6* Phycobilisomes (arrows) in *Nostoc* species. Courtesy of E. Gantt (37); with permission.

*Figure 7* Isolated phycobilisomes of *Nostoc* species: negative stain. Courtesy of E. Gantt, Smithsonian Institution, Radiation Biology Laboratory, Rockville, Md.

*Figure 8* Freeze-etching of the parasporal crystal of *Bacillus thuringiensis* var. *alesti.* Courtesy of S. C. Holt, University of Massachusetts, Amherst.

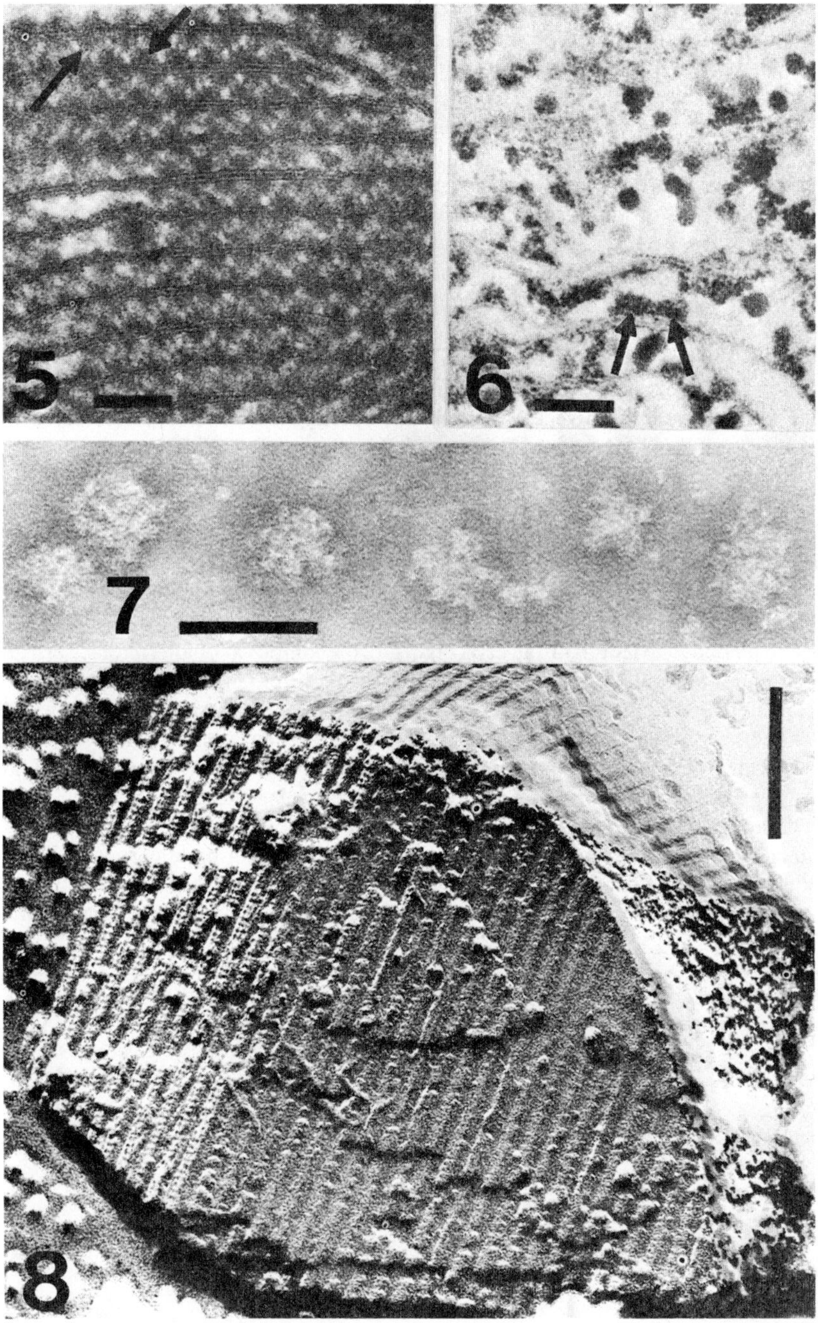
5
6
7
8

protein synthesis (142) and crystal formation may be initiated on the spore exosporium (118), or on cytoplasmic membrane invaginations (100).

The formation of the crystal is definitely linked to sporulation (84, 100, 142) and evidence indicates that the crystal protein may result from the over production of spore coat protein(s) (74, 119). In this regard, Santo & Doi (106) report crystal formation in a RNA polymerase mutant of *Bacillus subtilis* which is conditionally temperature sensitive only during sporulation (Figure 9). The crystal forms in 1–2% of the cells that do not form spores (85% of cells sporulate normally). The crystal subunits show a center to center repeat distance of 8.4 nm; the cross striation units averaged 8.5 nm by 8.5 nm. This material may be a spore protein.

Parasporal crystals have also been reported in clostridia. Pope et al (95) discovered a crystal lattice (250 nm by 160 nm by 130 nm) composed of rods (12 nm diameter) with a repeat distance of 15 nm in *Clostridium cochlearium* (Figure 10). This crystal was formed only in the sporangium. A second crystal was formed (6.5 nm periodicity) in both vegetative cells and sporangia. Norris (85) speculates that these crystals are of degenerate bacteriophage protein(s) which he has also noted in *B. thuringiensis.* More recently (20), parasporal paracrystalline inclusions (192 nm by 2,120 nm) have been found in *Clostridium perfringens* (Figure 11). They are formed only during spore morphogenesis and only by enterotoxin positive strains. It is theorized that the crystals may represent the enterotoxin.

An interesting intracytoplasmic axial fiber with a terminal structure was recently reported in a variant (rho) form of *Mycoplasma* (89). The fiber (40–120 nm wide) which extends the length of the cell (Figure 12) is composed of alternating dark and light bands with a banding periodicity of 12.0–14.5 nm (Figure 13). The structure is apparently composed of fibers laying parallel to the long axis. More recently (103) it has been shown that the fiber is a paracrystalline aggregate of fibrous protein (molecular weight 28,000 daltons) which can be disassembled and reassembled into the fiber; small amounts of other proteins may also be present.

Kim & Barksdale (65) reported the presence of a crystal in 10% of the cells of old cultures of bacterium 22 M (Figure 14). They consist of parallel rows of 7.5 nm in diameter polyhedral subunits, 2.0 nm apart and 3.0 nm between rows. These occur in cells showing degenerative processes and are not likely to be of viral origin (65).

*Figure 9* Crystal of RNA polymerase mutant of *Bacillus subtilis.* Courtesy of L. Santo (106); with permission.

*Figure 10* Parasporal crystal of *Clostridium cochlearium.* Courtesy of L. Pope (95); with permission.

*Figure 11* Paracrystalline inclusion in mutant 8–4 of *Clostridium perfringens.* Symbols: I, inclusion; OC, outer spore coat material; IC, inner spore coat material. Courtesy of C. L. Duncan (20); with permission.

*Figure 12* Axial fiber in a variant (rho) form of *Mycoplasma*: negative stain. Courtesy of J. E. Peterson (89); with permission.

*Figure 13* Segment of an isolated axial fiber of a variant (rho) form of *Mycoplasma*: negative stain. Marker bar equals 200 nm. Courtesy of J. E. Peterson (89); with permission.

*Figure 14* Crystal in bacterium 22 M. Courtesy of L. Barksdale (65); with permission.

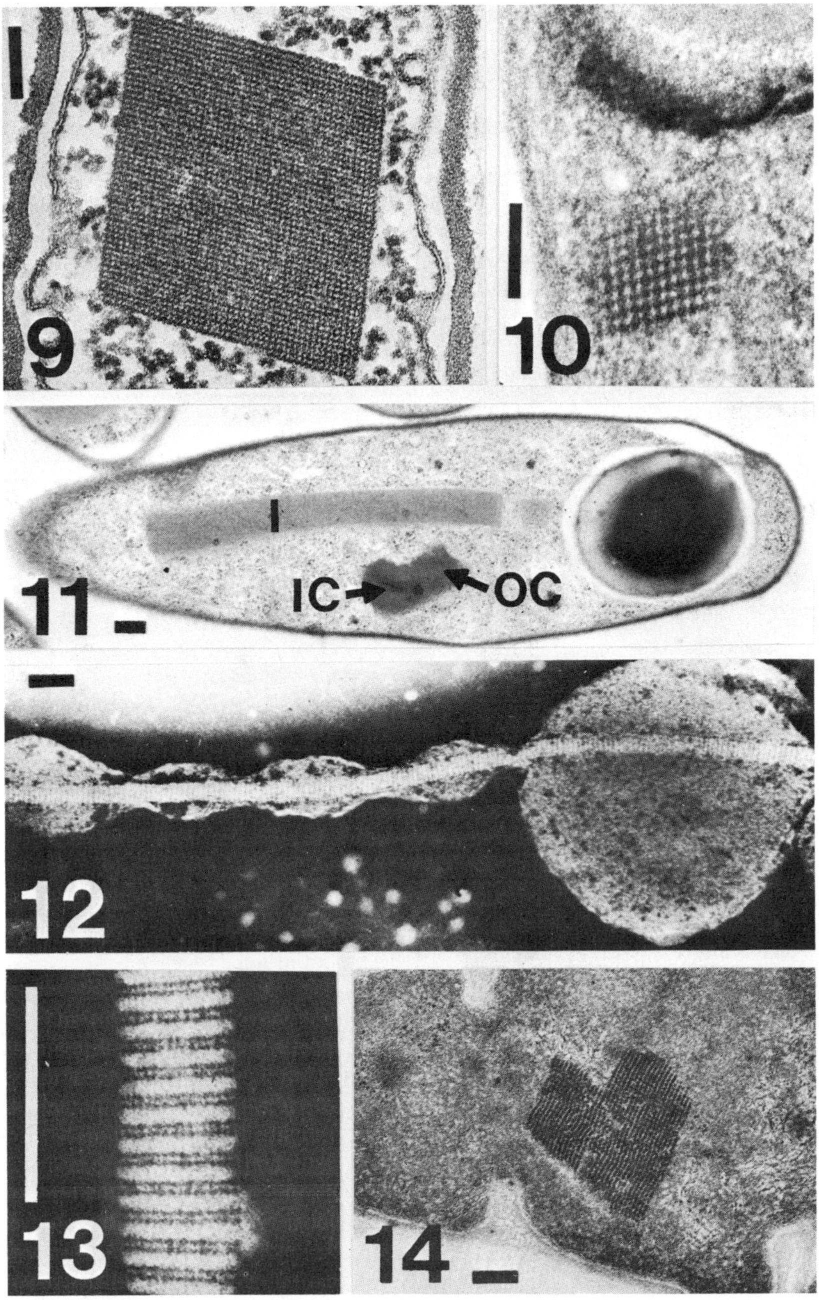
9
10
11
IC
OC
12
13
14

Crystalline inclusions have also been observed in the blue-green algae (6, 32, 59), in a root nodule endophyte (33), in the symbiotic bacteria of a leafhopper (67), and in *Thiobacillus intermedius* (113).

### *Tubules, Microtubules, and Raphidosomes*

These inclusions have been observed in a number of bacteria (12, 17, 55, 69, 88, 94, 97, 126, 140). They are variable in length in different organisms and sometimes in the same organism. Diameters from 9.0–40.0 nm have been reported (17, 55, 94, 126). Those of *Saprospira grandis* contain an outer sheath 23.0 nm in diameter (17). Some are formed only during cell lysis, are composed of lipid and protein, and are proposed to be reorganized mesosome or cytoplasmic membrane (69, 88, 126). Others are thought to be degenerative bacteriophage proteins (12, 17, 97). If some of these structures are shown not to be the result of a degenerative bacteriophage genome, their cellular function could prove interesting.

## MEMBRANE-ENCLOSED INCLUSIONS

The barrier surrounding all of these inclusions is of the nonunit membrane type, i.e. in thin section it appears as a single layer, 2.0–4.0 nm thick. Current evidence (poly-$\beta$-hydroxybutyrate, sulfur globules, gas vacuoles) indicates that the membrane is composed entirely of protein.

### *Polyglucoside (Glycogen) Granules*

Many prokaryotes have been shown to accumulate polyglucose; however, in most instances the polymer accumulates as a nonmembrane bound granule (see above). In several species of *Clostridium* [*Cl. botulinum* type E (5), *Cl. butyricum* (104), *Cl. pasteurianum* (71, 76), and *Cl. saccharobutyricum* (104)], the polyglucose granules appear to be surrounded by a single-layered membrane (Figure 15). Membrane-bound polyglucose granules have not been observed in *Clostridium tyrobutyricum* (105) and *Cl. botulinum* type A (5).

The granules first appear in the cells of early log phase cultures and become more numerous as the culture ages, reaching a maximum (ca 15% of cell dry weight) at the outset of sporulation (5, 71, 76, 122). Their initial appearance correlates well with the derepression of ADP-glucose pyrophosphorylase (71). The polymer appears to be of the amylopectin type (5, 34, 122) and molecular weights of 180,000 daltons have been recorded. Laishley et al (71) recently reported on the isolation and morphology of the granules (160–300 nm in diameter) of *Cl. pasteurianum.*

*Figure 15* Polyglucoside granules in *Clostridium pasteurianum.* Courtesy of E. J. Laishley (71). (Reproduced with permission of the National Research Council of Canada.)

*Figure 16* Poly-$\beta$-hydroxybutyrate granules *Thiobacillus (Ferrobacillus) ferrooxidans.* Courtesy of D. G. Lundgren, with permission (75a).

*Figure 17* Sulfur globules in *Chromatium weissii.* Marker bar equals 1 $\mu$m. Courtesy of G. L. Hageage, National Institute of Dental Research, Bethesda, Md.

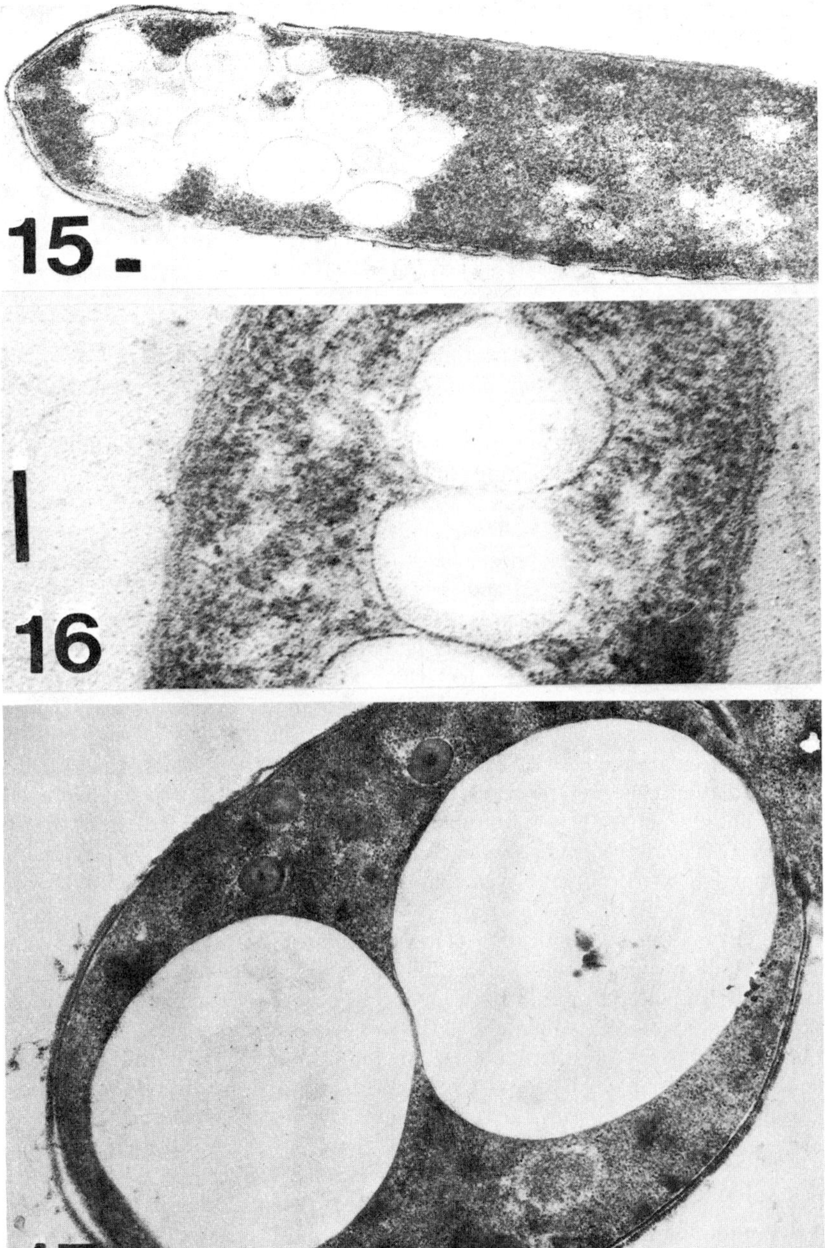
15
16
17

Freeze-etch studies revealed 12.0–16.0 nm in diameter projections in the granule matrix; these projections were hypothesized to be polymer fibrils.

Evidence indicates that the enzyme, granulose synthetase, is intimately associated with the granules (102). One could speculate that the enzyme may be an integral part of the granule membrane.

### *Poly-β-hydroxybutyrate Granules* (19)

The ability to accumulate poly-β-hydroxybutyrate (PHB) is common among the bacteria (19, 26, 48, 93, 121, 123, 133, 141) and has been reported in the blue-green algae (60, 61). PHB has recently been found to accumulate in sporulating cells of *Cl. botulinum* type E (26). As already noted, this organism has also been shown to deposit polyglucoside granules (5, 122).

The polymer accumulates, sometimes to greater than 50% of the cell dry weight (19), when carbon and energy sources are in excess. PHB is considered to be a cellular reserve of energy, or of carbon and energy (19).

The PHB is deposited in nonunit membrane-enclosed granules (Figure 16) which appear electron transparent in thin section (61, 133). Granule diameters of 100–800 nm (21, 25, 60, 141) have been reported and each granule may contain several thousand PHB molecules (25). The granules consist of 98% PHB, 2% protein, and trace amounts of lipid and phosphorous (19, 39). The surrounding membrane is 2.0–4.0 nm thick (2, 60, 133) and may arise from one layer of the cytoplasmic membrane (91). Dunlop & Robards (21), using freeze-etching, have recently demonstrated that the granules (240–720 nm in diameter) of *Bacillus cereus* consist of a central core (140–370 nm in diameter) which occupies less than 50% of the granule volume, an outer coat, and a surrounding membrane. This may indicate that the polymer is in different physical states within the granule.

The molecular weights of PHB vary to a great degree; values from 1,000 to 256,000 daltons have been reported (19). The variation may be the result of preparative techniques and/or organismic and growth state differences. Research indicates that the PHB in the granule is in a crystalline form (19, 25). The crystalline conformation of the polymer is a right-hand helix stabilized by carbonyl-methyl interaction (19).

The enzyme for polymerization of D-(–)-β-hydroxybutyryl CoA, PHB synthetase, and all or part of the depolymerizing complex (depending on the organism) are associated with the granules, presumably as part of the surrounding membrane (19, 38, 39). It is postulated that the PHB synthetase aggregates into a micellar form and the PHB is deposited within (25). The reutilization of the PHB, under conditions of energy and/or carbon starvation, involves a labile, protein, inhibitor factor (commonly associated with the granules); and activator, which counteracts the effect of the inhibitor; and the depolymerase (19, 38). The activator and depolymerase may or may not be associated with the granules (19). Barber & Nakata (2) have recently demonstrated that the initial step in the reutilization of PHB in *B. cereus* is the rupture of the granule membrane; a heat labile, trypsin sensitive protein was isolated. How this factor is involved in the above depolymerization complex remains to be elucidated. Monomers and dimers of β-hydroxybutyrate are the resulting products; the dimer is further hydrolyzed by dimer hydrolyase (19).

## *Sulfur Globules*

Sulfur globules are a distinctive feature of the *Thiorhodaceae* and of certain other apochlorotic sulfur bacteria (16, 19, 29, 40, 77, 99). The sulfur is deposited as the cells oxidize and grow in the presence of hydrogen sulfide. The sulfur globules disappear, i.e. the sulfur is oxidized, when hydrogen sulfide becomes limiting (77).

The globules are generally observed in thin sections as nonunit membrane-enclosed holes; the sulfur is removed during dehydration (Figure 17). They vary from 100 nm to over 1.0 μm in diameter and are most commonly deposited in invaginated pockets of the cytoplasmic membrane, i.e. they are inside the cell wall, but outside the cytoplasmic membrane (40, 77). Therefore, it may be erroneous to classify the sulfur globules as inclusions. However, the sulfur globules of *Thiovulum majus* (16, 29) and, in some instances, those of *Beggiatoa* and *Chromatium* (G. J. Hageage, personal communication) are found in the cytoplasm proper.

The globules have a monolayer membrane (16, 29, 40, 81, 99, 108) which consists of globular subunits, 2.5 nm in diameter (81), and is composed entirely of protein, molecular weight 13,500 daltons (109). The protein, solubilized by urea, reaggregated into sheets when the urea was removed by dialysis (109). Schmidt et al (109) speculated that the membrane provides binding sites for the enzymes responsible for sulfur metabolism.

Polarizing microscopy and X-ray diffraction studies on globules in intact cells or isolated (wet state) revealed the sulfur to be in liquid state (40, 41). During drying the sulfur passed through an unstable crystalline phase and was eventually converted to crystalline orthorhombic sulfur (40, 41).

## *Gas Vacuoles* (131, 132)

Gas vacuoles occur in many aquatic prokaryotic organisms including representatives of the blue-green algae, the photosynthetic green and purple sulfur bacteria, and a few other bacteria (Figures 2 and 18).

The gas vacuoles are complex organelles consisting of an array of substructures referred to as gas vesicles. The gas vesicles are hollow cylinders with conical ends (Figure 19). The diameter and length vary from 65–115 nm and 0.2–1.2 μm, respectively. The limiting barrier of the gas vesicle varies between 1.9 and 3.0 nm depending on the organism and the method of examination employed (thin-sectioning, shadow casting, X-ray diffraction). The vesicles have striated ribs, with a periodicity of 4.0–5.0 nm (depends on method of examination), at a right angle to the long axis of the vesicle (Figure 19). Therefore, the vesicle is proposed to be composed of either a stack of hoops or one to several continuous strands. It has been suggested that the vesicles are built of subunits 2.8–3.5 nm in diameter. This conclusion is supported by the observation of a beaded appearance in thin section when the vesicles are cut longitudinally at a right angle to the plane of the striated ribs.

X-ray diffraction studies also indicate subunits, but whether these are the same as those observed in electron microscopy remains to be proven.

The membrane appears to consist entirely of protein; phosphorous and galactose may occur in some species (68). The vesicles of the blue-green algae are partially soluble in 80% formic acid or phenol-acetic acid water and consist of a single protein species, 14,000–15,000 daltons mol wt. The gas vesicles of *Halobacterium halobium* are not soluble in the above reagents or guanidine hydrochloride, organic solvents, and pH extremes (68). Neither the blue-green alga or *Halobacterium* vesicles are soluble in detergents (28, 68).

The $pH_I$ of the blue-green alga vesicle protein is 7.0 and that of *H. halobium* is 4.0. The low $pH_I$ may reflect the phosphorous content of these vesicles (68). All of the vesicles thus far isolated have a predominance (30–33%) of amino acids with hydrophobic side chains. It has been hypothesized that the inner surface of the vesicle membrane is hydrophobic; the outer surface hydrophilic.

The membrane is rigid, i.e. it is not inflated with gas, impermeable to water, and freely permeable to all gasses. Its impermeability to water is attributed to the hydrophobic inner membrane surface. The vesicle appears to be a self-assembling structure; the body elongates after formation of the conical ends. The shape is determined by the subunit proteins.

The gas vacuoles may function in buoyancy provision, buoyancy regulation, light shielding, surface to volume regulation, or a combination of these functions.

### *Polyhedral Bodies (Carboxysomes)*

Inclusions with polygonal profiles (Figure 20) have been observed in the blue-green algae (32, 51, 59, 87, 139), and in many, but not all, of the nitrifying bacteria (80, 93, 127, 134) and thiobacilli (113, 133). They have also been observed in *Beggiatoa* (D. S. Hoare, personal communication). There are commonly several bodies per cell; 1–15 (4–6 most common) in *Thiobacillus neapolitanus* (112), 60–70 in older cells of *Thiobacillus thioparus* (113), and 200 in *Nitrococcus mobilis* (134).

As seen in thin section, the bodies are 90–500 nm in diameter (32, 51, 87, 112, 127, 134), have a granular substructure of medium electron density (87, 112, 139), are commonly located in the nucleoplasmic region of the cell (87, 112, 113), and appear to be bounded by a nonunit membrane 3.0–4.0 nm thick (87, 112, 134). A tripartite membrane less than 5.5 nm thick has been observed in some blue-green algae preparations (135).

The inclusions have been recently isolated from *T. neapolitanus* (111). By electron microscopy, the purified bodies (Figure 21) were shown to consist of a mass

*Figure 18* Freeze-etching of *Nostoc muscorum* showing gas vacuoles. Courtesy of J. R. Waaland, University of Washington, Seattle.

*Figure 19* Isolated gas vesicle from *Anabaena flos-aquae:* negative stain. Courtesy of A. E. Walsby (131); with permission.

*Figure 20* Polyhedral bodies (carboxysomes) in *Thiobacillus neapolitanus* J. M. Shively (113); with permission.

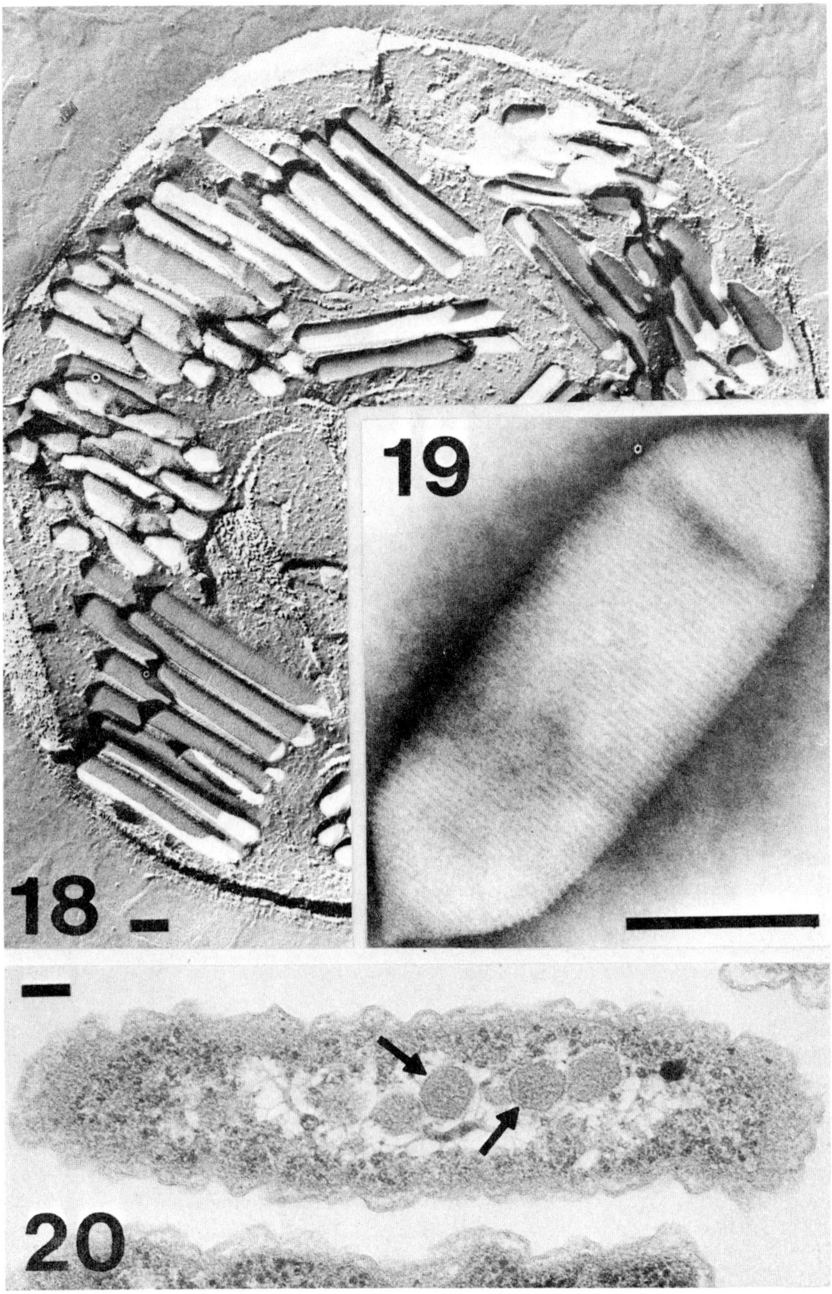
18
19
20

of 10 nm particles in a paracrystalline array surrounded by a membrane 3.5 nm thick (111, 112). The 10 nm particles (Figure 22) have been identified as ribulose-1,5-diphosphate carboxylase (111). Carboxysomes is the proposed name for the polyhedral bodies (111). The bodies are fragile and current assay conditions do not favor their stability. The presence of other components, e.g. other enzymes, remains to be established.

That the bodies from all the organisms are identical is still in doubt, but circumstantial evidence strongly supports this conclusion. All of the organisms utilize carbon dioxide as their sole source of carbon; in thin section the bodies all have essentially the same appearance; and negative stains of released but impure bodies of *Anacystis nidulans* (32) and *N. mobilis* (134) show a membrane-enclosed, paracrystalline array of particles. Research is in progress in this laboratory to prove the hypothesis.

It is tempting to propose that the bodies are active in carbon dioxide fixation, but alternatively they may be for enzyme storage. Bock & Heinrich (4) observed greater numbers of polyhedral bodies in cells of *Nitrobacter winogradskyi* stored for 200–300 days in the absence of nitrite than in reactivated cells; the loss of the bodies correlated with the degree of reactivation. Furthermore, as the reactivation proceeded the cell membranes became studded with particles resembling ribulose-1,5-diphosphate carboxylase. They also observed that 37% of the reactivated cells did not possess bodies. Remsen & Lundgren (98) published a micrograph of a *Thiobacillus (Ferrobacillus) ferrooxidans* cell which did not possess polyhedral bodies. If they are essential entities, why are they absent in some cells? It is also well known that in the blue-green algae, ribulose-1,5-diphosphate carboxylase synthesis is not repressed even in the presence of organic substrates, i.e. cultures grown in the dark with an organic substrate do not have reduced enzyme levels (7). Dark grown cells, even in the absence of carbon dioxide, have polyhedral bodies (51). One could theorize then, that since the cells do not have the ability to control ribulose-1,5-diphosphate carboxylase synthesis, the enzyme is packed away in a nonactive state until needed. The present evidence then favors a storage function, but critical experimentation needs to be undertaken. No information is available on how the bodies are assembled or disassembled.

## *Chlorobium Vesicles*

The chlorophyl, principally chlorobium chlorophyl, but also bacteriochlorophyl *a,* of the green photosynthetic bacteria is contained within vesicles (Figure 23) 30–40 nm wide by 100–150 nm long, which are bounded by a nonunit menbrane 2–3 nm

*Figure 21* Isolated carboxysomes of *Thiobacillus neapolitanus:* negative stain.

*Figure 22* Ribulose-1,5-diphosphate carboxylase from carboxysomes of *T. neapolitanus:* negative stain.

*Figure 23* Chlorobium vesicles in a ballistically opened cell of *Chloropseudomonas ethylicum:* negative stain. Courtesy of S. C. Holt (53); with permission.

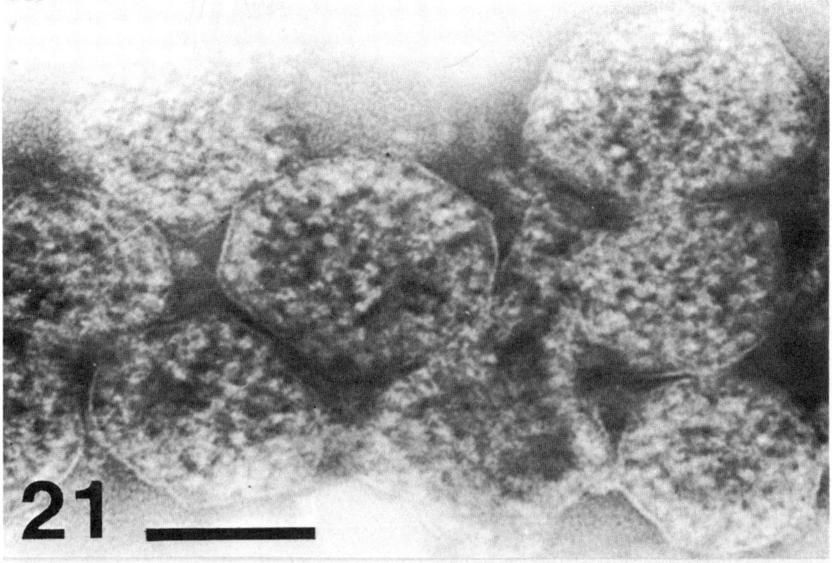
21

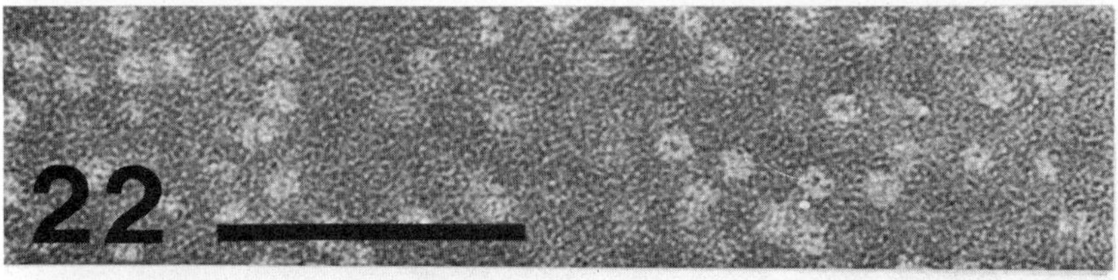
22

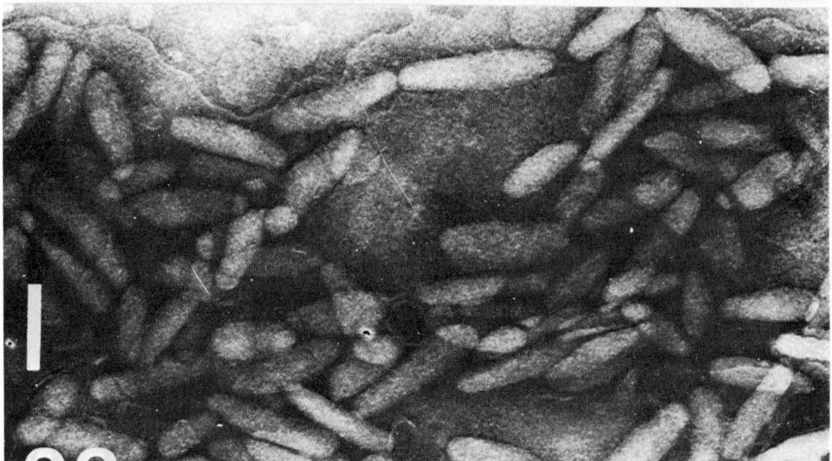
23

thick (13, 15, 52, 90). The vesicles immediately underly the cytoplasmic membrane and more or less completely line the internal periphery of the cell (13, 52, 53). The vesicles may appear either transparent or opaque in thin section depending on the embedding medium utilized (13). The vesicles themselves may be interconnected (52), but they have little, if any, association with the cytoplasmic membrane of the cell (15). Under normal growth conditions the vesicles constitute about 12% of the total cell dry weight (15); their number and their chlorophyl content is inversely proportional to the light intensity at which the cells are grown (53).

Some substructure has been observed. Cohen-Bazire et al (13) reported that the vesicles were filled with 1.0-2.0 nm wide fibrils laying parallel to the long axis of the vesicles. Circular particles, 9.0–10.0 nm in diameter, with a center hole and consisting of 5–6 subunits have also been seen (15).

On a dry weight basis, the vesicles are composed of 50% lipid, 30% protein, and 15% carbohydrate (15). Seventy-five percent of the vesicular lipid is in the chlorobium chlorophyl; the remaining 25% is glycolipid I, monogalactosyl diglyceride. Glycolipid I is not found in the cytoplasmic membrane of the cell where another glycolipid, glycolipid II, and all of the phospholipids reside. The vesicles have NADH- and NADPH-linked dye reductases, as do the cytoplasmic membranes, but lack the cytoplasmic membrane-associated enzymes, malic and succinic dehydrogenase (15). Fowler, et al (30) recently isolated a bacteriochlorophyl *a* reaction center complex from the vesicles of *Chlorobium limicola* and *Chlorobium thiosulfatophilum.* The polymeric complex with a minimum molecular weight of $1.5 \times 10^6$ daltons is composed of similar subunits and contains bacteriochlorophyl *a,* bchl-*a* protein, cytochrome 553, carotenoids, chlorophyl P-340, a small amount of chlorobium chlorophyl, and possibly other components. In this complex bacteriochlorophyl *a* alone absorbs light energy.

Obviously, the green photosynthetic bacteria have a much greater degree of structural and functional differentiation than do the other photosynthetic bacteria (90) or, for that matter, the blue-green algae (139).

## OTHER INCLUSIONS

Lipid deposits have been repeatedly reported in a number of bacteria and blue-green algae (138, 139). Many of these will probably be identified as poly-β-hydroxybutyrate, but the occurrence of other lipid deposits is entirely possible. Other inclusions in prokaryotes include the cylindrical bodies of *Trichodesmium erythraeum* (1) and *Symploca muscorum* (87); the membrane-associated protein inclusions of *Bacillus subtilis* (3); the striated organelles of *Halobacterium halobium* (11); the fibrillar organelle (16) and greenish bodies (50) of *Thiovulum majus;* the filamentous inclusions, spheroids, rosette-like inclusions, and intrathylakoidal granules of representatives of the blue-green algae (59); the large granulated body of *Corynebacterium* (63); the hydrocarbon inclusion of *Acinetobacter* (64); the calcium carbonate inclusions of *Achromatium* (120); and the ribosome studded inclusions of the myxospores of *Stigmatella arthantiaca* (128).

## CONCLUDING REMARKS

A wealth of information is available on the inclusion bodies of prokaryotes, but it is obvious that much remains to be revealed. With the availability of sophisticated experimental techniques, it is time to completely elucidate the structure of the inclusions, study the mechanisms of their assembly and disassembly, and fully assess their metabolic roles in the prokaryotic organisms.

### ACKNOWLEDGMENTS

I am deeply indebted to those who provided micrographs; to those who supplied prepublication information; to Clanton Black, University of Georgia, Athens, for his assistance with the literature survey; and to Sue Bogardus, Oya Yazar, and H. W. Raynall for their assistance in preparing the manuscript.

*Literature Cited*

1. Baalen, C. van, Brown, R. M. 1969. *Arch. Mikrobiol.* 69:79–91
2. Barber, L. C., Nakata, H. M. 1973. *Abstr. Ann. Meet. Am. Soc. Microbiol.* 73:50
3. Behme, R. J., Fitz-James, P. C. 1972. *J. Bacteriol.* 109:906–15
4. Bock, E., Heinrich, G. 1971. *Arch Mikrobiol.* 77:349–65
5. Brown, G. W. Jr., Pate, J. L., Sugiyama, H. 1971. *J. Bacteriol.* 105:1207–10
6. Butler, R. D., Allsopp, A. 1972. *Arch. Mikrobiol.* 32:283–99
7. Carr, N. G. 1973. In *Botanical Monographs. Vol. 9. The Biology of the Blue-Green Algae,* ed. N. G. Carr, B. A. Whitton, 39–65. Berkeley: Univ. California Press. 676 pp.
8. Carr, N. G., Sandhu, G. R. 1966. *Biochem. J.* 99:29P–30P
9. Chao, L., Bowen, C. C. 1971. *J. Bacteriol.* 105:331–38
10. Chapman, D. J. See Ref. 8, 162–85
11. Cho, K. Y., Doy, C. H., Mercer, E. H. 1967. *J. Bacteriol.* 94:196–201
12. Clark-Walker, G. D. 1969. *J. Bacteriol.* 97:885–92
13. Cohen-Bazire, G., Pfennig, N., Kunisawa, R. 1964. *J. Cell Biol.* 22:207–25
14. Craig, A. S., Williamson, K. I. 1972. *Arch. Mikrobiol.* 87:165–71
15. Cruden, D. L., Stanier, R. Y. 1970. *Arch. Mikrobiol.* 72:115–34
16. de Boer, W. E., La Riviere, J. W. M., Houwink, A. L. 1961. *Antonie van Leeuwenhoek J. Microbiol. Serol.* 27: 447–56
17. Delk, A. S., Dekker, C. A. 1972. *J. Mol. Biol.* 64:287–98
18. Dierksheide, W. C., Pfister, R. M. 1972. *Can. J. Microbiol.* 19:149–51
19. Doudoroff, M. 1966. *Curr. Aspects Biochem. Energ.,* 385–400
20. Duncan, C. L., King, G. J., Frieben, W. R. 1973. *J. Bacteriol.* 114:845–59
21. Dunlop, W. F., Robards, A. W. 1973. *J. Bacteriol.* 114:1271–80
22. Edwards, M. R., Gantt, E. 1971. *J. Cell Biol.* 50:896–900
23. Eigener, U., Bock, E. 1971. *Arch. Mikrobiol.* 81:367–78
24. Elbein, A. D., Mitchell, M. 1973. *J. Bacteriol.* 113:863–73
25. Ellar, D., Lundgren, D. G. 1968. *J. Mol. Biol.* 35:489–502
26. Emeruwa, A. C., Hawirko, R. Z. 1973. *J. Bacteriol.* 116:989–93
27. Evans, E. L., Allen, M. M. 1973. *J. Bacteriol.* 113:403–8
28. Falkenberg, P., Buckland, B., Walsby, A. E. 1972. *Arch. Mikrobiol.* 35:304–9
29. Fauré-Fremiet, E., Rouiller, C. 1958. *Exp. Cell Res.* 14:29–46
30. Fowler, C. F., Gray, B. H., Nugent, N. A., Fuller, R. C. 1973. *Biochim. Biophys. Acta* 292:692–99
31. Friedberg, I., Avigad, G. 1968. *J. Bacteriol.* 96:544–53
32. Gantt, E., Conti, S. F. 1969. *J. Bacteriol.* 97:1486–93
33. Gatner, E. M. S., Gardner, I. C. 1970. *Arch. Mikrobiol.* 70:183–96
34. Gavard, R., Milhaud, G. 1952. *Ann. Inst. Pasteur* 82:478–83
35. Glatron, M. F., Lecadet, M. M., Dedonder, R. 1972. *Eur. J. Biochem.* 30:330–38
36. Gould, G. W., Hurst, A., Eds. 1969.

*The Bacterial Spore*. New York: Academic. 724 pp.
37. Gray, B. H., Lipschultz, C. A., Gantt, E. 1973. *J. Bacteriol.* 116:471–78
38. Griebel, R. J., Merrick, J. M. 1971. *J. Bacteriol.* 108:782–89
39. Griebel, R. J., Smith, Z., Merrick, J. M. 1968. *Biochemistry* 7:3676–81
40. Hageage, G. J. Jr., Eanes, E. D., Gherna, R. L. 1969. *Bacteriol. Proc.* 69:38–39
41. Hageage, G. J. Jr., Eanes, E. D., Gherna, R. L. 1973. *J. Bacteriol.* 101: 464–69
42. Halvorson, H. O., Hanson, R., Campbell, L. L., Eds. 1971. *Spores,* Vol. 5. Washington, D.C.: Am. Soc. Microbiol. 471 pp.
43. Hanson, R. S., Peterson, J. A., Yousten, A. A. 1970. *Ann. Rev. Microbiol.* 24: 53–90
44. Hara, F., Akazawa, T., Kojima, K. 1973. *Plant Cell Physiol.* 14:737–45
45. Harold, F. M. 1963. *J. Bacteriol.* 86: 885–87
46. Harold, F. M. 1966. *Bacteriol. Rev.* 30:772–94
47. Healey, F. P. 1973. *CRC Crit. Rev. Microbiol.* 3:69–113
48. Heptinstall, J., Rittenhouse, H. G., McFadden, B. A., Shumway, L. K. 1972. *J. Bacteriol.* 110:363–67
49. Herbert, B. N., Gould, H. J., Chain, E. B. 1971. *Eur. J. Biochem.* 24:366–75
50. Hinze, G. 1913. *Ber. Deut. Bot. Ges.* 31:189–202
51. Hoare, D. S., Ingram, L. O., Thurston, E. L., Walkup, R. 1971. *Arch. Mikrobiol.* 78:310–21
52. Holt, S. C., Conti, S. F., Fuller, R. C. 1966. *J. Bacteriol.* 91:311–23
53. Ibid 349–55
54. Holt, S. C., Leadbetter, E. R. 1969. *Bacteriol. Rev.* 33:346–78
55. Iterson, W. van, Hoeniger, J. F. M., Zanten, E. N. van. 1967. *J. Cell Biol.* 32:1–10
56. Jensen, T. E. 1968. *Arch. Mikrobiol.* 62:144–52
57. Ibid 1969. 67:328–38
58. Jensen, T. E. 1970. *J. Cell Biol.* 47: 241A–42A
59. Jensen, T. E., Bowen, C. C. 1970. *Cytologia* 35:132–52
60. Jensen, T. E., Sicko, L. M. 1971. *J. Bacteriol.* 106:683–86
61. Jensen, T. E., Sicko, L. M. 1973. *Cytologia* 38:381–91
62. Jost, M. 1965. *Arch. Mikrobiol.* 50: 211–45
63. Kawata, T., Inoue, T. 1973. *J. Bacteriol.* 89:1613–14
64. Kennedy, R. S., Finnerty, W. R. 1971. *Bacteriol. Proc.* 71:165
65. Kim, K. S., Barksdale, L. 1969. *J. Bacteriol.* 98:1390–94
66. Kobayashi, Y., Siegelman, H. W., Hirs, C. H. W. 1972. *Arch. Biochem. Biophys.* 152:187–98
67. Korner, H. K., Feldhege, A. 1970. *Cytobiologia* 1:203–7
68. Krantz, M. J., Ballou, C. E. 1973. *J. Bacteriol.* 114:1058–67
69. Kuhrt, M., Pate, J. L. 1973. *J. Bacteriol.* 114:1309–18
70. Kurland, C. G. 1972. *Ann. Rev. Biochem.* 41:377–408
71. Laishley, E. J., MacAlister, T. J., Clements, I., Young, C. 1973. *Can. J. Microbiol.* 19:991–94
72. Lang, N. J. 1968. *Ann. Rev. Microbiol.* 22:15–46
73. Lang, N. J., Simon, R. D., Wolk, C. P. 1972. *Arch. Mikrobiol.* 83:313–20
74. Lecadet, M. M., Dedonder, R. 1971. *Eur. J. Biochem.* 23:282–94
75. Lefort-Tran, M., Cohen-Bazire, G., Pouphile, M. 1973. *J. Ultrastruct. Res.* 44:199–209
75a. Lundgren, D. G. 1972. In *Water Pollution Microbiology,* ed. R. Mitchell, 69–88. New York: Wiley. 416 pp.
76. Mackey, B. M., Morris, J. G. 1971. *J. Gen. Microbiol.* 66:1–13
77. Maier, S., Murray, R. G. E. 1965. *Can. J. Microbiol.* 11:645–55
78. Miller, M. M., Lang, N. J. 1968. *Arch. Mikrobiol.* 60:303–13
79. Mitruka, B. M., Costilow, R. N., Black, S. H., Pepper, R. E. 1967. *J. Bacteriol.* 94:759–65
80. Murray, R. G. E., Watson, S. W. 1965. *J. Bacteriol.* 89:1594–1609
81. Nicolson, G. L., Schmidt, G. L. 1971. *J. Bacteriol.* 105:1142–48
82. Niemeyer, R., Richter, G. 1969. *Arch Mikrobiol.* 69:54–59
83. Nomura, M. 1973. *Science* 179:864–73
84. Norris, J. R. 1969. *Spores,* ed. L. L. Campbell, 4:45–58. Washington, DC: Am. Soc. Microbiol. 335 pp.
85. Norris, J. R., Proctor, H. M. 1969. *J. Bacteriol.* 98:824–26
86. Orpin, C. G. 1973. *Arch. Mikrobiol.* 90:247–54
87. Pankratz, H. S., Bowen, C. C. 1963. *Am. J. Bot.* 50:387–99
88. Pate, J. L., Johnson, J. L. Ordal, E. J. 1967. *J. Cell Biol.* 35:15–35
89. Peterson, J. E., Rodwell, A. W., Rodwell, E. S. 1973. *J. Bacteriol.* 115: 411–25
90. Pfennig, N. 1967. *Ann. Rev. Microbiol.* 21:285–324

91. Pfister, R. M., Lundgren, D. G., Remsen, C. C. 1969. *Bacteriol. Proc.* 69:38
92. Pollard. E. C. 1955. In *Polysaccharides in Biology,* ed. G. F. Springer, 219–26. New York: Josiah Macy Jr. Foundation. 271 pp.
93. Pope, L. M., Hoare, D. S., Smith, A. J. 1969. *J. Bacteriol.* 97:936–39
94. Pope, L. M., Jurtshuk, P. 1967. *J. Bacteriol.* 94:2062–64
95. Pope, L. M., Yolton, D. P., Rode, L. J. 1968. *J. Bacteriol.* 96:1859–68
96. Priess, J. 1969. *Current Topics of Cellular Regulation,* ed. B. L. Horecker, E. R. Stadtman, 1:125–60. New York: Academic. 314 pp.
97. Reichenbach, H. 1967. *Arch. Mikrobiol.* 56:371–83
98. Remsen, C. C., Lundgren. D. G. 1966. *J. Bacteriol.* 92:1765–71
99. Remsen, C. C., Truper, H. G. 1973. *Arch. Mikrobiol.* 90:269–80
100. Ribier, J. 1971. *C. R. Acad. Sci. D* 273:1444–47
101. Robinow, C. F. 1960. In *The Bacteria. Vol. I. Structure,* ed. I. C. Gunsalus, R. Y. Stanier, 207–48. New York: Academic. 513 pp.
102. Robson, R. L., Robson, R. M., Morris, J. G. 1972. *Biochem. J.* 130:4P–5P
103. Rodwell, A. W., Peterson, J. E., Rodwell, E. S. 1973. *Ann. NY Acad. Sci.* 225:190–200
104. Rousseau, M., Hermier, J., Bergere, J. L. 1971. *Ann. Inst. Pasteur* 120: 23–32
105. Ibid 33–41
106. Santo, L. Y., Doi, R. H. 1973. *J. Bacteriol.* 116:479–82
107. Sayles, V. B. Jr., Aronson, J. N., Rosenthal, A. 1970. *Biochem. Biophys. Res. Commun.* 41:1126–33
108. Schmidt, G. L., Kamen, M. D. 1970. *Arch. Mikrobiol.* 73:1–18
109. Schmidt, G. L., Nicolson, G. L., Kamen, M. D. 1971. *J. Bacteriol.* 105: 1137–41
110. Shapiro, J. 1967. *Science* 155:1269–71
111. Shively, J. M., Ball, F., Brown, D. H., Saunders, R. E. 1973. *Science* 182: 584–86
112. Shively, J. M., Ball, F. L., Kline, B. W. 1973. *J. Bacteriol.* 116:1405–11
113. Shively, J. M., Decker, G. L., Greenawalt, J. W. 1970. *J. Bacteriol.* 101: 618–27
114. Sicko, L. M. 1972. *Electron Microscopy Soc. Am. Ann. Proc.* 6:218
115. Simon, R. D. 1971. *Proc. Nat. Acad. Sci. USA* 68:265–67
116. Simon, R. D. 1973. *J. Bacteriol.* 114: 1213–16
117. Simon, R. D. 1973. *Arch. Mikrobiol.* 92:115–22
118. Somerville, H. J. 1971. *Eur. J. Biochem.* 18:226–37
119. Somerville, H. J., Delafield, F. P., Rittenberg, S. C. 1968. *J. Bacteriol.* 96: 721–26
120. Starr, M. P., Skerman, V. B. D. 1965. *Ann. Rev. Microbiol.* 19:407–54
121. Stockdale, H., Ribbons, D. W., Dawes, E. A. 1968. *J. Bacteriol.* 95:1798–1803
122. Strasdine, G. A. 1968. *Can. J. Microbiol.* 14:1059–62
123. Tamura, T., Fujino, T., Kondo, M., Kotani, S. 1968. *Biken J.* 11:225–34
124. Terry, K. R., Hooper, A. B. 1970. *J. Bacteriol.* 103:199–206
125. Torjesen, P. A., Sletten, K. 1972. *Biochem. Biophys. Acta* 263:258–71
126. Ueda, M., Takagi, A. 1972. *J. Gen. Appl. Microbiol.* 18:81–98
127. Van Gool, A. P., Lambert, R., Laudelout, H. 1969. *Arch. Mikrobiol.* 69: 281–93
128. Voelz, H., Reichenbach, H. 1969. *J. Bacteriol.* 99:856–66
129. Voelz, H., Voelz, U., Ortigoza, R. O. 1966. *Arch. Mikrobiol.* 53:371–88
130. Walker, P. D. 1970. *J. Appl. Bacteriol.* 33:1–12
131. Walsby, A. E. 1972. *Bacteriol. Rev.* 36:1–32
132. Walsby, A. E. See Ref. 8, 340–52
133. Wang, W. S., Lundgren, D. G. 1969. *J. Bacteriol.* 97:947–50
134. Watson, S. W., Waterbury, J. B. 1971. *Arch. Mikrobiol.* 77:203–30
135. Wildman, R. B. 1969. *Studies on the nucleoplasm and the photosynthetic pigment system of blue-green algae.* PhD. Thesis. Iowa State Univ., Ames. 242 pp.
136. Wildman, R. B., Bowen, C. C. 1974. *J. Bacteriol.* 117:866–81
137. Wildman, R. B., Loescher, J. H. Unpublished manuscript
138. Wilkinson, J. F. 1959. *Exp. Cell Res. Suppl.* 7:111–30
139. Wolk, C. P. 1973. *Bacteriol. Rev.* 37: 32–101
140. Yamamoto, T. 1967. *J. Bacteriol.* 94: 1746–56
141. Young, H. L., Chao, F., Turnbill, C., Philpott, D. E. 1972. *J. Bacteriol.* 109: 862–68
142. Yousten, A. A., Rogoff, M. H. 1969. *J. Bacteriol.* 100:1229–36

# *LEISHMANIA* ❖1636

*R. S. Bray*
Medical Research Council Laboratories, Fajara, The Gambia

---

CONTENTS

INTRODUCTION ........ 189
THE OLD WORLD SPECIES ........ 190
*Leishmania infantum* ........ 190
*L. donovani* ........ 192
*L. tropica* ........ 195
*L. major* ........ 197
*L. aethiopica* ........ 198
THE NEW WORLD SPECIES ........ 199
*L. chagasi* ........ 199
*L. mexicana mexicana* ........ 200
*L. mexicana amazonensis* ........ 201
*L. braziliensis braziliensis* ........ 202
*L. braziliensis guyanensis* ........ 202
*L. braziliensis panamensis* ........ 203
*L. peruviana* ........ 204
*L. enriettii* ........ 204
*L. hertigi* ........ 204
THE *LEISHMANIA* OF LIZARDS ........ 205
TRANSMISSION ........ 205
FINE STRUCTURE ........ 206
BIOCHEMISTRY ........ 208
IMMUNOLOGY ........ 211

## INTRODUCTION

It has been ten years since the biology and ecology of the genus *Leishmania* (198) have been comprehensively reviewed. Certain aspects were covered by the World Health Organization (246) report of the traveling seminar to the USSR on leishmaniasis held in 1967. Apart from this report the previous review along the lines of the present review was that written by the greatest authority on the subject—the late Saul Adler (3). Since then much work on epidemiology and immunology with consequent effects upon taxonomy has been done, notably in Asiatic USSR, Iran, Sudan, Ethiopia, southern France, Senegal, British Honduras, Panama, Venezuela, and Brazil. This review will examine the past ten years since Adler's review (3) and attempt to fill any gaps in the latter which the passage of time may have revealed.

The layout reflects the interests and experience of the author which lie in the direction of geography and biology rather than clinico-pathology. Thus it is intended to treat the genus as two groups, the Old World species and the New World species, examining their ecologic and biologic facets in turn, without comment upon pathology, clinical manifestations, or chemotherapy unless particularly relevant to biology. Following this treatment of the species, the transmission and ultrastructural, immunologic, and biochemical aspects of the genus as a whole will be reviewed. This review will focus more on zoonotic aspects than that of Adler (3); this reflects the current trend of thinking about leishmaniasis.

## II. THE OLD WORLD SPECIES

### *1. Leishmania infantum Nicolle, 1908*

*L. infantum* (175) causes infantile visceral leishmaniasis or kala azar in man.

DISTRIBUTION

*Europe* Portugal, Spain, southern France, southern Italy, Corsica, Sardinia, Sicily, Yugoslavia, Hungary, Rumania, Bulgaria, Greece, Crete, European Turkey, Malta, southern European USSR, and Cyprus.

*Asia* Northern China, southern Asiatic USSR, Iran, Iraq, Turkey, Syria, Jordan, Israel, Lebanon, Kuwait, Yemen, southern Yemen, Afghanistan (?), and northern Pakistan (?).

*Africa* Morocco, Algeria, Tunisia, and Libya.

RESERVOIRS From the anthropocentric view the dog is the prime reservoir of the disease. However, the true home of *L. infantum* is more probably the fox (158, 194), the jackal (140, 141), the wolf (141), and the porcupine (*Hystrix hirsutirostris satumini*) (183). It seems probable that the dog first acquires the infection from such a wild source. Whether the organism is transmitted by sandflies from dog to dog is unknown but it seems probable, as in the inner areas of a city like Tashkent, where dogs are infected, the presence of jackals seems unlikely. However, it can happen that the distribution of infantile kala azar may be peri-urban as in Baghdad (226) where the dogs are not infected (36); here the jackal may be the reservoir and transmission is direct to man. It is thought that the organism is never transmitted by sandflies from man to man. The common rat (*Rattus rattus*) has been found infected in Yugoslavia (184).

It is relatively difficult to infect sandflies from patients with *L. infantum* infection but it is comparatively easy to do so from infected dogs (7, 8). In dogs it is frequently possible to isolate *L. infantum* from nasal secretions (80) but the significance of this observation to epidemiology is problematical.

It may be that *L. infantum* is particularly present in northwest China where 90 out of 15,873 dogs were found infected but in northeast China it may be confused with *Leishmania donovani* which is being transmitted from man to man by sandflies (252). The organism may persist in dogs long after treatment and after symptoms have disappeared (181).

VECTORS

*Europe* *Phlebotomus ariasi* and *P. major syriacus* are the main vectors while *P. simici, P. perfiliewi,* and *P. perniciosus tobbi* may be involved (144, 194). The involvement of *P. papatasi* is problematical.

*Asia* In northern China *P. chinensis chinensis* is the only known vector. Other subspecies such as *P. c. halepensis* and *P. c. longiductus,* as well as *P. causasicus* and *P. mongolensis,* may be involved in Soviet Asia and Iran (144, 183, 187). In Georgia, USSR, *P. kandelakii* is suspected (67). In the eastern Mediterranean area and some parts of southern USSR *P. major syriacus* also occurs and is a certain vector; again *P. p. tobbi* and *P. simici* may be involved (183, 231–233).

*Africa* *P. ariasi* is strongly suspected as is *P. longicuspis* and *P. p. perniciosus* in the northern African littoral. *P. perfiliewi* may also be involved (56, 61).

BEHAVIOR The parasite causes symptoms in children and is therefore detected primarily in them. Taub (228) reported that the serum of adults but not children had a lytic effect upon *L. infantum* promastigotes in vitro but this was not confirmed by the careful work of Ben Rachid (24) who found that all human serum had the lytic effect. Ulrich et al (241) have shown that this effect is general and is due to two heat labile factors present in the serum of man, guinea pigs, rabbits, rats, and hamsters. It is not known if children are the major hosts of the infected vector sandflies for some ecological reason of time and place, or whether adults somehow control the infection. The latter seems more likely as no one has noted any preferential feeding upon children by *P. ariasi* or *P. major.* The dog does not show any age factor in relation to disease. On inoculation into golden hamsters *(Mesocricetus auritus) L. infantum* behaves similarly to *L. donovani* about which more is known. Chinese hamsters *(Cricetulus griseus)* are less susceptible to *L. infantum* than to *L. donovani* (102).

Dedet (61) has attempted infection of gerbils *(Gerbillus pyramidum* and *Meriones shawi),* gerboas *(Jaculus orientalis),* and rats (*Rattus* spp.) intradermally or intraperitoneally with promastigotes. He has also attempted to infect a jackal *(Canis aureus)* intrahepatically with amastigotes. The gerbils inoculated intradermally became infected only at the site of the lesion but contracted generalized infections when inoculated intraperitoneally. Gerboas became either locally or generally infected when inoculated intradermally and rats developed generalized infection after intradermal inoculation. The jackal developed a visceral infection with little cutaneous involvement; the infection was less severe than that seen in dogs. In dogs the infection is severe with extensive cutaneous and visceral involvement (61, 107, 194). Popovic (189) showed that the ground squirrel *(Citellus citellus)* is susceptible.

Rioux and Golvan (194) have infected *P. ariasi* by feeding on an infected dog but only 3 out of 202 became infected and only one of those became infected in the anterior end of the alimentary canal. Experimental infection of *P. chinensis* from man yielded only 5 of 102 positive flies. Infected hamsters, however, successfully infected *P. chinesis, P. perniciosus,* and *P. major,* but infections in *P. mongolensis, P. argentipes, P. papatasi,* and *P. sergenti* were poor. Dogs were good donors also. This situation is, however, not as simple as it looks, as geographical strains of both parasite and sandfly may contribute complications. For a fuller discussion see Adler & Theodore (9) and Rioux & Golvan (194).

The organism is not always easy to isolate. Strains exist in culture from France (194), Tunisia (61), Crete (213), Malta, and Israel (1). Dedet & Lanotte (63) recommend a heart-brain-blood medium for heavy growth in culture of *L. infantum* of human origin. However, Bray (unpublished results) was completely unable to maintain *L. infantum* of Baghdad in any sort of culture. A few cycles of multiplication would occur and then the parasite would die out. Dedet & Lanotte (63) also had some difficulty in cultivating a canine strain of *L. infantum.* Dedet & Ben Osman (62) grew *L. infantum* in the chorio allantoic fluid of chick embryos. Gleiberman & Belova (87) were able to get *L. infantum* into tissue cultures of KEM, SCH, or Hep 2 cells; of kidney cells from monkeys, newborn dogs, cats, rabbits, guinea pigs, and man; and chick embryo skin muscle cells and mouse embryo cells. Invasion and multiplication were said to occur.

Foner (76) has preserved five strains of *L. infantum* promastigotes at –60°C in 10% glycerin.

TAXONOMY The name *L. infantum* (175) is given to the parasite of infantile visceral leishmaniasis of the Old World which has various members of the Canidae as reservoir hosts. The parasite does not differ in gross morphology from any other *Leishmania* spp. with the exception of *L. enriettii* and it is distinguished from the other *Leishmania* of the human viscera, *L. donovani,* by serology (3) and the infection of Canidae in nature. The problem remains of the parasite of northern China as stated previously. Undoubtedly *L. infantum* from Tunis grew poorly in *P. chinensis* as did Indian *L. donovani* (101). However, the dog is a reservoir host over much of northern China and this is commonly taken to define *L. infantum.*

Nicoli (174) uses *L. donovani infantum.* Adler (3), Lainson & Shaw (130), and Garnham (83) use *L. infantum.* Dedet (61) and Rioux & Golvan (194) use *L. donovani.* Obviously no general agreement has been reached as yet.

## 2. *Leishmania donovani (Laveran et Mesnil, 1903)*

*L. donovani* (142) causes visceral leishmaniasis or kala azar, and post-kala azar dermal leishmaniasis in all age groups on man in the Old World.

DISTRIBUTION

*Asia* Indian subcontinent, particularly Bengal, Assam and Bangladesh; Thailand, Burma, Sumatra, and Pakistan.

*Africa* Southern and middle Sudan, eastern and southern Ethiopia, Djibouti, Somalia, Kenya, northern Uganda, Chad, Dafur, Niger, Gambia, Republique Centrafricane, and Gabon.

RESERVOIRS In the Indian subcontinent the disease is an anthroponosis and man is the sole reservoir. In the Sudan and therefore probably western Ethiopia, Chad, Dafur, and Niger, the animals infected with *L. donovani* known so far are the common rat *(Rattus rattus)* and the spiny rat *(Acomys albigena)* in an urban situation where they probably do not represent a threat to man. In the important rural situation the following animals are infected: the Nile grass rat *(Arvicanthis niloticus),* the spiny rat, the Senegal genet *(Genetta genetta senegalensis),* and the Sudan serval *(Felis serval phillipsi)* (104). The presence of two carnivores in this group which feed commonly on rodents obviously raises the possibility that they acquired their infections by the consumption of infected rodents. There remains in the Sudan the suspicion that the jackal may be involved, as only 33 have been examined in the endemic zone and this might be insufficient to uncover a reservoir being infected by sandfly bite (104).

In Kenya, southern Ethiopia, and Somalia no reservoir has been demonstrated and the disease in man may be an anthroponosis. Strains of *L. donovani* (?) have been isolated from the viscera of 1 out of 161 ground squirrels *(Xerus rutilans)* and 3 out of 354 gerbils *(Tatera robusta)* (94) but these strains infected man only in the skin and only for a short time. They did not give rise to typical Kenyan kala azar (152).

VECTORS

*Asia* In Bengal, Assam, and Bangladesh *P. argentipes* is or was the vector. No pandemics of kala azar have occurred in these areas recently, as most house-haunting *P. argentipes* were destroyed by antimalarial spraying. The evidence at present is that the remaining *P. argentipes* population rarely feeds on man (207). In northern Pakistan it is possible that *P. chinensis* is a vector.

In central Sudan the vector is *P. langeroni orientalis.* It is also probably the vector in western Ethiopia, Chad, Dafur, and Niger (104; R. W. Ashford, E. McConnell, and R. S. Bray, unpublished observations). In the very south of Sudan at Kapoeta the vector may be *P. martini* which also occurs and is the probable vector in Karamoja in Uganda (253).

In Kenya and probably in southern Ethiopia, Somalia, and Djibouti the vector is *P. martini. P. vansomerenae* and *P. celiae* are probably also involved (152, 162).

BEHAVIOR With Sudanese strains a parasitemia is quite common in man; the nasal secretions are also infected (196). Parasites from India, Sudan, and Kenya have been inoculated into hamsters and their behavior there has been described on numerous occasions. The most recent of these descriptions has been that of Ott et al (177) using a Sudan strain and the reader is referred to this paper for references to other descriptions. Ilardi et al (106) have inoculated a strain of *L. donovani* into hamsters which had been splenectomized, X-irradiated, or treated with cortisone. All these treatments enhanced the hamster's susceptibility. Herman & Baron (97) have shown that interferon inducers (Poly I poly C, Newcastle disease virus, and *Escherichia coli* endotoxin) had no inhibitory effect upon the growth of *L. donovani* in hamsters.

In recent years some new hosts for experimental *L. donovani* infection have been tried. Sati (204) infected *Galago senegalensis* successfully and Packchanian & Kelly (178) infected *Peromyscus californicus.* Krampitz & Mühlpfordt (118) infected *Acomys cahirinus, Meriones libycus, Gerbillus gerbillus,* and *Saccostomus campestris.* None had heavy or lethal infections and all were less susceptible than hamsters. In the laboratory Stauber et al (221) and Stauber (222) infected the Sudanese reservoir *Arvicanthis niloticus niloticus* with a Sudanese strain and showed that it had the prime characteristics of a good reservoir host in that the infection was nonlethal and it persisted. Similar infections were obtained in *Tatera flaviceps, Acomys albigena, Mystromys albicaudatus, Mastomys natalensis ismailiae, Acomys cahirinus, Mus musculus, Meriones unquicalatus, Gerbillus gerbillus, G. pyramidum, Jaculus jaculus, Rattus rattus,* and the white mouse. Strains of parasites which had been in culture for any length of time were noninfectious. Rodents from Egypt were highly susceptible to Sudanese strains. *Tatera* from Sudan was highly susceptible. A Kenyan strain infected *Mastomys* but not *Acomys* (104).

Mansour et al (154) infected dogs with Sudanese and Kenyan strains of *L. donovani* but the infections were relatively low grade and they died out.

Lemma & Schiller (143) claimed to have grown amastigotes in a diphasic blood agar medium at 32 and 34°C but subsequently Wonde & Honigberg (250) have shown that these apparent amastigotes were the result of poor nutrition rather than temperature. Lupasco et al (145) and Holbrook & Stauber (103) have grown *L. donovani* promastigotes in the vitelline sac and the chorioallantois and amastigotes in the organs of 4–18 day-old chick embryos at 27 and 28°C. Little or no growth occurred at 37°C. No intracellular forms developed in the sac or chorioallantois. On intravenous inoculations most forms occurred intracellularly in the liver. These multiplied at temperatures up to 33°C. At 28°C some transformation to promastigotes occurred.

There have been numerous attempts to grow *L. donovani* in tissue cultures. Gleiberman & Belova (87) (see above) also grew *L. donovani* in the cells already mentioned. Lamy (136) and Lamy et al (137) have grown *L. donovani* as amastigotes in cells from a Sticker sarcoma from a dog (cell line 503). Invasion and multiplication occurred at 37°C and the organism was maintained for up to five months with up to three changes of cells. At 22°C growth occurred largely extracellularly, though some promastigotes were taken up by macrophages (using mouse macrophages); they converted to amastigotes at higher temperatures. Amastigotes converted to promastigotes only if the cell was dead. Some amastigotes multiplied even at 22–25°C.

Herman (95, 96) has grown *L. donovani* in macrophages of the peritoneal exudate from hamsters. Cotton rat serum in the medium gave rise to excessive fibroblastic growth. Some increase in amastigote numbers and in the number of cells infected occurred in the first week but after that the infection declined. Some growth of acriflavine-induced dyskinetoplastic amastigotes also occurred. Frothingham & Lehtimaki (81, 82) were able to keep strains of *L. donovani* alive in dog sarcoma cells for up to one year and some multiplication occurred. In human amniotic cells the parasite slowly died out. Intracellular amastigotes were the rule at 36°C. At 33°C both intracellular amastigotes and extracellular promastigotes occurred. At 28°C only extracellular promastigotes were seen. Similar observations have been made by Lupasco et al (146). Akiyama & McQuillan (11) found that while hamster macrophages could often degrade promastigotes of *L. donovani* in vitro, the dog sarcoma cell (line 503) was unable to do so.

Miller & Twohy (161) observed that the growth of *L. donovani* was inhibited in macrophages from immune animals as compared to macrophages from normal animals and that macrophages engulf promastigotes, flagellar end first. Akiyama & Haight (10), however, believe that macrophages take up the promastigotes from the posterior (nonflagellated) end.

Most et al (164) have preserved *L. donovani* at –70°C for four months. Chakraborty & Das Gupta (46) studied the mitotic cycle of *L. donovani* and found a sequence of 15.2 hr resting phase, 1.1 hr prophase, 3.9 hr metaphase, 0.9 hr anaphase, and 1.8 hr telophase and binucleate phase to make a total turnover time of 24 hr. There is no agreement about the number of chromosomes.

TAXONOMY *L. donovani* is the type species of the genus. Argument has centered around whether parasites from non-Bengali kala azar are *L. donovani. L. infantum* has been split off and Lainson & Shaw (129) have readopted the species *L. chagasi* for the parasite of New World kala azar.

There remain the points of whether the parasite of post-kala azar dermal leishmaniasis is the same as that of kala azar (33) and whether all strains recovered from man, animals, and sandflies in the Sudan are identical (5). In both cases serological methods have indicated that they are the same.

Some authors have recommended the use of the subspecies *L. donovani archibaldi* for the parasite of African kala azar (147). While I am sympathetic to the idea of giving the Sudan parasite separate status this cannot include the Kenya parasite which is patently different. There is every hope that this question can be solved in the near future by comparative studies on serology, enzyme variants, and the DNA buoyant density of strains from Bengali, Sudanese, and Kenyan kala azar. In the meantime it is logical to suppose that distinct characters might have arisen in parasites that are separated geographically and by the nature of their reservoir hosts and their vectors.

## 3. *Leishmania tropica (Wright, 1903)*

*L. tropica* (251) causes cutaneous leishmaniasis (oriental sore) in urban areas.

DISTRIBUTION It seems best to list the distribution of *L. tropica* in Asia by urban centers rather than by countries. An explanation of the restriction of area which will become apparent below will be given under the distribution of *L. major.*

*Europe* Portugal, Spain, southern France, Italy, Yugoslavia, Sardinia, Sicily, Greece, Bulgaria, and Crete.

*Asia* Turkey, Aleppo, Jericho, Damascus, Tripoli, Mosul, Baghdad, Tehran, Meshed, Erevan, Kirovabad, Tabriz, Shiraz, Kabul, Delhi, Cambay, Ashkabad, Merv, Samarkand, Bokhara, Balkh, Saudi Arabia, and southern Yemen.

*Africa* The oases towns of Morocco, Algeria, and Tunisia, e.g. Gafsa, Mila, Biskra, and Laghouat; the "tell" of Algeria and Tunisia, particularly around Constantine.

RESERVOIRS It is possible that *L. tropica* exists only in man and dogs as reservoirs. It may occasionally infect cats as well, presumably from dogs. As dogs become infected at the same time of the year as, or even a little later than, man and often lose their infections before man (there is a three-month transmission season), it seems unlikely that the dog is a reservoir for man. The opposite is possible. Either man is the major reservoir or some completely unknown reservoir exists in an urban environment. The attack rate must have been very high indeed 50 years ago in urban Aleppo, Jericho, and Baghdad and it is difficult to believe that the necessary infection rate in sandflies could have been achieved by feeding on old, healing, single sores on man. I feel inclined to believe that an urban reservoir is still to be found despite the negative evidence.

VECTORS

*Europe* In Italy across to Georgia and Armenia, USSR *P. perfiliewi* is a vector. *P. papatasi* is a suspected vector in most of its range.

*Asia* In Israel, Jordan, Lebanon, and western Syria the vector is *P. papatasi.* Somewhere in the Syrian desert *P. papatasi* gives way as a vector to *P. sergenti* which is the vector in Mosul, Baghdad, Kabul, Delhi, and Meshed (160, 176).

*Africa* *P. papatasi* is the suspected vector; *P. sergenti* and *P. chabaudi* may contribute.

BEHAVIOR In nature *L. tropica* normally causes a single, indolent, spontaneously healing, cutaneous lesion in both man and dogs. The organisms seem never to survive in the viscera (107, 208). It is transmitted in the summer months (191). The organism infects hamsters but has a low infectivity for white mice.

Gleiberman & Belova (87) were able to culture *L. tropica* in a wide variety of cells in tissue culture. Schaeffer et al (205) used *L. tropica* in their most interesting and successful work on continuous cultivation in a chemostat. Foner (76) was able to preserve successfully 18 out of 25 strains of *L. tropica* at –60°C. If Adler's strain "Zamira Salah" is true *L. tropica* then Coelho (52) succeeded in infecting *Lutzomyia longipalalpis* and *Lu. renei* from hamster lesions containing *L. tropica.* Development was largely confined to the midgut and hindgut.

TAXONOMY *L. tropica* (251) was first described from a girl from Armenia with a single urban-type lesion. It is assumed that she came from Erevan. Kozevnikov

(117) has listed the characteristics which separate the urban *L. tropica* from the rural zoonotic *L. major* (see also 32). There is also good serological evidence for this separation (14, 20). Bray & Rahim (40) showed that strains of *L. tropica* from Baghdad cutaneous leishmaniasis and leishmaniasis recidivans of man and from a dog were all identical by serological testing.

## *4. Leishmania major (Yakimov & Schockov, 1915)*

*L. major* (254) causes zoonotic cutaneous leishmaniasis largely in rural areas.

### DISTRIBUTION

*Asia* Rural Israel and Jordan; rural Turkmen, Kazak, Uzbek, USSR; and rural Iran (69, 70, 113, 167–171, 214, 258).

*Africa* Senegal, Mali, Sudan (139), Niger, northern Nigeria, Angola, and Namibia.

This distribution is based on the belief that *P. major* is the parasite of all rural Old World zoonotic cutaneous leishmaniasis, including that contracted from cricetids in the Jordan valley and from grass rats in Senegal. I feel that cutaneous leishmaniasis in Mali, the Sudan, and West Africa generally is rural and probably zoonotic. However, I have no proof that the cutaneous leishmaniasis of the North African oases is zoonotic, and I have considered the parasite from there as *L. tropica.*

RESERVOIRS In the USSR and Iran the major reservoir is the great gerbil *Rhombomys opimus* and less important reservoirs are *Meriones lybicus erythrourus, M. meridianus, Mus musculus, Spermophilopsis leptodactylus, Allactaga servertzovi, Erinaceus auritus,* and *Hemiechinus albulus* (69, 182, 183, 258). The predators of rodents in the USSR, the marbled polecat *(Vormela peregusna)* and the polecat *(Mustela hiralis),* have been found infected (68). In the Jordan valley of Israel and Jordan the major reservoir is the sand rat *Psammomys obesus;* less important is a gerbil *Meriones* sp. (92, 171). In Senegal and probably in Mali and the Sudan, the reservoir is *Arvicanthis niloticus* (43, 139).

VECTORS In the USSR and Iran the most important vector is *P. papatasi* because of its preference for man (168, 170, 201, 258). *P. caucasicus* is an undoubted vector but it may be more important in maintaining the infection among gerbils rather than transferring the infection to man (168, 214). Other sandflies that have been incriminated are *P. mongolensis* (70), *P. ansarii* (168, 170), and *P. andrejevi* (72). Also suspected is *P. alexandri.*

It seems probable that the vector in the Jordan valley is *P. papatasi.* The vector in West Africa is unknown but *P. duboscqi* (138), *P. bergeroti,* and *Sergentomyia clydei* have been suggested. *P. grovei* may be a vector in Namibia.

BEHAVIOR In the USSR and Iran the highest promastigote infections are found in late August and early September near Isfahan, Iran (166) and in August in Uzbek, USSR (258). In the gerbil burrows *S. arpaklensis* transmits lizard leishmaniae but the suspicion remains that it may occasionally transmit *L. major,* just as *P. caucasicus* may occasionally transmit lizard leishmaniae. When force-fed with promastigotes of *L. major* development in *P. papatasi* is anterior, while promastigotes of a strain from geckoes develop posteriorly. *S. arpaklensis* is less susceptible to *L. major* than to a gecko strain (200). Using serological tests Safyanova (201) showed that two of three strains from *P. papatasi* and two of two strains from *P. caucasicus* were *L. major,* while three of four strains from *S. arpaklensis* were from lizards. Using virulence to white mice as a criterion, Shishlyaeva-Matova et al (214) concluded that all strains isolated from *P. papatasi,* five of seven from *P. caucasicus,* and two of ten from *S. arpaklensis* were *L. major* but the strains from *S. arpaklensis* were of low virulence. If, as seems probable, the "Ein Geddi II" strain of Adler is a rural *Psammomys* derived strain, then Coelho (52) has infected *Lutzomyia longipalpis* and *Lu. renei* with *L. major.* Development was confined largely to the mid- and hind-guts.

Very high infection rates may be found among *Rhombomys opimus* in nature (nearly 100% has been mentioned). In Isfahan only the ears are infected (167) but in the USSR the nose may be infected and even the eyelids (182). The prevalence is highest in July (113). While the strains isolated from man are always virulent to mice, only two of six strains isolated from *R. opimus* were virulent (114). Dubrovsky et al (68) found that in areas of low infection rates gerbil ears did not show marked lesions and parasites were found in normal ear skin. Dubrovsky et al (69) found that infections in the ear of *Meriones libycus* were usually in intact skin. Eliseev & Kellina (73) found that *L. major* could persist for up to 25 months in the ear of *R. opimus.* Glazunova (86) attempted infection of hamsters with varying numbers of *L. major* promastigotes and found that 12,000 promastigotes were necessary to achieve a continuous infection. White mice are easily infected with *L. major.* Preston et al (190) showed that neo-natal thymectomy and whole body lethal irradiation of CBA mice increased the time and intensity of infection.

Serebryakov et al (210) in a most interesting piece of work showed it was possible to preserve *L. major* by lyophilization. Viability was maintained for at least one year.

TAXONOMY *L. major* has long been accepted at least as a subspecies of *L. tropica.* Recently Bray, Ashford & Bray (32) have put forward reasons for treating it as a full species. *L. major* is separated from *L. tropica* on immunological and serological grounds, as well as on defined nosological grounds (163). Bray & Rahim (40) separated Baghdadi strains from Iranian strains, all from cutaneous leishmaniasis. They were probably dealing with *L. tropica* from Baghdad and *L. major* from Iran.

### *5. Leishmania aethiopica Bray, Ashford & Bray, 1973*

*L. aethiopica* (32) causes cutaneous and diffuse cutaneous leishmaniasis of Ethiopia.

DISTRIBUTION Ethiopian highlands; Mount Elgon, Kenya; and possibly southern Yemen (19).

RESERVOIRS The rock hyraxes *(Procavia habessinica* and *Heterohyrax brucei).*

VECTORS *P. longipes* and *P. pedifer.*

BEHAVIOR The infection in the hyrax is confined almost entirely to the very tip of the nose which is the favored site for the bite of *P. longipes.* Bray & Bryceson (35) showed by serology that strains from normal cutaneous and diffuse cutaneous leishmaniasis of Ethiopia were identical. Ashford et al (19) similarly showed that strains from hyrax, *P. longipes, P. pedifer,* and man were all identical. *L. aethiopica* infects hamster skin with difficulty and only when freshly isolated. It does not infect white mice.

TAXONOMY Bray, Ashford & Bray (32) separated *L. aethiopica* on nosological, serological, and behavioral grounds. M. L. Chance (personal communication) has also shown that the bouyant density of the kinetoplastic DNA of *L. aethiopica* falls into a distinct group.

## III THE NEW WORLD SPECIES

### *1. Leishmania chagasi Marques da Cunha & Chagas, 1937*

*L. chagasi* (156) causes New World visceral leishmaniasis. The disease is usually one of infants and children.

DISTRIBUTION Argentina, Paraguay, Bolivia, Colombia, Venezuela, Salvador, Guatemala, Mexico, and Guadeloupe and the following states of Brazil: Minais Gerais, Goias, Espirito Santo, Mato Grosso, Alagoas, Sergipe, Bahia, Pernambuco, Paraiba, Rio Grande do Norte, Ceara, Maranhao, Piaui, and Para.

RESERVOIRS Three reservoirs would appear to exist—the dog, the wild fox or "raposa" *(Lycalopex vetelus),* and the crab-eating fox *(Cerdocyon thous)*—but their relative importance is in doubt. The dog is obviously the important reservoir in the semi-arid regions of Ceara, Rio Grande do Norte, and Paraiba states in Brazil and in Venezuela (e.g. 13, 58, 60, 235). In those same areas *Ly. vetelus* would seem to be important also in the rural situation but its contact with man must be less than that of the dog (57). Obviously the dog may be infected from *Ly. vetelus.* It seems doubtful if *Ly. vetelus* and a sandfly represent a nidus of infection. Lainson et al (131) found *C. thous* infected with *L. chagasi* in the wet forest areas of Para state. There is a school of thought which proposes that *C. thous* and *Ly. vetelus* are not true reservoirs because *L. chagasi* appears to be quite pathogenic to *Ly. vetelus* (59). However, the organism does not seem to be so pathogenic to *C. thous* (131, 237). Lainson & Shaw (129) believe that a "hitherto unsuspected animal" is the true source of *L. chagasi* infection and foxes, dogs, and man are new accidental hosts.

VECTORS The accepted major vector is *Lutzomyia longipalpis.* Pifano & Romero (186) found *L. chagasi* in the Turimiquire hills of Venezuela in the apparent absence of *Lu. longipalpis* and suspected *Lu. evansi.* Courmes et al (53) found a case of visceral leishmaniasis in Guadeloupe and suspected that *Lu. guadeloupensis* was the vector. Other vectors have been suspected at one time or another.

BEHAVIOR On inoculation into *C. thous, L. chagasi* infects the viscera but after seven months of observation little pathogenicity was evidenced (237). *L. chagasi* produces fatal visceral infections in hamsters. It is not always easy to cultivate as promastigotes. *L. chagasi* infects children to a considerably greater degree than it does adults. In dogs it behaves much as does *L. infantum.* See Adler & Theodore (9) for infection in sandflies.

TAXONOMY The taxonomic situation is not fully defined at present since the identity of strains from man, dogs, and foxes is not finally established. Work being done at the Liverpool School of Tropical Medicine on buoyant density of nuclear and kinetoplastic DNA and on the characterization of enzyme variants will, one hopes, be extended to establish the affinities of these strains. Comparisons with *L. donovani* and *L. infantum* will also need to be made. The parasite of visceral leishmaniasis from the semi-arid areas of Brazil and Venezuela has been confirmed as *L. chagasi* by Lainson & Shaw (130) but this may not be the end of the story. It is at least possible that further work will establish this parasite as *L. infantum* and that differences may exist among organisms from northeastern Brazil, northern Brazil, Venezuela, and Central America.

## 2. *Leishmania mexicana mexicana (Biagi, 1953)*

*L. m. mexicana* (25) causes a form of cutaneous leishmaniasis in the New World known as chiclero's ulcer or bay sore in southern Mexico and British Honduras. Occasionally it may cause diffuse cutaneous leishmaniasis (DCL) (155, 157, 179).

DISTRIBUTION This organism occurs in the forests of southern Mexico, British Honduras, Guatemala (probably Honduras to Panama), and the Sasardi area of Panama. Whether there is a southern limit for *L. m. mexicana* and a northern limit for *L. m. amazonensis* is pure conjecture.

RESERVOIRS Small forest rodents: *Ototylomys phyllotis, Heteromys desmarestianus, Nyctomys sumichrasti,* and *Sigmodon hispidus* (65, 135, 249). Williams (249) believes that *O. phyllotis* is the major reservoir and *H. desmarestianus* is the secondary reservoir.

VECTORS *Lu. olmeca* and perhaps *Lu. cruciata* (248, 249).

BEHAVIOR *L. m. mexicana* like *L. major* will infect the dermis of rhesus monkeys, hamsters, and white mice (123, 134). Mata et al (159) showed that all mice and hamsters became infected in the exposed dermis following infection by either the subcutaneous or the intraperitoneal route. Following infection, 85% of white mice and 75% of hamsters showed visceral infection. All these figures are somewhat higher than suggested by our experience with a strain isolated from a reservoir in British Honduras (Lainson & Bray, unpublished observations). With the discovery of *L. mexicana* ssp., presumably *L. m. mexicana,* in the Sasardi area of Panama in *Oryzomys, Proechimys, Marmosa, Agouti,* and *Diplomys* by Herrer (98) and Herrer et al (100), it may be that one mystery has been cleared up; that is the occurrence of organisms found in the heart blood of *Proechimys* by workers in the Gorgas Memorial Laboratories, Panama in 1957 (16). It may have been that *L. m. mexicana* appeared as an epizootic in the area at that time and that a visceralizing infection may have occurred in a few specimens of *Proechimys.* Torrealba et al (236) have found parasites presumably of the *L. mexicana* complex in the heart blood of *Heteromys,* and Disney (65) found a visceral infection of *L. m. mexicana* in a specimen of *Heteromys* with a heavily infected ear.

Gonzales & Biagi (88) infected six volunteers with 500 promastigotes of *L. m. mexicana.* Only one developed an ulcer but all the other five developed delayed hypersensitivity to leishmanin. The authors believed that subpatent infections had developed. Infection with and recovery from *L. braziliensis panamensis* protects man from infection with *L. m. mexicana* but the reverse is not true (124). *L. m. mexicana* grows well in tissue culture at not more than 36°C. It can be preserved at –75 or –180°C as either a promastigote or an amastigote (Bray & Lainson, unpublished observations). For development in sandflies see section on transmission.

TAXONOMY This species is well established from studies of serology, cross-immunity, and DNA buoyant density (38, 123; M. L. Chance, personal communication).

### *3. Leishmania mexicana amazonensis Lainson & Shaw, 1972*

*L. m. amazonensis* (130) sometimes causes cutaneous leishmaniasis in northern Brazil (Para, Amapa, and Mato Grosso states) and southern Venezuela. It may cause diffuse cutaneous leishmaniasis.

DISTRIBUTION This parasite occurs in Trinidad and in the forests of Amazonia from Para to Mato Grosso states and up at least to the Amazonian type forests of southern Venezuela. It probably occurs also in other South American countries, particularly Amazonian Peru and Colombia.

RESERVOIRS Forest rodents and marsupials: *Oryzomys capito, O. concolor, O. macconnelli, Proechimys guyannensis, Heteromys anamalus, Neocomys spinosus, Nectomys squamipis, Zygodontomys microtinus, Dasyprocta* spp., *Marmosa murina, Marmosa mitis, Caluromys philander,* and *Metachirus nudicaudatus* (115, 125–128, 130, 172, 173, 215, 234, 236; R. Lainson and J. J. Shaw, unpublished observations); probably *Kannabateomys* and *Cuniculus paca* (77).

VECTORS *Lutzomyia flaviscutellata* (125, 212).

BEHAVIOR The behavior in mice, hamsters, and NNN medium closely resembles that of the type subspecies. Both subspecies show no conspicuous growth in the hind triangle of the sandfly host as does *L. braziliensis* spp. Rhesus monkeys are susceptible and there is some cross-immunity between the two subspecies, if one accepts that L1 and L15 of Bray & Lainson (38) are *L. m. amazonensis* (123).

TAXONOMY By including *Z. microtinus* and *H. anamalus* among the reservoirs I have included Venezuela in the area of distribution of *L. m. amazonensis* (115, 236). Other work has convinced me that a single subspecies or species of *Leishmania* may cause single sore cutaneous leishmaniasis or diffuse cutaneous leishmaniasis (DCL). Lainson & Shaw (130) have shown that organisms recovered from most rodents, some single sore cutaneous leishmania of man, and all DCL of man in Brazil show the characteristics of *L. m. amazonensis.* I assume from this that DCL in Venezuela is caused by *L. m. amazonensis* and not by another sub-species—*Leishmania mexicana.* In any case I am certain that if *L. m. pifanoi* is a valid species it causes single sore cutaneous leishmaniasis in man as well as DCL, that it accounts for a zoonosis with the major reservoir in rodents, and that it is transmitted by *Lu. flaviscutellata* or a closely related species. Lainson (122) seems certain that the parasite recovered from *H. anamalus* in Trinidad is *L. m. amazonensis.*

### 4. *Leishmania braziliensis braziliensis Vianna, 1911*

*L. b. braziliensis* (243) causes cutaneous and mucocutaneous leishmaniasis.

DISTRIBUTION Brazil, Amazonian Peru, Ecuador, Bolivia, Venezuela, Paraguay, and Colombia.

RESERVOIRS *Oryzomys concolor* (128). According to Lainson (122) the reports of infections in *O. nigripes* and *Akodon arviculoides* by Forattini et al (78) are due also to *L. b. braziliensis.* Lainson (122) also reports a visceral infection in *Proechimys.* Obviously *L. b. braziliensis* and *L. m. amazonensis* overlap in their reservoir hosts.

VECTORS *Psychodopygus wellcomei,* possibly *Ps. paraensis* and *Ps. amazonensis* (132); probably also *Lu. migonei, Lu. intermedia, Lu. whitmani, Lu. anduzei* (122), and *Pintomyia pessoai* (79).

BEHAVIOR All reports of behavior of *L. b. braziliensis* prior to 1972 are compromised, as it seems probable that most refer to *L. m. amazonensis. L. b. braziliensis* by definition grows very poorly in NNN medium and raises only the most insignificant lesion with few parasites in the hamster's nose (130). Thus it is very difficult to maintain and study and may not have been studied in the past by anyone except the Belem group. Reports of visceralizing infections in mice or hamsters probably refer to *L. mexicana.*

TAXONOMY The identity of this species rests on the behavioral aspects laid out by Lainson & Shaw (130). Venezuelan strains do not conform to the criteria of Lainson & Shaw (130) so they may form distinct subspecies.

### 5. *Leishmania braziliensis guyanensis (Floch, 1954)*

*L. b. guyanensis* (75) causes cutaneous leishmaniasis known as bosch yaws, forest yaws, or pian-bois in the forests of the Guyanas.

DISTRIBUTION Amapa and Roraima states in Brazil, Surinam, French Guyana, and Guyana; possibly stretches south and west to Para and Amazonas states of Brazil and to southeast Venezuela.

RESERVOIRS Unknown.

VECTORS Probably *Lu. anduzei* which has been found to harbor promastigotes (247).

BEHAVIOR Bray & Mumford (39) were able to grow the parasite in NNN medium containing hamster or rat blood but not rabbit blood. R. Lainson (personal communication) has been unable to confirm this observation with strains from Amapa state. In our hands the parasite grew slowly and fairly sparsely in the nose of hamsters. Lainson & Shaw (130) note that the lesion in hamster nose or feet was fleshy with few parasites and with considerable cellular reaction. In sandflies this subspecies shows vigorous continuous growth in the posterior triangle of the gut at the same time as anterior development.

TAXONOMY The position of this subspecies still rests to a considerable degree on clinical grounds.

### 6. *Leishmania braziliensis panamensis Lainson & Shaw, 1972*

*L. b. panamensis* (130) causes cutaneous leishmaniasis, with occasional metastases, in Central America.

DISTRIBUTION Panama, Nicaragua, Costa Rica, possibly El Salvador, Honduras, and Colombia.

RESERVOIRS The major reservoir is the two-toed sloth, *Choeloepus hoffmanni* and to a lesser degree *Bradypus infuscatus.* Other reservoirs may be *Potos flavus, Bassaricyon gabbii,* and *Saguinus geoffroyi* (17, 18, 50, 99, 229).

VECTORS *Lu. trapidoi, Lu. gomezi, Lu. sanguinaria, Lu. panamensis,* and *Lu. ylephiletrix* have all been shown to contain promastigotes infective to hamsters and all are anthropophilic (51, 149; H. A. Christensen, personal communication).

BEHAVIOR The organism can be grown with reasonable facility in NNN medium (149) and can also infect the hamster nose with fair ease, giving rise to a fleshy lesion with moderate numbers of amastigotes. Growth in blood agar medium has been characterized by Rivero & Zeledon (195). On inoculation intraperitoneally into hamsters the organisms reappear in the cooler areas of the skin and do not infect the viscera successfully. Mice are not easy to infect (255). In Panama Thatcher et al (230) infected a variety of local animals with two strains of *L. b. panamensis.* They found *Sigmodon hispidis* and *Potos flavus* to be susceptible; *Tylomys panamensis, Proechimys semispinosus,* and *Bassaricyon gabbi* to be fairly resistant; and *Caluromys derbianus, Didelphis marsupialis,* and *Dasyprocta punctata* to be completely resistant. This subspecies also develops in the hind gut of sandflies as well as in the anterior portions.

TAXONOMY Strains of parasites recovered from Panama were shown by Schneider & Hertig (206) to share all the antigens demonstrable except for Shaw's strain (L7) from Achioti area. Bray & Lainson (38) showed that two serologically distinct strains occur in Costa Rica. One of these came from the coastal humid forested area and it may be that it is *L. m. mexicana,* though it was less exuberant in hamster lesions than other strains of *L. m. mexicana.* It is at least possible that three serologically distinct strains of *L. b. panamensis* exist.

### 7. *Leishmania peruviana Veles, 1913*

*L. peruviana* (242) causes the cutaneous disease known as uta in Peru.

DISTRIBUTION The high valleys of the west side of the Andes mountains in Peru.

RESERVOIR The dog.

VECTORS Thought to be probably *Lu. verrucarum* and *Lu. peruensis.*

BEHAVIOR Strains of this parasite are known in various laboratories in the form of promastigotes in NNN culture. I do not know of any reports of the parasite in hamsters. In dogs, in the wild particularly, the parasite causes small nodules or ulcers on the nose or lips. Parasites can be found in unbroken dog skin.

TAXONOMY Based on ecology (reservoir, the dog, and occurrence outside forests) and clinical signs and symptoms.

### 8. *Leishmania enriettii Muniz & Medina, 1948*

*L. enriettii* (165) causes cutaneous leishmaniasis of the guinea pig.

DISTRIBUTION Unknown.

RESERVOIRS Unknown.

VECTORS Unknown.

BEHAVIOR The behavior of this parasite in its only known host is well known (6, 41, 180). It causes a self-limiting cutaneous disease in guinea pigs. It may metastasize if the original inoculum of organisms contains above $10^5$ amastigotes. It does not cause a progressive infection in any animals other than the domesticated guinea pig and *Cavia aperea* (=*Corbaia aperea*) the wild guinea pig. The origin of this parasite remains a complete mystery.

TAXONOMY This is the only species of *Leishmania* to be immediately and easily differentiated on morphological grounds. The amastigotes measure twice the size of all other species, i.e. up to $7 \times 4\ \mu$.

### 9. *Leishmania hertigi (Herrer, 1971)*

*L. hertigi* (98) causes cutaneous leishmaniasis, usually without lesions, in the tree porcupine in Panama.

RESERVOIR The only known host is *Coendu rothschildi;* 83 of 94 studied were found to be infected in the wild.

VECTORS Unknown.

BEHAVIOR The organism is found predominantly in unbroken skin but may occur in spleen and liver. The organism may persist for at least 30 months in *C. rothschildi.* Hamsters are partially susceptible but the cotton rat, jerboas, and guinea pigs are not. The organism grows well on NNN medium.

TAXONOMY The organism is differentiated on the basis of the elongate amastigote, host specificity, and course of infection in *C. rothschildi.* There is said to be no cross-immunity to *L. b. panamensis* in that *L. b. panamensis* successfully infected hamsters recovered from *L. hertigi* infection. However, no attempt to test immunity to a challenge by *L. hertigi* was recorded (98).

## IV. THE *LEISHMANIA* OF LIZARDS

The group has been reviewed excellently by Belova (23) and there is little to add. The species have been listed by Garnham (83). However, a few points might be highlighted. Uptake of promastigotes of *L. adleri* by iguanid leucocytes and peritoneal exudate cells in vitro has been studied by Dollahan & Janovy (66). Phagocytosis occurred in a similar manner as with mammalian cells and species. Amastigotes occurred for a short time in cells at both 25 and 35°C. Up to 20% of *Gymnodactylus caspius* may be infected in the USSR (22). Cultivation is necessary for isolation and among 222 lizards shown to be positive for leishmaniae by culture, parasites were seen by direct examination of the viscera in only four. The parasite is present in the lizard as a promastigote. Nadim et al (169, 170) and Seyedi Rashti et al (209) have shown *S. sintoni* to be a vector in the Iranian Turkmen Sahara. Garnham's list (83) omits *L. hoogstraali* (150). Hoogstraal & Heyneman (104) state that B. McMillan showed that *S. clydei* fed avidly on lizards so it may be a vector of *L. hoogstraali.* Southgate & Manson-Bahr (220) consider *S. clydei* to be the vector of *L. adleri* of lizards and, as *S. clydei* also bites man, they consider that *L. adleri* may infect man fleetingly and give rise to the high incidence of delayed hypersensitivity to leishmanin in the areas free of human leishmaniasis which they had discovered.

## V. TRANSMISSION

The great discussions about transmission were over by the time Adler wrote his 1964 review. The conclusion was that the sandfly was the major vector, possibly the only means of transferring leishmaniae from vertebrate to vertebrate. Lainson & Southgate (133) repeated Berberian's observations that *Stomoxys* could transmit leishmaniae mechanically and leishmaniae were demonstrated in the nasal secretions of dogs (61, 80, 196), but these observations did little to disturb the general belief that sandflies are the sole important means of transmission.

Some further experiments have been made on the capacity of sandflies as vectors. Strangways-Dixon & Lainson (224) fed *Lu. apicalis, Lu. bispinosa, Lu. cruciata, Lu.*

*geniculata, Lu. ovallesi, Lu. panamensis, Lu. pessoana, Lu. shannoni,* and *Lu. ylephilator* on lesions in hamsters containing *L. mexicana mexicana.* While all became infected only *Lu. pessoana* transmitted the infection to man. Since then doubt as to the true identity of this sandfly has arisen and it is assumed not to be *Lu. pessoana.* It may have been *Lu. bispinosa.* Coelho (52) fed *Lu. longipalpis* and *Lu. renei* on lesions in hamsters or mice containing *L. chagasi, L. mexicana amazonensis* (= *L. braziliensis* No. 4 of Coelho), *L. m. mexicana, L. enriettii, L. tropica, L. major* (= *L. tropica* "Ein Geddi II" of Coelho), and a strain isolated from a case of espundia in Ceara state which must be presumed to be *L. braziliensis braziliensis.* Both sandfly species became infected with all species of *Leishmania.* All showed massive hind and mid gut infection for the first few days but only in the cases of *Lu. longipalpis* with *L. chagasi, Lu. longipalpis* and *Lu renei* with *L. m. mexicana, Lu. longipalpis* with *L. m. amazonensis,* and *Lu. longipalpis* and *Lu. renei* with *L. braziliensis,* did development of the parasite proceed to the proventriculus, cardia, pharynx, and buccal cavity after four days.

*L. m. amazonensis* also infected *Lu. intermedia, Lu. whitmani, Lu. sallesi, Lu. shannoni, Lu. arthuri, Lu. monticola, Lu. coelhoi,* and *Lu. cavernicola.* Transmission was effected only twice in 37 attempts using *Lu. longipalpis* and *Lu. renei* with *L. m. mexicana.* Williams (248) fed *Lu. cruciata* on hamster lesions containing *L. m. mexicana* and succeeded in transmitting the infection twice to a human volunteer.

At one time a suspicion arose among the workers at the Gorgas Memorial Laboratories, Panama, that *L. braziliensis panamensis* might develop in the hind-gut of its vectors and never move posteriorly. McConnell (149), however, found that only those promastigotes which had been recovered from anterior infections in wild-caught sandflies showed typical *L. b. panamensis* behavior in hamsters, and this was largely confirmed by Phyllis Johnson and Cecilia Eisenmann in an addendum to his paper. Nonetheless a very large number of unexplained infections are found in forest sandflies in Panama and R. Lainson (personal communication) believes that hind-gut infection plays an essential part in the development of *L. braziliensis* spp. in sandflies.

It would be wholly false, however, to believe that there is not an enormous amount of useful research still to be done in this field. Above all we do not know the mechanism of injection of the organism into the vertebrate. Until this is known there is no way to calculate the percentage of sandflies potentially infective in a population, and there is no way of calculating the attack rate. No unifying epidemiological theory is possible without this information, and at present it is impossible to approach an epidemiological situation in leishmaniasis with any preconceptions as to what might be the prevalence of leishmaniae in either vertebrate or invertebrate host.

## VI. FINE STRUCTURE

As all amastigotes and promastigotes look very much alike by conventional microscopy (except *L. enriettii* and that differs only by having a comparatively large amastigote), the results of electron microscopic studies have had an enhanced interest. Adler has summarized the knowledge gained from the electron microscope up to 1964. Since that time some major advances have been made. Rudzinska et al (199) and Creemers & Jadin (54) showed that part of the transformation process from amastigote to promastigote was a lengthening and elaboration of the mitochondrion, but this was questioned as Pham et al (185) and Bray et al (37) have demonstrated a long and tortuous mitochondrion in amastigotes. Since then Akiyama & McQuillen (11) have confirmed that the mitochondrion is extended during transformation from amastigote to promastigote. Tanikawa & Hojiro (227) claimed some disorganization in the cytoplasm of the host cell, but most electron photomicrographs seem to show this to be minimal (185, 197, 203). The question of a phagosome seems uncertain; Sanyal & Sen Gupta (203) demonstrated a vacuole in which *L. donovani* lay inside skin histiocytes, but Akiyama & Haight (10) using phase-contrast microscopy found that *L. donovani* may or may not lie inside a vacuole in macrophages.

It seems that the number of subpellicular microtubules in the amastigotes may be specific for each species. Garnham & Bird (84) found the number for *L. mexicana* to be 180–200, while Sanyal & Sen Gupta (203) found 80–120 in *L. donovani.* Angelopoulos (15) spread the microtubules of promastigotes of *Leishmania* by surface tension and found they radiated in all directions from a point near the flagellar base unlike the case in other trypanosomatids in which they spiraled. Safyanova et al (202) have found that the distance between microtubules differs as between mammalian and reptilian species.

Pham et al (185) found that *L. tropica* lacked any amount of rough endoplasmic reticulum but showed active pinocytosis of host cell cytoplasm. McAlpine (148) and Campo-Aasen (44) have demonstrated lysosomes in amastigotes of *L. donovani* and *L. braziliensis* s.l. thus confirming the observations of Rudzinska et al (199). According to McAlpine (148) it is a large structure lying between the flagellar pocket and the nucleus. Campo-Aasen et al (45) have demonstrated four isolated tubules in the reservoir region that may serve to anchor the subpellicular tubules to the flagellar apparatus. A curious invagination at the end of the amastigote distal to the flagellar pocket has been described by Pham et al (185) and Howells & Gardener (105). Creemers and Jadin (54, 108) have shown, during transformation from amastigote to promastigote, an increase in mitochondrial ridges at 1 hr and at 6 hr an increase in overall mitochondrial size, an increase in the empty space, and a concentration of the DNA fibrils to the center of the kinetoplast with a wider disposition of the cytoplasmic RNA granules.

Jadin & Creemers (54, 109) in a most interesting series of observations have shown that the rosettes of promastigotes found in cultures are due to a feeding process and not, as has sometimes been thought, to rapid division. In a rosette the promastigotes are directed flagellum inwards, and surround the granular debris of a dead promastigote upon which they are feeding. The granules are taken in through the flagellar pocket and are presumably pinocytosed. Aleman (12) demonstrated granules in the flagellar pocket similar to granules already present in the organism. No cytostome has been demonstrated, but a pair of tubules has been demonstrated adjacent to the flagellar pocket which may indicate an organelle of cytostome-like function (D. H. Molyneux, personal communication).

Cherepova (49) has shown that the promastigotes may contain pigment granules as well as lipid inclusions. Chatterjee & Sen Gupta (47) have demonstrated a band of amorphous material connecting the kinetoplast to the basal body. They also showed that the nuclear membrane may possess extensions which penetrate deep into the cytoplasm to form dilated vesicles. Sometimes two axonemes may be present in a single flagellar sheath. In *L. donovani* the kinetoplastic DNA is in the form of a coiled filament 20–50 Å wide. On division this coil elongates, then splits transversely inside the kinetoplastic membrane.

Bianchi et al (26) have described an endonuclear spindle but definitive studies on the nuclear division process are still lacking.

Wallace & Hertig (245) have used the morphology of the kinetoplastic DNA band to group flagellates recovered in Panama from sandflies. They found a group of six strains which showed a compact shortly delineated DNA band and which were equivalent to I, II, or uncertain categories of Schneider & Hertig (206). This group they felt were *L. mexicana*-like parasites. One strain (from *Lutzomyia sanguinaria*) had irregular fibers and masses of DNA which occupied most of a subcircular kinetoplast. They believe that this strain belongs to the monexenous genus *Leptomonas.* Rudzinska et al (199) and Akiyama & McQuillan (11) have shown two nucleoli in the amastigotes of *L. donovani* (Figure 1).

## VII. BIOCHEMISTRY

This is a much neglected aspect of the study of *Leishmania.* Two reviews exist, those of von Brand (27) and of Bell (21); the reader is referred to them for a general view. Simpson (217) has reviewed the structure and function of DNA of *L. tarentolae.* In recent years work has concentrated largely on biochemical variations in activity with temperature and transformation.

Using *L. enriettii* promastigotes, Greenblatt & Glaser (90) and Greenblatt & Wetzel (89) showed that raising the temperature to 30, 35, and 37°C caused an elevated respiration but a declining viability. Though phosphorus is taken up and the organisms respire and divide, inorganic phosphorus accumulates and leaks to the exterior. Permeability is increased 30 times but respiration increases only 2 times. There is loss of guanosine, uracil, hypoxanthine, ribose, and at least 13 amino acids. Lipid inclusions increase as 18 C fatty acids are increasingly incorporated. Transformation to oleic acid is mildly increased and to linoleic and linolenic acid considerably decreased. Korn & Greenblatt (116) have listed the fatty acids to be found in a culture of *L. enriettii.* Janovy and his colleagues (110–112, 188) have shown that respiration is increased as *L. donovani* transforms from amastigote to promastigote. They found too that respiration increases with temperature in the promastigotes of *L. donovani, L. tarentolae,* and *L. mexicana* with a peak at 35°C for *L. tarentolae* and *L. mexicana* and 37°C for *L. donovani.* The addition of glucose increased the oxygen uptake only of *L. tarentolae* while the addition of blood increased the oxygen uptake of *L. donovani* and *L. mexicana.* Aldolases (1–6 diphosphate aldolase EC4.1.2.b) from *L. tarentolae* and *L. adleri* were most active at 45°C and specific activity was highest in *L. tarentolae.* The same aldolase from *L. donovani* and *L. mexicana* was most active at 32°C. This result led Janovy (111) to investigate other enzymes to see of the greater tolerance to temperature on the part of the lizard strains was general and of evolutionary significance. Four dehydrogenases were studied in *L. donovani, L. mexicana,* and *L. tarentolae.* Not all were thermolabile though some were. Where thermolability of enzyme activity was present the species differences were most apparent. It was concluded that cutaneous *Leishmania* species were the most susceptible to the effect of homeothermic conditions and that this may on occasion also be the case with their enzyme systems.

Krassner (119, 120) has also studied the effect of temperature and transformation on *Leishmania.* He finds that heme is present in amastigotes but absent in promas-

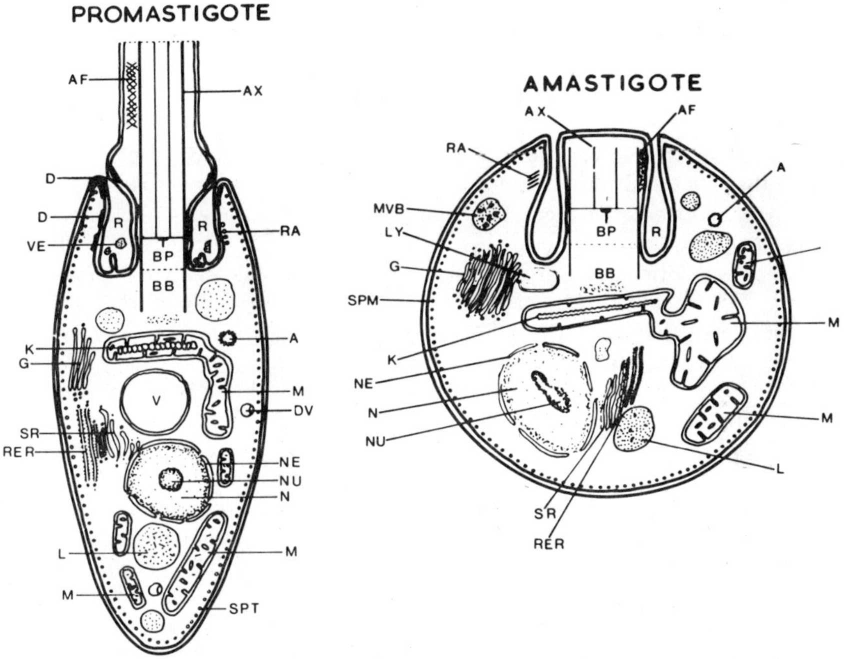


*Figure 1* A schematic representation of the fine structure of a promastigote and an amastigote. A = acanthosome; AF = accessory filament; AX = axoneme; BB = basal body; BP = basal plate; D = desmosome; DV = dense inclusion vesicle; G = golgi apparatus; I = invagination; K = kinetoplast; L = lipid; LY = lysosome; M = mitochondria; MVB = multivesiculate body; MT = subpellicular microtubules; N = nucleus; NE = nuclear envelope; NU = nucleolus; R = reservoir; RA = reservoir associated microtubules; RER = rough endoplasmic reticulum; SC = surface coat; SPM = subpellicular microtubules; SR = smooth reticulum; V = vacuole associated with nucleus; VE = vesicle.

tigotes, and that cytochromes are produced concurrently with the mitochondrial development during transformation from amastigote to promastigote. Present in the fully developed promastigote are succinic dehydrogenase, flavoproteins, and cytochromes *b* and *c* but not cytochrome oxidase. Fair & Krassner (74) found *L. tarentolae* aspartate aminotransferase (EC.2.6.1.1.) most active at 35°C but the alanic aminotransferase (EC.2.6.1.2.) most active at 29.5°C. Da Cruz & Krassner (55) grew *L. tarentolae* without organic sulphur using sodium sulphate instead. Mancilla et al (153) and Zeledon & De Monge (256) have studied general respiration and glucose respiration in promastigotes. $C^{14}$-labeled glucose when utilized by *L. enriettii* appears as carbon dioxide, protein, and acid metabolic products, and it was concluded that glycolysis and the Krebs cycle were the main pathways, while the pentose phosphate pathway was little used. Strains of *L. braziliensis* showing high multiplication rates and high infectivity and virulence for hamsters were also shown to have short lag phases, high respiratory rates and quotient, high nitrogen content, and high utilization of many substrates. Those with lower virulence, infectivity, and lag phase showed lower respiration. Inhibitors of respiration were iodacetate, arsenite, cyanide, azide, fluoracetate, and malanate. Von Brand et al (28) found that promastigotes consumed less glycerol compared to glucose as a substrate.

Voller et al (244) studied the uptake of 1,4 $C^{14}$ succinate and $C^{14}$ glucose. They found that almost all the glucose used went through the tricarboxylic cycle with glycolysis and transamination. They concluded that the Embden-Meyerhof pathways and Krebs cycle were being used. Chatterjee & Datta (48) found that labeled succinate was formed to a greater degree from (1–$C^{14}$) glucose than from (6–$C^{14}$) glucose. Ghosh & Datta (85) have concluded that the Embden-Meyerhof and Parnas pathways are more important than the shunt pathway. Krassner & Flory (121) found that proline stimulated oxygen uptake by *L. donovani* promastigotes and suggested that the proline-glutamate interconversion pathway was used.

Some studies have been made upon the action of drugs. De Jimenez & Ercoli (64) concluded that the action of Amphotericin B was not directed against succinic dehydrogenase. Trager & Rudzinska (239) showed that promastigotes of *L. tarentolae* require at least 10 $m\mu g/ml$ of riboflavin for optimal growth. If adequate riboflavin was present then acriflavin caused akinetoplasty but not death. Acriflavin altered the mitochondrion and kinetoplast, causing swelling of the cristae and loss of the structure of the DNA band. Trager (238) showed that *L. tarentolae* promastigotes required both folic acid and unconjugated pteridine. Simpson (216) studied the physiology of amastigote-promastigote transformation of *L. donovani.* He found a 5 to 7 times increase in the respiratory quotient after about 24 hr of transformation. Amastigote $QO_2$ was $0.29 \pm 0.01$ at 27°C as $\mu MO_2/min/10^7$ organisms and it was inhibited by cyanide, antimycin A, and sodium amytal, so presumably it was cytochrome dependent. Transformation was inhibited by actinomycin D, puromycin, and mitomycin C. Simpson & Braly (218) were able to synchronize DNA synthesis and therefore cell division of *L. tarentolae* by eliminating the S-phase cells with hydroxyurea. Synchronism was lost after two cycles. Stewart & Beck (223) found that a number of strains of *Leishmania* reacted with anti-DNA serum but not with antiserum against DNA linked to histone.

## VIII. IMMUNOLOGY

This area has gained enormously in knowledge in the past ten years. The sero-diagnosis of leishmaniasis has been reviewed by Bray (31) and the general subject reviewed by Dumonde & Preston (71). Some recent advances were outlined by Bray (30).

It is not proposed here to deal with sero-diagnosis but only with those highlights which have increased our knowledge of biologic and ecologic aspects of the genus.

Leishmaniasis has been shown to be a member of the growing group of diseases which depress the immune system. Serebryakov et al (211) infected subjects with *L. major* prior to a third inoculation with diptheria-pertussis-tetanus vaccine and showed that the subsequent immune reaction to diptheria was depressed. Adler (4) obtained a prolongation of skin graft acceptance in hamsters heavily infected with *L. donovani.* Avitaminosis due to lack of vitamin A, a known depressor of the immune reaction, allowed metastasis in guinea pigs infected with *L. enriettii* when normally fed guinea pigs showed no spread of the infection (151). Artificial suppression of the immune response using antilymphocyte serum, drugs, irradiation, and large infecting doses have all enhanced infection of the guinea pig with *L. enriettii* (42). Serological methods have been used for identification of strains, and by Simpson (216) to show that antigenic change occurs during amastigote-promastigote transformation. The Noguchi-Adler test (3) was used by Adler in identifying a strain from *P. martini* as Kenyan *L. donovani* (2) and used on Sudanese strains of *L. donovani* as already detailed. Since that time Safyanova and her colleagues have used the test extensively to differentiate between strains recovered from gerbil burrows. They have also developed a successful system for scoring the results (14). The technique has distinguished between *L. major, L. tropica,* and lizard strains (14, 201). Bray (29) developed an indirect hemagglutination test using cross-absorbed antisera for the identification of strains. The technique has been used on strains from cutaneous leishmaniasis of the Middle East (40), strains from cutaneous and visceral leishmaniasis of Ethiopia (19, 35), and strains of Bengali *L. donovani* (33) with the results already detailed in the various sections on taxonomy. A new test using excreted antigens from cultures shows some promise in differentiating groups (257).

An elegant technique for testing the serological affinities of various strains has been elaborated by Avakyan et al (20). They have labeled anti-sera with ferratin and added it to cultures of *Leishmania.* Thin sections of the promastigotes were then examined by electron-microscopy for evidence of agglutination by ferritin-labeled material. It was found that antiserum to *L. major* caused adherence in cultures of *L. major* and in one instance *L. tropica.* In the case of *L. tropica, L. adleri,* and a *Leishmania* from an agamid lizard the reaction was specific. A similar study by Strauss (225) showed a band of antibody between promastigotes which, however, did not fuse at lower antibody dilutions. At such dilutions promastigotes continued to grow as a mass of separate bonded organisms, not as a syncytium.

The effect of antisera upon parasites has been studied without anything very conclusive which might have an effect upon the life cycle being elicited. Rezai et al (193) have demonstrated a growth inhibiting factor in the serum of guinea pigs infected with and recovered from *L. enriettii* but it cannot as yet be taken that this is the mechanism of resistance to reinfection. Gunders & Yaari (93) have shown that the motility of promastigotes in an electric field is inhibited by immune serum.

It seems probable that effective immunity is bound up with both the antibody system and the cell-mediated immune system and both are necessary for rejection of the parasite. Bray (unpublished observations) has evidence of antibody or antigen-antibody complex assisting in the cytotoxic effect mediated by sensitized lymphocytes and macrophages in an infected tissue culture.

Evidence for the involvement of the cell-mediated immune system has come from the work of Bray & Bryceson (34), Bryceson et al (41), Tremonti & Walton (240), Bryceson et al (42), and Preston et al (190) who have shown that lymphocytes from animals recovering from *L. enriettii* infection and from cases of American cutaneous leishmaniasis respond to antigen by transformation and the production of mitogenic factor and macrophage migration inhibition factor. The unpublished results of Bray, Bryceson, Maini, Bowers, Holmes, and Dumonde have shown that in active and cured diffuse cutaneous leishmaniasis, active cutaneous leishmaniasis of Ethiopia, and kala azar the lymphocytes are not responsive to antigen, while they respond when taken from cases cured of cutaneous leishmaniasis.

Even in spontaneously cured cutaneous leishmaniasis resistance to reinfection is not absolute. Guirges (91) has reported eight cases of reinfection among 3420 patients with active disease, and Rahim & Tatar (192) and Ashford et al (19) have reported cases of reinfection. For contrast Manson-Bahr & Southgate (152) and Southgate (219) have reported that transient infection with *L. adleri* protects against further challenge by *L. adleri,* by a *Xerus* strain of presumed *L. donovani,* and by *L. donovani* of man.

## Acknowledgments

I am grateful to Dr. R. Lainson for his advice and for showing me the typescript of one of his reviews which was in press, to Dr. D. Molyneux and Dr. D. Bradley for allowing me to use material from working papers prepared by them for the seminar on leishmaniasis arranged by the Wellcome Trust in August 1973, and to Dr. R. W. Ashford for many useful discussions.

## *Literature Cited*

1. Adler, S. 1961. *Bull. Res. Counc. Isr. Sect. E* 9:166
2. Adler, S. 1963. *Isr. J. Exp. Med.* 11: 31–34
3. Adler, S. 1964. *Advan. Parasitol.* 2: 25–95
4. Adler, S. 1965. *Isr. J. Med. Sci.* 1:9–13
5. Adler, S., Foner, A., Montiglio, B. 1966. *Trans. Roy. Soc. Trop. Med. Hyg.* 60:380–86
6. Adler, S., Halff, L. 1955. *Ann. Trop. Med. Parasitol.* 49:37–41
7. Adler S., Theodore, O. 1932. *Proc. Roy. Soc. London Ser. B* 110:402–12
8. Adler, S., Theodore, O. 1935. *Proc. Roy. Soc. London Ser. B* 116:494–504
9. Adler, S., Theodore, O. 1957. *Ann. Rev. Entomol.* 2:203–26
10. Akiyama, H. J., Haight, R. D. 1971. *Am. J. Trop. Med. Hyg.* 20:539–45
11. Akiyama, H. J., McQuillan, N. K. 1972. *Am. J. Trop. Med. Hyg.* 21: 873–79
12. Aleman, C. 1969. *Exp. Parasitol.* 24: 259–64
13. Alencar, J. E. de. 1962. *Rev. Brasil. Malariol.* 14:367–70

14. Aliev, E. I., Safiyanova, V. M., Nadzhafov, A. Y., Gasanzade, G. B. 1972. *Med. Parazitol.* 41:531–36
15. Angelopoulos, E. 1970. *J. Protozool.* 17:39–51
16. *Ann. Rep. Gorgas Mem. Lab.* (Panama) 1957–1958
17. *Ann. Rep. Gorgas Mem. Lab.* (Panama) 1966–1967
18. *Ann. Rep. Gorgas Mem. Lab.* (Panama) 1968–1969
19. Ashford, R. W., Bray, M. A., Hutchinson, M. P., Bray, R. S. 1973. *Trans. Roy. Soc. Trop. Med. Hyg.* 67:568–601
20. Avakyan, A. A., Safiyanova, V. M., Koshelev, B. A. 1972. *Med. Parazitol.* 41:66–71
21. Bell, E. J. 1968. *Medicina Tropical,* ed. A. Anselmi, 109–32. Mexico City: Fournier
22. Belova, E. M. 1965. *Med. Parasitol. Parasit. Dis.* 34:349–51
23. Belova, E. M. 1971. *Bull. WHO* 44:553–60
24. Ben Rachid, M. S. 1967. *Arch. Inst. Pasteur Tunis* 44:155–61
25. Biagi, F. F. 1953. *Med. Mex.* 33:401–6
26. Bianchi, L., Rondanelli, E. G., Carosi, G., Gerna, G., Romero, E. 1969. *J. Parasitol.* 55:1091–92
27. Brand, T. von. 1966. *Rev. Biol. Trop.* 14:13–25
28. Brand, T. von, Tobie, E. J., Higgins, H. 1967. *J. Protozool.* 14:8–14
29. Bray, R. S. 1969. *Trans. Roy. Soc. Trop. Med. Hyg.* 63:378–82
30. Bray, R. S. 1972. *Brit. Med. Bull.* 28:39–43
31. Bray, R. S. 1974. *Immunology of Parasitic Diseases,* ed. E. H. Sadun, S. Cohen. Oxford: Blackwell Sci. Publ. In press
32. Bray, R. S. Ashford, R. W., Bray, M. A. 1973. *Trans. Roy. Soc. Trop. Med. Hyg.* 67:345–48
33. Bray, R. S., Ashford, R. W., Mukherjee, A. M., Sen Gupta, P. C. 1973. *Trans. Roy. Soc. Trop. Med. Hyg.* 67:125–30
34. Bray, R. S., Bryceson, A. D. M. 1968. *Lancet* iii:898–99
35. Bray, R. S., Bryceson, A. D. M. 1969. *Trans. Roy. Soc. Trop. Med. Hyg.* 63:524–27
36. Bray, R. S., Dabbagh, M. A. 1968. *J. Trop. Med. Hyg.* 17:46–48
37. Bray, R. S., Ellis, D. S., Bird, R. G. 1969. *Trans. Roy. Soc. Trop. Med. Hyg.* 63:10–11
38. Bray, R. S., Lainson, R. 1967. *Trans. Roy. Soc. Trop. Med. Hyg.* 61:490–505
39. Bray, R. S., Mumford, F. 1967. *J. Trop. Med. Hyg.* 70:23–24
40. Bray, R. S., Rahim, G. A. F. 1969. *Trans. Roy. Soc. Trop. Med. Hyg.* 63:383–87
41. Bryceson, A. D. M., Bray, R. S., Wolstencroft, R. A., Dumonde, D. C. 1970. *Clin. Exp. Immunol.* 7:301–41
42. Bryceson, A. D. M., Preston, P. M., Bray, R. S., Dumonde, D. C. 1972. *Clin. Exp. Immunol.* 10:305–35
43. Camerlynck, P., Ranque, P., Quilici, M. 1967. *Med. Trop.* 27:89–92
44. Campo-Aasen, I. 1970. *Med. Cutanea* 4:533–41
45. Campo-Aasen, I., Aleman, C., Convit, J. 1973. *Trans. Roy. Soc. Trop. Med. Hyg.* 67:122–24
46. Chakraborty, J., Das Gupta, N. N. 1962. *J. Gen. Microbiol.* 28:541–45
47. Chatterjee, S. N., Sen Gupta, P. C. 1970. *Ind. J. Med. Res.* 58:70–76
48. Chatterjee, T., Datta, A. G. 1973. *Exp. Parasitol.* 33:138–46
49. Cherepova, N. 1970. *Izv. Mikrobiol. Inst. Bulg. Akad. Nauk.* 21:265–76
50. Christensen, H. A., Herrer, A. 1972. *Trans. Roy. Soc. Trop. Med. Hyg.* 66:798–99
51. Christensen, H. A., Herrer, A., Telford, S. R. 1969. *J. Parasitol.* 55:1090–91
52. Coelho, M. de V. 1966. *Desenvolvimento de espécias do gênero Leishmania em espécies brasileiras de flebótomos do gênero Lutzomyia França 1924.* Tese. Inst. Nac. Endemias Rurais, Belo Horizonte, Minas Gerais
53. Courmes, E., Esudie, A., Fauvan, P., Monnerville, A. 1966. *Bull. Soc. Pathol. Exot.* 59:217–25
54. Creemers, J., Jadin, J. M. 1967. *Bull. Soc. Pathol. Exot.* 60:53–58
55. Da Cruz, F. S., Krassner, S. M. 1971. *J. Protozool.* 18:718–22
56. Danesco, P., Dedet, J. P., Ben Osman, F., Chadli, A. 1970. *Arch. Inst. Pasteur Tunis* 47:65–88
57. Deane, L. M. 1961. *Rev. Assoc. Med. Brasil* 7:161–69
58. Deane, L. M., Deane, M. P. 1954. *O. Hospital Rio de Janeiro* 45:419–21
59. Deane, L. M., Deane, M. P. 1962. *Rev. Inst. Med. Trop. Sao Paulo* 4:198–212
60. Deane, L. M., Deane, M. P. 1964. *Arq. Hig. Saude Pub.* 29:89–94
61. Dedet, J. P. 1969. *Epidemiologie de la leishmaniose viscerale en Tunisie. Etude des reservoirs de virus. Incidence et repartition de la leishmaniose canine.* Docteur de Spécialité thesis. Univ. Languedoc, Montpellier, France. 163 pp.

62. Dedet, J. P., Ben Osman, F. 1970. *Arch. Inst. Pasteur Tunis* 47:343–49
63. Dedet, J. P., Lanotte, G. 1969. *Arch. Inst. Pasteur Tunis* 46:69–81
64. De Jimenez, G., Ercoli, N. 1965. *Exp. Parasitol.* 17:302–8
65. Disney, R. H. L. 1964. *Trans. Roy. Soc. Trop. Med. Hyg.* 58:581
66. Dollahan, N. R., Janovy, J. 1973. *Exp. Parasitol.* 34:56–61
67. Dolmatova, A. V. 1965. *Med. Parasitol. Parasit. Dis.* 34:297–302
68. Dubrovsky, Y., Belova, E. M., Neronov, V. M. 1966. *Med. Parasitol. Parasit. Dis.* 35:275–81
69. Dubrovsky, Y. A., Neronov, V. M., Belova, E. M., Komarova, L. V. 1968. *Med. Parazitol.* 37:60–65
70. Dubrovsky, Y. A., Safiyanova, V. M. 1971. *Med. Parazitol.* 40:556–61
71. Dumonde, D. C., Preston, P. M. 1974. *Immunology of Parasitic Diseases,* ed. E. H. Sadun, S. Cohen. Oxford: Blackwell Sci. Publ. In press
72. Eliseev, L. N., Dergacheva, T. I., Kellina, O. A., Lavrova, M. Y., Strelkova, M. V. 1973. *Int. Congr. Trop. Med. Mal. 9th* (Abstr. of invited papers) 1:210
73. Eliseev, L. N., Kellina, O. I. 1964. *Med. Parasitol. Parasit. Dis.* 33:101–2
74. Fair, D. S., Krassner, S. M. 1971. *J. Protozool.* 18:441–44
75. Floch, H. 1954. *Arch. Inst. Pasteur Guyane Fr. Publ.* 328, 4 pp.
76. Foner, A. 1963. *Isr. J. Exp. Med.* 11:69
77. Forattini, O. P. 1960. *Rev. Inst. Med. Trop. Sao Paulo* 2:195–203
78. Forattini, O. P., Pattoli, D. G. B., Rabello, E. X., Ferreira, O. A. 1972a. *Rev. Saude Publ. Sao Paulo* 6:255–61
79. Forattini, O. P., Pattoli, D. G. B., Rabello, E. X., Ferreira, O. A. 1972b. *Rev. Saude Publ. Sao Paulo* 6:431–33
80. Fraga de Azevedo, J., Des Neves, V. M. 1963. *Ann. Parasitol. Hum. Comp.* 38:741–55
81. Frothingham, T. E., Lehtimaki, E. 1967. *Ann. J. Trop. Med. Hyg.* 16: 658–64
82. Frothingham, T. E., Lehtimaki, E. 1969. *J. Parasitol.* 55:196–99
83. Garnham, P. C. C. 1971. *Bull. WHO* 44:477–89
84. Garnham, P. C. C., Bird, R. G. 1962. *Sci. Rep. Ist. Super. Sanita.* 2:83–88
85. Ghosh, D. K., Datta, A. G. 1971. *Exp. Parasitol.* 29:103–9
86. Glazunova, Z. I. 1968. *Med. Parazitol.* 37:65–69
87. Gleiberman, S. E., Belova, E. M. 1964. *Med. Parasitol. Parasit. Dis.* 33: 650–54
88. Gonzales, H. A., Biagi, F. F. 1968. *Dermatol. Int.* 7:8–9
89. Greenblatt, C. L., Wetzel, B. K. 1966. *J. Protozool.* 13:521–31
90. Greenblatt, C. L., Glaser, P. 1965. *Exp. Parasitol.* 16:36–42
91. Guirges, S. Y. 1971. *Ann. Trop. Med. Parasitol.* 65:197–205
92. Gunders, A. E., Foner, A., Montilio, B. 1968. *Nature* 219:85–86
93. Gunders, A. E., Yaari, A. 1972. *Int. J. Parasitol.* 2:113–17
94. Heisch, R. B. 1963. *East Afr. Med. J.* 40:359–62
95. Herman, R. 1966. *J. Protozool.* 13: 408–18
96. Herman, R. 1968. *J. Protozool.* 15: 35–44
97. Herman, R., Baron, S. 1970. *Nature* 226:168–70
98. Herrer, A. 1971. *J. Parasitol.* 57:626–29
99. Herrer, A., Telford, S. R. 1969. *Science* 164:1419–20
100. Herrer, A., Telford, S. R., Christensen, H. A. 1971. *Ann. Trop. Med. Parasitol.* 65:349–58
101. Hindle, E. 1931. *Proc. Roy. Soc. London Ser.* B 108:366–83
102. Hindle, E., Thomson, J. G. 1928. *Proc. Roy. Soc. London Ser.* B 103:252–57
103. Holbrook, T. W., Stauber, L. A. 1972. *J. Protozool.* 19:490–93
104. Hoogstraal, H., Heyneman, D. 1969. *Am. J. Trop. Med. Hyg.* 18:1091–1210
105. Howells, R. E., Gardener, P. J. 1972. *Trans. Roy. Soc. Trop. Med. Hyg.* 66:336
106. Ilardi, A., Hashimoto, I., Fiorillo, P., Gugliemi, S. 1969. *Parassitologia* 11:161–69
107. Isayev, L. M. 1966. *Med. Parasitol. Parasit. Dis.* 35:259–62
108. Jadin, J. M., Creemers, J. 1966. *Ann. Soc. Belge Med. Trop.* 46:349–54
109. Jadin, J. M., Creemers, J. 1967. *Bull. Soc. Pathol. Exot.* 60:58–60
110. Janovy, J. 1967. *Exp. Parasitol.* 20: 51–55
111. Ibid 1972. 32:196–205
112. Janovy, J., Poorman, A. E. 1969. *Exp. Parasitol.* 25:276–82
113. Kalyakin, V. N. 1971. *Med. Parazitol.* 40:561–66
114. Kellina, O. I. 1965. *Med. Parasitol. Parasit. Dis.* 34:701–8
115. Kerdel-Vegas, F., Essenfeld-Yahr, E. 1966. *Trans. Roy. Soc. Trop. Med. Hyg.* 60:563
116. Korn, E. D., Greenblatt, C. L. 1963. *Science* 142:1301–3
117. Kozevnikov, P. V. 1963. *Am. J. Trop. Med. Hyg.* 12:719–24

118. Krampitz, H. E., Mühlpfordt, H. 1964. *Z. Tropenmed. Parasitol.* 15:269–78
119. Krassner, S. M. 1965. *J. Protozool.* 12:73–78
120. Ibid 1966. 13:286–89
121. Krassner, S. M., Flory, B. 1972. *J. Protozool.* 19:682–85
122. Lainson, R. 1974. *Bol. Of. Sanit. Panam.* In press
123. Lainson, R., Bray, R. S. 1966. *Trans. Roy. Soc. Trop. Med. Hyg.* 60:526–32
124. Lainson, R., Shaw, J. J. 1966. *Trans. Roy. Soc. Trop. Med. Hyg.* 60:533–35
125. Ibid 1968. 62:385–95
126. Ibid 1969a. 63:408–9
127. Ibid 1969b. 63:738–40
128. Ibid 1970. 64:654–57
129. Lainson, R., Shaw, J. J. 1971. *Ecology and Physiology of Parasites: A Symposium Held at University of Toronto, 19–20 Feb. 1970,* ed. A. M. Fallis, 21–56. Toronto: Univ. Toronto Press
130. Lainson, R., Shaw, J. J. 1972. *Brit. Med. Bull.* 28:44–48
131. Lainson, R., Shaw, J. J., Lins, Z. C. 1969. *Trans. Roy. Soc. Trop. Med. Hyg.* 63:741–45
132. Lainson, R., Shaw, J. J., Ward, R. D., Fraiha, H. 1973. *Trans. Roy. Soc. Trop. Med. Hyg.* 67:184–96
133. Lainson, R., Southgate, B. A. 1965. *Trans. Roy. Soc. Trop. Med. Hyg.* 59:716
134. Lainson, R., Strangways-Dixon, J. 1963. *Trans. Roy. Soc. Trop. Med. Hyg.* 57:242–65
135. Lainson, R., Strangways-Dixon, J. 1964. *Trans. Roy. Soc. Trop. Med. Hyg.* 58:136–53
136. Lamy, L. H. 1969. *Ann. Inst. Pasteur Paris* 117:545–55
137. Lamy, L. H., Samso, A., Lamy, H. 1964. *Bull. Soc. Pathol. Exot.* 57:16–21
138. Lariviere, M., Quenum, C., Abbonenc, E. 1961. *Bull. Soc. Med. Afr. Noire Langue Fr.* 6:431–35
139. Lariviere, M. et al 1965. *Bull. Soc. Med. Afr. Noire Langue Fr.* 10:237–38
140. Latyshev, N. I., Kryukova, A. P., Povalishina, T. P., Chernyshov, M. I. 1947. *Med. Parasitol. Parasit. Dis.* 5:5–6
141. Latyshev, N. I., Kryukova, A. P., Povalishina, T. P. 1951. *Prob. Regional, General Exp. Parasitol. Med. Zool. Moscow* 7:35–62
142. Laveran, A., Mesnil, F. 1903. *C. R. Acad. Sci.* 87:957–61
143. Lemma, A., Schiller, E. L. 1964. *Exp. Parasitol.* 15:503–13
144. Lewis, D. J. 1971. *Bull. WHO* 44: 535–51
145. Lupasco, G., Bossie-Agavriloaiei, A., Dincoulesco, M. 1963. *Arch. Roum. Pathol. Exp. Microbiol.* 22:167–72
146. Lupasco, G., Bossie, A., Dincoulesco, M., Epurean, E., Profeta, A. 1968. *Arch. Roum. Pathol. Exp. Microbiol.* 27:641–50
147. Lysenko, A. J. 1971. *Bull. WHO* 44: 515–20
148. McAlpine, J. C. 1970. *Trans. Roy. Soc. Trop. Med. Hyg.* 64:822–25
149. McConnell, E. 1963. *Exp. Parasitol.* 14:123–28
150. McMillan, B. 1965. *J. Parasitol.* 51: 336–39
151. Machado, J. O. L. 1969. *Bull. Soc. Pathol. Exot.* 62:689–95
152. Manson-Bahr, P. E. C., Southgate, B. A. 1964. *J. Trop. Med. Hyg.* 67:79–83
153. Mancilla, R., Naquira, C., Lanas, C. 1965. *Nature* 206:27–28
154. Mansour, N. S., Stauber, L. A., McCoy, J. R. 1970. *J. Parasitol.* 56:468–72
155. Marques, I. F. 1966. *Med. Cutanea* 1:287–92
156. Marques da Cunha, A., Chagas, E. 1937. *O. Hospital Rio de Janeiro* 11:148–52
157. Martinez Ruiz, J. L., Alvares Fuertes, G., Biagi, F. F. 1968. *Rev. Invest. Salud. Publ.* 28:107–18
158. Maruashvili, G. M., Bardzhadze, B. G. 1966. *Med. Parasitol. Parasit. Dis.* 35:462–63
159. Mata, A. D., Ruiz, C. B., Gasca, E. F., Morales, M. C. 1968. *Salud. Publ. Mex.* 10:159–71
160. Mesghali, A., Seyedi-Rashti, M. A., Nadim, A. 1967. *Bull. Soc. Pathol. Exot.* 60:514–18
161. Miller, H. C., Twohy, D. W. 1967. *J. Protozool.* 14:781–89
162. Minter, D. M., Wijers, D. J. B. 1963. *Ann. Trop. Med. Parasitol.* 57:24–31
163. Moskovskij, S. D., Southgate, B. A. 1971. *Bull. WHO* 44:491–97
164. Most, H., Alger, N., Yoeli, M. 1964. *Nature* 15:735–36
165. Muniz, J., Medina, H. 1948. *O. Hospital Rio de Janeiro* 33:7–25
166. Nadim, A., Amini, H. 1970. *Trop. Geogr. Med.* 22:476–78
167. Nadim, A., Faghih, M. 1968. *Trans. Roy. Soc. Trop. Med. Hyg.* 62:534–42
168. Nadim, A., Mesghali, A., Amini, H. 1968. *Trans. Roy. Soc. Trop. Med. Hyg.* 62:543–49
169. Nadim, A., Seyedi-Rashti, M. A., Mesghali, A. 1968a. *J. Trop. Med. Hyg.* 71:238–39
170. Nadim, A., Seyedi-Rashti, M. A.,

Mesghali, A. 1968b. *J. Trop. Med. Hyg.* 71:240–42
171. Naggan, L. et al 1970. *J. Infec. Dis.* 121:427–32
172. Nery-Guimaraes, F., Azevedo, M. 1964. *O. Hospital Rio de Janeiro* 66:279–85
173. Nery-Guimaraes, F., Costa, O. R. da 1964. *O. Hospital Rio de Janeiro* 66:287–91
174. Nicoli, R. M. 1963. *Bull. Soc. Pathol. Exot.* 56:408–16
175. Nicolle, C. 1908. *Arch. Inst. Pasteur Tunis* 3:3–26
176. Omar, A., Saboor, A., Amin, F. M., Sery, V. 1969. *Z. Tropenmed. Parasitol.* 20:293–302
177. Ott, K. J., Hanson, W. L., Stauber, L. A. 1967. *J. Parasitol.* 53:641–45
178. Packchanian, A., Kelly, L. 1965. *Tex. Rep. Biol. Med.* 23:767–75
179. Padilla, H. C., Lainez, N. H. 1968. *Med. Cutanea* 3:119–23
180. Paraense, L. W. 1953. *Trans. Roy. Soc. Trop. Med. Hyg.* 47:556–60
181. Poul, J., Pallas, P. 1962. *Arch. Inst. Pasteur Alger.* 40:329–35
182. Petrisceva, P. A. 1971. *Bull. WHO* 44:567–76
183. Petrishcheva, P., Zasukhin, D., Safyanova, V. Undated. *Human Diseases with Natural Foci,* ed. Y. N. Pavlovsky, 282–346. Moscow: Foreign Languages Publishing House
184. Petrovic, Z., Bordjoski, A., Savin, Z., Conic, V. 1973. *Int. Congr. Trop. Med. Mal. 9th.* Abstracts of communications, 2, 133
185. Pham, T. D., Azar, H. A., Moscovic, E. A., Kurban, A. K. 1970. *Ann. Trop. Med. Parasitol.* 64:1–4
186. Pifano, C. F., Romero, M. J. 1964. *Gac. Med. Caracas* 72:473–79
187. Ponirovsky, E. N. 1969. *Med. Parazitol.* 38:62–66
188. Poorman, A. E., Janovy, J. 1969. *Exp. Parasitol.* 26:329–35
189. Popovic, D. 1965. *Angew. Parasitol.* 6:181–85
190. Preston, P. M., Carter, R. L., Leuchars, E., Davies, A. J. S., Dumonde, D. C. 1972. *Clin. Exp. Immunol.* 10:337–57
191. Pringle, G. 1957. *Bull. Endem. Dis.* 2:41–76
192. Rahim, G. F., Tatar, I. H. 1966. *Bull. Endem. Dis.* 8:29–54
193. Rezai, H., Gettner, S., Behforouz, N. 1972. *J. Med. Microbiol.* 5:371–75
194. Rioux, J. A., Golvan, Y. J. 1969. *Épidémiologie des Leishmanioses dans le Sud de la France.* Monogr. Inst. Nat. Santé Rech. Méd., No. 37, Paris, 220 pp.
195. Rivero, N., Zeledon, R. 1966. *Rev. Biol. Trop.* 14:297–315
196. Rohrs, L. C. 1964. *Am. J. Trop. Med. Hyg.* 13:265–71
197. Rondanelli, E. G., Carosi, G., Cavalcanti, U., Sprovieri, G. 1971. *Parassitologia* 13:333–38
198. Ross, R. 1903. *Brit. Med. J.* II:1401
199. Rudzinska, M. A., D'Alesandro, P. A., Trager, W. 1964. *J. Protozool.* 11: 166–69
200. Safiyanova, V. M., Alekseev, A. N. 1967. *Med. Parazitol.* 36:580–86
201. Safyanova, V. M., 1966. *Med. Parasitol. Parasit. Dis.* 35:686–89
202. Safyanova, V. M., Avakyan, A. A., Aliev, E. I., Koshelev, B. A. 1973. *Progr. Protozool.,* 358:
203. Sanyal, A. B., Sen Gupta, P. C. 1967. *Trans. Roy. Soc. Trop. Med. Hyg.* 61:211–16
204. Sati, M. H. 1963. *Exp. Parasitol.* 14:52–53
205. Schaeffer, F. W., Bell, E. J., Etges, F. J. 1970. *Exp. Parasitol.* 28:465–72
206. Schneider, C. R., Hertig, M. 1966. *Exp. Parasitol.* 18:25–34
207. Sen Gupta, P. C. 1973. *Int. Congr. Trop. Med. Mal. 9th* (Abstr. of invited papers). 1:146
208. Seyedi-Rashti, M. A., Nadim, A. 1967. *Bull. Soc. Pathol. Exot.* 60:510–14
209. Seyedi-Rashti, M. A., Nadim, A., Naficy, A. 1971. *J. Trop. Med. Hyg.* 74:70–72
210. Serebryakov, V. A., Yusupov, K. A., Nu, G. V., Shishlyaeva-Matova, Z. S. 1967. *Med. Parasitol. Parasit. Dis.* 36:267–71
211. Serebryakov, V. A., Karakhodzhaeva, S., Dzhumaev, M. D. 1972. *Med. Parasitol.* 41:303–7
212. Shaw, J. J., Lainson, R. 1968. *Trans. Roy. Soc. Trop. Med. Hyg.* 62:396–405
213. Shaw, J. J., Voller, A. 1964. *Trans. Roy. Soc. Trop. Med. Hyg.* 58:349–52
214. Shishlyaeva-Matova, Z. S., Ny, G., Zvyagintseva, T. V. 1966. *Med. Parasitol. Parasit. Dis.* 35:266–70
215. Simoes Barbosa, F., Mills, D. A., Coura, J. R. 1970. *Rev. Soc. Brasil. Med. Trop.* 4:113–15
216. Simpson, L. 1968. *J. Protozool.* 15: 201–7
217. Simpson, L. 1973. *J. Protozool.* 20:2–8
218. Simpson, L., Braly, P. 1970. *J. Protozool.* 17:511–17
219. Southgate, B. A. 1967. *J. Trop. Med. Hyg.* 70:33–36

220. Southgate, B. A., Manson-Bahr, P. E. C. 1967. *J. Trop. Med. Hyg.* 70:29–33
221. Stauber, L. A., McConnell, E., Hoogstraal, H. 1966. *Exp. Parasitol.* 18:35–40
222. Stauber, L. A. 1973. *Int. Congr. Trop. Med. 9th* (Abstr. of invited papers). 1:138–39
223. Stewart, J. M., Beck, J. S. 1967. *J. Protozool.* 14:225–31
224. Strangways-Dixon, J., Lainson, R. 1966. *Trans. Roy. Soc. Trop. Med. Hyg.* 60:192–201
225. Strauss, P. R. 1971. *J. Protozool.* 18:147–56
226. Taj-Eldin, S., Nouri, L., Jawad, J., Falaki, N. 1969. *J. Fac. Med. Baghdad.* 11:7–15
227. Tanikawa, K., Hojiro, O. 1965. *Karume Med. J.* 12:148–54
228. Taub, J. 1956. *Bull. Res. Counc. Isr.* 6:55–57
229. Thatcher, V. E., Eisenmann, C., Hertig, M. 1965a. *J. Parasitol.* 51:1002–23
230. Thatcher, V. E., Eisenmann, C., Hertig, M. 1965b. *J. Parasitol.* 51:842–44
231. Theodore, O. 1958. *Fliegen Palaearkt. Reg.* 9c:1–55
232. Theodore, O. 1964. In *Zoonoses,* ed. J. van den Hoeden, 475–91. Amsterdam: Elsevier
233. Theodore, O. 1954. *Proc. Int. Congr. Entomol. 12th* 771–72
234. Tikasingh, E. S. 1969. *Trans. Roy. Soc. Trop. Med. Hyg.* 63:411
235. Torrealba, J. W. 1964. *Gac. Med. Caracas* 72:99–115
236. Torrealba, J. W., Gomez-Nunez, J. C., Ulloa, G. 1972. *Trans. Roy. Soc. Trop. Med. Hyg.* 66:361
237. Torrealba, J. W., Torrealba, J. F., 1964. *Gac. Med. Caracas* 72:117–18
238. Trager, W. 1969. *J. Protozool.* 16: 372–75
239. Trager, W., Rudzinska, M. A. 1964. *J. Protozool.* 11:133–45
240. Tremonti, L., Walton, B. C. 1970. *Am. J. Trop. Med. Hyg.* 19:49–56
241. Ulrich, M., Trujillo Ortiz, D., Convit, J. 1968. *Trans. Roy. Soc. Trop. Med. Hyg.* 62:825–30
242. Veles, L. R., 1913. *Bull. Soc. Pathol. Exot.* 6:545
243. Vianna, G. 1911. *Brasil Med.* 25: 411–12
244. Voller, A., Shaw, J. J., Bryant, C. 1963. *Ann. Trop. Med. Parasitol.* 57:404–8
245. Wallace, E. G., Hertig, M. 1968. *J. Parasitol.* 54:606–12
246. WHO 1971. *Bull. WHO* 44:471–584
247. Wijers, D. J. B., Linger, R. 1966. *Ann. Trop. Med. Parasitol.* 60:501–8
248. Williams, P. 1966. *Ann. Trop. Med. Parasitol.* 60:365–72
249. Williams, P. 1970. *Trans. Roy. Soc. Trop. Med. Hyg.* 64:317–64
250. Wonde, T., Honigberg, B. M. 1971. *Am. J. Trop. Med. Hyg.* 20:828–38
251. Wright J. H. 1903. *J. Med. Res.* 10:472–82
252. Wu, C. C. 1958. *Chin. Med. J.* 77:307–9
253. Wykoff, D. E., Barnley, G. R., Winn, M. M. 1969. *East Afr. Med. J.* 46:204–7
254. Yakimov, V. L., Schockov, N. F. 1915. *C. R. Soc. Biol.* 78:107–9
255. Zeledon, R., Blanco, E., DeMonge, E. 1969. *Acta Trop.* 26:136–55
256. Zeledon, R. De Monge, E. 1967. *J. Parasitol.* 53:937–45
257. Zuckerman, A., Schnur, L. F., Greenblatt, C. L., Montillo, B. 1973. *Progr. Protozool.,* 455
258. Zvyagintseva, T. V. 1968. *Med. Parazitol.* 37:570–74

# BACTERIAL GENETICS EXCLUDING *E. COLI*

❖1637

*Mark Levinthal*
Department of Biological Sciences, Purdue University, W. Lafayette, Indiana 47907

CONTENTS

INTRODUCTION .......... 219
MODES OF GENETIC EXCHANGE .......... 219
*Conjugation* .......... 220
STRUCTURE OF LINKAGE MAPS .......... 223
*Enteriobacteriaceae* .......... 224
GENE ARRANGEMENTS .......... 225

## INTRODUCTION

Enteric bacteria have long been the paradigm for bacterial genetics. In recent years, genetic systems have been developed for a wide variety of other bacteria. It is of interest to compare modes of genetic transfer. Such information has already been an aid in bacterial taxonomy and evolutionary relationships (75). In addition, a comparative study will shed light on the selective pressures leading to genome arrangements.

This review will consider the major conjugation systems in bacteria and the kinds of genome structures found. It will focus on gene arrangements and the genetic regulatory patterns emerging from such linkage relationships. Its aim is to convince the reader that genetics is not restricted to *Escherichia coli,* that the tools are available to do elegant genetics in other bacteria, and that one ought to do so.

## MODES OF GENETIC EXCHANGE

Three major mechanisms for gene transfer between bacteria are known. Conjugation requires cellular contact, following which all or part of the bacterial chromosome is transferred. Transformation is the process of gene transfer mediated by soluble DNA molecules; small discrete portions of the genome are transferred. A third mechanism of gene transfer is transduction. Bacteriophage can, in a variety of ways, incorporate small segments of the bacterial chromosome and transmit these to a recipient. Neither transformation nor transduction involve cell-to-cell contact and both do transmit similar-sized fragments of the genome, but the two processes are distinguished by the sensitivity of transformation to DNA-degrading enzymes.

The distribution of genetic transfer mechanisms among bacteria is presented in Table 1. Conjugation is limited to *Enterobacteriaceae* and related families, to *Pseudomonaceae* and some related families, and to some members of the order *Actinomycetales.* Transduction and transformation are more generally distributed.

## *Conjugation*

The mechanism of conjugation was reviewed recently by Curtiss (34). Sexuality in coliforms has been studied most intensively and is the paradigm for the field. The conjugal mechanism involves a unidirectional transfer from male to female of all or part of the donor's chromosome. The element responsible for sexual differentiation

**Table 1** Genetic exchange in bacteria

| Genus | Mode of Exchange | | |
|---|---|---|---|
| | Conjugation | Transduction | Transformation |
| *Acinetobacter* | | 134[a] | 76 |
| *Agrobacterium* | | | 78 |
| *Bacillus* | | 44 | 131 |
| *Escherichia* | 85 | 86 | |
| *Erwinia* | 27 | | |
| *Haemophilus* | | | 1 |
| *Klebsiella* | | 28 | |
| *Micromonospora* | 12 | | |
| *Mycobacterium* | 48 | 47 | |
| *Neisseria* | | | 2,106 |
| *Nocardia* | 16 | | |
| *Pasteurella* | 84,99 | | 54,136 |
| *Proteus* | | 29 | |
| *Pseudomonas* | 56,92 | 62 | |
| *Rhizobium* | 55,77 | 83 | 9 |
| *Rhodopseudomonas* | 97 | | |
| *Salmonella* | 148 | 149 | |
| *Serratia* | 11 | | |
| *Shigella* | 123 | 42 | |
| *Staphylococcus* | | 38,101 | 49 |
| *Streptococcus* | | | 52 |
| *Streptomyces* | 63 | | |
| *Thermoactinomyces* | | | 69,70 |
| *Xanthomonas* | | | 31,32 |
| *Vibro* | 13 | | |

[a]The number refers to the appropriate reference. A blank indicates that this mode of gene transfer has not been described.

is an extra chromosomal plasmid called the fertility factor, $F^+$. Novick (104) reviewed the fertility factor and other plasmids. As an episome, F can exist in two states, autonomous and integrated into the chromosome. When integrated (an Hfr strain) genetic material is transferred with high frequency and in an oriented manner. Genes proximal to the site of insertion of F are transferred first. The integrated F factor is transferred last, so that most recombinants are $F^-$ (recipients). The F factor can insert in many sites giving rise to a family of Hfr strains. The autonomous F factor is transferred with high frequency from donor to recipient. Such transfer is independent of the chromosome. However, $F^+$ strains will donate genetic material at low frequency. Such recombinants are $F^+$, but the episome transfer occurs independently of chromosome transfer.

The fertility factor from *Escherichia coli* K12 has been transferred throughout the enterics and allied genera (119). The *Salmonella typhimurium* genome has been extensively mapped with Hfr strains derived from the *E. coli* K12 factor (122). In all respects, the fertility factor behaves identically in *Salmonella* and in *E. coli.*

A well-characterized conjugation system exists in *Pseudomonas* (58, 60). As in the enterics, sexual differentiation exists and is mediated by a plasmid, FP (61). The linkage groups are transferred unidirectionally, in a linear manner from donor ($FP^+$) to recipient, although $FP^+ \times FP^+$ crosses are also fertile (59). Strains carrying $FP^+$ do not lose this sex factor spontaneously, or after treatment with acridines (59). While $FP^+$ can be transferred independently of the chromosome, it does not spread infectiously, as does $F^+$, and various strains transfer with differing efficiencies (128).

Recently, several mutant sex factors were isolated and studied. One class shows extended fertility (130). This mutation allows efficient chromosome transfer to males ($FP^+$) as well as females. In addition, the mutant sex factor is transmitted with high frequency to $FP^+$ strains and is dominant. The stable co-existence of both sex factors in such strains is demonstrated by the ability to isolate both $FP^+$ and extended fertility donors from newly infected recipient populations.

At least three classes of FP mutants with decreased fertility have been isolated. Loutit (89) described a strain derived from an $FP^+$ donor which was defective in both sex factor and chromosome transfer. In addition, these strains could not be reinfected with $FP^+$. Since more than one sex factor can exist in a cell, it appears that this class of mutations is dominant to the wild type. Two other classes of transfer-deficient mutants were described by Stanisich (127). One class, FPd will not donate either sex factor or chromosome, but will act as a recipient with the extended fertility donor for either sex factor or chromosomal genes. In strains carrying FPd and the extended fertility donor, extended fertility is dominant both for chromosome transfer and the ability to supply a function required for FPd plasmid transfer. Another class, FPs shows only a slight reduction in recombination frequency, but seems to have altered cell surface properties (see below).

The original sex factor, FP2, did not transfer all regions of the chromosome with high efficiency, therefore other sex factors were sought. One such sex factor, FP39, was isolated (109). FP39 transferred a terminal marker, *leu-38,* at a frequency a thousand times higher than FP2. Time of entry studies indicated FP39 has a point of origin 10 min from that of FP2. However, since the direction of transfer of FP2 and FP39 is the same and no markers are proximal to FP39 and distal for FP2, it is possible that the two sex factors have identical points of origin, but that chromosome entry is delayed 10 min. In all other properties, FP39 is identical to FP2. An approach toward isolating new donor strains is suggested by the ability to transfer R factors from *E. coli* to *Pseudomonas aeruginosa* and vice versa (132). In addition, these R factors promote conjugation with some markers being recovered at frequencies higher than observed with FP2 (129). Some transductants of *Pseudomonas putida,* using the generalized transducing phage pf16, harbor a defective prophage pfdm (24) replicating in an autonomous state. In certain cells carrying pfdm, conjugation occurs with the transfer of chromosomal markers as well as pfdm. Such recombinants are unstable and appear to be partial diploids. Another plasmid, CAM, has been shown to carry genes controlling camphor oxidation (114). The plasmid is transmissible and able to promote chromosome mobilization at a low frequency (126).

There has not been a clear demonstration of sex factor-determined surface structures analogous to the $F^+$ sex pili. However, *fer* mutants have been isolated in which a chromosomally located gene allows for increased ability to form recombinants (108). Strains carrying the *fer* mutation show an increased tendency at low pH, to agglutinate while strains harboring the mutant FPs sex factor show a lesser tendency under the same conditions (127). Such work supports the view that cell surface structures are involved in the conjugation process.

The development of an interrupted mating technique for *P. aeruginosa* (93) revealed a conjugation process very similar to that of the enteric bacteria. Selection for late entry markers yielded co-inheritance of proximal markers, and markers with similar times of entry were co-transducible (87, 88, 90, 91). In most cases, recombinants are haploid (57), but the FP39 sex factor appears to carry to the *leu-38* region of the chromosome (109). However, it is not yet clear that the FP sex factor must integrate into the chromosome to promote conjugation. Indeed, the evidence cited above suggests that more than one FP factor is present in each male and since each of these is independently transmissible, an extrachromosomal location is suggested.

A third conjugal system has been described for *Streptomyces coelicolor.* A recent review of this genetic system has appeared (66), but earlier reviews (65, 68) should be consulted for the theory and methodology of the genetic system. *Streptomyces* is an actinomycete and thus resembles the fungi in growing with multinucleate and branching hyphae which form a colony after several days. Aerial hyphae develop septa and form spores which are usually uninucleate. The spores can be collected and replated whereupon they germinate and form vegetative hyphae.

Hopwood (63) demonstrated recombination between genetically marked strains of *S. coelicolor.* Crosses were performed by mixing spores of appropriately marked strains on petri plates. Mating occurs between hyphae produced after germination and recombinants are selected for and analyzed by plating spores on selective media. While recombinants are usually the minority class, certain combinations of mating types produce recombinants efficiently, and such recombinants may constitute the entire spore progeny. In such cases, one can sample the recombinants by plating spores on nonselective media.

Crosses tended to give unequal numbers of complimentary recombinants (64), indicating a donor-recipient mating system and the formation of incomplete zygotes. Indeed, Sermonti & Casciano (125) showed that two mating types ($R^+$ and $R^-$) existed and that $R^+ \times R^-$ or $R^+ \times R^+$ crosses were fertile while $R^- \times R^-$ crosses were not. Later work (124) showed that the $R^+$ cell was the donor and the zygote was formed in the $R^-$ cell by progressive chromosome transfer from donor to recipient.

Mutagenesis of donor strains (NF) lead to the production of highly fertile strains (UF) (67). Analysis of NF X UF crosses showed that the UF strain contributed its entire chromosome to the zygote, while the NF donor contributed a population of fragments all of which contained a common region of the chromosome. All progeny were NF. The NF-contributed fragments formed a bidirectional gradient with markers having a decreasing probability of transfer as their distance from the common region increased. Such a gradient is not formed in NF X NF crosses where a random population of fragments is transferred. A third fertility type, IF, was distinguished, unlike the NF types, on the basis of being able to give rise to UF at high frequency.

The explanation of these results appears to be that the IF type harbors a plasmid SCPl (137) in the autonomous state. The NF strains ($R^+$) contain the plasmid in an integrated state, presumably at the common region, while the UF ($R^-$) recipient lacks the plasmid. Using IF strains, new donors were isolated (139). These new donors had differing patterns of marker donation and produced a unidirectional gradient of transfer to UF recipients.

The SCP1 plasmid is not the only determinant of fertility. Crosses between UF strains are fertile and have the appearance of a conjugal system (138), although such crosses are less fertile than IF X UF crosses. However, using strains with identical markers, while only varying which parent contains the SCP1, shows that this plasmid plays a role in gene transfer analogous to the $F^+$ of *E. coli.*

Thus, in three different conjugal systems involving major groups of unrelated bacteria certain generalizations emerge. In all, sexual differentiation exists—sexuality is controlled by a plasmid, which results in incomplete zygotes being formed in the recipient. However, these similarities may be superficial and it behooves us to understand the conjugal process in more detail in bacteria other than *E. coli.*

## STRUCTURE OF LINKAGE MAPS

A criterion of genetic relatedness of two species is similarity of the linkage map. Such a comparison requires detailed genetic analysis of large sections of the map and is usually confined to species having conjugation systems. However, one can obtain information from organisms extensively studied by transduction and transformation, and even (see below) from organisms where no known mode of genetic transfer is involved.

*Enteriobacteriaceae*

The genes of *E. coli* K12 and *Salmonella typhimurium* are arranged in a single, circular linkage group (120, 133). These two closely related organisms have almost identical gene sequences but certain differences exist. The *trp-cysB pyrF* segments are arranged in the same order in the two genera, but are inverted with respect to the rest of the genome (121). *Salmonella* is missing the *lac* genes and *proAB* is more closely linked to *proC* than in *E. coli* K12 (100). A smaller number of genes have been mapped in *E. coli* B (15), *E. coli* C (144), and *Salmonella abony* (95). So far no differences in the linkage arrangement have been detected. A mapping of eight scattered loci in *Erwinia* (27) shows the same order as *Escherichia* and *Salmonella.* The *Shigella flexneri* genetic map is also identical to the *E. coli* map (123).

A less related group to *E. coli* is *Proteus.* The genetics of *Proteus* have been reviewed recently (30). The *trp-cysB* region of *Proteus mirabilis* appears to be similar to *E. coli,* but other regions of the chromosome show differences. Several different species of *Proteus (P. mirabilis, P. vulgaris, P. rettgeneri,* and *P. morganii)* have similar linkage arrangements.

The linkage map of *S. coelicolor* is circular (68) and an analysis of *Streptomyces rimosus* (45) and *Streptomyces bikiensis* (22) shows their linkage groups identical to *S. coelicolor.* Although other actinomycetes show genetic recombination (see Table 1), not enough data has accumulated to compare linkage maps.

Since a conjugation system is not available for *Bacillus,* it is hard to assess the overall structure of the linkage group from transduction and transformation crosses. However, a combination of transduction analysis (39) and a technique of ordered gene replication (105) suggests that the linkage group of *Bacillus subtilis* is a single continuous structure. Furthermore, physical analysis of the early events in chromosome replication points to a circular chromosome (146, 147). Indeed autoradiographic analysis of replicating chromosomes strongly suggests a continuous circular structure (37). The fine structure of two regions of the *Bacillus* were examined in detail by transformation and found to be identical in *B. subtilis, Bacillus megaterium,* and *Bacillus niger* (118).

The original mapping data with *Pseudomonas aeruginosa* suggested that more than one linkage group existed (43), but more recent information (107) shows that all the genes may be arranged on a single linear chromosome. However, the possibility of a closed linkage group has not been tested. The gene arrangements in *P. putida* and *P. aeruginosa* were compared by transduction (25) and shown to be very similar.

Altenbern (3) developed a mapping method for *Staphylococcus* which depends on marker frequency induction by nitrosoguanidine in synchronously replicating cells. Using this method he found a single linear map for *Staphylococcus aureus* (4) and demonstrated similarities between the *S. aureus* gene orders and the gene orders of other species of *Staphylococcus* (5). He performed the same analysis with *Brucella abortus* and showed it also contained a single linkage group, but the gene orders were different from those of the Staphylococci (6). His technique is applicable to all bacteria and can yield reasonably detailed linkage relationships even in the absence of a known mode of genetic transfer.

All bacteria analyzed genetically have a single, haploid linkage group. In most, if not all cases, the linkage groups are closed. Closely related genera conserve linkage relationships. It would appear that gene orders are not random, but reflect a selective advantage; rearrangements are counter selected.

## GENE ARRANGEMENTS

A knowledge of the arrangement of genes on chromosomes allows us to infer the mechanism of genetic regulation. The initial observation by Demerec et al (36) of the clustering of functionally related genes in *S. typhimurium* suggested a genetic organization more complex than the gene. Later work in *Escherichia coli* by Jacob & Monod (73) led to the formulation of a new structural unit, the operon. As more mapping data accumulated Demerec (35) was able to generalize the Jacob-Monod model to genes other than *lac.* As more control units of *E. coli* and *S. typhimurium* were analyzed it became clear that not all of these constituted simple operons like the *lac, his,* and *trp.* In the *ilv* gene cluster, for example, although the structural genes are linked, it is divided into three control units (111–113). Maas (94) recognized that the genes for arginine biosynthesis were organized as a regulon (a group of genes linked as well as unlinked which respond to a common signal). Even in the *arg* regulon four structural genes are clustered and controlled by a single operator (23); the details (41, 74) of the control system are complicated.

An early analysis of the *Pseudomonas* linkage groups showed an absence of functionally related genes (59). However, the biodegradative pathways show a high degree of clustering. Close linkage was shown (115) for the enzymes of the β-ketoadipate pathway, but it is not clear that this arrangement has regulatory significance. Wheelis & Stanier (142) have shown that these closely linked loci are independently regulated. This situation is reminiscent of the *E. coli* K12 *ilv* gene cluster. The details of regulatory systems in *Pseudomonas* have yet to be worked out and may turn out to be different from those of enteric bacteria which would reflect the gene relationships. In this regard, one views with interest the work of Clarke and her associates (reviewed in 21) on the genetics and biochemistry of the aliphatic amidinase system. She has isolated and characterized several classes of regulatory mutants for this inducible system and has identified a regulatory gene closely linked to the structural gene.

The linkage groups of *Streptomyces* (66) show more clustering than *Pseudomonas* and less than *E. coli.* Six of the eight genes of the histidine pathway are clustered; the *trp* genes are in two clusters, some of the *aro* genes are clustered, and two of the three *ilv* genes are clustered. Other examples can be gleaned from the map.

*Bacillus* shows less clustering, but the *trp* genes are clustered (8, 19). Degradative pathways have not been studied in *Bacillus.* It would be of some interest to see if these are clustered.

Some regulatory systems have been studied in a number of different organisms. Such studies allow us to compare gene arrangements with modes of regulation and perhaps will allow some insight into the evolution of regulatory systems.

Tryptophan is synthesized from chorismate in five steps (for a review see 96). The flow of carbon through the pathway is controlled by endproduct inhibition of the first enzyme, anthranilate synthetase. Endproduct inhibition has been shown in *E. coli* (72), *S. typhimurium* (10), *Klebsiella aerogenes* (40), *B. subtilis* (102), *Bacillus alvie* (20), *Pseudomonas putida* (110), and *Chromobacterium violaceum* (141). Endproduct control is widely distributed among the bacteria.

The details of the regulation of enzyme synthesis for the tryptophan pathway are well worked out in *Salmonella* and *Escherichia.* The structural genes are clustered and under the control of a single operator. Upon limitation for tryptophan, derepression ensues until the level of tryptophan increases, and then the free amino acid combines with the product of *trpR* gene to stop transcription of the operon. A similar control pattern was observed in *Serratia marcescens* (71). A preliminary analysis of *Acinetobacter calco-aceticus* (135) shows that anthranilate synthetase is the only enzyme of the pathway which derepresses upon tryptophan limitation. In *B. subtilis,* the *trp* genes are clustered (19), but it is not clear they constitute a separate regulatory unit (143). Regulatory mutants analogous to the *trpR* mutants of *E. coli* have been isolated and, although these show several phenotypes, no class shows a coordinate response for all the enzymes (103).

In *Pseudomonas,* the *trp* genes are organized in two gene clusters (26). One group contains the genes (*trpABD*) for three enzymes and the second contains the genes for tryptophan synthetase. The *trpABD* cluster appears to be an operon under repression control by tryptophan and *trpR* mutations render their expression constitutive (53). Tryptophan synthetase formation is induced by substrate (33) and another unlinked gene (*trpC*) is not under any control (33). The regulatory gene(s) maps closely to the *trpABD* cluster (98)—an observation made in *B. subtilis* as well (103).

The histidine operon in *E. coli* (46, 51), *Salmonella typhimurium* (50), and *S. aureus* (79) is a contiguous set of genes. The details of the control system in *Salmonella* have been under intensive study for many years (see 50 for review). The operon will derepress when histidine is limiting, but the actual co-repressor is *his-tRNA.* Two classes of constitutive mutations have been isolated. Those unlinked by transduction to the histidine operon are involved in the production and modification of *his-tRNA:* adjacent to the structural genes, a second class of *cis* dominant operator mutations was isolated. The repressor gene has not yet been identified.

In *Streptomyces,* five genes are clustered, a sixth is close to the cluster, two others are clustered some distance away, and another, *hisD,* maps far away from the clustered genes (18). The *hisD* gene codes for the histidinol phosphate phosphatase while the *hisB* gene (located in the five-gene cluster) specifies the IGP-dehydrase (18). In *Salmonella* both activities are specified by the same gene. The same situation may have existed in *Streptomycetes* as the *hisD* is genetically distant from the others. However, the *hisD* gene does respond to histidine limitation, although noncoordinately with *hisA* and *hisB* (members of the cluster). The five-clustered histidine genes do form an operon. Synthesis of two of the enzymes is strictly coordinate. Of interest is a recent deletion mutation described by Russi et al (18) which genetically inactivated one gene of the *his* operon, but phenotypically could not express the remaining four genes. Derivative strains which could express *hisA* (growth on histidinol) appeared and these turned out to be extensions of the original deletion. These strains were no longer under histidine control. An analogous situation occurred in *Salmonella* (7). These events suggest that the five-gene cluster is under the control of an operator gene. Another observation is the sensitivity of the wild type to L-2,4-diamino butyric acid (DAB) (117). DAB mimics histidine and is a false feedback inhibitor of the first enzyme (pyrophosphorylase). However, DAB also prevents the utilization of L-histidinol (HOL). Since the activity of pyrophosphorylase does not require histidinol utilization, one might suppose that DAB and HOL are transported by a common carrier. However, the deletion mutation which renders HOL dehydrogenase constitutive is resistant to the action of DAB. Therefore, DAB must also interfere with regulation. Some evidence (17) in *Streptomyces* suggests that *his-tRNA* is involved in repression. DAB might be activated (like the analog triazolealanine) but this seems unlikely. On the other hand, since DAB interacts with the pyrophosphorylase, perhaps the pyrophosphorylase has a role in the control process.

In *Salmonella,* Goldberger and his associates (80, 81) demonstrated that genetic and chemical modifications of the pyrophosphorylase produced alterations in the repression process. The purified enzyme will bind the co-repressor, *his-tRNA* (14, 140) and bind specifically to *his* DNA in vitro (82). In addition, one regulatory mutation has been isolated which maps in the pyrophosphorylase structural gene (116) and several other different classes are currently being studied in my laboratory. If *Streptomyces* has the same mode of regulation by a structural gene product as *Salmonella,* it will be of interest, because the present mapping evidence in *Streptomyces* suggests that the pyrophosphorylase structural gene is not part of the five-gene cluster.

The recent work of Levinthal et al (87) demonstrated the central role of threonine deaminase as a positive regulatory element for all three *ilv* biosynthetic enzyme operons, as well as in the control of the three-branched chain amino-acyl-tRNA synthetases. The work on *ilv* and *his* suggests a possible explanation for the observation that the structural gene for the first enzyme of the pathway always maps adjacent to the operator. Such is the case even in regulons in *E. coli.* If the first enzyme is also involved in regulation of enzyme synthesis, it is not unreasonable to suppose that such regulation is exerted by binding of the enzyme to the operator region. Some suggestions have been made (145) that the present genetic code reflects a chemical interaction between codons and amino acids, reflecting a primitive protein synthetic system where amino acids interacted directly with the DNA. One might conceive of operator genes emerging as a tandem duplication of the first enzyme's structural gene and then mutating to a form where it served as a promoter. It might still retain enough chemical homology with the primary structure of the first enzyme to recognize it and thus be an operator locus. It is extremely interesting to learn about operator-first enzyme gene arrangements in bacteria other than *E. coli* to test this hypothesis. The genetics of regulation may turn out to be an important indicator of evolutionary relationships among the bacteria.

ACKNOWLEDGMENTS

I wish to thank Drs. R. F. Goldberger, H. E. Umbarger, and L. S. Williams; Ms. Maxine Levinthal, Ms. Christine A. Gritzmacher, and Mr. Thomas Newman for many hours of stimulating discussion on various aspects of this paper. I also thank Ms. Cindy Maxwell for her help in the preparation of the manuscript.

*Literature Cited*

1. Alexander, H. E., Leidy, G. 1951. *J. Exp. Med.* 93:234–59
2. Alexander, H. E., Redman, W. 1953. *J. Exp. Med.* 97:17–31
3. Altenbern, R. A. 1968. *Biochem. Biophys. Res. Commun.* 25:346–53
4. Altenbern, R. A. 1971. *Can. J. Microbiol.* 17:903–9
5. Ibid 1973. 19:105–8
6. Ibid 109–12
7. Ames, B. N., Hartman, P. E., Jacob, F. 1963. *J. Mol. Biol.* 7:23–42
8. Anagnostopoulos, C., Crawford, I. P. 1961. *Proc. Nat. Acad. Sci. USA* 47: 378–86
9. Balassa, R. 1960. *Nature* 188:246–47
10. Bauerle, R. H., Margolin, P. 1966. *Cold Spring Harbor Symp. Quant. Biol.* 31:203–14
11. Belser, W. L., Bunting, M. I. 1956. *J. Bacteriol.* 72:582–92
12. Beretta, M., Betti, M., Polsinelli, M. 1971. *J. Bacteriol.* 107:415–19
13. Bhaskaran, K., Iyer, S. S. 1961. *Nature* 189:1030–31
14. Blasi, F., Barton, R. W., Kovach, J. S., Goldberger, R. F. 1971. *J. Bacteriol.* 106: 508–13
15. Boyer, H. 1966. *J. Bacteriol.* 91: 1767–74
16. Brownell, G. H., Walsh, R. S. 1970. *J. Bacteriol.* 104:79–91
17. Carere, A., Russi, S. 1970. *G. Bot. Ital.* 104:349–56
18. Carere, A., Russi, S., Bignami, M., Sermonti, G. 1973. *Mol. Gen. Genet.* 123:219–24
19. Carlton, B. C., Whitt, D. D. 1969. *Genetics* 62:445–53
20. Catena, A., DeMoss, R. D. 1970. *J. Bacteriol.* 101:476–88
21. Clarke, P. H. 1970. *Advan. Microbiol. Physiol.* 4:179–221
22. Coats, J. H., Roeser, J. 1971. *J. Bacteriol.* 105:880–87
23. Cunin, R., Elseviers, D., Sand, G., Freundlich, G., Glandsdorff, N. 1969. *Mol. Gen. Genet.* 106:32–47
24. Chakrabarty, A. M., Gunsalus, I. C. 1969. *Proc. Nat. Acad. Sci. USA* 64: 1217–23
25. Chakrabarty, A. M., Gunsalus, I. C. 1970. *J. Bacteriol.* 103:830–32
26. Chakrabarty, A. M., Gunsalus, C. F., Gunsalus, I. C. 1968. *Proc. Nat. Acad. Sci. USA* 60:168–74
27. Chatterjee, A. K., Starr, M. P. 1973. *J. Bacteriol.* 116:1100–6
28. Clark, C. M. 1961. *Nature* 190:194
29. Coetzee, J. N. 1961. *Nature* 189:946–47
30. Coetzee, J. N. 1972. *Ann. Rev. Microbiol.* 26:23–54
31. Corey, R. R., Starr, M. P. 1957. *J. Bacteriol.* 74:141–45
32. Ibid 146–50
33. Crawford, I. P., Gunsalus, I. C. 1966. *Proc. Nat. Acad. Sci. USA* 56:717–24
34. Curtiss, R. III 1969. *Ann. Rev. Microbiol.* 23:69–136
35. Demerec, M. 1964. *Proc. Nat. Acad. Sci. USA* 51:1057–60
36. Demerec, M., Blomstrand, I., Demerec, Z. E. 1955. *Proc. Nat. Acad. Sci. USA* 41:359–64
37. Dennis, E. S., Wake, R. G. 1967. *Replication and Recombination of Genetic Material,* ed. W. J. Peacock, R. D. Brock, 61. Canberra: Aust. Acad. Sci.
38. Dowell, C. E., Rosenblum, E. D. 1962. *J. Bacteriol.* 84:1071–75
39. Dubnau, D., Goldthwaite, C., Smith, I., Marmur, J. 1967. *J. Mol. Biol.* 27: 163–85
40. Egan, A. F., Gibson, F. 1966. *Biochim. Biophys. Acta* 130:276–87
41. Elseviers, D., Cunin, R., Glansdorff, N., Baumberg, S., Ashcroft, E. 1972. *Mol. Gen. Genet.* 117:349–58
42. Falkow, S., Schneider, H., Baron, L. S., Formal, S. B. 1963. *J. Bacteriol.* 86: 1251–58
43. Fargie, B., Holloway, B. W. 1965. *Genet. Res.* 6:284–99
44. Francis, A. E., Rippon, J. E. 1949. *J. Gen. Microbiol.* 3:425–33
45. Friend, E. J., Hopwood, D. A. 1971. *J. Gen. Microbiol.* 68:187–97
46. Garrick-Silversmith, L., Hartman, P. E. 1970. *Genetics* 66:231–44
47. Gelbart, S. M., Juhasz, S. E. 1970. *J. Gen. Microbiol.* 64:253–54

48. Gelbart, S. M., Juhasz, S. E. 1973. *Antonie van Leeuweuhoek J. Microbiol. Serol.* 39:1–10
49. Gillissen, G. 1958. *Naturwissenschaften* 45:297
50. Goldberger, R. F., Kovach, J. S. 1972. *Curr. Top. Cell. Reg.* 5:285–308
51. Goldschmidt, E. P., Cater, M. S., Matney, T. S., Butler, M. A., Greene, A. 1970. *Genetics* 66:219–29
52. Griffith, F. 1928. *J. Hyg.* 27:113–59
53. Gunsalus, I. C., Gunsalus, C. F., Chakrabarty, A. M., Sikes, S., Crawford, I. P. 1968. *Genetics* 60:419–35
54. Henriksen, S. D. 1962. *Acta Pathol. Microbiol. Scand.* 55:496
55. Heumann, W. 1968. *Mol. Gen. Genet.* 102:132–44
56. Holloway, B. W. 1955. *J. Gen. Microbiol.* 13:572–81
57. Ibid 15:221–24
58. Holloway, B. W. 1969. *Bacteriol. Rev.* 33:419–43
59. Holloway, B. W., Fargie, B. 1960. *J. Bacteriol.* 80:362–68
60. Holloway, B. W., Krishnapillai, V., Stanisich, V. 1971. *Ann. Rev. Genet.* 5:425–46
61. Holloway, B. W., Jennings, P. A. 1958. *Nature* 181:855–56
62. Holloway, B. W., Van de Putte, P. 1968. *Nature* 217:459–60
63. Hopwood, D. A. 1957. *J. Gen. Microbiol.* 16:ii–iii
64. Hopwood, D. A. 1961. *Sci. Rep. Ist. Super. Sanita* 1:463–66
65. Hopwood, D. A. 1967. *Bacteriol. Rev.* 31:373–403
66. Hopwood, D. A., Chater, K. F., Dowding, J. E., Vivian, A. 1973. *Bacteriol. Rev.* 37:371–405
67. Hopwood, D. A., Harold, R. J., Vivian, A., Ferguson, H. M. 1969. *Genetics* 62:461–77
68. Hopwood, D. A., Sermonti, G. 1962. *Advan. Genet.* 11:273–42
69. Hopwood, D. A., Wright, H. M. 1971. *Heredity* 27:83–86
70. Hopwood, D. A., Wright, H. M. 1970. *J. Gen. Microbiol.* 71:383–88
71. Hutchinson, M. A., Belser, W. L. 1969. *J. Bacteriol.* 98:109–16
72. Ito, J., Yanofsky, C. 1966. *J. Biol. Chem.* 41:4112–17
73. Jacob, F., Monod, J. 1961. *J. Mol. Biol.* 3:318–56
74. Jacoby, G. A. 1972. *Mol. Gen. Genet.* 117:337–48
75. Jones, D., Sneath, P. H. A. 1970. *Bacteriol. Rev.* 34:40–81
76. Juni, E., Janik, A. 1969. *J. Bacteriol.* 98:281–88
77. Kaushik, B. D., Venkataraman, G. S. 1972. *Folia Microbiol. Prague* 17: 393–95
78. Klein, D. T., Klein, R. M. 1956. *J. Bacteriol.* 72:308–13
79. Kloos, W. E., Pattee, P. A. 1966. *J. Gen. Microbiol.* 39:195–207
80. Kovach, J. S., Berberich, M. A., Venetianer, P., Goldberger, R. F. 1969. *J. Bacteriol.* 97:1283–90
81. Kovach, J. S., Phang, J. M., Ference, M., Goldberger, R. F. 1969. *Proc. Nat. Acad. Sci. USA* 63:481–88
82. Kovach, J. S. et al 1972. *Abstr. Ann. Meet. Am. Soc. Microbiol.,* 169
83. Kowalski, M. 1971. *Plant Soil* Special volume: 63–66
84. Lawton, W. D., Morris, B. C., Burrows, T. W. 1968. *J. Gen. Microbiol.* 52:25–34
85. Lederberg, J., Tatum, E. L. 1946. *Nature* 158:558
86. Lennox, E. S. 1955. *Virology* 1:190–206
87. Levinthal, M., Williams, L. S., Levinthal, M., Umbarger, H. E. 1973. *Nature New Biol.* 246:65–68
88. Loutit, J. S. 1969. *Genet. Res.* 13:91–98
89. Ibid 14:103–9
90. Loutit, J. S., Marinus, M. G. 1969. *Genet. Res.* 12:37–44
91. Loutit, J. S., Marinus, M. G., Pearce, L. E. 1968. *Genet. Res.* 21:139–45
92. Loutit, J. S., Pearce, L. E. 1965. *J. Bacteriol.* 90:425–30
93. Loutit, J. S., Pearce, L. E., Marinus, M. G. 1968. *Genet. Res.* 12:29–36
94. Maas, W. K. 1961. *Cold Spring Harbor Symp. Quant. Biol.* 26:183–92
95. Mäkelä, P. H. 1963. *Genetics* 48:423–29
96. Margolin, P. 1971. *Metabolic Regulation,* ed. H. J. Vogel, 389–446. New York: Academic
97. Marrs, B. 1974. *Proc. Nat. Acad. Sci. USA.* In press
98. Maurer, R., Crawford, I. P. 1969. *Genetics* 61 (suppl. No 2/part 2)S:39
99. McMahon, P. C. 1971. *J. Gen. Microbiol.* 69:105–15
100. Miyake, T., Demerec, M. 1959. *Nature* 83:1586
101. Morse, M. L., LaBelle, J. W. 1962. *J. Bacteriol.* 83:775–80
102. Nester, E., Jensen, R. A. 1966. *J. Bacteriol.* 91:1594–1603
103. Nester, E. W., Jensen, R. A., Nasser, D. S. 1969. *J. Bacteriol.* 97:83–94
104. Novick, R. P. 1969. *Bacteriol. Rev.* 33:210–35
105. O'Sullivan, A., Sueoka, N. 1967. *J. Mol. Biol.* 27:349–58
106. Otero, R. B. 1972. *Experientia* 28: 484–85

107. Pemberton, J. M., Holloway, B. W. 1972. *Genet. Res.* 19:251–60
108. Pemberton, J. M., Holloway, B. W. 1972. *Aust. J. Exp. Biol. Med. Sci.* 50:577–88
109. Pemberton, J. M., Holloway, B. W. 1973. *Genet. Res.* 21:263–72
110. Queener, S. W., Gunsalus, I. C. 1969. *Bacteriol. Proc.* 61
111. Ramakrishnan, T., Adelberg, E. A. 1965. *J. Bacteriol.* 89:654–60
112. Ibid 661–64
113. Ratzkin, B., Arfin, S., Umbarger, H. E. 1972. *J. Bacteriol.* 112:131–38
114. Pheinwald, J. G., Chakrabarty, A. M., Gunsalus, I. C. 1973. *Proc. Nat. Acad. Sci. USA* 70:885–89
115. Rosenberg, S., Hegeman, G. D. 1969. *J. Bacteriol.* 99:353–55
116. Rothman-Denes, L., Martin, R. G. 1971. *J. Bacteriol.* 106:227–37
117. Russi, S., Carere, A., Siracusano, A., Ballio, A. 1973. *Mol. Gen. Genet.* 123:225–32
118. Saito, H., Takahashi, H., Ikeda, Y. 1973. *Genetics of Industrial Microorganisms,* ed. Z. Vanek, Z. Hostalek, J. Cudlin, 89–94. Prague: Academica
119. Sanderson, K. E. 1971. *Advan. Genet.* 16:35–51
120. Sanderson, K. E. 1972. *Bacteriol. Rev.* 36:558–86
121. Sanderson, K. E., Hall, C. A. 1970. *Genetics* 64:215–28
122. Sanderson, K. E., Ross, H., Ziegler, L., Mäkelä, P. H. 1972. *Bacteriol. Rev.* 36:608–37
123. Schneider, H., Falkow, S. 1964. *J. Bacteriol.* 88:682–89
124. Sermonti, G., Bandiera, M., Spada-Sermonti, I. 1966. *J. Bacteriol.* 91:384–92
125. Sermonti, G., Casciano, S. 1963. *J. Gen. Microbiol.* 33:293–301
126. Shaham, M., Chakrabarty, A. M., Gunsalus, I. C. 1973. *J. Bacteriol.* 116: 944–49
127. Stanisich, V. A. 1973. *Genet. Res.* 22: 13–24
128. Stanisich, V. A., Holloway, B. W. 1969. *Genetics* 61:327–39
129. Stanisich, V. A., Holloway, B. W. 1971. *Genet. Res.* 17:169–72
130. Ibid 19:91–108
131. Spizizen, J. 1958. *Proc. Nat. Acad. Sci. USA* 44:1072–78
132. Sykes, R. B., Richmond, M. H. 1970. *Nature* 226:952–54
133. Taylor, A. L., Trotter, C. D. 1972. *Bacteriol. Rev.* 36:504–24
134. Twarog, R., Blouse, L. E. 1968. *J. Virol.* 2:716–22
135. Twarog, R., Liggins, G. L. 1970. *J. Bacteriol.* 104:254–63
136. Tyeryar, F. J. Jr., Lawton, W. D. 1969. *J. Bacteriol.* 100:112–13
137. Vivian, A. 1971. *J. Gen. Microbiol.* 69:353–64
138. Vivian, A., Hopwood, D. A. 1970. *J. Gen. Microbiol.* 64:101–17
139. Ibid 1973. 76:147–62
140. Vogel, T., Meyers, M., Kovach, J. S. Goldberger, R. F. 1972. *J. Bacteriol.* 112:126–29
141. Wegman, J., Crawford, I. P. 1968. *J. Bacteriol.* 95:2325–38
142. Wheelis, M. L., Stanier, R. Y. 1971. *Genetics* 66:245–66
143. Whitt, D. D., Carlton, B. C. 1968. *Biochem. Biophys. Res. Commun.* 33: 636–42
144. Wiman, M., Bertani, G., Kelly, B., Sasaki, I. 1970. *Mol. Gen. Genet.* 197: 1–31
145. Woese, C. 1967. *The Genetic Code,* 179–88. New York: Harper & Row
146. Yoshikawa, H. 1967. *Proc. Nat. Acad. Sci. USA* 58:312–16
147. Yoshikawa, H. 1970. *J. Mol. Biol.* 47:403–8
148. Zinder, N. D. 1960. *Science* 131:924–26
149. Zinder, N. D., Lederberg, J. 1952. *J. Bacteriol.* 64:679–99

# SLOW VIRUS DISEASES ❖1638

*David A. Fuccillo, Jerome E. Kurent, and John L. Sever*
Infectious Diseases Branch, National Institute of Neurological Diseases and Stroke, National Institutes of Health, Bethesda, Maryland 20014

## CONTENTS

INTRODUCTION .......... 232
CONVENTIONAL AND UNCONVENTIONAL AGENTS OF SLOW DISEASE .......... 232
VIROLOGICAL AND CLINICOPATHOLOGICAL FINDINGS IN CHRONIC INFECTIONS OF THE CENTRAL NERVOUS SYSTEM .......... 233
*Chronic Infections of the Human CNS with Conventional Agents* .......... 233
*Subacute sclerosing panencephalitis* .......... 233
*Progressive multifocal leukoencephalopathy* .......... 237
*Chronic Infections of the Human CNS with Unconventional Agents* .......... 238
*Kuru* .......... 238
*Creutzfeldt-Jakob disease* .......... 238
*Chronic Infections of the Animal CNS with Conventional Agents* .......... 240
*Visna* .......... 240
*Lymphocytic choriomeningitis virus* .......... 242
*Chronic Infections of the Animal CNS with Unconventional Agents* .......... 243
*Scrapie* .......... 243
*Transmissible mink encephalopathy* .......... 245
THE POSSIBLE ROLE OF VIRUSES IN CHRONIC DEGENERATIVE DISEASES OF UNKNOWN ETIOLOGY .......... 245
*Multiple Sclerosis* .......... 247
*Guillain-Barré Syndrome* .......... 248
*Amyotrophic Lateral Sclerosis* .......... 248
*Parkinson's Disease* .......... 249
*Presenile Dementias* .......... 250
SPECIAL FEATURES OF SLOW VIRUS DISEASE .......... 250
*General Considerations* .......... 250
*Host-Related Factors in Slow Virus Infections* .......... 250
*Genetic factors* .......... 250
*Immunological factors* .......... 252
*Virus-Related Factors* .......... 254
*Long incubation period* .......... 254
*Viral persistence* .......... 254
*Antigenicity of agents* .......... 255
VIRUS-HOST INTERACTIONS AND THE PATHOGENESIS OF SLOW DISEASE .......... 256
*Cellular and Organ Specificity* .......... 256
*Transmissibility and Range of Host Susceptibility* .......... 257
*Viral Replication* .......... 258
THE FUTURE OF SLOW VIRUS RESEARCH .......... 259

# I. INTRODUCTION

The concept of slow virus infections was first introduced by Sigurdsson less than 20 years ago in his classic descriptions of scrapie, visna, maedi, and pulmonary adenomatosis, as transmissible chronic diseases of Icelandic sheep (172). These disorders are characterized by an insidious onset, chronic and unrelenting progressive course, and inexorably fatal outcome. Since then, additional slow virus infections have been described in humans and domestic animals.

Numerous excellent reviews have dealt with many aspects of slow virus infections (8, 38, 47, 55, 58, 60, 96, 108, 164, 185). This presentation attempts to synthesize conclusions which have been drawn from more recent investigations, and will be restricted to infections which involve the central nervous system. Consideration will also be given to the possible viral etiology of chronic degenerative diseases of unknown or obscure causation. Emphasis will be placed on recent developments in the area of specific host and virus factors as determinants of slow disease, and, when possible, virus-host interactions at the cellular level shall be stressed.

It has been observed that while virologists may refer to slow virus diseases, and while slow virologists may certainly exist, it is highly doubtful that there are in fact any slow viruses (51). The term slow refers to the clinical course of the disease in question, rather than to basic properties of the inciting agent.

# II. CONVENTIONAL AND UNCONVENTIONAL AGENTS OF SLOW DISEASE

The agents of slow virus diseases can be divided into conventional and unconventional (Table 1). The conventional agents resemble classic viruses, and include measles virus (subacute sclerosing panencephalitis), papovaviruses (progressive multifocal leukoencephalopathy), visna virus (visna), and arenoviruses (lymphocytic choriomeningitis). All of these agents replicate in vitro and induce cytopathic effects (CPE) under appropriate conditions; all are antigenic, and with rare exception, are associated with inflammatory lesions of the central nervous system (CNS). In contrast, the unconventional agents of scrapie, kuru, Creutzfeldt-Jakob disease, and transmissible mink encephalopathy have not yet been demonstrated by electron microscopy, nor do they induce unequivocal in vitro CPE. The scrapie agent replicates in vitro, as determined by dilution experiments. Attempts to demonstrate antigenicity either by artificially stimulating animals inoculated with diseased tissue fractions, or by directly testing infected animals for neutralizing antibody, have been uniformly unsuccessful. Considering scrapie agent as the prototype of unconventional agents, there is little evidence that it has a nucleic acid genome, and this is assumed to be true for the other related unconventional agents. It should be noted, however, that this view is based primarily upon inactivation studies of relatively unpurified scrapie preparations. Since the protective effect of contaminating tissue materials against many harsh treatments is a well-known phenomenon, highly purified scrapie material must be utilized before this conclusion can be accepted without reservation. The agent is considered to be extremely resistant to a wide range of physicochemical treatments that would quickly inactivate most viruses. Its basic biochemical composition is unknown, and infectivity is uniquely associated with plasma membrane fractions of disrupted, infected cells.

## III. VIROLOGICAL AND CLINICOPATHOLOGICAL FINDINGS IN CHRONIC INFECTIONS OF THE CENTRAL NERVOUS SYSTEM (CNS)

### *A. Chronic Infections of the Human CNS with Conventional Agents*

Table 2 is a compilation of the chronic infections of the human CNS with conventional agents.

1. SUBACUTE SCLEROSING PANENCEPHALITIS (SSPE) SSPE (Dawson's inclusion body encephalitis, Van Bogaert's subacute sclerosing leukoencephalitis, Pette and Dorings panencephalitis) is a rare disease of children and young adults. Its estimated frequency is 1 per 1,000,000 in the United States (168). It occurs more frequently in males than females (4 to 1), and 85% of the cases are children from rural areas (93). Once characteristic clinical features are observed diagnosis is confirmed by the demonstration of measles antibody in the cerebrospinal fluid (CSF) (95).

Evidence that SSPE results from chronic measles virus infection is now extensive, and the isolation of rubeola virus from SSPE brain biopsies and autopsy specimens has been accomplished by several different laboratories (92, 155). Antigenic identity between SSPE virus isolates, wild measles virus strains, and the Edmonston vaccine strain has been demonstrated. However, neutralizing antibody titers of SSPE patients' sera were found to be four to eight times lower against SSPE isolates than against a wild measles virus strain (94). In general, the biological characteristics of SSPE isolates more closely resemble those of laboratory adapted vaccine strains of measles, than those of the wild virus. Recent biochemical studies suggest that differences may exist between the 18S RNA of SSPE virus-infected cells and measles virus-infected cells (202). Whether such findings reflect basic biological differences between the SSPE virus and wild rubeola virus, or simply represent modifications resulting from long-term in vivo residence and propagation of virus within brain cells, remains to be determined.

The pathogenesis of SSPE is not well understood. The availability of an animal model would be a valuable adjunct in the study of the pathogenesis of this disease. Information derived from the study of such a model might provide a rationale for therapeutic trials in this uniformly fatal disorder. It has recently been demonstrated that a latent measles infection of the newborn hamster brain can be established if the animal has a high level of maternally transmitted measles neutralizing antibody before receiving the intracerebral inoculation (195). Animals without antibody developed acute encephalitis. When these chronically infected hamsters were treated with cyclophosphamide, the majority developed persistent myoclonic tremors, and virus was isolated from their brains for at least ninety days postinoculation. In another investigation, weanling hamsters inoculated intracerebrally with SSPE virus

**Table 1** The agents of slow virus disease

| Property | Conventional (Example: measles virus in subacute sclerosing panencephalitis) | Unconventional (Example: scrapie and other agents of transmissible spongiform encephalopathies) |
|---|---|---|
| 1. Morphology | Identifiable virus structure and substructure by electron microscope | Demonstration of virus not accomplished |
| 2. Antigenicity | Stimulate production of specific antibody in naturally infected host, and in artificially immunized animals | Specific antibody not demonstrable in infected host or artificially immunized animals |
| 3. Biochemical composition | Virus composed of basic nucleocapsid consisting of protein, plus either RNA or DNA, with or without lipid envelope | Biochemical composition unknown |
| 4. Mode of replication | Generally analogous to the virus family of which it is a member | Unknown, but various hypotheses have been suggested, including that of the replicating membrane; replicating polysaccharide; and nuclear histone, among others |
| 5. In vitro characteristics | Produced CPE under appropriate conditions, and are inhibited by known metabolic inhibitors of viral replication | CPE not produced, even though replication occurs in appropriate tissue culture systems |

**Table 1** (Continued)

| Property | Conventional (Example: measles virus in subacute sclerosing panencephalitis) | Unconventional (Example: scrapie and other agents of transmissible spongiform encephalopathies) |
|---|---|---|
| 6. Minimal infectivity requirements | Naked virion capable of initiating infection | Infectivity uniquely associated with plasma membrane fraction of disrupted, infected cells (i.e. chemical disruption of plasma membrane may result in total loss of infectivity) |
| 7. Sensitivity to physicochemical agents | Susceptible to most known virucidal agents | Resistant to a wide range of physicochemical exposure |
| 8. Natural host range | Restricted | Relatively restricted |
| 9. Experimental transmission | Limited success—Visna (Icelandic sheep), LCM (Rats & Mice), SSPE (Hamsters), and PML—None | Long incubations. Transmitted to some laboratory animals and/or a few subhuman primates |
| 10. Salient neuropathological features | Relatively characteristic for each disease. In general, inflammation (except in immunologically-compromised hosts, as in PML), and may demonstrate demyelination and the presence of viral inclusions (SSPE and PML); budding virus (visna, LCM); or viral crystalline aggregates (PML) | Extremely similar, including neuronal vacuolation and astrocytic proliferation in the gray matter. Primarily noninflammatory in nature |

**Table 2** Chronic infections of the human CNS with conventional agents

| Disease | Virus | Hosts affected | Incubation period | Clinical signs | Major findings |
|---|---|---|---|---|---|
| Subacute sclerosing panencephalitis | Measles virus | Human | Range: 2–20 yr Mean: 6 yr | Behavioral changes, mental deterioration, myoclonic jerks, loss of vision, coma | CSF measles antibody titers; measles-like virus isolated from CNS; perivascular infiltration; microglial nodules; paramyxovirus-nucleocapsids in nuclei and cytoplasm of neurons and glial cells; characteristic EEG |
| Progressive multifocal leukoencephalopathy | Papovavirus (SV 40; JC virus) | Human | unknown | Memory loss; dysarthria; incoordination | Widespread, patchy, confluent demyelination; large bizarre astrocytes; intranuclear inclusions in oligodendrocytes |

at 21 to 22 days of age developed a chronic neurological disease characterized by myoclonus in some animals (23). When virus was inoculated into younger, suckling animals, acute encephalitis developed. It was impossible to culture virus from brains of chronically infected animals by conventional virological methods, but using co-cultivation techniques, as successfully utilized in SSPE isolations, virus could be isolated up to 81 days after inoculation. These observations strongly suggest that immune mechanisms may be key determinants in the pathogenesis of chronic measles infection of the brain, as will be discussed later.

2. PROGRESSIVE MULTIFOCAL LEUKOENCEPHALOPATHY (PML) PML is a rare central nervous system disorder of man first described in 1958 (9), and characterized primarily by demyelinative lesions. With rare exceptions, patients who contract PML have severe secondary immunodeficiency states resulting from lymphoproliferative disorders, such as Hodgkin's disease, and chronic lymphocytic leukemia, sarcoidosis, or miliary tuberculosis (163). However, there have been reports of primary PML (43). The first clue suggesting a viral component to PML was the electron microscopic demonstration of oligodendrocyte nuclei containing particles resembling papova virions (204, 205). Since then papovavirus has been isolated in cultures of human fetal spongioblasts (148). Two serologically distinct isolates have been recovered: one which is indistinguishable from SV-40 (197, 198), and another which represents a new agent, the JC virus (148). However, most PML brains studied show evidence of JC virus rather than SV-40, and a recent report has summarized the pertinent findings (139). There is some indication that the clinical picture of PML associated with these two agents may differ according to which one is involved, in that SV-40 may be associated with more protracted disease.

Although demyelinating disease has not been transmitted to laboratory animals with PML isolates, there is evidence indicating an etiological relationship between papovavirus and PML (139).

Viral antigen is most concentrated in cells surrounding demyelinated foci, and virions have been observed within oligodendrocytes (205). These cells, which are the myelin-forming elements of the CNS, are depleted within areas of demyelination. Papovaviruses in association with PML brains may exceed $10^7$ to $10^9$ virions per gram of tissue. Furthermore, papovaviruses have not been identified in normal human brain, or in other pathological conditions of humans, except in warts.

Upwards of 70% of 400 normal adults tested had hemagglutinating antibody to JC virus (147). This suggests that PML does not result from infection by a highly lethal or exotic virus. The highest rate of seroconversion appeared to occur before 14 years of age, further supporting the ubiquity of that agent. Antibody to SV-40 virus also occurs with variable frequency in human populations (169, 170). The critical question of whether either of these two agents assume residence in normal brains, inciting the neuropathologic process of PML only under very specific circumstances, as in an immunologically compromised host, is unknown.

The possible association of PML, a degenerative disease of the brain, and malignancy has stimulated a great deal of interest (205). The fact that giant astrocytes usually seen in the lesions of PML cannot be distinguished from malignant astrocytes of pleomorphic glioblastomas is consistent with an oncogenic potential of isolated papovaviruses. It has been recently reported that 83% of newborn hamsters inoculated with JC virus developed malignant gliomas within six months. Virus was not recoverable from cultured tumor cells, but could be rescued when tumor cells were fused with permissive cells (193).

## *B. Chronic Infections of the Human CNS with Unconventional Agents*

Table 3 provides a listing of the chronic infections of the human CNS with unconventional agents.

1. KURU Kuru was the first chronic degenerative disease of the human CNS to be transmitted to an experimental animal (58). This disease was originally discovered to be endemic among the Foré people, a tribe in the eastern highlands of New Guinea (56). The name kuru means to shiver, and refers to the tremors noted in this disease.

The clinical and pathological picture of kuru in man is analogous to the other transmissible spongiform encephalopathies, namely Creutzfeldt-Jakob Disease (CJD), scrapie, and Transmissible Mink Encephalopathy (TME). Clinically, kuru is characterized by progressive ataxia, tremors, emotional lability, and mental deterioration, usually terminating in death within six to nine months (91). All of the spongiform encephalopathies are atypical in that they elicit no inflammatory response, nor leave any of the classic hallmarks of viral infection, such as inclusion bodies or glial nodules (120). There are no febrile phases in the disease and no abnormalities of the CSF, serum, or peripheral blood cells. To date, no antigenic properties of any of the transmissible agents of spongiform encephalopathies have been found (66).

Kuru primarily affects children and adult females, and until the successful transmission of this disease in 1966, it had been considered a heredofamilial disorder of the CNS. The decline in the incidence of kuru now observed reflects the elimination of the practice of cannibalism among the Foré people since 1957. This completely interrupted the natural transmission of the disease (60). Transmission resulted from self-inoculation of the women and their infants during the mourning ritual when highly infective brain was handled before cooking. Infection probably occurred via cutaneous and conjunctival routes of inoculation. In recent years, kuru has occurred in less than one third of the victims than it did during the early years of investigation. The disease is virtually absent among children under 12 years of age (69).

Chimpanzees inoculated with human brain suspensions from kuru victims developed a stereotyped neurological disease within 10 to 59 months (70). They showed neuropathological changes remarkably similar to those observed in human kuru victims (8).

2. CREUTZFELDT-JAKOB DISEASE CJD, a rare presenile dementia, was originally described by Creutzfeldt in 1920 and Jakob in 1921. Most victims are between the ages of 35 and 65. Males and females are affected equally. Most cases are sporadic, but there are several pedigrees in which multiple family members have

**Table 3** Chronic infections of the human CNS with unconventional agents

| Disease | Virus | Hosts affected | Incubation period | Clinical signs | Major findings |
|---|---|---|---|---|---|
| Kuru | Infectious agent passes filters with pore size of 220 nm | Human chimpanzee New World monkeys Old World monkeys | 9–240 months | Incoordination, progressive ataxia, tremors, loss of emotional control, dementia | Progressive vacuolation in the dendritic and axonal processes of the neurons, and to a lesser extent in astrocytes and oligodendrocytes; extensive astroglial hypertrophy and proliferation, ends in status spongiosus of gray matter; no inflammatory reaction or primary demyelination. PAS—positive plaques in cerebellum |
| Creutzfeldt-Jakob Disease | Infectious agent passes filters with pore size of 220 nm | Human chimpanzee New World monkeys Old World monkeys domestic cat | 4–47 months | Progressive dementia, ataxia, myoclonus | Similar to kuru; cortex, basal ganglia most prominently affected as well as changes in thalamus, cerebellum, brain stem, and spinal cord |

been affected over several generations (131). Both sporadic and familial cases have been successfully transmitted to subhuman primates. The disease resembles kuru both clinically and neuropathologically (8) and it has been suggested that they may have identical etiologies.

Since the initial successful transmission of CJD to chimpanzees, a total of 14 of 26 CJD cases have been inoculated into 42 chimpanzees, 18 of which developed the disease (69). Peripheral and intracerebral routes of inoculation of brain tissue produced essentially the same disease, although the incubation period was longer after peripheral inoculation. More recently spider and squirrel monkeys have also developed CJD after inoculation, with incubation periods ranging from 23 to 29 months (71).

Electron microscopic studies of the spongiform encephalopathies have been unrevealing in the search for virus particles. One study, however, described two types of virus-like particles in biopsy tissues from two patients with CJD (192). The larger of the particles resembled myxoviruses of the murine and avian tumor types. However, particles of this general type have also been seen in brains from patients with a variety of unrelated diseases, including cerebral degeneration, Tay-Sachs, and Schilder's disease (20, 74, 75). The smaller particle resembled the papovavirus-like particles found in PML, although there was no evidence of intranuclear particles.

A human brain culture from a patient with CJD transformed spontaneously after 60 days (89). Virus particles morphologically similar to oncogenic RNA viruses were present in the transformed cells. The 110th subculture of these cells still contained virus particles (90). Inoculation of the transformed cell line has not induced CJD in primates after 20 months of observation. It was suggested that this agent is probably not etiologically related to CJD.

## *C. Chronic Infections of the Animal CNS with Conventional Agents*

Table 4 provides a list of the chronic infections of the animal CNS with conventional agents.

1. VISNA Visna, first reported in 1935, is a subacute viral encephalomyelitis of Icelandic sheep. It was completely eradicated by 1951. Visna virus is serologically identical to the agent causing maedi, a slow pulmonary infection of Icelandic sheep (187). Zwoegerziekte, a neurological disease occurring in the Netherlands, is comparable to visna, and may be caused by a similar virus (36). Although it has been suggested that visna is the encephalitic form of the lung disease, further study is necessary to identify the pathogenetic factors which determine the major organ system involved (81).

Visna is readily transmitted by intracerebral inoculation of brain material obtained from diseased sheep; the incubation period may extend from several months to years (173, 174). The virus has been propagated in cultures of sheep choroid plexus or sheep testes cells. Virus replication in cell culture produced CPE characterized by multinucleated syncytia appearing within several days post-inoculation, followed by complete disintegration of the cell culture several days later (175).

Visna virus is a RNA-containing virus with a lipid envelope, replicating by budding from the plasma membrane (32, 183). Morphologically, it resembles agents

**Table 4** Chronic infections of the animal CNS with conventional agents

| Disease | Virus | Hosts affected | Incubation period | Clinical signs | Major findings |
|---|---|---|---|---|---|
| Visna | 70–100 nm myxovirus-like | Sheep | months to years | Ataxia, paresis of hind legs progressing to total paralysis | Patchy demyelination; meningoleukoencephalomyelitis; high titered serum neutralizing antibody with persistent virus; marked pleocytosis with increased gamma globulin in CSF |
| Lymphocytic choriomeningitis | 50 nm arenovirus | Mouse Rat | days to months | Death preceded by convulsive diathesis | Brain has marked mononuclear cell infiltration in meninges, ependyma, and choroid plexus; virus induced immune-mediated pathology |

of the myxovirus group (125, 186). Two types of particles have been observed: one contains a dense core enclosed by a single membrane; the other is a somewhat larger form without a core, enclosed by a double membrane. Visna virus may be inactivated by chloroform, ether, trypsin, formaldehyde, heat, or ultraviolet radiation (184).

The virion has a sedimentation coefficient of 64S, and also contains a RNA-dependent DNA polymerase (reverse transcriptase) (86, 124, 178). It has been stressed that visna virus shares many features with known oncogenic viruses, and indeed it has caused transformation of murine cell cultures (180). In this latter situation, classic viral CPE does not occur, and evidence of complete virus was not detectable in cells or supernatant fractions. However, when such transformed lines were co-cultivated with normal sheep testes cells, virus was subsequently rescued and identified as the visna agent. It retained the capacity to transform mouse cells. The implications of this important observation are unknown, but it demonstrates that viral carcinogenesis and slow virus infections may share important pathogenetic mechanisms, since the agents of both may have the capacity to incorporate viral genome into host cells.

The possible relationship of visna virus to human neurological disease has been considered, and it has been proposed that visna may be a useful model for the study of human subacute and chronic demyelinating disease (85). It has also been suggested that subacute lesions of visna may be indistinguishable from the acute lesions of multiple sclerosis, but no direct evidence in support of an etiological relationship has been described (172).

2. LYMPHOCYTIC CHORIOMENINGITIS VIRUS (LCM) LCM infection in mice may occur as a slow virus infection of the CNS (100). This infection has served as a model of the virus carrier state, and of virus-induced immune-mediated pathology. In nature, the virus is indigenous to mice who may harbor it for life, and vertically transmit it to succeeding generations. Intracerebral inoculation of adult mice with LCM virus produces a rapidly fatal generalized infection showing characteristic CNS pathology. However, mice infected transplacentally or inoculated shortly after birth develop a persistent infection with no damage to the host. After 10 months of age, many of the inoculated mice develop a progressive disease involving the CNS. These animals have high levels of LCM virus in the brain, blood, and other tissues. Serological methods failed to detect antibodies, and for years this infection was thought to represent a state of immunological tolerance. Recently, however, LCM carrier mice have been shown to produce antibodies (99). The antibody response results in a large accumulation of antigen-antibody complexes in the kidneys which leads to chronic glomerulonephritis and death (144).

Electron microscopy of infected tissues shows pleomorphic virions containing electron-dense granules budding from cell membranes. They have been given the name arenovirus (165).

Little is known about the relationship between the virions seen by electron microscopy, and infectivity tests or the various antigens demonstrated by serological techniques. Intact virus and complement-fixing (CF) antigens appear to be immunologically distinct from one another. Animals inoculated with soluble CF antigen are not protected against challenge with infectious virus (98). Whether CF antigen circulates freely in the persistently infected mouse, or is complexed with antibody, is unknown. However, CF antigen can be readily solubilized from infected cells or tissues and remains in the liquid phase after centrifugation. Evidence is available that the lesions in LCM-infected mice are immune-mediated. However, elucidation of the precise mechanisms involved in viral persistence and in the selected destruction of rodent cerebellum presents an area for further investigation (31). A relationship of an autoimmune phenomenon and disease in infected LCM mice could be comparable to a number of pathological disorders of man, such as glomerulonephritis in systemic lupus erythematosus.

### *D. Chronic Infections of the Animal CNS with Unconventional Agents*

Table 5 is a compilation of the chronic infections of the animal CNS with unconventional agents.

1. SCRAPIE Scrapie is one of four transmissible subacute spongiform virus encephalopathies, which also include TME, kuru, and CJD (68). All are caused by undefined transmissible agents which can be detected only by animal inoculation after extensive incubation periods. As mentioned, they are all characterized by chronic, progressive, ultimately fatal neurological diseases. Scrapie is the colloquial name given to a disease of sheep, and denotes a persistent tendency of affected animals to scratch or scrape against fixed objects. The disease was first recognized in Scotland nearly two centuries ago, but has spread to Canada, Australia, and the United States in recent years. It does not represent a significant economic problem at present. Since certain breeds of sheep have demonstrated a high incidence of disease, while others are totally resistant, it had been proposed that vertical transmission is controlled by an autosomal recessive gene (37). It has also been suggested that scrapie may occur as an intrauterine infection (54). Spread of the natural disease probably occurs by contact, although the specific routes are unknown (19). Despite the proposed genetic influence, scrapie has been experimentally transmitted to a wide range of diverse and unrelated animal species, and the agent clearly has the capacity to cross wide biological barriers (70, 71).

In spite of the vast amount of work done with scrapie, it has not been completely possible to characterize the transmissible agent. Electron microscopic studies of diseased tissues have failed to provide clues as to the identity of the scrapie agent (27). It is remarkably resistant to formalin, heat, and fluorocarbons (103), and to virucidal levels of ultraviolet radiation (54) and ionizing irradiation (49). These observations have led to suggestions that the agent is not a virus, but instead a self-replicating membrane, polysaccharide (72), or a small nucleic acid core with polysaccharide coat (1). Most recently, it has been suggested that the scrapie agent is a viroid, a term designating a class of naked infectious RNA molecules causing a variety of plant diseases (39, 40).

**Table 5** Chronic infections of the animal CNS with unconventional agents

| Disease | Virus | Hosts affected | Incubation period | Clinical signs | Major findings |
|---|---|---|---|---|---|
| Scrapie | Infectious agent passes filters with pore size of 30 nm | Sheep, goat, mouse, rat, gerbil, mink, cynomolgus and squirrel monkey, skunk, hamster | 30–60 months | Ataxia, tremors, hyperexcitability, incoordination | Similar to kuru with some PAS-positive doubly refractile birifrigent amyloid plaques; subcortical regions particularly medulla affected; vacuolation of nerve cells outstanding |
| Transmissible mink encephalopathy | Infectious agent passes filters with pore size of 50 nm | Mink, skunk, raccoon, ferret, hamster, goat, sheep, albino ferret, Old World monkey, New World monkey | 4–48 months | Slowly progressive locomotor incoordination; excitability, convulsions | Similar to scrapie; cerebrum most prominently affected especially its more rostral parts; marked astrogliosis and spongy degeneration of the gray matter |

Attempts to detect immunological responses by various techniques have been unsuccessful (54). Antibody formation is not suppressed in infected animals, since they respond normally when immunized with other antigens (62). Interferon synthesis is not induced by scrapie infection (110). The prominent feature of the histopathological lesions supports the negative immunological findings in that the disease produces a degenerative process with the absence of an inflammatory reaction.

The agent replicates in vitro without evidence of CPE. Cultures passed up to 41 times, representing a dilution well in excess of the original inoculum, still contained infectious material (29).

2. TRANSMISSIBLE MINK ENCEPHALOPATHY TME was first recognized about 25 years ago in U.S. ranch mink, but the disease was not described until 1965 (84). Perpetuation of the natural disease is not well understood. The disease may be transmitted under laboratory conditions by subcutaneous or intraperitoneal inoculation, or by feeding infectious material to a variety of animals (22, 70).

Clinicopathological findings combined with the lack of demonstrable humoral and cellular host responses are reminiscent of scrapie, and it has been proposed that TME is the mink equivalent of scrapie in sheep and mice (47, 130).

Various animal species have been infected with TME (70). However, clinical disease did not develop in cats, calves, or chickens, even though the agent persisted in their lymphoid tissues for up to two years (127). The infective agent was found in many organs of terminally infected mink, with the highest infectivity in the brain. Cell cultures of brain retain infectivity after as many as eight passages. Electron microscopy has failed to reveal the etiological agent (128). The physical and chemical properties of the agent are similar to those of scrapie. It is partly sensitive to ether, phenol, and pronase, but relatively resistant to 10% formalin and ultraviolet radiation (128).

Recently it was found that circulating lymphocytes from infected animals were noninfectious, although the transmissible agent could be demonstrated within intact lymphoid organs. The lack of immunological response in these animals, therefore, could not be the result of infection of circulating lymphocytes (129).

The transmission of TME to primates suggests that a closer relationship to the human spongiform encephalopathies may exist, and the transmission to skunk and raccoon could indicate a natural reservoir in wild animals for human disease (71, 185).

## IV. THE POSSIBLE ROLE OF VIRUSES IN CHRONIC DEGENERATIVE DISEASES OF UNKNOWN ETIOLOGY

Since the experimental transmission of the human spongiform encephalopathies to subhuman primates (59, 70), the recovery of measles virus from SSPE (92), and the isolation of papovaviruses from PML brains (197, 205), there has been a renewed effort to determine if other subacute and chronic degenerative diseases of the CNS

**Table 6** Possible chronic viral infections of the human CNS

| Disease | Virus suspected | Clinical signs | Major findings |
|---|---|---|---|
| Multiple sclerosis | Measles virus? other paramyxovirus? | Incoordination, dysarthria, nystagmus, paraplegia | Acute foci of primary demyelination associated with infiltrates of lymphocytes and macrophages scattered throughout the CNS; chronic sclerotic plaques completely demyelinated with gliosis, shadow plaque with partial demyelination |
| Guillain-Barre syndrome | Echovirus? EB virus? mumps? rubeola? other viruses? also *Mycoplasma pneumoniae* | Polyneuritis, ascending paralysis | Foci of primary demyelination associated with infiltrates of lymphocytes and macrophages scattered throughout the peripheral nervous system |
| Amyotrophic lateral sclerosis | Poliovirus? rabies virus? | Muscular atrophy; dysarthria; muscle fasciculations | Motor neuron cell loss in spinal cord and lower brain stem with degeneration of pyramidal tracts. Guam ALS-classic ALS lesions with neurofibrillary tangles in brain |
| Parkinsonism | | | |
| A. idiopathic | ? | Akinesia and bradykinesia; muscular rigidity; tremor | Neuronal loss in basal ganglia and brainstem; hyaline inclusions (Lewy body) |
| B. postencephalitic | Influenza virus? | Same as above | Same as above |
| C. Parkinson-dementia complex of Guam | ? | Bradykinesia; rigidity; dementia | Neuronal loss widespread throughout brain; neurofibrillary tangles |
| Presenile dementia (Alzheimer's disease and Pick's disease) | ? | Memory loss; dysarthria; disorientation; dementia | Diffuse neuronal degeneration of cerebral cortex. 1. Alzheimer: senile plaques and neurofibrillary tangles. 2. Pick: ballooned neurones and argentophilic Pick bodies |

have viral etiologies (Table 6). Several such neurological disorders of humans are candidates for possible viral causation.

Arguments favoring a viral etiology for these disorders consist primarily of epidemiological, immunological, or pathological evidence. A review of the most important of these conditions follows:

### *A. Multiple Sclerosis (MS)*

The original report of measles antibody occurring in the CSF of MS patients (2) focused attention on the possible etiological role of measles virus in this chronic demyelinating disease of humans. Subsequent serological investigations have supported this original finding (26), and while other viruses have also been implicated to a lesser degree, the measles association is still the strongest relationship. Recently, measles (48) and parainfluenza type-1 (181) viruses were reported to have been isolated from passaged MS brain explant cultures, but these reports have not yet been confirmed. Electron microscopic studies of acute MS lesions have demonstrated intracellular virus-like particles (41, 161, 194). It may be that they represent a nonspecific host response to cellular injury, since they are seen in other unrelated disorders (41).

Epidemiological evidence provides the strongest argument for an infectious basis for MS. The disease is generally most common in northern latitudes (16, 119). Migration studies have also determined that the propensity to develop MS is almost certainly acquired before 15 years of age (3, 119). Transmission experiments have been unrewarding, although the induction of a scrapie-like illness in sheep inoculated with MS brain suspensions after many months of incubation represents an interesting, albeit questionable, observation which needs confirmation (150). The occurrence of MS in laboratory personnel working with swayback of sheep is an interesting but unexplained observation which occurred many years ago (24).

Study of the cellular immunity of MS patients may provide important information concerning the pathogenesis of MS. Recent work has suggested that the lymphoreticular cells of the MS patient may have an inability to recognize measles antigen, and other lipid-containing viruses (28, 191). The addition of transfer factor obtained from immune donors to the in vitro system has restored immunocompetence to the deficient cells, and thus it has been suggested that transfer factor therapy may be a rational approach to the treatment of MS (191).

Although the pathogenesis of SSPE and MS are almost certainly different, there are important parallels between these two disorders. Both conditions may have increased IgG in the CSF, and oligoclonal IgG has also been demonstrated in the CSF (25, 121). However, such patterns are occasionally found in other diseases of infectious or immunological etiology (25, 121). Some MS patients have measles antibody in CSF, but SSPE patients always have antibody and in much greater quantity than do MS patients (95, 189). In both conditions immunoglobulins are produced locally in diseased brain (188). At this time the most significant data in support of a viral etiology for MS is the presence of measles antibody in CSF of some MS patients. It is to be hoped that future imaginative studies will provide additional clues to solve the enigma of this intriguing disease.

## *B. Guillain-Barré Syndrome (GBS)*

The GBS, or postinfectious polyradiculitis, has been associated with a multitude of infectious agents, including mumps, influenza, rubeola, enteroviruses, varicella-zoster, Epstein-Barr (EB) virus, and *Mycoplasma pneumoniae* (33, 50, 78, 82, 122, 123, 134, 190). It has also been observed in association with numerous immunization procedures, including tetanus antitoxin, smallpox, rabies, and poliomyelitis vaccines, and more recently with the mumps and rubella vaccines (82, 134, 166). The more consistent associations have been with the enteroviruses, EB virus, and *M. pneumoniae* infections. Echo viruses have been isolated from the CSF of patients with GBS, and increases in serum antibody titers were also noted coincident with neurological dysfunction (190).

For a number of years there have been reported epidemiological associations between acute and subacute CNS disorders, and infectious mononucleosis. Recent work has demonstrated the relationship of the EB virus with infectious mononucleosis (14, 78), and has thus permitted serological correlations between this virus and the GBS. In a recent study, patients with the GBS were found to have high levels of antibody to EB virus, as compared to age-matched controls (78). In another study, peripheral white blood cells from GBS patients were found to have an increased tendency to become continuous self-proliferating lines (14). When examined by electron microscopy, these cells contained herpes-like viral particles resembling EB virus. Inoculation of hamsters with these cells failed to produce neurological disease, however.

Elevated *M. pneumoniae* CSF antibody levels have been associated with the GBS (122, 177), and there is also one reported isolation of *M. pneumoniae* from the CSF of a patient with this disorder (50). It is estimated that up to 7% of patients hospitalized with *M. pneumoniae* infections may develop some type of subacute CNS disorder, including the GBS (177). Although the pathogenesis of CNS disease associated with *M. pneumoniae* is unknown, it has been shown that antibody to this agent cross-reacts with human brain antigen (13). A significant percentage of patients infected with *M. pneumoniae* have complement-fixing antibrain antibody in the serum which may be removed by adsorption with mycoplasma antigen (13). Although *Mycoplasma neurolyticum* and *Mycoplasma gallisepticum* elaborate neurotoxins thought to be pathogenetically important in neurological disease of lower animals, no such toxin has been discovered in the case of *M. pneumoniae* (176).

In view of the variety of infectious agents associated with GBS, this syndrome may represent a nonspecific hyperimmune response, demyelinating in nature. However, much work remains to be done before such an hypothesis can be readily accepted.

## *C. Amyotrophic Lateral Sclerosis (ALS)*

ALS occurs primarily as a sporadic disease, but 5 to 10% of all cases occur in families and are believed to be associated with an autosomal dominant mode of inheritance (142). Certain foci of ALS also occur in other parts of the world in exceedingly high frequencies, as among the native Guam population (17), and on the Kii peninsula in Japan (171).

ALS is a fatal chronic degenerative disorder affecting the motor neurons of the spinal cord and brain, with a primarily noninflammatory neuropathology. Death and drop-out of motor neurons of affected CNS tissues and demyelination of the motor tracts are hallmarks of this disorder (87, 88). The predilection of poliovirus for anterior horn cells makes it a logical choice as a possible candidate for the etiology of ALS. Proponents of such an association might suggest chronic poliovirus infection of the motor neuron as the underlying pathogenetic mechanism. Although direct evidence for such an association is lacking, it has been suggested that ALS patients gave a history of antecedent paralytic poliomyelitis at rates up to ten times that observed in controls (159). The association is also supported by the existence of a syndrome following documented paralytic poliomyelitis by fifteen years, or more, where the patient demonstrates a slowly progressive, relatively benign, motor neuron disease, not totally unlike that seen with classic ALS (7, 138). It is possible that this may represent reactivation of an old latent poliovirus infection, or simply an increased rate of cellular decompensation by elements previously injured by the virus many years earlier. These patients should obviously be studied for the presence of poliovirus antibodies in their CSF, and when possible, for poliovirus antigen in affected neural tissues.

Intraneuronal inclusion bodies indistinguishable from those seen in rabies have been described in ALS patients, but the likelihood that they may represent non-specific findings has been suggested (87, 88).

The successful transmission of ALS to rhesus monkeys was first reported by Russian investigators (203), but the study of pathological tissues and affected animals by a United States delegation to Russia failed to document their findings (15, 105). Furthermore, inocula prepared in collaboration with these investigators did not induce CNS disease in animals inoculated in the United States (68). Since then, an additional report has appeared in the Russian literature, again claiming the successful transmission of ALS to rhesus monkeys in subsequent experiments (61).

Recently, C-type virus particles have been found to cause motor neuron disease as well as lymphoproliferative disorders in a wild mouse colony in California (63, 143). This model is currently under investigation.

ALS, as seen in Guam, occurs at rates more than 50 times those seen in the United States (17). Furthermore, neurofibrillary tangles are seen in the brains of virtually 100% of ALS patients in Guam (171). This finding is complicated since a significant proportion of normal individuals in Guam also have these tangles. The significance of these structures is unknown. A percentage of ALS cases also occurs in conjunction with the Parkinson-dementia complex (171). The extraordinarily high incidence of these diseases among the Guam natives is consistent with an infectious etiology, or some toxic environmental exposure. However, a genetic contribution should also be considered.

### *D. Parkinson's Disease*

Idiopathic Parkinson's disease, paralysis agitans, represents a significant cause of chronic neurological disease in the adult population, and is the most common form of Parkinsonism. Its etiology is unknown. The postencephalitic variant of Parkinsonism which occurred as a complication of von Economo's encephalitis could indicate a possible infectious basis (133). Recently, influenza virus antigen was demonstrated in brains of postencephalitic Parkinson patients by the fluorescent antibody technique (64). Tissue culture investigation of these brains was not reported, but would constitute an important step in identifying a virus etiology for this variant of Parkinson's disease. Although similar immunological evidence does not exist to suggest an infectious basis for idiopathic Parkinson's disease, it has been proposed that it may also be caused by persistent influenza virus in the CNS, possibly as a defective virus (52). Viral seroepidemiological studies and tissue culture investigation of Parkinsonism patients would be most worthwhile.

### *E. Presenile Dementias*

The presenile dementias occur as a group of disorders affecting middle-aged adults, having an insidious onset, and no clear etiology (132). They may occur in familial patterns, but most are sporadic cases. CJD, as a presenile dementia, has been shown to be transmissible, although Alzheimer's disease and Pick's disease, as the main constituents of this category, have not been successfully transmitted. Many specimens have been inoculated into subhuman primates, and now must await the lapse of suitable incubation periods (68).

## V. SPECIAL FEATURES OF SLOW VIRUS DISEASE

### *A. General Considerations*

In studying the complex and inadequately understood virus-cell relationship, the possibility emerges that virtually all viruses studied in vitro can either convert to, or be experimentally manipulated to exist as agents of chronic persistent infections (141). The clinical spectrum of slow virus infections probably results at least in part from host-related factors, but more likely from a combination of host and virus-related influences. Accordingly, attempts to separate completely host from parasite factors may be futile. But certain host variables may be more consistently associated with some slow virus infections than with others. These shall be briefly reviewed.

### *B. Host-Related Factors in Slow Virus Infections*

1. GENETIC FACTORS Following the discovery of kuru, a subacute degenerative disorder of the CNS occurring in the highlands of New Guinea, it was initially felt that this represented a genetic affliction (12, 57). Victims of this disease were most often adult females and children, but a precise mode of genetic transmission had not been established. Members of other groups married to, or in close contact with the Foré people, did not contract kuru. In spite of the unequivocally proven infectious nature of kuru, and of the more than 2500 cases studied, no evidence refutes the possibility that a single gene may be responsible for the expression of this disease. Such a gene would be dominant in the adult female and male, but only partially penetrant in the adult male. It would produce disease with an earlier and more acute

onset in children having the homozygous condition (53). More recent investigations of blood groups and serum proteins in which the Foré people were compared with their unrelated neighbors continue to suggest that a genetic determinant may possibly govern expression of disease (118, 201).

CJD, a closely related spongiform encephalopathy, occurs primarily as a sporadic disease, but there are several pedigrees in which multiple family members have been affected over several generations. The distribution of cases is consistent with an autosomal dominant inheritance (131). Perhaps the precise relationship between kuru and CJD and genetic tendencies may be explainable in terms of a recently proposed hypothesis (52). It has been speculated that the original source of the kuru agent may have been a case of CJD occurring among the Foré, and later transmitted as a consequence of the mourning ritual. The disease would then be perpetuated in a pseudogenetic pattern reflecting the familial patterns of the tribal ceremony. It has also been suggested that the kuru agent may represent the modification of a known human virus. The cannibalistic mourning rites of the Foré would have caused it to be passed from human to human serially by ingesting brain, thus selecting for enhanced neurotropism (52).

The expression of scrapie in both sheep and mice has been thought to depend upon a particular genetic allele imparting susceptibility to the host. Natural scrapie in Great Britain has been explained completely in genetic terms, with the expression of clinical scrapie dependent upon homozygosity for an autosomal recessive gene (153). Additional support for possible genetic contributions to slow virus disease expression comes from the range of host susceptibility observed in experimental transmission. In general, marked specificity is seen; although scrapie causes disease in most breeds of sheep tested, breeds do vary in relative susceptibility, and some are completely resistant (153). Although a variety of rodents are susceptible to scrapie, guinea pigs and rabbits are not (70).

Significant genetic influences upon the expression of visna in sheep probably exist. Visna is considered to have been imported into Iceland during the early 1930s in a small flock of apparently healthy Karakul sheep from Germany (73). After the importation of those animals, visna became a recognized disease of Icelandic sheep. Neither visna nor maedi, the pulmonary analog of visna, had ever been observed in Karakul sheep, either in Iceland or in the flocks currently maintained in Germany (179). There is little reason to doubt that Icelandic sheep differ considerably genetically from other European breeds, since Icelandic sheep were brought into that country by settlers more than 1000 years ago, and have lived in relative isolation since (149). Numerous early attempts to transmit visna infection to a variety of laboratory and domestic animals, including non-Icelandic sheep, have been unsuccessful. Most recently, however, evidence of CNS infection in American lambs inoculated with visna virus has been presented (140).

While a possible genetic component of SSPE has been suggested, a recent report describing proven SSPE in only one of two identical twins represents strong evidence against a significant genetic contribution to that disorder (199). The living unaffected twin has no serological evidence of SSPE, nor any other of its laboratory or clinical stigmata.

Aleutian disease of mink is a transmissible slow disease discovered in ranch mink (76, 158). The term Aleutian has reference to the animal's gun metal gray color, similar to that of the Aleutian fox. The gene for this color is inherited as an autosomal recessive trait designated "aa," and mink with the Aleutian color are afflicted with the disorder. Features of this disease include some of those observed in connective tissue disorders of man, and the disease may also be a model for multiple myeloma (158). As with most other slow virus diseases with possible genetic components, the precise mechanisms which predispose such animals to disease expression are unknown. It is of interest, however, that the mortality rates vary among genotypes, according to whether "aa," "Aa," or "AA" mink are involved. Mink with "aa" usually die within 150 days, while over half of "Aa" and "AA" animals live a year or more (158).

2. IMMUNOLOGICAL FACTORS PML, a chronic and fatal neurological disease characterized by focal areas of cerebral demyelination, primarily affects older individuals suffering from a variety of lymphoproliferative disorders of malignant origin, as well as miliary tuberculosis or sarcoid (75, 205). Although the PML-immunodeficiency association may represent one of the strongest relationships existing between host susceptibility and propensity to slow virus disease, the questions it has stimulated far outnumber the solutions it has provided. PML is a very rare disease, in spite of the fact that medically immunosuppressed patients, as well as those with secondary immunodeficiencies, far outnumber those afflicted with this slow disease. If exposure to JC virus and SV-40 virus are as common as seroepidemiologic evidence would indicate, how can it explain the comparative rarity of PML? Does only a small percentage of exposed individuals harbor virus in the brain, available to induce disease later under certain conditions? Must residence of virus in the brain coincide with the onset of the immunodeficient state? The isolation of numerous and diverse viral agents from normal subhuman primate brains (59, 189) raises the question of whether there is a normal viral flora of the human brain.

There are other slow virus diseases which are characterized by unusual immunological features. SSPE is noteworthy in this regard in that afflicted patients usually have exaggerated serum antibody responses to rubeola virus. Hemagglutination inhibition and complement-fixing antibody to this agent are also detectable in the CSF (95). Detection of measles antibody in CSF combined with appropriate clinical and electroencephalographic findings is virtually pathognomonic for this disorder. It is not known whether these abnormal antibody responses to measles virus represent the host reaction to chronic stimulation of antibody synthesizing clones due to persistent viral antigen, or alternatively signify the production of biologically ineffective immunoglobulins.

Based on experimental models of chronic measles infection of the hamster brain, it has been suggested that the SSPE patient may have a deficiency of the cell-mediated immune system, rendering him unable to eliminate viral antigen (23, 195). Alternatively, a blocking factor has been demonstrated in the plasma and CSF of SSPE patients, which has the ability to suppress normal lymphocytes in vitro, rendering them incapable of recognizing measles antigen (167). The blocking factor may be a complex of immunoglobulin and measles virus antigen. The factor is ten times as concentrated in CSF as in plasma. If this blocking factor is fully characterized, and its pathogenetic role demonstrated, it would represent the first instance in which a blocking factor is centrally involved in the pathogenesis of a human disease.

Approximately 95% of IgG found in CSF of SSPE patients is probably due to local synthesis in the brain (188). Presumably it comes from perivascular mononuclear cells in the brain and meninges. Although it is not known if such antibody damages brain cells of the SSPE patient harboring measles antigen, the immunolysis of HeLa cells infected with measles virus has been demonstrated with measles antibody and complement (135). This mechanism could presumably also occur in vivo. Theoretically, antibody could be directed against released virus containing fragments of the infected cell plasma membrane, or could be directed against the cell itself which has been antigenically altered by virus infection. The possible pathogenetic role of measles antibody in the SSPE patient is complicated by reports of SSPE patients with hypogammaglobulinemia (83, 200), and the occurrence of SSPE-like neuropathology in a child with a combined immunodeficiency syndrome (5).

SSPE may reflect a generally depressed cell-mediated immune system, or a specific defect in cell-mediated immunity against measles virus (126). This has indirect support in that measles infection temporarily suppresses cellular immune mechanisms against a variety of unrelated antigens (45). There are conflicting reports regarding the cellular immune mechanism in SSPE patients (137). One study of four such patients demonstrated impaired delayed hypersensitivity to a variety of skin test antigens including measles virus, and also showed slow rejection of skin allografts (65). In another investigation, eight SSPE patients had positive skin test responses to *Candida,* while those to measles antigen were negative (104). Two of three patients tested became sensitized to dinitrochlorobenzene. These results must be interpreted with caution, since it is known that an adverse nutritional status, as seen in end-stage SSPE patients, may depress delayed hypersensitive reactions (11).

In all naturally occurring cases of visna virus infection, CSF pleocytosis is noted, and an elevation in CSF gamma globulin may also be present (149). The specificity of the increased gamma globulin has not been described, and it is known that visna virus persists in the presence of high titered neutralizing antibody. This is consistent with the claim that the immune response in visna is deficient as compared with that in other viral infections (157). In this disorder, neutralizing antibodies are usually observed well in advance of clinical disease, and it has been proposed that an antigen-antibody reaction occurs on the surface of infected CNS cells, causing cell destruction and secondary demyelination (79, 149). Visna virus has the property of causing cell fusion and subsequent cell disintegration in vitro, even when virus does not replicate (21, 85). In protracted experimental visna disease, if a reisolated virus is compared with the original strain used for inoculation, it is found that sera obtained early in the disease are unable to neutralize the reisolated agent as well as the original one (80). This situation has some analogy to that of SSPE, where the patient has a diminished ability to neutralize SSPE virus isolates when compared with wild measles (94, 154). These alterations of virus strain, occurring over prolonged incubation periods in the host, are also analogous in that the SSPE isolates usually resemble vaccine strains of measles virus, rather than the wild type (93). As with SSPE, it has been suggested that a search for serum blocking factors might be worthwhile. Again, in both SSPE (34, 35) and visna (5), virus may be demonstrated within CSF cells.

## *C. Virus-Related Factors*

As mentioned, it is difficult to separate host from virus factors in slow disease. Such a division, though arbitrary, has been made to facilitate an understanding of the relative contributions of host and parasite to the evolution of slow disease. Some of these features, and the special problems relating to their study, are the following:

1. LONG INCUBATION PERIOD Slow virus diseases, by definition, are characterized by very long incubation periods, lasting from months up to 20 years or more, as in human kuru. The events occurring during this interim are poorly understood. The critical primary interactions between host and virus may occur many years before the first detectable clinical manifestations are noted. Animal transmission has enabled investigators to study infected tissues in a sequential fashion, beginning with inoculation and ending with death. Most retrievable information obtained directly from human slow virus disease, however, has been limited to pathological descriptions of end-stage tissues. Very little is known concerning the pathologic sequences in the human brain, although one may infer this from animal investigations. The study of unconventional agents, in particular, is hampered by an inability to recognize them in infected tissues. Furthermore, the futility of attempting to reconstruct the complex interactions taking place over a period of months to years prior to development of clinical disease is self-evident.

2. VIRAL PERSISTENCE All slow virus diseases are characterized by agents which persist in host tissues throughout most, if not all, of the clinical disease. Virtually all of the meaningful laboratory data attributing a viral etiology to slow disease depends upon this property. Persistence may be demonstrated by morphologically identifiable virions, as in SSPE, PML, visna, and LCM, or by the transmission of disease, as with scrapie, TME, kuru, and CJD. The demonstration of viral persistence as a consistent feature of slow virus diseases does not imply an understanding of their pathogenesis, and certainly not of their successful prevention and treatment. A knowledge of the precise mechanisms involved, and the means of terminating or modifying the relationship will be important requirements if this is to be achieved.

Persistence of viral antigen within host cells does not necessarily imply a deleterious effect on the parasitized elements. Consider the classic example of LCM infection of the rodent CNS, in which fatal neurological disease can be prevented by immunosuppressive treatment with a variety of chemical and physical agents (31). Not until the host mounts an immunological attack against the LCM virus does tissue destruction ensue (31, 144, 145). Unfortunately, most persistent viral infections, many of which are associated with slow disease, have not been defined to the extent of the LCM system. It is often assumed that if one were to rid the host of persistent viral antigen, the underlying basis for slow disease might likewise be eliminated.

The nature of the unconventional agents of slow disease is so poorly understood that it is difficult to think in terms of their mechanisms of persistence. Immunosuppressive treatments given to mice infected with scrapie had no effect on the incubation period or pathologic development. This suggests that immunological mechanisms neither contribute to the pathogenesis of scrapie, nor play any significant role as defense against the agent (67). If the agent of scrapie resembles a small fragment of nucleic acid in intimate contact with a portion of plasma membrane (52), it would probably have little or no antigenic properties. It would not be recognized by the host's immunological surveillance system, thus explaining its persistence in a wide range of tissues.

Although substantive evidence is lacking to explain viral persistence in slow disease caused by conventional agents, a number of possibilities might account for this phenomenon. As discussed, a defect in the cell-mediated immunological system of the SSPE patient has been postulated (65). The recent demonstration of a serum and CSF blocking factor in these patients (167) represents an alternative mechanism to explain failure of the SSPE patient to eliminate chronic viral infection. Both possibilities must be further explored.

The problem of viral persistence in visna has been studied less extensively than in SSPE, but it has been suggested that viral antigen within mononuclear cells of the CSF may explain this phenomenon (5). In view of antigenic changes in visna virus following extended residence in the sheep CNS, perhaps the infected animal loses the capability it once had to eliminate the original infecting strain. As previously noted, a similar situation may exist in the SSPE patient, in that isolated SSPE viruses more closely resemble vaccine strains than wild virus. Analogous to the situation postulated with visna, perhaps the SSPE patient also loses the ability to eliminate virus because of its prolonged residence in the SSPE brain, and presumed changes in antigenic and biological character. Measles virus may possibly reach the CNS even in uncomplicated infections, as noted by electroencephalographic changes in patients with natural measles infection (151), or given measles vaccine (137, 152).

In the PML, patient, it is easier to account for a mechanism of viral persistence, since the majority of these patients have immune deficiencies (205). Most of their underlying deficiencies primarily affect the cellular immune system. Since this is a significant component of the immunological surveillance system in recovery from virus infection (4), perhaps papovavirus persistence is a result of a grossly ineffective antiviral mechanism. Other possibilities certainly exist, however.

3. ANTIGENICITY OF AGENTS All conventional viruses are antigenic; they stimulate the proliferation of immunocompetent lymphoreticular cells and elicit the production of specific antiviral antibody. Specific clones recognize viral antigen upon subsequent exposure, and thus assume a host-protective function. To what extent the host immune system malfunctions, and fails to eliminate virus, is not

known in the cases of SSPE and visna. The PML patient probably manifests diseases because of a deficient immune system.

Both the SSPE (95) and the visna-affected (149) host produce antibody to their respective viruses, often in greatly exaggerated quantities. The PML victim may likewise produce antibody to the papovavirus infecting him, but usually not at increased levels (139). One patient with SV-40 in her brain demonstrated an eight-fold rise in antibody titer to that agent during her clinical course, whereas this has not been observed in JC virus PML (139).

Efforts to demonstrate antigenicity of the unconventional agents have been futile. There is no indication that they are able to provoke any trace of immunological response in the infected or artificially immunized host, nor to produce interferon (110). As recently reviewed, many classic immunological methods to detect antibody in affected subjects have been employed, including complement fixation, neutralization, precipitation, gel diffusion, and direct and indirect fluorescent antibody techniques (60, 120). All have been uniformly unsuccessful, even though the affected animals have unimpaired immunological and interferon responses when tested with known antigens. Mouse spleen and kidney tissue suspensions from scrapie-infected mice have also been unsuccessfully used in neutralization tests, and attempts to demonstrate incomplete antibody or antigen-antibody complexes have failed. However, the cell-mediated component of the immune system has not been studied in detail.

Perhaps, as speculated, the actual activating agent in the transmissible spongiform encephalopathies is a small, or helper, molecule rather than a conventional viral particle (52). This would not be expected to elicit the immune response generally observed with complete virions.

## VI. VIRUS-HOST INTERACTIONS AND THE PATHOGENESIS OF SLOW DISEASE

The understanding of basic pathogenetic mechanisms involved in slow virus disease is still fragmentary. With most such infections the precise cellular specificity of infection, if any, is unknown. The infectivity of unconventional agents is demonstrable in many pathologically unaffected non-neural tissues, as well as the CNS, in which primary pathological changes occur. Reticuloendothelial tissues, in particular, are a fertile source of these agents. Evidence has been presented that the scrapie agent first replicates in tissues such as spleen, and only secondarily reaches the brain, where it may then be found for an extended period of time before clinical disease develops (42).

It is apparent that the host range of susceptibility to unconventional agents is much more extensive than originally suspected, as described in a recent review (70).

These general areas of study, and the special problems associated with them, form the subject of the following discussion.

### *A. Cellular and Organ Specificity*

The information available concerning the pathogenesis of unconventional slow virus diseases is derived primarily from their transmissibility to a wide variety of laboratory and domestic animals, and particularly to the smaller species. Unfortunately little data exist regarding specific host-destructive mechanisms operating at the cellular and molecular levels. It has been suggested that scrapie infection of the CNS causes neuronal degeneration by an indirect route, that is, by disturbances of astrocytic-neuron regulatory mechanisms following infection involving the astrocytes (42). These cells typically hypertrophy and proliferate, and in doing so may adversely affect homeostatic mechanisms of the neurons with which they are in intimate physical contact by foot processes. Whatever the underlying pathogenetic mechanisms, there is no evidence of acute neuronal destruction.

Biochemical study of mouse scrapie brain has demonstrated no abnormalities in RNA and protein metabolism, and total contents of dry matter, protein, and nucleic acid do not differ from normal mouse brains (136). However, radioisotope study of scrapie brain demonstrated an enhanced rate of DNA synthesis not observed in other organs, including the spleen (115, 117). Although there was an increased rate of DNA synthesis or turnover in glial cells, there was no increase in total DNA. DNA synthesis was not considered to represent replication of the scrapie agent, and so the precise interpretation of this observation remains obscure (116).

In both PML and SSPE, intracellular virions have been demonstrated within CNS cells, including oligodendrocytes (196). Interference with the metabolism of this cell presumably leads to disruption and loss of integrity of the cell membrane which, in fact, constitutes myelin. Demyelination is a characteristic feature of both disorders, although it is not the sole neuropathological alteration.

SSPE virus has been isolated from lymph nodes of affected patients; this is consistent with a possible extra-neural site of viral replication in lymphoid organs (97). Similar search for PML viral antigen in extra-neural tissues has been unsuccessful (139), although an exhaustive study has not been conducted.

Cellular pathology with visna occurs in the CNS with the appearance of meningeal and subependymal infiltrates. Myelin degeneration occurs secondary to extensive microglial infiltrations which have a tendency to necrose and cavitate (149).

## *B. Transmissibility and Range of Host Susceptibility*

Knowledge of the complete spectrum of hosts capable of supporting infection by the agents of slow disease would be useful. The conventional agents appear to have a limited range of natural host susceptibility. Thus, SSPE and PML are afflictions restricted entirely to man as natural host. Disease somewhat similar to SSPE has been produced in cynomolgus monkeys (156), calves and lambs (182), ferrets (111), and hamsters (23, 195). Visna, a well-characterized RNA virus sharing many physicochemical and biological properties with oncogenic viruses, produces clinical disease only in Icelandic sheep. Visna virus infection causes subclinical inflammatory lesions in the brains of experimentally inoculated American lambs (140).

The unconventional agents of scrapie, kuru, CJD, and TME produce very similar neuropathological lesions both in naturally infected hosts and experimental animals (8, 120). The comparative neuropathology and overall similarity of clinical disease support the theory that all the transmissible spongiform encephalopathies may be manifestations of infection by a single agent, or very similar agents.

A recent report has summarized the results of transmission studies and indicates that all four spongiform encephalopathies are transmissible to at least some species of Old and New World monkeys (70). Although the incubation period of CJD in man is estimated to be four to five months, CJD tissues inoculated into chimpanzees caused clinical disease in 11 to 26 months. Recently, clinical and pathological criteria for CJD developed in a corneal transplant recipient 18 months after the operation (41a). Post-mortem study of the donor, who had a neurological disorder, revealed CJD after the transplant had been performed. Natural kuru in man, with an estimated incubation period of 60–240 months, caused disease in the chimpanzee in 10–59 months. The domestic cat is also susceptible to experimental inoculation with CJD tissues, manifesting clinical disease within 30 months following inoculation (70). This latter observation raises the possibility of domestic and wild animals serving as natural reservoirs for viruses of slow disease in man (18, 182). It is also of great interest that familial CJD has recently been transmitted to the chimpanzee (46), and suggests the possibility that other familial chronic degenerative disorders of man, having obscure or unknown etiologies, may also be of infectious origin.

Visna is readily transmissible to Icelandic sheep, but not to other animals. PML, with a probable etiological association with papovaviruses, has not been experimentally transmitted. The oncogenicity of the JC isolate for hamsters, while of great interest, does not demonstrate the transmissibility of PML (193). Perhaps future attempts to transmit PML will utilize highly concentrated and purified preparations for inoculation.

The relative ease by which spongiform encephalopathies are transmitted compared to slow diseases caused by conventional agents, may be significant. Perhaps host factors may be more important determinants of disease caused by conventional agents than is the case with the unconventional agents.

## *C. Viral Replication*

While innumerable elegant experiments have demonstrated the intricate biochemical mechanisms involved in the replication of animal and bacterial viruses, no such descriptions exist for the unconventional agents of slow disease. The perplexing features of the scrapie agent have led to the question whether it should be classified as a virus (6, 102), even though it is filtrable, transmissible, and self-replicating. It has been suggested that the agent is a replicating membrane, polysaccharide, or protein (1, 6, 72, 77). It has also been stated that the scrapie agent may not have a nucleic acid genome (6). Such notions do not follow the dicta of classical virology. They have probably resulted from frustration with efforts to characterize an agent which has defied analysis. These earlier hypotheses are in contrast to one recently proposed, which suggests that the scrapie agent is a viroid (40), a term designating naked infectious RNA noted to cause a variety of plant diseases (39). The diversity of these currently held views attests to the paucity of leads in the identification and characterization of the unconventional agents.

Barring some breakthrough, an understanding of the nature of the unconventional agents may be at some distance in the future. However, until these agents have been exhaustively studied, and every reasonable possibility that they contain some remnant of classic viral material has been eliminated, there is no urgency to seek new biological systems to account for them. It has been stated that even considering the most unusual properties of the scrapie agent, it is not inconceivable that classic viruses with atypical properties may be involved (67). The recent isolation and characterization of the viruses of Aleutian mink disease (112), and hepatitis A (44) and B (160) support this notion.

As mentioned earlier, scrapie-infected mouse brain has demonstrated an increased rate of DNA synthesis, and organ cultures of brain material from scrapie mice have shown marked tendencies for continued cell growth and multiplication not observed in normal tissues. Multiplication of the agent seemed closely linked with division of the infected cells (30). At the macroscopic level, a number of important variables are recognized which affect the preclinical period of experimental scrapie, and have been reviewed (185). These include the size of the inoculum, route of administration, previous passage, history of the agent, species differences, and, in the mouse, even strain differences between donor and recipient. These data, plus genetic predispositions serving as determinants of clinical scrapie, indicate that this infection represents a very complex host-agent interaction.

In SSPE it is believed that defective viral particles may play an important role in persistence in brain cells. A number of questions have been raised regarding the nature of SSPE infection, as well as that occurring in PML (10). The recognized prerequisite for fusion or co-cultivation of SSPE or PML-infected brain explant cultures with indicator cells for induction of virus may be evidence for its defective nature. It is not known whether defective virus particles initiate the chronic infection, or whether they arise secondarily as a result of prolonged residence in the host. A question has been whether the etiologic agents of slow infections may arise from activated viral genes contained within cellular genomes (10). Such a relationship would be analogous to the oncogenes of RNA tumor viruses (101). That some agents of slow disease share common biological mechanisms with oncogenic viruses is demonstrated by the ability of visna virus to transform murine cell tissue cultures (180), and by the presence of a reverse transcriptase enzyme (124, 178).

The exact role that PML-associated papovaviruses occupy in the total biology of infected hosts is not understood. The giant astrocytes associated with papovaviruses in this disorder are indistinguishable from those in malignant glioblastomas. One must wonder if any relationship exists between these viruses and the underlying malignant disorders which frequently precede the onset of PML.

## VII. THE FUTURE OF SLOW VIRUS RESEARCH

At the Workshop and Symposium on Slow, Latent, and Temperate Virus Infections held at the National Institutes of Health in 1965, it was observed that the sole criterion to establish the presence of scrapie virus was the induction of scrapie with infected cells (57). Since then, although nearly a decade has passed, less stringent criteria for the demonstration of the unconventional agents have not been developed. This limitation has dictated the slow progress in certain areas of slow virus research. An otherwise straightforward virus titration often measured in days for most conventional viruses may take from months to years for the unconventional agents. These titrations require an in vivo indicator system since they must be conducted with living susceptible hosts. Inoculated animals must be maintained over a prolonged time period. The possibility of nonspecific deaths, as by bacterial infection, constantly looms as a potential threat to the successful completion of long-term studies.

Probably the greatest obstacle impeding the progress of slow virus research is the inability to characterize the unconventional agents of slow disease. Until some biochemical, immunological, or histochemical marker is identified, research in vital areas of slow disease has arrived at a temporary stalemate.

Tissue culture searches for unconventional agents in brain explant cultures are complicated by the isolation of numerous viruses now known to inhabit subhuman primate brains as latent inapparent infections (59, 89). Their relationship, if any, to slow disease is difficult to ascertain.

A better appreciation of host-predisposing factors should be attempted, such as the influence of genetic constitution on disease expression. Further search for aberrant immunological reactions of pathogenetic significance should be conducted. Indeed, there is strong evidence suggesting such a role for the immune system, as discussed earlier.

Perhaps the greatest challenges are represented by the vast spectrum of chronic degenerative disorders of man which occur in either sporadic or heredofamilial patterns. Most are in desperate need of etiological description. It is conceivable that at least some members of this group are caused by agents no longer present in, or recoverable from, diseased tissues. Accordingly, successful recovery of virus and experimental transmission would not be possible (106). These infections occur among lower animals. Examples include mumps-induced obstructive hydrocephalus (107, 109), cerebellar hypoplasia caused by feline panleukopenia virus (113, 114), and bluetongue virus-induced encephalopathies (146, 162). These defects are often noninflammatory in nature, and resemble classic defects of embryogenesis.

## Acknowledgments

We gratefully acknowledge the assistance in the preparation of this manuscript provided by Nelva Reckert, Rebecca Gilbert, and Renee Traub.

*Literature Cited*

1. Adams, D. H. 1970. *Pathol. Biol.* 18:559–77
2. Adams, J. M., Imagawa, D. T. 1962. *Proc. Soc. Exp. Biol. Med.* 111:562–66
3. Acheson, E. D. 1968. *Multiple Sclerosis: A Reappraisal,* ed. D. McAlpine, C. E. Lumsden, E. D. Acheson, chap. 2. Edinburgh: Livingstone. 415 pp.
4. Allison, A. C. 1967. *Brit. Med. Bull.* 23:60–65
5. Allison, A. C. 1972. *J. Clin. Pathol.* 25:121–31 Suppl.
6. Alper, T., Cramp, W. A., Haig, D. A., Clarke, M. C. 1967. *Nature* 214:764–66
7. Anderson, A. D., Levine, S. A., Gellert, H. 1972. *Lancet* 2:1061–63
8. Asher, D. M. et al 1973. *Symp. Int. Congr. Primatol., 4th* 4:43–90
9. Astrom, K. E., Mancall, E. L., Richardson, E. P. Jr. 1958. *Brain* 81:93–111
10. Barbanti-Brodano, G. 1972. *Ann. Inst. Pasteur* 123:553–63
11. Bellanti, J. 1971. *Immunology,* chap. 9. Philadelphia: Saunders. 584 pp.

12. Bennett, J. H., Rhodes, F. A., Robson, H. N. 1959. *Am. J. Hum. Genet.* 11: 169–87
13. Biberfeld, G. 1971. *Clin. Exp. Immunol.* 8:319–33
14. Birnbaum, G. 1973. *Arch. Neurol.* 28: 215–18
15. Brody, J. A. et al 1965. *Science* 147: 1114–16
16. Brody, J. A. 1972. *Lancet* 2:173–76
17. Brody, J. A., Chen, K. 1969. *Motor Neuron Diseases,* ed. F. H. Norris, L. T. Kurland, 61–79. New York: Grune & Stratton. 407 pp.
18. Brody, J. A., Detels, R. 1970. *Lancet* 2:500–1
19. Brotherston, J. G., Renwick, C. C., Stamp, J. T., Zlotnik, I., Pattison, I. H. 1968. *J. Comp. Pathol.* 78:9–17
20. Bouteille, M., Guazzi, G. C., Masselin, S., Houdart, R., Delarue, J. 1966. *Presse Med.* 74:2353–54
21. Bune, R. P., Harter, D. H. 1969. *J. Neuropathol. Exp. Neurol.* 28:185–94
22. Burger, D., Hartsough, G. R. 1965. *J. Infec. Dis.* 115:393–99
23. Byington, D. P., Johnson, K. P. 1972. *J. Infec. Dis.* 126:18–26
24. Campbell, A. M. G. et al 1947. *Brain* 70:50–58
25. Castaigne, P. et al 1972. *Multiple Sclerosis: Progress in Research,* ed. E. J. Field, T. M. Bell, P. R. Carnegie, 3: 152–58. Amsterdam: North-Holland. 273 pp.
26. Cathala, F., Brown, P. 1972. *J. Clin. Pathol.* 25:41–151
27. Chandler, R. L. 1968. *Brit. J. Exp. Pathol.* 49:52–59
28. Ciongoli, A. K. et al 1973. *Lancet* 2: 1146
29. Clarke, M. C., Haig, D. A. 1970. *Res. Vet. Sci.* 11:500–1
30. Clarke, M. C., Haig, D. A. 1970. *Nature* 225:100–3
31. Cole, G. A., Gilden, D. H., Monjan, A. A., Nathanson, N. 1971. *Fed. Proc.* 30:1831–41
32. Coward, J. E., Harter, D. H., Morgan, C. 1970. *Virology* 40:1030–38
33. Dayan, A. D., Ogul, E., Graveson, G. S. 1972. *J. Neurol. Neurosurg. Psychiat.* 35:170–75
34. Dayan, A. D., Stokes, M. I. 1971. *Lancet* 1:891–92
35. Ibid 1973. 1:177–79
36. De Boer, G. F. 1970. *J. Immunol.* 104:414–22
37. Dickinson, A. G., Meikle, V. N. H. 1971. *Mol. Gen. Genet.* 112:73–79
38. Dietzman, D., Horta-Barbosa, L. 1973. In *Brenneman's Practice of Pediatrics,* chap. 43. New York: Harper
39. Diener, T. O. 1972. *Advan. Virus Res.* 17:295–312
40. Diener, T. O. 1972. *Nature* 235:218–19
41. Dubois-Dalcq, M., Schumacher, G., Sever, J. L. 1973. *Lancet* 2:1408–11
41a. Duffy, P. et al 1974. *N. Engl. J. Med.* 290:692–93
42. Eklund, C. M., Kennedy, R. C., Hadlow, W. J. 1967. *J. Infec. Dis.* 117: 15–22
43. Faris, A. A., Martinez, A. J. 1972. *Arch. Neurol.* 27:357–60
44. Feinstone, M., Kapikian, A. F., Purcell, R. H. 1973. *Science* 182:1026–28
45. Fenner, F., White, D. O. 1970. In *Medical Virology,* chap. 7. New York: Academic. 390 pp.
46. Ferber, R. A. et al 1974. *Proc. Int. Congr. Neurol., 10th, Barcelona, September 1973.* Amsterdam: Excerpta Medica
47. Field, E. J. 1969. *Int. Rev. Exp. Pathol.* 8:129–239
48. Field, E. J., Cowshall, S., Narong, H. K., Bell, T. M. 1972. *Lancet* 2:280–81
49. Field, E. J., Farmer, F., Caspary, E. A., Joyce, G. 1969. *Nature* 226:90–91
50. Fleischhauer, P. et al 1972. *Deut. Med. Wochenschr.* 97:678–82
51. Gajdusek, D. C. 1971. *Am. J. Clin. Pathol.* 56:320–32
52. Gajdusek, D. C. 1973. In *Slow Virus Infection: Report of the 64th Ross Conference on Pediatric Research.* Columbus, Ohio: Ross Laboratories. 52 pp.
53. Gajdusek, D. C., Alpers, M. 1972. *Am. J. Hum. Genet.* 24:(6 Suppl.)1–38
54. Gajdusek, D. C., Gibbs, C. J. Jr. 1968. *Res. Publ. Assoc. Res. Nerv. Ment. Dis.* 44:254–80
55. Gajdusek, D. C., Gibbs, C. J. Jr. 1971. *Nature* 230:588–91
56. Gajdusek, D. C., Zigas, V. 1957. *N. Engl. J. Med.* 257:974–78
57. Gajdusek, D. C., Gibbs, C. J. Jr., Alpers, M., Eds. 1965. *Slow, Latent, and Temperate Virus Infections,* NINDS Monograph No. 2, US Govt. Print. Off. 489 pp.
58. Gajdusek, D. C., Gibbs, C. J. Jr., Alpers, M. 1966. *Nature* 209:794–96
59. Gajdusek, D. C., Rogers, N., Gibbs, C. J. Jr., Alpers, M. 1969. *Ann. NY Acad. Sci.* 162:529–50
60. Gajdusek, D. C., Gibbs, C. J. Jr. 1973. *Perspect. Virol.* VIII:279–311
61. Gardashian, A. M., Khondkarian, O. A., Bunina, T. L., Popova, L. M.,

Katkin, S. G. 1970. *Vestn. Akad. Med. Sci.* 9:80–83
62. Gardines, A. C., Marucci, A. A. 1969. *J. Comp. Pathol.* 79:233–35
63. Gardner, M. B. et al 1973. *J. Nat. Cancer Inst.* 51:1243–54
64. Gamboa, E. et al 1973. Pap. presented at *Am. Neurol. Assoc. Ann. Meet., 98th, Montreal, Canada, June 11–13*
65. Gerson, K. L., Haslam, R. H. A. 1971. *N. Engl. J. Med.* 285:78–82
66. Gibbs, C. J. Jr. 1967. *Curr. Top. Microbiol. Immunol.* 40:44–58
67. Gibbs, C. J. Jr. 1972. See Ref. 52, 18–24
68. Gibbs, C. J. Jr., Gajdusek, D. C. 1972. *J. Clin. Pathol.* 25:132–40
69. Ibid 84–96
70. Gibbs, C. J. Jr., Gajdusek, D. C. 1973. *Science* 182:67–68
71. Gibbs, C. J. Jr., Gajdusek, D. C. 1972. *Nature* 236:73–74
72. Gibbons, R. A., Hunter, G. D. 1967. *Nature* 215:1041–43
73. Gislason, G. 1947. *Dep. Agr. Publ.*, 235–57; Reykjavik, Iceland
74. Gonatas, N. K., Martin, J., Evangelista, I. 1967. *J. Neuropathol. Exp. Neurol.* 26:369–76
75. Gordon, W. S., Astrom, K. E., Mancall, E. L., Richardson, E. P. Jr. 1958. *Brain* 81:93–111
76. Gorham, J. R., Leader, R. W., Padgett, G. A., Burger, D., Henson, J. B. See Ref. 57, 279–85
77. Griffith, J. S. 1967. *Nature* 215:1041–44
78. Grose, C., Feorino, P. M. 1972. *Lancet* 2:1285–87
79. Gudnadottir, M., Palsson, P. A. 1965. *J. Immunol.* 95:1116–20
80. Gudnadottir, M. 1971. Cited by Palsson, P. A. *J. Clin. Pathol.* 115–20
81. Gudnadottir, M., Palsson, P. A. 1967. *J. Infec. Dis.* 117:1–6
82. Gunderman, J. R. 1973. *Am. J. Dis. Child.* 125:834–35
83. Hanissian, A. S., Jabbour, J. T., DeLamerens, S. Garcia, J. H., Horta-Barbosa, L. 1972. *Am. J. Dis. Child.* 123:151–55
84. Hartsough, G. R., Burger, D. 1965. *J. Infec. Dis.* 115:387–92.
85. Harter, D. H., Choppin, P. W. 1967. *Virology* 31:279–88
86. Harter, D. H., Robenkranz, H. S., Rose, H. M. 1969. *Proc. Soc. Exp. Biol.* 131:927–33
87. Hirano, A. See Ref. 57, 23–27
88. Hirano, A., Malamud, N., Kurland, L. T., Zimmerman, H. M. See Ref. 17, 51–60
89. Hooks, J. J., Gibbs, C. J. Jr., Chopra, H., Lewis, M., Gajdusek, D. C. 1972. *Science* 176:1420–22
90. Hooks, J. J., Gibbs, C. J. Jr., Gajdusek, D. C. 1973. *Science* 179:1019–20
91. Hornabrook, R. W. 1968. *Brain* 9: 53–74
92. Horta-Barbosa, L., Fuccillo, D. A., Sever, J., Zeman, W. 1969. *Nature* 221: 974
93. Horta-Barbosa, L. et al 1970. *Proc. Soc. Exp. Biol. Med.* 132:272–77
94. Horta-Barbosa, L. et al 1970. *Proc. Soc. Exp. Biol. Med.* 134:17–21
95. Horta-Barbosa, L. et al 1971. *Pediatrics* 47:782–83
96. Horta-Barbosa, L., Fuccillo, D. A., Sever, J. L. 1971. *J. Am. Med. Assoc.* 218:1185–88
97. Horta-Barbosa, L., Hamilton, R., Wittig, B., Fuccillo, D. A., Sever, J. L. 1971. *Science* 173:840–41
98. Hotchin, J. 1971. *Am. J. Pathol.* 64: 747–69
99. Hotchin, J., Benson, L., Sikora, E. 1969. *J. Immunol.* 102:1128–35
100. Hotchin, J. 1969. *Proc. Int. Congr. Virol., 1st, Helsinki* 1968:109–12
101. Huebner, R. J., Todaro, G. J. 1969. *Proc. Nat. Acad. Sci. USA* 64:1087–94
102. Hunter, G. D. See Ref. 5, 152–55
103. Hunter, G. D. 1970. In *Proc. Int. Congr. Neuropathol., 6th, Paris,* pp. 802–17
104. Jabbour, J. T., Roane, J. A., Sever, J. L. 1969. *Neurology* 19:929–31
105. Johnson, R. T. 1969. See Ref. 17, 280–85
106. Johnson, R. T. 1972. *N. Engl. J. Med.* 287:599–604
107. Johnson, R. T., Johnson, K. P. 1968. *J. Neuropathol. Exp. Neurol.* 27:591–606
108. Johnson, R. T., Johnson, K. P. 1969. In *Recent Advances in Neurology*, ed. F. Plum, 33–78. Philadelphia: Davis. 254 pp.
109. Johnson, R. T., Johnson, K. P., Edmond, C. J. 1967. *Science* 157:1066–67
110. Katz, M., Koprowski, H. 1968. *Nature* 219:639–40
111. Katz, M., Rorke, L. B., Masland, W. S., Barbanti-Brodano, G., Koprowski, H. 1970. *J. Infec. Dis.* 121:188–95
112. Kenyon, A. J., Gandu, J. E., Lopez, C., Good, R. A. 1973. *Science* 179:187–89
113. Kilham, L., Margolis, G., Colby, E. D. 1967. *Lab. Invest.* 17:465–80
114. Kilham, L., Margolis, G., Colby, E. D. 1971. *J. Am. Vet. Med. Assoc.* 158: 888–901
115. Kimberlin, R. H. 1969. *Res. Vet. Sci.* 10:392–94
116. Kimberlin, R. H., Anger, H. S. 1969. *J. Neurochem.* 16:543–48

117. Kimberlin, R. H., Hunter, G. D. 1967. *J. Gen. Virol.* 1:115–24
118. Kitchen, F. D., Bearn, A. G., Alpers, M., Gajdusek, D. C. 1972. *Am. J. Hum. Genet.* 24:S72–S85
119. Kurtzke, J. F. 1972. See Ref. 25, 208–28
120. Lampert, P. W., Gajdusek, D. C., Gibbs, C. J. Jr. 1972. *Am. J. Pathol.* 68: 626–46
121. Laterre, E. C., Callewaert, A., Heremans, J. F., Sfaello, Z. 1970. *Neurology* 20:982–90
122. Lerer, R. J., Lalavsky, S. M. 1973. *Pediatrics* 52:658–68
123. Lidin-Janson, G., Strannegard, O. 1972. *Brit. Med. J.* 2:572
124. Lin, F. H., Thormar, H. 1970. *J. Virol.* 6:702–4
125. Lin, F. H., Thormar, H. 1970. *Virology* 42:1140–43
126. Lischner, H. W., Sharma, K. M., Grover, W. D. 1972. *N. Engl. J. Med.* 286:786–87
127. Marsh, R. F., Burger, D., Hanson, R. P. 1969. *Am. J. Vet. Res.* 30:1637–42
128. Marsh, R. F., Hanson, R. P. 1970. *Infec. Immunol.* 2:727–30
129. Marsh, R. F., Miller, J. M., Hanson, R. P. 1973. *Infec. Immunol.* 7:352–55
130. Marsh, R. F., Pan, I. C., Hanson, R. P. 1970. *Infec. Immunol.* 2:727–30
131. May, W. W., Itabashi, H. H., De Jong, R. N. 1968. *Arch. Neurol.* 19:137–49
132. Merritt, H. H. 1969. *A Textbook of Neurology,* 450–54. Philadelphia: Lea & Febiger. 4th ed. 844 pp.
133. Ibid 93–97
134. Miller, H. G., Stanton, J. B., Gibbons, J. L. 1956. *Quart. J. Med.* 25:427–97
135. Minagawa, T., Yamada, M. 1971. *Jap. J. Microbiol.* 15:341–50
136. Mould, D. L., Dawson, A. M., Slater, J. S., Zlotnik, I. 1967. *J. Comp. Pathol.* 77:393–403
137. Moulias, R. L., Reinert, D. H., Goust, J. M. 1971. *N. Engl. J. Med.* 285:1090
138. Mulder, D. M., Rosenbaum, R. A., Layton, D. C. 1972. *Mayo Clin. Proc.* 47:756–61
139. Narayan, O., Penney, J. B., Johnson, R. T., Herndon, R. M., Weiner, L. P. 1973. *N. Engl. J. Med.* 289:1278–82
140. Narayan, O., Silverstein, A., Price, D., Johnson, R. 1974. *Science* 183:1202–3
141. Nathanson, N., El Dadah, A. H., Price, W. H. See Ref. 17, 254–63
142. Norris, F. H., Kurland, L. T. Eds. 1969. *Motor Neuron Diseases.* New York: Grune & Stratton. 407 pp.
143. Officer, J. E. et al 1973. *Science* 181: 194–97
144. Oldstone, M. B. A., Dixon, F. J. 1969. *J. Exp. Med.* 129:483–505
145. Ibid 1970. 131:1–19
146. Osburn, B. I. et al 1971. *Lab. Invest.* 25:206–10
147. Padgett, B. L., Walker, D. L. 1973. *J. Infec. Dis.* 127:467–70
148. Padgett, B. L., Walker, D. L., ZuRhein, G. M., Eckroade, R. J., Dessel, B. H. 1971. *Lancet* 1:1257–60
149. Palsson, P. A. 1972. *J. Clin. Pathol.* 25: 115–20
150. Palsson, P. A., Pattison, I. H., Field, E. J. See Ref. 57, 55–63
151. Pampiglione, G. 1964. *Brit. Med. J.* 2: 1296–1300
152. Pampiglione, G., Griffiths, A. H., Bramwell, E. C. 1971. *Lancet* 2:5–8
153. Parry, H. B. 1969. In *Scrapie Seminar, US Dep. Agr. Publ. ARS.* 93–107, 117–35, 153–71, 300–40
154. Payne, F. E., Baublis, J. V. 1973. *J. Infec. Dis.* 127:505–11
155. Payne, F. E., Baublis, J. V., Itabashi, H. H. 1969. *N. Engl. J. Med.* 281:585–89
156. Perier, O., Thiry, L., Vanderhaeghen, J. J., Pelc, S. 1968. *Neurology* 18: 138–43
157. Petursson, G. See Ref. 103, 831–32
158. Porter, D. C., Larsen, A. E. 1968. *Perspect. Virol.* VI:173–87
159. Poskanzer, D. C., Cantor, H. M., Kaplan, G. S. See Ref. 17, 286–90
160. Prince, A. M. 1968. *Proc. Nat. Acad. Sci. USA* 60:814–21
161. Prineas, J. 1972. *Science* 178:760–63
162. Richards, W. P. C., Cordy, D. R. 1967. *Science* 156:530–31
163. Richardson, E. P. Jr. 1961. *N. Engl. J. Med.* 265:815–23
164. Roos, R., Gajdusek, D. C., Gibbs, C. J. Jr. 1973. *Brain* 96:1–20
165. Rowe, W. P. 1970. *J. Virol.* 5:651–52
166. Sagman, D. L. 1972. *J. Am. Med. Assoc.* 221:301
167. Sell, K. W., Thurman, G. B., Ahmed, A., Strong, D. M. 1973. *N. Engl. J. Med.* 288:215–16
168. Sever, J. L., Zeman, W. 1968. *Neurology* 18:1–192
169. Shah, K. V. 1972. *Am. J. Epidemiol.* 95:199–206
170. Shah, K. V. et al *J. Nat. Cancer Inst.* 48:557–61
171. Shiraki, H. See Ref. 17, 80–84
172. Sigurdsson, B. 1954. *Brit. Vet. J.* 110: 7–9, 255–70, 307–22, 341–54
173. Sigurdsson, B., Palsson, P. A., Grimsson, H. 1957. *J. Neuropathol. Exp. Neurol.* 16:389–403

174. Sigurdsson, B., Palsson, P. A., van-Bogaert, L. 1962. *Acta Neuropathol.* 1:343–62
175. Sigurdsson, B., Thormar, H., Palsson, P. A. 1960. *Arch. Gesamte Virusforsch.* 10:368–81
176. Steele, J. C., Gladstone, R. M., Thanasophon, S., Fleming, P. C. 1969. *Lancet* 2:710–13
177. Sterner, G., Biberfeld, G. 1969. *Scand. J. Infec. Dis.* 1:203–8
178. Stone, L. B., Scolnick, E., Takemoto, K., Aaronson, S. A. 1971. *Nature* 229: 257–58
179. Straub, O. C. 1970. *Berl. Münch. tierärzt. Wochenschr.* 83:357–60
180. Takemoto, K., Stone, L. B. 1971. *J. Virol.* 7:770–75
181. Ter Meulen, V., Koprowski, H., Iwasaki, Y., Kackell, Y. M., Muller, D. 1972. *Lancet* 2:1–5
182. Thein, P. et al 1972. *Arch. Neurol.* 27:540–48
183. Thormar, H. 1961. *Virology* 14:463–75
184. Thormar, H. 1965. *Res. Vet. Sci.* 6: 117–29
185. Thormar, H. 1971. *Z. Neurol.* 199: 1–23, 151–66
186. Thormar, H., Cruickshank, J. G. 1965. *Virology* 25:145–48
187. Thormar, H., Helgadottir, H. 1965. *Res. Vet. Sci.* 6:456–65
188. Tourtellotte, W. W., Parker, J. A., Herndon, R. M., Cuadros, C. V. 1968. *Neurology* 18:117–21
189. Tourtellotte, W. W. 1971. In *Immunological Disorders of the Nervous System,* ed. L. P. Rowland, 112–55. Baltimore: Williams & Wilkins. 470 pp.
190. Urano, T., Kawerse, T., Kodairo, K. 1970. *Pediatrics* 45:294–95
191. Utermohlen, V., Zabriskie, J. B. 1973. *Lancet* 2:1146–47
192. Vernon, M. L. et al 1970. *Lancet* 1: 964–67
193. Walker, D. L., Padgett, B. L., ZuRhein, G. M., Albert, A. A., Marsh, R. F. 1973. *Science* 181:674–76
194. Watanabe, I., Okazaki, H. 1973. *Lancet* 2:569–70
195. Wear, D. J., Rapp, F. 1971. *J. Immunol.* 107:1593–98
196. Weiner, L. P., Johnson, R. T., Herndon, R. M. 1973. *N. Engl. J. Med.* 288: 1103–9
197. Weiner, L. P. et al 1972. *N. Engl. J. Med.* 286:385–90
198. Weiner, L. P. et al 1972. *J. Virol.* 10:147–49
199. Whitaker, J. N., Sever, J. L., Engel, W. K. 1972. *N. Engl. J. Med.* 287:864–66
200. White, H. H., Kepes, J. H., Kirkpatrick, C. H., Schuinke, R. N. 1972. *Arch. Neurol.* 26:359–65
201. Wiesenfeld, S. L., Ferber, R. A., Hargunding, H. C., Gajdusek, D. C. 1974. *Am. J. Hum. Genet.* In press
202. Yeh, J. 1973. *J. Virol.* 12:962–68
203. Zil'ber, L. A. et al 1963. *Bull. WHO* 29:449–56
204. Zu Rhein, G. M., Chou, S. M. 1965. *Science* 148:1477–79
205. Zu Rhein, G. M. 1969. *Progr. Med. Virol.* 11:185–247

# PERSISTING BACTERIOPHAGE INFECTIONS, LYSOGENY, AND PHAGE CONVERSIONS

❖1639

*Lane Barksdale and Sheldon B. Arden*
Department of Microbiology, New York University School of Medicine, New York, N.Y. 10016

CONTENTS

INTRODUCTION .......... 265
*Related Terminology* .......... 266
*Range of Coverage* .......... 268
LYSOGENY .......... 268
*Inducibility of Lysogenic Bacteria* .......... 272
*Elimination of Prophages from Lysogenic Bacteria: "Curing"* .......... 274
*Variations in the Patterns of Lysogeny* .......... 275
THE PHAGE CARRIER STATE, PSEUDOLYSOGENY .......... 276
*Condition 1: Phage Infection Limited by Available Receptors on Bacterial Cell* .......... 277
*Condition 2: Loss of Receptors Due to the Action of Virolysin (Endolysin)* .......... 278
*Condition 3: The Accumulation of Mutant $\phi^{vir}$ in a Population of Bac ($\phi$)* .......... 279
MODEL PHAGE CONVERSIONS .......... 280
*Bacteriophages $\epsilon^{15}$ and $\epsilon^{34}$ and the Conversion of O-Antigens in Salmonella anatum* 280
*Corynebacteriophages and Diphtherial Toxin* .......... 284

## INTRODUCTION

Bacteriophages persist in one of two general ways in nature: as prophages of temperate viruses integrated into the bacterial genome [or the closely associated bacterial membrane replicatory system (100, 151)] or as persistent viral infections (carrier state[1], pseudolysogeny) in which phage multiplies in a fraction of the bacterial

[1]The editors of *The Bacteriophage λ* (124) have defined carrier as: "Bacteria that harbor a specified phage or other dispensable genetic element. Originally the term designated bacterial cultures that were persistently contaminated with phage but from which uninfected cells could be recovered readily (as opposed to lysogenic cultures)." Here we are using the *original* definition. We are principally concerned with new findings from nature and what they mean, and so we agree with Hayes who said (121): "In practice the existence of lysogeny should be judged by rather rigorous criteria of its stability, since interaction of some virulent phages with their hosts may superficially simulate the condition."

population. Either of these conditions may bring about real and/or *apparent* changes in characteristic properties of the bacterial population. Such changes may be due to the expression of prophage genes, of vegetative viral genes, or to modifications which lead to the induction of cryptic bacterial genes. They are all *phage conversions.* In reviewing the literature on phage conversions we find that persistent bacteriophage infections have sometimes been mistakenly equated with lysogeny and that changes found in such phage-infected populations have been called *lysogenic conversions.* There seems to be a widespread idea that the mixing of temperate bacteriophage and suitable bacteria has but one outcome: lysogeny. While the lysogenic state is very common in nature, in the laboratory lysogenization is not always the most common outcome of temperate bacteriophage infection. Nor are all temperate phages capable of inducing the lysogenic state. We have therefore felt the need to include here a summary of the characteristics which separate lysogeny from the nonlysogenic perpetuation of phage (persisting bacteriophage infections, pseudolysogeny, carrier states) and to include models from the literature of those changes in bacterial genotype or phenotype which may be associated with each kind of persisting association.

### *Related Terminology*

Every now and then terminology gets to be overlapping and needs pruning. The initiators of this sort of change logically should be textbook writers and their readers; sometimes, perhaps, a reviewer or two. All of the terms used for describing mechanisms of bringing about genetic changes in bacteria are not necessary. We feel that those that help the student should be the ones we keep. Those superfluous to understanding what is meant should be dropped. Terms important for understanding the genetic changes which can be brought to bacteria include, in order of their discovery: (*a*) *mutation;* (*b*) *transformation* (88, 135, 282), which deserves special standing because of its role in the development of all genetics; (*c*) *transduction* (240), transformation mediated by dud bacteriophage particles (this term is retained because of its usefulness with regard to the to transfer of plasmids, prophages, and bacterial genes); (*d*) *conjugation* (1,68,224); and (*e*) *lysogenization* (see Figure 1) with its concomitant changes. Each, with the exception of the transfer of plasmids, if successful, ultimately results in recombination with the bacterial chromosome or fixation to the closely allied membrane replicating system. When plasmids (transferred by conjugation) behave according to definition they replicate in the cytoplasm. The cytoplasm has been plasmidized. Presumably such plasmids can be eliminated by growth of the host cell in the presence of acridine orange or ethidium bromide (44, 125).

Here we have included neither specialized transduction nor episomes. Viruses are defined by their genes. Plasmids are not viruses even though viruses and plasmids have been known to exchange segments of DNA (174). Should plasmids and viruses by such exchanges switch their natures, one categorically becomes the other. Lambda *dg,* $\lambda^{bio}$, $\lambda^{+}$, $\lambda^{vir}$, $\phi 80$, $\beta^{tox+}$, $\epsilon^{15}$ or $P2^{+}$ are all bacteriophages defined by their genes. Nothing is gained or made more clear by calling them transducers and certainly one of them is no more specialized (specialized transduction) than the other. Each is an identifiable genetic entity and therefore specialized no more or less

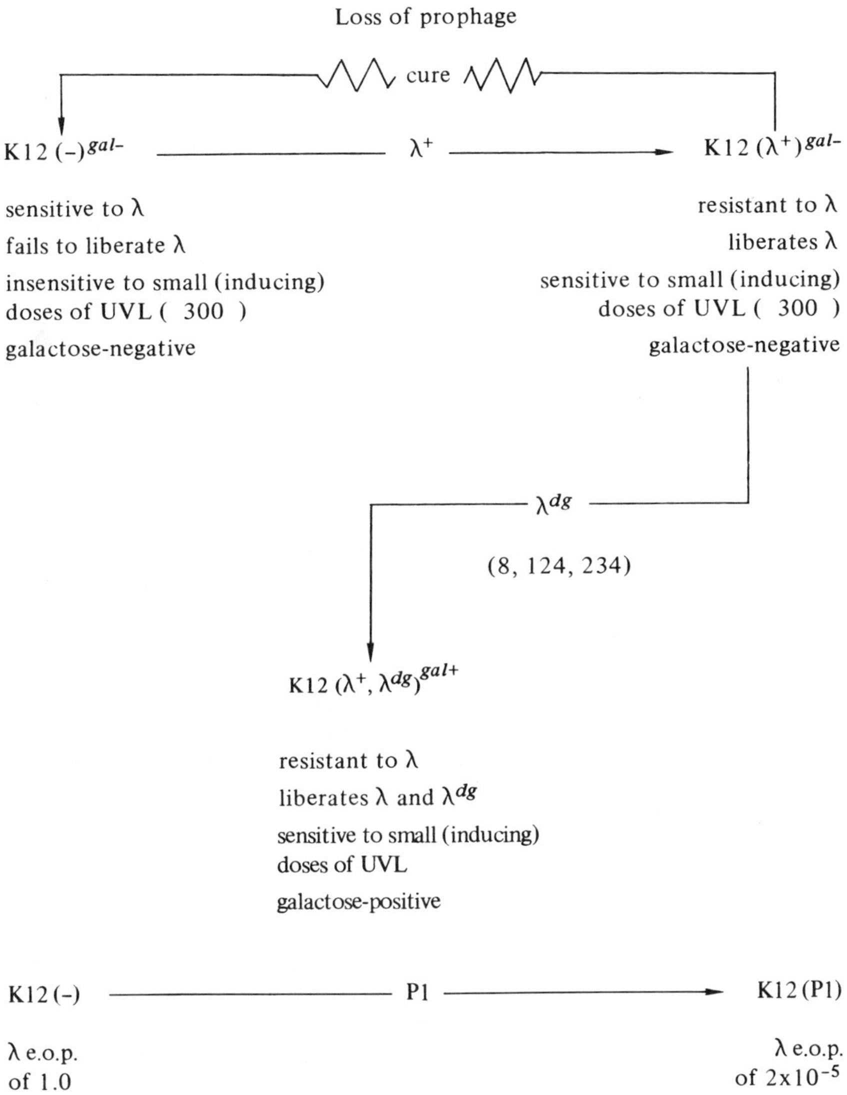


*Figure 1* Properties associated with nonlysogenic *Escherichia coli* K12(⁻) and the lysogenic derivatives *E. coli* K12($\lambda^+$), *E. coli* K12($\lambda^+$, $\lambda^{dg}$), and *E. coli* K12(P1). Following infection by temperate phage the majority of infected bacteria are lysed. A minority are lysogenized and survive as stable lysogens. Lambda *dg* is often lost from the double lysogen, K12($\lambda^+$, $\lambda^{dg}$). Lambda *dg* is unstable because, in its polymerization into being, the *E. coli* galactose region (the *coli* genes for the synthesis of galactokinase, galactose-1-P-uridyl transferase, and UDP-galactose epimerase) has replaced essential phage functions (6, 162–164), thus creating a defective phage which cannot survive outside of the laboratory. When such bacterial-viral hybrid genomes retain information for essential viral functions they survive as stable prophages: e.g. $\lambda^{bio}$ (209, 304), $\phi 80^{tryp}$ (70, 217–219), P1CM (174, 175). P1 brings to K12(P1) a restriction and modifying system as an adjunct property of lysogeny (7, 181).

than other comparable genomes. Knowing what $\lambda^{dg}$ (see Figure 1) is genetically is the important point. To know fully the genetics of $\lambda^{dg}$, $\lambda^{+}$, or any other prophage one must, of course, eventually have a map of it as well as a map of where it sits. Wild-type temperate phages are capable of fixing to and replicating with the nucleocytoplasmic membrane system. For some phages the site is intrachromosomal, for others it is epi- or, perhaps, intramembranal (evidence not yet available). Replicons (151) which are capable of replication either within the chromosome or within the cytoplasm are best described for what they are, not as episomes but as a specific sequence of DNA replicating in the cytoplasm, attached to the cytoplasmic membrane system or integrated into the bacterial chromosome.

### *Range of Coverage*

In Table 1 are summarized selected reports of phage-associated changes found in a variety of Gram-positive and Gram-negative bacteria. While this is not an exhaustive listing, coupled with information in the footnotes, it should serve as a useful guide to reported phage conversions. For reasons set out in the next two sections, we have been unable in many cases to determine the exact manner in which phage was perpetuated in the bacterial clones reported to have been modified. Notable exceptions are to be found, e.g. in the study by Winkler et al with staphylophages (serological group F) and conversion of *Staphylococcus aureus* to loss of $\beta$ toxin where criteria supporting the existence of lysogeny have been clearly established (303). Only a few of the many reported cases of phage conversion in *Salmonella* have been listed by us (see Table 1). For additional information the reader is referred to papers by LeMinor (183, 185), Stocker (275, 276), Uetake (293–295), Iseki (143–146), and others (see also footnote j in Table 1).

The two model conversions presented here have been chosen because they represent the most illuminating studies of phage conversions on record. Many of their potentialities for giving us new information, originally outlined in 1959 (19), now seem to have been realized. For this realization the communal nature of scientific endeavor, extolled by Echols (85), has been a key contributing factor. The reliance of all concerned on the findings of the bacteriophage $\lambda$ community (124); on the investigators of phages P1 (136), P2 (32), P22 (190), and T7 (3, 279); and on the explorers of the lipopolysaccharides and endotoxins of Gram-negative bacteria is obvious, and our general knowledge is the better for it.

## LYSOGENY

Lysogeny is the perpetuation of prophages (124, 203) as part of the bacterial replicating system. When a bacterium incorporates the genome of a temperate bacteriophage into its chromosome [e.g. coliphages $\lambda^{+}$ (124) or $P2^{+}$ (32) or corynebacteriophage $\beta^{+}$ (25)] or into the closely associated replicating machinery of the bacterial membrane system [e.g. coliphages $\lambda^{N}$ (193, 266, 267), P1 (37, 136)] it becomes lysogenic. It has been lysogenized; it carries a phage genome as prophage. Therefore, in the change from the nonlysogenic to the lysogenic state every bacterium becomes converted to the capacity to liberate phage and to an immunity to

Table 1 Phage conversions in Gram-positive and Gram-negative bacteria[a]

| Bacterium | Phage(s), $\phi$ | Effect(s) reported | References |
|---|---|---|---|
| *Bacillus megatherium* | 1*pt*, 3 | Change in colonial morphology | 141 |
| *Clostridium botulinum* | | | |
| type C | CE$\beta$ | Type $C_1$ toxin is made | 85a, 85b, 86, 87 |
| type D | DE$\beta$ (=1D$^{tox^+}$) | Type D toxin is made | 137–139 |
| *Corynebacterium diphtheriae* type *mitis*, strains C4 and C7 | $\beta^{tox^+}$ | Diphtherial toxin[b] is made | 92, 93 |
| *Corynebacterium ovis*, strain 21, and *Corynebacterium ulcerans*, strain 298G | 76c/ovis 21 [= $Z^{tox^+}$ (10)] | Diphtherial toxin is made | 221 |
| *Mycobacterium smegmatis* | | | |
| strain 607 (= SN10) | D29 | Lipase detected[c] | 155 |
| strains SN2, SN10, SN14 | B4, Bo1, Bo13, D29, $R_1$, Roy | R ⟶ S with changes in colonial morphology, growth rate, and enzymic activities[d] | 38, 156, 159, 160, 207, 208, 299, 301 |
| strain 607 | D29, B4 | Changes in somatic antigens | 154 |
| *Staphylococcus aureus* | | | |
| strain S57 | $\phi$ from group A | Leucocydin of Panton-Valentine is made | 297 |
| S57, BSS | $\phi$'s from group F (e.g. $\phi$ D) | Repression of synthesis of $\beta$ toxin: staphylokinase is made | 75–79, 303 |

[a] The reader should consult original references in order to decide the phage-host relationships responsible for these changes. With rare exceptions the required evidence, as outlined in this review, for deciding the actual role of the phage in the reported conversion is lacking. Some papers claiming a lysogenic conversion report curing of the lysogenic condition by subculturing in the presence of Tween 80®, oxalate, antiphage serum, or acridine orange. The first three obviously have to do with mechanisms for perpetuating phage which involve readsorption and reinfection. The latter presumably eliminates phage by preventing the maturation of vegetative phage in the host cytoplasm. In none of these cases does lysogeny seem to be involved.

[b] Wild-type *C. diphtheriae* actively reduces nitrates to nitrites. A dubious species, *Corynebacterium belfanti*, differs from *C. diphtheriae* in being unable to reduce nitrates. It has been reported that lysogenization of *C. belfanti* with $\beta^{tox^+}$, derived from $C4_s$ $(\beta)^{tox^+}$, yields a *C. belfanti* having the capacity to produce diphtherial toxin and the ability to reduce nitrates (115, 119). The converted *C. belfanti's* had the antigenic properties of *C. diphtheriae*, $C4_s$ $(\beta)^{tox^+}$ (N. B. Groman, personal communication). The details of the experiments leading to this multigenic conversion are lacking. Nitrate reductase-negative mutants of *C. diphtheriae* are readily obtainable and, following lysogenization with $\beta^{tox^+}$, they remain unable to reduce nitrates. Further, *C. belfanti*, strain 1030, when lysogenized with $\beta^{tox^+}$, retains its inability to reduce nitrates (9, 11, 107).

[c] Also reported in *M. fortuitum* (155).

[d] R ⟶ S = rough to smooth colony change. For additional information see reference 161 (pp. 204–209, 215–226, 227–243). Similar changes reported in *Mycobacterium fortuitum* (69) and in *Mycobacterium phlei* (69, 157, 158).

**Table 1** (continued)

| Bacterium | Phage(s), $\phi$ | Effect(s) reported | References |
|---|---|---|---|
| *Staphylococcus aureus* | | | |
| Phage group IV | 42D | Enterotoxin A is made | 58 |
| strains 2003, 2017 | L2043 | $\alpha$-toxin is made[e] | 78 |
| Group III (strain 39x35) | L54a | Inhibition of lipase activity | 83, 84 |
| Type 80/81 | $\phi$'s from Type 80 and 52/52A/80/81 complex | Failure to hydrolyze tween 80 | 258, 259 |
| 655 "cured" | 655 | R ⟶ S with changes in antibiotic and phage sensitivities and inhibition of coagulase activity | 152 |
| SA13, SA14, SJ37 | 71, 81, 97 | $\delta$ toxin is made | 60 |
| type 80 | $\phi$'s from type 52/52A/80 | Changes in phage type[f] | 12 |
| *Streptococcus pyogenes* group A strain $T25_3$ | $\phi^{T12g1}$ | Scarlantinal (= erythrogenic) toxin is made[g] | 34, 56, 94, 313 |

[e] Also see reference 36.

[f] For additional information on changes in phage types in *S. aureus* see references 67, 257, 260.

[g] *Streptococci* of group *A*: In 1926, Cantacuzene & Bonciu (56) reported that filtrates from cultures of scarlatinal streptococci rendered certain nonscarlatinal streptococci agglutinable by antiscarlatinal (convalescent) serum. This newly gained property they characterized as "une agglutinabilite specifique et hereditairement persistante." A year later, Frobisher & Brown (94), using strains of streptococci carrying distinctive combinations of markers (mannitol fermentation, or not, protease production, or not, liberation of a soluble hemolysin, or not, and the ability to produce scarlatinal toxin, or not), grew pairs of scarlatinal and nonscarlatinal strains together and then reisolated each and examined the nonscarlatinal strains for the acquisition of the capacity to produce scarlatinal toxin. In another set of experiments these investigators grew nonscarlatinal strains in the presence of a sterile (Berkfeld V) filtrate derived from a scarlatinal strain. By each method nonscarlatinal strains appeared to acquire the capacity to produce a scarlatinal toxin. The capacity was short-lived and was readily lost on subculture of the modified strains. Bingel (34) reported having confirmed the experiments of Frobisher and Brown. In his work the converted nonscarlatinal strains produced antigen specifically reactive with antiscarlatinal sera. The converted strains did not lose their capacity to make scarlatinal antigen(s) until after 16 subcultures. He was able to eliminate the capacity to convert in both naturally occurring and converted scarlatinal strains by treatment with antiscarlatinal serum. The loss was permanent. Ten years ago Zabriskie (313) reported that a nonscarlatinal *Streptococcus pyogenes*, strain $T25_3$, could be lysogenized with a phage, $\phi^{T12g1}$, derived from a scarlatinal strain. He indicated that the *Str. pyogenes* (T12g1) was inducible and that it produced an erythrogenic toxin. Growth of the strain in the presence of antiphage serum failed to affect its capacity to produce the toxin. It has been pointed out that this is an interesting system (312, 314, 315), but to date it has been neither extended nor confirmed by others. While Zabriskie has stated that his work confirms that of Frobisher and Brown, the way in which the strains of those authors lost the capacity to make erythrogenic toxin(s) suggests that those investigators were *not* dealing with lysogenic bacteria. Further, their converted strains

**Table 1** (continued)

| Bacterium | Phage(s), $\phi$ | Effect(s) reported | References |
|---|---|---|---|
| *Escherichia coli* | | | |
| C | P2 | Increased sensitivity to 5-fluorodeoxyuridine | 31, 33 |
| K12 | $\lambda^{bio}$, $\lambda^{dbio}$[h] | *bio*- to *bio*+ | 209, 304 |
| K12 | $\phi$ $80^{pt}$, $\phi$ $80^{dt}$ | *tryp*- to *tryp*+ | 70, 217–219 |
| K12 and *Shigella dysenteriae* | P1 | DNA modification and restriction | 7, 181 |
| | $P1^{dl}$ | *lac*- to *lac*+ | 2, 90, 202 |
| K12, *Salmonella typhi, Pasturella pseudotuberculosis, Pasteurella pestis* | $P1^{CM}$, $P1^{dCM}$ | Chloramphenicol $(CM)^s$ to $Cm^r$ | 174, 175, 177 |
| *Pseudomonas aeruginosa* | | | |
| strain 1 | D3 | Changes in somatic antigens and loss of ability to adsorb phage D3[i] | 130 |
| *Rhizobium trifolii* | | | |
| strain SU297 | 7, *7cr* | Changes in somatic antigens and loss of ability to adsorb phages 7, *7cr*, and 8 | 26 |
| *Salmonella bredeney* | | | |
| (group B) | 27 | 0-factors 1, 4, 12 to 1, 4, 12, *27B* | 15, 182, 187, 188, 272 |
| *Salmonella cholerae suis* | | | |
| (group $C_1$) | 14(6, 7) | 0-factors $6_2$, 7 to $6_2$, (7), *14* | 95, 96, 184 |
| *Salmonella durham* | | | |
| (group G) | 37 | 0-factors 13, 23, 36 to *1*, 13, 23, 36, *37*[j] | 186, 273 |
| *Shigella flexneri* | | | |
| types I and II | V | 0-antigens 1 or 2 to 5[k] | 98 |
| *Vibrio fetus* | | | |
| strain V-2673 | VFP-13 | serotype V to I | 237 |

lost their capacity to produce scarlatinal toxin when cultivated in the presence of antitoxin. With one or the other of these findings Cantacuzene, Frobisher and Brown, and Bingel seem in agreement.

The simplest way to examine or screen for the expression of a particular phage gene is not by going through the elaborate routine of producing a lysogenic strain. What one wants to know is whether or not $\phi^{T12g1}$ carries information required for the synthesis of erythrogenic toxin. It should be a simple matter to obtain a virulent mutant of $\phi^{T12g1}$ (supposedly carrying the gene for the synthesis of erythrogenic toxin) and to examine the synthesis of erythrogenic toxin in one cycle of virus growth in the non-scarlatinal strain of streptococcus, $T25_3$. The results of such an experiment should lead to an unambiguous answer as to the role of $\phi^{T12g1}$ in the synthesis of erythrogenic toxin.

[h] Lambda *dg* is described in text and in Figure 1.

[i] Also see reference 196.

[j] Conversions of salmonella antigens far exceed all other conversions studied. For those not listed above nor included in the text see references 27, 89, 122, 143–145, 183, and 185.

[k] For additional information on changes in somatic antigens in *Sh. flexneri* see references 97, 142, and 216.

that liberated phage. The acquisition of these two properties is the *sine qua non* of all lysogenic conversions (see Figure 1). In addition, many temperate bacteriophages carry genes which effect the synthesis of what are clearly bacterial products, such as the lipopolysaccharides of *Salmonella*, or products of unknown function, such as bacterial toxins. Lysogenic conversions, then, involve the integration into the bacterial replicating system of a particular linkage group of genes which in the process of integration and in the process of excision act as a unit—that unit is a viral genome (32, 124, 190, 263). The stability of lysogeny depends upon the silencing of the expression of many genes related to viral function. The unsilenced genes required for this effect are viral. Additional viral genes serving no viral function may also be expressed. Thus the converting gene responsible for O-antigen 1 carried by phage P22 in *Salmonella typhimurium* (275, 276, 316) remains turned on in the prophage state. One cannot, however, equate the expressions of these converting genes with the existence of the prophage state, for they are fully expressed by infecting temperate phage, clear-plaque mutants, and virulent mutants in the vegetative state (18, 294, 316). Misunderstanding this point has lead to difficulties where carrier clones were confused with lysogenic clones. Lysogenization in the laboratory seldom takes place in one step. One plates out a mixture of temperate phages and bacteria. After incubation the plates contain some killed bacteria, some colonies with sensitive cells, some colonies with sensitive cells and infected cells, a small percentage of colonies of lysogenic cells, some colonies containing lysogenic and sensitive cells, and a very rare colony of resistant cells (bar mutants). From these one has to recover, reclone, and characterize the lysogenic strain being sought. Obviously, one needs to know the nature of each survivor. Most important here are the lysogenic survivors. The lysogenic state is stable to repeated subculture. In lysogeny of the λ type inducibility (see induction below) is a key characteristic. The lysogenic state is unaffected by cultivation in specific antiphage serum. It is in this way that lysogenic clones may be distinguished from stable carrier clones (see Figure 2).

### *Inducibility of Lysogenic Bacteria*

The discovery by Lwoff, Siminovitch & Kjeldgaard (205) that exposure of lysogenic *Bacillus megatherium* to small doses of ultraviolet light (UVL) was followed by the production of bacteriophage by almost every cell in the population (the induction of lysogenic cells to lysis) has provided a tool for probing the molecular basis of lysogeny and for characterizing lysogenic populations. Other conditions may also lead to induction: e.g. exposure to mitomycin C (239), fluoropyrimidines (210), shifts in temperature (192), etc. Whether or not the basis for the excision of prophage is the same for all of these inducing agents remains to be determined. Literature relevant to the process of induction has recently been exhaustively reviewed by Ernest Borek and the late Ann Ryan (42). Wild-type temperate phages fall into three classes with regard to induction: (*a*) those that are readily inducible on exposure to UVL such as coliphage $\lambda^+$ or corynebacteriophage $\beta^+$; (*b*) those which show a slight increase in phage following irradiation as is the case for coliphage P1 (59);

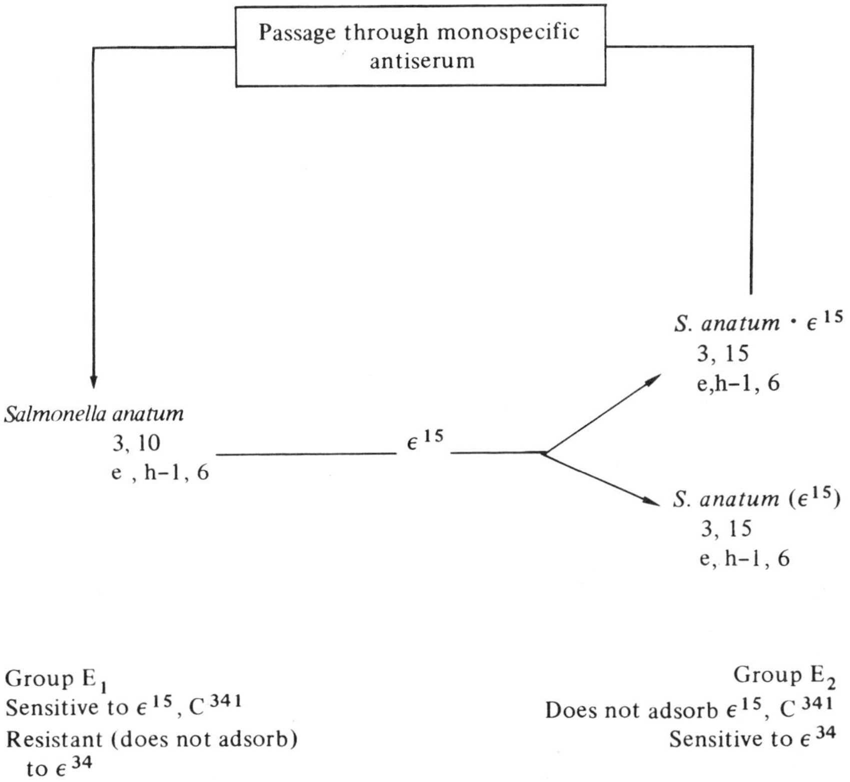


*Figure 2* Antigenic changes (phage conversion) brought to clones of *Salmonella anatum* (3, 15; e, h-1, 6) carrying phage $\epsilon^{15}$. Such phage conversions result in elimination of receptor sites for $\epsilon^{15}$. For a discussion of this closing of the door following infection, see text. Passage of carrier clone, *S. anatum*·$\epsilon^{15}$ (3, 15; e, h-1, 6), through certain antibacterial sera results in the elimination of phage and a return of *S. anatum* (3, 15; e, h-1, 6) (53, 294, 295). The original source of $\epsilon^{15}$ was a naturally occurring lysogen *Salmonella newington* (3, 10; e, h-1, 6) ($\epsilon^{15}$). The $\epsilon^{15}$ phages have not been mapped and nothing is known regarding their immunity regions or the genetic control of lysogenization. Whether or not *c* mutants of $\epsilon^{15}$ exist and are comparable to *c* mutants of λ or $\beta^{tox+}$ is not known. In the *S. anatum* (3, 15; e, h-1, 6) ($\epsilon^{15}$), made in the laboratory and reported to be curable by passage through antiserum (see text), it is assumed that spontaneously cured cells, lacking factor 15, become enriched in the supernatant because they escape agglutination by monospecific serum.

and (*c*) those which are not induced at all, as in the case of coliphage P2. It is clear that phage $\lambda^+$ and phage $P2^+$ behave very differently in response to UVL. The plaguing fact about the properties of $\lambda^+$ and $P2^+$ is that both are chromosomally integrated. The shut-off of their phage functions involves the synthesis of specific repressor by each (32, 124). Both undergo spontaneous induction, but one responds to inducing agents and one does not. When bacteria carrying both $\lambda^+$ and $P2^+$ are exposed to UVL, induction of both phages takes place (32). Thus, 23 years after its discovery, the mechanism(s) of induction remain(s) elusive. When an investigator is concerned with establishing a case for lysogenic conversion, information regarding inducibility of his lysogen offers a useful marker. For example, a purported *Corynebacterium diphteriae* ($\beta^+$) is resistant to free phage $\beta^+$, is inducible with UVL, and produces toxin. It retains these same properties following cultivation in anti-$\beta$ serum[2]. These are the proofs needed to establish the fact that the culture is indeed lysogenic and that toxin production is associated with that lysogeny. That phage $\beta^+$ in all of its lysogenizing attributes follows the $\lambda$ model is indeed fortuitous.

## *Elimination of Prophages from Lysogenic Bacteria: "Curing"*

Prophages may be viewed as the true wild types of temperate phage genomes. The stability of these wild types in nature is an impressive aspect of natural selection. Thus, while it is easy to cure pseudolysogenic bacteria of phage, it is often difficult to cure lysogenic bacteria of their prophages. Currency should not be given to claims of curing in the absence of absolute proof that lysogeny existed prior to the application of the methods of cure. The Park-Williams 8 strain of *C. diphtheriae*, $PW8_r(P)^{tox+}$, has been maintained in continuous culture under a variety of conditions in many different laboratories since 1896 (244). Being a rough strain, it does not adsorb phage homologous to the prophage it carries. Thus, curing followed by reinfection does not figure in the stability of its lysogeny. A recent examination of five substrains of this bacterium from laboratories around the world showed them all to be lysogenic and toxinogenic (176). Here then is a lysogenic strain which cannot be reinfected once it loses its prophage. [In that respect it is like the rough lysogenic *Salmonella enteritidis* by which Burnet & McKie (54) originally established evidence for the anlage of lysogenizing bacteriophages.] $PW8_r(P)^{tox+}$ has remained stably lysogenic for 77 years on record and perhaps, for 77,000 years or more not on record. Bertani & Bertani (32) have pointed out that the Lisbonne and

[2]Anderson & Cowles (4) have reported that passage of $C4_s(\beta)^{tox+}$ through medium containing anti-$\beta^c$ serum or in animals immune to toxin resulted in the emergence of nonlysogenic, nontoxinogenic strains. More recently, Carne, Bagnall & Massey (57) have reported curing of three of nine lysogenic strains of *Corynebacterium ovis* and four of eight strains of *Corynebacterium ulcerans* following incubation in vivo in diffusion chambers contained in peritoneal cavities of fowls and turkeys. These results are very different from our own experience with the strains of *C. diphtheriae*, $PW8_r(P)^{tox+}$, $C7_s(\beta)^{tox+}$, and $C4_s(\beta)^{tox+}$. Assuming that spontaneous curing might occur at a rate of $10^{-6}$ or $10^{-7}$, we find it difficult to understand what could give the small number of cured cells such a selective advantage that they could emerge as the major or only population. Neither of these authors offers much information on this point.

Carrere strain of *Escherichia coli* (194, 195) is still lysogenic after 41 years. So in Gram-negative and Gram-positive bacteria there are examples that lysogeny is a very stable state. On the other hand curing following irradiation with UVL is common in *Salmonella typhimurium* (317). In Figure 1 it is indicated that K12(λ) can be cured of its lysogeny. E. M. Lederberg inadvertently cured K12(λ) of prophage λ when, in her search for bacterial mutants, she irradiated it with heavy doses of UVL. In fact it was the nibbled condition of K12(–) survivor cells, then called W-158, which lead the Lederbergs to λ (178, 179). Lambda is the model lysogenizing phage. It forms turbid plaques and much of the turbidity is attributable to surviving lysogens, K12(λ)s. Its discovery came at a suitable time for ushering in the study of genetics of temperate phage(s), now so magnificently summed up in *The Bacteriophage λ* (124). The key to the λ-type lysogeny is the turbid plaque. The ultimate basis for the turbid plaque is a specific λ-repressor protein (248, 249) synthesized by transcription from prophage $\lambda^+$. $\lambda^c$ (clear mutants) make less repressor. A multiplicity of them is required to effect lysogenization. $\lambda^{vir}$, mutants which lyse K12($\lambda^+$), are unable to bind repressor.

## *Variations in the Patterns of Lysogeny*

It is now clear that all lysogeny does not follow the model of λ lysogeny. For example, June Rothman Scott has shown that coliphage P1, unlike λ, has the genes controlling lysogeny mapping separately about its chromosome (263), that it occupies a site in the membrane replicating system outside of the host chromosome (37, 136), and that it is only slightly inducible with UVL (59). In addition, as shown in Figure 1, cells lysogenized with prophage P1 acquire the capacity to restrict and to modify the DNA of λ and certain other coliphages (7, 181). When the P1 genome loses and/or exchanges with the host some of its genes (*dl* mutants) it possibly integrates into the *E. coli* chromosome (136). $P1^{cry}$, harboring DNA from a resistance transfer factor with an affinity for the *lac* region of the *E. coli* chromosome, locates in the *pro-lac* region (136, 264). Coliphage P2 may occupy any of several chromosomal sites (32), is noninducible with UVL (30, 32), and brings to the cell a sensitivity to small amounts of 5-fluorodeoxyuridine (31, 33). Coliphage P22 of *S. typhymurium* occupies a site in the bacterial chromosome between *pro* A and *pro* C (190). In addition to bringing immunity to the lysogenic cell, its presence prevents (excludes) the development of certain other infecting viruses (251, 298). Further, its presence results in the turning on of the synthesis of O-factor 1 [α-glucose-(1, 6)/-galactose-], a characteristic hapten of certain bacterial (*Salmonella*) lipopolysaccharide side chains (see Table 1). Thus, each group of temperate phages exhibits some distinctive properties regarding the clustering of related gene functions about their chromosomes, the number of and/or the places they sit in the lysogenic cell, and the mechanisms operating to insure their stability in that cell. Furthermore, they differ in the essentially bacterial syntheses which their presence may effect. For example, in contrast to the effect of prophage P22 on *Salmonella* O-factors, prophage $\lambda^{dg}$ is a λ genome which has replaced a region of its chromosome with the *E. coli* genes governing the utilization of galactose (see Figure 1). The presence of $\lambda^{dg}$ in a *gal–* cell enables that cell to utilize galactose. This is a perfect example of the acquisition of a bacterial biosynthetic capacity through lysogenization, where the genes involved are known to be bacterial genes.

## THE PHAGE CARRIER STATE, PSEUDOLYSOGENY

Just as it is now apparent that one cannot generalize about the specific behavior of phages responsible for the lysogenic state, so there are no broad generalizations that hold for the kinds of bacterial viruses which persist nonlysogenically in nature and the mechanisms for their persistence. The ways are as varied as the means of replication of RNA and DNA bacteriophages and the ample physiologic and genetic variations of bacterial host cells. For example, spore-forming bacteria (*Bacillus cereus* and *Bacillus subtilis*) may be lysogenic in the perpetuation of bacteriophage (203) or they may carry an injected virulent phage genome through to the spore state where it enjoys the immunity to heat enjoyed by other genomic material encased in the spores (43, 148, 170, 222, 270, 271, 280). Thus the carry-over of phage by bacterial spores can no longer be taken as certain evidence of lysogeny (73).

While single-stranded RNA and DNA phages have not yet been implicated in either genotypic nor phenotypic modifications of bacterial clones, they eventually may be so implicated, for representatives of each are capable of initiating persistent infections without destroying the bacterial populations. Thus single cells of *E. coli* K12 (Hfr, $F^+$, or F') infected with the DNA phages, fd (126, 128) or M13 (129), or the RNA phage, fr (128), continue to divide as copies of phage are liberated. Lysis of the cell is the exception rather than the rule. Whether or not the permeability of the cell liberating such small phages is very different from that of the intact cell has not been reported (127, 211). In these phage-host systems the leaking out of bacteriophage has at last been found (71).

The bacterial viruses important thus far in phage-induced modifications of bacteria are bacteriophages containing double-stranded DNA. The phages involved in the carrier state are *lytic* phages. They may be *obligately lytic* like T3 and T7, or *virulent mutants* (e.g. $\lambda^{vir}$, $\beta^{vir}$) or certain *clear-plaque mutants* (e.g. $\lambda^{c}$, $\beta^{c}$) of temperate phages. Once the genetics of temperate phages became better understood the term virulent ceased to have the polar (virulent vs temperate) meaning it once had with reference to the T-even phages. From the standpoint of the potentials of or the mutational range of their genomes, the T phages are *obligately lytic,* i.e. there is for them no finite probability of giving rise to mutants capable of lysogenizing host bacteria. Their relationship with the host cell is one which eventually leads to lysis and ranges from the pattern exhibited by T2 which can multiply in inactivated (nonviable) bacteria (5, 123) to T3 and T7 which require more of their hosts (3, 120). While vegetative T3, following infection, may wait two or three bacterial divisions before bringing about lysis of the cell containing it, eventual lysis does occur (91). In contrast to obligately lytic phages such as T2, T3, and T7, the wild-type temperate phages exist in nature as prophages: phage genomes integrated into the replicating machinery of the host bacterium. There are a number of lysogenic members of most bacterial genera and so it is not surprising that the majority of bacteriophages which have been discovered are temperate. In this review virulent will be used to describe lytic mutants of temperate phages which are of lowered capability or incapable of becoming integrated into the host cells' replication systems. These lytic phages are commonly generated as virulent mutants of wild-type temperate phages. While the behavior of such virulent phages is superficially similar to that of obligately lytic phages, the biosynthetic processes involved in their lytic cycles and their relation to their wild-type progenitors sets them apart from the prototypes of those obligately lytic phages, originally assembled by Demerec & Fano (72) under the designations T1–T7.

Bacterial populations manifest several conditions which prevent them from being wiped out by infecting bacteriophages. These same conditions insure the perpetuation of the phages. The following are three mechanisms of interaction giving rise to pseudolysogeny or the carrier state.

### *Condition 1: Phage Infection Limited by Available Receptors on Bacterial Cell*

(*a*) There exist only a few receptor sites per bacterium and therefore a fixed but low probability of infection per cell. Some phages are being made but at the expense of only a fraction of the bacterial population. [See one-step growth curves of T7•Sh on *E. coli* B, a cell with many receptors, and on *Shigella dysenteriae* R134, a cell with few receptors, presented by Li et al (191).] (*b*) A phage-sensitive bacterium, s, gives rise to a resistant (no receptors) mutant, r, at a rate sometimes as high as $10^{-3}$ to $10^{-4}$ per bacterium per generation [see Baker, Goebel & Perlman (16) regarding mutation of *Shigella sonnei* II to *Sh. sonnei* I and the associated change in its sensitivities to T3, T4, and T7]. Nonlysogenizing phages readily enter into a carrier state with such bacteria.

Certain strains of *Corynebacterium diphtheriae,* such as C4, establish a carrier relationship with $\beta^c$. [The B phage of reference 92 has been shown by Holmes (131) to be $\beta^c$.] C4•$\beta^c$ grows as slightly nibbled colonies and is toxinogenic. When recovered following injection into the skin of a guinea pig or following passage through an anti-$\beta$ serum, it is no longer C4•$\beta^c$. It is now C4 and is nontoxinogenic. Irradiation (UVL) of liquid cultures of C4•$\beta^c$ results in a lowering of, not an increase in, the levels of free $\beta^c$. These results lead to the conclusion that C4•$\beta^c$ is a carrier clone. Here then is an example of pseudolysogeny where the marker in a nonlysogenizing phage is the gene also carried by a wild-type temperate (lysogenizing) phage. Because *tox* is expressed in both lysing and lysogenic cells, such a marker cannot be used safely as an index to lysogeny. This means that experiments which are dependent on a prophage marker such as *tox* rather than on prophage itself for determining the presence and/or absence of the lysogenic state do not accomplish their goal. For as pointed out, genomes which lack the ability to integrate as prophages may carry and express such a marker gene.

### *Condition 2: Loss of Receptors Due to the Action of Virolysin*[3] *(Endolysin)*

Early infected cells of Condition 1a (above) produce enough receptor-destroying endolysin to render much of the population resistant (no receptors) so that the population is always a mixture of sensitive (phage producing) and enzyme-rendered resistant cells. Loss of the normal permeability properties of the bacterial population results in a profound modification of the bacterial phenotype.

A model system of modifications involving apparent but not real genetic changes in lactose-negative, mannitol-negative, maltose-negative *Sh. dysenteriae* was studied by Li and his associates (191). *Sh. dysenteriae* grows as clear colonies on MacConkey's lactose agar. However, clones of *Sh. dysenteriae* carrying coliphage T7 (*Sh. dysenteriae*•T7) formed bright red colonies on MacConkey's plates. Sometimes the early colonies were composed of red and white sectors and with time the white sectors slowly turned red. The authors showed that whether the stocks of T7 were made on $lac^+$ or $lac^-$ bacteria was of no consequence. This remarkable change in *Sh. dysenteriae*•T7 gave the appearance of a pleiotropic mutation, for the *Sh. dysenteriae*•T7 clones not only became lactose-positive, they became mannitol- and maltose-positive as well. Li and his associates pursued the cryptic nature of *Sh. dysenteriae* with regard to its *lac* operon (29) and showed that *Sh. dysenteriae* carries the gene, *Z*, for $\beta$-galactosidase but lacks the *Y* gene controlling the permease system found in *E. coli.* In crosses between $Z^-Y^+$ *E. coli* (with a deletion in the *Z* gene) and $Z^+Y^-$ *Sh. dysenteriae* they obtained recombinants which were $Z^+Y^+$ and grew on lactose plates as normal $lac^+$ colonies. They clearly demonstrated that the permeation of cells of *Sh. dysenteriae*•T7 clones was entirely different from those of uncontaminated *Sh. dysenteriae* and that this difference was brought about by T7 endolysin (see Footnote 3) which renders *Sh. dysenteriae* into osmotically sensitive, spheroidal cells lacking phage receptors. Not only did small inducer molecules gain entrance to these cells but larger molecules such as $\beta$ -galactosidase were readily secreted by them. While *Sh. dysenteriae* growing on Ouchterlony plates containing anti-*E. coli* $\beta$-galactosidase serum forms no antigen-antibody bands of precipitation, on the same plates *Sh. dysenteriae*•T7 forms readily visible bands which fuse with those formed from crystalline $\beta$-galactosidase (*E. coli*) and its antibody. That this leakage of macromolecules is rather general is suggested by the fact that when *Sh. dysenteriae* and *Sh. dysenteriae*•T7 are compared on Ouchterlony plates containing antitoxin prepared against the neurotoxin of *Sh. dysenteriae,* only the carrier clones produce precipitable amounts of neurotoxin (20).

The stability of the *Sh. dysenteriae*•T7 clones was impressive. Li reported that after 57 single colony isolations and restreakings the clones still yielded some $lac^+$

[3]Whether T7 lysozyme (279) or the N-acetylmuramyl-L-alanine amidase (140), which cleaves wedges of lipoprotein-DAP-D-glut-L-ala from the walls of *E. coli* K12, strain E309, or both, account(s) for most of the endolysin activity is not yet known. It remains to be determined whether the lysozyme activity and the amidase activity are one and the same.

colonies. The $lac^+$ colonies always contained T7, whereas the $lac^-$ colonies did not. However, the suspension of a $lac^+$ colony in anti-T7 serum and subsequent restreaking on MacConkey's plates always resulted in the loss of T7 and the return to the $lac^-$ state. The capacity of antiphage serum to eliminate phage-induced changes seen here is the key to pseudolysogeny. In experiments involving a known bacteriophage and a genetically unknown recipient it seems important to be sure that the observed change in the presence of the phage is not simply the unmasking of some cryptic property in the host. In other words, the ruling out of phenotypic modifications due to the presence of phage would seem a requisite prior to entertaining notions of genotypic modifications due to the phage, especially in the case of transduction and lysogenic conversion experiments. This precaution seems necessary.

That changes such as those investigated by Li are general is suggested by the reports of Coetzee for *Proteus* (61) and that for *Brucella abortus* by Jones, McDuff & Wilson (153).

### *Condition 3: The Accumulation of Mutant $\phi^{vir}$ in a population of Bac($\phi$)*

A bacterial culture, *Bac*($\phi$), is lysogenic for temperate phage $\phi^+$ and therefore is immune to superinfection by occasional particles of $\phi^+$ which accumulate in the milieu. However, prophage $\phi^+$ mutates at a fixed frequency to $\phi^{vir}$ which lyses *Bac* ($\phi$). The replication of $\phi^{vir}$ brings about a persisting viral infection in the *Bac*($\phi$) culture. Mutation to virulence is such a rare event as to be considered a two-stage process in coliphage $\lambda^+$, corynebacteriophage $\beta^+$, and the W phage of *Bacillus cereus* (223), but is a common single-step mutation in the case of corynebacteriophage $1^+$ (131), some *Pseudomonas* phages (150), and phage P22 of *Salmonella typhimurium* (51, 52). The puzzling nature of Condition 3 has been dwelt upon at length by Baess with regard to a strain of *Mycobacterium fortuitum* derived from an abscess in a human subject (14). An example from Coetzee & Hawtrey (61) demonstrates how a persisting infection with such a virulent phage mutant modifies the bacterial phenotype so that its fermentation properties are changed.

These authors studied a lysogenic strain, P57, of *Proteus mirabilis* which was sucrose negative. It could be shown, however, that supernates from broken open cells of this strain were able to dissimilate sucrose. Thus, the strain was in fact cryptic with regard to sucrose. A mutant of the wild-type prophage of the P57($\phi$) strain was shown to form persistent complexes with P57($\phi$) and these P57($\phi$)•$\phi^{vir}$ grew as sucrose-positive colonies. Passage of the sucrose-positive clones through $\phi$-specific antiserum resulted in their becoming sucrose-negative. Coetzee and Hawtrey found another serologically distinct strain of *Proteus* phage which also formed sucrose-positive carrier clones with strain P57. Phage-free virolysin was shown to be capable of rendering P57 clones sucrose positive as were certain concentrations of bile salts. A variation on the condition under discussion is that of lysogenic strains, a percentage of whose cells are induced following infection with phage homologous to the carried prophage. [For discussion, see McCloy (223).] Conceivably, such cultures could manifest modifications of their phenotypes.

# MODEL PHAGE CONVERSIONS

## *Bacteriophages $\epsilon^{15}$ and $\epsilon^{34}$ and the Conversion of O-Antigens in Salmonella anatum*

*S. anatum* [3, 10] belongs to group $E_1$ and is characterized by O-factors[4] 3,10 and flagellar antigens e, h-1, 6 of the Kauffmann & White scheme (169). When this salmonella is infected with phage $\epsilon^{15}$, either as a fatal infection, by forming a carrier clone (*S. anatum*•$\epsilon^{15}$), or presumably, by becoming lysogenic [*S. anatum* ($\epsilon^{15}$)], its O-factors change from 3, 10 to 3, 15 and this places it in group $E_2$. *S. anatum* [3, 15] is serologically indistinguishable from wild-type *Salmonella newington* ($\epsilon^{15}$) [3, 15] from which the phage $\epsilon^{15}$ was originally recovered (146).

In 1948 Bruner & Edwards (53) briefly reported that the cultivation of *S. anatum* [3, 10] in semisolid medium containing antiserum (which had been adsorbed with salmonella having antigens O-3, 15) resulted in the emergence (outgrowth) of an antigenically different salmonella, *S. newington* [3, 15]. Growth of *S. newington* in the presence of "absorbed 3, 15 serum" resulted in a change to *S. anatum* [3, 10]. The authors referred to their finding as a transformation. Iseki & Sakai (146) soon showed that the antigenic shift from O-3, 10 to O-3, 15 was related to certain bacteriophages obtained from salmonella of group $E_2$. They indicated that while O-antigens changed, flagellar antigens did not. Further, they made it clear that monospecific sera, adsorbed with dead bacilli, were effective in reversing the changes. These findings were confirmed and considerably extended by Uetake, Nakagawa & Akiba (295) who found it difficult to explain the behavior of antiserum in reversing this group of phage conversions which they assumed to involve the lysogenic state. The interaction of *S. anatum* [3, 10], $\epsilon^{15}$, and $\epsilon^{15vir}$ was carefully studied by Uetake, Luria & Burrous (294). Uetake has reviewed conversions in salmonella (293) and with his group has recently proposed sites for $\epsilon^{15}$ and $\epsilon^{34}$ in *S. anatum* (220).

[4]For a given species of *Salmonella,* the smooth strain, s, represents the full expression of O-antigen specificity. This smoothness is a hydrophylic condition made possible by certain genes governing lipopolysaccharide (LPS) syntheses. The O-specificities (O-factors) are haptens of the side chains of the LPS, occurring as terminal substituents, terminal sugars, or interchain repeating units (19, 274). The anomeric configuration of a particular repeating unit of the side chain may be a feature essential for the antigenic behavior of that unit. O-factors, plus antigenically distinguishable flagellar antigens (flagellins) of motile strains, determine the chemotypes and/or serotypes of the scheme of Kauffmann & White (169). The O-factors through their parent LPS [region I of Luderitz et al (201)] have continuity with the core [region II: phosphate, N-acetyl glucosamine, galactose, heptose, ketodeoxyoctanoate, ethanolamine, and phosphate] and Lipid A [region III: pyrophosphate bridges connecting $\beta$-1, 6-linked disaccharide units of glucosamine esterified by lauric, palmitic, and 3-D-myristoxymyristic acids and having amino groups with substituents of 3-dihydroxymyristic acid] which is tied into protein of the cell wall. For details regarding the relation of the O-antigen side chains to overall LPS of the cell envelope see Luderitz et al (199), Luderitz, Staub & Westphal (200), Nikaido (236), Luderitz, Westphal, Staub & Nikaido (201), Makela & Stocker (206), Osborne (238), and Wright & Kanegasaki (308a). Numbers in [ ] denote O antigens.

An interesting aspect of infection of *S. anatum* [3, 10] by $\epsilon^{15}$ is the shut-off in the synthesis of the receptors by which $\epsilon^{15}$ gained entry into the cell. Investigations directed at determining the mechanism(s) by which receptor synthesis is shut off in *S. anatum,* newly infected with $\epsilon^{15}$, have come from Uetake, Luria & Burrous (294), Uchida, Robbins & Luria (285), and Robbins in collaboration with various members of his group. These extensive investigations have not only revealed the amazing mechanics of the 3, 15 conversion, but in so doing have also provided major contributions to the chemistry of lipopolysaccharide (LPS) biosynthesis (307, 308) in salmonellas and to establishing the fact that interchain polysaccharide repeating units (as O-factors and as phage receptors) can function as antigenic determinants. The basic observations regarding the phage conversion of *S. anatum* by $\epsilon^{15}$ are given in Figure 2. Following infection, the cell gradually loses its receptors for $\epsilon^{15}$, concomitantly develops a susceptibility to $\epsilon^{34}$, begins to synthesize antigen-15 and, from its cell surfaces, antigen-10 gradually disappears. Presumably this happens whether the outcome of infection is the lysogenic or the carrier state. When Robbins & Uchida (255, 256) first began to look into the biochemical and genetic processes underlying this remarkable phage conversion, not even the chemical equivalencies of factors 3, 10, and 15 were known. In 1963, Uchida, Robbins & Luria (285) furnished the evidence upon which factor-3 was eventually equated with a unit of D-mannosyl-L-rhamnose occurring as an integral part (reading from the exterior of the cell toward the cell wall) of 6-β-D-mannosyl-1,4-α-L-rhamnosyl-1,3-O-acetyl-α-D-galactosyl⟶ repeating unit in a side chain of somatic lipopolysaccharide. The immunodominant sugar appears to be mannose (285). [Recently, Kanegasaki & Wright (166) and Takeda & Uetake (281) have described a phage tail-associated, $\epsilon^{15}$-induced receptor destroying enzyme, an endorhamnosidase, which cleaves the α-linkage between rhamnose and galactose liberating the disaccharide, rhamnosyl-mannose, and other random cleavage products.] Factor-10 is the O-acetyl group of the O-acetyl-α-D-galactosyl fragment. In the shift from LPS side chains reacting with sera which detect antigens 3 and 10 to LPS side chains reactive with anti-3 and anti-15 sera, the O-acetyl groups (factor 10) are lost and the linkage between the repeating units of the LPS which were α now become β. The steriochemical effect of this change in linkage is reflected immunochemically as a new antigen, 15, reactive with factor-specific (anti-15) antiserum. The evidence which shows that the mechanisms underlying the shifts involve inactivation (inhibition) of one host cell enzyme and the active synthesis of a β-linking polymerase under the direction of $\epsilon^{15}$ genes derives from the work of Robbins and co-workers as follows. As already pointed out, the hapten which is responsible for the emergent specificity of factor 10 is the acetyl substituent on the galactosyl portion of the trisaccharidic repeating unit. The transacetylase which puts this O-acetyl group in place is a product of the bacterial genome (254). In the conversion from *S. anatum* [3, 10] to *S. anatum* [3, 15], antigen 10 disappears. Its synthesis is suppressed and this suppression is brought about by wild-type $\epsilon^{15}$. This conclusion has been reached by Robbins et al (254) who have found mutants of $\epsilon^{15}$ whose presences do not suppress the transacetylase. So much for the disappearance of haptenic factor 10. The O-side chain repeating unit made by *S. anatum* [3, 15]$\cdot\epsilon^{15}$ is 6-β-D-mannosyl-1,

4-α-L-rhamnosyl-1,3-β-D-galactosyl⟶ (49, 253, 256, 285). Thus the haptenic aspect which emerges as O-15 is the anomeric configuration of the galactosyl portion of the trisaccharidic repeating unit, α as in *S. anatum* [3, 10] and β in *S. anatum* [3, 15] •$\epsilon^{15}$. Using a mutant of *S. anatum* having temperature sensitive α-polymerizing enzyme and therefore unable to produce α-polymer at 39°C, Losick & Robbins (198) showed that when they infected it with $\epsilon^{15}$, the mutant salmonella produced β-polymer at the sensitive temperature. This and other experiments indicate that $\epsilon^{15}$ gene directs the synthesis of the β-polymer. It was known from earlier studies (256, 285) that the amount of α-polymer in the cells drops soon after infection, and in the cells that survive infection there is no evidence of α-polymerizing activity. Cells of *S. anatum*•$\epsilon^{15}$, which have lost their phage, simultaneously lose the β-polymerizing activity and again synthesize their α-polymerase. Clearly, the host genetic control for synthesis of α-polymerase is always present. What is the mechanism of suppression? Bray & Robbins (50) isolated a group of $\epsilon^{15}$ mutants which after infection of *Salmonella anatum* failed to bring about the synthesis of antigen 15 (β-gal). A number of these mutant phages also suppressed or markedly depressed the synthesis of man-rham-α-ac-gal side chains, suggesting that the effect of $\epsilon^{15}$ on the disappearance of the α-polymerase is attributable to a phage function distinct from mere synthesis of β-polymerase. Subsequently, Losick (197) isolated, both from *S. anatum* newly infected with or carrying phage $\epsilon^{15}$, a trypsin-sensitive inhibitor capable of blocking the activity of the α-polymerizing enzyme but not that of the β-enzyme. Thus, the converting ability of $\epsilon^{15}$ can be attributed to: 1. a suppression of a transacetylase responsible for the existence of antigen 10, 2. the production of an inhibitor of the converted cells' α-linking polymerase, and 3. the continued synthesis from infection to and during the carrier state of a β-linking polymerase (see Figure 3).

When the O-side chain synthesis of *S. anatum* [3, 15] •$\epsilon^{15}$ is initiated by phage genes, the specific receptors to which the phage adsorbed prior to infection disappear. This closing off of the entrance way comes about with the cessation of the synthesis of mannosyl-rhamnosyl repeating units α-linked to galactose. In the case of $\epsilon^{34}$, superinfecting *S. anatum* ($\epsilon^{15}$) to yield the double lysogen *S. anatum* ($\epsilon^{15}$, $\epsilon^{34}$), it too shuts off the synthesis of its receptor site. $\epsilon^{34}$ genes bring about the attachment of glycosyl units to β-galactosyl residues through intermediate uridine diphosphoglucose (284, 305, 306) and a $C_{55}$-polyisoprenoid alcohol carrier lipid (305). The product, factor 34, assumes its position in the side chain as O-α-D-glucosyl/-1,4-linked to the galactosyl unit of 6-β-D-mannosyl-1,4-α-L-rhamnosyl-1,3-β-D-galactosyl⟶ (256, 285). Its presence sterically modifies the side chain so that factors 3, 15 (man-rham-β-gal) no longer can serve as a receptor for $\epsilon^{34}$ (306) (see Figures 2 and 3).

Boyd (47, 48) has pointed out that among lysogenic strains of *Salmonella typhimurium* there are those which can adsorb liberated phages homologous to their prophages and there are those which cannot. He has presented this information regarding certain A-phages: A1, A2, and A5 adsorb to their homologous lysogens; A3 and A4 do not. Following lysogenization by A3 or A4 the host stops making receptors for the infecting phage. This phenomenon finds its best understood models

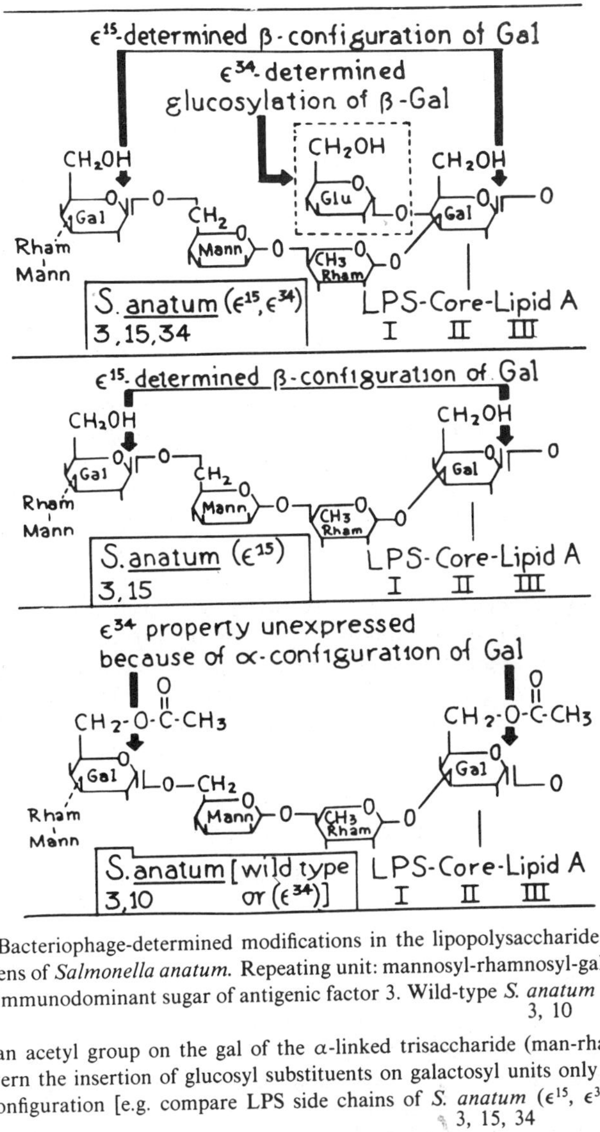


*Figure 3* Bacteriophage-determined modifications in the lipopolysaccharide side chains of the O-antigens of *Salmonella anatum.* Repeating unit: mannosyl-rhamnosyl-galactosyl-. Mannose is the immunodominant sugar of antigenic factor 3. Wild-type *S. anatum*$_{3, 10}$ and *S. anatum*$_{3, 10}$ ($\epsilon^{34}$) have an acetyl group on the gal of the $\alpha$-linked trisaccharide (man-rham-gal). Phage $\epsilon^{34}$ can govern the insertion of glucosyl substituents on galactosyl units only when they are in the $\beta$ configuration [e.g. compare LPS side chains of *S. anatum*$_{3, 15, 34}$ ($\epsilon^{15}$, $\epsilon^{34}$), upper, with *S. anatum*$_{3, 10}$ ($\epsilon^{34}$), lower]. Epsilon-15 controls: 1. the suppression of the bacterial transacetylase responsible for antigen 10 (the acetyl of acetyl-galactose), 2. the production of an inhibitor of the bacterial cell's $\alpha$-linking polymerase, and 3. the synthesis of a $\beta$-linking polymerase. Each of the LPS side chains through its parent LPS is linked to that part of the cell envelope called the *core* which, in turn, through Lipid A, is tied to the protein of the cell wall. Roman numerals I, II, and III refer to the three regions of the cell envelope described by Luderitz et al (201), and defined in Footnote 4. For original sources see text. Drawing by James E. Ziegler after an earlier diagram (20) based on the work of Robbins & Uchida (256).

in $\epsilon^{15}$ and $\epsilon^{34}$. The meaning of the shut-off of the synthesis of receptors for the phage and for the bacterium is very different. For the phage it is not good. Temperate phages are most effectively perpetuated as prophages. Conditions of infection decide whether the outcome will be lysis or lysogeny. Reduction to prophage is far from an obligatory event. The more phage the greater the chance of establishing lysogeny. In any lysogenizing experiment the host cells are growing and, therefore, in various stages of cell division. Consequently, accumulation of temperate phage in a clone of bacteria, following primary infection, influences the chances of infection. Where clear mutants of phage (hypoproducers of repressor) are concerned the increase in the probability of a lysogenic vs a carrier outcome of infection is a function of multiplicities of infection. However, no matter how much phage is around it is ineffective in the absence of receptors. Thus, the receptorless state engendered by $\epsilon^{15}$ or $\epsilon^{34}$ or any other phages equipped with similar converting capabilities, operates far less in favor of the phage (especially for superinfection or secondary infection which might result in lysogeny) than in favor of the bacterium. For the bacterium it has one very special advantage. For the sake of discussion let us consider a wild-type *Salmonella newington* [3, 15] carrying prophage $\epsilon^{15}$. In 1953 Boyd (46) indicated that wild-type (temperate) salmonella phages frequently gave rise to lytic and/or inducing mutants which destroyed the lysogenic cell (see Condition 3 and also reference 223). When this happens in a population which depends on lysogenic immunity for its insusceptibility to phages homologous to carried prophage, the cell is destroyed. When the same sort of mutation arises in *S. newington* [3, 15] the cell is protected because it has no receptors for $\epsilon^{15vir}$. Thus, in this light, the shut-off condition offers special protection to the lysogenic cell and, therefore, to its carried prophage as well.

## *Corynebacteriophages and Diphtherial Toxin*

In 1950 in a laboratory of the Department of Public Health and Preventive Medicine at the University of Washington, Seattle, an effort was made to enhance the amounts of diphtherial toxin diffusing from diptheria bacilli into agar gels (Elek plates) by adding lytic bacteriophage to the corynebacteria being examined. As is usual with in vitro tests for toxinogenicity, cultures of nontoxinogenic and toxinogenic diphtheria bacilli were included on each plate. It happened that among old plates that remained on the bench after tests were completed, some of the negative controls turned positive. In 1951–1952 Freeman and Morse (92, 93) reported that exposure of phage-sensitive, but not phage-resistant, nontoxinogenic diptheria bacilli to a filtered lysate of phage B (283) resulted in the outgrowth of toxinogenic *Corynebacterium diphtheriae.* This change could be induced in nontoxinogenic bacilli of distinct antigenic types. The nontoxinogenic strains prior to exposure to phage could be shown to contain no toxin. Passage of phage-modified strains through antiphage serum in no way altered their capacity to produce toxin (93).

This remarkable discovery came seven years after the demonstration that the transforming principle of the pneumococcus was almost certainly DNA (13), five years after the demonstration of genetic recombination in *Escherichia coli* (180), and one year after a reawakening of an interest in lysogeny (204). Freeman's findings were promptly confirmed (23, 24, 111, 112). From Freeman's stock of phage B a turbid plague-forming phage $\beta$ was isolated. With it two separate strains of nontoxinogenic *C. diphtheriae,* $C4_s$ and $C7_s$, were converted to yield the inducible, toxinogenic, lysogenic strains $C4_s(\beta)^{tox+}$ and $C7_s(\beta)^{tox+}$ and the conversion rates were calculated and reported (24, 25). Groman succeeded in curing $C4(\beta)^{tox+}$ of its prophage by superinfection with a virulent mutant of $\beta$ (113), thus demonstrating that elmination of prophage from lysogenic, toxinogenic *C. diphtheriae* resulted in the loss of toxinogenicity. What was not appreciated at this time was the fact that clear plaque-forming phage B, in the process of lysing nontoxinogenic *C. diphtheriae,* initiated the synthesis of toxin (18, 22). Later the reduction on paper of phage B to synonymy with phage $\beta$ (113) tended to obscure this fact. B is $\beta^c$ (131, 268), a phage which does not lysogenize under conditions of low multiplicity. Following Zinder's report in 1957 (316) that in lysing *Salmonella typhimurium*•P22, as well as in lysogenic *S. typhimurium* (P22), antigen 1 (a converted antigen) was made, it became obvious that converting genes are expressed during vegetative replication of phage (18, 275, 294). Matsuda (212), using a virulent mutant of $\beta$, $\beta^{vir}$, obtained yields of toxin in one cycle of virus growth which were equal to the best yields possible with the PW8 strain (176, 244). Groman (118) and Barksdale (17) independently assembled $tox^+$ and $tox^-$ corynebacteriophages, some of which were co-immune and some hetero-immune (131, 132). At this time the capacity to produce toxin was designated $tox^+$ (17). Corynebacteriophage $\beta^{tox+}$ is a DNA virus (212) whose twin helical length is equivalent to about $2.2 \times 10^7$ daltons [Wolfson and Dressler, as credited by Gill, Uchida & Singer (106)]. Groman found a temperate phage $\gamma^{tox-}$ which was related to $\beta^{tox+}$ and he and Eaton obtained recombinants of the two (116, 117). Holmes worked out the details of a mating system for corynebacteriophages and succeeded in mapping the *tox* gene (131). This rudimentary map of $\beta$ has been considerably extended by Singer (268, 269) using a number of temperature-sensitive (*ts*) mutants. Matsuda (213) has described additional *ts* mutants of $\beta$ and these have been reexamined and their colinearity with other markers has been presented by Singer (268) (see Figure 4 and Table 2). Holmes has also shown that the gene $tox^+$ is distributed among a considerable variety of corynebacteriophages differing both serologically and genetically (132). Thus *tox* does not only occur in phages closely related to $\beta$. He constructed a hybrid phage, essentially like $\beta$ except for an absence of the *tox* gene, and found it to be, in its viral functions, indistinguishable from $\beta^{tox+}$. Further, Uchida pointed out that several mutants which coded for atoxic analogues (cross reacting proteins, *crm*'s) of toxin seemed unimpaired in their phage functions (286, 287). Therefore, *tox,* which Matsuda (212) had shown to be a gene expressed early (7–14 min) in the vegetative multiplication of $\beta^{vir}$, serves no essential viral function. Toxin appears to be made on the cytoplasmic membrane (292). The time for its total synthesis has been estimated by Uchida and Yoneda to be 3 min and for its release, 30 sec (291). John Murphy, by programming the *E. coli* protein synthesizing system of Zubay (296, 318) with $\beta^c$ DNA, has succeeded in effecting the synthesis of measurable amounts of toxin in the test tube. While corynebacterial extracts could not be so programmed, they did respond to $\lambda^{plac}$ DNA by producing the $\beta$-galactosidase of *E. coli* (235a). This

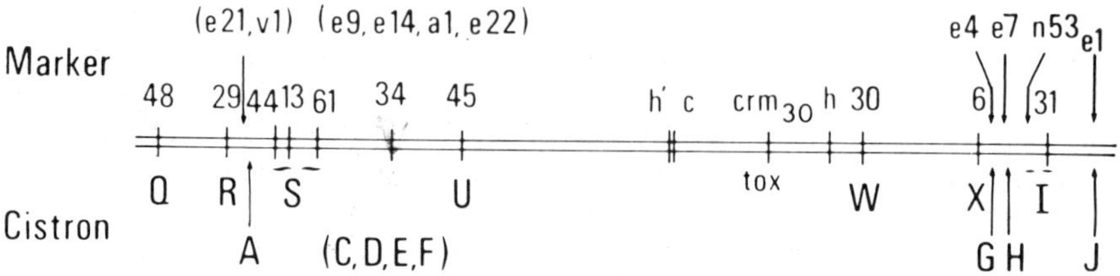


*Figure 4* A provisional map of corynebacteriophage $\beta$: Singer (268) has proposed this composite genetic map of phage $\beta$. The inner markers, *ts* mutants of $\beta^+$, were mapped by two and three factor crosses. The outer markers, the *ts* mutants of $\beta^{vir}$ (212), isolated by Matsuda (213), were mapped by three factor crosses only. $\beta^{vir}$ *ts* markers in parentheses were not ordered with respect to near $\beta$*ts* markers. Complementation groups defining cistrons are indicated by capital letters below the map. For definition of markers see Table 2.

**Table 2** Genetic markers of corynebacteriophage $\beta$[a]

| Marker | Cistron | Description | References |
|---|---|---|---|
| *h* | | Extended host range | 131 |
| *h'* | | Extended host range | 131 |
| *c* | | Clear plaques | 131 |
| *v*1 | | Required for virulence | 268 |
| *tox*, $crm_{30}$[b] | *tox* | Toxin and toxin-*crm*'s[c] | 17, 131, 287 |
| *ts e*21 | A | DNA synthesis | 213, 215 |
| *ts*48, 29, 44, 13, 61, 34, 45 | Q, R, S, (T)[d], U | Head synthesis or assembly | 268, 269 |
| *ts e*9, *e*14, *a*1, *e*22 | C, D, E, F | Head synthesis or assembly(?) | 213 |
| *ts* 30, 6, 31 | W, X, I | Tail synthesis or assembly | 268, 269 |
| *ts e*4, *e*7, *n*53, *e*1 | G, H, I, J | Tail synthesis or assembly(?) | 213 |
| *df* | (V)[b] | Head and tail joining | 226 |

[a] Adapted from R. A. Singer (268).
[b] Should also apply to $crm_{45}$, $crm_{197}$, etc (286, 288).
[c] *crm* = nontoxic proteins (*crm*'s) coded by modified *tox*.
[d] Provisional cistron assignments.

synthesis of toxin in an *E. coli* system has recently been confirmed by Lightfoot & Iglewski (193a).

The need for phages which would code for altered toxins (*crm*'s) was recognized early. Holmes reported that he had available no phage mutants which made altered toxin protein and pointed out the need for such mutants for ascertaining whether or not *tox* was the structural gene for diphtherial toxin (131). Matsuda and Barksdale had earlier screened a large number of *tox*⁻ diphtheria bacilli for *crm*'s of toxin and found none (unpublished data). Tsuyoshi Uchida (286, 287) succeeded in obtaining mutants of phage $\beta$ which made altered toxin proteins (*crm*'s), thus furnishing the first evidence that *tox* is the structural gene for diphtherial toxin.

In the 1950s in three separate laboratories it was found that some host cells, carrying $tox^+$ phages, failed to make detectable amounts of toxin (19, 114, 245). Interestingly, in the intervening decade or more this matter has not been further investigated. For information tangential to this problem see Matsuda, Kanei & Yoneda (214).

The expression of *tox* is affected by the environment in a way which has not been reported for converting genes of such bacteriophages as $\lambda^{dg}$, P22, or $\epsilon^{15}$. The levels of iron in media in which diphtherial toxin is being synthesized may cause a marked reduction in the amounts of toxin produced (242, 247). Yoneda has studied the iron-binding capacity of diphtheria bacilli (311). Under conditions optimal for toxin production the curtailment by iron may be as high as 95%. No matter how high the iron concentration, some toxin is made (235). A cell which is undergoing phage-induced lysis makes about 10,000 molecules of toxin per cell (21, 212). Iron may suppress the release of toxin from such cells by about 90%. Matsuda and Barksdale (unpublished data) found that different *mitis* strains of *Corynebacterium diphtheriae,* growing with inhibitory amounts of iron (10 $\mu$g iron/ml) made amounts of toxin averaging out to about 200 molecules per cell. The question has been one of whether toxin is made only in certain cells such as those in which phage multiplication (with or without lysis inhibition) is taking place or is it made all of the time in all of the cells. Gill, Uchida & Singer, without regard to iron concentration (106), have carried out a series of experiments with cells carrying marked $\beta$ prophages and marked superinfecting phages. These experiments have shown that the *tox* gene can be expressed in three states of the $\beta$ genome: (*a*) as nonreplicating, nonintegrated intracellular phage; (*b*) as replicating vegetative phages; and (*c*) as repressed integrated prophages. What remains is to make sense out of this regarding the iron story. Perhaps the key is to be found in Matsuda's experiment in which every cell is known to be making both phage and toxin, but iron-rich cells make only 10% of the possible yield of toxin (212). The iron effect, in that case, seems to be on the release of toxin involving some sort of feedback control. Uchida & Yoneda have provided data to support the idea that toxin is made on the cytoplasmic membrane (292). The difficulties with membrane studies have been emphasized by Siegel & Schaechter (265). Raynaud et al have confirmed and refined earlier experiments which show that toxin does not accumulate in diphtheria bacilli (252). If the peeling off of toxin is required for the synthesis of more toxin, then any ultrastructure which blocks or limits or prevents toxin molecules from leaving the cytoplasmic membrane would inhibit toxin production. Kwang-Shin Kim has shown that the laminations of the cell wall of iron-rich $PW8_r(P)^{tox+}$ are different from those of iron-starved cells, and he and M. -A. Laneelle have found a remarkable difference in bound and free lipids of iron-rich and iron-poor cells (unpublished data; 173). The electron micrographic and chemical studies taken together point to an effect of iron on the peptidolipid of the outer envelope and therefore upon the permeability of the cell envelope. If indeed iron affects the release of toxin through its stabilizing effect upon the peptidolipid of the outer envelope, then cells which lack the cell envelope should make toxin in the presence of what ordinarily would be inhibitory concentrations of iron. For example, iron should have no effect on the synthesis of toxin by protoplasts.

The product of the gene, *tox*, is a protein of a molecular weight of about 62,000 (101), which is lethal for man, guinea pigs, rabbits, and birds in doses of 130 ngm per kilogram of body weight (22, 302). Mice and rats are singularly resistant to toxin. Aside from its toxicity and its ability to fix to mammalian cells, no other biological activity is known for the intact toxin molecule. No enzymic activity has been found for toxin per se. In 1957 Lennox & Kaplan (189) reported several cultured animal cells which were sensitive to diphtherial toxin. Strauss & Hendee (278) and Strauss (277) showed that HeLa cells, following exposure to diphtherial toxin: (*a*) continued glycolysis and aerobic respiration at a normal rate for several hours; (*b*) suffered no effect on oxidative phosphorylation; (*c*) seemed to be blocked in protein synthesis, as evidenced by a decline in the ability to incorporate radioactive methionine; and (*d*) developed visible blebs within 4 hr and underwent obvious destruction 7 hr post intoxication. Because low temperatures blocked intoxication of HeLa cells, a means was available to these investigators to examine the initial steps in the interaction of toxin and cells. Adsorption of toxin by the cell was very rapid.

Sensitivity to toxin as a genetic marker has been found to be dominant in hybrid cells (74) so that toxin cannot be used as a selective agent for singling out specific toxin-resistant heterokaryons. Investigations into the response of mammalian cells to toxin have been extended by the Moehrings, Kuchler & Solotorovsky (231). The Moehrings have continued looking into the effects of toxin at various levels in sensitive and resistant mammalian cells (227–230), and with Stinebring (232) have confirmed the findings of Yabrov (309, 310) regarding a somewhat protective effect of interferon when administered with diphtherial toxin. They extended these findings showing that homologous interferon relieved the intoxication of human KB, mouse, and chicken fibroblast cells in culture. Their results suggested that the effect of interferon was at the level of the cell membrane. The effect of toxin on the synthesis of polio virus in HeLa cells has been examined by Duncan & Groman (81, 82). Following up an earlier observation of Kim & Groman (171, 172), that ammonium ion and certain amines were capable of reversing the effects of toxin in mammalian cells, these authors found that there was an appreciable reversal of toxicity for polio virus synthesis in HeLa cells when the amine was added as late as 15 min following initial exposure to toxin. A study of the effects of diphtherial toxin on Swiss mice and implanted cancerous cells (Ehrlich ascites tumor cells) has recently been reported by Buzzi & Maistrello (55). It has long been known that mice are relatively tolerant of diphtherial toxin. In the mouse both Ehrlich ascites and solid tumor growths were found to be inhibited by toxin. Their sensitivities were dose-dependent, but levels which completely eliminated them caused neurological changes in the mice.

Gibson & Harris have found that toxin blocks the activity of the aminoacyl-tRNA transferring enzymes in cell-free protein synthesizing systems from heart muscle

(99). The specific target organ(s) hit by toxin in bringing death to an animal is not yet known. Bonventre and his group have addressed themselves to studies on the action of toxin in the guinea pig (39–41, 45, 261). Baseman et al, using $^{125}I$-labeled toxin, toxoid, and BSA injected into guinea pigs, concluded that there was no evidence for any "particular affinity of toxin for muscle tissue or for a 'target' organ" (28).

In 1960, following up the observations of Strauss & Hendee (278), Kato & Pappenheimer (168) and, in 1962, Kato (167) offered additional evidence for an effect of toxin on mammalian protein synthesis. Collier & Pappenheimer (65) found that NAD was required for the inhibition by "toxin" of protein synthesis in a cell-free system (from HeLa cells and rabbit reticulocytes). Toxin is written in quotation marks here for, as will become clear later, the effect being studied in in vitro systems was due to a fragment of toxin rather than to the intact toxin molecule itself. Later, Collier (62) and Goor & Pappenheimer (109) showed that "toxin" specifically inactivated elongation factor 2 (EF2, aminoacyl transferase II, translocase II), the soluble translocase involved in mRNA-directed growth of polypeptide chains. Goor, Pappenheimer & Ames (110), Gill et al (104), and Gill, Pappenheimer & Baseman (103) next found that nicotinamide could reverse the action of "toxin." In 1968, Honjo et al (134) showed that "toxin" catalyzes the transfer of ADP-ribose from NAD to EF2, thereby bringing about the inactivation of EF2. In the reaction, a stoichiometric amount of nicotinamide was released (see Figure 5). These authors also pointed out that the ribosome-dependent guanosine triphosphatase activity associated with EF2 was also inactivated in the "toxin"-induced ADP ribosylation reaction. Goor & Maxwell (108) found that the ADP ribosylation occurred between 0–40°C, being maximal at 20°C, and the adenosine diphosphoribosylaminoacyl transferase II (EF2:ADPR) bond stabilized at 90°C for 15 min in 5% trichloracetic acid. Adenine proved to be an effective inhibitor of the ADP ribosylation reaction (165). Raeburn et al (250) demonstrated that EF2 from rat liver underwent ADP ribosylation by "toxin." In 1969, John Collier made it clear that classical diphtherial toxin was not itself responsible for the inactivation of protein synthesis in vitro (63, 66), but rather the active agent was a soluble fragment of toxin, called by Collier a subunit (now termed fragment *A*). Collier found considerable support for his discovery in existing, isolated reports (35, 147). The nomenclature of the toxin fragments is coordinately presented in the papers of Gill & Dinius (101), Gill & Pappenheimer (102), Collier & Kandel (64), and Drazin, Kandel & Collier (80) (see Figure 5). These fragments are comparable to the L and H chains discovered independently by Michel et al (225). In Figure 5 the toxin molecule is shown before and after being separated into two fragments, *A* (molecular weight 24,000) and *B* (molecular weight 38,000). Collier's observation that the EF2 ribosylating activity of purified diphtherial toxin was attributable to a contaminating fragment of the toxin molecule (Fragment *A*) marked the beginning of research on the tertiary structure of the diphtherial toxin. This work has gone on independently in the laboratories of John Collier and in the laboratories of A. M. Pappenheimer Jr. and D. Michael Gill. The outstanding accomplishments of the latter have recently been reviewed (105, 241).

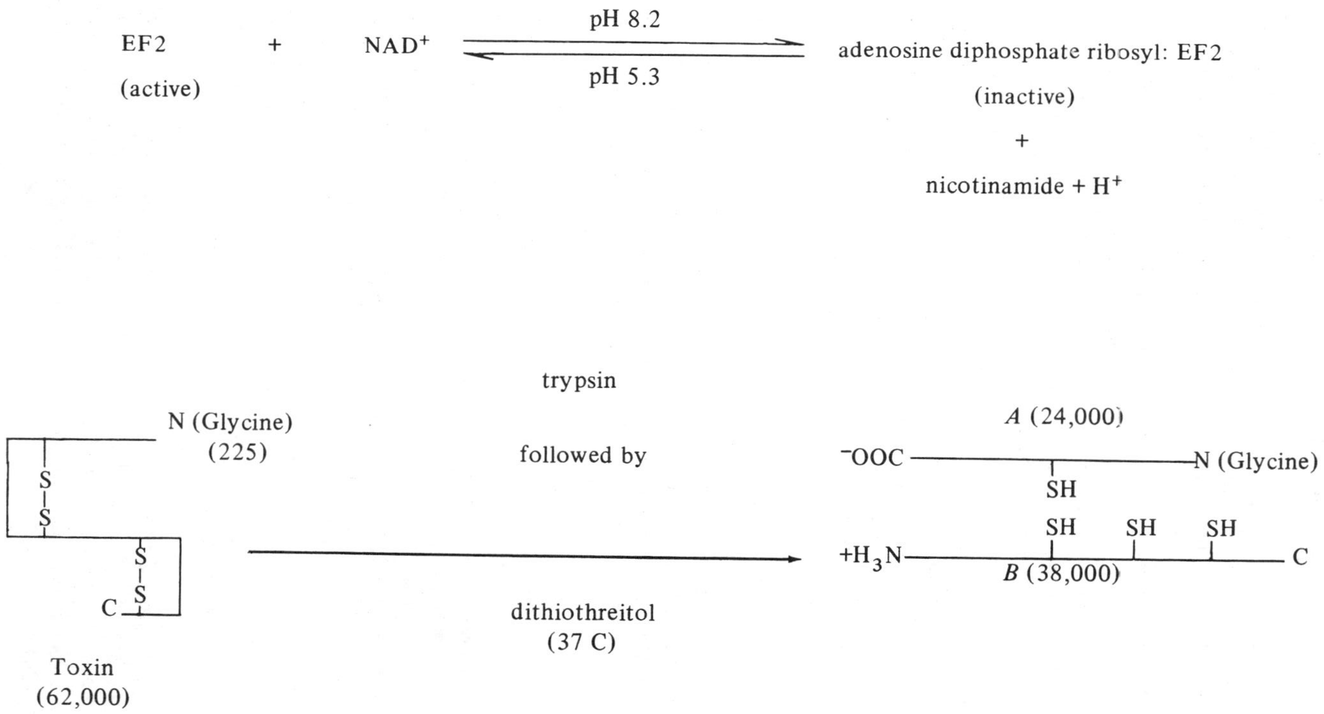


*Figure 5* Upper: The ribosylation reaction, catalyzed by fragment *A* of diphtherial toxin [after Honjo et al (133, 134) and Collier et al (63, 66)], which inactivates elongation factor 2, the soluble translocase in the mRNA-directed growth of polypeptide chains (see text). Lower: Schematic illustration of the breaking (by trypsinization and reduction) of the polypeptide chain of diphtherial toxin into amino terminal and carboxy terminal fragments. [After Pappenheimer & Gill (241); see also Kandel, Collier & Chung (165)].

Mild treatment of diphtherial toxin with trypsin produces a number of toxin molecules having nicks in their peptide backbones, but still held together by disulfide bridges. These nicks appear to occur at one or another of the arginines in an arginine-rich bend in the toxin molecule, see Figure 5 (R. Drazin, R. J. DeLange, J. Kandel, R. J. Collier, and D. W. Chung, personal communication). Reducing the S-S bridges in the nicked molecules of toxin with dithiothreitol (Cleland's reagent) allows the separation of soluble *A* fragments and hydrophobic *B* fragments (see Figure 5). All of the ADP ribosylation activity, once ascribed to the toxin molecule, is attributable to fragments *A* (63, 241).

In a recent paper Kandel, Collier & Chung (165) have shown that the *A* fragment of toxin slowly catalyzes the hydrolysis of the nicotinamide-ribose linkage of $NAD^+$:

$$NAD^+ + H_2O \rightleftharpoons ADPR + \text{nicotinamide} + H^+$$

Fragment *A* has a single binding site for $NAD^+$, and the binding is rapidly reversible. The authors found no evidence that a covalent ADPR-fragment *A* intermediate was formed. Rather it seems that in the absence of EF2 water is the acceptor molecule. The binding site interacts with both the adenine and the nicotinamide moieties of $NAD^+$. From their work and that of others (108, 133) the authors conclude that $NAD^+$ binds initially to fragment *A* during the transfer of ADPR to EF2. At present the importance of the glycohydrolase activity cannot be fully assessed. An awareness of its existence has, however, given information regarding the initial interaction between fragment *A* and $NAD^+$ leading to:

$$NAD^+ + EF2 \rightleftharpoons ADPR\text{-}EF2 + \text{nicotinamide} + H^+$$

Intact toxin does not participate in the inactivation of EF2 in vitro. The "isolated" *A* fragment has no toxic effect upon animals or animal cells (see Table 3). Uchida's experiments with the atoxic proteins (*crm*'s) synthesized by $\beta^{crm_{45}}$ and $\beta^{crm_{197}}$ (286, 287) indicate that mutation in the *tox* gene leads to two useful classes of atoxic *crm*'s: those which have a modified *A* moiety and those in which the *B* moiety of the toxin molecule is altered. Those with an altered *A* moiety, in addition to being nontoxic, yield *A* fragments incapable of bringing about the inactivation of EF2. Uchida, Pappenheimer & Harper (288, 290) used the trypsin-dithiothreitol treatment for fragmenting nontoxin $crm_{45}$ and nontoxin $crm_{197}$ into their respective *A* and *B* components. Mixtures were then made of the products of the two mutant proteins and the mixtures dialyzed against 0.01 M phosphate buffer for 24 hr at 0°C. After suitable fractionation, hybrid molecules having full toxic activity were obtained. Since only the *A* fragment of $crm_{45}$, $A_{45}$, showed ADP-ribosylating activity and since both proteins were nontoxic, it was concluded that the new molecules with toxic activity were the hybrid molecules, $A_{45} \cdot B_{197}$ (see Table 3). It had been suggested that toxin fixes to the cell by the *B* moiety and that, thereafter, the *A* portion gains entry into the cell where it intoxicates through its capacity to inactivate EF2. The supporting evidence for this hypothesis comes from competitive adsorption (fixation) experiments employing HeLa cells and various *crm*'s, especially $crm_{197}$ (149, 289) and, to some extent, from immunological data (243). This

**Table 3** Some biological properties of diphtherial toxin, toxoid, and mutant toxin proteins[a]

| Protein | Molecular weight | Toxicity for guinea pigs, HeLa cells | $NAD^+$: EF2–ADPR transferase activity (ADP ribosylation, EF2 inactivation) | Blocks toxin fixation to HeLa cells |
|---|---|---|---|---|
| Toxin | 62,000 | + | – | |
| $crm_{45}$ | 45,000 | – | – | – |
| $crm_{197}$ | 62,000 | – | – | + |
| Fragment *A* | 24,000 | – | + | – |
| Hybrid $A_{45}{\cdot}B_{197}$ | 62,000 | + | – | |
| Toxoid | 62,000 | – | – | – |

[a] Toxin is a single polypeptide chain (101) consisting of an amino terminal end (segment *A*), separable from the carboxyl end (segment *B*) at an arginine rich (see text), trypsin-sensitive region. Fragment *A* ≈ soluble products of varying lengths resulting from the nicking of the arginine rich region with trypsin, followed by reduction of a disulfide bond. Fragment *B*, the C terminal portion of molecular weight 38,000, exhibits hydrophobic behavior and remains to be further characterized. Toxoid is toxin rendered nontoxic by formalinization under alkaline conditions. The $crm_{45}$ is a "toxin" with an incomplete *B* segment (286); $crm_{197}$ is a "toxin" with an altered *A* segment. Hybrid $A_{45}{\cdot}B_{197}$ molecules were generated from mixtures of trypsin-nicked, thiol reduced $crm_{45}$ and $crm_{197}$ (288, 290). For glycohydrolase activity of fragment *A*, see text. Data assembled from references 64, 80, 101, 105, 241, 287, 288.

general breakthrough into the structure of toxin protein and its probable mode of action is indeed exciting.

Some information in support of the model of the toxin molecule (shown in Figure 5) can be gained from consideration of the behavior of toxoid in relation to fragments *A* and *B*, $crm_{45}$, $crm_{197}$, and the intact toxin molecule (243). Toxoid, a formalinized product of toxin, successfully immunizes against diphtherial toxin. It reacts with diphtherial antitoxin to form specific toxoid-antitoxin precipitates and its antibody neutralizes toxin in vivo. Today, toxoid and/or its antibody are responsible for eliminating death, the age old signal for diphtheritic infections. Toxoid is incapable of blocking adsorption of toxin to HeLa cells (289). It has long been assumed that the conversion to toxoid renders the toxic site of diphtherial toxin nontoxic but leaves it antigenic. In the model of diphtherial toxin which emerges from the data here reviewed, innocuous toxoid is effective because it induces the production of antibodies which block the adsorption of the carboxy terminus of toxin to the animal cell. There is no evidence that the proposed toxic site, sector *A*, is of any immunological consequence in this story. Sector *A*, the source of the fragment which inactivates EF2, is cryptic in the toxin molecule. The biologically active segment of diphtherial toxin is the carboxyl terminal end which emerges as fragment *B* following trypsinization and thiol reduction. In the model presented by Gill, Pappenheimer, and co-workers (105. 241) [for which Collier's discovery was so important (63, 66)] in order for toxin to intoxicate, proteolytic and reductive events on or about the cell surface must be so coordinated as to: 1. fix the carboxy terminus of toxin to the cell and 2. assure the entry of fragment *A* into the cell. Strong support for this model could come from the construction of an artificial toxin molecule. The possibility of constructing such a toxin composed of an *A* fragment coupled to an unrelated transport (adsorbing, fixing) portion analogous to *B* fragment seems not too remote. Its very toxicity would incriminate fragment *A* as the component responsible for the lethal effects of diphtherial toxin. Further, antibody to it should protect against the constructed toxin molecule and not against diphtherial toxin. This would leave no doubt about the role of the *B* fragment in getting *A* into the cell. The report of Samagh & Gregory (262), using antilactate dehydrogenase antibody conjugated (by *p,p'*-difluoro-*m,m'*-dinitrodiphenylsulphone) to diphtherial toxin as a means of introducing toxin into toxin-resistant Ehrlich ascites tumor cells, suggests a possibly unrelated carrier for fragment *A.* Conjugates of toxin and antibody have been reported by Moolten & Cooperband (233) and by Philpott, Bower & Parker (246).

ACKNOWLEDGMENTS

We thank Kwang-Shin Kim for help in preparing the figures and we are grateful to Geraldine Hodgson for help with the manuscript. Work from our laboratory was aided by Public Health Service grant AI-01071 from the National Institute of Allergy and Infectious Diseases.

*Literature Cited*

1. Achtman, M. 1973. *Curr. Top. Microbiol. Immunol.* 60:80–123
2. Adams, J. N., Luria, S. E. 1958. *Proc. Nat. Acad. Sci. USA* 44:590–94
3. Adams, M. H. 1959. *Bacteriophages.* New York: Interscience. 592 pp.
4. Anderson, P. S. Jr., Cowles, P. B. 1958. *J. Bacteriol.* 76:272–80
5. Anderson, T. F. 1948. *J. Bacteriol.* 56: 403–10
6. Arber, W. 1958. *Arch. Sci.* 11:259–338
7. Arber, W., Dussoix, D. 1962. *J. Mol. Biol.* 5:18–36
8. Arber, W., Kellenberger, G., Weigle, J. 1957. *Schweiz. Z. Allg. Pathol. Bakteriol.* 20:659–65
9. Arden, S. B., Barksdale, L. 1970. *Bacteriol. Proc.* 1970:V239 (Abstr.)
10. Ibid 1971. 1971:V83 (Abstr.)
11. Arden, S. B., Barksdale, L. In preparation
12. Asheshov, E. H., Rippon, J. E. 1959. *J. Gen. Microbiol.* 20:634–43
13. Avery, O. T., MacLeod, C. M., McCarty, G. 1944. *J. Exp. Med.* 79: 137–58
14. Baess, I. 1971. *Acta Pathol. Microbiol. Scand.* 79:428–34
15. Bagdian, G., Luderitz, O., Staub, A. M. 1966. *Ann. NY Acad. Sci.* 133:405–24
16. Baker, E. E., Goebel, W. F., Perlman, E. 1949. *J. Exp. Med.* 89:325–38
17. Barksdale, L. 1955. *C. R. Acad. Sci.* 240:1831–33
18. Barksdale, L. 1958. *J. Gen. Microbiol.* 18:x–xi
19. Barksdale, L. 1959. *Bacteriol. Rev.* 23: 202–12
20. Barksdale, L. 1964. *The Streptococcus, Rheumatic Fever and Glomerulonephritis,* ed. J. W. Uhr, 70–82. Baltimore: Williams & Wilkins
21. Barksdale, L. 1970. *Bacteriol. Rev.* 34:378–422
22. Barksdale, L., Garmise, L., Horibata, K. 1960. *Ann. NY Acad. Sci.* 88: 1093–1108
23. Barksdale, W. L., Pappenheimer, A. M. Jr. 1953. *Proc. Fed. Soc. Biol. Med.* 12:435–36
24. Barksdale, W. L., Pappenheimer, A. M. Jr. 1953. *Int. Congr. Microbiol., 6th, Roma* 3:457
25. Barksdale, W. L., Pappenheimer, A. M. Jr. 1954. *J. Bacteriol.* 67:220–32

26. Barnet. Y. M., Vincent, J. M. 1970. *J. Gen. Microbiol.* 61:319–25
27. Baron, L. S., Formal, S. B., Washington, O. 1957. *Virology* 3:417–25
28. Baseman, J. B., Pappenheimer, A. M. Jr., Gill, D. M., Harper, A. A. 1970. *J. Exp. Med.* 132:1138–52
29. Beckwith, J. R., Zipser, D., Eds. 1970. *The Lactose Operon.* New York: Cold Spring Harbor Lab. 437 pp.
30. Bertani, G. 1951. *J. Bacteriol.* 62: 293–300
31. Bertani, L. E. 1964. *Biochim. Biophys. Acta* 87:631–40
32. Bertani, L. E., Bertani, G. 1971. *Advan. Genet.* 16:199–237
33. Bertani, L. E., Levy, J. A. 1964. *Virology* 22:634–40
34. Bingel, K. F. 1949. *Deut. Med. Wochenschr.* 127:703–6
35. Bizzini, B., Prudhomme, R. O., Turpin, A., Raynaud, M. 1963. *Bull. Soc. Chim. Biol.* 45:925–32
36. Blair, J. E., Carr, M. 1961. *J. Bacteriol.* 82:984–93
37. Boice, L. B., Luria, S. E. 1963. *Virology* 20:147–57
38. Bonicke, R., Saito, H. 1970. *Bull. Int. Union Tuberc.* 43:217–25
39. Bonventre, P. F. 1973. *Infec. Immunity* 7:556–60
40. Bonventre, P. F., Imhoff, J. G. 1966. *J. Exp. Med.* 124:1107–22
41. Ibid 1967. 126:1079–86
42. Borek, E., Ryan, A. 1973. *Progress in Nucleic Acid Research and Molecular Biology,* ed. J. N. Davidson, W. E. Cohn, 13:249–300. New York: Academic
43. Bott, K., Strauss, B. 1965. *Virology* 25:212–25
44. Bouanchaud, D. H., Scavizzi, M. R., Chabbert, Y. A. 1969. *J. Gen. Microbiol.* 54:417–25
45. Bowman, C. G., Bonventre, P. F. 1970. *J. Exp. Med.* 131:659–74
46. Boyd, J. S. K. 1953. *Symp. Soc. Gen. Microbiol.* 2:119–48
47. Boyd, J. S. K. 1954. *J. Pathol. Bacteriol.* 68:311–14
48. Boyd, J. S. K. 1954. *Nature* 173: 1050–51
49. Bray, D., Robbins, P. W. 1967. *Biochem. Biophys. Res. Commun.* 28: 334–39
50. Bray, D., Robbins, P. W. 1967. *J. Mol. Biol.* 30:457–75
51. Bronson, M. J., Levine, M. 1971. *J. Virol.* 7:559–68
52. Bronson, M. J., Levine, M. 1972. *Virology* 47:644–55
53. Bruner, D. W., Edwards, P. R. 1948. *J. Bacteriol.* 55:449
54. Burnet, F. M., McKie, M. 1929. *Aust. J. Exp. Biol. Med. Sci.* 6:277–84
55. Buzzi, S., Maistrello, I. 1973. *Cancer Res.* 33:2349–53
56. Cantacuzene, J., Bonciu, O. 1926. *C. R. Acad. Sci.* 182:1185–87
57. Carne, H. R., Bagnall, B. G., Massey, G. M. 1973. *Brit. J. Exp. Pathol.* 54: 566–70
58. Casman, E. P. 1965. *Ann. NY Acad. Sci.* 128:124–31
59. Christensen, J. R., Werner, E. R. 1969. *J. Virol.* 3:448–49
60. Clecner, B., Sonea, S. 1966. *Rev. Can. Biol.* 25:145–48
61. Coetzee, J. N., Hawtrey, A. O. 1962. *Nature* 194:1196–97
62. Collier, R. J. 1967. *J. Mol. Biol.* 25: 83–98
63. Collier, R. J., Cole, H. A. 1969. *Science* 164:1179–82
64. Collier, R. J., Kandel, J. 1971. *J. Biol. Chem.* 246:1496–503
65. Collier, R. J., Pappenheimer, A. M. Jr. 1964. *J. Exp. Med.* 120:1019–39
66. Collier, R. J., Traugh, J. A. 1969. *Cold Spring Harbor Symp. Quant. Biol.* 34:589–94
67. Comtois, R. D. 1960. *Can. J. Microbiol.* 6:491–502
68. Curtiss, R. III. 1969. *Ann. Rev. Microbiol.* 23:69–136
69. Damsker, B., Sonea, S. 1970. *Rev. Can. Biol.* 29:331–38
70. Deeb, S. S., Okamoto, K., Hall, B. D. 1967. *Virology* 31:289–95
71. Delbruck, M. 1946. *Biol. Rev.* 21:30–40
72. Demerec, M., Fano, U. 1945. *Genetics* 30:119–36
73. den Dooren de Jong, L. E. 1931. *Zentralbl. Bakteriol. Parasitenk. Infektionskr. Abt. 1 Orig.* 120:1–15
74. Dendy, P. R., Harris, H. 1973. *J. Cell Sci.* 12:831–37
75. deWaart, J., Grootsen, C., Zeegers, B. J. H., Winkler, K. C. 1963. *Antonie van Leeuwenhoek J. Microbiol. Serol.* 29: 324
76. deWaart, J., Winkler, K. C., Grootsen, C. 1962. *Nature* 195:407–8
77. Dobardzic, R., Sonea, S. 1970. *Experientia* 26:1022–23
78. Dobardzic, R., Sonea, S. 1971. *Ann. Inst. Pasteur* 120:42–49
79. Dobardzic, R., Sonea, S., Cote, J. R. 1970. *Rev. Can. Biol.* 29:1–6
80. Drazin, R., Kandel, J., Collier, R. J. 1971. *J. Biol. Chem.* 246:1504–10
81. Duncan, J. L., Groman, N. B. 1967. *J. Exp. Med.* 125:489–500

82. Duncan, J. L., Groman, N. B. 1969. *J. Bacteriol.* 98:963–69
83. Duval-Iflah, Y. 1972. *Can. J. Microbiol.* 18:1491–97
84. Duval-Iflah, Y., Rousseau, M., Expert, D. 1971. *C. R. Acad. Sci.* 273:246–49
85. Echols, H. 1972. *Ann. Rev. Genet.* 6:157–90
85a. Eklund, M. W., Poysky, F. T. 1972. *Appl. Microbiol.* 24:108–13
85b. Eklund, M. W., Poysky, F. T. 1974. *Appl. Microbiol.* 27:251–58
86. Eklund, M. W., Poysky, F. T., Reed, S. M. 1972. *Nature New Biol.* 235:16–17
87. Eklund, M. W., Poysky, F. T., Reed, S. M., Smith, C. A. 1971. *Science* 172:480–82
88. Erickson, R. J. 1970. *Curr. Top. Microbiol. Immunol.* 53:149–99
89. Escobar, M. R., Edwards, P. R. 1964. *Bacteriol. Proc.* RT10 (Abstr.)
90. Franklin, N. C., Luria, S. E. 1961. *Virology* 15:299–311
91. Fraser, D. 1957. *Virology* 3:527–53
92. Freeman, V. J. 1951. *J. Bacteriol.* 61: 675–88
93. Freeman, V. J., Morse, I. U. 1952. *J. Bacteriol.* 63:407–14
94. Frobisher, M., Brown, J. H. 1927. *Bull. Johns Hopkins Hosp.* 41:167–73
95. Fuller, N. A., Etievant, M., Staub, A. -M. 1968. *Eur. J. Biochem.* 6:525–33
96. Fuller, N. A., Staub, A. -M. 1968. *Eur. J. Biochem.* 4:286–300
97. Giammanco, G. 1968. *Ann. Inst. Pasteur* 114:63–76
98. Giammanco, G., Natoli, D. 1969. *Ann. Inst. Pasteur* 117:16–25
99. Gibson, K., Harris, P. 1973. *J. Mol. Cell. Cardiol.* 5:185–89
100. Gilbert, W., Dressler, D. 1968. *Cold Spring Harbor Symp. Quant. Biol.* 33:473–84
101. Gill, D. M., Dinius, L. L. 1971. *J. Biol. Chem.* 246:1485–91
102. Gill, D. M., Pappenheimer, A. M. Jr. 1971. *J. Biol. Chem.* 246:1492–95
103. Gill, D. M., Pappenheimer, A. M. Jr., Baseman, J. B. 1969. *Cold Spring Harbor Symp. Quant. Biol.* 34:595–602
104. Gill, D. M., Pappenheimer, A. M. Jr., Brown, R., Kurnick, J. T. 1969. *J. Exp. Med.* 129:1–21
105. Gill, D. M., Pappenheimer, A. M. Jr., Uchida, T. 1973. *Fed. Proc.* 32:1508–15
106. Gill, D. M., Uchida, T., Singer, R. A. 1972. *Virology* 50:664–68
107. Goldzimer, E., Arden, S. B., Barksdale, L. 1968. *Bacteriol. Proc.* 1968:V94 (Abstr.)
108. Goor, R. S., Maxwell, E. S. 1970. *J. Biol. Chem.* 245:616–23
109. Goor, R. S., Pappenheimer, A. M. Jr. 1967. *J. Exp. Med.* 126:899–912
110. Goor, R. S., Pappenheimer, A. M. Jr., Ames, E. 1967. *J. Exp. Med.* 126: 923–39
111. Groman, N. B. 1953. *J. Bacteriol.* 66: 184–91
112. Groman, N. B. 1953. *Science* 117: 297–99
113. Groman, N. B. 1955. *J. Bacteriol.* 69: 9–15
114. Groman, N. B. 1956. *Virology* 2:843–44
115. Groman, N. B. 1960. *Proc. Ann. Biol. Colloq. Oreg. State Univ.* 21:41–46
116. Groman, N. B., Eaton, M. 1955. *J. Bacteriol.* 70:637–40
117. Groman, N. B., Eaton, M., Booher, Z. K. 1958. *J. Bacteriol.* 75:320–25
118. Groman, N. B., Memmer, R. 1958. *J. Gen. Microbiol.* 19:634–44
119. Gundersen, W. B., Henriksen, S. D. 1959. *Acta Pathol. Microbiol. Scand.* 47:173–81
120. Hausmann, R. 1973. *Ann Rev. Microbiol.* 27:51–67
121. Hayes, W. 1968. *The Genetics of Bacteria and their Viruses,* 448. New York: Wiley. 2nd ed.
122. Hellerqvist, C. G., Lindberg, B., Svensson, S., Holme, T., Lindberg, A. A. 1970. *Carbohyd. Res.* 14:17–26
123. Herriot, R. G. 1951. *J. Gen. Physiol.* 34:761–64
124. Hershey, A. D., Ed. 1971. *The Bacteriophage Lambda.* New York: Cold Spring Harbor Lab. 792 pp.
125. Hirota, Y. 1960. *Proc. Nat. Acad. Sci. USA* 46:57–64
126. Hoffmann-Berling, H., Durwald, H., Beulke, I. 1963. *Z. Naturforsch.* 186: 893–98
127. Hoffmann-Berling, H., Kaerner, H. C., Knippers, R. 1966. *Advan. Virus Res.* 12:329–70
128. Hoffmann-Berling, H., Maze, R. 1964. *Virology* 22:305–13
129. Hofschneider, P. H., Preuss, A. 1963. *J. Mol. Biol.* 7:450–51
130. Holloway, B. W., Cooper, G. N. 1962. *J. Bacteriol.* 84:1321–24
131. Holmes, R. K., Barksdale, L. 1969. *J. Virol.* 3:586–98
132. Holmes, R. K., Barksdale, L. 1970. *J. Virol.* 5:783–94
133. Honjo, T., Nishizuka, Y., Hayaishi, O. 1969. *Cold Spring Harbor Symp. Quant. Biol.* 34:603–8
134. Honjo, T., Nishizuka, Y., Hayaishi, O., Kato, I. 1968. *J. Biol. Chem.* 243: 3553–55
135. Hotchkiss, R. D., Gabor, M. 1970. *Ann. Rev. Genet.* 4:193–224

136. Ikeda, H., Tomizawa, J. 1968. *Cold Spring Harbor Symp. Quant. Biol.* 33:791–98
137. Inoue, K., Iida, H. 1970. *Jap. J. Microbiol.* 14:87–89
138. Inoue, K., Iida, H. 1971. *Rep. Hokkaido Inst. Public Health* 21:26–29. (In Japanese)
139. Inoue, K., Iida, H. 1971. *Jap. J. Med. Sci. Biol.* 24:53–56
140. Inouye, M., Arnheim, N., Sternglanz, R. 1973. *J. Biol. Chem.* 248:7247–52
141. Ionesco, H. 1953. *C. R. Acad. Sci.* 237:1794–95
142. Iseki, S., Hamano, S. 1959. *Proc. Jap. Acad.* 35:407–12
143. Iseki, S., Kashiwagi, K. 1955. *Proc. Jap. Acad.* 31:558–63
144. Ibid 1957. 33:481–85
145. Iseki, S., Matsumoto, T. 1959. *Proc. Jap. Acad.* 35:626–31
146. Iseki, S., Sakai, T. 1953. *Proc. Jap. Acad.* 29:127–31
147. Iskierko, J. 1965. *Med. Dosw. Mikrobiol.* 17:217–23. In Polish
148. Ito, J., Meinke, W., Hathaway, G., Spizizen, J. 1973. *Virology* 56:110–22
149. Ittelson, T. R., Gill, D. M. 1973. *Nature* 242:330–32
150. Jacob, F. 1950. *C. R. Acad. Sci.* 231: 1585–87
151. Jacob, F., Brenner, S., Cuzin, F. 1963. *Cold Spring Harbor Symp. Quant. Biol.* 28:329–48
152. Jollick, J. D. 1972. *Microbios* 6:97–100
153. Jones, L. M., McDuff, C. R., Wilson, J. B. 1962. *J. Bacteriol.* 83:860–66
154. Jones, W. D. Jr., Beam, R. E. 1969. *Can. J. Microbiol.* 15:1112–14
155. Jones, W. D. Jr., David, H. L. 1970. *Am. Rev. Resp. Dis.* 102:818 20
156. Jones, W. D. Jr., White, A. 1968. *Can. J. Microbiol.* 14:551–55
157. Juhasz, S. E. 1967. *Nature* 214:518–20
158. Juhasz, S. E. 1968. *J. Gen. Microbiol.* 52:237–41
159. Juhasz, S. E. 1970. *Ann. NY Acad. Sci.* 174:847–51
160. Juhasz, S. E., Gelbart, S., Harize, M. 1969. *J. Gen. Microbiol.* 56:251–55
161. Juhasz, S. E., Plummer, G., Ed. 1970. *Host-Virus Relationships in Mycobacterium, Nocardia and Actinomyces.* Springfield, Ill.: Thomas. 271 pp.
162. Kaiser, A. D. 1962. *J. Mol. Biol.* 4: 275–87
163. Kaiser, A. D., Hogness, D. S. 1960. *J. Mol. Biol.* 2:392–415
164. Kalckar, H. M., Kurahashi, K., Jordan, E. 1959. *Proc. Nat. Acad. Sci. USA* 45:1776–86
165. Kandel, J., Collier, R. J., Chung, D. W. 1974. *J. Biol. Chem.* 249:2088–97
166. Kanegasaki, S., Wright, A. 1973. *Virology* 52:160–73
167. Kato, I. 1962. *Jap. J. Exp. Med.* 32:335–43
168. Kato, I., Pappenheimer, A. M. Jr. 1960. *J. Exp. Med.* 112:329–49
169. Kauffmann, F. 1972. *Serological Diagnosis of Salmonella-Species. Kauffmann-White Schema.* Baltimore: Williams & Wilkins. 126 pp.
170. Kawakami, M., Landman, O. 1968. *J. Bacteriol.* 95:1804–12
171. Kim, K., Groman, N. B. 1965. *J. Bacteriol.* 90:1552–56
172. Kim, K., Groman, N. B. 1965. *J. Bacteriol.* 90:1557–62
173. Kim, K. S., Laneelle, M. -A., Barksdale, L. 1971. *Bacteriol. Proc.* 1971:G51 (Abstr.)
174. Kondo, E., Mitsuhashi, S. 1964. *J. Bacteriol.* 88:1266–76
175. Ibid 1966. 91:1787–94
176. Lampidis, T., Barksdale, L. 1971. *J. Bacteriol.* 105:77–85
177. Lawton, W. D., Molnar, D. M. 1972. *J. Virol.* 9:708–9
178. Lederberg, E. M. 1951. *Genetics* 36:560
179. Lederberg, E. M., Lederberg, J. 1953. *Genetics* 38:51–64
180. Lederberg, J., Tatum, E. L. 1946. *Cold Spring Harbor Symp. Quant. Biol.* 11:113–14
181. Lederberg, S. 1957. *Virology* 3:496–513
182. Le Minor, L. 1962. *Ann. Inst. Pasteur* 103:684–706
183. Ibid 1963. 105:879–96
184. Ibid 1965. 109:505–15
185. Ibid 1968. 114:49–62
186. Le Minor, L., Ackermann, H. W., Nicolle, P. 1963. *Ann. Inst. Pasteur* 104: 469–76
187. Le Minor, L., Le Minor, S., Nicolle, P. 1961. *Ann. Inst. Pasteur* 101:571–89
188. Le Minor, L., Staub, A. -M. 1966. *Ann. Inst. Pasteur* 110:834–48
189. Lennox, E. S., Kaplan, A. S. 1957. *Proc. Soc. Exp. Biol. Med.* 95:700–2
190. Levine, M. 1972. *Curr. Top. Microbiol. Immunol.* 58:135–36
191. Li, K., Barksdale, L., Garmise, L. 1961. *J. Gen. Microbiol.* 24:355–67
192. Lieb, M. 1966. *J. Mol. Biol.* 16:149–63
193. Lieb, M. 1970. *J. Virol.* 6:218–25
193a. Lightfoot, H. N., Iglewski, B. H. 1974. *Biochem. Biophys. Res. Commun.* 56: 351–57
194. Lisbonne, M., Carrere, L. 1922. *C. R. Soc. Biol.* 86:569–70
195. Ibid 1923. 88:724–26

196. Liu, P. V. 1969. *J. Infec. Dis.* 119: 237–46
197. Losick, R. 1969. *J. Mol. Biol.* 42: 237–46
198. Losick, R., Robbins, P. W. 1967. *J. Mol. Biol.* 30:445–55
199. Luderitz, O. et al 1973. *J. Infec. Dis.* 128 (Suppl):S17–S29
200. Luderitz, O., Staub, A. -M., Westphal, O. 1966. *Bacteriol. Rev.* 30:192–255
201. Luderitz, O., Westphal, O., Staub, A. -M., Nikaido, H. 1971. *Microbial Toxins,* ed. G. Weinbaum, S. Kadis, S. J. Ajl, IV:145–233. New York: Academic
202. Luria, S. E., Adams, J. N., Ting, R. C. 1960. *Virology* 12:348–90
203. Lwoff, A. 1953. *Bacteriol. Rev.* 17: 269–337
204. Lwoff, A., Gutman, A. 1950. *Ann. Inst. Pasteur* 78:711–39
205. Lwoff, A., Siminovitch, L., Kjeldgaard, A. 1950. *Ann. Inst. Pasteur* 79:815–59
206. Makela, P. H., Stocker, B. A. D. 1969. *Ann. Rev. Genet.* 3:291–322
207. Mankiewicz, E. 1961. *J. Gen. Microbiol.* 24:63–68
208. Mankiewicz, E., Liivak, M., Dernuet, S. 1969. *J. Gen. Microbiol.* 55:409–16
209. Manly, K. F., Signer, E. R., Radding, C. M. 1969. *Virology* 37:177–88
210. Marcovich, H., Kaplan, H. S. 1963. *Nature* 200:487–88
211. Marvin, D. A., Hohn, B. 1969. *Bacteriol. Rev.* 33:172–209
212. Matsuda, M., Barksdale, L. 1967. *J. Bacteriol.* 93:722–30
213. Matsuda, M., Kanei, C., Yoneda, M. 1971. *Biken J.* 14:119–30
214. Ibid 365–68
215. Ibid 1972. 15:111–14
216. Matsui, S. 1958. *Jap. J. Microbiol.* 2: 153–58
217. Matsushiro, A. 1961. *Biken J.* 4:141–44
218. Matsushiro, A. 1963. *Virology* 19: 475–82
219. Matsushiro, A., Sato, K., Kida, S. 1964. *Virology* 23:299–306
220. Matsuyama, T., Uetake, H. 1972. *Virology* 49:359–67
221. Maximesco, P., Pop, A., Oprisan, A., Potorac, E. 1968. *Arch. Roum. Pathol. Exp. Microbiol.* 27:733–50
222. McCloy, E. 1953. *Int. Congr. Microbiol., 6th, Roma* 3:490
223. McCloy, E. 1958. *J. Gen. Microbiol.* 18:198–220
224. Meynell, G. G. 1973. *Bacterial Plasmids, Conjugation, Colicinogeny and Transmissible Drug-Resistance.* Cambridge, Mass.: MIT Press. 164 pp.
225. Michel, A., Zanen, J., Monier, C., Crispeels, C., Dirkx, J. 1972. *Biochim. Biophys. Acta* 257:249–56
226. Miller, P. A., Pappenheimer, A. M. Jr., Doolittle, W. F. 1966. *Virology* 29: 410–25
227. Moehring, J. M., Moehring, T. J. 1968. *J. Exp. Med.* 127:541–54
228. Moehring, T. J., Moehring, J. M. 1968. *J. Bacteriol.* 96:61–9
229. Moehring, T. J., Moehring, J. M. 1972. *Infec. Immunity* 6:487–92
230. Ibid 493–500
231. Moehring, T. J., Moehring, J. M., Kuchler, R. J., Solotorovsky, M. 1967. *J. Exp. Med.* 126:407–22
232. Moehring, T. J., Moehring, J. M., Stinebring, W. R. 1971. *Infec. Immunity* 4:747–52
233. Moolten, F. L., Cooperband, S. R. 1970. *Science* 169:68–70
234. Morse, M. L., Lederberg, E. M., Lederberg, J. 1956. *Genetics* 41:758–79
235. Mueller, J. H. 1941. *J. Immunol.* 42: 343–51
235a. Murphy, J. R., Pappenheimer, A. M. Jr., De Borms, S. T. 1974. *Proc. Nat. Acad. Sci. USA* 71:11–15
236. Nikaido, H. 1968. *Advan. Enzymol.* 31:77–124
237. Ogg, J. E., Chang, W. 1972. *Am. J. Vet. Res.* 33:1023–29
238. Osborn, M. J. 1969. *Ann. Rev. Biochem.* 38:501–38
239. Otsuji, N., Sekiguchi, M. Iijima, T., Takagi, Y. 1959. *Nature* 184:1079–80
240. Ozeki, H., Ikeda, H. 1968. *Ann. Rev. Genet.* 2:245–78
241. Pappenheimer, A. M. Jr., Gill, D. M. 1973. *Science* 182:353–58
242. Pappenheimer, A. M. Jr., Johnson, S. J. 1936. *Brit. J. Exp. Pathol.* 17:335–41
243. Pappenheimer, A. M. Jr., Uchida, T., Harper, A. A. 1972. *Immunochemistry* 9:891–906
244. Park, W. H., Williams, A. W. 1896. *J. Exp. Med.* 1:164–85
245. Parsons, E. I. 1955. *Proc. Soc. Exp. Biol. Med.* 90:91–93
246. Philpott, G. W., Bower, R. J., Parker, C. W. 1973. *Surgery* 73:928–35
247. Pope, C. G. 1932. *Brit. J. Exp. Pathol.* 13:218–23
248. Ptashne, M. 1967. *Proc. Nat. Acad. Sci. USA* 57:306–13
249. Ptashne, M. 1967. *Nature* 214:232–34
250. Raeburn, S., Collins, J. F., Moon, H. M., Maxwell, E. S. 1971. *J. Biol. Chem.* 246:1041–48
251. Rao, R. N. 1968. *J. Mol. Biol.* 35: 607–22

252. Raynaud, M., Turpin, A., Mangalo, R., Bizzini, B., Pery, R. 1954. *Ann. Inst. Pasteur* 87:599–616
253. Robbins, P. W., Bray, D., Dankert, M., Wright, A. 1967. *Science* 158:1536–42
254. Robbins, P. W., Keller, J. M., Wright, A., Bernstein, R. L. 1965. *J. Biol. Chem.* 240:384–90
255. Robbins, P. W., Uchida, T. 1962. *Fed. Proc.* 21:702–10
256. Robbins, P. W., Uchida, T. 1962. *Biochemistry* 1:323–35
257. Rosenblum, E. D., Jackson, J. L. W. 1960. *Tex. Rep. Biol. Med.* 18:654–61
258. Rosendal, K., Bulow, P. 1965. *J. Gen. Microbiol.* 41:349–56
259. Rosendal, K., Bulow, P., Jessen, O. 1964. *Nature* 204:1222–23
260. Rountree, P. M. 1959. *J. Gen. Microbiol.* 20:620–33
261. Saelinger, C. B., Imhoff, J. G., Bonventre, P. F. 1973. *Proc. Soc. Exp. Biol. Med.* 142:41–45
262. Samagh, B. S., Gregory, K. F. 1972. *Biochim. Biophys. Acta* 273:188–98
263. Scott, J. R. 1968. *Virology* 36:564–74
264. Ibid 1970. 40:144–51
265. Siegel, P. J., Schaechter, M. 1973. *Ann. Rev. Microbiol.* 27:261–82
266. Signer, E. R. 1969. *Nature* 223:158–60
267. Signer, E. R. 1970. *Virology* 40:624–33
268. Singer, R. A. 1973. *Virology* 55:347–56
269. Ibid 357–62
270. Sonenshein, A. L. 1970. *Virology* 42: 488–95
271. Sonenshein, A. L., Roscoe, D. H. 1969. *Virology* 39:265–76
272. Staub, A. -M., Bagdian, G. 1966. *Ann. Inst. Pasteur* 110:849–60
273. Staub, A. -M., Girard, R. 1965. *Bull. Soc. Chim. Biol.* 47:1245–68
274. Staub, A. -M., Tinelli, R., Luderitz, O., Westphal, O. 1959. *Ann. Inst. Pasteur* 96:303–32
275. Stocker, B. A. D. 1958. *J. Gen. Microbiol.* 18:ix
276. Stocker, B. A. D., Staub, A. -M., Tinelli, R., Kopacka, B. 1960. *Ann. Inst. Pasteur* 98:505–23
277. Strauss, N. 1960. *J. Exp. Med.* 112: 351–59
278. Strauss, N., Hendee, E. D. 1959. *J. Exp. Med.* 109:144–63
279. Studier, F. W. 1972. *Science* 176: 367–76
280. Takahashi, I. 1964. *J. Bacteriol.* 87: 1499–502
281. Takeda, K., Uetake, H. 1973. *Virology* 52:148–59
282. Tomasz, A. 1969. *Ann. Rev. Genet.* 3:217–32
283. Toshach, S. 1950. *Can. J. Pub. Health* 41:332–36
284. Uchida, T., Makino, T., Kurahashi, K., Uetake, H. 1965. *Biochem. Biophys. Res. Commun.* 21:354–60
285. Uchida, T., Robbins, P. W., Luria, S. E. 1963. *Biochemistry* 2:663–68
286. Uchida, T., Gill, D. M., Pappenheimer, A. M. Jr. 1971. *Nature New Biol.* 233:8–11
287. Uchida, T., Pappenheimer, A. M. Jr., Greany, R. 1973. *J. Biol. Chem.* 248: 3838–44
288. Uchida, T., Pappenheimer, A. M. Jr., Harper, A. A. 1972. *Science* 175:901–3
289. Uchida, T., Pappenheimer, A. M. Jr., Harper, A. A. 1973. *J. Biol. Chem.* 248:3845–50
290. Ibid 3851–54
291. Uchida, T., Yoneda, M. 1967. *Biken J.* 10:121–28
292. Uchida, T., Yoneda, M. 1967. *Biochim. Biophys. Acta* 145:210–13
293. Uetake, H. 1964. *Ann. Rep. Inst. Virus Res., Kyoto Univ.* 7:38–55
294. Uetake, H., Luria, S. E., Burrous, J. W. 1958. *Virology* 5:68–91
295. Uetake, H., Nakagawa, T., Akiba, T. 1955. *J. Bacteriol.* 69:571–79
296. Urm, E., Yang, H., Zubay, G., Kelker, N., Maas, W. 1973. *Mol. Gen. Genet.* 121:1–7
297. van der Vijver, J. C. M., van Es-Boon, M., Michel, M. F. 1972. *J. Virol.* 10: 318–19
298. Walsh, J., Meynell, G. G. 1967. *J. Gen. Virol.* 1:581–82
299. Ward, A. J., Bates, J. H. 1969. *Bacteriol. Proc.* 1969:V297 (Abstr.)
300. Weigle, J. J., Delbruck, M. 1955. *J. Bacteriol.* 62:301–18
301. White, A., Foster, F., Lyon, L. 1962. *J. Bacteriol.* 84:815–18
302. Wilson, G. S. 1967. *The Hazards of Immunization,* 39–42. London: Athlone
303. Winkler, K. C. et al 1965. *J. Gen. Microbiol.* 39:321–33
304. Wollman, E. L. 1963. *C. R. Acad. Sci.* 257:4225–26
305. Wright, A. 1971. *J. Bacteriol.* 105: 927–36
306. Wright, A., Barzilai, N. 1971. *J. Bacteriol.* 105:937–39
307. Wright, A., Dankert, M., Fennessey, P., Robbins, P. W. 1967. *Proc. Nat. Acad. Sci. USA* 57:1798–1803
308. Wright, A., Dankert, M., Robbins, P. W. 1965. *Proc. Nat. Acad. Sci. USA* 54:235–41
308a. Wright, A., Kanegasaki, S. 1971. *Physiol. Rev.* 51:748–84

310. Ibid 1967. 9:692–706
311. Yoneda, M., Ishihara, H. 1960. *Biken J.* 3:11–26
312. Zabriskie, J. B. 1964. *The Streptococcus, Rheumatic Fever and Glomerulonephritis,* ed. J. W. Uhr, 53–70. Baltimore: Williams & Wilkins
313. Zabriskie, J. B. 1964. *J. Exp. Med.* 119:761–79
314. Zabriskie, J. B. 1966. *Ann. Rev. Med.* 17:337–50
315. Zabriskie, J. B., Read, S. E., Fischetti, V. A. 1972. *Streptococci and Streptococcal Diseases. Recognition, Understanding, and Management,* ed. L. W. Wannamaker, J. M. Matsen, 99–118. New York: Academic
316. Zinder, N. D. 1957. *Science* 126:1237
317. Zinder, N. D. 1958. *Virology* 5:291–326
318. Zubay, G., Morse, D. E., Schrenk, W. J., Miller, J. H. M. 1972. *Proc. Nat. Acad. Sci. USA* 69:1100–3

# MYCOPLASMAS AND RICKETTSIAE IN RELATION TO PLANT DISEASES

❖1640

*K. Maramorosch*[1]
Institute of Microbiology, Rutgers University, New Brunswick, New Jersey 08903

CONTENTS

INTRODUCTION .......... 301
DEFINITIONS .......... 303
*Mollicute-Like Organisms (MLO)* .......... 303
*Spiroplasma* .......... 303
*Rickettsia-Like Organisms (RLO)* .......... 304
MYCOPLASMATALES .......... 304
*SPIROPLASMA CITRI* .......... 306
*Characteristics* .......... 306
*Cultivation* .......... 306
*Relation to Insect Vectors* .......... 307
*Comparison Among Spiroplasma, Mycoplasma, and Acholeplasma* .......... 308
CORN STUNT SPIROPLASMA .......... 308
*Electron Microscopy* .......... 309
*Optical Microscopy* .......... 309
*Serology* .......... 310
MOLLICUTE-LIKE ORGANISMS (MLO) .......... 311
*Morphology* .......... 311
*Intracellular Growth* .......... 312
*Natural Degeneration* .......... 313
*Association with Viruses* .......... 313
*Dual Infections: MLO and Viruses* .......... 314
*Response to Antibiotics* .......... 316
RICKETTSIA-LIKE ORGANISMS (RLO) .......... 317
CONCLUSIONS .......... 318

## INTRODUCTION

The objective of this review of mycoplasmas in relation to plant diseases, as requested, is to prepare a critical chapter and to aim its content at microbiologists.

[1]Work on mycoplasma-like agents of plant diseases was sponsored by NSF grants GB-11861 and GB-29280.

To accomplish these aims required an evaluation of work carried out primarily by plant pathologists and entomologists, and a presentation in terms that would be meaningful to microbiologists. Consequently this review is not a complete list of all published reports, but rather an analysis of certain selected papers. It is expected that the focusing of attention at some confused and controversial aspects and conclusions will stimulate future work by microbiologists in this important and exciting field.

In 1967 it was first recognized that insects, as well as plants, can be infected by wall-less microorganisms that differ from walled bacteria (50, 97, 133). It became apparent that there exists a large and unique group of prokaryotes which are pathogenic to insects as well as to plants. These diseases agents appeared to belong to the class Mollicutes. The main reason for the lack of earlier recognition of mollicutes as disease agents of insects and plants was their ability to pass through filters that retained bacteria. Thus, they were grouped together with filterable viruses, even though they differ chemically and morphologically from viruses. Crucial tests for their identification require cultivation and comparison with other known microorganisms. Although several laboratories have carried out such attempts, to date only one mollicute infecting insects and plants has been properly identified and made available to type culture collections for comparison with established forms.

The discovery of microorganisms in sieve elements of plants with four different yellows-type diseases was first announced by Doi et al in 1967 (50). The nature of these microorganisms was carefully considered and their morphological resemblance to mycoplasmas, as well as to PLT (psittacosis-lymphogranuloma-trachoma) agents, was pointed out. The authors did not favor one or the other group and they left open the possibility that L-forms of bacteria were involved. The companion paper from the same laboratory, by Ishiie et al (97), described the temporary remission of one of the diseases, when tetracycline antibiotics, but not penicillin, were applied. Furthermore, electron microscopy of treated, recovering plants showed the gradual disappearance of the mycoplasma-resembling bodies. Several weeks after tetracycline treatments ceased, the plants succumbed to the disease, indicating that the cure was only temporary, or incomplete. Electron microscopy of such plants with relapse of disease revealed the reappearance of the microorganisms in phloem cells. The authors of these papers concluded, therefore, that the unit membrane-bounded bodies—containing ribosome granules and DNA-containing strands in nuclear areas, and susceptible to tetracycline but not to penicillin—were most likely the causative agents of the yellows-type plant diseases.

Extensive English abstracts of both papers were soon supplemented by widely distributed mimeographed translations of the complete text. The third short paper by Nasu et al (133) described the presence of similar microorganisms in rice yellow dwarf diseased plants, as well as in leafhopper vectors of the disease agent. The influence of these reports was immense. Scores of papers appeared from all over the world, some failing to give credit to the original discoverers, and others carefully following the same procedures and describing numerous mycoplasma diseases of plants. During the past 7 years over 70 distinct plant diseases, affecting some 300 genera of plants, were added to the still increasing list of diseases believed to be caused by mollicute-like organisms (MLO). Since the term "mycoplasma" has been used by plant pathologists at the turn of the century to describe a hypothetical fungal structure, its use caused some confusion at first. The etymology of the word and the justification for its use in bacteriology have been discussed recently (106). For reasons outlined below under the section on definitions, the term mycoplasmas used in the title of this review will not be used to denote agents of plant diseases. Recently, in addition to the disease agents characterized by unit membranes and grouped together as MLO, a new group of walled microorganisms was recognized; this group, resembling rickettsiae, is described in the present chapter as rickettsia-like organisms (RLO). A partial list of earlier reviews, combining MLO and RLO, has been assembled (2, 4, 6, 7, 17, 25, 32, 38, 42, 63, 77, 92, 93, 95, 98, 104, 117, 118, 120, 127, 131, 141, 151, 156, 165, 166).

## DEFINITIONS

Most reports during the past seven years combined MLO and RLO, considering them as a single group of disease agents and usually describing them as mycoplasma-like or as plant mycoplasma agents. Authors were concerned with aspects of ultrastructure of MLO in plants and insect vectors, attempts to isolate and cultivate MLO in cell-free media, and effects of antibiotics on diseased plants and insect vectors. Some authors did not bother to define MLO and accepted the view that the newly recognized pathogens were members of the family Mycoplasmataceae.

In the present review MLO and RLO are of necessity ill-defined and these terms are somewhat reminiscent of the fungi imperfecti. The reason for the poor definition is obvious. There is no possibility to characterize accurately disease agents that have not yet been properly isolated and cultured.

For the purpose of this review, the agents associated with yellows-type plant diseases will be characterized and defined as follows.

### *Mollicute-Like Organisms (MLO)*

This term is applied to pleomorphic microorganisms, bounded by unit membranes, 8–10 nm in thickness, with RNA granules (ribosomes) and DNA strands in the nuclear region. Many MLO have been found susceptible to tetracycline application in vivo. This has been demonstrated by applying various tetracycline antibiotics via plant roots, and subsequently observing the deterioration of MLO and their final disappearance, as visualized by electron microscopy of thin sections of phloem cells. Remission of disease is less reliable, since such remission, except for flower formation, has also been induced, to a certain degree, by compounds that do not seem to affect MLO. Known vectors of MLO include leafhoppers, planthoppers, and psyllids.

### *Spiroplasma*

Spiroplasma is a vernacular name (39, 44) given to certain MLO that are characterized by a spiral form, in addition to the typical MLO shape. The spiral form is discernible in dark field and phase contrast microscopy. The first and so far the only cultured spiroplasma is *Spiroplasma citri,* the causative agent of citrus-stubborn disease. Another spiroplasma, now known to be related to *S. citri* but not yet cultured in cell-free media, is associated with, and believed to be the agent of, the corn stunt disease.

### *Rickettsia-Like Organisms (RLO)*

This term is applied to pleomorphic microorganisms, possessing a definite cell wall, 20–25 nm in thickness, which is often rippled. The RLO seem susceptible to penicillin in vivo. Their internal structure resembles that of rickettsiae and they do not belong to the Mollicutes. In some plant diseases they have been found associated with the phloem, and in other diseases with the xylem.

## MYCOPLASMATALES

In order to place the MLO and RLO in proper perspective, taxonomic data about the class Mollicutes and the order Mycoplasmatales are summarized below. These data are from the most recent classification by Freundt (57, 58).

The order Mycoplasmatales Freundt belongs to the class Mollicutes (Edward and Freundt) that comprises prokaryote microorganisms with pliable cell membranes. It is not yet possible to define Mollicutes in terms of properties shared by all members of the class, that would clearly distinguish them from cell-defective L-forms of bacteria. Collectively, fundamental morphological, biochemical, and physiological differences provide ample evidence that Mollicutes are phylogenetically and taxonomically unrelated to the class Bacteria. Only one order, Mycoplasmatales, now belongs to the class Mollicutes, so that the description of the class and the order do not differ.

Two families and two genera of uncertain affiliation have been described up to now. Since numerous plant pathogens have been called plant mycoplasmas, it seems worthwhile to list the taxonomic characteristics of the Mycoplasmatales in detail, so as to compare them with MLO. It is hoped that this will also help in preventing the continuation of the nonscientific use of the term mycoplasma-like in the plant pathological literature.

Members of the order Mycoplasmatales are prokaryotic organisms, bounded by a single triple-layered membrane, 7–10 nm thick (14, 15). They lack a true cell wall and are incapable of synthesizing cell wall precursors, such as muramic and diaminopimelic acids. They form small, sometimes even ultramicroscopic cells, 200 nm in diameter, highly pleomorphic, coccoid to filamentous, with a tendency to form branched myceloid structures. Their mode of reproduction is still uncertain. They are Gram-negative and usually are nonmotile. They can be grown on artificial, cell-free media of diverse complexity. On solid media they form minute colonies and grow into the media usually with characteristic 'fried egg' appearance. Most species are completely resistant to penicillin. Their growth and metabolism are specifically inhibited by antibody. They may be saprophytic, parasitic, or pathogenic.

In the Mycoplasmataceae, cholesterol or other sterols are required for growth. Urea is not hydrolyzed. Temperature range is 22–41°C, with an optimum at 36–37°C at pH 7. All species are sensitive to 1.5% digitonin. Susceptibility to antibiotics is variable, particularly to certain macrolides, such as erythromycin. Usually thallium acetate is tolerated at 1:2000–1:4000. The G + C content of DNA ranges from 23–40 moles %. At least 32 species have been well characterized and properly named. Such naming, according to international agreement, requires deposition in a type culture collection. In the same family there are also well-defined groups which have not yet been assigned a valid name. The T-strains which hydrolyze urea and are highly susceptible to erythromycin, as well as organisms which have no validly published names or for which no cultures are available, have been placed in the *species incertae sedis.*

The second family, Acholeplasmataceae, comprises Mollicutes that do not require sterol for growth. Otherwise they resemble Mycoplasmataceae. They are more susceptible to osmotic shock at 37°C than the Mycoplasmataceae. In addition to the Mycoplasmataceae and Acholeplasmataceae, two genera of uncertain family affiliation are now recognized in the order Mycoplasmatales. They are *Thermoplasma* Darland, Brock, Samsonoff, and Conti 1970 (37), and *Spiroplasma* Saglio, L'Hospital, Lafleche, Dupont, Bové, Tully, and Freundt 1973 (148).

*Thermoplasma* differs antigenically, as shown by metabolic inhibition and by double immunodiffusion tests, from *Acholeplasma* and *Mycoplasma. Thermoplasma* does not require sterol, it is a strict aerobe, and it is a true saprophyte. Its optimum growth temperature is 59°C, no growth occurs at 37 or 65°C, and optimum pH is about 1–2. The organism is Gram-negative (11).

*Spiroplasma,* not yet grouped into a family, is characterized by pleomorphic cells, from spherical or slightly ovoid to helical and branched nonhelical filaments. Only nonhelical and round cells occur in agar cultures. These forms are 120 nm in diameter. Their mode of reproduction is unknown. The Gram-positive staining, as well as an additional outer layer of short projections of the triple layer membrane-bounded cells, is the distinctive feature of *Spiroplasma.* The projections or the bounding membrane often appear periodic. Helical filaments are motile with a rapid rotary screw-type motion, and a slow undulation. No flagella, axial filaments, or other organelles of locomotion have been demonstrated. On solid media, *Spiroplasma* forms typical 'fried egg' colonies. Turbidity is produced in broth cultures. *Spiroplasma* produces acid from glucose and mannose.

Surprisingly, for a plant pathogen, there is a growth requirement for cholesterol or possibly other sterols. Conventional mycoplasma media, with 10% yeast extract and 20% horse serum, with 7% sorbitol, 1% tryptose, 1% sucrose, 0.1% fructose, and 0.1%glucose were used initially, but adapted cultures are less fastidious. *Spiroplasma* is a facultative anaerobe that grows best in 5% $CO_2$ in nitrogen, with a sharp temperature optimum at 32°C. Erythromycin 0.16–0.32 g/m, tetracycline 20–40 mg/ml, neomycin 20–40 mg/ml, amphotericin 15–25 mg/ml, and thallium acetate 1230–2560 mg/ml completely inhibit the growth. The G + C content of DNA is 25–26 moles %, and the genome size is $10^9$ daltons.

## *SPIROPLASMA CITRI*

### *Characteristics*

Since *Spiroplasma citri* is the only cultured plant-pathogenic member of the class Mollicutes and at the same time the only MLO properly identified, additional details deserve to be mentioned here. This pathogen is distinct from all the described members of the order Mycoplasmatales, even though in many respects it resembles the classical mycoplasmas. The colonial and cellular morphology, the ultrastructure in thin sections, the filterability, the requirement for cholesterol in cell-free media, the absolute resistance to penicillin, the inhibition of growth by antibody, the lack of reversion to bacterial forms, the low guanine and cytosine content of cellular DNA, the small genome size, and the cultural properties on solid agar media, mentioned earlier, parallel the characteristic features of Mycoplasmatales. The unique features of *S. citri* that distinguish this mollicute from L-phase bacterial variants as well as from all known members of the genera *Mycoplasma* or *Acholeplasma* are the production of helical and motile filaments at the logarithmic phase of growth, the Gram-positive staining, and the presence of a temporary wall-like coating, 55–90 nm thick. The finding of a tailed bacteriophage in almost all isolates has been considered unique by some workers (18, 30, 31). *S. citri* is extremely sensitive to lysis by osmotic shock (143). Membranes obtained by this method show the typical particle-studded fracture faces in freeze-etched preparations (143). The major phospholipid of the membrane is phosphotidyl glycerol, accompanied by significant, 15–35 $\mu$g/mg amounts of membrane protein.

*S. citri* produces typical 'fried egg' colonies on solid agar media and such cultured forms reveal the presence of filaments and rounded forms, but do not suggest the presence of helices (31). A possible explanation for the lack of helices comes from the observation, under dark field microscopy, of loss of helicity upon the addition of glutaraldehyde. The microorganisms were bounded by a single, often asymetric membrane, sometimes with a vaguely defined outer layer. Helices were observed when 3.5% glutaraldehyde or 10% formalin were used for fixation at pH 7. Striking helices were observed in freeze-dried preparations (44, 48, 49). It seems conceivable that in optimal growth conditions in liquid media helices form frequently but do not form at all, or only rarely, on solid media.

### *Cultivation*

The first published accounts of *S. citri* cultivation came from two groups: Saglio et al in France (146) and Fudl-Allah et al in the United States (59, 61, 62). These reports were followed by very extensive work in several laboratories (18, 24, 30, 31, 36, 60, 143, 147) and the results are summarized below.

*S. citri* is unquestionably the first MLO obtained in pure culture. This statement might shock some readers of earlier reviews that dealt with up to 20 different plant-pathogenic species of mycoplasmas, presumably isolated and cultured in cell-free media. Unfortunately, the authors of earlier reports, who claimed successful isolation and cultivation of MLO, had neglected to follow the accepted international rules pertaining to the identification of members of the class Mollicutes. Even worse, their work could not be confirmed by reliable mycoplasma experts. Some of the earlier, unconfirmed claims have been reviewed (117). Additional attempts have been published since (13, 46, 64, 67, 68, 78, 102, 103, 105, 108, 117, 136, 137, 141, 155, 162). In sharp contrast to these unconfirmed claims, there is now excellent evidence for the belief that *S. citri* is a plant-pathogenic Mollicute, distinct from the members of the other genera of this class.

Cultured *S. citri* has been obtained first from stubborn-diseased citrus leaves and seed coats, and more recently from several species of leafhoppers (*Cicadellidae*) collected in California in an area where stubborn disease of citrus is prevalent (E. C. Calavan, personal communication; 24). *S. citri* has not been found in healthy citrus. Electron microscopy of diseased plant material revealed the presence of MLO in the phloem, but healthy material was consistently free from MLO. Since 1971 the microorganisms have been consistently isolated by Bové and co-workers in France (18) in 39 out of 45 experiments using stubborn-diseased plant material; they were never found in healthy controls. No Mycoplasma or Acholeplasma contaminations were found in the liquid or solid media used in these tests. Material from Morocco, R8-A2, provided the type strain of *S. citri,* now deposited in the ATCC as #27556. The California strain yielded the second isolate, ATCC #27563. Recently Daniels et al in England (36) obtained stubborn-diseased material from Israel and isolated *S. citri,* which was used in the first successful inoculation of plants. The leafhopper *Euscelis plebejus* was injected with the cultured pathogen and confined to white cover plants.

After several days, the plants showed signs of a yellows-type disease and *S. citri* was reisolated from these diseased plants (36). Noninoculated *E. plebejus,* as far as could be ascertained, did not produce any disease when confined to control plants. In recent tests (M. J. Daniels, personal communication) *E. plebejus* inoculated with *S. citri* was confined to healthy citrus seedlings and stubborn disease symptoms were reproduced in exposed plants. The above tests, if confirmed, provide the first evidence that *S. citri* is not merely associated with stubborn disease, but is actually the causative agent of stubborn disease. It provides the first instance of a properly isolated and taxonomically defined Mollicute that constitutes a veritable plant pathogen.

## *Relation to Insect Vectors*

The natural vector of *S. citri* is still unknown. Recently the common vector of sugar beet curly top agent in the western United States, the leafhopper *Circulifer tenellus* Baker, was found to be a natural carrier (not a transmitting vector, however) of *Spiroplasma citri* (24). Cultured *S. citri* from leafhoppers collected near stubborn-diseased citrus in Riverside, California, appeared identical to the California isolate (ATCC #27556) from citrus (I. M. Lee, G. Cartie, E. C. Calavan, and G. H. Kaloostian, personal communication). There is a strong suspicion that *S. citri* may have noncitrus plant hosts in California (24). This hypothesis is strengthened by the reported induction of an experimental disease in white clover, mentioned earlier (36). Further tests in the Mediterranean area might result in the incrimination of *E. plebejus, C. tenellus,* and/or other leafhoppers as vectors of *S. citri.*

It is of interest that *S. citri* can be acquired by various leafhoppers either through feeding, or through injection. The leafhoppers *Dalbulus maidis* De L. & W. and *Macrosteles fascifrons* Stål, efficient vectors of MLO agents of corn stunt and aster yellows, respectively, were injected with *S. citri* that presumably multiplied and attained high titers in these nontransmitting insects (167). Retention of MLO in nonvectors has been reported as early as 1952 (116) for the agents of aster yellows and corn stunt, acquired by injection, or by feeding *M. fascifrons* and *D. maidis* on diseased plants. Such retention did not render the insects infective, however. *Acholeplasma laidlawii* and *Acholeplasma granularum* presumably can multiply in these insects when introduced artificially (167). It has been demonstrated that *A. laidlawii* and *Mycoplasma gallisepticum* can enter a living plant via roots and be recovered from leaves (111), but in such plants there was no indication of an increase in titer. *S. citri* acquired through plant roots can only be recovered from leaves in less than 20% of samples (112).

### *Comparison Among Spiroplasma, Mycoplasma, and Acholeplasma*

In liquid media, *Spiroplasma* forms characteristic helical filaments, but on agar the 'fried egg' colonies of the three microorganisms are similar. *Spiroplasma* possesses rotary motility (39) despite the absence of demonstrable organelles and it has a layer of outside surface projections adherent to the cytoplasmic membrane. Another feature, the infection by a bacteriophage of type B morphology, was considered unique (31) because other viruses of Mollicutes described until now were of different morphology (72). Besides, all isolates from Morocco as well as from California seemed to carry this bacteriophage. The impression was created that the virus infection was a permanent association. The recent isolate from Israel (36) was free from such infection, thus dispelling the earlier assumption. The observed motility of *S. citri* suggests the presence of a fragile, contractile mechanism, that can only operate in optimal conditions. The microorganism loses its motility and helicity in aging broth cultures and does not possess it in agar (30). Other mycoplasmas have also been reported motile (23) but in a gliding fashion. Perhaps the unique surface projections of *S. citri* play a role in its movement. These projections are reminiscent of those seen in several negatively stained species of mycoplasmas (31) and in T-strains (12). The projections might also play a role as phage receptor sites.

## CORN STUNT SPIROPLASMA

The agent causing corn stunt disease has been reported isolated and cultured in a cell-free medium (27, 28). A critical analysis of the data was made in 1971 by Davis & Whitcomb (42) who discussed this, and similar claims of successful MLO cultivation, in the spirit of constructive comments. These authors concluded that the results could be interpreted as long-term maintenance, but that the corn stunt agent was not consistently isolated, passed through a sufficient number of serial subcultures with appropriate dilutions, or cloned and subcultured. Today there is no doubt that no veritable culture of the corn-stunt agent has been obtained and that the report was premature. Attempts to confirm this work have consistently failed to yield veritable cultures (13, 155). No representative prototype strain has been produced and deposited in a type culture collection. In fact, extensive attempts made by Davis and Whitcomb to obtain such cultures (personal communication to M. Klein) resulted only in retention of infectivity for limited, not prolonged, periods.

## *Electron Microscopy*

Since cultures of the corn stunt agent have not been available, work has concentrated on characterization of the agent in thin sections of plant and insect vector material (74, 75, 119, 150). In plants, filamentous forms, up to 2000 nm in length, were observed—while in vectors the MLO resembled cross sections of cultured Mollicutes, such as *Mycoplasma* and *Acholeplasma* species.Negative staining was applied to crude extracts prepared from diseased plant material and it was asserted that forms, characteristic for negatively stained mycoplasmas, were found only in diseased, but not in healthy material (47, 74). The authors used 2% phosphotungstic acid at pH 7 and claimed to have found characteristic filamentous structures of even caliber, often attached to spherical bodies. No mention was made of the occurrence of similar bodies in negatively stained juice from healthy plants. It is now known that healthy plant material contains structures that resemble negatively stained mycoplasmas (172). The artifacts do not appear, however, when plant extracts are treated with fixatives during extraction. Negative staining with phosphotungstic acid is known to alter the morphology of phospholipid membranes and the technique, as usually used, does not lend itself to the characterization of Mollicutes in crude extracts that contain other cellular material. According to Cole et al (31), this difficulty can be overcome only when the suspect microorganism can be serially propagated in artificial media. Wolanski (172) pointed out that one occasionally sees filamentous structures in negatively stained extracts from old infected corn plants with corn stunt, that may represent the helical filaments. As pointed out by several investigators (31, 172, 173) the problem of mycoplasma-like artifacts in host materials had not been overcome in the published work. Since the corn stunt agent has not been serially propagated in cell-free media, negative staining for its detection is of little value. The same comment applies to other MLO. Nevertheless, the observation of filaments that emerged from the main body of the corn stunt agent (28, 49) might not have been due to an artifact (172).

## *Optical Microscopy*

Crude extracts from diseased corn plants examined by dark field microscopy, showed the presence of short, helical filaments and small, round bodies (44). Filament lengths usually ranged from 2–4 μm, but in extracts from old diseased plants they were sometimes much longer. The helices showed motility (43) reminiscent of spirochetes and of the same kind of motility as *S. citri.* One type of motility was a rapid screw motion, which could lead to a back-and-forward progress; the second was a slow undulation and bending of filaments. Such helices were not observed in extracts from insect vectors, however (K. Maramorosch, unpublished data). Thicker sections observed by electron microscopy, and, more strikingly, freeze-etched preparations of diseased corn material (48) showed clearly the helical appearance of the microorganisms in plants.

Helical filaments, resembling those in broth cultures of *Spiroplasma citri,* were seen not only in dark field, but also in phase contrast microscopy in the sap expressed from corn (*Zea mais*) plants infected with corn stunt (47). Under phase contrast the filaments appeared 3–12 μm in length and about 25 nm in diameter. The amplitude of the spirals was approximately 0.4 μm and spherical bodies, 400–600 nm in diameter, were often seen attached to the filaments. Results of freeze-etching observations further supported these findings, revealing the three-dimensional aspects and details of surface structure of helical filaments within phloem cells of infected plants. Unfortunately the authors also relied, in their original report (47), on negative staining of crude juice, expressed from infected plants.

The resemblance between *S. citri* and the helical forms observed in corn stunt-infected plants under phase contrast, dark field, and electron microscopy, gave rise to speculation that these two kinds of microorganisms might be related forms. The helices were not found in corn stunt transmitting leafhopper vectors and they were abundant in older diseased plants and in extracted plant juice. It seems likely that the helices are formed under certain conditions that prevail in plant sap, but not in insect vectors. The two environments, the phloem sap of the corn plant and the cytoplasm of the invertebrate animal cell, might perhaps be roughly comparable to the liquid broth environment and the solid agar substrate, respectively. The related *S. citri* Mollicute does form helices in optimal growth conditions in liquid media, but not in agar.

It is usually assumed that the only instances in which helical forms were observed are those of *S. citri* and the corn stunt agent. However, such helical forms have also been noticed and reported in *Nicotiana rustica* infected with the agent of aster yellows (85). In this material helical forms occurred extremely rarely, compared to the rather common appearance in corn stunt-infected *Z. mais.* We have checked the working hypothesis that, perhaps, helices appear in monocotyledonous plants more frequently than in dicotyledonous. Onion (*Allium cepa*) seedlings were infected with aster-yellows agent by means of *Macrosteles fascifrons* vectors and thin sections of diseased plants were examined (K. Maramorosch and H. Hirumi, unpublished data). We found that the MLO profiles were similar to those in dicotyledonous host plants of the aster-yellows agent and that helical forms were as infrequent as in *N. rustica.* No spiral forms were observed in expressed onion sap (B. S. Skowronski, unpublished observations). This supports the view that the presence of frequent helical forms is a characteristic feature of *S. citri* and of the corn stunt agent. It is not, however, a unique feature of spiroplasmas and it might be characteristic of many plant-pathogenic MLO, frequent in some, and rare in others.

## *Serology*

The first evidence that MLO can be identified specifically by serological tests was provided by Marchoux et al (126). Crude extracts from corn stunt-infected plants were recently used in a similar manner and it was reported that of six antigens that were detected, four were found unrelated to antigens in healthy material (109). It has not been established in these tests whether the findings were indicative of MLO or of byproducts formed in diseased plants.

A rapid slide test has been developed recently for detecting the presence of antibodies against *S. citri*. The test (113) was based on a significant reduction of spiral forms in the presence of specific antibodies as viewed by dark field microscopy. This rapid test revealed that *S. citri* is antigenically related to the corn stunt MLO, but not to the MLO of aster yellows.

The serological relation between *S. citri* and the corn stunt MLO was also demonstrated by growth inhibition and precipitin tests (164). Growth-inhibiting antibodies directed against *S. citri* were first observed three to four weeks after the first immunization of rabbits receiving corn stunt agent. Growth inhibition was also observed with homologous antibody to *S. citri*, but not with antiserum obtained from rabbits receiving healthy corn antigen. Further evidence for the serological relation between *S. citri* and the corn stunt MLO came from precipitin ring tests. There was low immunological reactivity between serum and antigens in heterologous precipitin tests, whereas in the homologous *S. citri* combination the reactivity was high. This suggests, but does not prove, that the two microorganisms may share a number of different antigenic determinants.

In conclusion, it now seems that the causative agents of citrus stubborn disease and of corn stunt might belong to the same, or to closely related genera. It is likely, but not proven, that the corn stunt MLO is a member of the genus *Spiroplasma*. The MLO of aster yellows, where helices are formed very rarely (85), shows no serological or other relationship to *Spiroplasma* (113) and has to await further characterization and classification.

Plant pathologists have been using the vernacular term spiroplasma to describe the two serologically related agents, the MLO of corn stunt and *Spiroplasma citri*. This term might be condoned, provided one keeps in mind that it is only on the basis of an assumption, and not proper characterization, that these disease agents are grouped together.

## MOLLICUTE-LIKE ORGANISMS (MLO)

### *Morphology*

The plant- and insect-infecting MLO have been studied very extensively by thin section electron microscopy of tissues removed from diseased plants, and, to a lesser extent, insect vectors. These MLO represent a unique group of prokaryotes, always pathogenic to plants, but only rarely pathogenic to insect vectors.

The most extensive morphologic study of an MLO was that of the ultrastructure of the aster-yellows agent. It was among the first four MLO described in 1967 by the Japanese team (50). In order to lay a sound background for the morphological characterization of this and other MLO agents, an intensive study of nearly 3000 thin sections was made in our laboratory (83–85) to ascertain whether features ascribed to MLO of different plant diseases were sufficiently distinct to be considered as species specific, or whether all such features occur in a single type of MLO within one plant. The cytoplasmic components of MLO, seen in ultrathin sections are similar to those of *Mycoplasma* or *Acholeplasma* components. The cells are bounded by a unit membrane, there are ribosome granules, randomly distributed, and there is fibrillar nuclear material. The width of the limiting membrane of MLO, 8–10 nm, also corresponds with that of other Mollicutes. Profiles from thin sections indicate further similarities, such as a loose cytoplasm with well-defined ribosomes and nuclear material, or compact electron-dense cytoplasm with barely distinguishable nuclear material. Boatman (14) analyzed electron micrographs of two MLO-infecting leafhopper organs and found that they appeared particularly prone to show a dispersed cytoplasm and condensed nuclear material.

Other studies (75, 82, 119, 153) showed that the MLO in vectors appear quite similar to those in plants, except for the already mentioned frequency of, or appearance of, helices in plants (with corn stunt) as opposed to insect vectors. As already pointed out, helical forms have not yet been observed in insect vectors, nor in any other Mollicutes, except *Spiroplasma citri* and the MLO of corn stunt. In other aspects the ultrastructural characteristics of plant- and insect-infecting MLO in thin sections correspond to the basic criteria of the morphology of most vertebrate-infecting species of Mollicutes.

Osmotic fragility of MLO accounts for their morphological alteration, which makes difficult the interpretation of their ultrastructure. Growth conditions also influence pleomorphism and add to the confusion. The study of thin sections of aster-yellows MLO was based entirely on materials excised from plants grown under natural conditions and no artificial media were influencing the morphological characteristics of the MLO. Therefore variations in ultrastructure observed in the study can be ascribed to natural alterations. No physical factors, such as centrifugation, filtration, or rinsing, were applied. The only alterations were those usually accepted in studying the ultrastructure of biological properties by thin-sectioning techniques of electron microscopy.

Earlier descriptions of MLO, as well as those of well-defined Mollicutes, described so-called elementary bodies, that were sometimes believed to represent stages in the replication cycle. In MLO, very small spherules with or without internal substances, ranging from 30–80 nm, were frequently observed. These spherules probably represent transverse sections of the filaments and filamentous bodies. They are too small to contain the entire genome and thus they could not represent cross sections through spherical elementary bodies (130).

In general features the morphology of MLO in sieve tube elements, where these microorganisms grow in the phloem sap, resembles the morphology of other Mollicutes propagated in liquid media.

## *Intracellular Growth*

In addition to sieve tube elements, MLO occur also in phloem parenchyma cells (19, 35, 50, 70, 74–76, 79, 84, 114, 152, 175). Intracellular growth of MLO in such cells has been compared to the growth of Mollicutes on solid agar media (83). The growth of MLO inside living cells that contain normal cell organelles is sometimes considered a feature distinguishing MLO from other Mollicutes that grow on cells, but not within cells. The ability of MLO to grow intracellularly is not limited to phloem parenchyma cells of plants. In invertebrate hosts of the respective MLO species, ultrathin sections have also revealed the presence of these Mollicutes within the animal cell cytoplasm.

Certain differences in morphological features have been observed in MLO in phloem parenchyma cells. Colony type accumulations of tightly packed MLO were frequently observed in the cytoplasm (84). The colonies of aster-yellows MLO consisted of a single type of spherical or ovoid cells. No filaments or chain forms, budding, or binary fission were seen. The intracytoplasmic growth appears to continue until the phloem parenchyma cells are fully packed with MLO. Certain morphological variations, such as mushroom- or horseshoe-shaped forms, were also observed. It is feasible to assume that MLO multiplication in the phloem parenchyma cell cytoplasm differs from that in the liquid environment of sieve tube elements.

### *Natural Degeneration*

Ultrastructural abnormalities interpreted as degeneration were observed within phloem tissues of yellows-diseased plants (79, 83). The abnormalities comprised swelling of MLO, granulation, condensation of the cytoplasmic contents, formation of inclusion bodies, rupture of plasma membranes, and formation of cellular debris. These degenerative changes in spherical as well as in filamentous forms occurred not only in sieve elements but also in phloem parenchyma cells and companion cells. The changes resembled the degenerative stages described in liquid cultures of certain Mycoplasmatales (16, 115). Deposition of callose resulted in increased fluorescence (80).

### *Association with Viruses*

In recent years several viruses have been described in cultured species of Mollicutes and often listed as Mycoplasmatales viruses (72, 144). Of three viruses isolated from *Acholeplasma laidlawii,* two were shown to contain DNA, and the third, not yet fully characterized, was probably also a DNA virus. The capsid of one, MV-1, was helical, while the capsid of another, MV-L3, was cubic. The three viruses differed in plaque size.

In contrast, the virus associated with *S. citri,* not yet well characterized because of the lack of an indicator strain, resembled closely classical, tailed bacterial viruses of type B (20). No chemical analysis has been carried out and it is not yet known whether this virus contains DNA or RNA. The virus was seen attached to filaments of *S. citri* (31), with numerous incomplete phage heads on, or within, filaments. The phage head was usually hexagonal in profile, measuring approximately 50 nm in diameter. Individual capsomeres were approximately 8 nm wide with a central hole of 4 nm in diameter. The tail, 75–85 nm in length, probably noncontractile, showed 20–25 cross-striations. It is not known at present whether the *S. citri* virus that differs so strikingly from the known viruses of *Acholeplasma* is present in a state of lysogeny, or whether it represents a carrier state or pseudolysogeny (31), as suggested by the presence of numerous empty heads and polyheads. Its association with Moroccan and Californian isolates, but not with the latest isolate from Israel

(36), demonstrates that tailed bacteriophage-type viruses, as well as helical or cubical symmetry-type viruses, can infect wall-less Mollicutes.

In addition to the virus of the cultured *Spiroplasma citri,* electron microscopy has revealed rod-shaped, virus-like particles associated with several MLO, fixed within sieve elements of diseased plants. Ploaie (139, 141) described rod-shaped particles associated with the clover dwarf MLO. Giannotti et al (66) described rod-shaped particles associated with deteriorating MLO in three phyllody-infected species of plants and suggested that they might be viruses. Virus-like particles have been described in association with corn stunt MLO (74), but similar particles have been seen in control material. Allen (1) reported bacilliform virus-like particles associated with aster-yellows MLO. These particles seemed to align themselves on a dense membrane-like structure but no changes in the MLO were noted. Hirumi & Maramorosch (83) observed rod-shaped virus-like particles associated with aster-yellows MLO. It was found that tubular particles surrounded degenerating MLO in a large vacuole of a phloem parenchyma cell. Virus-like particles were claimed to occur in *Dalbulus elimatus,* but not in *Dalbulus maidis* leafhoppers that carried corn stunt MLO (74). These particles were described from cross sections of the brain, ventral ganglia, salivary glands, Malpighian tubules, and intestinal tracts (74). It is likely that these particles represented a normal cell component, rather than a virus.

Since MLO diseases of plants were earlier believed to be caused by viruses, the hypothesis that MLO are merely virus carriers, or vectors, has had certain appeal to plant pathologists (6, 7). There is no evidence to support this assumption, however, and there is ample evidence to refute such a hypothesis. The chemotherapy of MLO diseases in which both MLO and virus-like particles have been observed, resulted in remission of disease and disappearance of MLO, but not disappearance of virus-like particles (121, 122). The disappearance of MLO, following tetracycline treatment, accompanied by the remission of disease symptoms in practically all MLO diseases in which such tests have been carried out, supports the view that MLO itself, and not in conjunction with viruses, nor the viruses themselves, are the actual etiologic agents of these diseases. The recent demonstration that cultured *S. citri,* without bacteriophage infection, can induce citrus-stubborn disease (M. J. Daniels et al, unpublished observations) proves this contention.

It ought to be stressed here that the nature of the different virus-like particles observed in several MLO within plant cells has not been determined, because none of these MLO have been grown in cell-free media until now. If the particles represent viruses, as seems indicated by their morphology and size, one might speculate on their role in diseased plants and insect vectors. Could they be employed in future control of certain MLO diseases?

### *Dual Infections: MLO and Viruses*

Combined virus and MLO infections have been described in several instances (8, 9, 21, 26, 86) and summarized recently by Banttari & Zeyen (10). Oat-blue dwarf virus in combination with aster-yellows MLO causes a naturally occurring disease and both agents are transmitted by the same leafhopper vector, *Macrosteles fascifrons*

(8, 9). Dual infection results in external symptoms that do not occur in plants infected by either pathogen singly. The virus and MLO were usually found by electron microscopy in different phloem cells, and only rarely within the same cell. The same two disease agents are now being studied in the invertebrate host and vector, *M. fascifrons,* where both multiply before rendering the leafhopper infective (E. E. Banttari, personal communication). An association of MLO and virus in the cells of the salivary gland and in other organs of the vector has not yet been demonstrated.

The tristeza virus of citrus has been reported associated with MLO in *Citrus reticulata* (26). Severe disease symptoms result from such dual infection, while no conspicuous symptoms develop when the plants are infected by either the virus, or the MLO, alone. Occasionally both agents were observed by electron microscopy within a single phloem cell, but more commonly different cells contained the different types of pathogens.

*Cajanus cajan* witches'-broom disease from the Dominican Republic was studied by electron microscopy and the presence of MLO and of rhabdo-type virus particles reported in naturally infected plants (36). Recently, a second instance of a similar association was reported from Puerto Rico (124, 125). In both instances, MLO and rhabdo-type virus particles usually occurred in adjoining cells of the phloem. No close relationship between the two pathogens was found in dually infected plants. The vector or vectors of the two agents remain unknown.

*Opuntia tuna monstrosa* is the name of a horticultural variety of *Opuntia tuna.* It is now known that an MLO disease changes the robust *O. tuna* into the tiny ornamental plant. The infection results in the formation of numerous small adventitious branches. The natural mode of MLO transmission from cactus to cactus has not yet been determined and a leafhopper or psyllid vector might eventually be discovered. At present the only known means of transmitting the MLO is by grafting. Electron microscopy revealed that, in addition to MLO, there appeared in phloem cells of *O. tuna monstrosa* rod-shaped virus-like particles (121). At first it was not known whether the ornamental form required the combined action of MLO and virus, or only that of one of these agents. The question was solved by tetracycline treatment and subsequent electron microscopy observation of thin sections from plants that recovered temporarily. Remission of witches'-broom for up to 14 months occurred after tetracycline application (122). As expected, virus particles were not affected by the antibiotic treatment and were found in plant tissues of healthy appearing cacti, but MLO vanished a few days after the roots of *O. tuna monstrosa* were placed in a water solution of tetracycline hydrochloride. It was concluded that MLO alone was responsible for the *monstrosa* characteristics (122).

What is the biologic significance of viruses of MLO and of other Mollicutes? I would like to quote Clyde who pondered this question recently (29): "The discovery of the Mycoplasmatales viruses begs the question of the biologic significance of this unique group of infectious agents. Postulating parallels with bacterial viruses, one would expect that new tools have become available to analyze mycoplasma genetics; the new viruses could relate also to mycoplasma pathogenicity, as in the case of several bacterial diseases. Until the time that a virus-free indicator cell line is available, it is hazardous to assume that the appearance of lytic areas in indicator cell lawns exposed to test samples proves the presence of viruses in the samples. Investigators engaged in surveys of this sort must be prepared to characterize presumed new viruses by classical methods, and to demonstrate some biologic link between the isolates and their donor organisms. Meanwhile, the true biologic significance of this fascinating group of microbial parasites remains enigmatic."

### *Response to Antibiotics*

Tests with antibiotics have provided a simple means by which certain MLO diseases have been distinguished from virus diseases. The first report by Ishiie et al in 1967 (97) described in great detail the procedure, results, and conclusions reached. Plants were first immersed in a water solution containing tetracyclines at 1:100 or 1:1000 ppm, and then similarly treated at weekly intervals, sometimes via root immersion, at other times by spraying leaves of diseased plants. Electron microscopy observations demonstrated the disappearance of MLO from treated plants. Phytotoxicity was noted in almost all instances. This toxicity was often overlooked by those who used tetracyclines for MLO disease treatments during subsequent years. Only limited tests have been carried out to ascertain whether the tetracycline antibiotics, applied via roots and/or via leaves, actually entered the plants and whether they remained active. When such tests were made with aster-yellows diseased plants (100) it was established that no detectable amounts of tetracyclines were acquired via sprayed leaves or through soil drenching. These findings were confirmed with the MLO of clover phyllody disease, believed to be a strain of aster-yellows MLO (154). Extensive data on antibiotic spectra of MLO of aster yellows were presented (41) but evaluation of the results is difficult since there was no attempt made by the authors to ascertain the actual uptake and retention of antibiotic activity in treated plants. Tests were also reported with insect vectors of aster-yellows MLO and the observation made that transmission of MLO was impaired, or delayed, by tetracyclines, but not by penicillin (167). When vectors that acquired MLO, but did not yet become infective, were fed on plants treated with tetracyclines, the MLO incubation in such vectors was protracted. The tests, even though crude and poorly designed, strengthened the evidence that MLO are the actual causative agents of the aster-yellows disease. In addition, these tests confirmed the much more elaborate and accurate tests performed earlier in Japan and summarized recently (5). A group of workers from 13 institutions, coordinated by K. Yora of Tokyo University, tested the effects of tetracyclines on several MLO diseases, including aster yellows, mulberry dwarf, rice yellow dwarf, and potato witches'-broom in 1968. Tetracycline, chlortetracycline, dimethylchlortetracycline, and oxytetracycline were used. In some instances dimethylchlortetracycline, hexametaphosphate, and some other salts and chelates of tetracyclines were tested. Results of these very extensive tests were later confirmed, in general, by workers in the United States, France, Portugal, Czechoslovakia, India, and Canada (3, 16, 22, 33, 34, 40, 45, 51, 54–56, 73, 94, 96, 99, 102, 107, 110, 128, 129, 132, 134, 142, 149, 157–160, 163, 168, 174). The Japanese team concluded that tetracyclines did not permanently cure MLO-diseased plants, but caused temporary remission. When applied immediately before or after experimental inoculation of plants, infection was delayed or occasionally prevented. Several macrolides and other antibiotics, aside from tetracyclines, were tested and found ineffective. In this context the results obtained by Klein et al (101) might be discussed, as these authors observed improved plant growth, following the application of certain sulfa drugs to aster-yellows infected plants. The criteria of disease remission are subjective and might require more scrutiny in the future, to separate such remission as improved growth, or increased formation of chlorophyll, from the formation of normal-appearing flowers. Incidentally, in tests performed with chlortetracycline, in which aster-yellows diseased plants temporarily recovered and produced normal-appearing flowers (102), no viable seed has been obtained (M. Klein, personal communication). Since sterility is a common feature of MLO diseases of plants, it would seem worthwhile to propose, as a criterium for complete cure of an MLO disease, the obtaining of viable seed from treated plants. Until now, no compounds that would achieve this goal have been reported.

The extensive Japanese tests underscored the fact that treatment of plants in advanced stages of MLO diseases was much less effective than treatment during earlier phases of disease. Tetracycline uptake occurred through roots rather than through foliage, and repeated root immersion of hydroponically cultured plants was more effective than root immersion followed by foliage spraying. The effectiveness of various tetracycline antibiotics differed only slightly and the effects on transmission of MLO by insect vectors were not as distinct as in plants. A very interesting observation was made concerning the possible induced tolerance to tetracyclines. Symptoms once suppressed reappeared occasionally even when repeated antibiotic applications were being continued (5).

## RICKETTSIA-LIKE ORGANISMS (RLO)

The recognition that certain plant yellows disease agents are not among the unit membrane-bounded microorganisms designated in this review as MLO, dates back to an obscure paper by Giannotti et al (65) in which the authors described a walled bacterium-like organism in thin sections of dodder (*Cuscuta subinclusa*). The authors did not implicate rickettsiae specifically and described the microorganism as a bacterium so that little notice was made of this discovery by plant pathologists. The report has been overlooked when it was speculated for the first time that rickettsiae might someday be found as plant disease agents (42).

In 1972 an observation was made in our laboratory of microorganisms in the xylem of ratoon-stunted sugar cane from Puerto Rico (138). Further study of thin sections from this material led to the conclusion that the microorganisms were not MLO, but rather a small bacterium or a rickettsia (123). Since there was no evidence that the observed rickettsia-like organism was the causative agent of sugar cane ratoon stunt, the detailed observations were presented as a suggestion that rickettsiae might be found in diseased plants. Several other reports of RLO associated with different plant diseases have been published recently. In all instances, electron microscopy revealed the presence of microorganisms possessing a cell wall, as opposed to the unit membrane-bounded MLO (140). In addition, in the instance of clover club leaf disease, it was found that plants treated with penicillin showed remission of disease symptoms (170, 171). Pierce's disease symptoms were suppressed with tetracycline antibiotics (89).

While all MLO disease agents seem confined to phloem tissues, the RLO have been observed either in the phloem, or in the xylem tissues in specific diseases, but never in both phloem and xylem. The xylem-confined RLO have been found associated with sugar cane ratoon stunt (123, 138, 161), Pierce's disease of grapevine (71, 88), phony peach (90, 91, 135), and in the prune scalding disease (E. W. Kitajima and J. Fernandez-Valiela, personal communication). A recent report described bacteria in the xylem of sugar cane ratoon stunt that might be similar or identical to the RLO if and when properly compared (70). It is surprising that no reference has been made by the authors of the latter report of the earlier claim of the senior author (69) that ratoon stunt disease is definitely a virus disease and that tetracycline antibiotics had no effect on disease remission.

The phloem-limited RLO have been described in malformation of *C. subinclusa* (65), in citrus greening (145), in witches'-broom of willow (87), in clover club leaf (169, 171), and in little leaf of *Sida cordifolia* (81). An RLO disease of cereals (140) is probably in the same group. The morphological differences between RLO and MLO in thin sections of phloem, when fixation and staining procedures are identical, are illustrated in Figure 1. The distinct presence of a cell wall, as compared to a unit membrane, as well as the differences in the internal structure, are apparent. The cell wall of RLO is composed of two triple-layered parts, separated by an area approximately 20–25 nm in thickness. The outer wall is often rippled. Elongated forms and an internal structure characteristic of bacteria (123) and different from that of MLO, have been described by most authors. In the instance of penicillin-treated clover club leaf-diseased plants, no data have been presented on the effect of the antibiotic on RLO in the phloem.

It seems worthwhile to point out that the *Drosophila paulistorum* sterility factor, earlier described as mycoplasma-like (52, 53, 120), has a definite cell wall and is, therefore, similar to RLO and not to MLO. The etiologic agent of cytoplasmic incompatibility in *Culex pipiens* (176, 177), identified as *Wolbachia pipiens,* is also susceptible to antibiotic treatment and, morphologically, is rickettsia-like.

## CONCLUSIONS

The MLO diseases, sometimes described as plant mycoplasma diseases, are an ill-defined group at present. As far as is known, the only MLO that has been isolated and properly characterized, *Spiroplasma citri,* is a member of the class Mollicutes, but not a member of the family Mycoplasmataceae. Other MLO agents have been poorly characterized and no proper taxonomical classification is possible at this time. The agent of citrus-stubborn disease, *S. citri,* has been grown in cell-free media, properly characterized, and deposited in a type culture collection. The MLO of corn stunt appears related to *S. citri,* not only because of its morphological features that resemble the agent of citrus-stubborn disease, but more so because of results of serological tests. The MLO of aster yellows apparently differs serologically

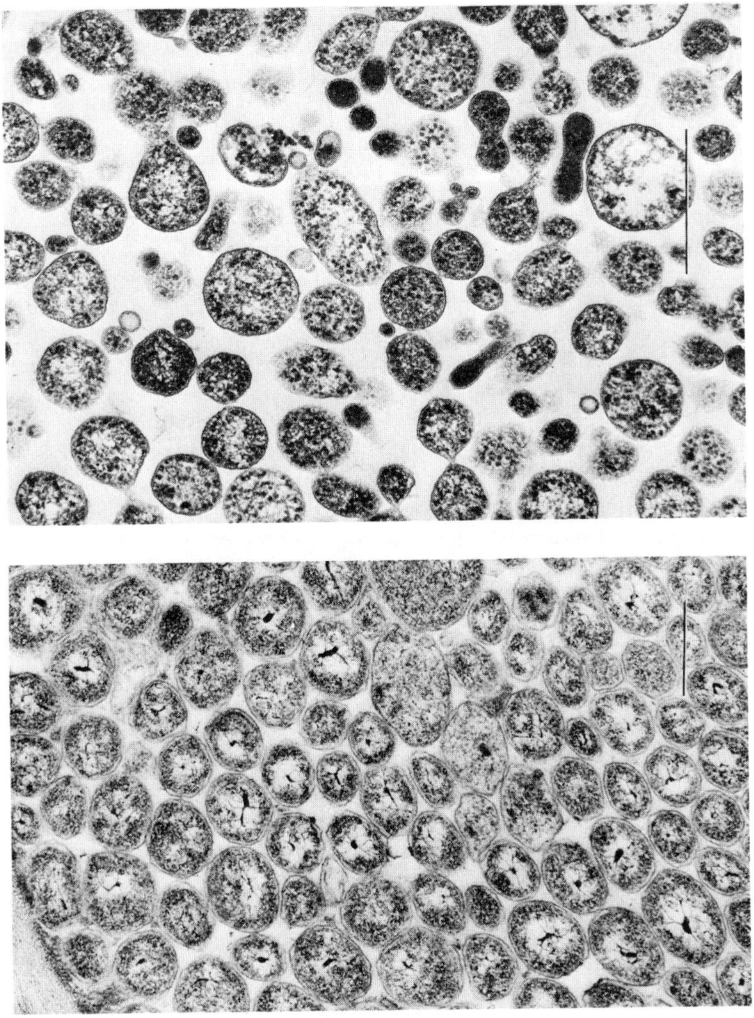

*Figure 1* Comparison between identically prepared cross sections of phloem cells from plants with MLO and RLO infection. Top: MLO of aster yellows in *Nicotiana rustica*; note pleomorphic bodies which are from 60–800 nm in diameter, of diverse electron density, with ribosome granules, with strands in nuclear region, having a unit membrane approximately 10 nm in thickness. Bar equals 500 nm. Bottom: RLO of *Sida cordifolia* witches'-broom disease; note fairly uniform, rounded bodies which are 300–800 nm in diameter, of medium electron opacity, with dispersed ribosomal and condensed nuclear material, and with distinct cell wall approximately 20 nm in thickness. Bar equals 500 nm. Original electron micrographs courtesy of H. Hirumi.

from *S. citri* and corn stunt MLO. Electron microscopy does not permit the distinction between various species of MLO that cause different, distinct plant diseases. Practically all forms of MLO described as characteristic for different yellows-type diseases have been observed to occur in a single plant experimentally infected with aster-yellows MLO. Nevertheless, electron microscopy can be used to distinguish the wall-less MLO from the walled, rickettsia-like organisms (RLO) recently discovered in plants.

In vivo chemotherapy with tetracycline antibiotics has been used successfully in distinguishing several plant MLO and RLO diseases from plant virus diseases. It can serve as a diagnostic tool, but less so in the cure or prevention of MLO diseases. The criteria for disease remission in plants have not been well defined and chemotherapy, not combined with electron microscopy, can be misleading in diagnosing MLO infection. When tetracycline applications are followed by MLO destruction in phloem cells of plants, as well as remission of disease, strong evidence is provided for MLO etiology of a disease (174). Treatment of insect vectors with tetracycline antibiotics gives less reliable results than treatment of plants. The RLO of plant diseases seem susceptible not only to tetracyclines, but also to penicillin, so that diagnosis can sometimes be made by penicillin alone. Electron microscopy has revealed some xylem-limited, and other phloem-limited RLO. Their distinct cell walls, 20–25 nm thick, place them outside the class Mollicutes. If RLO should be proven to belong to the Rickettsiales, hope for their eventual cultivation in cell-free media would be slimmer than hope for their cultivation if they were MLO. Viruses and virus-like particles of diverse morphology have been observed associated with MLO in plant cells in vivo, and with *S. citri* in vitro.

*Literature Cited*


1. Allen, T. C. 1972. *Virology* 47:491–93
2. Amici, A., Grancini, P., Osler, R., Refatti, E. 1972. *Riv. Patol. Veg.* 8: 21–50
3. Amin, P. W., Jensen, D. D. 1971. *Phytopathology* 61:696–702
4. Anonymous. 1972. A list of plant mycoplasma diseases in foreign countries. *Plant Prot.* 26:184–89
5. Asuyama, H., Iida, T. T. 1973. *Ann. NY Acad. Sci.* 225:50
6. Atanasoff, D. 1969. *Biol. Zentralbl.* 88: 571–74
7. Atanasoff, D. 1972. *Phytopathol. Z.* 74: 342–48
8. Banttari, E. E., Zeyen, R. J. 1970. *Phytopathology* 60:1282
9. Banttari, E. E., Zeyen, R. J. 1972. *Virology* 49:305–8.
10. Banttari, E. E., Zeyen, R. J. 1973. *Ann. NY Acad. Sci.* 225:503–8
11. Belly, R. T., Brock, T. D. 1972. *J. Gen. Microbiol.* 73:465–69
12. Black, F. T., Birch-Andersen, A., Freundt, E. A. 1972. *J. Bacteriol.* 111: 254–59
13. Blasingame, D. J. 1972. *Isolation and subculture of plant mycoplasma, and the effect of antibiotics on the organism in vivo and electron microscope studies of infected cells.* Phd thesis. Univ. Microfilms, Ann Arbor, Michigan. 97 pp.
14. Boatman, E. S. 1973. *Ann. NY Acad. Sci.* 225:172–80
15. Boatman, E. S., Kenny, G. E. 1970. *J. Bacteriol.* 101:262–77
16. Borges, M., Martins, M. M. 1972. *Agronomia Lusitana* 33:443–53
17. Bos, L. 1970. *Gewasbescherming* 1: 45–54
18. Bové, J. -M. et al 1973. *Ann. NY Acad. Sci.* 225:462–70
19. Bowyer, J. W., Atherton, J. G. 1970. *Aust. J. Biol. Sci.* 23:115–25
20. Bradley, D. E. 1967. *Bacteriol. Rev.* 31:230–314
21. Brcak, J., Kralik, O. 1969. *Biol. Plant.* 11:95–96

22. Brcăk, J., Kralik, O., Limberk, J., Ulrychova, M. 1969. *Biol. Plant.* 11:470–76
23. Bredt, W. 1973. *Ann. NY Acad. Sci.* 225:246–50
24. Calavan, E. C. 1973. New developments on stubborn disease. *Int. Org. Citrus Virol. Newslett.* 9:3 (Mimeographed)
25. Casper, Von R. 1969. *Nachrichtenbl. Pflanzenschutzdienst DDR* 21:177–82
26. Chen, M. -h., Kiyakawa, T., Matsui, C. 1972. *Phytopathology* 62:663–66
27. Chen. T. -A., Granados, R. R. 1970. *Phytopathology* 60:573
28. Chen, T. -A., Granados, R. R. 1970. *Science* 167:1633–36
29. Clyde, W. A. Jr. 1973. *Ann. NY Acad. Sci.* 225:159–60
30. Cole, R. M., Tully, J. G., Popkin, T. J., Bové, J. -M. 1973. *Ann. NY Acad. Sci.* 225:471–93
31. Cole, R. M., Tully, J. G., Popkin, T. J., Bové, J. -M. 1973. *J. Bacteriol.* 115: 367–86
32. Cousin, M. -T. 1972. *Le Selectionneur Francais* 15:1–27
33. Cousin, M. -T., Moreau, J. P. 1972. *Troisieme Congres de l'Union Phytopathologique Mediterraneenne, Oeiras—Portugal,* pp. 19–28
34. Cousin, M. -T., Staron, T. 1969. *Ann. Phytopathol.* 1:267–74
35. Cousin, M. -T., Ruegg, E. F., Kartha, K. K. 1972. *C. R. Acad. Sci.* 274: 538–41
36. Daniels, M. J. et al 1973. *Nature* 244: 523–24
37. Darland, G., Brock, T. D., Samsonoff, W., Conti, S. F. 1970. *Science* 170: 1416–1618
38. Darpoux, H. 1971. *Phytoma* 23:16–23
39. Davis, R. E. 1973. *Plant Dis. Rep.* 57:333–37
40. Davis, R. E., Whitcomb, R. F. 1969. *Phytopathology* 59:1556
41. Davis, R. E., Whitcomb, R. F. 1971. *Infec. Immunity* 2:201–8
42. Davis, R. E., Whitcomb, R. F. 1971. *Ann. Rev. Phytopathol.* 9:119–54
43. Davis, R. E., Worley, J. F. 1972. *Phytopathology* 62:752–53
44. Ibid 1973. 63:403–8
45. Davis, R. E., Whitcomb, R. F., Steere, R. L. 1968. *Science* 161:793–95
46. Davis, R. E., Whitcomb, R. F., Purcell, R. 1970. *Phytopathology* 60:573–74
47. Davis, R. E., Whitcomb, R. F., Chen, T. -A., Granados, R. R. 1972. In *Ciba Found. Symp. Pathogenic Mycoplasmas,* pp. 205–25
48. Davis, R. E., Worley, J. F., Whitcomb, R. F., Ishijima, T., Steere, R. L. 1972. *Science* 176:521–23
49. Davis, R. E., Worley, J. F., Whitcomb, R. F., Ishijima, T., Steere, R. L. 1972. *Phytopathology* 62:494
50. Doi, Y., Terenaka, M., Yora, K., Asuyama, H. 1967. *Ann. Phytopathol. Soc. Jap.* 33:259–66
51. Ehrenfeld, R. K. 1970. *Agr. Tec. Chile* 30: 43–50
52. Ehrman, L., Kernaghan, R. P. 1971. *J. Hered.* 62:67–71
53. Ehrman, L., Williamson, D. L. 1969. *Genetics* 62:193–99
54. Filer, T. H. 1973. *Plant Dis. Rep.* 57:341–43
55. Frederick, R. J., Klein, M., Maramorosch, K. 1971. *Plant Dis. Rep.* 55: 223–26
56. Freitag, J. H., Smith, S. H. 1969. *Phytopathology* 59:1820–23
57. Freundt, E. A. 1973. *Ann. NY Acad. Sci.* 225:7–13
58. Freundt, E. A. 1974. In *Bergey's Manual.* Baltimore: Williams & Wilkins. 8th ed. In press
59. Fudl-Allah, A. E. A., Calavan, E. C. 1972. *Phytopathology* 62:758
60. Ibid 1973. 63:256–59
61. Fudl-Allah, A. E. A., Calavan, E. C., Igwegbe, E. C. K. 1971. *Phytopathology* 61:1321
62. Ibid 1972. 62:729–31
63. Ghosh, S. K., Raychaudhuri, S. P. 1972. *Curr. Sci.* 41:235–41
64. Ghosh, S. K., Raychaudhuri, S. P., Chenulu, V. V., Varma, A. 1972. *Abstr. Symp. Mycoplasmal Dis. Chandigarh. Indian Nat. Sci. Acad. New Delhi,* 40 pp.
65. Giannotti, J., Vago, C., Marchoux, G., Duthoit, J. -L. 1970. *C. R. Acad. Sci.* 271:2118–19
66. Giannotti, J., Devauchelle, G., Vago, C. 1970. *Int. Congr. Microbiol., 10th, Mexico,* Abstr., p. 222
67. Giannotti, J., Vago, C., Sassine, J., Czarnecky, D. 1971. *C. R. Acad. Sci.* 272:1776–78
68. Giannotti, J., Marchoux, G., Leclant, F., Morvan, C. 1972. *Troisieme Congress de l'Union Phytopathologique Mediterraneenne, Oeiras—Portugal,* 21–28
69. Gillaspie, A. G. Jr. 1970. *Phytopathology* 60:1448–50
70. Gillaspie, A. G. Jr., David, R. E., Worley, J. F. 1973. *Plant Dis. Rep.* 57: 987–90
71. Goheen, A. C., Nyland, G., Lowe, S. K. 1973. *Phytopathology* 63:341–45
72. Gourlay, R. N. 1973. *Ann. NY Acad. Sci.* 225:144–48

73. Granados, R. R. 1969. *Phytopathology* 59:1556
74. Granados, R. R. 1969. *Contrib. Boyce Thompson Inst.* 24:173–87
75. Granados, R. R., Maramorosch, K., Shikata, E. 1968. *Proc. Nat. Acad. Sci. USA* 60:841–44
76. Granett, A. L. 1973. *Abstr. Int. Congr. Plant Pathol., 2nd,* 645
77. Hampton, R. O. 1972. *Ann. Rev. Plant Physiol.* 23:389–418
78. Hayflick, L., Arai, S. 1973. *Ann. NY Acad. Sci.* 225:494–502
79. Hiruki, C., Dijkstra, J. 1973. *Neth. J. Plant Pathol. 79:112–21*
80. Hiruki, C., Dijkstra, J. 1973. *Abstr. Int. Congr. Plant Pathol., 2nd,* 240
81. Hirumi, H., Kimura, M., Maramorosch, K., Bird, J. 1974. *Phytopathology* 64:In press
82. Hirumi, H., Maramorosch, K. 1969. *J. Virol.* 3:82–84
83. Hirumi, H., Maramorosch, K. 1972. *Phytopathol. Z.* 75:9–26
84. Ibid 1973. 77:71–83
85. Hirumi, H., Maramorosch, K. 1973. *Ann. NY Acad. Sci.* 225:201–22
86. Hirumi, H., Maramorosch, K., Hichez, E. 1973. *Phytopathology* 63:202
87. Holmes, F. O., Hirumi, H., Maramorosch, K. 1972. *Phytopathology* 62: 826–28
88. Hopkins, D. L., Mollenhauer, H. H. 1973. *Science* 179:298–300
89. Hopkins, D. L., Mortensen, J. A. 1971. *Plant Dis. Rep.* 55:610–12
90. Hopkins, D. L., French, W. J., Mollenhauer, H. H. 1973. *Phytopathology* 63: 443
91. Hopkins, D. L., Mollenhauer, H. H., French, W. J. 1973. *Phytopathology* 63: 1422–23
92. Horne, R. W. 1972. *Ciba Found. Symp. Pathogenic Mycoplasmas,* pp. 39–66
93. Horvath, J. 1970. *Növenytermeles* 19: 327–37
94. Huhtanen, D. P., Converse, R. H. 1971. *Phytopathology* 61:1137–39
95. Hull, R. 1971. *Rev. Plant Pathol.* 50:121–30
96. Igwegbe, E. C. K., Calavan, E. C. 1973. *Phytopathology* 63:1044–48
97. Ishiie, T., Doi, Y., Yora, K., Asuyama, H. 1967. *Ann. Phytopathol. Soc. Jap.* 33:267–75
98. Kitajima, E. W., Costa, A. S. 1970. *Cienc. Cult. Sao Paulo* 22:351–63
99. Klein, M., Frederick, R. J., Maramorosch, K. 1971. *Phytopathology* 61:130
100. Ibid 1972. 62:111–15
101. Klein, M., Frederick, R. J., Maramorosch, K. 1973. *Ann. NY Acad. Sci.* 225:522–30
102. Kleinhempel, H., Lehmann, W., Spaar, D. 1971. *Fortschrittsber. Landwirt. Nahrungsgüterwirt* 9:3–78
103. Kleinhempel, H., Müller, H. M., Spaar, D. 1972. *Arch. Pflanzenschutz* 8:361–70
104. Kleinhempel, H., Müller, H. M., Spaar, D. 1972. *Nachrichtenbl. Pflanzenschutzdienst DDR* 26:1–3
105. Kleinhempel, H., Müller, H. M., Spaar, D. 1973. *Abstr. Int. Congr. Plant Pathol., 2nd,* 641
106. Krass, C. J., Gardner, M. W. 1973. *Int. J. Syst. Bacteriol.* 23:62–64
107. Lin, S. -C, Lee, C. -S. 1964. *Sugarcane Pathol. News* 3:2–3
108. Lombardo, G., Pignattelli, P. 1970. *Ann. Microbiol.* 20:83–88
109. McBeath, J. H., Chen, T. -A. 1973. *Phytopathology* 63:803
110. McCoy, R. E. 1972. *Plant Dis. Rep.* 56:1019–21
111. McIntosh, A. H., Maramorosch, K. 1973. *Ann. NY Acad. Sci.* 225:330–33
112. McIntosh, A. H., Maramorosch, K. 1973. *Abstr. Int. Congr. Plant Pathol., 2nd,* 642
113. McIntosh, A. H., Skowronski, B. S., Maramorosch, K. 1974. *Phytopathol. Z.* In press
114. Maillet, P. -L., Gourret, J. -P., Hamon, C. 1968. *C. R. Acad. Sci.* 266:2309–11
115. Maniloff, J. 1970. *J. Bacteriol.* 102: 561–72
116. Maramorosch, K. 1952. *Phytopathology* 42:663–68
117. Ibid 1972. 62:1230–31
118. Maramorosch, K. 1974. *Indian Nat. Acad. Sci., Bahadur Shah Zalar Marg, New Delhi.* Proceeding of Symp. at Chandigarh. In press
119. Maramorosch, K., Shikata, E., Granados, R. R. 1968. *Trans. NY Acad. Sci.* 30:841–55
120. Maramorosch, K., Granados, R. R., Hirumi, H. 1970. *Advan. Virus Res.* 16:135–93
121. Maramorosch, K., Klein, M., Wolanski, B. S. 1972. *Phytopathology* 62:497
122. Maramorosch, K., Klein, M., Wolanski, B. S. 1972. *Experientia* 28:362–63
123. Maramorosch, K., Plavsic-Banjac, B., Bird, J., Liu, L. J. 1973. *Phytopathol. Z.* 77:270–73
124. Maramorosch, K., Hirumi, H., Kimura, M., Bird, J., Vakili, N. G. 1974. *FAO Plant Prot. Bull.* 22:In press
125. Maramorosch, K., Hirumi, H., Kimura, M., Bird, J., Vakili, N. G. *Phytopathology* 64:In press

126. Marchoux, G., Giannotti, J., Quiot, J. -B., Marou, J., Vago, C. *Acad. Agr. Fr.* 55:191–96
127. Marchoux, G., Leclant, F., Giannotti, J., Cadilhac, B. 1972. *Troisieme Congres de l'Union Phytopathologique Mediterraneenne, Oeiras—Portugal,* pp. 43–52
128. Martinez, A. L., Nora, D. M., Armedilla, A. L. 1970. *Plant Dis. Rep.* 54:1007–9
129. Moreau, J. -P., Cousin, M. -T., Staron, T., Faivre-Amiot, A. 1972. *Ann. Phytopathol.* 2:239–43
130. Morowitz, H. J., Wallace, D. C. 1973. *Ann. NY Acad. Sci.* 225:62–73
131. Müller, H. M., Kleinhempel, H., Spaar, D., Müller, H. J. 1973. *Advan. Phytopathol. Pflanzenschutz* 9:95–104
132. Nariani, T. K., Raychaudhuri, S. P., Viswanath, S. M. 1971. *Curr. Sci.* 40:552
133. Nasu, S., Sugiura, M., Wakimoto, T., Iida, T. 1967. *Ann. Phytopathol. Soc. Jap.* 33:343–44
134. Nyland, G. 1971. *Phytopathology* 61: 904–5
135. Nyland, G., Goheen, A. C., Lowe, S. K., Kirkpatrick. H. C. 1973. *Phytopathology* 63:1275–78
136. Pereira, A., Lima, G., Oliveira, B. S. Jr. 1971. *Arq. Inst. Biol. Sao Paulo* 38: 191–200
137. Petru, E., Limberk, J., Ulrychova, M., Brcak, J. 1971. *Biol. Plant.* 13:391–95
138. Plavsic-Banjac, B., Maramorosch, K. 1972. *Phytopathology* 62:498–99
139. Ploaie, P. G. 1971. *Rev. Roum. Biol. Ser. Bot.* 16:3–6. Transl. *Rev. Plant Pathol.* 1972. 51:223
140. Ploaie, P. G. 1973. *Abstr. Proc. Int. Congr. Plant Pathol., 2nd,* 643
141. Ploaie, P. G. 1973. *Micoplasma si bolile proliferative la plante.* Bucharest: Ceres. 178 pp. (In Romanian)
142. Rao, P. S. et al 1972. *Abstr. Symp. Mycoplasmal Dis. Chandigarh. Indian Nat. Sci. Acad. New Delhi,* p. 26
143. Razin, S., Hasin, M., Neeman, Z., Rottem, S. 1973. *J. Bacteriol.* 116:1421–35
144. Robertson, J., Gomersall, M., Gill, P. 1972. *J. Microbiol.* 18:1971–72
145. Saglio, P., Lafleche, D., Bonissol, C., Bové, J. -M. 1971. *Physiol. Veg.* 9: 569–82
146. Saglio, P., Lafleche, D., Bonissol, C., Bové, J. -M. 1971. *C. R. Acad. Sci.* 272:1387–90
147. Saglio, P., Lafleche, D., L'Hospital, M., Dupont, G., Bové, J. -M. 1972. *Ciba Found. Symp. Pathogenic Mycoplasmas,* pp. 187–203
148. Saglio, P. et al 1973. *Int. J. Syst. Bacteriol.* 23:191–204
149. Schwarz, R. E., Van Vuuren, S. P. 1971. *Plant Dis. Rep.* 55:747–50
150. Shikata, E., Maramorosch, K. 1969. *Phytopathology.* 59:1559
151. Shikata, E., Maramorosch, K., Ling, K. C. 1969. *FAO Plant Prot. Bull.* 17:121–28
152. Sinha, R. C., Paliwal, Y. C. 1969. *Virology* 39:759–67
153. Ibid 1970. 40:665–72
154. Sinha, R. C., Peterson, E. A. 1972. *Phytopathology* 62:377–83
155. Skowronski, B. S., Maramorosch, K., McIntosh, A. H. 1974. *Plant Dis. Rep.* 58:In press
156. Spaar, D., Kleinhempel, H., Müller, H. M. 1972. *Arch. Pflanzenschutz* 8: 175–88
157. Staron, T., Cousin, M. -T., Kollmann, A. 1969. *Ann. Phytopathol.* 1:465–66
158. Staron, T., Kollmann, A., Cousin, M. -T., Faivre-Amiot, A., Moreau, J. -P. 1970. *Ann. Phytopathol.* 2:547–53
159. Story, G. E. 1969. *Investigation of papaya viruses and association of a mycoplasma-like organism with the bunchy top disease of Carica papaya L. in the Dominican Republic.* Ph.D. Thesis No. 69–14, 163. Univ. Microfilms, Ann Arbor, Michigan, pp. 935b–936b
160. Tahama, Y., Shikata, E., Murayama, D. 1972. *Bull. Hiroshima Agr. Coll.* 4: 198–207
161. Teakle, D. S., Smith, P. M., Steindl, D. R. L. 1973. *Aust. J. Agr. Res.* 24: 869–74
162. Terenaka, J., Otsuka, K. 1973. *Bull. Coll. Agr. Utsunomiya Univ.* 8:11–19
163. Thirumalachar, M. J. 1972. *Abstr. Symp. Mycoplasmal Dis. Chandigarh. Indian Nat. Sci. Acad. New Delhi*
164. Tully, J. G., Whitcomb, R. F., Bové, J. -M., Saglio, P. 1973. *Science* 182P: 827–29
165. Vago, C., Giannotti, J. 1972. *Physiol. Veg.* 10P:87–101
166. Whitcomb, R. F., Davis, R. E. 1970. *Ann. Rev. Entomol.* 15:405–64
167. Whitcomb, R. F., Davis, R. E. 1970. *Infec. Immunity* 2:209–15
168. Whitcomb, R. F., Tully, J. G. 1973. *Abstr. Int. Congr. Plant Pathol., 2nd,* 647
169. Windsor, I, M., Black, L. M. 1972. *Phytopathology* 62:1112
170. Ibid 1973. 63:1139–48
171. Ibid 44–46
172. Wolanski, B. S. 1973. *Ann. NY Acad. Sci.* 225:223–35

173. Wolanski, B. S., Maramorosch, K. 1970. *Virology* 42:319–27
174. Wolanski, B. S., Klein, M., Maramorosch, K. 1971. *Phytopathology* 61:917
175. Worley, J. F. 1970. *Phytopathology* 60:284–92
176. Yen, J. H., Barr, A. R. 1971. *Nature* 232:657–58
177. Yen, J. H., Barr, A. R. 1973. *J. Invertebr. Pathol.* 22:242–50

# VIRUS-INDUCED MODIFICATION OF CELLULAR MEMBRANES RELATED TO VIRAL STRUCTURE

❖1641

*Daniel B. Rifkin*[1] *and James P. Quigley*
Department of Chemical Biology, The Rockefeller University, New York, N.Y. 10021 and Department of Microbiology, SUNY-Downstate Medical Center, Brooklyn, N.Y. 11203

*All nature is but art unknown to thee,*
*All chance, direction which thou canst not see;*
*All discord, harmony not understood . . .*

Alexander Pope
1733

CONTENTS

INTRODUCTION .......... 325
ARBOVIRUSES .......... 327
RHABDOVIRUSES .......... 330
RNA TUMOR VIRUSES .......... 333
MYXOVIRUSES .......... 336
PARAMYXOVIRUSES .......... 339
HERPES VIRUSES .......... 341
POX VIRUSES .......... 343
SUMMARY AND DISCUSSION .......... 345

## INTRODUCTION

During the last few years it has become apparent that animal viruses can be used as probes for examining eukaryotic cell membranes. Many of these viruses derive their envelopes from pre-existing cellular membranes and, to a certain extent, can be thought of as fragments of cellular membrane. As derivatives of membranes,

[1]Supported by NIH Grant CA-13138 and Faculty Research Award No. PRA-99 from the American Cancer Society.

however, the animal viruses have certain features which make them unique tools. They can be purified relatively simply and to a degree which is difficult to obtain with other subcellular membranous structures. They contain few macromolecular components, all of which can be characterized by present techniques. Many animal viruses inhibit cellular biosynthetic processes during their own replication, and, therefore, viral membrane biogenesis can be studied against a low or nonexistent background of cell-directed synthesis. Finally, different animal virus types appear to utilize different components of the cellular membrane system; thus the selection of a given virus may yield membranous particles derived from the host cell's nuclear membrane, plasma membrane, or endoplasmic reticulum.

The information which can be gained from the study of animal viruses and their interactions with host cell membranes is quite diverse. The flow of both protein and lipid into the newly forming virus particles can be followed in order to explore the organization and modification of membranes. Moreover, those viruses which form their membranes de novo present the experimenter with the unique opportunity to study membrane biogenesis under conditions where no cellular membrane serves as precursor. Analysis of the process of budding might yield information about the physical requirements for the production of new viral membrane structures since certain physical parameters such as surface tension, radius of curvature, and lipid packing must be considered in understanding the formation of particles the size of viruses. The lipid composition of particular cellular membranes can be determined by examining those viruses which bud from the membrane of interest, since the lipid content of enveloped viruses closely resembles that of their membrane of origin. The study of experimentally induced changes in cellular membrane lipids is greatly facilitated also, since the changes can be monitored far more easily by examining purified viruses released from the treated cells than by isolating the host cell membranes themselves. The modification of cell membranes by viruses also may yield information on the mechanism of membrane fusion and the molecules required for fusion to take place. Finally, viral modification of cellular membranes may account for certain of the abnormal patterns of cell growth and cell-cell recognition seen in vitro.

Therefore, we thought it appropriate to write a critical review of the literature dealing with the following general areas: 1. the effects of viral infection on the composition of cellular membranes, and 2. the relationship between the composition of the cell membrane and that of viruses which derive from them. A description of the major groups of viruses and a short summary of the salient aspects of their structure and replication has been presented in order to lay the foundation for more pertinent literature. In addition Table 1 lists the viruses discussed and the major groups to which they belong. Only those changes in cellular membranes related to structural features of the virus have been considered. Thus, much of the immunological work describing the appearance of new surface antigens on virally infected or transformed cells has not been discussed. Likewise, certain studies on virally induced alterations of cellular metabolism, which apparently have only indirect effects on cellular membranes, have not been reviewed.

**Table 1** Major subgroups and their constituents

| | Virus subgroup | | | | | | |
|---|---|---|---|---|---|---|---|
| | Arbo | Rhabdo | Oncorna | Myxo | Paramyxo | Herpes | POX |
| viruses: | Sindbis | Vesicular Stomatitis | Rous Sarcoma | Influenza | SV5 | Herpes Simplex | Vaccinia |
| | Semliki Forest | Rabies | BAI | | NDV | Pseudorabies | |
| | | | AMV | | Measles | | |
| | | | Rauscher Leukemia | | Mumps | | |

## ARBOVIRUSES

The arboviruses are among the smallest of the enveloped RNA viruses (38). They are composed of 6–8% RNA, 30% lipid, and 65% protein (94). These viruses have a diameter of 400–700 Å (1, 77) as determined by electron microscopy. They possess a nucleoprotein core surrounded by a lipid-containing membrane. The viral membrane is covered with morphologically identifiable spikes. The protein composition of arboviruses is relatively simple compared to that of other RNA viruses as there are only three structural proteins in the intact virion. One is associated with the internal core structure, while the other two are the glycoproteins which constitute the spikes on the surface of the virion (19, 111, 114, 126, 127).

Unlike many other enveloped RNA viruses whose internal structure becomes visible only when the virion begins to bud from the cell plasma membrane, the RNA and the internal protein of the arboviruses coalesce to form morphologically visible particles in the host cell cytoplasm (1). These nucleoids then migrate either to the inner surface of the plasma membrane (group A arboviruses) (1, 42, 47, 52, 83) or to the membranes of cytoplasmic vacuoles (group B arboviruses) (41, 77). The nucleoid buds through the appropriate membrane and thus is enveloped by a host cell membrane. Brown, Waite & Pfefferkorn (14) have examined sindbis virus maturation by freeze-fracture techniques. They have proposed that the high affinity of viral nucleocapsid for surface membranes is the driving force for the extrusion of the viral particle through the membrane. The authors state that "a wave of capsomere-membrane interactions would work its way around the nucleocapsid until the membrane was brought into contact with itself at the base of the virion."

It is not known whether the nucleocapsid migrates to specific regions of the plasma membrane prior to budding or whether the migration is nonspecific, with budding occurring at random points on the plasma membrane. Direct visualization of the cell surface by freeze-fracture and surface-replica techniques indicates that the budding of sindbis virus is not random but occurs preferentially at specific areas of the cell surface (9, 14). If unique regions for budding on the plasma membrane exist, the recognition of these areas by the viral nucleocapsid must involve either specific protein-protein or protein-lipid interactions. The data in support of these possibilities will be discussed below.

At some time prior to the final step in the maturation of the virion there must be a migration of cellular proteins out of the budding area of the membrane, since a mature sindbis virion is devoid of any cellular structural proteins and contains only the three structural proteins of the virus (19, 111, 114, 126, 127). The absence of cellular proteins in a specific region of the surface membrane may serve as a recognition site for the nucleocapsid. However, it is not clear whether the loss of cellular membrane proteins occurs prior to the association of the nucleocapsid with the inner surface of the plasma membrane, or concomitantly with or possibly as a result of this association. It also is possible that the expulsion of cellular proteins occurs late in the morphogenesis of the budding virus (14) and is not involved in nucleocapsid recognition.

It has been shown that newly synthesized viral glycoproteins are associated with the cell plasma membrane early after infection. Bose & Brundige (13) fractionated cellular membranes from sindbis virus-infected cells and demonstrated that labeled viral glycoproteins were found to be associated specifically with surface membranes as early as 4 hr post-infection. The early presence of viral envelope glycoproteins in the surface membrane fraction suggests that these proteins possibly modify the membrane prior to viral envelopment. It would be of interest to perform similar studies on the membrane association of the proteins of the group B arboviruses, since these viruses are reported to mature at the surface of internal cytoplasmic membranes (1, 42, 47, 52, 83). At early times after infection, there should be viral glycoproteins associated with the internal membranes rather than the plasma membrane.

The presence of viral glycoproteins on the cell surface membrane (13) may provide the recognition sites for the nucleocapsid in those areas which will be the budding sites for the virus. Detailed studies on the isolated sindbis virion, however, have shown that direct protein-protein interactions between the nucleocapsid protein and the viral glycoproteins probably do not occur since the two glycoproteins do not penetrate the lipid bilayer of the viral membrane. The two experimental approaches which have yielded data to support this conclusion involve treatment of virus with proteolytic enzymes (19) and examination of purified virions by X-ray diffraction (50). Compans (19) has shown that intact sindbis virus can be subjected to bromelain digestion under conditions which do not destroy the integrity of the viral membrane. Externally located viral glycoproteins are completely removed by exposure to this proteolytic enzyme. No portion of either of the two membrane polypeptides remains after treatment. Therefore, it seems that the glycoproteins are attached to the surface of the viral membrane and do not penetrate the lipid bilayer. Harrison et al (50) have studied the X-ray diffraction patterns of sindbis virus particles, and from the resulting density profile these authors conclude that there is little or no protein spanning the lipid bilayer. Moreover, it appears that the hydrophilic portions of the lipid bilayer are in direct contact with the protein of the nucleocapsid on one side and the viral glycoproteins on the other.

The fact that viral proteins do not span the lipid bilayer (19, 50) poses an interesting problem. If the arbovirus nucleocapsid does recognize specific regions of host cell membrane when budding begins (9, 14), then it might only be recognizing lipid differences within the plasma membrane since the nucleocapsid protein does not interact directly with the envelope proteins (19, 50). A modification of host cell membranes by viral infection resulting in the formation of a recognition site thus may be mediated through specific lipid-lipid and lipid-protein interactions.

Pfefferkorn & Hunter (94) analyzed the phospholipids and neutral lipids of sindbis virus and found a high content of sphingomyelin and cholesterol in the virus compared to that in the whole cell. Although unexplained at the time, the enrichment in these two lipids, subsequently found for a number of enveloped viruses, probably reflects the plasma membrane origin of the viral envelope.

David (32) examined the phospholipid and fatty acid composition of sindbis virus grown in both BHK cells and chick embryo fibroblasts (CEF). The data were compared to that of the whole cells and the respective isolated plasma membranes. The phospholipid compositions of sindbis virions isolated from the two different host cells were shown to be similar. The phospholipid composition of the BHK-derived virus was strikingly similar to that of the BHK plasma membrane, except for the absence of a minor phospholipid, phosphatidyl inositol, in the virus preparations. In the case of CEF-derived virus, the phospholipid composition did not appear to reflect the composition of the host cell plasma membrane. However, the CEF plasma membrane preparation did not exhibit the characteristic increase in sphingomyelin content and decrease in phosphatidyl choline content found in many plasma membrane preparations (93). These observations suggest that the CEF plasma membrane preparation may not have been as pure as the BHK plasma membrane preparation.

A similar comparison of viral and cellular fatty acids, also reported by David (32), indicates that the compositions of different fatty acid classes were similar for the CEF-derived and BHK-derived virus preparations. Again, the composition of the virus did not reflect the composition of the CEF plasma membrane, but it did appear to resemble that of the BHK plasma membrane. It was suggested in these studies that the selectivity of the virus for a certain lipid composition reflected the specific lipid affinities of the arbovirus envelope proteins. In order to examine the question further, David (32) analyzed the fatty acid compositions of sindbis virus and vesicular stomatitis virus, a rhabdovirus, grown in the two different host cells. The two viruses have distinctly different polypeptide compositions. When CEF were used as the host cells, the fatty acid compositions of the two viruses were different. When BHK cells were employed, the fatty acid compositions of the viruses were nearly identical. Thus, although both the phospholipid and fatty acid data from the CEF system and the viruses grown in these cells were consistent with the suggestion that a part of the viral lipid composition results from viral protein selectivity, the data from BHK cells indicated that the host cell determined almost exclusively the lipid composition of the enveloped viruses. This apparent discrepancy has yet to be resolved.

Renkonen and co-workers have studied the lipid composition of another group A arbovirus, Semliki Forest Virus (102). Their studies show that the phospholipid and cholesterol composition of the virus closely resembles that of the host cell plasma membrane and is distinct from the phospholipid and cholesterol compositions of the whole cell and of the endoplasmic reticulum. Additional studies from the same laboratory demonstrate that each type of phospholipid has a specific pattern of fatty acids which is unique for that phospholipid class. When the fatty acids from each type of phospholipid are examined in virus, plasma membrane, endoplasmic reticulum, and whole cells, the viral fatty acid pattern is found to resemble most closely that of the plasma membrane. This type of analysis is more extensive and, therefore, more convincing than the simple analysis of a single fatty acid composition in a given membrane. The data from Renkonen et al (102) thus suggest that the lipid composition of the virus is determined by the host cell plasma membrane. These fatty acid analyses should be extended to the study of a single type of virus grown in different host cells and different types of virus grown in a single host cell, as in David's studies (32). It is of interest to note that Laine et al (73) estimated that there were about 25 polar lipid molecules for one envelope protein molecule in an arbovirus. Therefore, each of the minor lipids, not exceeding 4% of the total lipid, were present in less than equimolar amounts when compared to the virus envelope proteins. Since these minor components taken together form a sizable fraction of the viral lipids, the calculations of Laine et al imply a certain nonspecificity in lipid affinities of viral envelope proteins.

## RHABDOVIRUSES

The rhabdoviruses are enveloped RNA-containing viruses with a unique bullet-shaped structure (38), approximately 680 Å in diameter and 1750 Å long. The envelope of the virion is covered with 100 Å long projections. After infection and passage of vesicular stomatitus virus (VSV) at high multiplicities, noninfectious interfering particles, called T particles, are produced (38). These spherical structures, 650 Å in diameter, contain all of the viral proteins but possess only one third of the amount of viral RNA present in infectious particles. In the discussion which follows we shall not consider T particles, since under normal conditions they are either absent or represent only a small proportion of the virus population.

Purified VSV is composed of 3% RNA, 64% protein, 13% carbohydrate, and 20% lipid (80, 81). The viral envelope appears to be acquired from the host cell plasma membrane as the virion buds through the cell surface (38). There are reports that a second membrane exists immediately beneath the viral envelope (38) but these observations remain to be confirmed by biochemical techniques and chemical analysis. The viral RNA is associated with a specific set of proteins and the resulting complex appears as a striated, coiled nucleocapsid within the interior of the virus particle (38).

The organization of the proteins of rhabdoviruses (15, 48, 64, 65, 68, 79, 132, 134, 135), as exemplified by VSV, is generally the same as that found for a number of other enveloped viruses. A glycoprotein (G) is located on the outer surface of the virion and presumably forms the membrane spikes. A nonglycosylated protein (N) is associated with the nucleocapsid. A second nonglycosylated polypeptide (S) is associated with the viral membrane and can be selectively released from the virus by detergent treatment. It is possible that S lines or partially covers the internal surface of the viral membrane, as has been postulated for the "M" protein of the myxovirus, influenza (see below).

Wagner and his collaborators have found that the viral structural proteins are synthesized at or near sites which reflect their final association with intracellular components (133, 136). The nucleocapsid protein N is synthesized in the cytoplasm and can be found in cellular membrane fractions only 1–2 hr following a radioactive pulse. After a relatively short radioactive pulse the glycoprotein G is associated predominantly with a smooth membrane fraction which is enriched in plasma membrane marker enzymes. These results imply that the G protein may be synthesized in close proximity to its insertion site on the surface membrane. The N protein, however, is apparently synthesized on soluble polyribosomes, becomes associated with the viral progeny RNA, and then migrates to the surface membrane. The nonglycosylated viral membrane protein, S, is found complexed with the endoplasmic reticulum and to a lesser extent with smooth membrane. Cohen et al (18), however, showed that protein S could bind strongly to uninfected cell plasma membranes in vitro. Thus the presence of protein S in isolated membranes from infected cells does not necessarily indicate its in vivo site of synthesis, and its nature and role remain uncertain. Cohen et al (18) further demonstrated that the isolated spike protein G does not bind to uninfected cell membranes in vitro and is detectable in infected cell plasma membranes less than 5 min after a radioactive pulse. David (33) has examined the rate of incorporation of the S and G proteins into the host cell plasma membrane. He suggests that the two proteins must be synthesized close to or complexed with the cell surface membrane because of the short time (30 sec) required for their synthesis and incorporation into the plasma membrane. The interpretation of all of these studies is difficult since the purity of the various membrane fractions was not accurately known, and therefore, the reported distribution of viral protein in specific cellular membrane fractions must be considered with some caution. It is clear from these studies, however, that the analysis of viral membrane proteins in a cell system in which host protein synthesis is inhibited provides a model for examining the biogenesis of specific membrane structures.

Printz & Wagner (98) have described a temperature sensitive mutant of VSV, Ts-52, which may provide information on the conformational requirements for the insertion of proteins into a biological membrane. During infection with Ts-52, at the nonpermissive temperature, protein G is neither incorporated into the viral or host cell membrane, nor is it glycosylated. Normal cellular glycosylation reactions continue to function normally in the Ts-52–infected cells, as judged by glycolipid synthesis. The study of other viral systems has shown that glycosylation of viral membrane proteins occurs after insertion of the protein into the membrane. Therefore, it appears that the conformation of protein G at the restrictive temperature, in Ts-52–infected cells, prevents its insertion into the cell membrane and precludes its glycosylation. The relationship of the defectiveness of protein G to other virally induced cell membrane modifications, such as the association of protein M with infected cell membranes and the association of nucleocapsid with the surface membrane, should be examined in the mutant-infected cells.

The lipids of two strains of VSV and of their host cells have been examined by McSharry & Wagner (80). They grew a specific strain of vesicular stomatitis virus, $VS_{Ind}$, in two separate host cells, L-cells and chick embryo cells. No significant differences could be found in the relative proportions of neutral lipids and phospholipids or in the cholesterol:phospholipid molar ratios for the $VS_{Ind}$ virus grown in the two cell types. By contrast, differences were found in the lipid profiles of two strains of VSV, $VS_{Ind}$ and $VS_{NJ}$, differing by a single protein component, if they were both grown in L-cells. From these experiments McSharry & Wagner (80) concluded that a given virus determines to some extent which lipids are incorporated into the viral envelope. The authors suggest that viral proteins might be involved in rearranging pre-existing cellular lipids to form specific lipoprotein complexes that would make up the viral envelope. However, somewhat contradictory data are found in the same report (80). When $VS_{Ind}$ virus and $VS_{NJ}$ virus were grown in chick embryo cells instead of L-cells as described above, the overall lipid composition was strikingly *similar* for the two viruses. In addition, when $VS_{NJ}$ virus was grown in L-cells and chick embryo cells and analyzed, the total neutral lipid, total phosphilipid and the cholesterol:lipid molar ratio, was quite *different* for virus purified from the two different host cells. The latter results suggest that the lipid composition of a budding virus is largely determined by the host cell, in contrast to the conclusion of McSharry and Wagner that specific viral proteins can determine the lipid arrangement in the virion.

The role of sterols in the membrane envelope of VSV was examined by Bates & Rothblat (5). They showed that when L-cells were grown in the absence of serum cholesterol, the immediate biosynthetic precursor of cholesterol, desmosterol, was the only sterol found in the cell membranes. Moreover, desmosterol was the sole sterol found in vesicular stomatitis virus grown in such cholesterol-starved L-cells. Virus grown in L-cells which had a constantly changing cholesterol:desmosterol ratio contained a mixture of the two sterols, but the virus was enriched in cholesterol compared to the host cell. Viral stability, growth, and plaquing efficiency were found not to be affected by the changing sterol composition. These experiments suggest that a cell culture system in which the composition and biosynthesis of a major cellular and viral lipid can be manipulated and possibly inhibited by the use of sterol analogues may provide insights into the requirements of sterols for membrane structure and biosynthesis.

Rabies virus was analyzed for total lipid composition by Schlesinger et al (110). Both the extracellular and intracellular viruses had similar lipid compositions, and both were found to contain relatively high levels of cholesterol and sphingomyelin. Since the intracellular virus is supposedly not derived from the cell surface membrane, but rather synthesized de novo in the cytoplasm, its high content of cholesterol and sphingomyelin may reflect a specific structural or stabilizing requirement for these two lipids in the intact virion. It has been assumed in the past that a high cholesterol and sphingomyelin content in virus was simply an indication of a surface membrane origin for the viral envelope. The results on the lipid content of intracellular rabies virus, whose synthesis is presumably independent of the plasma membrane, implies a more fundamental role for these two lipids in enveloped viruses.

## RNA TUMOR VIRUSES

The RNA tumor or oncorna viruses are composed of 64% protein, 2% RNA, 6% carbohydrate, and 31% lipid (100). The virions are approximately 1000 Å in diameter and are spherical (38). The oncorna viruses possess a nucleoprotein core surrounded by a lipoprotein envelope derived from host cell membranes (38). Glycoprotein spikes are situated on the external surface of the viral membrane (104). A hydrophobic protein (46) is located on the internal side of the viral membrane (104) and may function to coat the internal face of the viral envelope in a similar manner to the M protein of paramyxo and myxo viruses (see below).

The RNA tumor viruses are classified into three groups, A, B, and C, by morphological criteria (8). The A type appears to bud from internal membranes and is only found intracellularly. The B and C types secure their membranes by budding through the host cell's plasma membrane. B-type particles can be distinguished from C-type particles by the eccentric position of the electron opaque core of the former when compared to the centrally positioned nucleoid of the latter.

The elucidation of the early events in viral assembly has been unsuccessful largely because of the temperate, or noncytocidal, nature of the RNA tumor viruses (38). Studies have shown that the synthesis of virus-specific macromolecules accounts for less than 0.3% of the total cellular biosynthetic activity (103). In addition, the synthesis of viral RNA and proteins is sensitive to actinomycin D (38). Thus there is no simple way of observing viral development since the processes of viral maturation are well hidden within the background of normal cellular activity.

The mechanism by which specific viral proteins and RNA migrate to the cytoplasmic surface of the plasma membrane and are assembled to form the ribonucleoprotein core is poorly understood. The internal structure of the oncorna viruses becomes morphologically detectable only as the core proteins and nucleic acid begin to condense immediately before they bud through the surface membrane (8). It may be that the synthesis of these molecules is concerted and takes place in specific regions juxtaposed to the plasma membrane. Fleissner (39) has shown an association of the internal proteins of Rous sarcoma virus (RSV) with the membranes of the endoplasmic reticulum of nonvirus-producing transformed hamster cells. It would be interesting to compare the proteins in the plasma membranes of such cells and of virus-producing cells. The possible role of membrane-associated viral proteins in the production (or nonproduction) of virions may be elucidated by such studies.

During the time of nucleoprotein assembly and virus extrusion dramatic changes must be occurring within those areas of the plasma membrane from which the virus will bud, since the mature virion has abstracted little, if any, cellular protein (40, 59, 104). The newly acquired viral membrane appears to contain only virus specific proteins (40, 59, 104). The exact mechanism of cellular protein removal from the membrane bilayer prior to budding is not known.

While no host structural proteins are found associated with the purified virus, small amounts of host-specific enzymes are contained in the virion. Early studies indicated that a membrane-bound ATPase, derived from the host cell, was present in isolated avian myeloblastosis virus particles (12). The amount of enzymatic activity associated with the virus was dependent upon the host cell used for virus growth. Cells which contained high levels of ATPase produced virus particles containing relatively high enzymatic activity, while cells which had low ATPase levels produced virions with little or no detectable activity. These observations suggest that the presence of ATPase in these virions is simply nonspecific encapsulation of host-cell proteins by the virus rather than specific selection of a cellular protein necessary for viral membrane structure or function. The nonspecific nature of the small amounts of cellular proteins found in association with purified virions also is suggested by the study of Mizutani & Temin (82). These workers demonstrated that glycolytic enzymes such as hexokinase and lactate dehydrogenase were present in virions of Rous sarcoma virus.

Viral glycoproteins are inserted into or onto the cell surface membrane during or just prior to budding. The mechanism and sequence of the insertion of specific viral glycoproteins is poorly understood. Gelderblom et al (45) used ferritin labeled antibodies to show that the viral envelope antigens are located on the surface of the host cell plasma membrane in discrete regions, some of which appear to be sites of virus budding. However, since these experiments were not done under single cycle growth conditions, it is impossible to distinguish the proteins of budding virions from the proteins of virus particles adsorbed to the cell surface.

The viral glycoproteins located on the outer surface of the virion, and presumably on the outer surface of the infected cell, do not penetrate the lipid bilayer of the viral envelope to any extent. This conclusion is based on the observation that these proteins can be removed in their entirety by protease treatment of whole virions with no apparent disturbance of the viral membrane (104). These observations are similar to those described for arboviruses (19).

Although the budding process is accompanied both by the insertion of virus-specific proteins and the deletion of cellular proteins, the lipids of the cell membrane do not appear to undergo such dramatic rearrangements. In its characteristic increased content of sphingomyelin and cholesterol and decreased content of phosphatidyl choline, RSV has been shown to resemble qualitatively the lipid composition of the plasma membrane rather than that of the whole cell (76, 100). Rao et al (101), however, reported a quantitative difference between BAI avian tumor virus lipids and those of the host cell plasma membrane. They suggested that the viral lipid was incorporated from different subcellular elements. This conclusion is probably incorrect because of impurities in the plasma membrane preparation. The low values of sphingomyelin and cholesterol that they report for the cell membrane (101) is in disagreement with the elevated levels of these lipids found in most preparations of plasma membrane (93).

The resemblance of the lipids of the viral envelope to those of host cell plasma membrane is in accordance with morphological evidence suggesting that the virus acquires its envelope by budding through the plasma membrane of the cell (28). Furthermore, the biosynthetic rate, turnover rate, and specific activity of individual phospholipids in RSV and host-derived membranes have been shown to be similar (99, 100), indicating a direct precursor role for cellular plasma membrane lipids. Additional evidence that viral lipids are derived directly from host cells comes from studies comparing the phospholipid composition of two different host cell plasma membranes with that of a single type of virus grown in both cell types (99). These studies demonstrate that isolated quail cell plasma membranes have a lower sphingomyelin and phosphatidylethanolamine content and a higher phosphatidylcholine content than isolated chick cell plasma membranes. The phospholipid composition of purified RSV grown in the two cell types exactly reflects these host cell differences: lower sphingomyelin and phosphatidylethanolamine content and a higher phosphatidylcholine content are found in virus from quail cells than in virus from chick cells.

The studies with RSV-infected chick and quail cells (99, 100) also demonstrate that, although the lipid composition of the virus qualitatively reflects that of the host cell plasma membrane, there are quantitative differences in the distribution of the individual lipids. The virus contains a significantly higher proportion of sphingomyelin and cholesterol (free and esterfied) and a lower proportion of phosphatidylcholine than does the isolated host cell plasma membrane. These differences are not the result of a gross change in lipid composition and metabolism brought about by viral infection, since normal, uninfected cells have a phospholipid and cholesterol composition that is indistinguishable from that of virally infected cells. The biosynthetic rates and metabolic stability of normal cell phospholipids also are similar to those of the infected cells (99). In addition, the observed lipid variations are large enough so that they do not appear to be a reflection of differences in the relative purity of the virus and the plasma membrane. Similar variations in lipid composition between virus and plasma membrane also have been reported for six separate types of RNA viruses grown in the same cell type (100). Since all of these viruses mature by budding from the plasma membrane these lipid differences may reflect a fundamental property of cell membranes and budding enveloped viruses (see discussion).

The fatty acids of the Rauscher leukemia virus and host cells were analyzed by Johnsen & Mora (62). They demonstrated that the composition of the different fatty acid classes in the virus was similar to that of the host cell with a few striking differences. Linoleic acid was present in considerable amounts in the purified virus but not in the infected cells. Cellular membrane fractions were not isolated and analyzed, and this would be necessary in order to confirm this considerable enrichment in the virus of a specific fatty acid.

While it is currently fashionable to consider that neoplastic transformation caused by the RNA tumor viruses is dependent upon alterations in the cell surface membrane, it appears unlikely that these changes are related to the appearance of viral structural proteins in the cell membranes. Certain differences in membrane structure of normal and transformed cells have been described but there is no evidence to relate these changes to specific viral structural proteins (137). On the other hand, there is evidence, beyond the scope of this review, that viral transformation induces the production of other molecules which may affect cell membrane structure and function (91, 92, 131).

## MYXOVIRUSES

The myxoviruses are generally spherical particles having a diameter of 800–900 Å, although filamentous forms do exist (38). Influenza virus, the most widely studied myxovirus, is composed of approximately 0.9% RNA, 5–8% carbohydrate, 20% lipid, and 63% protein (23). The organization of the influenza virion is similar to that of other membrane viruses. Two glycoproteins, a hemagglutinin and a neuraminidase, form a layer of spikes on the external surface of the virion and are anchored to the viral envelope (27, 112). The viral envelope is a lipid bilayer derived from the host cell surface membrane (4, 24). A hydrophobic protein, the M, or membrane, protein, is located in the interior of the virus (23, 27, 46). It is thought that this protein lines the internal surface of the viral membrane. The M protein in turn surrounds the viral nucleocapsid which is composed of viral RNA and a specific nucleocapsid protein.

Compositional and architectural changes occur at the surfaces of cells infected with influenza virus. Viral hemagglutinin and neuraminidase accumulate there and can be visualized using a combination of electron microscopy together with various immunological techniques (35, 84). The distribution of the viral glycoproteins at the cell surface has been reported to be uniform (35, 84). However, this conclusion is not based on single-cycle growth studies, and thus the even distribution of viral antigen may be the result of readsorption of virus particles. On the other hand biochemical studies of virus isolated from cells labeled with amino acids prior to infection indicate that no host protein is incorporated into budding virions (27, 54). This implies that the distribution of viral protein at the cell surface may not be purely random.

A report by Seto & Rott (113) indicates that if antibodies to viral neuraminidase are present during the growth of fowl plague virus, no infectious virus is released from the cell. Thus, this viral enzyme may be necessary for budding and release of nascent virus.

The relative stability of influenza virus, compared to other enveloped viruses, has permitted a large number of physical and biochemical studies to be performed on the isolated virion. These studies have revealed that the proteins of influenza virus do not span the lipid bilayer of the viral envelope. Data obtained by X-ray diffraction studies (49) and limited proteolytic digestion (27) of intact virions have demonstrated the absence of any protein within the lipid phase. However, the polar groups of the envelope lipids seem to be in close apposition to the proteins on either side of the bilayer, the glycoproteins on the outer surface of the envelope and the M protein on the inner surface. The hydrophobic nature of the M protein [it is the only viral protein that can be extracted into chloroform-methanol (46)] may account for its association with the lipid bilayer. The nature of the binding of the glycoproteins to the bilayer remains uncertain since Landsberger et al (75, see below) have used electron spin resonance techniques to show that the glycoproteins do not penetrate the viral membrane.

Compans (20) has studied the intracellular sites of synthesis of influenza viral proteins and their subsequent association with subcellular fractions using density gradient fractionation. The nucleoprotein is found associated primarily with an intermediate density fraction consisting of a mixture of smooth membranes, rough membranes, and heterogeneous material. The glycoproteins, on the other hand, are localized in the rough microsomal fraction shortly after synthesis and subsequently with a smooth membrane fraction. This passage of carbohydrate-containing proteins from rough to smooth membranes has been described previously for the synthesis of cellular secretory proteins (118). Moreover, Compans (21) recently demonstrated that the individual sugar residues on the viral glycoproteins are added in a stepwise fashion, glucosamine being added at the rough membrane state, and fucose being added at the smooth membrane stage. This phenomenon also has been shown to occur during the synthesis of cellular glycoproteins in other systems (6, 138).

The M protein is found associated with a smooth membrane fraction which may contain plasma membrane (20). It is possible that the M protein serves as a nucleation site for virus maturation on the inner surface of the plasma membrane. It is not clear, however, whether the site of attachment of the M protein to the plasma membrane determines or is determined by the glycoproteins on the outer surface of the budding region of the membrane.

Compans & Caliguiri (22) have reported that viral and host proteins from influenza-infected cells may co-exist in cytoplasmic membranes. They have performed experiments similar to those of Heine & Roizman (51) with Herpes virus-infected cells (see below). Rabbit antiviral antiserum was incubated with membrane vesicles prepared by dounce homogenization from cells labeled with $^{3}H$-amino acids pre-infection and $^{14}C$-amino acids post-infection. Both isotopes remained associated with the treated vesicles and sedimented to a higher buoyant density than those isotopes associated with vesicles not exposed to the antiserum. These results implied that both cellular and viral proteins could be found in the same vesicle. However, Compans & Caliguiri (22) found that this shift in density could, in fact, be produced by serum from rabbits which had not been immunized to viral proteins. Thus the shift in density of the membrane fractions containing both $^{14}C$ and $^{3}H$ was not necessarily dependent upon binding of antiviral antibodies to viral proteins and, therefore, does not exclude the possibility that there are two populations of vesicles present: one which contains only host proteins labeled with $^{3}H$, and one containing only viral proteins labeled with $^{14}C$.

Since Morgan et al (86) first showed that influenza virus appears to acquire its envelope from the cell surface by a budding process, a number of workers have examined the lipids of myxoviruses. These studies have indicated that the lipid composition of the virion depends upon the lipid composition of the host cell, the growth and environmental conditions of the infected cell, and the types and configuration of viral envelope proteins. Kates et al (66) showed that when influenza virus is grown in two different host cells the fatty acid and the phospholipid patterns of the virion reflect those of the host cell in which it is grown. In addition, when virus is grown in cells which have been labeled with $^{32}PO_4$ before infection, all the viral phospholipids, with the exception of phosphatidic acid, have specific activities very similar to the corresponding phospholipids in the host cell. These results indicate that the virus quantitatively incorporates cellular lipid components synthesized by the host cell before infection.

Frommhagen et al (43) and Kates et al (66) have shown that virus grown in chick embryos has a higher proportion of sphingomyelin than do the host cells. Kates et al (66) also have reported that the neutral lipids of the virus closely resemble the neutral lipids of a nuclear membrane fraction. On the basis of this finding they have suggested that a large part of the viral envelope might have a nuclear membrane origin. However, no plasma membrane fraction was isolated for comparison in these studies, nor was the nuclear membrane fraction examined for the possible contamination with surface membrane.

A number of workers have examined host cell-induced modifications of the myxovirus envelope. Studies by Simpson & Hauser (119) showed that the sensitivity of isolated myxoviruses to phospholipases could be modified by changing the nature of the host cell or its nutritional supplements. Studies by Blough et al (11) indicated that treatment of host cells with vitamin A caused a rearrangement of acidic phospholipids within the envelope of the virus grown in such cells. It thus appears from these studies and those of Kates et al (66) that the host cell directly affects the lipid composition of the virion.

Tiffany & Blough (129), however, postulated that influenza viral envelope proteins might be responsible for influencing the composition of cellular membrane lipids at the site of viral release. These workers demonstrated that viruses with antigenically related envelope proteins showed a greater similarity in their fatty acid composition than those of unrelated strains. They suggested that a given envelope protein, possibly having a different amino acid sequence than a protein from an unrelated strain, would direct the rearrangement or exchange of existing membrane lipids in the vicinity of that protein in order to achieve a sterically favorable conformation of lipids. In these, as in other studies of this type, it is difficult to assess the meaning of the reported differences or similarities in lipid composition, since all of the experiments are performed in ovo. Under these conditions cytocidal effects of different virus strains during multiple infectious cycles cannot be adequately controlled. Isolation of virus from single cycle-infected cells at relatively short periods of time, as performed in tissue culture, could provide a more controlled comparison of subcellular structures and viruses.

In recent studies, Landsberger et al (75) used electron spin resonance to examine the relationship between the viral envelope spike proteins and the lipid bilayer in influenza virus. These workers incorporated spin label analogues of steroids and fatty acids, labeled at positions both proximal and distal to the hydrophilic part of the fatty acid chain, into the lipid bilayer of influenza virus. Complete removal of the glycoprotein spikes by protease treatment had no detectable effect on the viral lipid organization, as monitored by the various spin label probes. Since such a large change in membrane structure as spike removal occurred with no detectable alteration of lipid structure, Landsberger et al concluded that the spikes or envelope proteins do not penetrate the lipid bilayer and are not directly involved in determining the organization of the lipid bilayer.

## PARAMYXOVIRUSES

The paramyxoviruses comprise the most extensively studied group of enveloped viruses. They include measles, mumps, sendai, SV5, and Newcastle disease virus (38). The paramyxoviruses are generally spherical, with a large variation in diameter occurring within a virus type (38). Filamentous forms similar to those seen with the myxoviruses occur with certain members of this group (38). The typical paramyxovirus consists of a coiled nucleocapsid, composed of RNA and protein, surrounded by a lipoprotein envelope (38). Situated on the outer surface of the envelope are glycoprotein spikes (16, 38). The chemical composition of a typical paramyxovirus, SV5, is 1.7% RNA, 73% protein, 20% lipid, and 6% carbohydrate (69).

The organization of the proteins of the paramyxoviruses appears to be similar to that found in other enveloped viruses. The viral genome is associated with a nonglycosylated protein (16) and this complex forms the nucleocapsid. The nucleocapsid is surrounded by a second, low molecular weight nonglycosylated protein. This protein may be equivalent to the M protein of influenza virus and thus possibly lines the inner surface of the viral membrane. All of the viral glycoproteins are external to the viral membrane and form the spikes or projections observed in electron micrographs of purified virus (38, 75, 87).

Little is known about the intracellular sites of synthesis of paramyxovirus proteins. Electron microscopic studies have demonstrated the formation of nucleocapsids in the cytoplasm of infected cells and their subsequent concentration directly beneath specific areas of plasma membrane (26). These areas of the plasma membrane can be distinguished by the presence of viral glycoproteins. Purified paramyxovirus contains only viral proteins and no host cell proteins (69). Thus the aggregation of viral structural proteins into discrete regions of the cell membrane occurs with the loss of host cell proteins from these areas.

The most dramatic result of the modification of host cell membranes by parainfluenza viruses is cell fusion (17, 26, 96). It appears that this phenomenon is related to the presence of specific viral proteins and is not dependent on virus multiplication, since UV-inactivated virus can induce cell fusion when added directly to cells. The proteins responsible for inducing fusion in SV5- and sendai-infected cells are glycoproteins which have recently been identified (58, 109). Since these viral proteins can be isolated in pure and active form it may be possible to use them as probes for elucidating the mechanism of virally induced cell fusion.

The extent of virally induced cell fusion depends on the particular host cell type. Holmes et al (55, 56) have found rather striking differences in the capacity of SV5 virions to induce fusion in BHK21-F cells and in monkey kidney cells. Infection of BHK21-F cells induces rapid fusion and little virus production, while infection of monkey kidney cells induces high virus titers but little fusion. Holmes et al have suggested that the differing propensities of monkey kidney cells and BHK21-F to SV5-induced fusion might be related to the lipid compositions of the plasma membranes of these cells. They showed that monkey kidney cell plasma membranes had a significantly higher cholesterol:phospholipid ratio than that of BHK21-F plasma membranes (56). It remains to be established why a higher cholesterol:phospholipid ratio would prevent membrane fusion. Results from other laboratories indicate that the gross lipid composition of plasma membranes is not a major determinant of cellular susceptibility to fusion (95, 97). Further evidence for the influence of the cell type in virally induced fusion is provided by the fact that established cell lines and tumor cells fuse more readily than do the corresponding primary cells (97). This observation is not fully understood.

The lipids of two paramyxoviruses, Sendai and NDV, have been studied in detail by Blough & Lawson (10). They demonstrated that although the two viruses have similar phospholipid compositions and similar cholesterol:phospholipid ratios, their fatty acid compositions differ significantly. It was suggested that the changes found in the fatty acyl chains of different viruses, propagated from the same cell type, were determined by the differences in the structures of the envelope proteins of the two viruses. Tiffany & Blough (130) extended these studies by analyzing the fatty acid compositions of various strains of a single virus, NDV. They explained the observed differences in the relative amounts of saturated and unsaturated fatty acids in the BL, Milano, and Sato strains of NDV by suggesting that the envelope proteins of these three viruses were distinct. However, since they could detect no differences in the proteins by immunological or biochemical methods, these workers suggested that undetectable differences, possibly in amino acid sequence, must account for the fatty acid differences. It should be noted that both of the studies described (10, 130) are based on in ovo propagated virus and, therefore, the purified viruses are not derived from a single cycle of infection. Possibly the virus isolates represent a heterogeneous population of virus particles produced during various stages of a multiple cycle infection and thus possess a correspondingly heterogeneous content of fatty acids.

In contrast to Blough and co-workers, Landsberger et al (74) have suggested that viral envelope proteins are probably not involved in determining the structure and composition of the lipid bilayer of a paramyxovirus envelope. This conclusion was based on electron spin resonance (esr) studies in which a paramyxovirus (SV5) and a myxovirus (influenza) which have completely different polypeptide compositions, were analyzed following isolation from two different host cells. The rigidity of the two viral membranes, which depends largely on the lipid composition, was spectrally indistinguishable when the viruses were grown in the same host cell. However, when the same virus was grown in two host cells, which differ in their lipid composition, the esr spectral splitting showed significant differences.

Klenk & Choppin (69–72), in an excellent series of papers, examined the phospholipid, cholesterol, glycolipid, and fatty acid composition of SV5 virus grown in four different host cells and two types of serum. Comparisons were made between the virus and the plasma membranes of the respective host cells. It was demonstrated that the lipid composition of the virus strongly reflects the lipid composition of the host cell plasma membrane. Although the virus may bring about some selective rearrangement of specific lipids, the virion appears to acquire the lipid pattern of the host cell plasma membrane when it buds from the cell surface.

## HERPES VIRUSES

The herpes viruses are large complex DNA-containing viruses with a diameter of 1400–2100 Å (38). Purified herpes simplex virus particles contain approximately 6.5% DNA, 70% protein, 1.6% carbohydrate, and 22% phospholipid (108). The molecular weight of the DNA of most herpes viruses is between 60 and 90 million daltons.

Morphological studies have shown that the herpes viruses are composed of a series of concentric layers (89). The innermost component consists of a group of proteins organized into a rod-like structure which passes through the middle of a doughnut-shaped complex of viral DNA. The viral core of DNA and protein is in turn surrounded by a layer of capsid proteins arranged in the form of an icosahedron. Located between the icosahedral nucleocapsid and the viral membrane envelope is a layer of filamentous proteins called the tegument.

The initial steps of viral maturation occur in the nucleus of the infected cell where the progeny DNA and specific structural proteins coalesce to form the core, tegument, and surrounding capsid (105). In most types of herpes infection the nucleocapsid plus tegument proteins become enveloped at the inner lamella of the nuclear membrane as the particle buds into the perinuclear space (31, 90, 115, 117, 124). Although there are reports of herpes viruses obtaining their membranes from other cellular structures (89), the primary source of envelope for infectious particles appears to be the inner nuclear membrane. Enveloped particles accumulate in both the perinuclear space and within the endoplasmic reticulum, which appears morphologically continuous with the perinuclear space (89). It is not clear how virions move from this region of the cell to the extracellular space. One view is that the endoplasmic reticulum is continuous with the extracellular space and, therefore, virus is released simply by migrating along the endoplasmic reticulum (116). Morgan et al (85), however, believe that pieces of the endoplasmic reticulum that contain virus particles break off and form intracellular vesicles. These vesicles are then transported to the surface of the cell and liberate their contents into the extracellular space.

Cellular protein synthesis is inhibited shortly after herpes infection while viral proteins continue to be made in the cell cytoplasm (122). The capsid and core proteins migrate from their cytoplasmic sites of synthesis into the nucleus for assembly (122). Other viral proteins are inserted into various cellular components including the plasma and nuclear membranes and the smooth endoplasmic reticulum (121, 123). Spear & Roizman have shown that the viral proteins are glycosylated following their insertion into membranes (123). These newly glycosylated proteins are strongly associated with the various cellular membrane fractions since extensive membrane purification and washing fail to remove them (123). A detailed comparison of newly synthesized intracellular glycoproteins and purified virion glycoproteins by gel electrophoresis and immunological analyses suggests that they are identical (107). Roizman and his collaborators also have shown that as viral proteins become associated with cell membranes, there is no concurrent expulsion of cell-determined membrane proteins (51, 106). Thus host proteins made prior to infection and newly synthesized viral proteins coexist in the plasma membrane following infection. This observation is of interest, since the purified herpes virus, like other viruses which derive their envelope from host cell membranes, contains no cellular proteins (122).

Heine & Roizman (51) have further explored the question of viral and cellular protein coexistence in membranes. They have demonstrated that small membrane vesicles prepared from infected cells contained viral proteins as well as cellular proteins. In these experiments they incubated membrane fragments with antiviral antiserum, and subjected the resulting complexes to equilibrium density centrifugation. After exposure to antiserum the vesicles prepared from infected cells were found to have a higher density than vesicles from uninfected cells or those from infected cells which were not treated with viral antiserum. The vesicles from infected cells contained both cellular proteins, which had been prelabeled with radioactive amino acids before infection, and viral proteins which were complexed with the viral antibodies. The vesicles had approximately the same dimensions (1600 Å) needed for potential viral envelopes. These results suggest that cellular membranes do not contain regions or patches of any appreciable size which contain only viral proteins. However, since the virus derives its membrane from the inner nuclear membrane of the host cell (31, 90, 115, 117), the relationship of the viral proteins in the plasma membrane to the actual structure and development of the viral membrane remains obscure. It is obviously important to perform similar experiments with vesicles prepared from purified nuclear membranes to determine if a similar coexistence of viral and cellular proteins occurs in a specific membrane fraction which is known to be a precursor of the viral envelope. It also should be noted (see above) that similar experiments with vesicles prepared from influenza-infected cells cast some doubt as to whether antiviral antibodies are complexing with the viral proteins (22).

Infection of cells in culture by herpes virus provides a striking example of the effects of cellular membrane modification by viral proteins. Uninfected cells in culture tend to be dispersed evenly, covering the surface of the culture vessel. Cells infected with herpes virus, by contrast, tend to aggregate and in some instances fuse with each other. Ejercito et al (37) have called this phenomenon the "altered social behavior" of cells. Individual strains of herpes virus induce various cellular responses which include the formation of cellular aggregates of different sizes and different degrees of karyocytosis (37, 128). In all cases the behavior of the infected cells is genetically determined by the virus, although the cell type may modulate the response (107, 125). The change in behavior of the infected cells can be correlated with the appearance of new cell surface antigens which cross react with antibodies produced against viral structural proteins (67). Moreover, when cells are infected simultaneously by two different virus strains, one of which is dominant over the other in altering the interactions of the infected cells, the viral proteins found in a smooth membrane fraction of the infected cells resemble those found upon infection of cells with the dominant virus by itself. Thus the insertion of viral proteins into cellular membranes has been suggested as an explanation for the altered social behavior of infected cells (67). Additional viral or cell mutants are required in order to correlate alterations in the behavior of infected cells with the presence of specific proteins.

The lipids of herpes virus and infected cell membranes have not been as extensively studied as the proteins. Ben-Porat & Kaplan (7) reported that the phospholipid composition of purified pseudorabies virus resembles that of the inner nuclear membrane of the host cell. They found that the virion and inner nuclear membrane possess high levels of sphingomyelin and low levels of phosphatidyl choline relative to those of the outer nuclear membrane and cytoplasmic membrane fractions. It was suggested that these results confirmed the morphological evidence that the inner nuclear membrane is the source of the viral envelope (7). The amount of sphingomyelin and phosphatidylcholine in the membrane envelope of herpes virus is reminiscent of that found for other viruses, which acquire their envelope by budding through the surface membrane. Since the inner nuclear membrane fraction examined by Ben-Porat and Kaplan was isolated apparently free of any other cytoplasmic membranes, a relatively high content of sphingomyelin and low content of phosphatidylcholine in the viral membrane may indicate a specific lipid requirement for maturation of all enveloped viruses. The neutral lipid content of the nuclear membranes was not analyzed and it would be of interest to compare the cholesterol contents of the inner nuclear membrane and the herpes virus membrane since high cholesterol values have been shown to be a characteristic of viruses which acquire their envelope from the cell surface membrane (93).

The studies of Ben-Porat & Kaplan (7) showed an increase in the incorporation of $^{32}P$, $^{3}H$-choline, and $^{3}H$-inositol into phospholipids after pseudorabies infection. The increase was especially marked in the nuclear fraction. Approximately two or three times more $^{3}H$-choline label was found in the sphingomyelin of the infected cell nuclear membrane than in that of the uninfected cell. These results differ from those reported by Asher et al (3), who found no change in the rate and amount of $^{3}H$-choline incorporation after infection of cells with herpes simplex virus. These apparently conflicting results may be due to differences in the physiological conditions of the respective host cells. Further studies should be performed to resolve this discrepancy.

## POX VIRUSES

The poxviruses are the largest of the animal viruses. They are composed of DNA (3.2%), protein (92%), carbohydrate (0.2%), and lipid (5%) (29, 36, 53, 120, 139). The large amount of DNA, $160 \times 10^6$ daltons (63, 78), gives the virus the potential to direct the synthesis of a great number of proteins. Vaccinia, a representative poxvirus, is composed of a dumbbell-shaped nucleoprotein core, two protein-containing lateral bodies juxtaposed to the indented regions of the core, and a lipoprotein envelope (29, 30, 61, 63).

In a detailed series of papers Moss and his collaborators (44, 88) have demonstrated that vaccinia infection is associated with the biosynthesis of a number of unique glycoproteins which are distinct in their electrophoretic mobility and carbohydrate composition from the glycoproteins of uninfected cells. A majority of these virally induced glycoproteins are found associated with a crude cellular membrane fraction. In contrast to the infected cell, purified virions contain only a single glycoprotein in the viral envelope (44, 57, 88). This glycoprotein is absent in uninfected cells and can be distinguished from other virally induced cellular glycoproteins on the basis of molecular weight, carbohydrate composition, and size of the oligosaccharide. Thus, during the synthesis of the viral membrane, this glycoprotein is selected and specifically incorporated into the virion structure.

Ichihashi & Dales (60) described two virus-induced proteins in vaccinia-infected cells which may be related to certain of the proteins described by Moss et al (88). These are a hemagglutinin and a fusion-inducing protein responsible for polykaryocytosis (60). The hemagglutinin induced upon vaccinia infection is unusual in that it is found evenly distributed on the surfaces of cells, except in those regions where virus is being released. Moreover, it is not found associated with mature virions. This is in contrast to most other virus-infected cells where the hemagglutinin is found associated only with mature virions and those regions of the cell surface which have been modified to serve as a part of the viral membrane (25, 34). The fusion-inducing protein has been shown to be associated with the internal membranes of vaccinia-infected cells as well as with mature virions. This protein has not been identified nor has its role in viral maturation been defined.

Appleyard et al (2) have reported that an antigenic difference exists between extracellular and intracellular rabbit pox virus. Extracellular virus possesses an antigen also present on the surfaces of infected cells, while intracellular virus lacks this protein. No work has been done to relate this work to the proteins described by Ichihashi & Dales (60) or Moss et al (88).

The envelope of the vaccinia virus, the best characterized of the pox viruses, resembles cellular membranes in its general chemical composition and morphology (29). However, the pox viruses are unique among the enveloped animal viruses in that their membrane apparently is not derived from pre-existing membranes of the host cell, but is synthesized de novo in specific regions or factories in the cytoplasm (29, 30, 61). The viral membrane first appears in these discrete regions of the cytoplasm as small trilaminar segments coated with spike-like projections. These membranous foci appear to grow outward from all sides, subsequently enclosing the viral core (29). At no time during this early membrane development is there any observed continuity between cellular membranes and the viral membranes (29).

Additional membrane development occurs when the virions migrate to the centrosphere region of the cell, where they become enveloped by cisternae of the Golgi complex. Thus the virus is internalized into a double membrane vesicle, the outer component of which is part of the smooth-surfaced Golgi complex. This interaction between viral and host cell membranes appears to be quite specific (29, 30). It seems possible that certain of the membrane glycoproteins described by Moss and collaborators (61, 82) may act as receptors for viral recognition of Golgi membranes. It would therefore be of interest to determine the specific intracellular membrane locations of the virally induced glycoproteins to assess their possible role as receptors in viral envelopment. The enveloped virus particle migrates along the Golgi cisternae to the surface of the cell (29, 30). Fusion takes place between the cell's plasma membrane and the outer cisternal membrane of the enveloped virus, liberating a mature virus particle into the extracellular fluid. The release of mature virus represents an early event in the infective process, since at later times (14–24 hr post-infection) only naked virus or partially enveloped virus accumulates in the cell. The envelopment of virus by elements of the Golgi complex and subsequent fusion and release of mature virions also appear to cease late after infection.

Since the vaccinia envelope shows no continuity with any cellular membranes during its formation, it has been presumed that the viral membrane lipids are synthesized de novo. Dales & Mosbach (29) demonstrated that radioactive choline, employed as a precursor of membrane lecithin, is incorporated into virus at a four- to eightfold faster rate in *post-infection*–labeled cultures than in cultures labeled previous to infection. Thus developing virus preferentially incorporates nascent phospholipid into its envelope. It also was demonstrated that the fatty acid composition of viral lipids was quantitatively different from that of cellular microsomal membrane lipids (29). The specific composition of the individual phospholipid species in the viral membrane, however, has not been determined, nor has it been compared to the relative amounts of individual phospholipids in specific cellular membranes. Such studies might confirm the presumed uniqueness of the viral membrane.

## SUMMARY AND DISCUSSION

In the past few years the structure of many enveloped viruses has been well characterized because of and in conjunction with the development of relatively new techniques in the fields of protein biochemistry, immunology, and electron microscopy. Techniques used in peripheral fields of study, such as X-ray crystallography and electron spin resonance spectroscopy, have also aided in the elucidation of viral substructure. It has been shown that many enveloped viruses have a number of structural features in common, though the viruses differ greatly in biological activity. The viruses are usually composed of a nucleoprotein core surrounded or enveloped by a lipoprotein membrane. Incorporated into the lipoprotein envelope of the virus are a number of highly specific proteins. These proteins are usually glycosylated and possibly serve as receptor molecules defining both the immunological properties and the host range of the virus. A ubiquitous feature of these viruses is a lipoprotein envelope similar in structure to cellular membranes.

This review has shown that the biogenesis of these viruses, unlike their structural features, is not clearly understood at the molecular level, but only at the morphological level. Not only are the biochemical steps in virus maturation poorly understood, but the viral effects on cellular membranes remain to be clearly defined. However, because these viruses are membranous in nature, and because they are relatively simple structures, they can serve as unique model systems in the study of membrane structure, function, and biogenesis.

The morphogenesis of all the enveloped viruses, with the possible exception of the pox viruses, is dependent on their direct association with subcellular membrane elements of the host cell. The pox virus literature indicates that the membranes of these viruses are synthesized de novo and that no observed continuity exists between cellular membranes and the pox virus envelope during its formation. There does, however, appear to be a specific involvement of the golgi membranes for the intracellular processing of pox virions. All other virus types exhibit an intimate and morphologically detectable association with specific cellular membranes at some time during their formation. In addition, the incorporation of specific virally coded proteins into host cell membranes appears to be a requirement for the maturation of these viruses. Since these incorporated proteins are membrane proteins by definition, the study of their biosynthesis and subsequent insertion into a given membrane has yielded interesting information on the structural organization of membranes.

The viral envelope proteins of the rhabdo, arbo, myxo, paramyxo, oncorna, and herpes viruses are all glycoproteins that are inserted into a cellular membrane prior to its conversion into a viral membrane. The role of these proteins as possible receptors or recognition sites for the integration of other subviral elements has been suggested by a number of workers. The envelope glycoproteins of myxoviruses, paramyxoviruses, and oncornaviruses have been shown to be located specifically on the external surface of the mature virion and are not anchored within the lipid bilayer. The biosynthesis of these glycoproteins has been shown in a number of cases to occur in close proximity to the membranes in which they will be incorporated. The mode of biosynthesis and glycosylation of viral envelope proteins appears to be strikingly similar to that of specific cellular proteins. It appears that the biogenesis and function of these glycoproteins are similar for many if not all of the enveloped viruses discussed. Detailed studies on the amino acid sequence, carbohydrate composition, and binding properties of these proteins remain to be performed, but it would not be surprising if a number of structural and biochemical similarities were exhibited among the envelope glycoproteins of the many different viruses.

The existence of another type of viral membrane protein has been described for myxo, oncorna, paramyxo, and rhabdo viruses. This protein is a nonglycosylated, hydrophobic protein that is believed to line the internal surface of the viral membrane. It has been found strongly associated with specific cellular membranes in infected cells immediately following a radioactive pulse. Whether the binding of this protein to plasma membrane occurs prior to or subsequent to the insertion of the viral glycoprotein into that membrane has not yet been determined.

The relationship of the glycosylated and nonglycosylated viral membrane proteins to each other and to the modification of cellular membranes induced by the single or concomitant presence of these proteins is a difficult question to answer. The use of specific mutants such as TS-52 mutant of VSV should allow one to determine directly the function of either or both proteins in the biogenesis of membrane viruses.

A third type of viral structural protein that is involved in the infectious cycle of the enveloped viruses is the nucleocapsid protein or proteins. It has been shown that these proteins are synthesized in a different manner from the viral membrane proteins. They appear to be synthesized on soluble polyribosomes and are not found in association with cellular membranes until late in the infectious cycle. They then coalesce with viral nucleic acid and appear in juxtaposition to those areas of the cell membrane from which the virus will bud. The mode of recognition of these membrane areas by the nucleocapsid is somewhat uncertain. It appears, however, that the nucleocapsid only becomes associated with those membranes that possess viral envelope antigens. The nucleocapsid protein cannot directly interact with the viral envelope glycoprotein since neither protein spans the lipid bilayer. The recognition may be mediated by host membrane changes brought about either by the presence of the viral envelope glycoprotein or possibly by the presence of the nonglycosylated viral membrane protein. If one assumes that within the infected cell the nonglycosylated protein is present on one side of a membrane bilayer while the glycoprotein is present on the opposite side, as is the case in the intact virion, then the nucleocapsid can directly interact only with the nonglycosylated membrane protein. Studies on intact virions have indicated that the membrane protein is in close proximity to the nucleocapsid. Thus the modification of the infected cell membrane that creates the nucleocapsid recognition site simply may be the presence of the membrane protein at that site. In vitro studies on the binding properties of purified viral membrane protein with isolated nucleocapsids might resolve this point. However, it should be noted that sindbis virus does not possess a nonglycosylated membrane protein and thus the presence of such a protein may not be an absolute requirement for the biogenesis of enveloped viruses.

One other possible method of recognition may involve the absence of cellular protein in specific areas of the plasma membrane. Since it is known that the mature virion does not possess any cellular proteins, the expulsion of cellular proteins must occur at some time prior to budding. The exact mechanism of this expulsion is unknown. The membrane-associated synthesis of viral envelope protein and its early and rapid association with surface membrane may be a determinant of cellular protein extrusion from those areas of the membrane. The absence of cellular protein and any resulting changes in the membrane may form the recognition site for the nucleocapsid. This possibility necessitates that the expulsion of cellular protein from the membrane be a relatively early event in the final stages of virus maturation. Conversely, the absence of cellular protein does not necessarily imply that an active expulsion takes place. There may exist, within the surface membrane, areas or regions that at a given time are devoid of cellular protein. Viral protein may selectively bind to these areas and the remaining viral substructures may coalesce in these regions to form the budding virion. Morphological studies demonstrate, however, that particles seen on the surface of freeze-etched membranes, which are believed to be cell membrane proteins, are present until the last stages of budding.

It has been suggested that a lipid rearrangement occurs in the membrane at the site of budding, and that this rearrangement may constitute a part of the recognition site. Various types of rearrangements have been postulated based on reported differences between specific cellular membranes and intact virions. These include alterations in fatty acid composition, changes in cholesterol: phospholipid molar ratio, changes in cholesterol ester composition, general shifts in the composition of individual phospholipids, and the loss of specific phospholipids such as phosphatidyl inositol and phosphatidic acid. A number of workers have suggested that the viral envelope glycoproteins determine, to some extent, these lipid rearrangements in the cell, implying that these viral glycoproteins indirectly determine the formation of a recognition or nucleation site. One must also consider the possibility that reported differences between the lipid composition of viral membranes and those cellular membranes which are the proposed precursors of the viral envelope may be due simply to the relative purity of the isolated membranes. This would suggest that the viral lipid composition is identical to the cellular membrane's lipid composition and implies that specific lipid rearrangements do not occur. In line with this suggestion, many studies have indicated that the lipid composition of a given host cell membrane is the major, if not the sole, determinant of the lipid composition of the viral envelope.

An alternative hypothesis is that any given cellular membrane has a certain heterogeneity in its lipid composition. This could take the form of a dynamic heterogeneity brought about by the diffusion of lipids and proteins—such that at physiological temperatures, lipid existed in a fluid state within intact cellular membranes. Alternatively it could take the form of static heterogeneity in which lipids and proteins were arranged in a mosaic pattern along the cell surface. Any given region of the surface membrane, therefore, might be quantitatively different from the overall isolated plasma membrane, whose reported composition would represent only an average statistical value. Thus viral nucleocapsids might preferentially migrate to and bud from selected areas within this heterogeneity that were, for example, enriched in sphingomyelin, cholesterol, and certain fatty acids, and diminished in phosphatidyl choline and phosphatidyl inositol. One can envision a number of reasons why this might occur. It may be that the viral budding process can take place only where local differences in the physical properties of the membrane, such as the packing of lipid molecules, radius of curvature, or surface tension, fit the structural requirements of the mature virus particle. Studies on structurally incomplete virions and virions isolated from Vitamin A-treated cells indicate that abnormalities in the lipid packing of their envelopes are the result of differences in their lipid compositions. It appears from these studies and from electron spin resonance studies that relatively high values of cholesterol and sphingomyelin are needed for tightly packed, thermodynamically stable virus particles. In addition, it has been shown that the presence of high levels of sphingomyelin and cholesterol occurs in virions which acquire their envelope intracellularly from nonsurface membranes. Therefore, the elevated presence of these two lipids is not just an indication of surface membrane origin but suggests that they might be necessary for viral envelopment. Thus, the selection of cellular lipids by a virus might not only be determined by protein-lipid interactions but might also be dictated by the overall architecture of the virion. Similarities in the lipid compositions of a number of different viruses may be a reflection of similarities in their structures. Differences in the lipid compositions between a given virus and the plasma membrane of its host cell may be the consequences of a selection by the virus of those lipids which can best accommodate the structural requirements of a budding virion as contrasted to the structural requirements of the whole cell.

This hypothesis is consistent with the available data and with the fluid and/or mosaic model of biological membranes (120a). The study of enveloped viruses can serve as a probe for quantitatively examining these and other models.

ACKNOWLEDGMENTS

The authors gratefully acknowledge Drs. S. Rohrlich, D. Loskutoff, and M. Rifkin for their critical reading of the manuscript and their excellent suggestions.

*Literature Cited*

1. Acheson, N. H., Tamm, I. 1967. *Virology* 32:128–43
2. Appleyard, G., Hapel, A. J., Boulter, E. A. 1971. *J. Gen. Virol.* 13:9–17
3. Asher, Y., Heller, M., Becker, Y. 1969. *J. Gen. Virol.* 4:65–76
4. Bächi, T., Gerhard, W., Lindeman, J., Mühlethaler, K. 1969. *J. Virol.* 4: 769–76
5. Bates, S. R. Rothblat, G. H. 1972. *J. Virol.* 9:883–40
6. Bennett, G., Leblond, C. P. 1970. *J. Cell Biol.* 46:409–16
7. Ben-Porat, T., Kaplan, A. S. 1971. *Virology* 45:252–64
8. Bernhard, W. 1958. *Cancer Res.* 18: 491–509
9. Birdwell, C. R., Strauss, E. G., Strauss, J. H. 1973. *Virology* 56:429–38
10. Blough, H. A., Lawson, D. E. M. 1968. *Virology* 36:286–92
11. Blough, H. A., Weinstein, D. B., Lawson, D. E. M., Kodicek, E. 1967. *Virology* 33:459–66
12. Bolognesi, D. P., Obara, T. 1970. *Comp. Leuk. Res. Biblo. Haematatol.* 36: 126–39
13. Bose, H. R., Brandige, M. A. 1972. *J. Virol.* 9:785–91
14. Brown, D. T., Waite, M. R. F., Pfefferkorn, E. R. 1972. *J. Virol.* 10:524–36
15. Burge, B. W., Huang, A. S. 1970. *J. Virol.* 6:176–87
16. Chen, C., Compans, R. W., Choppin, P. W. 1971. *J. Gen. Virol.* 11:53–57
17. Choppin, P. W., Klenk, H. D., Compans, R. W., Caliguiri, L. A. 1971. *Perspect. Virol.* 7:127–58
18. Cohen, G. H., Atkinson, P. H., Summers, D. F. 1971. *Nature* 231:121–23
19. Compans, R. W. 1971. *Nature* 228: 114–16
20. Compans, R. W. 1973. *Virology* 51: 56–70
21. Ibid 55:541–45
22. Compans, R. W., Caliguiri, L. A. *Negative Strand Viruses,* ed. R. D. Berry, B. W. J. Mahy. New York: Academic. In press
23. Compans, R. W., Choppin, P. W. 1971. *Comparative Virology.* New York: Academic
24. Compans, R. W., Dimmock, N. J. 1969. *Virology* 39:495–515
25. Compans, R. W., Harter, D. H., Choppin, P. W. 1967. *J. Exp. Med.* 126: 267–76
26. Compans, R. W., Holmes, K. V., Dales, S., Choppin, P. W. 1964. *Virology* 30: 411–26
27. Compans, R. W., Klenk, H. D., Caliguiri, L. A., Choppin, P. W. 1970. *Virology* 42:880–89
28. Courington, D., Vogt, P. K. 1967. *J. Virol.* 1:400–14
29. Dales, S., Mosbach, E. H. 1968. *Virology* 35:564–83
30. Dales, S., Siminovitch, L. 1961. *J. Biophys. Biochem. Cytol.* 10:475–503
31. Darlington, R. W., Moss, L. H. 1968. *J. Virol.* 2:48–55
32. David, A. 1971. *Virology* 46:711–20
33. David, A. 1973. *J. Mol. Biol.* 76:135–48
34. Duc-Nguyen, H. 1968. *J. Virol.* 2: 494–506
35. Duc-Nguyen, H. Rose, H. M., Morgan, C. 1966. *Virology* 28:404–12
36. Easterbrook, K. B. 1967. *J. Virol.* 1: 643–58
37. Ejercito, P. M., Kieff, E. D., Roizman, B. 1968. *J. Gen. Virol.* 3:357–64
38. Fenner, F. 1968. *The Biology of Animal Viruses,* Vol. I. New York: Academic
39. Fleissner, E. 1970. *J. Virol.* 5:14–21
40. Ibid 1971. 8:778–85
41. Filshie, B. K., Rehacek, J. 1968. *Virology* 34:435–43
42. Friedman, R. M., Levin, J. G., Grimley, P. M., Berezesky, I. K. 1972. *J. Virol.* 10:504–14
43. Frommhagen, L. H., Knight, C. A., Freeman, N. K. 1959. *Virology* 8: 176–97
44. Garon, C., Moss, B. 1971. *Virology* 46:233–46

45. Gelderblom, H., Bauer, H., Graf, T. 1972. *Virology* 47:416–25
46. Gregoriades, A. 1973. *Virology* 54: 369–83
47. Grimley, P. M., Berezesky, I. K., Friedman, R. M. 1968. *J. Virol.* 10:504–14
48. Gyorgy, E., Sheehan, M., Sokol, F. 1971. *J. Virol.* 8:649–55
49. Harrison, S., Compans, R. W. 1973. Personal communication
50. Harrison, S. C., David, A., Tumblatt, J., Darnell, J. E. 1971. *J. Mol. Biol.* 60:523–28
51. Heine, J. W., Roizman, B. 1973. *J. Virol.* 11:810–13
52. Higashi, N., Matsumoto, A., Tabata, K., Nagatomo, Y. 1967. *Virology* 33: 55–69
53. Hoagland, G. L., Smadel, J. E., Rivers, T. M. 1940. *J. Exp. Med.* 71:737–50
54. Holland, J. J., Kiehn, E. O. 1970. *Science* 167:202–5
55. Holmes, K. V., Choppin, P. W. 1966. *J. Exp. Med.* 124:501–20
56. Holmes, K. V., Klenk, H. D., Choppin, P. W. 1969. *Proc. Soc. Exp. Biol. Med.* 131:651–57
57. Holowczak, J. A. 1970. *Virology* 42: 87–99
58. Homma, M., Ohuchi, M. 1973. *J. Virol.* 12:1457–65
59. Hung, P. P., Robinson, H. L., Robinson, W. S. 1971. *Virology* 43:251–60
60. Ichihashi, Y., Dales, S. 1971. *Virology* 46:533–43
61. Ichihashi, Y., Matsumoto, S., Dales, S. 1971. *Virology* 46:507–32
62. Johnson, M., Mora, P. T. 1967. *Virology* 31:230–37
63. Joklik, W. K. 1962. *J. Mol. Biol.* 5:264–76
64. Kang, C. Y., Prevec, L. 1969. *J. Virol.* 3:404–13
65. Ibid 1970. 6:20–27
66. Kates, M., Allison, A. C. Tyrell, D. A. J., James, A. T. 1961. *Biochim. Biophys. Acta* 82:455–66
67. Keller, J. M., Spear, P. G., Roizman, B. 1970. *Proc. Nat. Acad. Sci. USA* 65: 865–71
68. Kelley, J. M., Emerson, S. U., Wagner, R. R. 1972. *J. Virol.* 10:1231–35
69. Klenk, H. D., Choppin, P. W. 1969. *Virology* 37:155–57
70. Ibid 38:255–68
71. Ibid 1970. 40:939–47
72. Klenk, H. D., Choppin, P. W. 1970. *Proc. Nat. Acad. Sci. USA* 66:57–64
73. Laine, R., Kettunen, M. L., Gahmberg, C. G., Kaariainen, L., Renkonen, O. 1972. *J. Virol.* 10:433–38
74. Landsberger, F. R., Compans, R. W., Choppin, P. W., Lenard, J. 1973. *Biochemistry* 12:4498–4503
75. Landsberger, F. R., Lenard, J., Paxton, J., Compans, R. W. 1971. *Proc. Nat. Acad. Sci. USA* 68:2579–83
76. Marion, P. L. 1969. *The phospholipids of normal and virus-infected chick fibroblasts and lipid-containing viruses.* PhD thesis. Univ. of California, Berkeley
77. Matsumura, T., Stollar, V., Schlesinger, R. W. 1971. *Virology* 46:344–55
78. McCrea, J. F., Lipman, M. P. 1967. *J. Virol.* 1:1037–48
79. McSharry, J. J., Compans, R. W., Choppin, P. W. 1971. *J. Virol.* 8:722–29
80. McSharry, J. J., Wagner, R. R. 1971. *J. Virol.* 7:59–70
81. Ibid 412–15
82. Mizutani, S., Temin, H. M. 1971. *J. Virol.* 8:409–16
83. Morgan, C., Howe, C., Rose, H. M. 1961. *J. Exp. Med.* 113:128–43
84. Morgan, C., Rifkind, R. H., Rose, H. M. 1962. *Cold Spring Harbor Symp. Quant. Biol.* 27:57–66
85. Morgan, C., Rose, H. M., Holden, M., Jones, E. P. 1959. *J. Exp. Med.* 110: 643–56
86. Morgan, C., Rose, H. M., Moore, D. H. 1956. *J. Exp. Med.* 104:171–81
87. Mountcastle, W. E., Compans, R. W., Caliguiri, L. A., Choppin, P. W. 1970. *J. Virol.* 6:677–84
88. Moss, B., Rosenblum, E. N., Garon, C. 1971. *Virology* 46:221–32
89. Nahmias, A. J., Roizman, B. 1973. *N. Engl. J. Med.* 289:667–74
90. Nii, S., Morgan, C., Rose, H. M. 1968. *J. Virol.* 2:517–36
91. Ossowski, L., Quigley, J. P., Kellerman, G. M., Reich, E. 1973. *J. Exp. Med.* 138:1056–64
92. Ossowski, L. et al 1973. *J. Exp. Med.* 137:112–26
93. Patton, S. 1970. *J. Theor. Biol.* 29: 489–91
94. Pfefferkorn, E. R., Hunter, H. S. 1963. *Virology* 20:433–45
95. Poste, G. 1970. *Advan. Virus Res.* 16:303–56
96. Poste, G. 1972. *Int. Rev. Cytol.* 33:157–252
97. Poste, G., Reeve, P., Alexander, D. J., Terry, G. 1972. *J. Gen. Virol.* 17:133–36
98. Printz, P., Wagner, R. R. 1971. *J. Virol* 7:651–62
99. Quigley, J. P., Rifkin, D. B., Reich, E. 1972. *Virology* 50:550–57
100. Ibid 1971. 46:106–16

101. Rao, P. R., Bonar, R. A., Beard, J. W. 1966. *Exp. Mol. Pathol.* 5:374–88
102. Renkonen, O., Kaarainen, L., Simons, K., Gahmberg, C. G. 1971. *Virology* 46: 318–26
103. Rifkin, D. B. Unpublished observation
104. Rifkin, D. B., Compans, R. W. 1971. *Virology* 46:485–89
105. Roizman, B. 1969. *Curr. Top. Microbiol. Immunol.* 49:1–79
106. Roizman, B., Spear, P. G. 1971. *Science* 171:298–300
107. Roizman, B., Spring, S. B. 1967. *Proceedings of the Conference on Cross Reacting Antigen and Neoantigens,* ed. J. J. Trenton, 85–96. Baltimore, Md.: Williams & Wilkins
108. Russell, W. C., Watson, D. H., Wildy, P. 1963. *Biochem. J.* 87:26–38
109. Scheid, A., Choppin, P. W. Unpublished observations
110. Schlesinger, H. R., Wells, H. J., Hummeler, K. 1973. *J. Virol.* 12:1028–30
111. Schlesinger, M. J., Schlesinger, S., Burge, B. W. 1972. *Virology* 47:539–41
112. Schulze, I. T. 1970. *Virology* 42: 890–904
113. Seto, J. T., Rott, R. 1966. *Virology* 30:731–37
114. Shapiro, D., Brandt, W. E., Cardiff, R. D., Russell, P. K. 1971. *Virology* 44:108–24
115. Shipkey, F. H., Erlandson, R. A., Bailey, R. B. et al 1967. *Exp. Mol. Pathol.* 6:39–67
116. Schwartz, J., Roizman, B. 1969. *Virology* 38:42–49
117. Siegert, R., Falken, D. 1966. *Arch. Gesamte Virusforsch.* 19:230–49
118. Siekevitz, P., Palade, G. E. 1958. *J. Biophys. Biochem. Cytol.* 4:557–66
119. Simpson, R. W., Hauser, R. E. 1966. *Virology* 30:684–97
120. Smadel, J. E., Lavin, G. I., Dubois, R. J. 1940. *J. Exp. Med.* 71:373–89
120a. Singer, S. J., Nicolson, G. L. 1972. *Science* 175:720–31
121. Spear, P. G., Keller, J. M., Roizman, B. 1970. *J. Virol.* 5:123–31
122. Spear, P. G., Roizman, B. 1968. *Virology* 36:545–55
123. Spear, P. G., Roizman, B. 1970. *Proc. Nat. Acad. Sci. USA* 66:730–37
124. Spear, P. G., Roizman, B. 1972. *J. Virol.* 9:143–59
125. Spring, S. B., Roizman, B. 1968. *J. Virol.* 2:979–85
126. Stollar, V. 1969. *Virology* 39:426–38
127. Strauss, J. H., Burge, B. W., Darnell, J. E. 1969. *Virology* 37:367–76
128. Terni, M., Roizman, B. 1970. *J. Infec. Dis.* 121:212–16
129. Tiffany, J. M., Blough, H. A. 1969. *Science* 163:573–74
130. Tiffany, J. M., Blough, H. A. 1970. *Proc. Nat. Acad. Sci. USA* 65:1105–12
131. Unkeless, J. C. et al 1973. *J. Exp. Med.* 137:85–111
132. Wagner, R. R., Heine, J. W., Goldstein, G., Schnaitman, C. A. 1971. *J. Virol.* 7:274–77
133. Wagner, R. R., Kiley, M. P., Snyder, R. M., Schnaitman, C. A. 1972. *J. Virol.* 9:672–83
134. Wagner, R. R., Schnaitman, T. A., Snyder, R. M., Schnaitman, C. A. 1969. *J. Virol.* 3:611–18
135. Wagner, R. R., Schnaitman, T. A., Snyder, R. M. 1969. *J. Virol.* 3:395
136. Wagner, R. R., Snyder, R. M., Yamazaki, S. 1970. *J. Virol.* 5:548–58
137. Wickus, G. G., Robbins, P. W. 1973. *Nature* 245:65–67
138. Zagury, D., Uhr, J. W., Jamieson, J. D., Palade, G. E. 1970. *J. Cell Biol.* 46:52–63
139. Zwartouw, H. T. 1964. *J. Gen. Microbiol.* 34:115–23

# CYCLIC AMP IN PROKARYOTES

❖1642

*H. V. Rickenberg*[1]
National Jewish Hospital and Research Center and Department of Biophysics and Genetics, University of Colorado School of Medicine, Denver, Colorado 80206

CONTENTS

INTRODUCTION .......... 353
THE OCCURRENCE OF cAMP IN PROKARYOTES .......... 354
EFFECTS OF cAMP .......... 354
*Effects of Exogenous cAMP on the Synthesis of Proteins* .......... 354
MECHANISM OF ACTION OF cAMP IN STIMULATING THE SYNTHESIS OF PROTEINS .......... 357
*Effect on Transcription vs Effect on Translation* .......... 357
*cAMP-Activated Protein Kinases* .......... 359
*Catabolite Gene Activator Protein* .......... 359
REGULATION OF THE CELLULAR CONCENTRATION OF cAMP IN PROKARYOTES .......... 362
*Cellular Pools of cAMP and Release of cAMP* .......... 362
*Adenyl Cyclase* .......... 363
*cAMP Phosphodiesterase* .......... 364
CONCLUDING REMARKS .......... 365

## INTRODUCTION

Sutherland and his associates discovered adenosine 3',5'-cyclic monophosphate (cAMP) in 1957 as an intermediate in the hyperglycemic effect of epinephrine and glucagon (84). Since then it has been shown that cAMP mediates the effects of a variety of hormones and other biologically active agents. cAMP is found in all animal cells. Its occurrence in higher plants has been the subject of debate; recent evidence (19, 112) indicates that cAMP is formed in plants and it has been suggested (39) that in plants too, cAMP mediates the effects of hormones. cAMP has been found in the green alga *Chlamydomonas reinhardii* (4) and in the prokaryotic blue-green alga *Anacystis nidulans* (H. V. Rickenberg and E. Spitz, unpublished observations).

[1]The author's research is supported by Public Health Service grant No. AM-11046 from the National Institute of Arthritis and Metabolic Diseases.

The occurrence of cAMP in bacteria was first reported in 1963 when the cyclic nucleotide was observed in *Brevibacterium liquefaciens* (69) and in *Escherichia coli* (61). The more recent finding by Perlman & Pastan (77) and Ullman & Monod (108), that exogenous cAMP partially overcame catabolite repression in *E. coli,* stressed the physiological importance of the nucleotide in bacteria and attracted the attention of molecular biologists who proceeded to explore the mode of action and metabolism of cAMP in bacteria.

## THE OCCURRENCE OF cAMP IN PROKARYOTES

The occurrence of cAMP or, at least, of one of the two enzymes which catalyze its formation and hydrolysis has been demonstrated directly in only relatively few prokaryotes. These, in addition to the organisms mentioned in the preceding section, include *Serratia marcescens* (70), *Alcaligenes faecalis* (49), *Erwinia carotovora* (49), *Arthrobacter citreus* (49), *Arthrobacter globiformis* (49), *Micrococcus lysodeikticus* (49), *Micrococcus flavus* (49), *Corynebacterium equi* (49), *Nocardia erythropolis* (49), *Streptococcus salivarius* (53), *Bacillus licheniformis* (27), and *Caulobacter crescentus* (3). This paucity of information is not to be construed as indicating a limited distribution of the cyclic nucleotide in prokaryotes. Rather it reflects the probably justifiable assumption that as basic a mechanism of control as that represented by the cAMP system is likely to be ubiquitous also in prokaryotes and hence not in need of repeated demonstration. It also reflects the relative intricacy of the assay for cAMP and the enzymes of its metabolism. That cAMP is widely distributed and quite possibly universal in occurrence, also in prokaryotes, is suggested by the large number of microbial activities affected in different organisms by either exogenous cAMP or by manipulations known to change endogenous levels of cAMP. Such activities will be discussed in subsequent sections.

It has been stated that *Lactobacillus plantarum* (96) and *Bacillus megaterium* (98) are devoid of cAMP, adenyl cyclase, and cAMP phosphodiesterase. However, work in the laboratory of H. V. Rickenberg (unpublished observations) led to the conclusion that cAMP is formed by the two organisms, albeit at concentrations significantly lower than those found in *E. coli,* for example.

Little is known about the occurrence of guanosine 3',5'-cyclic monophosphate (cGMP) in prokaryotes. This dearth of information also reflects the technical difficulties encountered in the assay of that compound. cGMP has been found in *B. licheniformis* (27) and in *E. coli* (R. W. Bernlohr, personal communication) at concentrations very much lower than those of cAMP. In *B. licheniformis* cGMP is present during exponential growth and disappears at the end of the period of active cell division whereas cAMP appears only after the end of growth (27).

## EFFECTS OF cAMP

### *Effects of Exogenous cAMP on the Synthesis of Proteins*

As stated earlier, in *E. coli* exogenous cAMP overcomes both the severe transient (71) and the less severe steady-state catabolite repression (60) of the synthesis of

$\beta$-galactosidase caused by the presence of glucose in the medium. This fact suggested that the cyclic nucleotide played a regulatory role particularly relevant to the phenomenon, at that time ill-understood, of catabolite repression. Confirmatory evidence for this view came from the finding that cAMP abolished or alleviated the catabolite repression of the formation of a number of bacterial proteins. Some of these are listed in Table 1; this compilation is undoubtedly incomplete and it may be assumed that wherever the formation of a bacterial protein is controlled by catabolite repression, cAMP plays a regulatory role in the synthesis of that protein. Most of the enzymes enumerated in Table 1 catalyze reactions which are clearly catabolic in their end effects. There are exceptions to this generalization; thus guanosine-5'-monophosphate reductase does not catalyze a catabolic reaction and the synthesis of the enzyme is not subject to catabolite repression (10). The activities of the antibiotic-inactivating enzymes chloramphenicol acetyl transferase and streptomycin adenylyl transferase (43) also do not contribute to catabolism, although they are regulated by catabolite repression and cAMP.

It may be argued that cAMP, by its regulation of the synthesis of certain proteins, controls cellular functions which are not essential to the organism under all conditions of growth. A case in point may be the synthesis of so-called secondary metabolites (109), including antibiotics, formed typically only after bacterial growth has slowed or stopped. To the author's knowledge a thorough study of the involvement of cAMP in the synthesis of secondary metabolites has not been made. The finding (38) that the synthesis of the enzyme phenoxazinone synthase which catalyzes the formation of the chromophoric portion (actinocin) of actinomycin in *Streptomyces antibioticus,* is severely repressed by glucose, is of interest in this context.

The morphogenetic effects of cAMP are particularly noteworthy. Thus cAMP is required for the formation of flagella in coliform bacteria (33, 114) and exogenous dibutyryl cAMP (and to a lesser degree cAMP) under certain conditions hastens the morphological differentiation that is part of the normal life cycle of *C. crescentus* (99).

Table 2 lists miscellaneous effects of cAMP on bacteria. Clearly most, and probably all, of these effects are mediated by a role of cAMP in stimulating the synthesis of proteins and the only reason for a separate listing here is that at the time of writing the specific protein affected had not been identified. The one case where the activity, rather than the synthesis, of a protein is affected, is that of the NADP-linked malic enzyme of *E. coli* where cAMP stimulates activity (95). It appears that the case of the malic enzyme is indeed exceptional. Whereas in eukaryotes cAMP modulates the activities of a number of enzymes, especially of enzymes which catalyze reactions of energy metabolism (90), in prokaryotes 5'-AMP, rather than cAMP, acts as allosteric effector (24, 37, 59, 113).

In summary of this section, it may be stated that in prokaryotes cAMP exerts its effects primarily by a stimulation of the synthesis of a number of proteins which are not required or functional under all conditions of growth. Furthermore, the role of cAMP in bacteria is clearly regulatory but not essential. This conclusion is reinforced by the recent finding (18) that mutants of *E. coli* with a deletion in the *cya* gene, which codes for adenyl cyclase, have not lost an essential function.

Table 1 Synthesis of proteins controlled by cAMP

| Protein | Organism | Reference |
|---|---|---|
| Proteins coded by *lac* operon | *Escherichia coli* | e.g. 30, 58, 77, 78, 108, 118 |
| Proteins coded by *gal* operon | *E. coli* | 30, 68, 110 |
| Proteins coded by *ara* operon | *E. coli* | 58, 65, 104, 119 |
| Tryptophanase | *E. coli* | 29, 30, 73, 77 |
| D-serine deaminase | *E. coli* | 30, 63 |
| Threonine deaminase (degradative) | *E. coli* | 100 |
| Glycerokinase | *E. coli* | 30 |
| Glutamate dehydrogenase | *E. coli* | 83 |
| Glutaminase A[a] | *E. coli* | 83 |
| Glutamine synthetase | *E. coli* | 83 |
| Glutamate synthase[a] | *E. coli* | 83 |
| Thymidine phosphorylase | *E. coli* | 30 |
| Pseudouridylate synthetase | *E. coli* | 105 |
| Guanosine-5′-monophosphate reductase | *E. coli* | 10 |
| Chloramphenicol acetyl transferase | *E. coli* | 32, 34, 43 |
| Streptomycin adenylyl transferase | *E. coli* | 43 |
| Flagellar proteins | *E. coli* | 114 |
| Enzyme II for fructose of PEP phosphotransferase system | *E. coli* | 30 |
| Repressor required for lysogenization by lambdoid phage | *E. coli* | 42, 76, 115 |
| Proteins coded by *ara* operon | *Salmonella typhimurium* | 12 |
| Enzymes required for utilization of mannitol | *S. typhimurium* | 11 |
| Repressor required for lysogenization by phage P22 | *S. typhimurium* | 47 |
| Histidase[b] and proteins of *lac* operon | *Klebsiella aerogenes* | 82 |
| Cholinesterase | *Pseudomonas aeruginosa* | 41 |
| Luciferase | *Photobacterium fischeri* | 66 |
| "Translocators" for $C_6$-tricarboxylic acid anions | *Azotobacter vinelandii* | 86 |

[a]The effect of cAMP on the formation of these enzymes is unusual in that cAMP inhibited; the mechanism of the inhibition which requires an intact CAP gene, is not understood.

[b]The role of cAMP in the regulation of the synthesis of histidase is complex; the reader is referred to the original publication.

**Table 2** Diverse effects of cAMP

| Phenomenon affected | Organism | Reference |
|---|---|---|
| Chemotaxis | *Escherichia coli* | 33 |
| Anaerobic growth | *E. coli* | 75 |
| Oxidative phosphorylation | *E. coli* | 44 |
| Activity of NADP-specific malic enzyme | *E. coli* | 95 |
| Competence for transformation by DNA | *Hemophilus influenzae* | 111 |
| Formation of prodigiosin | *Serratia marcescens* | U. Winkler, personal communication |
| Formation of somatic antigens and certain cell wall components | *Vibrio cholerae* | T. Yokata and S. Kuwahara, personal communication |
| Production of enterotoxin | *V. cholerae* | M. Ohashi, personal communication |
| Differentiation[a] | *Caulobacter crescentus* | 99 |

[a] Diburyryl cAMP was employed.

## MECHANISM OF ACTION OF cAMP IN STIMULATING THE SYNTHESIS OF PROTEINS

### *Effect on Transcription vs Effect on Translation*

The demonstration that cAMP is required for the effective synthesis of β-galactosidase and tryptophanase in *E. coli* raises the question of whether the cyclic nucleotide facilitates the transcription of the respective operons or whether it exerts its effect on the translation of the mRNAs into protein.

In the case of the *lac* operon, evidence for an effect of cAMP on the process of transcription comes from several sources. Silverstone et al (101, 102) and Eron & Block (36) showed that an intact promoter of the *lac* operon was essential for the sensitivity of that operon to catabolite repression and to control by cyclic cAMP. When, in certain mutants in which the *lac* promoter had been deleted, the residual *lac* operon was fused genetically to the catabolite repression-insensitive *trp* (biosynthesis of tryptophan) operon, such that the synthesis of the *lac* proteins now depended on the *trp* promoter, the synthesis of the *lac* proteins became insensitive to catabolite repression. Similarly in a number of *lac* promoter mutants (7, 72, 102) synthesis of the proteins coded by *lac* no longer requires cAMP or the catabolite gene activator protein (cf. below), whereas the syntheses of catabolite repressible proteins coded by other operons retain their sensitivity in these strains.

Evidence that initiation of transcription is the site of action of cAMP also comes from experiments in which initiation, RNA chain elongation, and translation of the proteins of the *lac* operon were separated chronologically by the use of inhibitors (51). In the same experiments it was demonstrated that cAMP had no effect on the stability of the mRNA.

The observation by Simon & Apirion (103) that high concentrations of exogenous cAMP are required for the synthesis of β-galactosidase and other catabolite-repressible enzymes in a temperature-sensitive (Ts) mutant of *E. coli* is still unexplained. The Ts mutation does not map near the *lac* operon or the gene specifying CAP (see below); it appears that the mutation causes increased RNase activity at 43°C. The concentration of endogenous cAMP and the synthesis of *lac* messenger, as measured by hybridization, are not affected. However, in the absence of exogenous cAMP, inactive protein which cross-reacts with antibody against β-galactosidase is formed at 43°C.

Claims (e.g. 1) that catabolite repression of the proteins coded by the *lac* operon, as well as the reversal of catabolite repression by cAMP, occurred at the level of translation are probably in error and can perhaps be explained on the basis of the use of presumptive inhibitors of transcription which, however, blocked transcription only partially under the conditions of the experiments. By the same token an early report (73) suggesting that cAMP acted at the level of translation in stimulating the synthesis of tryptophanase in *Escherichia coli* may be discounted. It has been suggested (28) that the ability of cAMP to block the uptake of proflavine, one of the inhibitors employed to stop the synthesis of tryptophanase mRNA, could explain, at least in part, the erroneous conclusion that cAMP affected the translation of the tryptophanase messenger. However that may be, recently published findings (29, 50, 85) suggest that cAMP exerts its effect predominantly at the level of transcription. Experiments in the reviewer's laboratory in which tryptophanase was induced in the presence of chloramphenicol and protein synthesis permitted after resuspension of the bacteria in preconditioned medium (13) containing rifampicin, led to the conclusion that in the case of tryptophanase too, cAMP exerted its effect *exclusively* at the level of transcription (M. Tecklenburg and H. V. Rickenberg, unpublished observations). An effect of cAMP on transcription, but not on translation, has also been demonstrated in other bacterial systems such as in the case of the threonine deaminase (100) and of the proteins specified by the *gal* (68) and *ara* (65) operons of *E. coli.*

A finding originally thought relevant to a role of cAMP in the translation of mRNA was the observation (57) that cAMP bound to G factor (a protein which participates in the translocation of the nascent polypeptide chain) and that this binding was dependent on GTP and was inhibited by fusidic acid. However, it was shown later (14) that purified G factor does not bind cAMP and it is assumed that the binding reported originally was due to a contaminating cAMP-binding protein, possibly CAP (cf. below). At the time of this writing, there is no convincing evidence that cAMP influences the translation of mRNA in prokaryotes. This situation differs from that found in eukaryotes where, admittedly, somewhat inconclusive evidence indicates that cAMP may affect the synthesis of different proteins at either the level of transcription or translation.

### *cAMP-Activated Protein Kinases*

By analogy with the mode of action of cAMP in eukaryotes, it might be thought that in prokaryotes, too, cAMP exerted its effects by a stimulation of protein kinases. Kuo & Greengard (56) reported on the occurrence of a cAMP-stimulated protein kinase in *E. coli.* They employed histone as phosphate acceptor and found that cAMP stimulated phosphorylation approximately threefold; the stimulation was dependent on $MnCl_2$. To the reviewer's knowledge, these findings have not been confirmed. Khandelwal et al (53a) found protein kinases in oral streptococci. Certain of the protein kinases were stimulated by cAMP; others were slightly inhibited. Eightfold stimulation by 5 $\mu$M cAMP was obtained with a pellet preparation derived from *Streptococcus salivarius* with histone type III as substrate. There is no evidence at this time for a regulatory role of protein kinases in prokaryotes.

### *Catabolite Gene Activator Protein*

It appears that, at least in *E. coli,* cAMP exerts its effect on transcription by binding to a protein which, in turn, interacts with DNA. The occurrence of this protein was first reported by Zubay and his collaborators (116, 118) who named it CAP (catabolite gene activator protein) and shortly thereafter by Pastan and his associates (35) who prefer the acronym CRP (cAMP receptor protein). CGA and CR have also been employed to describe the same protein. To avoid confusion the term CAP will be employed in this review irrespective of the nomenclature used in the original publications.

The discovery and elucidation of the mode of action of CAP were aided by the development of a preparation for the DNA-directed in vitro synthesis of $\beta$-galactosidase (117); cAMP stimulated the synthesis of $\beta$-galactosidase in this system (21). Furthermore, the stimulation required the presence of a protein not found in certain mutants (35, 118) which had been selected on the basis of their pleiotropic inability to utilize a number of sources of carbon including lactose, arabinose, maltose, mannitol, and glycerol. Such mutants fall into two classes: in one group the multiple defect can be remedied phenotypically by the addition of cAMP to the medium; such mutants are defective in adenyl cyclase (79). The second class of mutants (35, 97, 118) does not respond to cAMP and is deficient in CAP.

Zubay and his collaborators (118) isolated and purified CAP on the basis of its ability to stimulate the synthesis of $\beta$-galactosidase in a cell-free preparation derived from a mutant in which exogenous cAMP failed to overcome the pleiotropic defect in carbohydrate utilization. Phage $\phi$80*dlac* containing a normal *lac* operon served as source of DNA. Pastan and his colleagues (35) isolated and purified CAP on the basis of its ability to bind tritiated cAMP at 1°C. They found several cAMP binding proteins in *E. coli* extracts; one of the proteins stimulated the synthesis of $\beta$-galactosidase in an in vitro system. This particular cAMP-binding protein occurred both in the supernatant fluid and in the pellet when a crude extract of *E. coli* was submitted to centrifugation at 100,000 X g about one third of the binding activity sedimented with the ribosomes from which it could be extracted by washing with 0.5 M KCl (35). CAP and its mode of action have been studied in Zubay's and

Pastan's laboratories and the following account is based on the generally similar findings obtained by the two groups of workers.

The gene coding for CAP has been mapped at 64 min on the *E. coli* chromosome and is co-transducible with the genes determining sensitivity to streptomycin (*str*) and spectinomycin (*spc*); the order seems to be *cap-str-spc*. The $cap^+/cap^-$ diploid has the wild-type phenotype (80).

Experiments designed to detect CAP on the basis of immunological cross-reactivity with antibody against purified *E. coli* CAP indicate the occurrence of the protein in *Salmonella typhimurium, Klebsiella aerogenes, Proteus mirabilis, Photobacterium fischeri,* and *Caulobacter crescentus* (weak cross-reactivity). Extracts obtained from a variety of other species bound cAMP (6).

The CAP protein is a dimer with subunits of 22,500 daltons. The association constant for the binding of cAMP by CAP, as determined by equilibrium dialysis, is approximately $10^{-5}$ M cAMP. There appears to be only one site for cAMP binding per protein molecule of 45,000 mol wt. Of a large number of compounds tested, only cyclic GMP competes with cAMP for binding; cyclic GMP also inhibits the stimulation of the synthesis of $\beta$-galactosidase in a cell-free system. [However, a mutation mapping in, or very close to, the CAP locus and resulting in the synthesis of an altered CAP has been identified (93). Unlike in the case of the wild-type CAP, the binding of *either* cAMP *or* cGMP activates the mutant CAP.] There are four free sulfhydryl groups per native dimer; CAP is quite basic with its isoelectric point at pH 9.1; its amino acid composition has been determined (5).

CAP exerts its stimulation of transcription by binding to DNA (55), specifically by binding to the promoters (i.e. the sites which also bind RNA polymerase) of operons controlled by catabolite repression. CAP has no detectable protein kinase activity (74). Riggs, Reiness & Zubay (88), using a membrane filtration technique, found that purified CAP bound to phage λh80*dlac* DNA. Some binding occurred in the absence of cAMP; binding, however, was greatly enhanced by cAMP with half-maximal binding at $2 \times 10^{-5}$ M cAMP. The dependence of the binding of CAP to DNA on the concentration of cAMP was quantitatively similar to the dependence of the in vitro synthesis of $\beta$-galactosidase on the concentration of cAMP. The binding of CAP to DNA was nonspecific, however, with respect to the source of the DNA under the conditions of the experiment.

A highly resolved system for the in vitro transcription of the *lac* operon was employed by de Crombrugghe et al (31). It consisted of DNA from transducing phage carrying the *lac* operon, RNA polymerase, CAP, cAMP, purified *lac* repressor protein, and an inducer of *lac*. The *lac* mRNA synthesized was assayed by hybridization with DNA from the appropriate phage. Synthesis of *lac* mRNA which hybridized with the correct strand of *lac* DNA required the presence of CAP and cAMP in the incubation mixture. The synthesis was inhibited by purified *lac* repressor and this inhibition, in turn, was overcome by addition of inducers of the *lac* operon. Both CAP and cAMP are needed for the formation of a rifampicin-resistant complex of the DNA and RNA polymerase. Guanosine tetraphosphate in the presence of CAP and cAMP, but not in their absence, inhibited *lac* transcription; the mechanism of this inhibition is not understood.

De Crombrugghe and his collaborators suggested that the promoter of the *lac* operon had two discrete binding sites, one for the RNA polymerase and a second one for the CAP-cAMP complex and that the occupation of the latter site by the complex was required for the effective binding of the RNA polymerase to its site on the DNA molecule. Genetic evidence for the existence of two distinct sites within the *lac* promoter, which display the suggested functions, was obtained by Beckwith's group (9).

*Gal* mRNA was synthesized in a system similar to the one employed for the synthesis of *lac* messenger except that phage λp*gal* was employed as the source of DNA (68). In this particular case the combination of CAP and cAMP stimulated total RNA synthesis as well as *gal*-specific RNA synthesis. It appears that in the absence of the termination factor, rho, RNA polymerase initiates at the *gal* promoter and reads through into the phage genes.

It has been reported (92) that, unlike its in vitro synthesis, the formation of galactokinase in vivo is largely independent of cAMP and CAP. Mutants defective in either adenyl cyclase, CAP, or both of these proteins, were employed. The authors suggest that the cell-free systems lack factors which in the intact bacterium permit the efficient expression of the *gal* operon even in the absence of cAMP and CAP.

The constitutive synthesis of β-galactosidase, due to mutations at either I or O loci, retains its sensitivity to catabolite repression and is regulated by the CAP-cAMP system. This observation suggested the discreteness of the sites at which the operon-specific *lac* repressor exerted negative control and CAP-cAMP effected positive regulation. The assumption is borne out by the experiments discussed in the preceding sections which showed that CAP binds to the promoter whereas the repressor binds to the operator (40). However, the separation between the sites of positive and negative control may not be as clear-cut in all cases. Thus Nakanishi et al (64) found that in a transcription system which consisted of λp*gal* DNA, RNA polymerase, cAMP, and CAP, the *gal* repressor competed with RNA polymerase and CAP-cAMP. A preincubation complex formed by the DNA template, RNA polymerase, CAP, and cAMP was resistant to inhibition by *gal* repressor. Conversely, incubation of the DNA template with *gal* repressor prior to the addition of RNA polymerase, CAP, and cAMP prevented the formation of a preinitiation complex. The authors suggested that in the case of *gal* the operator and promoter regions overlapped. A similar situation may obtain in certain promoter mutants of the *lac* operon where the mutation has caused either a deletion, bringing promoter and operator into abnormally close juxtaposition, or where the mutation has led, perhaps, to the formation of a new promoter close to the operator (23).

There is convincing evidence then that the interaction of CAP and the promoter facilitates the binding between the promoter and RNA polymerase which precedes initiation of transcription. Although a certain heterogeneity of CAP is not rigorously excluded, it seems unlikely that there are as many different CAPs as there are operons regulated by catabolite repression. It follows that the promoters of such operons must have in common certain nucleotide sequences which are recognized by CAP in the presence of appropriate concentrations of cAMP. Evidence compatible with this assumption comes from a recent report by Sankaran & Pogell (94). The authors found that acridine orange and ethidium bromide, which are known to intercalate between the bases of the DNA double helix, preferentially inhibited the induction of catabolite repressible enzymes such as β-galactosidase and acid hexose phosphatase in *Escherichia coli* and O-demethylpuromycin methyltransferase in *Streptomyces alboniger.* cAMP overcame the inhibition by acridine orange. β-galactosidase synthesis in a promoter mutant, insensitive to catabolite repression, was also largely resistant to acridine orange, whereas the synthesis of tryptophanase remained sensitive. The implication of these findings is that the promoters of catabolite sensitive operons are particularly sensitive to intercalating compounds; this sensitivity presumably reflects the occurrence of nucleotide sequences iterated in all promoters of operons regulated by catabolite repression and cAMP.

A related problem concerns the quantitative aspects of the control of different catabolite repression-sensitive operons. Specifically, one may ask: does the maximal rate of transcription of every operon, controlled by catabolite repression, occur at the same concentration of cAMP (given a saturating concentration of operon-specific inducer where such is required)? Or, alternatively, is there a hierarchy of sensitivities with Operon A requiring a higher concentration of cAMP for its maximal rate of transcription than Operon B? The fact that, for example, the induction of tryptophanase in *E. coli* is more sensitive to catabolite repression and less responsive to exogenous cAMP than is the induction of β-galactosidase (15), suggests indeed a differential sensitivity to endogenous cAMP.

Lis & Schleif (58) compared the effects of cAMP on the synthesis of β-galactosidase and on ribulokinase (as representative of the *ara* operon) both in a cell-free system and in vivo. They found that the induction of the ribulokinase consistently required a significantly higher concentration of cAMP than did the induction of β-galactosidase. The numerical values describing the (exogenous) cAMP concentrations required for the half-maximal rates of synthesis of the two enzymes in vivo may not be very meaningful since residual barriers to permeability and the presence of a cAMP phosphodiesterase make it difficult to estimate the effective intracellular concentration of cAMP. Nonetheless it is clear that the *lac* and *ara* operons differ significantly in their sensitivity to cAMP. It would be of evident interest to extend these studies. Ideally they might be performed in mutants devoid of cAMP phosphodiesterase activity and constitutive, by loss of the operon-specific repressors, for the expression of the operons under examination. This is important in view of the possibility of an overlap between promoter and operator sites in certain operons (23, 64). Constitutivity would also obviate a consideration of possible effects of cAMP on the transport of the inducer.

## REGULATION OF THE CELLULAR CONCENTRATION OF cAMP IN PROKARYOTES

### *Cellular Pools of cAMP and Release of cAMP*

Clearly, if cAMP is to exert the multiplicity of regulatory functions described in the preceding sections, then the cellular concentration of cAMP must itself be subject to control by cultural conditions. And, in fact, a regulatory role of cAMP in prokaryotes was first suggested by Makman & Sutherland (61) when they observed that the exhaustion of the source of carbon from the medium led to a rapid increase in the cellular concentration of cAMP in *E. coli* and that, conversely, the addition of a source of carbon to a starved culture brought about the equally rapid release of the cAMP into the medium. The rapidity of the changes and experiments in which chloramphenicol inhibited the synthesis of protein indicated that the regulation of the cellular concentration of cAMP did not involve de novo synthesis of protein. These findings have been confirmed and extended. For example, Buettner et al (20) found that the cellular concentration of cAMP in *E. coli* varied with the source of carbon in the sense that the cAMP concentration was 20-fold higher in bacteria growing on L-proline, a poor source of carbon, than during growth on glucose, a good source of carbon. The readdition of glucose to a starving culture caused a very rapid decline in cellular cAMP and the amount of cAMP which appeared in the medium was greatly in excess of that in the bacteria at the time of the addition of the glucose; the bacteria continued to synthesize and release cAMP into the medium even after the intracellular accumulation had ceased (20). The observation (61) that, under conditions of starvation for carbon, the bacteria synthesized and released into the medium an amount of cAMP that corresponded to a conversion of the total pool of ATP extant in the bacteria at the onset of starvation, was also confirmed in the reviewer's laboratory. The cellular concentration of ATP under these conditions decreased by about one half. The gradual breakdown of RNA and limited proteolysis accounted for the synthesis of cAMP (M. Tecklenburg and H. V. Rickenberg, unpublished observations).

It may be remarked parenthetically that the determination of the cellular concentration of cAMP in bacteria requires great care. Experiments in the reviewer's laboratory have shown that harvesting of bacteria by centrifugation for the assay of cAMP leads to highly variable results. Rapidity of separation of the bacteria from the medium seems essential and is achieved by filtration of 0.5–2.0 ml samples through membrane filters, followed by immersion of the filters in hot 0.1 N HCl.

Thus it may be considered as established that the cellular concentration of cAMP varies with conditions of growth and, in particular, with the energetic state of the cell.

It is obvious that the regulation of the cellular concentration of cAMP can be effected at the level of the adenyl cyclase, or of the cAMP phosphodiesterase, or by a change in the rate of release of cAMP from the bacteria. A combination of effects at all three levels is, of course, not excluded. That release of cAMP into the medium plays an important role in the setting of cellular concentrations of cAMP has already been pointed out; how the release of cAMP is controlled is not known. Unfortunately the same ignorance prevails with respect to the regulation of the activities of the adenyl cyclase and the cAMP phosphodiesterase.

### *Adenyl Cyclase*

The first prokaryotic adenyl cyclase to be partially purified was that of *Brevibacterium liquefaciens.* Hirata & Hayaishi (45, 46) found the soluble enzyme to require

$Mg^{2+}$ and pyruvate, or some other α-keto-monocarboxylic acid, for activity. Recent observations by Chiang & Cheung (25) indicate that in its native state the adenyl cyclase of *B. liquefaciens* may be associated with the bacterial membrane; their partially purified preparation had the characteristics of a lipo-glycoprotein. The enzyme was reversibly activated by pyruvate and DL-lactate and this activability was abolished by treatment of the enzyme with neuraminidase, phospholipase A, or phospholipase C.

The occurrence of a particulate, but readily solubilizable, adenyl cyclase in *E. coli* was reported by Braná (16), Ide (48), and Tao and his collaborators (106, 107). The latter workers purified the enzyme about 1000-fold and found it to have a molecular weight of 110,000, a pH optimum of 9.0–9.5, and an absolute requirement for $Mg^{2+}$. The adenyl cyclase showed normal Michaelis-Menten kinetics with a $K_m$ of $4.5 \times 10^{-4}$ M and it was inhibited by NaF and pyrophosphate (106); GTP was a competitive inhibitor and cGMP was formed at about 10% of the rate of cAMP (107). Among a large number of compounds tested a few stimulated and a few inhibited activity slightly when employed at unphysiologically high concentrations (48). It would probably be premature to conclude from these negative findings that the adenyl cyclase of *E. coli* is not regulated; conceivably the enzyme loses its regulatory properties upon dissociation from the membrane. Perhaps a combination of an in vivo assay of the adenyl cyclase (81) with the use of bacteria rendered permeable to potential effectors of the enzyme will throw light on its regulation.

Mutants of *E. coli*, defective in adenyl cyclase, are readily selected (79) on the basis of their pleiotropic inability to utilize a number of carbohydrates. The *cya* locus has been mapped at 75 min on the *E. coli* chromosome between *ilv* and *metE* (18, 114).

Khandelwal & Hamilton (52, 53) found that the adenyl cyclase of *Streptococcus salivarius* was heterogeneous in size; they purified one of the fractions approximately 3000-fold and tested the effects of a number of metabolic intermediates on the activity of the enzyme. AMP inhibited with a $K_i$ of 2.5 mM; hexose phosphates at concentrations below 1 mM activated and at higher concentrations inhibited the adenyl cyclase.

Clark & Bernlohr (26, 27) found both the adenyl and guanyl cyclases of *Bacillus licheniformis* to be membranal and to require $Mn^{2+}$ for activity. The two enzymes differed in their behavior during fractionation and in their pH optima. Ide (49) surveyed 21 bacterial species for adenyl activity; he failed to detect activity in several bacilli.

### *cAMP Phosphodiesterase*

The occurrence of a cAMP phosphodiesterase in *E. coli* was first reported by Braná & Chytil (17) who found the enzyme to be soluble. Later, Nielsen et al (67) purified the enzyme about a hundred-fold; it had a molecular weight of 30,000, a $K_m$ of 0.5mM and a pH optimum of 7; it was specific for 3',5'-cAMP. The partially purified enzyme required the presence of a reducing compound and of either $Fe^{2+}$ or an iron-carrying protein for activity. In crude extracts reduced pyridine nucleotides activated the enzyme effectively, suggesting the possibility that the redox potential of the bacteria might play a regulatory role. Contrary to an earlier report (2), theophylline did not appear to inhibit the *E. coli* enzyme.

Okabayashi & Ide (70) purified a soluble cAMP phosphodiesterase of *Serratia marcescens* over 1000-fold. This enzyme had a molecular weight of 51,000, a $K_m$ of 0.5 mM, a pH optimum of 7.5–8.5, and it was stimulated by $Fe^{2+}$, $Ca^{2+}$, and $Ba^{2+}$. It was inhibited by theophylline. The enzyme catalyzed the hydrolysis of several 3',5'-cyclic nucleotides. The occurrence of membranal cAMP and cGMP phosphodiesterases in *B. licheniformis* has been reported (27).

The role of cAMP phosphodiesterases in the regulation of bacterial cAMP metabolism is open to question. Strains of *E. coli,* defective in cAMP phosphodiesterase, are more resistant to catabolite repression than are strains with normal cAMP phosphodiesterase and also have slightly, but consistently, higher levels of cellular cAMP (20, 62). That cAMP phosphodiesterase is not the primary site of regulation, however, is shown by the fact that even in a strain lacking the enzyme, levels of cAMP still differed with the source of carbon on which the bacteria were grown (20).

There is no convincing evidence at this time that either adenyl cyclase or cAMP phosphodiesterase play a major role in the control of cellular levels of cAMP in prokaryotes. Therefore the possibility that regulation is exerted primarily by release of cAMP from the cell, must be considered. As pointed out earlier, however, the failure to detect modulation of adenyl cyclase activity may be due to the dissociation of the enzyme from the membrane and attempts to reconstitute a membranal environment (e.g. by use of lipids or detergents) for the assay of adenyl cyclase might prove rewarding. The possibility that adenyl cyclase is regulated by the energy charge of the cellular adenylate pool (8) might also be considered. Such a mechanism of control would have escaped detection since it would require the simultaneous presence of several nucleotides in certain ratios during the assay of the enzyme. Chapman et al (22) showed that in *E. coli* the energy charge declined from a value of 0.8 during growth to 0.5 during starvation for carbon.

A recent observation (91) on the effect of infection of *E. coli* by the small, doubled-stranded DNA phage N4 may provide tangential information on the regulation of bacterial cAMP pools. Infection by the phage leads to a rapid and, apparently, preferential loss of the ability of the bacteria to synthesize catabolite-repressible enzymes. cAMP can overcome this effect and a mutant of N4 has been obtained which fails to shut off the synthesis of the catabolite-repressible enzymes. The identification of the product of the mutant phage gene and of its function might cast some light on the regulation of cAMP levels in noninfected bacteria also.

## CONCLUDING REMARKS

The ubiquity of cAMP suggests evolutionary antiquity; it may profit the student of evolution, especially, to compare the function and mechanism of action of the cyclic nucleotide in prokaryotes and eukaryotes. There are both similarities and differences. Thus it appears that cAMP coordinates, in both bacteria and multicellular organisms, the mobilization of potential reserves of carbon and energy when readily available sources become limiting. It seems that in bacteria cAMP exerts its effects predominantly on the synthesis of proteins, whereas in multicellular organisms the cyclic nucleotide affects both the formation and the activities of proteins. This is to be expected in view of the transitoriness of the individual cell in a bacterial culture, as contrasted with the relative longevity of a majority of the cells in the p.ıricellular organism. By the same token, the control of the metabolism of cAMP is different in the unicellular prokaryote, which is not in need of supercellular regulation, and the component cell of the complex organism which is subject to a multiplicity of integrative controls. In bacteria the cellular concentration of cAMP is regulated by the energetic needs of the cell: the level of cAMP is low when the production of energy exceeds the biosynthetic requirements for energy; conversely, the level of cAMP rises when the bacterium is starved for carbon. Whether or not such a simple relationship also obtains in the individual eukaryotic cell, when for example, grown in tissue culture, is not known to the reviewer. However, control of cAMP levels in multicellular organisms is predominantly intercellular, organismal, and hormonally regulated; cAMP reacts as "Second Messenger" (89) to hormonal signals.

Thus in unicellular organisms both the metabolism of cAMP and the role of cAMP in metabolism are confined perforce to the individual cell, whereas in multicellular eukaryotes the cellular concentration of cAMP responds predominantly to intercellular hormonal signals and cAMP exerts its effect within the target cell.

An interesting situation is found in the slime mold *Dictyostelium discoideum* which has a multicellular (pseudoplasmodial) as well as a unicellular stage in its life cycle. Here cAMP plays a dual role; it acts as *intracellular* effector of metabolism (H. V. Rickenberg, unpublished observations) and, very much as in bacteria, starvation for a source of carbon stimulates the formation of cAMP. cAMP then acts as "First Messenger" (54), as the *intercellular* signal (primitive hormone?) which triggers the transition from the amoeboid, single-celled to the multicellular stage in the life cycle. The role of cAMP in affecting the transition between the two stages makes it tempting to speculate on a possible role of starvation, as mediated by cAMP, in both the evolution of cellular specialization and of multicellularity.

A study of the differences between the mechanisms by which cAMP regulates transcription in prokaryotes and eukaryotes may prove instructive and throw light on the evolution of the genetic apparatus. The relatively simple interaction between cAMP, CAP, and the prokaryotic DNA, as compared with the complex and presently still hypothetical interaction between cAMP, protein kinase(s), and nuclear protein(s) reflects, perhaps, the differences between the naked prokaryotic DNA and the complex eukaryotic chromatin.

*Literature Cited*

1. Aboud, M., Burger, M. 1970. *Biochem. Biophys. Res. Commun.* 38:1023–32
2. Ibid 1971. 43:174–82
3. Agabian, N., Rosen, O. M., Shapiro, L. 1972. *Biochem. Biophys. Res. Commun.* 49:1690–98
4. Amrhein, N., Filner, P. 1973. *Proc. Nat. Acad. Sci. USA* 70:1099–1103
5. Anderson, W. B., Schneider, A. B., Emmer, M., Perlman, R. L., Pastan, I. 1971. *J. Biol. Chem.* 246:5929–37
6. Anderson, W. B., Pastan, I. 1973. *Biochim. Biophys. Acta* 320:577–87
7. Arditti, R., Grodzicker, T., Beckwith, J. 1973. *J. Bacteriol.* 114:652–55
8. Atkinson, D. E., Walton, G. M. 1967. *J. Biol. Chem.* 242:3239–41
9. Beckwith, J., Grodzicker, T., Arditti, R. 1972. *J. Mol. Biol.* 69:155–60

10. Benson, C. E., Brehmeyer, B. A., Gots, J. S. 1971. *Biochem. Biophys. Res. Commun.* 43:1089–94
11. Berkowitz, D. 1971. *J. Bacteriol.* 105: 232–40
12. Bhattacharya, A. K., Chakravorty, M. 1971. *J. Bacteriol.* 106:107–12
13. Bilezikian, J. P., Kaempfer, R. O. R., Magasanik, B. 1967. *J. Mol. Biol.* 27:495–506
14. Bodley, J. W., O'Dea, R. F., Gordon, J., Goldberg, N. D. 1971. *J. Biol. Chem.* 246:3618–22
15. Botsford, J. L., De Moss, R. D. 1971. *J. Bacteriol.* 105:303–12
16. Braná, H. 1969. *Folia Microbiol.* 14: 185–89
17. Braná, H., Chytil, F. 1965. *Folia Microbiol.* 11:43–46
18. Brickman, E., Soll, L., Beckwith, J. 1973. *J. Bacteriol.* 116:582–87
19. Brown, E. G., Newton, R. P. 1973. *Phytochemistry* 12:2683–85
20. Buettner, M. J., Spitz, E., Rickenberg, H. V. 1973. *J. Bacteriol.* 114:1068–73
21. Chambers, D. A., Zubay, G. 1969. *Proc. Nat. Acad. Sci. USA* 63:118–22
22. Chapman, A. G., Fall, L., Atkinson, D. E. 1971. *J. Bacteriol.* 108:1072–86
23. Chen, B. et al 1971. *Nature New Biol.* 233:67–70
24. Chen, G. S., Segel, I. H. 1968. *Arch. Biochem. Biophys.* 127:175–86
25. Chiang, M. H., Cheung, W. Y. 1973. *Biochem. Biophys. Res. Commun.* 55: 187–92
26. Clark, V. L., Bernlohr, R. W. 1972. *Biochem. Biophys. Res. Commun.* 46: 1570–75
27. Clark, V. L., Bernlohr, R. W. 1972. *Spores V,* ed. H. O. Halvorson, R. Hanson, L. L. Campbell, 167–73. Washington, DC: Am. Soc. Microbiol.
28. Conde, F., del Camo, F. F., Ramirez, J. M. 1971. *FEBS Lett.* 16:156–58
29. Dahl, R., Wang, R. J., Morse, M. L. 1971. *J. Bacteriol.* 107:513–18
30. De Crombrugghe, B., Perlman, R. L., Varmus, H. E., Pastan, I. 1969. *J. Biol. Chem.* 244:5828–35
31. De Crombrugghe, B. et al 1971. *Nature New Biol.* 231:139–42
32. De Crombrugghe, B., Pastan, I., Shaw, W. V., Rosner, J. L. 1973. *Nature New Biol.* 241:237–39
33. Dobrogosz, W. J., Hamilton, P. B. 1971. *Biochem. Biophys. Res. Commun.* 42:202–7
34. Dottin, R. P., Shiner, L. S., Hoar, D. I. 1973. *Virology* 51:509–11
35. Emmer, M., de Crombrugghe, B., Pastan, I., Perlman, R. 1970. *Proc. Nat. Acad. Sci. USA* 66:480–87
36. Eron, L., Block, R. 1971. *Proc. Nat. Acad. Sci. USA* 68:1828–32
37. Fraenkel, D. G., Pontremoli, S., Horecker, B. L. 1966. *Arch. Biochem. Biophys.* 114:4–12
38. Gallo, M., Katz, E. 1972. *J. Bacteriol.* 109:659–67
39. Giannattasio, M., Macchia, V. 1973. *Plant Sci. Lett.* 1:259–64
40. Gilbert, W., Müller-Hill, B. 1967. *Proc. Nat. Acad. Sci. USA* 58:2415–21
41. Gilboa-Garber, N., Zakut, V., Mizrahi, L. 1973. *Biochim. Biophys. Acta* 297: 120–24
42. Grodzicker, T., Arditti, R. R., Eisen, H. 1972. *Proc. Nat. Acad. Sci. USA* 69:366–70
43. Harwood, J., Smith, D. H. 1971. *Biochem. Biophys. Res. Commun.* 42: 57–62
44. Hempfling, W. P., Beeman, D. K. 1971. *Biochem. Biophys. Res. Commun.* 45:924–30
45. Hirata, M., Hayaishi, O. 1965. *Biochem. Biophys. Res. Commun.* 21: 361–65
46. Hirata, M., Hayaishi, O. 1967. *Biochim. Biophys. Acta* 149:1–11
47. Hong, J. -S., Smith, G. R., Ames, B. N. 1971. *Proc. Nat. Acad. Sci. USA* 68: 2258–62
48. Ide, M. 1969. *Biochem. Biophys. Res. Commun.* 36:42–46
49. Ide, M. 1971. *Arch. Biochem. Biophys.* 144:262–68
50. Immken, L., Apirion, D. 1972. *Genetics* 70:175–80
51. Jacquet, M., Kepes, A. 1969. *Biochem. Biophys. Res. Commun.* 36:84–92
52. Khandelwal, R. L., Hamilton, I. R. 1971. *J. Biol. Chem.* 246:3297–3304
53. Khandelwal, R. L., Hamilton, I. R. 1972. *Arch. Biochem. Biophys.* 151: 75–84
53a. Khandelwal, R. L., Spearman, T. N., Hamilton, I. R. 1973. *FEBS Lett.* 31:246–50
54. Konijn, T. M. 1972. *Advan. Cyclic Nucleotide Res.* 1:17–31
55. Krakow, J. S., Pastan, I. 1973. *Proc. Nat. Acad. Sci. USA* 70:2529–33
56. Kuo, J. F., Greengard, P. 1969. *J. Biol. Chem.* 244:3417–19
57. Kuwano, M., Schlessinger, D. 1970. *Proc. Nat. Acad. Sci. USA* 66:146–52
58. Lis, J. T., Schleif, R. 1973. *J. Mol. Biol.* 79:148–62
59. Maeba, P., Sanwal, B. D. 1968. *J. Biol. Chem.* 243:448–50

60. Magasanik, B. 1961. *Cold Spring Harbor Symp. Quant. Biol.* 26:249–56
61. Makman, R. S., Sutherland, E. W. 1965. *J. Biol. Chem.* 240:1309–14
62. Monard, D., Janeček, J., Rickenberg, H. V. 1969. *Biochem. Biophys. Res. Commun.* 35:584–91
63. McFall, E. 1973. *J. Bacteriol.* 113: 781–85
64. Nakanishi, S., Adhya, S., Gottesman, M. E., Pastan, I. 1973. *J. Biol. Chem.* 248:5937–42
65. Nakazawa, T., Yokota, T. 1973. *J. Bacteriol.* 113:1412–18
66. Nealson, K. H., Eberhard, A., Hastings, J. W. 1972. *Proc. Nat. Acad. Sci. USA* 69:1073–76
67. Nielsen, L. D., Monard, D., Rickenberg, H. V. 1973. *J. Bacteriol.* 116: 857–66
68. Nissley, S. P., Anderson, W. B., Gottesman, M. E., Perlman, R. L., Pastan, I. 1971. *J. Biol. Chem.* 246:4671–78
69. Okabayashi, T., Ide, M., Yoshimoto, A. 1963. *Arch. Biochem. Biophys.* 100: 158–59
70. Okabayashi, T., Ide, M. 1970. *Biochim. Biophys. Acta* 220:116–23
71. Paigen, K. 1966. *J. Bacteriol.* 91: 1201–9
72. Pastan, I., Perlman, R. L. 1968. *Proc. Nat. Acad. Sci. USA* 61:1336–42
73. Pastan, I., Perlman, R. L. 1969. *J. Biol. Chem.* 244:2226–32
74. Pastan, I., Perlman, R. L. 1972. *Advan. Cyclic Nucleotide Res.* 1:11–16
75. Patrick, J. M., Dobrogosz, W. J. 1973. *Biochem. Biophys. Res. Commun.* 54:555–61
76. Pearson, M. L. 1972. *Virology* 49:605–9
77. Perlman, R., Pastan, I. 1968. *Biochem. Biophys. Res. Commun.* 30:656–64
78. Perlman, R. L., Pastan, I. 1968. *J. Biol. Chem.* 243:5420–27
79. Perlman, R. L., Pastan, I. 1969. *Biochem. Biophys. Res. Commun.* 37: 151–57
80. Perlman, R. L. et al 1970. *Cold Spring Harbor Symp. Quant. Biol.* 35:419–23
81. Peterkofsky, A., Gazdar, C. 1973. *Proc. Nat. Acad. Sci. USA* 70:2149–52
82. Prival, M. J., Magasanik, B. 1971. *J. Biol. Chem.* 246:6288–96
83. Prusiner, S., Miller, R. E., Valentine, R. C. 1972. *Proc. Nat. Acad. Sci. USA* 69:2922–26
84. Rall, T. W., Sutherland, E. W., Berthet, J. 1957. *J. Biol. Chem.* 224:463–75
85. Ramírez, J. M., Conde, F., Del Campo, F. F. 1972. *Eur. J. Biochem.* 25:471–75
86. Reuser, A. J. J., Postma, P. W. 1973. *Eur. J. Biochem.* 33:584–92
87. Rickenberg, H. V., Hsie, A. W., Janeček, J. 1968. *Biochem. Biophys. Res. Commun.* 31:603–8
88. Riggs, A. D., Reiness, G., Zubay, G. 1971. *Proc. Nat. Acad. Sci. USA* 68:1222–25
89. Robison, G. A., Butcher, R. W., Sutherland, E. W. 1968. *Ann. Rev. Biochem.* 37:149–74
90. Robison, G. A., Butcher, R. W., Sutherland, E. W. 1971. *Cyclic AMP.* New York: Academic. 531 pp.
91. Rothman-Denes, L. B., Haselkorn, R., Schito, G. C. 1972. *Virology* 50:95–102
92. Rothman-Denes, L. B., Hesse, J. E., Epstein, W. 1973. *J. Bacteriol.* 114:1040–44
93. Sanders, R., McGeoch, D. 1973. *Proc. Nat. Acad. Sci. USA* 70:1017–21
94. Sankaran, L., Pogell, B. M. 1973. *Nature New Biol.* 245:257–60
95. Sanwal, B. D., Smando, R. 1969. *Biochem. Biophys. Res. Commun.* 35: 486–91
96. Sayhoun, N., Durr, I. F. 1972. *J. Bacteriol.* 112:421–26
97. Schwartz, D., Beckwith, J. R. 1970. *The Lac Operon,* ed. D. Zipser, J. Beckwith, 417–22. Cold Spring Harbor, NY: Cold Spring Harbor Lab. Quant. Biol. 437 pp.
98. Setlow, P. 1973. *Biochem. Biophys. Res. Commun.* 52:365–72
99. Shapiro, L., Agabian-Keshishian, N., Hirsch, A., Rosen, O. M. 1972. *Proc. Nat. Acad. Sci. USA* 69:1225–29
100. Shizuta, Y., Hayaishi, O. 1970. *J. Biol. Chem.* 245:5416–23
101. Silverstone, A., Magasanik, B., Reznikoff, W., Miller, J., Beckwith, J. 1969. *Nature* 221:1012–14
102. Silverstone, A. E., Arditti, R. R., Magasanik, B. 1970. *Proc. Nat. Acad. Sci. USA* 66:773–79
103. Simon, M., Apirion, D. 1972. *Genetics* 71:1–18
104. Singer, J., Englesberg, E. 1971. *Biochim. Biophys. Acta* 249:498–505
105. Solomon, L. R., Breitman, T. R. 1971. *J. Bacteriol.* 107:535–42
106. Tao, M., Lipmann, F. 1969. *Proc. Nat. Acad. Sci. USA* 63:86–92
107. Tao, M., Huberman, A. 1970. *Arch. Biochem. Biophys.* 141:236–40
108. Ullman, A., Monod, J. 1968. *FEBS Lett.* 2:57–60
109. Weinberg, E. D. 1970. *Advan. Microbiol. Physiol.* 4:1–44
110. Wetekam, W., Staack, K., Ehring, R. 1971. *Mol. Gen. Genetics.* 112:14–27
111. Wise, E. M. Jr., Alexander, S. P., Pow-

ers, M. 1973. *Proc. Nat. Acad. Sci. USA* 70:471–74
112. Wood, H. N., Lin, M. C., Braun, A. C. 1972. *Proc. Nat. Acad. Sci. USA* 69: 403–6
113. Wood, W. A. Gunsalus, I. C. 1949. *J. Biol. Chem.* 181:171–82
114. Yokota, T., Gots, J. S. 1970. *J. Bacteriol.* 103:513–16
115. Yokota, T., Kasuga, T. 1972. *J. Bacteriol.* 109:1304–6
116. Zubay, G. 1969. *Fogarty Int. Center Proc.* 4:231–35
117. Zubay, G., Lederman, M. 1969. *Proc. Nat. Acad. Sci. USA* 62:550–57
118. Zubay, G., Schwartz, D., Beckwith, J. 1970. *Proc. Nat. Acad. Sci. USA* 66: 104–10
119. Zubay, G., Gielow, L., Englesberg, E. 1971. *Nature New Biol.* 233:164–65

# MICROSCOPES, MICROSCOPY, AND MICROBIOLOGY

❖1643

*Robert Barer*
Department of Human Biology and Anatomy, University of Sheffield,
Sheffield S10 2TN, Great Britain

CONTENTS

INTRODUCTION .......... 371
OPTICAL MICROSCOPES .......... 372
*Absorption* .......... 372
*Refraction* .......... 373
ELECTRON MICROSCOPES .......... 376
MICROSCOPES AND MICROSCOPY .......... 377
IMPROVEMENTS IN MICROSCOPY .......... 377
*Resolution* .......... 378
*Spatial resolution* .......... 378
*Resolution in depth, depth of field, and penetration* .......... 379
*Chemical resolution* .......... 381
*Contrast* .......... 386
THE FUTURE .......... 387

## INTRODUCTION

It is no accident that the development of microscopy and microbiology have often been closely interlinked. Microbiology begins where the naked eye reaches its limit; even a comparatively crude microscope opens up a new world of life. Antonie van Leeuwenhoek, who first described protozoa in 1675 and bacteria in 1683, used only simple microscopes equipped with single uncorrected lenses of very short focal length. Almost two centuries later Charles Darwin took only a simple microscope on the voyage of the *Beagle.* Today the compound optical microscope is used routinely in almost every microbiological laboratory and many have access to a variety of special optical microscopes, as well as to one or more types of electron microscope.

Progress in optical microscopy has been particularly rapid during the past thirty years and this is probably a good moment to take stock. One should distinguish between microscopes and microscopy. The development of optical microscopes is bound to slow down, simply because there are few basic optical principles that have not been applied at the microscopic level. Virtually every type of optical method of analysis now has its microscopical counterpart.

## OPTICAL MICROSCOPES

All optical analytical methods depend on the absorption, refraction, or reflection of light.

### *Absorption*

This is the basis of probably the most widely used of all methods of biological microscopy. What, for want of a better term, we may call conventional microscopy depends on the differential absorption of light by parts of a specimen. The specimen in its natural state is usually refractile and more or less transparent but the uptake of various dyes by different components may lead to color contrasts that the eye can readily appreciate. Occasionally the natural specimen itself contains pigments such as chlorophyll derivatives, carotenoids, etc that may facilitate identification without artificial aids, but unfortunately the extreme thinness of many microbiological specimens may not ensure good contrast even when they are naturally pigmented. Chemists apply the principle of light absorption in several ways, varying from simple colorimetry to spectrophotometry. At the microscopical level we can compare the depth of staining or pigmentation between two specimens or against a standard projected into the field of view. A more refined method is to measure the light absorption (absorbance or optical density) photoelectrically at a selected wavelength, or over a wide range of wavelengths, and in this way plot an absorption spectrum. Microspectrophotometric techniques have been used in the ultraviolet, visible, and infrared regions of the spectrum (17, 46, 52, 65). The heterogeneous nature of most microscopic specimens has led to further sophistication, rarely required in chemical spectrophotometry. Images can be scanned electronically so that the absorbance at each point is measured and summed or integrated to give a result proportional to the total mass of absorbing material. Finally, the distribution of absorbance can be analyzed, usually by means of some form of computer, leading to the technique of pattern recognition. The usual aim of such methods is the automatic recognition and counting of cell types with only minimal operator intervention (21, 36, 38, 47, 58, 66).

Another method that depends basically on the absorption of light is luminescence microscopy, which can be subdivided into fluorescence and phosphorescence microscopy. Certain substances have the ability to re-emit some of the energy of the light they absorb in the form of light of the same, or more commonly, longer wavelength. Fluorimetry and phosphorimetry are common analytical methods in both their simple and spectrophotometric forms. It has become quite common to measure not merely the spectrum of the emitted light but that of the light absorbed (excitation spectrum). The latter should in principle be identical with the absorption spectrum, but it is often possible to measure the excitation spectrum of a substance present in much lower amount than is required for a true absorption spectrum.

Fluorescence microscopy is now a common and important method. Phosphorescence microscopes do exist but have been little used. Fluorescence microspectrophotometry is still mainly exploited in only a few specialized laboratories (48, 50, 63, 64).

### *Refraction*

Methods depending on the refractile properties of the specimen are of particular interest to biologists because most of their specimens exhibit local variations in these properties. Since the eye is only sensitive to the variations in the intensity of the light it receives, the image of a transparent object such as a living cell is essentially invisible. Thus in order to study cells they must either be stained (and therefore usually killed) or some means must be found of converting variations in refractive index and thickness into variations in light intensity.

An inefficient way of doing this is to close down the substage iris diaphragm very considerably, at the same time putting the object slightly out of focus. These procedures accentuate the effects of slight variations in optical path (product of refractive index and thickness) through the object and enhance interference and diffraction effects at discontinuities. The result is that invisible variations in optical path are converted to visible variations in intensity. Unfortunately, the relationship between these two sets of variations is complex and unpredictable so that image interpretation is difficult; another objection is that reducing the condenser aperture results in a fairly serious loss in resolution. This method really depends on the optical imperfections of the system (since a perfect optical image of a transparent system would be invisible) and the image is to some extent a caricature of the object. However, it is a good deal better than nothing at all, as many generations of microscopists have been forced to admit.

Another well-known technique that depends on refractive index discontinuities is dark-ground illumination; this has been in vogue in microbiology, especially for the detection of organisms such as spirochetes. Here the principle is to observe the light scattered or diffracted by the edges of the object. This can be regarded as the microscopical equivalent of the techniques of nephelometry and light-scattering, though it is not usually employed for the same purposes. One advantage of dark-ground illumination is the high contrast conferred by a bright object against a dark background. Under such conditions the limit of visibility is set by the brilliance of the light source. The development of modern laser sources might well revive interest in dark-ground illumination for work on living motile organisms.

Interest in biological interference microscopy really developed as a result of the discovery of an entirely new principle that was to revolutionize the study of living cells. In the early 1930s the Dutch physicist F. Zernike introduced a new method for testing optical systems, which he called phase contrast. He foresaw its potential in biology and attempted, at first with little success, to get the microscope manufacturers interested. Although the phase contrast method was originally conceived as a macroscopic physical tool, it would probably have attracted limited attention had it not been adapted to the microscope, and it is doubtful whether its discoverer would have been awarded the Nobel Prize in 1953.

Phase contrast is essentially an interference method. In classical interferometers, interference is produced between two sets of waves originating from the same light source and recombined after traversing different paths (4, 5, 18, 22, 31, 49, 52). If a transparent (refractile) object is placed in one light path it will alter the relative phases of the two waves, resulting in a shift of interference fringes or a change in light intensity. In phase contrast, however, interference occurs between two waves, one incident on the object and the other originating from the object itself as a result of diffraction. This is basically the mechanism of all image formation (with nonluminous objects). In conventional microscopy the phase relationships between the two sets of waves is such that the resultant wave for a transparent object has the same amplitude or intensity as the incident wave. In other words, the object is invisible against the background. Zernike's achievement was to recognize that if the two sets of waves could be separated and altered in phase relative to one another the resultant intensity would be changed so that parts of the transparent object could appear either brighter or darker than the background (4, 5, 22, 49). The variation in light intensity is a function of the optical path difference through the object, as it is in ordinary interferometry. The optical path difference can be defined as $\phi = (n_o - n_m)\, t$ where $n_o$ is the refractive index of the object, $n_m$ that of the surrounding medium, and $t$ the thickness of the object. The relationship between the light intensity $I$ at a point on the image and the corresponding optical path difference is given by an expression of the form

$$I = a - b \cos \phi - c \sin \phi$$

It might be thought that photometry of the image could be used to measure $\phi$ and ultimately the refractive index and thickness of an object. Unfortunately the practical means of achieving phase contrast leads to an incomplete separation of the (altered) incident and diffracted waves so that the two sets partially overlap. The relationship between intensity and path difference is distorted so that quantitative measurements are difficult. It was because of this and other defects that interest was renewed in other forms of microscope interferometry.

The purest form of interference microscope combines two separate microscope systems illuminated from a common light source by means of a beam splitter. One system contains the specimen, the other a blank reference slide. The images are recombined by another beam splitter in such a way as to produce interference phenomena—either a system of fringes or a uniform background if one of the fringes is spread out to fill the entire field of view. The refractile specimen appears either as a displacement or kinking of the fringe system or as an image of varying intensity against the uniform background. Such a system is expensive and difficult to construct and adjust. Simpler systems have been designed using only a single microscope in which two light paths originating from a common source are made to recombine and interfere. One light path passes through the specimen, the other mainly or entirely through the adjacent clear background.

Some types of interference microscopes can be used for quantitative measurement of optical path and hence the refractive index or thickness of the specimen, or sometimes both, can be derived. Though phase contrast is not generally suitable for such measurements, it can be used as a very delicate null method for determining refractive index. Very simply, since $\phi = (n_o - n_m)\ t$, if we make the refractive index of the mounting medium equal to that of the specimen, i.e. $n_m = n_o$, $\phi$ becomes zero no matter what the thickness of the specimen may be. Since the image intensity is a function of $\phi$, it will assume a value equal to that of the background illumination so that the image will disappear. The same technique of immersion refractometry can be employed with an interference microscope, or indeed with every other method of microscopy intended for observing transparent objects, but phase contrast is particularly convenient and sensitive, and is relatively cheap (4, 5, 49).

In most interference microscopes it is usual to make the separation between the two light paths as large as possible but in the differential type of interference microscope the separation is kept deliberately small, usually of the order of the resolving power of the system (22, 31, 40). Under these conditions the interference effects are sensitive to the rate of change or gradient of optical path rather than to the optical path itself. Sudden changes in refractive index or thickness are thus greatly enhanced. A particularly interesting feature is a pseudo three-dimensional effect. If we consider a spherical or cylindrical object of uniform refractive index, the gradient of optical path will be positive at one edge and negative at the opposite edge. Thus one edge will appear darker than the background, the other brighter, or if the field is colored, the two edges will differ in color from each other and from the background. This can lead to a striking enhancement of contrast; structures within a cell will appear as hills or craters according to local variations in optical path. However, it is important to remember that it is variation in optical thickness and not true thickness that is being demonstrated. Unless the specimen has an entirely uniform refractive index the image does not give a simple representation of surface structures alone. Great caution is required in interpreting the appearance of a differential contrast image and in general the technique is a qualitative rather than a quantitative one (42).

An old and familiar method for studying transparent specimens of a very special type involves the use of a polarizing microscope. If the specimen contains molecules or micelles in an orientated or regular arrangement it may be possible to detect birefringence (1, 4, 51, 65). A crystalline or paracrystalline region viewed at a suitable orientation between two crossed polarizers will appear bright against a dark background. However, apart from cell walls and chloroplasts such highly oriented regions are too rare or too small in most microorganisms for the method to have much application.

It was stated earlier that virtually every method of optical analysis now has its microscopical counterpart. The list given above is certainly not comprehensive but it covers most methods likely to be useful. The main important macroscopic methods not mentioned include Raman spectroscopy, emission spectroscopy, optical rotation and optical rotatory dispersion, and linear and circular dichroism. The appropriate technology at the microscopic level either exists already (1, 63, 64) or could probably be developed. The smallness of some of these effects and the difficulties of interpretation may make it hardly worthwhile devoting too many resources or too much time for a doubtful return.

## ELECTRON MICROSCOPES

As we shall see, a fundamental problem in optical microscopy is the limited resolving power. The ultimate limit is set by the wavelength ($\lambda$) of the light used and is approximately $\lambda/2$ or about 0.25 $\mu$m for visible light. Since this limit is not much less than the order of size of the smallest bacteria, an improvement in resolution of at least one order of magnitude is desirable. To achieve this by optical microscopy would require the use of ultra-shortwave ultraviolet light, overlapping the long wave X-ray region. Problems regarding suitable sources and optical materials could arise and the system would have to be used in a vacuum. This region of the spectrum has scarcely been investigated for microscopy but some attempts have been made to construct true X-ray microscopes using mirrors working at glancing incidence. Unfortunately, theoretical calculations show that the aberrations inherent in such systems are unacceptable. The realization that charged particles have wavelike properties and that a beam of such particles can be focused by electromagnetic fields made it possible to construct electron microscopes. The difficulties associated with the electron microscope—the high cost, the very high degree of mechanical and electrical stability required, and the possibility that the electron beam might damage or destroy the specimen—could have proved daunting but for the realization that even a crude electron microscope would be almost bound to have a very high resolving power. The wavelength associated with an electron beam accelerated through a potential of 60,000 V is 0.005 nm or about $10^{-5}$ that of visible light. If we could make an electron microscope with lenses as good as those in a modern optical microscope, a resolution of about 0.0025 nm would be theoretically possible. This should be compared with atomic dimensions which are about 0.2 nm. Unfortunately it is not, and is never likely to be, possible to correct the aberrations of electron lenses to the same high degree possible for optical lenses. Indeed, even the best electron lens is only equivalent to an optical lens stopped down to an aperture of about *f*/60 or NA 0.008! Under these conditions the best resolution obtainable with a conventional transmission electron microscope (TEM) is about 0.2 to 0.5 nm depending on the type of specimen.

Image formation in the TEM depends very little on true absorption but mainly on differential electron scattering. When high velocity electrons pass close to a positively charged nucleus they are deviated through an angle. The total deviation or scattering depends on the atomic number Z of the nucleus and the number of nuclei encountered, but usually the angular deviation is small. Many of the scattered electrons will be deflected beyond the limiting aperture of the objective and will thus not contribute to the final image. The object details responsible for the scattering will thus appear darker than the background. Although true phase contrast and interference electron microscopes have been constructed (29, 37, 43, 59), they appear at present to have little application in most types of biological work. Phase contrast effects are, however, quite important in the ordinary use of the TEM. They occur as a result of slight defocusing or because of excessive lens aberrations. In other words, as with the optical microscope, intensity variations can arise from the imperfections of the optical system.

In recent years several new forms of electron microscopes have come into more or less general use. They include the scanning electron microscope (SEM) which can be used in a variety of imaging modes; the high voltage electron microscope (HVEM); and several types of analytical electron microscopes (AEM) and microprobes. Some of these will be referred to later.

## MICROSCOPES AND MICROSCOPY

The variety of microscopes now available to biologists is indeed formidable and it is possible to extract a very large amount of useful information. It is important to remember that no single method tells us everything about the specimen—each examination must be regarded as an experiment that yields a little information. The value of combining different methods cannot be overemphasized; the specimen must be subjected to an attack from every possible angle. Quite apart from the correct use of an instrument, the selection of the most appropriate method of specimen preparation may be of crucial importance. Many of the most spectacular advances, particularly in biological electron microscopy have been made possible by seemingly trivial technological steps. One could almost argue that the glass knife was as important a landmark as the electron microscope itself! Fixation, embedding, staining, or shadowing can be every bit as important as resolution.

In many investigations the microscope itself may be the spearhead, but the auxiliary equipment such as special light sources, monochromators, photometric devices, counters, and so on may provide essential reinforcements. Modern instrumentation can produce so many units of information as to make it impossible to collect and analyze the results without sophisticated data processing equipment. It is for this reason that more and more scanning systems linked to computers are being developed (21, 38, 58, 66). Clearly, even if the microscope itself is capable of relatively little further development—and this may well be true of the optical microscope—the development and use of ancillary equipment and new specimen preparation methods, which are essential parts of the art of microscopy, have an almost unlimited potential.

## IMPROVEMENTS IN MICROSCOPY

Perhaps the first thing that springs to mind in discussing improvements in microscopy is some method of increasing resolving power. Clearly this is a matter of great importance, particularly in microbiology where most of the structural elements are extremely small. However, it is possible to become obsessed with the crude idea of spatial resolution to the exclusion of other important attributes. Contrast, for example, can be just as important as resolution in some circumstances. To put it simply, it is no good resolving something unless it can be seen! A familiar example is that if one wants to study a transparent living cell by conventional optical microscopy it is no use setting up the instrument for giving a high quality high resolution absorption image because the specimen would be almost invisible. One has to throw away a good deal of resolution and make use of optical artifacts in order to achieve some degree of contrast. At the other extreme, electron microscopes are now just about capable of resolving single atoms but low contrast is likely to be a serious problem. Even if the problem of contrast could be solved, that of recognition remains, because one grey dot looks very much like any other!

### *Resolution*

To think of resolving power purely in terms of spatial resolution is altogether too restrictive. Nowadays one has to think in terms of chemical, temporal, and contrast resolution as well. However, while it may be relatively easy to express spatial resolution numerically, it is less easy to do so for the other types.

SPATIAL RESOLUTION This is an expression of the ability of an optical system to distinguish fine detail in the image. It is usually restricted to lateral resolution in the plane of focus. There are many ways of considering lateral resolving power; the two classical methods are that of Ernst Abbe, which treats the case of a periodic object or grating, and that of Lord Rayleigh, which considers the minimum distance required between two luminous points for their images to be recognized as separate. Each yields a formula of the type

$$\text{minimum resolvable distance } r = \frac{k\lambda}{\text{NA}}$$

where $\lambda$ is the wavelength, NA the numerical aperture of the objective, and $k$ a constant depending on the nature of the assumptions made; $k$ is usually given as 0.5 for the Abbe theory or 0.61 in Rayleigh's treatment. The exact value of $k$ or $r$ is of less importance than the general nature of the formula which shows the dependence on wavelength and NA.

The numerical aperture (NA) is defined as $\text{NA} = n \sin \alpha$, where $n$ is the refractive index of the medium between the specimen and the objective and $\alpha$ is the semi-angle of the cone of rays subtended at the objective aperture by a specimen point. The maximum conceivable cone of rays accepted by a lens would be 180° ($\alpha = 90°$) in which case $\text{NA} = n$. For an immersion oil of usual refractive index this gives a maximum NA of about 1.52. In practice a lens cannot accept a 180° cone of rays so $\alpha$ has to be slightly less, giving a maximum NA of about 1.40. For work with visible light, it appears that we have reached the limit of useful lateral resolving power. The possibility of using radiations of shorter wavelength has already been mentioned, but the difficulties in establishing a really useful gain make this hardly worthwhile.

The situation in electron microscopy is very different because of the tiny NA of present-day objectives. A major factor in limiting NA is the presence of aberrations, especially spherical aberration. Aberration correction in electron lenses is very difficult but some progress has been made and modest advances may be foreseen (53). However, even this would not necessarily improve matters in practice. The problems of thermal and mechanical drift, electrical instability, the need to support the specimen, and, above all, some method of obtaining adequate contrast, all remain to be faced.

One difference between optical and electron microscopy is that in the former the method of specimen preparation may affect contrast but has relatively little effect on resolution. The same is not true in electron microscopy. Biologists are familiar with the fact that for really high resolution very thin specimens are required. A rough rule is that the resolution is of the order of one tenth of the specimen thickness (at 50 kV working voltage). Thus to achieve a modest resolution of 1 nm an exceptionally thin section (10 nm) is needed. Metal shadowing and positive or negative staining methods are little better. Evaporated metal films tend to form granular or crystalline deposits of the order of 1 nm in size and the same is true of the commonly used electron stains. It is evident that for cellular work at least the biologist has little need to worry about the inadequacies of his electron microscope so far as resolution is concerned! The resolving power of the electron microscope may still be very far from the theoretical limit but it may well be approaching the practical limit.

There remains, of course, the possibility of improving electron microscope resolution by working at shorter wavelengths, i.e. higher voltage. Within recent years several high voltage electron microscopes (HVEM) have been developed, working at anything up to 3 MV (19, 20, 55). Such instruments raise many problems of size, cost, radiation damage, specimen preparation, and contrast and in fact their main advantage from the biological point of view is likely to be greater penetration and the ability to examine relatively thick specimens rather than better lateral resolution.

RESOLUTION IN DEPTH, DEPTH OF FIELD, AND PENETRATION These factors are interrelated but are not easy to discuss. In practice the microscopist looking at a specimen that is not perfectly flat or infinitely thin wants to know how far an object detail can deviate from the plane of best focus without loss of resolution. Various formulae based on either wave optics or geometrical optics are usually given (35) but the difference is probably not as great as has been supposed. The tolerable variation in the object plane is given by a formula of the type depth of field $\Delta = Dr/NA$, where $r$ is the minimal (lateral) resolvable distance and D a constant. For an optical lens of high NA the depth of field is of the same order as the lateral resolution; in other words we obtain what is virtually an optical section.

As the NA gets smaller, $r$ increases, as does the ratio $\Delta/r$, so that the depth of field increases both absolutely and relatively to the minimal resolvable distance. High resolving power and large depth of field are essentially incompatible in optical microscopy. The situation in electron microscopy is complicated by the presence of severe aberrations but similar considerations apply. However, since the NA usually lies between 0.001 and 0.01 the depth of field is several hundred times the minimal resolvable distance, so that the entire thickness of an ordinary thin section is accommodated.

The scanning electron microscope (SEM) and HVEM require special consideration in relation to the study of thick specimens. Image formation in the ordinary SEM differs in important respects from that in the conventional TEM. A narrow beam or probe of electrons is focused onto the surface of the specimen and is made to scan the specimen in a regular pattern of lines or raster. When the beam strikes the specimen, high energy electrons may be reflected; low energy secondary electrons, X rays, or light may be emitted; electrons may be absorbed; or currents may flow. Of major interest in biology is the emission of secondary electrons. These are attracted towards a positively charged grid and then accelerated towards a solid scintillator maintained at a positive potential of about 12 kV. Light is emitted by the scintillator and is conducted along a light pipe to be detected by a photomultiplier. The fluctuations in the photomultiplier current are used to generate an image on a television tube, each image point corresponding with a point on the scanning raster. Resolution depends on several factors. The size of the scanning spot is clearly important. In principle, since the spot is produced by demagnifying the image of an electron source by an electron lens system, spot sizes of the order of resolution of a conventional TEM are possible, i.e. less than 1 nm. In practice, however, it is usually necessary to use long focal length lenses which give a practical spot size approaching 10 nm in diameter. The primary electrons may penetrate quite considerable distances (up to 1 $\mu$m) into the specimen and secondary electrons may be emitted from an area greater than that of the spot. Some backscattered electrons do originate from the area of the spot itself but those from outside it reduce resolution and contribute to a general background of electronic noise rather similar to glare in optical microscopy. Quantum noise is rarely important in optical microscopy unless sensitive electronic devices are used to detect or measure weak light signals, but in electron microscopy statistical fluctuations in electron emission may become an important limiting factor. This is true of the SEM where the number of electrons falling on the area of the spot is small enough to make random fluctuations obvious. Further electronic noise is generated in the photomultiplier and amplifier systems. Signal to noise ratio has to be taken into account in discussing resolution. The ratio can be improved by averaging, either by using a long-delay phosphor in the viewing screen or by taking long photographic exposures.

Taking these and other factors into consideration, the practical limit of resolution for commercial SEMs is about 10 nm for suitable specimens. The SEM helps to fill the gap between the optical microscope and TEM, but its main virtue is to provide a new type of contrast and the ability to study the surface structure of irregular objects over a depth that is large compared with the resolving power. This ability arises from the method of image formation. If we imagine the scanning spot focused on a given part of the specimen the brightness of the corresponding image point depends on the number of secondary electrons collected by the detector system. Parts of the specimen surface that are inaccessible to the electron beam or are shielded from the detector will appear relatively dark. The number of secondary electrons collected depends also on the inclination of the surface to the beam. An irregular surface thus produces an image varying in brightness. The image resembles that seen by an eye looking down the electron beam. When the whole surface is scanned a picture depending on the surface contours is produced and this is interpreted as a pseudo three-dimensional image (26, 41).

The SEM cannot compete with the TEM in revealing microbial ultrastructure; its strength resides in revealing three-dimensional relationships. This is a somewhat unfamiliar field in microbiology but already there have been several studies on the structure of bacterial colonies, the effects of antibiotics on cell walls, the structure of L phase and mycoplasma, the surface of bacterial spores, bacteria and fungi in infected tissues, and protozoa. An extensive bibliography on biomedical applications is available (9).

A major advantage of the HVEM is that relatively thick specimens can be studied by transmission microscopy. A fundamental problem is that a thick specimen produces energy loss in the electron beam so that the transmitted electrons move with different velocities and are not brought to a common focus. This is equivalent to chromatic aberration in optical microscopy. This effect causes resolution to be limited by specimen thickness (15). At higher voltages, however, the energy loss relative to thickness is much less, so that at 1000 kV the same resolution can be achieved for a specimen about ten to twenty times as thick as at 100 kV. The resolving power for a thin specimen should be considerably improved because of the reduction in wavelength, but spherical aberration and stabilization problems get worse and limit performance (7, 19, 20). However the ability to examine specimens up to several hundred nanometers in thickness is important, especially in microbiology. Increased penetration is unfortunately accompanied by reduced contrast and it is evident that new methods of specimen preparation are going to be of critical importance. Some of these problems and applications are discussed in a recent symposium (55).

In order to exploit the information in depth provided by both the SEM and HVEM it is desirable to use stereo imaging techniques. These involve taking two photographs of the same specimen after tilting through an angle of a few degrees, then recombining the images in a special viewer or projector. Such stereo images are a great help to image interpretation and enable measurements of height or differences in level to be made (8).

CHEMICAL RESOLUTION This aspect is increasing in importance. Light microscopists were at first simply concerned with seeing things, later with improving contrast and differentiating various parts of the specimen by staining methods, and more recently with demonstrating the distribution of specific chemical substances or groups by chemical reactions carried out at the microscopic level. Out of these beginnings the field of histochemistry has developed. Mere identification has not been enough; attempts have been made to quantify these methods. One approach has been to measure the light absorption of a component or of a colored reaction product. Microspectrophotometry began in the ultraviolet region when it was realized that nucleic acids exhibited strong absorption peaks at ca 260 nm and proteins at ca 280 nm. Caspersson and his school (12) exploited these properties and using a quartz ultraviolet microscope were able to indicate the important role of RNA in protein synthesis, for example. The possibilities, techniques, and errors of UV microspectrophotometry have been extensively reviewed (23, 61, 65). Microbiological applications have been relatively few and mostly qualitative rather than quantitative (28, 34) but there may be a case for further exploitation.

It is in the visible region of the spectrum that most recent work has been carried out. The problem here is to develop a specific color reaction in which it can be shown that under conditions of microscopic measurement the absorbance at any point of the image is proportional to the mass of absorbing material. This is in fact difficult to prove, as conditions in fixed and dried cells are very different from those in dilute solution. Nevertheless, it is generally accepted that some histochemical methods, for example, the Feulgen method for DNA, give valid quantitative results that are in good agreement with biochemical estimations (32, 46, 52, 65). Two further problems must be considered in relation to chemical resolution. First, what is the smallest object whose absorbance can be measured correctly, and second, to what extent is it possible to estimate one component out of a mixture such as may occur in biological specimens? It might be thought that one could measure absorbance over an area equivalent to the limit of lateral resolution. However, this is not so because even a so-called perfect lens does not image a point of light as a point but as a central disk surrounded by concentric rings which become progressively fainter (Airy disk pattern). Most of the light is concentrated into the central disk but some is spread far more widely, especially if aberrations are present. It is difficult to give an estimate of photometric resolution but the error is likely to become small with objects of diameter about 2 to 4 wavelengths, i.e. considerably greater than the resolution limit with a high aperture objective.

With regard to the resolution of different components, this depends on the nature of the absorption spectrum. Most dyes and organic compounds that absorb UV or visible light have relatively broad nonspecific absorption spectra so that if two colored components were present separation might be difficult unless the absorption maxima were widely separated. Again the relative amounts and specific absorptivity of the components might be important. In the UV, nucleic acids absorb maximally at about 260 nm, proteins at about 280 nm. Unfortunately, the protein peak usually appears as an inflection or shoulder on the downward slope of the nucleic acid curve, making accurate determinations of protein content difficult.

The use of cytophotometric methods in microbiology has been limited because of the small size of the objects to be measured. In principle a good deal of useful information could be obtained but measurements at a single point of the image are tedious and inaccurate. A basic problem in absorption measurements of most heterogeneous objects is that the mass of absorbing material is proportional not to the intensity of the transmitted light but to the absorbance, defined as the logarithm of the ratio of the intensity of the transmitted light to that of the incident light. Averaging intensity over a large heterogeneous area gives quite erroneous results. A new generation of scanning instruments is available in which the image is automatically scanned by a small spot, the absorbance at each point is measured, and the integrated absorbance, proportional to the mass of absorbing material present, is calculated. The scanning mode gives improved photometric accuracy but this is still limited by the size of the object relative to that of the scanning spot (6, 24, 38).

Fluorescence microscopy has a high potential chemical resolution but this again may be limited by the small dimension of microbiological structures and the consequent low image intensity. Apart from bacteriochlorophylls, porphyrins, and other pigments, few substances naturally present in microorganisms are likely to show visible fluorescence and the main hope lies in specific staining methods. There are now many histochemical fluorescence methods, including equivalents for the Feulgen (DNA) and PAS (polysaccharides) methods. Microfluorimetry offers many attractions as a quantitative method, especially in microbiology. Unlike the situation in absorptiometry the mass of fluorescent material is basically proportional to the light intensity. There is thus no need to determine absorbance at each point and then integrate; the total mass, even in a heterogeneous object, can be determined by one simple measurement of light intensity. There are other problems if absolute measurements are required; the light source must be stable and fluorescence intensities must be compared with that emitted by a standard specimen; photochemical decomposition may result in fading of fluorescence. Requirements are less stringent for comparative estimations and, of all the optical methods of analysis, this may well turn out to be the most promising in microbiology (27, 64, 65).

The use of fluorescent-labeled antibodies is now an important and widespread method in microbiology and requires little discussion (27, 39). The difficulties in the way of making this a quantitative method are similar to those already mentioned but some progress has been made (27). The possibility of distinguishing different types of antigens in microorganisms has already been realized (11, 14, 60) and one can perhaps begin to speak of immunochemical resolution. It is unlikely that such resolution can ever be great in light microscopy but immunolabeling methods are being widely used in electron microscopy. Here the antibody is conjugated with substances such as ferritin which contains iron or with other organic compounds containing heavy elements such as mercury, uranium, or iodine.

Just as some substances exhibit luminescence when irradiated with light so do others when exposed to an electron beam (cathodoluminescence). This phenomenon can be investigated by a simple modification of the SEM in which the light emitted is conducted directly to a photomultiplier. Many fluorescent substances are also cathodoluminescent and the possibility exists of developing chemical or immunochemical resolution techniques combined with fairly high spatial resolution. The SEM is particularly well adapted to the study of surface structure and since surface antigens are of special importance an immunoluminescence microscope of this sort could be very worthwhile. Many technical problems, especially low image intensity and tendency to fade, remain to be solved, however.

Considerable interest has been aroused by the development of analytical systems based on electron optics. One of the best established instruments is the electron probe microanalyzer or microprobe. This depends on the fact that when a beam of high velocity electrons encounters matter, characteristic X rays are generated. An electron is ejected from its atomic orbit and is replaced by one from a higher orbit. The energy difference between the orbits appears as an X-ray photon of definite wavelength. The X-ray spectrum of an atom is thus composed of easily distinguishable sharp lines. The spectrum can be analyzed either after diffraction at a curved crystal set for a given wavelength or after collection of all the emitted X rays by a solid state detector. The latter detects X-ray quanta as a series of pulses; the height of each pulse is proportional to the quantum energy so that by analyzing the height of the pulses the wavelength distribution can be deduced (25, 57).

Elements of atomic number 8 or over can be assayed fairly easily but systems for lighter elements are being developed. The type of information obtainable depends on the specimen thickness. In a thick specimen the electrons undergo scattering and energy loss but may excite quite a large volume of tissue. The penetration and resolution will depend on the density of the specimen. Electron scattering becomes relatively less important with decreasing thickness and with ultrathin sections the resolution depends on the diameter of the probe spot. This in turn governs the energy available for excitation and the resolution is thus limited by the amount of X-ray emitting element. The present limit is of the order of $10^{-16}$g, though this might be improved by one or even two orders. The local weight fraction of an element can be measured to 1 in $10^4$, i.e. 100 ppm, and in thin specimens the mass of element per unit volume and total mass per unit area can also be found. Microprobes can be used either statically, making measurements at one point of the specimen, or the beam can be made to scan the specimen in the form of a raster as in the SEM. Indeed, efficient X-ray detectors are now available for some SEMs and an X-ray image corresponding to a given wavelength can be displayed. The limiting factor in such instruments is the size of the scanning spot. This is rarely less than 0.1 μm for a conventional microprobe or 0.01 μm for an SEM. However, because of the spread of electrons within the specimen the minimal diameter for achieving X-ray resolution is about 1 μm, i.e. poorer than the resolution of a good optical microscope. A unique instrument that combines high lateral resolving power with optimal X-ray resolution is the electron microscope micro-analyzer (EMMA) constructed by Associated Electrical Industries. This is essentially a TEM in which a special mini-lens is provided for focusing a very fine beam (0.001 μm or 1 nm diameter) onto the specimen. The electron image approaches that of a conventional TEM in resolution and the X-ray resolution may be better than 0.1 μm. This instrument makes it possible to observe ordinary thin sections and to carry out elemental analyses on selected small areas (13, 57, 62). Clearly it could be of great potential interest in microbiology.

*Mass and concentration* Many of the methods mentioned above are aimed at deriving the mass or concentration of some specific component such as a nucleic acid or an inorganic ion. In many problems a knowledge of total (nonspecific) mass or concentration may be important in itself or for providing an essential baseline against which the amount of a specific constituent may be measured. Refractometry and interferometry can provide such information. The image intensity in a phase contrast or interference microscope is a function of optical path difference (phase change) defined by $\phi = (n_o - n_m)t$. It has been shown that a linear relationship exists between the refractive index of a solution $n_s$ and the concentration of solute. Thus $n_s = n_m + \alpha C$ ($n_m$ = refractive index of medium or solvent, $C$ = concentration in g/100 ml, $\alpha$ is a characteristic constant). Assuming that a similar relationship holds for a protoplasmic object, $n_o = n_m + \alpha C$, whence $\phi = \alpha Ct$. If the object has a projected area $A$, $\phi A = \alpha CtA = \alpha CV$ ($V$ = volume) = $100\alpha\ M$ ($M$ = dry mass) and finally $M/A = \phi/100\alpha$, i.e. the dry mass per unit area is proportional to $\phi$. Phase contrast and interference microscopy thus give an image that is basically a contour map of dry mass variation. A spot measurement of $\phi$ gives the dry mass at a given point but to measure the total dry mass of a heterogeneous object, such as a cell, the measurement has to be integrated over the total projected area. Scanning instruments are now available for carrying out such measurements comparable to those that measure integrated absorbance (6, 33, 52, 54). Phase contrast, while not easily adaptable to the measurement of $\phi$, can be used as a sensitive null method for measuring refractive index. Since this parameter varies linearly with concentration, the latter can be derived. Such calculations assume that a definite value for $\alpha$ can be assigned to protoplasm. Fortunately it can be shown that $\alpha$ is approximately constant for most proteins and the error in assuming a value of 0.0018 for protoplasm is unlikely to be great (4, 5, 18, 49). The sensitivity or mass resolution of these methods is high. Refractive index can be measured quite easily to an accuracy of 0.001, corresponding to a concentration of 0.5% protein; higher accuracy can be achieved in favorable circumstances. Modern instruments can measure phase changes to about $\lambda/1000$, corresponding to a mass of less than $10^{-14}$ g/$\mu m^2$. Many examples of the applications of phase and interference microscopy to microbiology are to be found in the literature (5, 44, 49).

Electron microscopy can also be used to measure total dry mass (2, 3). Theory shows that when an electron beam falls on a specimen the proportion of electrons scattered depends on the local dry mass. The electron micrograph, like a phase contrast or interference image, is essentially a map of mass distribution. By suitable exposure and photometry of the micrograph the local mass can be deduced. The sensitivity is ultimately limited by lateral resolution but the mass of single ribosomes, about $10^{-18}$g, has been measured.

*Temporal resolution* The ability to study time-dependent phenomena is high for most optical methods but low for electron microscopy. Certainly if it is a question of observing living cells, optical methods offer the only practical solution. Phase contrast has helped to elucidate many aspects of bacterial cytology. The interactions between microorganisms and cells as in phagocytosis, the structural changes resulting from the action of antibiotics, and aspects of cell division have all been investigated under conditions greatly superior to those available before its discovery. Phase and interference microscopy are among the very few methods capable of yielding quantitative measurements on living cells.

The temporal resolution of phase and interference microscopy is limited only by the speed of recording methods. For quantitative work the time needed to make a measurement is the limiting factor. Temporal resolution in electron microscopy is a very different matter. One can, as in light microscopy, examine different members of a cell population at a series of time intervals and attempt to piece together a sequence of events. The time element can also be introduced by labeling methods, especially autoradiography, at either the light or electron microscope level. The pitfalls of such methods are fairly obvious. The small size of microorganisms make the achievement of temporal resolution combined with high spatial resolution a matter of urgency. More than thirty years ago M. von Ardenne claimed that some spores were capable of germination after examination in the electron microscope. Since then numerous attempts have been made to develop environmental chambers in which specimens could be examined without the need for complete dehydration.

This field has recently been reviewed (30). The majority of environmental chambers have either a sealed atmosphere between two thin films or a gas saturated atmosphere with water vapor flowing continuously over the specimen. Among the problems to be overcome are heating and irradiation damage of the specimen and poor contrast. The latter arises partly from the thickness of the specimen but possibly also from the presence of water, which seems to scatter electrons strongly. Other limiting factors may be blurring of the image and loss of resolution as a result of cell motility, or on a smaller scale, protoplasmic streaming, Brownian movement, and so on. The combination of the HVEM with an environmental chamber would seem promising in view of the ability to penetrate relatively thick specimens. One of the earliest experiments with the Toulouse HVEM was to observe living bacteria in an environmental chamber. It was claimed that some of these bacteria underwent further growth when cultured after removal from the chamber (19). However, some aspects of these experiments are open to criticism and no clear confirmation is yet available. Success is theoretically possible especially if highly resistant organisms, such as *Micrococcus radiodurans,* are selected. The use of the SEM in the transmission mode may be even more promising than the HVEM for studying thick specimens. Electrons scattered by the specimen can be collected over a wide angle and since these do not have to be imaged by a lens, chromatic aberration becomes unimportant. The resolution is mainly dependent on spot size. Using an environmental chamber under these conditions, it has been claimed (56) that living, even motile, microorganisms have been observed, but no comments were made on subsequent survival. Temporal resolution in the SEM might be less than in the HVEM because of the time taken to scan the specimen. Looking at the results obtained so far it must be admitted that the images of living cells are of poor quality and have added little of real value to microbiology or elsewhere. Despite this pessimistic appraisal ultimate success could be so rewarding as to justify further efforts.

### *Contrast*

Throughout this discussion we have been concerned with different forms of resolution. In principle, some forms of resolution can be discussed without reference to contrast but in practice the two are very much interrelated. That is why microscopy, as well as the microscope, is of such importance, for microscopy is very often concerned with contrast. Sometimes the contrast is specific in nature: a histochemical method may stain only part of a cell, birefringent or fluorescent areas can be demonstrated, or X-ray emission images can be displayed corresponding to the distribution of individual elements. Selective labeling, such as autoradiography and immunolabeling, fall into similar categories. Other contrast method are nonspecific or require further analysis. Phase constrast and interference microscopy, many positive and negative staining techniques in electron microscopy, shadowing and replica methods either alone or combined with freeze-fracturing or freeze-etching often reveal variations in physical properties such as height, thickness, density, and mass, but these are not easily related to variations in chemical composition. All visual methods of microscopy involve the ability of the eye to resolve differences in relative light intensity or contrast. One must try to define the minimal change in a physical or chemical property that results in a just detectable change in relative light intensity in the image. Nonvisual methods bring in different problems such as the response of photographic materials, the number of grey levels of a photoelectric device, the signal to noise ratio, integration time, and so on.

## THE FUTURE

One aim of this survey has been to try to get away from the narrow idea that the only improvement in microscopy is related to spatial resolution. Admittedly this is an important requirement in microbiology but we have to accept that physical limitations make any dramatic improvement unlikely. Certainly so far as optical microscopy is concerned it seems that for extended objects at least, we have come to the end of the road. Improvements in this field undoubtedly lie in the development of methods of chemical resolution, contrast enhancement, and image processing and analysis. Future generations of optical microscopes are unlikely to embody any new principles but they may be coupled to a range of mechanical and electronic devices that make for easy and rapid operation, measurement, data storage, and analysis. In other words, the future lies in microscopy rather than microscopes; we shall not be able to do anything very different from what can be done at present but we shall be able to do it more easily and much more quickly. Optical microscopy is advancing into the computer age (21, 36, 45, 47, 66).

The situation in electron microscopy is different. Here the theoretical potentialities are nowhere near realized. That does not mean that progress is likely to be rapid. The very nature of electron microscopes is such that to try out a new device often requires a very long period for development and construction. The cost of commercial exploitation may be prohibitive. We talk glibly of high voltage instruments and sophisticated microanalyzers but how many biological laboratories are going to be able to afford such things? The main hope is that laboratories concerned with metals and materials will have sufficient use for such devices to justify their construction and allow their occasional use by biologists. Once again salvation may lie in microscopy rather than microscopes. If we could develop methods of cutting better and thinner serial sections, of improving contrast, and of demonstrating specific chemical components, we could go a long way further towards attaining the practical limit of resolving power and the amount of useful information that could be collected would be enormous. A resolution of 0.5 nm is in the size range of fairly small molecules and one wonders if many biologists really need to go much farther unless they have some means of identifying what they see. Indeed the possibility of observing biological molecules under the electron microscope without serious damage has been doubted (10).

It is dangerous to predict how any subject will develop. The indications are that the conventional TEM will continue to have a useful future and will become more reliable and easier to use. Commercial pressures are already forcing manufacturers to provide a number of rather expensive accessories, such as equipment for microanalysis or for scanning transmission electron microscopy (STEM). While such accessories cannot be expected to reach the level of performance of special-purpose instruments, they may provide a reasonable solution for the average biological laboratory, if care is taken to ensure that the range of problems can be dealt with adequately. All too often biologists have been hypnotized by manufacturers' claims into thinking that an instrument will solve their problems at the touch of a button, when in fact biological conditions make a meaningful solution difficult or impossible. In microanalysis, for example, it is one thing to claim to be able to measure the distribution of sodium or potassium but quite another to claim that this represents the distribution of such diffusible elements in life. To do this will almost certainly require a tremendous amout of work on specimens prepared and maintained at very low temperatures. This technology would probably be beyond the reach of most biological laboratories.

The exciting aim of studying living cells under the electron microscope will no doubt continue to stimulate interest in the HVEM and STEM and indeed even the HVSTEM but cost-effectiveness will become a critical issue. The STEM seems to be promising, especially if equipped with more efficient electron sources. Using a specially constructed STEM equipped with a field-emission cold cathode source, Crewe and his co-workers have taken photographs of uranium atoms bound in molecules (16). Commercial versions of such an instrument would probably be prohibitively expensive but simpler versions might be useful for studying thick sections with good resolution and would have all the flexibility and range of methods available with the first generation of SEMs.

Finally, as with optical microscopy we can expect increasing automation, data processing, and computerization. Whether the increasing complexity and cost of such equipment will ultimately be self-defeating remains to be seen.

*Literature Cited*


1. Allen, R. D., Brault, J. W., Zeh, R. M. 1966. *Advances in Optical and Electron Microscopy 1,* ed. R. Barer, V. E. Cosslett, 77–114. London: Academic
2. Bahr, G. F. 1966. *Introduction to Quantitative Cytochemistry,* ed. G. L. Wied, 137–51. New York: Academic
3. Bahr, G. F., Zeitler, E., Eds. 1965. *Symposium on Quantitative Electron Microscopy.* Baltimore: Williams & Wilkins
4. Barer, R. 1959. *Analytical Cytology,* ed. R. C. Mellors, 169–272. New York: McGraw-Hill. 2nd ed.
5. Barer, R. 1966. *Physical Techniques in Biological Research,* ed. A. W. Pollister, 111A:1–56. New York: Academic. 2nd ed.
6. Barer, R., Smith, F. H. 1972. *New Sci.* 1972:380–83
7. Beeston, B. E. P. 1973. *J. Microsc.* 98:402–16
8. Boyde, A. 1973. *J. Microsc.* 98:452–71
9. Boyde, A., Jones, S. J., Bailey, E. 1973. *Scanning Electron Microscopy/1973,* ed. O. Johari, I. Colvin, 698–734. Chicago: Ill. Inst. Technol. Res. Inst.
10. Breedlove, J. R., Trammell, G. T. 1970. *Science* 170:1310–13
11. Caldwell, W. J., Stulberg, C. S., Peterson, W. D. 1966. *J. Bacteriol.* 92:1177
12. Caspersson, T. O. 1950. *Cell Growth and Cell Function.* New York: Norton
13. Chandler, J. A. 1973. *J. Microsc.* 98: 359–78
14. Cole, R. M. 1965. *Bacteriol. Rev.* 29: 326
15. Cosslett, V. E. 1956. *Brit. J. Appl. Phys.* 7:10
16. Crewe, A. V., Wall, J., Longmore, J. 1970. *Science* 168:1338–40
17. Danielli, J. F., Ed. 1958. *General Cytochemical Methods* 1. New York: Academic
18. Davies, H. G. 1958. See Ref. 17, 55–161
19. Dupouy, G. 1968. *Advances in Optical and Electron Microscopy 2,* ed. R. Barer, V. E. Cosslett, 167–250. London: Academic

20. Dupouy, G. 1973. High voltage microscopy symposium at EMCON 1972. *J. Microsc.* 97:3–27
21. Evans, D. M. D. 1970. *Cytology Automation.* Edinburgh: Livingstone
22. Francon, M. 1961. *Progress in Microscopy.* Oxford: Pergamon
23. Freed, J. J. 1969. *Physical Techniques in Biological Research,* ed. A. W. Pollister, 95–167. IIIC. New York: Academic 2nd ed.
24. Goldstein, D. J. 1971. *J. Microsc.* 93: 15–42
25. Hall, T. A. 1971. *Physical Techniques in Biological Research 1A,* ed. G. Oster, 157–275. New York: Academic
26. Hearle, J. W. S., Sparrow J. T., Cross, P. M. 1972. *The Use of the Scanning Electron Microscope.* Oxford: Pergamon
27. Holborow, E. J. 1970. *Standardization in Immunofluorescence.* Oxford: Blackwell
28. Janicek, L., Svihla, G. 1967. *Microscope* 15:500–10
29. Johnson, H. M., Parsons, D. F. 1973. *J. Microsc.* 98:1–17
30. Joy, R. T. 1973. *Advances in Optical and Electron Microscopy 5,* ed. R. Barer, V. E. Cosslett, 297–352. London: Academic
31. Krug, W., Rienitz, J., Schulz, G. 1964. *Contributions to Interference Microscopy.* London: Hilger & Watts
32. Leuchtenberger, C. 1958. See Ref. 17, 219–78
33. Lomakka, G. 1965. *Acta Histochem. Suppl.* 6:393–96
34. Malmgren, B., Hedén, C. G. 1947. *Acta Pathol. Microbiol. Scand.* 24:417–96
35. Martin, L. C. 1966. *Theory of the Microscope.* London: Blackie
36. Mendelsohn, M. L., Mayall, B. H., Prewitt, J. M. S., Bostrom R. C., Holcomb, W. G. 1968. See Ref. 19, 77–150
37. Mollenstedt, G., Buhl, R. 1957. *Phys. Blätter* 13:357
38. Montgomery, P. O'B. 1962. *Ann. NY Acad. Sci.* 97:329–526
39. Nairn, R. C., Ed. 1969. *Fluorescent Protein Tracing.* Edinburgh: Livingstone. 3rd ed.
40. Nomarski, G. 1955. *J. Phys. Radium* 16:95
41. Oatley, C. W. 1972. *The Scanning Electron Microscope.* Cambridge: Univ. Press.
42. Padawer, J. 1968. *J. Microsc.* 88:305–49
43. Parsons, D. F. Ed. 1970. *Some Biological Techniques in Electron Microscopy.* New York: Academic
44. Payne, J. I., Sehgal, S. N., Gibbons, N. E. 1960. *Can. J. Microbiol.* 6:9–15
45. Piller, H. See Ref. 30, 95–114
46. Pollister, A. W., See Ref. 23, 201–51
47. Preston, K., See Ref. 30, 43–93
48. Rigler, R. 1966. *Acta Physiol. Scand.* 67:Suppl. 267, 1–122
49. Ross, K. F. A. 1967. *Phase Contrast and Interference Microscopy for Cell Biologists.* London: Arnold
50. Rost, F. W. D., Pearse, A. G. E. 1971. *J. Microsc.* 94:93–105
51. Ruch, F., See Ref. 5, 57–86
52. Sandritter, W., Kiefer, G., Eds. 1965. *Acta Histochem. Suppl.* 6
53. Septier, A., See Ref. 1, 204–74
54. Smith, F. H. 1972. *Microscope* 20: 153–60
55. Swann, P. R., Ed. 1973. High Voltage Microscopy Symposium at EMCON 1972. *J. Microsc.* 97:1–268
56. Swift, J. A., Brown, A. C. 1970. *J. Phys. E* 3:924–26
57. Symposium on Microanalytical Techniques in the Electron Microscope 1973. *J. Microsc.* 99:123–233
58. Tolles, W. E., Ed. 1969. *Ann. NY Acad. Sci.* 157:1–530
59. Unwin, P. N. T. 1973. *J. Microsc.* 98: 299–312
60. Walker, P. D., Batty, I. 1965. *J. Appl. Bacteriol.* 28:194
61. Walker, P. M. B., See Ref. 17, 163–217
62. Weavers, B. 1973. *Histochem. J.* 5: 173–93
63. West, S. S., See Ref. 58, 111–22
64. West, S. S., See Ref. 46, 253–321
65. Wied, G. L., Ed. 1966. *Introduction to Quantitative Cytochemistry.* New York: Academic
66. Wied, G. L., Bahr, G. F., Eds. 1970. *Automated Cell Identification and Cell Sorting.* New York: Academic

# BUDDING BACTERIA ❖1644

*Peter Hirsch*
Institut für Allgemeine Mikrobiologie der Universität, D-23 Kiel, Germany

---

CONTENTS

INTRODUCTION ........ 392
TOWARD A DEFINITION OF BUDDING ........ 392
*Types of Budding Processes Observed in Bacteria* ........ 393
*Budding for multiplication* ........ 393
*Budding for cell or hyphal branching* ........ 393
*Budding for sporulation and spore germination* ........ 394
*Bacterial Forms Resembling Budding Stages* ........ 395
*Comparison to Fungal Budding* ........ 396
*Definitions for Bacterial Budding* ........ 397
SURVEY OF BUDDING BACTERIA (TAXONOMY AND PHYSIOLOGY) ........ 397
*Hyphomicrobium* ........ 399
*Hyphomonas* ........ 407
*Pedomicrobium* ........ 408
*New Hyphal Budding Bacteria* ........ 410
*Rhodomicrobium* ........ 410
*Ancalomicrobium* ........ 415
*Ancalochloris* ........ 416
*Prosthecomicrobium* ........ 416
*Prosthecochloris* ........ 417
*Star-Shaped Bacteria* ........ 417
*Planctomyces* ........ 418
*Pasteuria* ........ 419
*Blastobacter* ........ 420
*Methylosinus* ........ 421
*Naumanniella* ........ 422
*Budding Cocci and Siderococcus* ........ 422
*Seliberia* ........ 423
*Mycococcus and Nocardioform Organisms* ........ 424
*Geodermatophilus and Blastococcus* ........ 425
*Bacterial Protoplasts and L Forms* ........ 426
*Mycoplasma, Acholeplasma, and Thermoplasma* ........ 426
*Metallogenium* ........ 428
*Caulococcus and Kusnezovia* ........ 429
GENOMES OF BUDDING BACTERIA ........ 430
*Base Ratios and DNA Homology Studies* ........ 430
*The Nuclear Apparatus and Genome Size* ........ 430
*Pure Culture Storage and Genetic Stability* ........ 432

MORPHOGENESIS AND LIFE CYCLES .......... 433
*Definitions and General Remarks* .......... 433
*Pleomorphy and Development of Hyphal Bacteria* .......... 433
*Cell Polarity* .......... 434
*Life Cycles* .......... 434
ECOLOGICAL OBSERVATIONS AND INTERPRETATIONS .......... 436
*Natural Habitats* .......... 436
*Parasites of Budding Bacteria* .......... 437
*Some Ecological Consequences of Budding* .......... 437
*Budding Bacteria as Indicators for Environmental Quality* .......... 437
SUMMING UP AND CONCLUSIONS .......... 438

## INTRODUCTION

Bacteria, by definition, divide by fission which is preceded by distinct cell wall growth that increases the length or diameter of their cells. Bud formation prior to the fission process is, then, just a special case of distinct wall growth; namely, one in which the parental wall is locally weakened to allow wall and membrane growth in only one very small area. Thus, most or all of the wall and membrane of an initially substantially smaller "daughter cell" are newly made. A bud is commonly thought of as a small, often spherical, structure attached to a larger and mature "mother cell."

Budding, or the formation of structures resembling buds, is quite common among microorganisms. However, only certain forms produce buds *regularly* before cell division; these organisms can be called "truly budding." Little is known about the biology and relationships among these truly budding bacterial forms. Many of them have not been cultured, and taxonomically they represent groups of great diversity. This review proposes to show and evaluate the present state of knowledge of the often very "unusual," truly budding bacteria.

Budding bacteria as a group have been reviewed by Schmidt (222), Starr & Skerman (246), Zavarzin (287), and Henrici & Johnson (96). Additionally, selected budding bacteria have been discussed by Hirsch (104, 105), Zavarzin (289), Kelly (132), and Pfennig (194).

The absence of pure culture studies and general lack of information gives rise to many problems regarding identification and nomenclature. For the purpose of this publication, the taxonomy and nomenclature of Bergey's Manual (8th edition) (31) are used.

## TOWARD A DEFINITION OF BUDDING

The first observation of bacterial buds was made by Stutzer & Hartleb (249) who described "thin filaments with terminal knobs" on *Hyphomicrobium vulgare.* However, budding was not recognized as such until some 35 years later (96, 133). It is surprising that even now we still know very little about this phenomenon. Too many different structures and processes fall within the commonly used criterion of a bud as "a local protuberance that is smaller than the cell forming it" (42, 76, 84, 287).

Therefore, we will first differentiate between those budding processes resulting in cell multiplication, and those for the purposes of hyphal or cell branching, sporulation, or spore germination. Then we will discuss structures which resemble bacterial budding.

## *Types of Budding Processes Observed in Bacteria*

BUDDING FOR MULTIPLICATION There are at least six different ways of budding, leading to cell multiplication (Figure 1), which can be found in various groups of otherwise unrelated bacteria (Table 1). In all cases, the initial structure is substantially smaller than the mother cell producing it.

BUDDING FOR CELL OR HYPHAL BRANCHING Bacterial cells, such as *Pelodictyon clathratiforme* (197), or hyphal extensions, such as in *Hyphomicrobium*

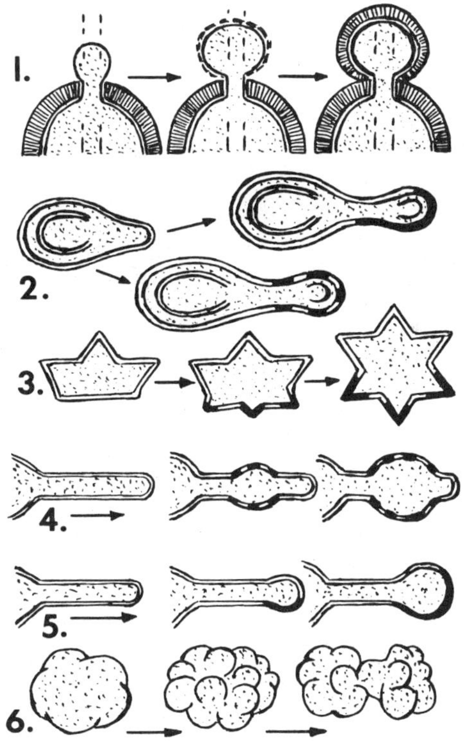


*Figure 1* Major types of budding processes observed in bacteria are the following: 1. *Planctomyces, Pasteuria, Mycococcus;* 2. terminal swelling of *Rhodopseudomonas, Nitrobacter;* 3. *Prosthecomicrobium, Ancalomicrobium,* star-shaped forms; 4. intercalary bud formation of *Pedomicrobium* and *Rhodomicrobium;* 5. terminal budding of hyphae—*Hyphomicrobium, Hyphomonas,* and *Pedomicrobium;* 6. Lobe formation of *Sulfolobus* and *Nitrosolobus.*

**Table 1** Distribution of major types of budding processes among bacteria

| Genus | Types of budding processes (see Figure 1) | | | | | | Genus | Types of budding processes (see Figure 1) | | | | | |
|---|---|---|---|---|---|---|---|---|---|---|---|---|---|
| | 1 | 2 | 3 | 4 | 5 | 6 | | 1 | 2 | 3 | 4 | 5 | 6 |
| *Hyphomicrobium* | | | | (+) | +[a] | | *Planctomyces ferrimorula* | + | | | | | |
| *Hyphomonas* | | | | | + | | *Siderococcus* | + | | | | | |
| *Pedomicrobium* | | | | + | + | | *Seliberia* | + | | | | | |
| *Rhodomicrobium* | | | | + | + | | *Mycococcus* | + | | | | | |
| *Ancalomicrobium* | | | +? | | | | *Geodermatophilus* | | | | | +? | |
| *Prosthecomicrobium* | | | + | | | | *Blastococcus* | | | | | +? | |
| *Ancalochloris* | | | + | | | | L-forms | + | | | | | |
| *Prosthecochloris* | | | + | | | | *Chlamydia* | + | | | | | |
| *Nitrobacter* | | + | | | | | *Mycoplasma* | + | | | +? | | |
| *Rhodopseudomonas* | | + | | | | | *Acholeplasma* | + | | | +? | | |
| *Gallionella* | | +? | | | | | *Thermoplasma* | + | | | +? | | |
| *Sulfolobus* | | | | | | + | *Spiroplasma* | | | | +? | | |
| *Nitrosolobus* | | | | | | + | *Metallogenium* | + | | | + | | |
| *Planctomyces* | + | | | | | | *Caulococcus* | + | | | + | | |
| *Pasteuria* | + | | | | | | *Kusnezovia* | ? | | | ? | | |
| *Planctomyces guttaeformis* | + | | | | | | | | | | | | |
| *Blastobacter* | + | | | | | | | | | | | | |
| *Methylosinus* | + | +? | | | | | | | | | | | |
| *Naumanniella* | + | | | | | | | | | | | | |

[a]+ = present; (+) = found rarely.

(249), *Rhodomicrobium* (60), or *Pedomicrobium* (6), have been reported to form branches through a true budding process. Similar branching is found in actinomycetes and in cyanobacteria (*Mastigocladus* sp.). Information on the predetermination of the budding site is still lacking for most of these organisms. In *P. clathratiforme,* buds originating laterally or near the cell poles give rise to the characteristic network of cells (197).

BUDDING FOR SPORULATION AND SPORE GERMINATION A recent electron microscopic study of *Micromonospora chalcea* clearly demonstrated that single, lateral spores directly bud out from the hypha (150). The germination of various types of actinomycete spores has been termed "budding" and is probably similar in mechanism to hypha formation by *Hyphomicrobium* and other related Gram-negative bacteria; a local swelling leading to annular wall growth results in the formation of a tubular cell extension of constant diameter. Budding of spores after the initial germination stages has also been described in detail for *Dermatophilus dermatonomus* (211). It was suggested that the spore wall had locally lost its tensile strength and was distended by osmotic pressure until stretched in a thin sheet over the resulting bud of protoplasm.

### *Bacterial Forms Resembling Budding Stages*

While most bacteria divided by cross septation followed by fission, some organisms have been observed to constrict between the two sister cells. Such constrictions can either be artifacts or quite real, as in *Achromatium,* where both sister cells often remain tethered together for a long time. Organisms with constrictive cell division may resemble budding stages, especially when forming "mini-cells," as reported for *Flavobacterium acidurans* (162) and motile, marine bacteria (146).

Johnson & Weisrock (128) described a pleomorphic, Gram-negative bacterium from Indian Ocean bottom mud at 400 m depth. Rod-shaped or coccal cells of 1.0 to 2.5 μm diameter were often joined by slender filaments up to 2 μm long. Because of a certain morphological similarity to *Hyphomicrobium* spp., the authors named the organism *Hyphomicrobium indicum,* although budding was only assumed to occur and the physiology was quite different from *H. vulgare,* the type species. A detailed study of this organism revealed neither a physiological nor a genetic relationship to several *Hyphomicrobium* strains (153; P. Hirsch, unpublished observations). There was no indication of budding but generally pleomorphic, constrictive multiplication was found.

Uneven cell division, i.e. an asymmetric site of septum formation, may also resemble budding stages as in *Asticcacaulis excentricus* (201); aggregating, star-forming bacteria from the Baltic Sea (163); or *Clostridium* (= *Granulobacter*) *pectinovorum* (124). The latter formed polar, bud-like cells which did not multiply, but could convert to normal viable rods. A certain resemblance to budding exists in the case of *Escherichia coli* miniature cells (2) or those formed by *Bacillus subtilis* (208). However, mini-cells have a diameter similar to that of the parent cell.

Uneven division may well result from unipolar cell wall growth as observed with *E. coli* B/r by Adler & Hardigree (3). Uneven division was also common among sedentary, freshwater bacteria growing on submerged electron microscope grids (115).

It is noteworthy that budding for multiplication has not been found in any cyanobacteria ("blue-green algae"). The formation of "gonidia" by *Chamaesiphon* spp. (237) or *Cyanophanon* spp. (71, 75) appears to be an uneven cell division. But Geitler (66) investigated "exospores" of two *Chamaesiphon* spp. which were definitely smaller and narrower than the parent cells. The mother cell body was not "used up" in this pinching-off process. Geitler (68) described a yeast, *Torulopsidosira,* with chains of barrel-shaped cells as producing buds on either cell pole along the main chain axis. He pointed out a considerable size variation and similarity to *Nostoc* or *Anabaena.* Later a grayish-green pigmentation and identity with *Isocystis pallida,* a thermotolerant cyanobacterium, were recognized (69). The presence of chlorophyll *a* was demonstrated by red UV fluorescence (5) and the budding was questioned. Bud-like structures observed occasionally could have resulted from unbalanced growth or cell wall damage.

Several investigators reported cell wall changes that lead to the formation of buds or branches. Depletion of $Mn^{2+}$ in cultures of *Brevibacterium ammoniagenes* (182), addition of 5% peptone (containing much glycine) to *Azotobacter vinelandii* (269) or of myxin to *E. coli* (248), even growth near the temperature minimum [6–9°C (121)], or an increasing radiation (203), resulted in budding. Buds also appeared in aging cultures of Gram-negative bacteria, probably due to unbalanced growth. Devidé (52) found this to be true for *Thiogloea ruttneri,* a colorless, sulfur-depositing bacterium. Budding morphological variants of old *Spirillum serpens* cells led Bisset (33) to assume that *Rhodomicrobium vannielii* was derived from this *Spirillum.*

Structures resembling buds often may have been artifacts or contaminants, as in the case of *Gallionella.* Investigators have long postulated that the twisted stalk fibers were alive. The stalk was thought to be the organism, and the bean-shaped, terminal cells observed occasionally were claimed to be accidentally attached bacteria (18, 19, 21, 92, 147, 267). However, end cells are easily lost by rough preparation techniques (45, 213, 250). P. Hirsch and J. M. Krul (unpublished observations) verified statistically the normal presence of bean- or kidney-shaped cells on undisturbed *Gallionella* stalk tips. The stalk fibers, apparently organic in nature, can be encrusted with ferric oxide hydrate. An organic core was present in sectioned stalk fibers (156). From diffraction and nuclear gamma-resonance studies it was concluded that the iron compounds present on the fibers have no crystal structure and that the iron atoms were strongly bound to a core structure (156). Globular structures, or terminal knobs, on branched stalk fibers resembling minute buds were interpreted as reproductive stages. Rohrer (213) referred to them as "secondary incrustations of globular shape." The real identity of such buds remains uncertain, but an acceptable explanation was offered by Walsh & Mitchell (273), who discovered an acid-tolerant, iron-oxidizing *Metallogenium* in *Gallionella* enrichments. Contamination of many *Gallionella* cultures with such a filterable and budding organism would account for the budding of *Gallionella* stalk fibers described.

## *Comparison to Fungal Budding*

Fungi appear to vary in budding mechanisms as much as bacteria do. For most bacterial budding types a morphological counterpart can be found among budding fungi: *Sterigmatomyces* spp. (38, 65) are easily mistaken for large hyphomicrobia. *Planctomyces bekefii,* now recognized as a bacterium, was originally described as a fungus (73).

Two different mechanisms of bud formation occur in yeasts. *Saccharomyces cerevisiae, Torulopsis glabrata,* or *Paracoccioides brasiliensis* have early budding stages where the wall bulges out with layers of increased density and stainability (37, 42, 228). The wall changes structurally in a large area. Thus, an appreciably large part of the bud wall must be derived from the mother cell. In the presence of fluorescein-conjugated concanavalin A as a tracer, *S. cerevisiae* deposits new mannan mainly near the distal tip of the growing bud, an area where newly synthesized glucan was also "inserted into the existing wall fabric" (255). Although initially a large wall area was altered, bud walls later grew apically only.

The second mechanism of bud formation, observed in *Rhodotorula glutinis* (254), *Cryptococcus neoformans* (76), or *Phialophora dermatitidis* (84), is described as follows: ". . . bud initiation is characterized by a blastic rupture of the outer portion of the yeast or hyphal wall and the emergence of a bud protuberance through the resulting opening. The wall of the emerging bud is continuous with only an inner wall layer of the parental yeast or hypha. The outer, ruptured portion of the parental wall typically forms a collar around the constricted emergence region of the developing bud . . ." (84).

Budding in many other fungi, as in *Phlyctidium scenedesmii,* or in algae, as in *Protosiphon botryoides* (44), may follow a similar pattern.

### *Definitions for Bacterial Budding*

For the purpose of this review, a process of new cell formation in a bacterium will be considered to be a truly budding process, if the following criteria apply: (*a*) Morphological: the new cell must be initially substantially smaller in size (i.e. narrower and shorter) than the mother cell. Even after separation, this usually holds true. (*b*) Developmental: all or most of the bud wall must be newly synthesized, although the age distribution pattern in the bud wall can vary in different organisms. Usually, buds are preformed before they become nucleated. Also, spherical and small buds increase in cell diameter during cell wall growth, contrary to elongation of rod-shaped nonbudding bacteria. (*c*) Functional: budding must be the *only* mode of new cell formation. A bud is the creation, by the mother cell, of a new space outside, into which the new cell constituents either have to migrate or where they have to be formed de novo. Thus budding does not necessarily describe a mode of cell separation (multiplication), but rather one of new cell wall formation.

In the following survey only those budding bacteria will be discussed for which these definitions apply. Although some *Rhodopseudomonas* and *Nitrobacter* spp. initiate multiplication by a budding-type process, this should be more properly termed "swelling" of a cell pole or particular surface area. Here the new cell arises partially out of the parent cell. Therefore, these will not be discussed in detail here. The same applies to the lobed *Sulfolobus* and *Nitrosolobus* spp. with local, hemispherical wall swellings and compartimentalization of DNA before division. *Sulfolobus* strain 98–3 daughter cell aggregates have different sizes during and after the constrictive aggregate division (36).

## SURVEY OF BUDDING BACTERIA (TAXONOMY AND PHYSIOLOGY)

Morphological types and variations observed among budding bacteria are diagrammed in Figure 2. Many additional forms observed, but so far undescribed, have been omitted. For detailed information on specific genera or species the reader is referred to the following survey. Table 2 presents budding forms according to expected relationships.

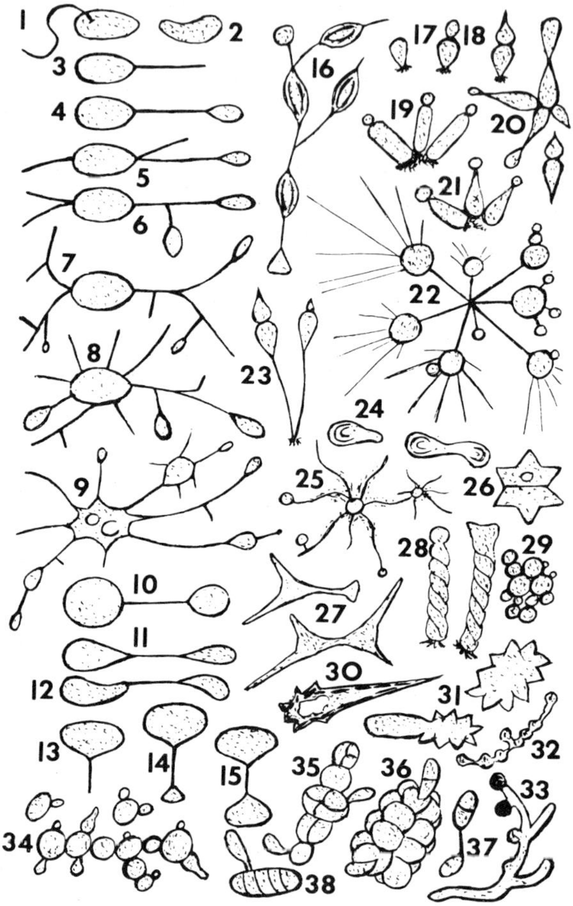


*Figure 2* Morphological types observed among budding bacteria are pictured here. The organisms are not drawn to comparable size: 1–7—*Hyphomicrobium, Pedomicrobium, Rhodomicrobium, Hyphomonas;* 8–9—*Pedomicrobium;* 10—*Hyphomicrobium, Hyphomonas, Rhodomicrobium, Pedomicrobium;* 11–12—*Hyphomicrobium, Pedomicrobium;* 13–15—mushroom-shaped bacterium; 16—*Rhodomicrobium;* 17–18—*Pasteuria;* 19,21—*Blastobacter, Methylosinus;* 20—*Planctomyces guttaeformis;* 22—*Planctomyces bekefii;* 23—*Planctomyces* sp.; 24—*Rhodopseudomonas* in part, *Nitrobacter;* 25—*Metallogenium;* 26—star-shaped bacteria; 27—*Ancalomicrobium;* 28—*Seliberia;* 29—*Planctomyces ferrimorula, Methanococcus;* 30—*Ancalochloris;* 31—*Prosthecomicrobium, Prosthecochloris;* 32—*Mycoplasma, Acholeplasma, Thermoplasma;* 33—*Micromonospora;* 34—*Mycococcus;* 35–38—*Geodermatophilus, Blastococcus.*

**Table 2** Genera of budding bacteria grouped according to expected relationships

I. GRAM-NEGATIVE FORMS

A. Organisms with cellular appendages ("prosthecae")
1. Hyphal bacteria: *Hyphomicrobium, Hyphomonas, Pedomicrobium, Rhodomicrobium*
2. Bacteria with tapered appendages: *Ancalomicrobium, Prosthecomicrobium, Ancalochloris,* star-shaped bacteria
3. Polarly swelling bacteria: *Rhodopseudomonas* in part, *Nitrobacter, Gallionella* (?)
4. Lobed bacteria: *Sulfolobus, Nitrosolobus*

B. Organisms with (probably) excreted appendages ("stalks")
5. Attaching forms: *Planctomyces/Blastocaulis*

C. Organisms without appendages
6. Cells tapered: *Pasteuria, Planctomyces* in part
7. Cells rod-shaped: *Blastobacter, Methylosinus, Naumanniella*
8. Cells spherical: *Planctomyces* in part, *Siderococcus*
9. Cells spirally twisted: *Seliberia*

II. GRAM-POSITIVE FORMS (ACTINOMYCETES)

10. Cells with irregular septation and motile swarmers: *Geodermatophilus, Blastococcus, Mycococcus* (without swarmers)
11. Organisms with spore formation by budding: *Micromonospora*

III. ORGANISMS LACKING A RIGID CELL WALL

A. Rigid wall temporarily absent: *Chlamydia*
12. bacterial L-forms and protoplasts

B. Rigid cell wall absent: mycoplasmas and related forms
13. Organisms pleomorphic and with low GC content: *Mycoplasma, Acholeplasma, Thermoplasma*
14. Organisms depositing Fe or Mn compounds onto cell surface: *Metallogenium, Caulococcus, Kusnezovia*

## *Hyphomicrobium*

The type species, *Hyphomicrobium vulgare,* has small rods with pointed ends and polar filaments that carry terminal knobs (249). A pellicle is formed on liquid media, and a preference for some unusual C or N sources has been pointed out. Subsequent reisolation and identification of *H. vulgare* has been claimed (133, 161, 286), but in all of these cases only the morphological characters of filament and bud formation were used for the identification, rather than the organism's physiology. Contrary to the type species, the new isolates were said to grow on peptone, to reduce nitrate, and to be unable to utilize mannitol. Indeed, subcultures of these isolates have now been studied in great detail and will be described as new *Hyphomicrobium* species. But four recent isolates of the author were more closely related to *H. vulgare* and one of these will be proposed as a neotype culture (P. Hirsch, in preparation).

*Hyphomicrobium neptunium* Leifson 1964, the second species described, came from a seawater sample. It is placed in this genus only because of its morphological similarity to *H. vulgare.* But recent studies of DNA-DNA homologies within *Hyphomicrobium* strains (164) reveal closer relationships to *Hyphomonas polymorpha,* a potential pathogen which also morphologically resembles *H. vulgare* (202).

A budding organism causing deposition of manganese compounds in hydroelectric pipelines and referred to as "*Hyphomicrobium* T37" was found to be morphologically similar to *Pedomicrobium* spp. (264). This latter genus was characterized by polar or lateral formation of one to several hyphae (6). The presence of such properties in T37, as well as in new, aquatic *Pedomicrobium* isolates, together with the virtual absence of them in 130 other hyphomicrobia, should place strain T37 among the pedomicrobia. *H. vulgare* thus remains the only valid species of *Hyphomicrobium* described so far. A large number of additional cultures isolated and studied in recent years have not been formally described (15, 108, 111, 240, 286).

Enrichment procedures for hyphomicrobia usually take advantage of their preference for C1 compounds such as methanol or formate (15, 111, 240, 286). The ability to develop in dilute media, or even distilled water, has also been used, as well as the resistance of many *Hyphomicrobium* strains to CO (99, 111). One enrichment procedure specific for *Hyphomicrobium* spp. (15, 240) takes advantage of their ability to denitrify with methanol and nitrate (110). The use of methylamine as the H-donor gave similar results (15). Growth with methylamine, nitrate, and low $pO_2$ was already observed by Hirsch & Conti (109).

The use of methanol in the enrichment results in growth of hyphomicrobia with a tendency to aggregate as rosettes. Presence of nitrite or ammonia and absence of any added carbon source will yield completely different types. Isolation of a *Hyphomicrobium* (strain MHS-7) from a seawater sample stored in the laboratory was reported by G. T. Sperl (personal communication). Carbon sources had not been added, and hyphomicrobia were obtained by hanging glass slides into the sample.

Hyphomicrobia were observed, but not isolated, many times. They appeared in soil suspensions or enrichments (7, 191, 247, 268); methane or natural gas favored the development of some *Hyphomicrobium* populations (1, 94). An association of hyphomicrobia with realgar ($As_2S_2$) was noted in percolation columns (64). These organisms here apparently constituted a normal part of the realgar microflora.

Freshwater hyphomicrobia were found in lakes (95, 116), brooks (116), springs (116), acid bog water (224, 225), forest marl ponds (P. Hirsch, unpublished observations), water distribution pipes (K. Ormerod, personal communication), acid mine drainage water (64), or borewell water (230). They also occur frequently in aquarium water and laboratory water baths (116). The demonstration of *Hyphomicrobium*-like microorganisms by scanning electron microscopy of lake detritus is especially noteworthy (184). Although capable of growing in very dilute media, hyphomicrobia are also found in sewage sludge or polluted streams (133, 243). There are numerous accounts of budding, hyphal bacteria from the marine environment. Mevius (161) and Hirsch & Rheinheimer (116) isolated them from brackish water of the Elbe River. Seawater samples incubated in the laboratory invariantly yield these organisms (85, 116). The organisms also attach to submerged slides or electron microscope grids, even at a depth of 300 m or more (136, 157). Hyphomi-

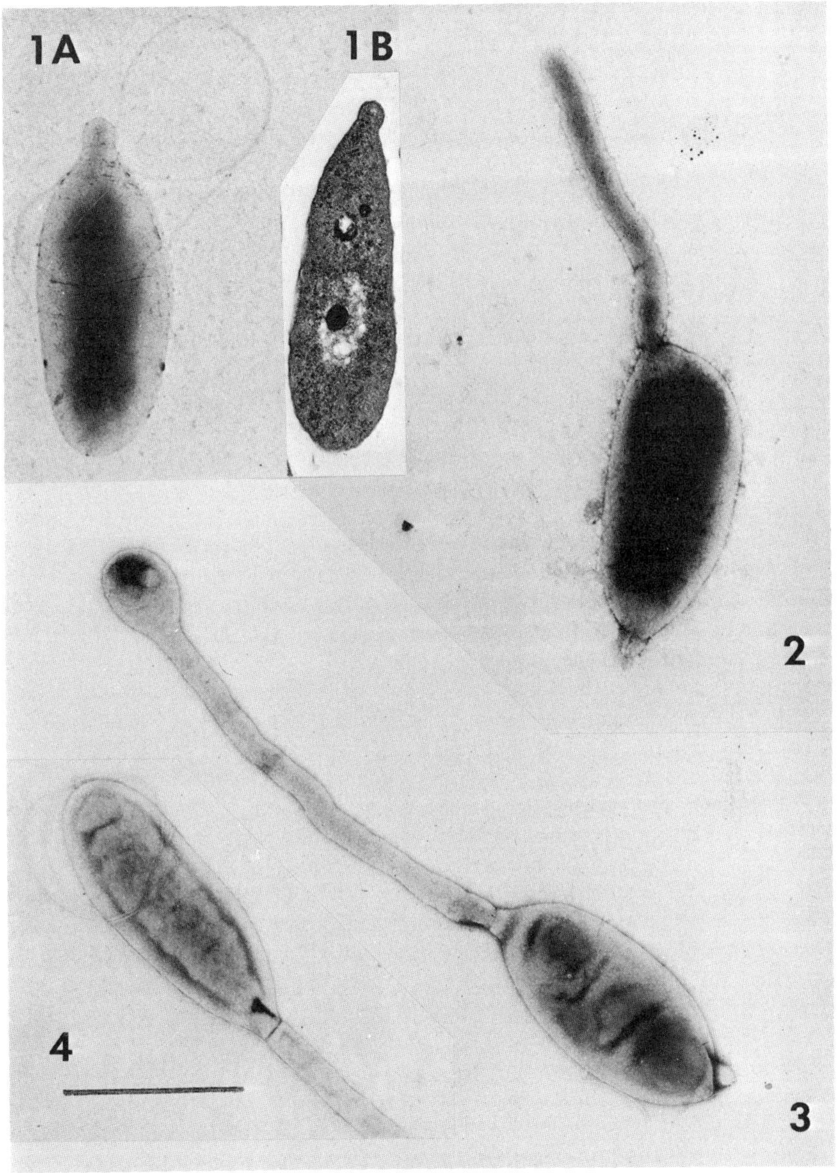


*Figure 3* The stages in the life cycle of *Hyphomicrobium* sp. B-522 are the following: 1a. swarmer cell, negatively stained; 1b. swarmer cell, thin section; 2. stalk growing stage; 3. formation of young bud; 4. bud during septation. 1a and 2–4: phosphotungstic acid negative stains. Magnification bar represents 1 $\mu$m.

crobia live in algal jellies (116, 262). The freshwater red alga, *Kyliniella latvica* Skuja 1926, harbors hyphomicrobia in its slime layer; they are arranged perpendicularly to the main filament axis (67, 70, 235).

One wonders whether temporary morphological similarity would justify classifying an organism with the hyphomicrobia. While investigating the effects of palmitate (0.1 mM) and/or elaidate on growth and fatty acid composition of a *Mycoplasma*, forms remarkably similar to hyphomicrobia developed. They had branched hyphae and buds (212). The pleomorphy of hyphomicrobia has been of great interest to all investigators since its discovery (Figure 3). The cell width and numbers, the length of hyphae, hyphal branching, incidence of bud formation, rosette formation, and site(s) of hyphal outgrowth have been linked to environmental conditions, growth rates, cell age, or types and concentrations of C, N, or phosphate sources (108). Rapid growth under favorable conditions ($CH_3OH$; $CH_3NH_2 \cdot HCl$; $NH_4^+$, 30°C, dark incubation) resulted in the formation of large cells with short and thick hyphae and few hyphal branches. Growth without added C or N sources gave small cells with thin hyphae over 100 $\mu$m long (108, 286). Cells from changing environments showed bipolar hyphal outgrowth; those grown under more stable conditions had one hypha only (P. Hirsch, unpublished observations).

The question whether the mother cell or the hypha constitutes the viable cell is lastly determined by the normal site of DNA location. Kingma-Boltjes (133) attempted to cut off hyphae of agar-grown cells, but he failed because of the great strength and flexibility of these appendages. No other experiments have been made to date. But hyphae alone cannot be viable since rodless hyphae are not found in normally growing cultures, while mother cells or swarmers without hyphae are common. DNA staining with Feulgen or Giemsa techniques (166, 286) clearly shows DNA in all mother cells but usually fails to indicate its presence in hyphae. Thus the basic viable units of hyphomicrobia are the rod-shaped portions.

The shape of mother cells appears to be species-specific. *H. vulgare* cells are pointed rods (249). Cells of later isolates from methanol enrichments were reported to be pear- or drop-shaped, while the isolate of Mevius (161) had a bean-shape and one pointed pole and resembled a grape seed. Other organisms were found to be normally nearly spherical (Hirsch, unpublished observations). *Hyphomicrobium* swarmer cells have one to three polarly or subpolarly inserted, short flagella (133, 145, 265, 286). Uhlken (265) obtained the highest number of motile swarmers with Mevius' strain by flooding agar growth with sterile medium and allowing swarmer formation to proceed for 1 hr.

The formation of aggregates (rosettes) by methanol-utilizing strains has been observed repeatedly (48, 133, 286); rosette formation was found to be due to monopolar excretion of a "holdfast" by young, swarmer cells (48).

Fine structural studies of *Hyphomicrobium* and *Rhodomicrobium* hyphae demonstrated the presence of cytoplasmic membranes, a dense peptidoglycan layer, and Gram-negative cell walls (48). A "stalk" originating by excretion had been postulated previously (96). Mevius' strain had checkered hyphae when studied by electron microscopy. The dense areas he observed may have been artifacts. Fixation conditions suitable for the larger mother cell may have been detrimental for the thin hyphae. *Hyphomicrobium* strains from soil formed a turbidity in liquid media and the cells had tubular, membranous invaginations (48). These tubules could be interconnected and distributed throughout the whole cell. They contained a fine granular matrix similar to that in the periplasmic space. Older cells had one or more large storage granules of poly-$\beta$-hydroxybutyrate, ("PHB") bounded by one single-track, stainable layer (74, 108, 110).

Pure culture preservation of C1-utilizing hyphomicrobia was comparatively simple. Most strains survived on methylamine agar at 5°C in the dark for over six months. Lyophilization or cold storage in buffered glycerol (205) were equally satisfactory. But some brackish water forms grew only for one generation on solid media and had to be kept in liquids (Hirsch, unpublished observations).

For C1-utilizing hyphomicrobia a mineral salts medium "337" with $NH_4^+$ and trace elements has been used successfully; methylamine • HCl (0.05 M) or methanol (0.5% v/v) were excellent carbon and energy sources (40, 93, 102, 109, 111, 116, 129, 164). A slight modification used by Moore & Hirsch (164) had less $Na_2HPO_4$ and less trace elements. L. Ockander (personal communication) suggested addition of Na-gluconate, 5 g/l, and L-lysine•HCl, 0.3 g/l. Brackish water strains preferred $NO_3^-$ to $NH_4^+$ for optimal growth (109, 164).

Growth of hyphomicrobia in batch cultures has been investigated by Hirsch & Conti (109). A derivative of Mevius' isolate ("NQ"), a pellicle-forming strain, had to be homogenized for inoculation. Optimal growth yields (~1.15 g protein/l) were obtained in 96 hr by vigorously aerating the culture supplemented with $CH_3NH_2$•HCl (100 mM). Soil isolates forming a turbidity in liquid media showed only little growth stimulation by aeration. Comparison of protein contents and turbidity ($OD_{420}$) was difficult during later stages of growth because of formation of PHB as a storage product.

Doubling times of 6.9 and 9.8 hr were reported for *Hyphomicrobium* X when grown at 30°C on methanol or ethanol (93). The doubling time for the first generation of *Hyphomicrobium* B-522 was approximately 14.5 hr when grown on agar slides or agitated in liquid media containing methylamine or methanol (112, 165). A *Hyphomicrobium* utilizing methanol grew with generation times as short as 4.7 hr in $O_2$– and pH-controlled fermenter cultures when $CH_3OH$ was the carbon substrate (281). At low dissolved oxygen levels, the stoichiometry of $O_2$ utilization varied with respect to cell yield; the maximum specific growth rate obtained depended on the initial concentration of methanol.

An influence of light on some *Hyphomicrobium* strains consisted of less attachment to glass surfaces and a lower growth yield (109). Normal laboratory illumination prevented all or most attachment to the illuminated side of a culture vessel, and this was not a temperature effect. Pellicle-forming strains (NQ, Mev) were more affected than those producing turbidity. Growth inhibition by constant illumination has also been observed with agar slide cultures (133). Preliminary action spectra obtained with defined filters indicated two areas in the visible spectrum which were effective: ~420 and ~568 nm (M. Jaffe and P. Hirsch, unpublished observations). Similar results were obtained when hyphomicrobia were allowed to attach to and grow on cover slips placed in a glass slide growth chamber onto which a spectrum was projected. Attachment and cell clumping were strongly affected in the two wave-length ranges mentioned above (D. E. Caldwell and P. Hirsch, unpublished observation).

Data on the composition of *Hyphomicrobium* cells are still scant. A cell wall analysis of soil isolate B-522 and of *Hyphomicrobium neptunium* showed similarities between both organisms, as well as characteristics of Gram-negative bacteria (129). Both walls contained $\alpha,\epsilon$-diaminopimelic acid and muramic acid. A pure peptidoglycan could only be isolated from the *Hyphomonas* strain when sodium dodecylsulfate was used for lipoprotein removal; this indicated some structural differences. The total lipid content of B-522 walls or of *Hyphomonas* was 23.1 or 26.4% (dry wt), respectively. In these wall preparations B-522 contained significantly more amino sugars and phosphorus.

The lipid composition of four hyphomicrobia (NQ-521, ZV-580, H-526, and M-552) was somewhat unusual (74, 88). In NQ-521 as a representative strain, phosphatidyl-N,N-dimethyl ethanolamine ("PDME") was the major P-lipid (36% of P-lipid phosphorus), and a trace of phosphatidyl-N-methyl ethanolamine ("PME") was found. Phosphatidyl choline ("PC," lecithin; 29%), phosphatidyl ethanolamine ("PE," 23%), and phosphatidyl glycerol (10%) were also present, but cardiolipin, plasmalogen, or sterols were absent from methylamine-grown cells. The methyl donor in PE methylation steps to PME and PDME to PC was S-adenosyl-L-methionin with an apparent $K_m$ of $1.9 \times 10^{-5}$ M in cell-free extracts. These findings were correlated with the formation of internal membranes (48) in these strains.

The *Hyphomicrobium* and *Nitrobacter* fatty acid composition was found to be similar (17); 92% of the fatty acids in extractable lipids of log-phase *Hyphomicrobium* NQ-521 or *Nitrobacter* spp. were vaccenic acid (11.0–18.1), which was also found to comprise 90% of the fatty acids of *Rhodomicrobium vannielii* (186) or *Rhodopseudomonas* strains (283). In methanol-grown *Hyphomicrobium* NQ-521 and in nitrite-oxidizing *Nitrobacter agilis* or *Nitrobacter winogradskyi* a 19-C cyclopropane fatty acid occurred during the stationary phase.

The base composition and some characteristics of *Hyphomicrobium* genomes are discussed below. Other common components of hyphomicrobia were polyphosphate granules which could be stained with Loeffler's methylene blue. They evaporated rapidly in the electron microscope beam (Hirsch, unpublished observations).

Methanol- or methylamine-grown hyphomicrobia (NQ-521, MEV-533) had several cytochrome types (absorption peaks in nanometers in dithionite-reduced vs air-oxidized difference spectra: *b* (562, 530, 429), *c* (551, 522, 418), and *a* (608,–, 446) (114). In CO-reduced vs reduced spectra two CO-binding hemeproteins were detected: an $a/a_3$ (589, –, 430; troughs at 606 and 447) and *o* (567, 532, 420; trough at 555). The relative concentrations of these cytochrome-*c* oxidases were markedly dependent on culture age and aeration. In this connection the remarkable tolerance by hyphomicrobia to CO should be mentioned (99). In Warburg experiments, oxygen uptake of strain NQ-521 was stimulated by $CO/O_2$ (9:1); this occurred with or without other carbon sources present.

Cytochromes of the *b, c,* and *a* type were also detected in methanol-grown *Hyphomicrobium* sp. isolated by G. A. Zavarzin. Maxima were at 600–610, 552, and

523 nm, with a shoulder at 563 nm (177). Types of carbon sources utilized for growth were studied with pellicle-forming strains NQ-521 and Mev-533. There was a distinct preference for C1 compounds (109), especially methanol or methylamine•HCl. Growth also occurred on ethanol or glycerol. Carbon sources utilized only after prolonged incubation time were formamide, hydantoate, acetate, acetamide, lactate, glycerate, serine, malate, succinate, aspartate, or glutamate. Absence of detectable growth on oxalate was in contradiction to previous reports (134, 161). In a recent comparative study of 80 hyphomicrobia (Hirsch, unpublished observations) many additional carbon compounds were tested as growth substrates. Most strains utilized the C1 compounds offered, except for methane and CO. C2 compounds were utilized by only a few cultures. C3 compounds normally did not sustain growth, the exception being glycerol, pyruvate, and perhaps in a few cases, propionate. However, successful enrichment for hyphomicrobia from pond water using 0.1% lactate was reported (116). Growth on C4, C5, or C6 compounds varied with groups of cultures tested. Hyphomicrobia isolated as denitrifiers, i.e. with a C1 compound and $NO_3^-$, only grew well on methanol, methylamine, or formate and developed poorly on C2 compounds (93; G. T. Sperl, personal communication).

The biochemistry of formate utilization by hyphomicrobia has been investigated in some detail (130, 134, 161, 175, 176). The low efficiency of free energy utilization (5–10%) seemed to indicate chemolithotrophy (161). Also, $^{14}CO_2$ was incorporated into amino acid "backbones" rather than in ninhydrin-sensitive carboxyl groups (161, 175). However, presence in formate-grown cells of an active carboxydismutase has never been shown (144). Recently, a pyridine nucleotide-linked formic dehydrogenase was found in formate-grown *Hyphomicrobium* B-522, but growth on formate was slow (D. Hoare, personal communication).

Microbial utilization of methanol has received considerable attention. Substrate affinities for $CH_3OH$ and $CH_4$ were determined for a mixed culture of pseudomonads (95%) and hyphomicrobia (5%) growing on methane. The mechanism and effects of intermediate methanol formation were of interest here (282). In pure culture the *Hyphomicrobium* had a high $K_m$ for methanol ($8.33 \times 10^{-6}$ M). This would enable the organism to constantly remove methanol to levels at which it was not inhibitory for the methane-oxidizing pseudomonads.

G. T. Sperl (personal communication) has found a soluble $NH_4^+$-dependent and pyridine nucleotide-independent primary alcohol dehydrogenase in *Hyphomicrobium* WC and B-522, as well as in *Pseudomonas*. This enzyme is linked to a pteridine, possibly a new derivative of lumazine (2,4-dihydroxypteridine). The cofactor is unstable in light. The enzyme acts best on methanol, but less well on ethanol, propanol, butanol, or amyl alcohol (D. Hoare, personal communication). It also catalyzes the oxidation of formaldehyde (hydrated) to formate. The antigenic relationships of this enzyme to those of other methanol or methane-utilizing bacteria was tested (187). The enzyme of *Hyphomicrobium* B-522 gave reactions indicating complete identity to that of *Methylosinus sporium* and *Methylosinus trichosporium*, two budding methylotrophs with peripheral membranes. An early stable product of methanol assimilation by methanol-grown hyphomicrobia was found to be serine, just as in the case of *Pseudomonas* AM1 (54, 144, 175). Other rapidly labeled compounds were aspartate, malate, glycollate, and glycine in experiments with methanol-grown *Hyphomicrobium* (Mevius' isolate) and $^{14}CH_3OH$ (144). After the oxidation of methanol (or other reduced C1 compounds) to the level of THF-linked formaldehyde, serine was formed by combination of this tetrahydrofolate-linked C1 unit with glycine. Conversion of serine into phosphoenolpyruvate, and fixation of $CO_2$ to form oxaloacetate were other important reactions (210). Some enzymatic evidence was lacking, however, and the origin of the C2 acceptor unit (glycin) remained unknown. Using labeled succinate with *Pseudomonas* AM1, Salem, Large & Quayle (217) indicated that the C2 unit might arise from cleavage of a C4 skeleton. Promptly reported was the finding of an inducible malate lyase (ATP cleaving, CoA-acetylating) in methylamine-grown *Pseudomonas* MA and *Hyphomicrobium* WC (98). This provided a route of acetyl CoA and glyoxylate synthesis. The enzyme was also found in *Hyphomicrobium* X and *Pseudomonas* MS (216). Detailed evidence for such a serine pathway in *Hyphomicrobium* X (methanol-grown) has now been obtained (93). The high specific enzyme activities found allowed the following conclusions (Scheme 1): 1. serine is formed from glycine and $N^{5,10}$-methylene tetrahydrofolate; 2. serine is converted into phosphoenolpyruvate via 2-phosphoglycerate (and not via 3-phosphoglycerate); 3. malate lyase (CoA, ATP) provides acetyl CoA and one glyoxylate for glycine regeneration; and 4. a second glyoxylate molecule arises from isocitrate lyase activity. The organism can thus synthesize C3 compounds from methanol and $CO_2$, the main drain of carbon for cellular synthesis being at the site of 3-phosphoglycerate. It was also noted that AMP inhibited glycerate phosphomutase; addition of 0.6 mM ATP resulted in a 2.5-fold stimulation, however. The authors concluded that this could represent a

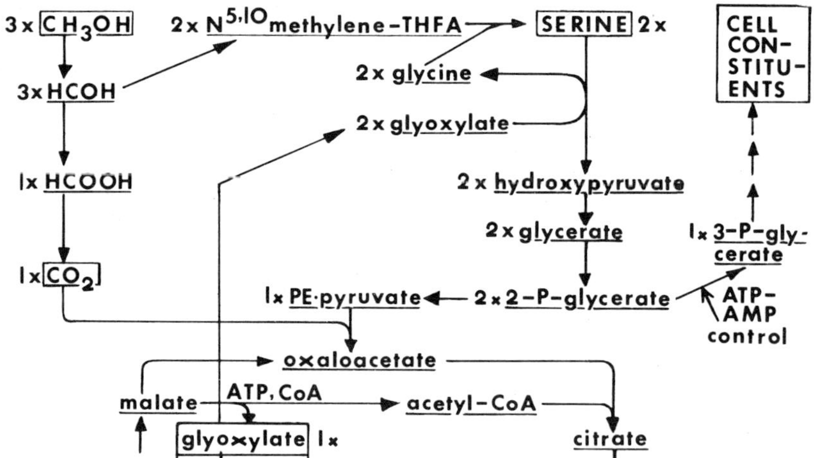


*Scheme 1* Reactions allowing growth of hyphomicrobia on methanol according to data given by Harder, Attwood & Quayle (93).

regulatory control mechanism at the AMP/ATP level. With sufficient ATP available, the flow of carbon could be guided into carbohydrate synthesis. The synthesis of malate synthase and isocitrate lyase was found to be noncoordinate in *Hyphomicrobium* X and *Pseudomonas* MA (29).

Methylamine-grown *Hyphomicrobium* NQ-521-Gr appeared to contain a heat-stable amine dehydrogenase similar to the one described from extracts of *Pseudomonas* AMl (P. Large, personal communication). The enzyme was inhibited by semicarbazide, and could not be found in hyphomicrobia (D-524 or H-526) or in *Pseudomonas aminovorans.* Meanwhile a detailed study of this enzyme has been published (63). When grown on trimethylamine, *Hyphomicrobium* NQ extracts contained 1. a mixed-function secondary amine oxidase system similar to that of *P. aminovorans* (62, 143), and 2. an NADPH-dependent, trimethylamine-oxidizing system (143). Contrary to the former enzyme, the latter was resistant to CO and $CN^-$; the product was indentified as trimethylamine-N-oxide. The metabolism of C2 compounds by hyphomicrobia has obtained little attention (16, 93). Ethanol supported growth of all denitrifying strains, while acetate was utilized by only 30% of the isolates. Inability to grow with C3, C5, or C6 compounds was explained by these authors by the absence or low activity of the pyruvate dehydrogenase complex.

Strains incapable of utilizing acetate were thought to lack the activating enzyme system. Ethanol appeared to be metabolized via acetaldehyde to form acetyl CoA; the TCA cycle and glyoxylic acid by-pass were functional. Doubling times of 9.8 hr were obtained with 0.5% v/v of ethanol as the carbon and energy source. *Hyphomicrobium* NQ and several soil isolates utilized most of the following nitrogen sources: $NH_2^+$, $NH_2OH$, $NO_2^-$, $NO_3^-$ formamide, urea, hydantoate, methylamine, acetamide, or aspartate (108, 110). A comparison of growth yields indicated specific nitrogen preferences by some strains (109). Most of 80 hyphomicrobia tested for oligonitrophily grew without any nitrogen source added in the presence of methanol (Hirsch, unpublished observations).

A strange inhibitory effect of some amino acids was noted (Hirsch, unpublished observations). Growth of most C1 hyphomicrobia was inhibited by D,L-threonine, D,L-phenylalanine, L-tryptophane, or L-glutamine. Similar observations were reported for *Rhodomicrobium vannielii* (60). The overall cell morphology was markedly influenced by the type and concentration of nitrogen compounds offered. The effect of aeration on the growth of three hyphomicrobia was investigated. Vigorous aeration of pellicle-forming strains NQ and MEV resulted in a tenfold growth yield, as compared to nonaerated controls. While strains growing as turbidity (B-522) were not significantly stimulated by aeration, shaken cultures of NQ ceased to grow unless aerated or supplied with $NO_3^-$ (109).

## *Hyphomonas*

Isolation of budding bacteria from nasal mucoid of a sinus-infected patient is surprising since the hyphomicrobia known so far are nonpathogenic (202). Although resembling *Hyphomicrobium* cells, these bacteria are physiologically quite different. They grow best at 37°C on coagulated serum, blood agar ($\alpha$-hemolysis), Loewenstein-Jensen agar, Dorset egg medium, etc. Pathogenicity against mice cannot be established. There is no growth on mineral salts media with a variety of C sources, which normally support growth of hyphomicrobia.

The base ratios of two variant strains, an S or R form, fell into the range of C1 hyphomicrobia (153), but DNA-DNA homology existed only with strain Le-670 ("*Hyphomicrobium neptunium*") (164). One wonders whether *H. neptunium* would not be better placed in the genus *Hyphomonas* (107). *Hyphomonas polymorpha* (S or R) and *H. neptunium* were different, though. The former organisms grew at 30–37°C in the presence of 5% NaCl, utilized D,L-glutamate, dilute urine, starch, or gelatine, while the latter species was negative in these tests but could grow at 15°C (Hirsch, unpublished observations).

## *Pedomicrobium*

Some budding, hyphal bacteria were observed to decompose organomineral humus complexes (6). Such organisms developed after three to four weeks in 1.5% agar prepared from an "organomineral gel" and water (288), but only enrichment cultures were obtained. The organisms resembled *Hyphomicrobium vulgare* or *R. vannielii* but lacked photosynthetic pigments. Their distinguishing characters were: 1. formation, under some conditions, of one to four branching hyphae which could arise laterally and give the cell a pleomorphic appearance (6, 11, 12; T. V. Aristovskaya, personal communication); 2. the hyphal outgrowth from still small, attached and immature buds (6); 3. the often highly branched mycelium; and 4. the lack of motile cells. Besides the iron-depositing type species, *Pedomicrobium ferrugineum*, a second species, *Pedomicrobium manganicum*, which deposited manganese compounds, was found on the same plates. Both organisms grew only in the presence of "organomineral complexes of fulvinic acids with sesquioxides," but not without added carbon sources. Unfortunately, the original cultures were lost. Recently in the author's laboratory, R. Gebers obtained pedomicrobia using Aristovskaya's procedures. A rare third species, *Pedomicrobium podsolicum*, often produced buds directly from the mother cell (8). Iron, as well as manganese compounds, were deposited. *P. manganicum var. sachalinicum* was described on the basis of a more oval cell shape (90). This variety, and colonies of a coccoid *Pedomicrobium* depositing manganese compounds grew well on a purely mineral medium with manganese carbonate.

The occurrence in natural waters of pedomicrobia has been widely recognized (100, 102, 106, 116, 140, 174, 226, 227, 231, 259, 261–264). Pure cultures obtained from brackish or freshwater differed in the site of primary ferric hydroxide deposition (100); morphologically they resembled the soil forms. Terminal buds on hyphae were sometimes attached with the long axis perpendicular to the hypha (140).

Pure cultures of brackish-water forms (103) grew well with $CH_3NH_2{\cdot}HCl$ or urea and at a $pO_2$ of 1–2%. They required seawater medium with 4% total salinity. Deposition occurred mainly on the hyphae (100). J. T. Staley (personal communication) obtained freshwater pedomicrobia with a 0.01% peptone medium containing Hutner's basal salts and vitamins. All aquatic pedomicrobia developed reddish-brown colonies. *Actinomyces ferrugineus* (174), from Swedish ponds, also deposits ferric hydroxide on its hyphae and may be a *Pedomicrobium*.

The aquatic pedomicrobia obtained by Hirsch (103) morphologically resembled hyphomicrobia when grown on mineral media with $CH_3NH_2{\cdot}HCl$. This raised the question of whether these pedomicrobia were sufficiently different to be recognized as a separate genus. Out of more than 100 strains of hyphomicrobia from various sources, only two soil isolates occasionally produced a lateral hypha on their mother cells. Contrary to this, *all* ferric hydroxide-depositing "pedomicrobia" from aquatic sources had a high percentage of cells with several lateral hyphae. Thus this *Pedomicrobium* appearance is normally absent from the hyphomicrobia.

A remarkable amount of work on aquatic pedomicrobia has been published recently (24–26, 259–264). Freshwater hydroelectric pipelines in Tasmania rapidly accumulate thick wall deposits containing approximately 20% manganese and large numbers of budding, hyphal bacteria. An astonishing degree of pleomorphy was observed even in pure cultures of a strain, T37, when grown with methanol as the C source.

On mineral medium 337 (108) with 0.02% $MnSO_4{\cdot}4H_2O$ ("MH") there were hyphomicrobial cells (the "classical *Hyphomicrobium* facies") with one polar flagellum, a little-branched hypha, and motile, pear-shaped buds. But on Pringsheim's mineral medium with 0.002% $MnSO_4{\cdot}4H_2O$ and 0.005% yeast extract ("PC medium"), or even on MH medium with methylamine, the cells had bizarre shapes and several short and richly branched hyphae which projected out from all over the cell surface (the "*Pedomicrobium* facies"). The author could confirm these observations when cultivating strain T37 in his laboratory. Interestingly, the buds did not change their pear shape, indicating "normality" of growth conditions. In turn, C1 hyphomicrobia exhibited a fair degree of pleomorphy depending on the type of C or N source, concentration of $PO_4^{3-}$, age of culture, etc (108). But this pleomorphy concerned length, branching, and number of *polarly* grown hyphae and *not* so much the mother cell. It thus is obvious that there are indeed budding bacteria with an occasional hyphomicrobial appearance but with a normally different cell shape and polarity, as well as different physiology and ecology. Even young *Rhodomicrobium vannielii* cells can initially resemble hyphomicrobia, yet one would not question the validity of the former genus. The existence of a genus *Pedomicrobium* should now be proven by collecting comparative data on pure cultures and investigating their genomes.

*Pedomicrobium* T37 frequently attaches to surfaces (262). Electrophoretic pH-mobility curves indicated a negatively charged surface due to dissociated carboxyl groups. For attachment, a mucilage (capsule, holdfast) was postulated but not demonstrated.

In laboratory experiments manganese oxide deposition could be shown to be due to living pedomicrobia (261). However, in pure culture, strain T37 rapidly lost its ability to oxidize. Several investigators (R. Schweisfurth, personal communication; G. A. Zavarzin, personal communication) observed phosphate interference with manganese oxidation. Medium 337 MH used for strain T37 had a high phosphate concentration.

In an attempt to quantitate morphological changes during nonsynchronous growth of *Pedomicrobium* T37, a population index "Pi" was defined as ratio of total number of colony-forming units over total number of cells (24). A drop of Pi below one thus indicated increasing complexity of form, i.e. more cells remained connected after maturation to form larger aggregates. However, a serious problem arises from such an approach. The individual "cells," recognized as such, must be nucleated to be counted for meaningful results, yet *Hyphomicrobium* studies (166) showed that preformed buds can reach a substantial size before nucleation. Observations of Pi during the development of a batch culture of T37 showed that swarmer cells were formed initially while at a later stage the organisms "consolidated" to larger aggregates by forming more intercalary, nonmotile buds.

Information on metabolic activities of pedomicrobia is still scarce. Soil and aquatic isolates deposit iron and/or manganese compounds. Manganese oxidation by a *"Hyphomicrobium"* observed recently (268) could have been performed by a *Pedomicrobium* sp. Although aerobic, soil forms grew better at reduced $pO_2$ (6). Poly-$\beta$-hydroxybutyrate was stored (264), and at least some aquatic forms grew on Cl compounds (25). Both $NH_4^+$ and $NO_3^-$ can be utilized as N source.

Pedomicrobia are ubiquitous; they occur worldwide in podzolic soils (6, 12, 14, 90, 91, 231; R. Gebers, personal communication), in freshwater (103, 116, 140, 226, 260), or in brackish water (100).

### *New Hyphal Budding Bacteria*

With more refined phase microscopy and new observation techniques, several other budding bacteria have been found. A mushroom-shaped organism isolated from pond water formed short, tube-like protrusions with terminal buds (279). The aerobic organism was catalase-, oxidase-, and cytochrome-positive and utilized a number of sugars (acid production), sugar alcohols, or organic acids as carbon and energy source. Formate, acetate, and propionate were utilized, but not methanol, urea, or hydrogen. On yeast extract agar much slime was produced. Besides these physiological differences from hyphomicrobia, a fundamental morphological characteristic was observed on slide cultures; the cells divided only after the bud had reached the size of the mother cell, i.e. two morphologically equal sister cells were the fission product. Another, similar form was isolated. It grew best on liquid media with a low concentration of organic compounds (172).

An unusual organism isolated from a temporary pond by adding 0.005–0.01% peptone to a sample (T. A. Babinchak, personal communication) is shown in Figure 4.4. Mushroom-shaped cells produce thin hyphae with branches. There probably exist in nature large numbers of similar, budding bacteria which await their isolation. "Square" bacteria with one budding hypha projecting out from each corner (140) or bag-shaped types resembling a *Hydra* with several hyphae growing out from one directly budding pole have also been observed.

## *Rhodomicrobium*

Duchow & Douglas (60) described *R. vannielii* as a photosynthetic, budding, hyphal bacterium with a morphology nearly identical to that of hyphomicrobia (Figure 4.5). Actually, photosynthetic rhodomicrobia may have been observed long before (27, 204). Forms shown, and called *Chromatium* spp., had buds and "bridges" between the cells. Four isolates obtained originally (60) came from a shallow, eutropic pond

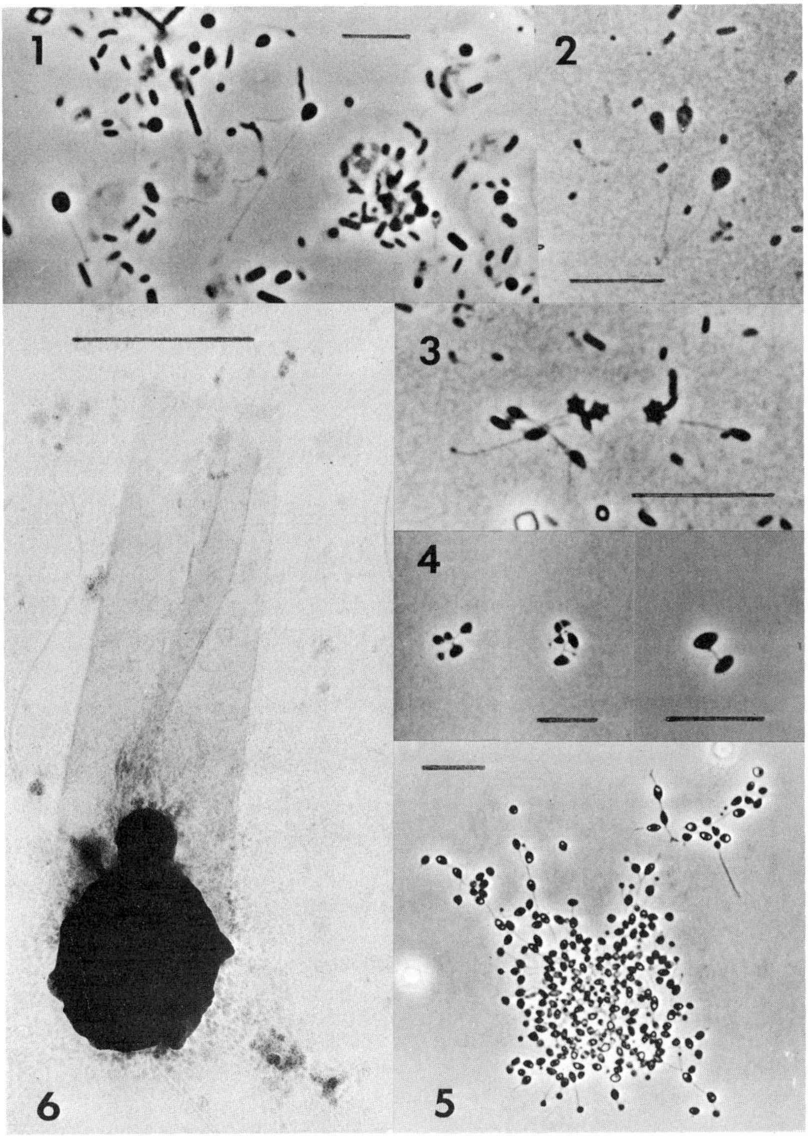


*Figure 4* Some selected budding bacteria are the following: 1 and 2—*Planctomyces* sp. on glass slide exposed to lake water. Note bud on middle cell in Figure 4.2. 3—Star-shaped bacteria from oxygen-rich stream containing humic acids. 4—Mushroom-shaped bacterium isolated by Babinchak from a temporary puddle. 5—*Rhodomicrobium* sp. from river water. 6—A budding, iron-depositing coccus from pond water. Figure 4.1—5: life phase contrast micrographs (bars = $\mu$m). Figure 4.6: electron micrograph (bar 1 $\mu$m).

in the Japanese Tea Garden, in Seattle, Washington. One of these, ATCC 17100, is now the neotype culture (198).

With different enrichment conditions, a large number of new isolates have been obtained since then (32). Generally, acetate, ethanol, or succinate were suitable H-donors, the light intensity had to be low, and a pH of 6.0 was optimal. None of these cultures has been formally described, although some were quite different from the original organism. Base ratios reported are shown in Table 4. Thus the genus remains monotypic.

Most investigators grew rhodomicrobia in liquid media, or, for the purpose of isolation, in solid agar "shake tubes." H. Biebl (personal communication) grew them on agar plates stored in illuminated, anaerobic desiccators. Growth of single colonies (within agar) was excellent when *R. vannielii* was brought together with *Hyphomicrobium* B-522 and *Thiopedia* sp. in two-dimensional, steady-state agar diffusion gradients of $Na_2S$ and $CH_3NH_2{\cdot}HCl$ (39, 40). Colonies appeared only in the limited area where concentrations of these compounds were favorable. Cells from rapidly growing colonies were spindle-shaped, slender, and had long hyphae, while those remaining in a resting state were almost spherical.

Microaerophilic, dark growth of rhodomicrobia has been possible by adding ascorbate (0.1%) to the medium (196). In agar-shake cultures most strains of *R. vannielii* or *Rhodopseudomonas viridis* grow pigmented below the surface, and nonpigmented on the surface. In a defined medium *Rhodomicrobium* C-2859 had a doubling time of 5.3 hr (256). This medium contained, besides mineral salts, the following additions (mg/ml): lactate (1.8), aspartic acid (0.1), riboflavin (0.001), bicarbonate (0.5), and $Na_2S{\cdot}9H_2O$ (0.1). The necessity of bicarbonate has been questioned (61), since organic compounds served readily as a source of reducing power and carbon: $CO_2$ was increasingly released into the atmosphere above the culture, as measured by gas chromatography.

Pfennig (195) stressed the importance of a low pH for *R. vannielii* (pH 6.0) and *Rhodopseudomonas acidophila* (pH 5.5). Hydrogen donors utilized by rhodomicrobia additionally to those studied previously (60) were: caprylate, succinate, fumarate, malonate, pyruvate, and yeast extract (195); also $\beta$-hydroxy-butyrate (120) or, slowly, methanol and methylamine (40, 111).

Contrary to previous reports, Duong (61) found that an isolate from a Michigan hardwater lake grew well with most sugars or polymer carbohydrates tested (0.2% w/v). Stimulation of adaptation to these compounds by a trace of acetate added with the inoculum was assumed. The absence, from the test medium, of any added bicarbonate, differed from test conditions employed by other investigators. Lack of $HCO_3^-$ was also given as a reason for poor growth on lower alcohols.

Hydrogen and $HCO_3^-$ were found to support growth in the light when tested on a mineral medium with $NH_4^+$ (195), but Hoare & Hoare (120) could not duplicate this observation. A necessity of combined nitrogen for adaptation to photooxidation of hydrogen has been demonstrated (61); with $N_2$ there was no growth under these conditions.

Pelargonate, glycolate, oxalate, benzoate, aspartate, glutamate, or arginine were not used as H-donors. All lower, straight chain primary alcohols tested were active substrates for an alcohol dehydrogenase of *Rhodomicrobium vannielii*—except for methanol. The enzyme was constitutive; it had NADP as co-enzyme and a pH optimum of 10.2. The greatest affinities were observed with C3, C4, and C5 compounds (218).

Few other enzymatic studies of *Rhodomicrobium* have been reported. A glyceraldehyde 3-phosphate dehydrogenase (NAD-dependent) was detected (238). As in other photosynthetic bacteria and cyanobacteria, rhodomicrobia synthesize arginine from glutamate via acetylated intermediates. N-acetylglutamate phosphokinase (specifically inhibited by arginine) and a trans-acetylase (L-glutamate specific) have been reported. A pyruvate decarboxylase active in *Rhodopseudomonas palustris* was absent from *R. vannielii* (206). Photoevolution of hydrogen was inhibited by nitrogen (120) and $N_2$ is fixed (148).

A *Rhodomicrobium* sp. from a hardwater lake grew well on N-free mineral medium supplemented with 0.2% acetate and 0.0002% yeast extract (61). The generation time of 10.5 to 12.6 hr was nearly equal whether grown with $N_2$ or 0.1% $NH_4Cl$. Factors affecting light-dependent acetylene reduction were optimal with 0.3% acetate and 10% acetylene in argon. $N_2$ fixation was initially slightly delayed by 0.0005% $NaNO_3$ or $NH_4Cl$ but not by yeast extract in this concentration. Real suppression of $N_2$ fixation occurred at ten- to a hundred-fold higher concentrations of these nitrogen compounds, but $N_2$ fixation could not be completely arrested at any of the concentrations tested.

Hydrogenase reducing methylene blue, but not inorganic compounds, was found in rhodomicrobia (285). Two different enzymes, one catalyzing photoreduction of $CO_2$, and one photoproduction of $H_2$, were postulated by Hoare & Hoare (120).

*R. vannielii* contained cytochromes of the following types (nm; reduced vs oxidized): *b* (563, 530, 423), *c* (553, 521, 423), $c_2$ (550, 522, 414), and a CO-binding heme protein (570, 538–543, 414; CO red vs red) (168). Breakage by pressure gave four fractions, one of which consisted mainly of hyphae, had a very low bacteriochlorophyll:protein ratio, and contained most of the cytochromes *b*-563 and *c*-553, as well as the CO-binding heme protein. Another fraction with a tenfold higher ratio contained the cytochrome *c*-550.

A peculiar, light-stimulated $O_2$ uptake of *Rhodomicrobium* cell suspensions, cell-free extracts, or fractions was observed (167, 169). The CO-binding heme protein apparently acted as terminal oxidase in this dark respiration. Cell extraction with iso-octane resulted in an increased, light-induced $O_2$ uptake, indicating an involvement of quinone(s) in the electron transport. However, this effect may have been due to a nonenzymatic process. Morita, Olson & Conti concluded that *Rhodomicrobium* had cytochromes some of which underwent both light-induced and oxygen-induced oxidation; others which were only light-oxidized, and still others that were only oxidized by oxygen. The first type was only half as prevalent as the other two (170).

When grown anaerobically in the light, *R. vannielii* and *R. palustris* contained low concentration of ubiquinone Q-10 (43). The concentration of Q-10 and bacteriochlorophyll was highest in the presence of malate. A co-enzyme Q-9 was isolated and crystallized from a new isolate (186). Bacteriochlorophyll *a* was identified in

*R. vannielii* (127, 271). Carotenoids were found to be β-carotene (47, 215, 271) and members of the spirilloxanthin series with rhodopin as the major component (215). β-carotene as a minor component has also been found in *Rhodopseudomonas acidophila* (223). An unidentified pteridine with blue fluorescence occurred in light-grown cells of *R. vannielii* at a concentration of 0.5 μg/mg dry wt (152).

P-lipids and fatty acids of *R. vannielii* have been investigated in some detail (185, 186, Table 3). Most conspicuous was the striking similarity to *Rhodopseudomonas palustris* (283). Vaccenic acid (C-18:1) accounted for 90% of the total fatty acids of the lipid fraction of *R. vannielii,* which was similar to results obtained from hyphomicrobia.

Lactate-grown cells of *R. vannielii* contained 0.2% of cell dry weight as poly-β-hydroxybutyrate (PHB) (186). Fine structural evidence for the presence of storage granules has been given (48, 78, 257). The formation and presence of PHB in acetate-grown cells has been reported (119).

**Table 3** Lipid composition of *Rhodomicrobium vannielii* (185, 186)

| Compound | Percent of dry weight in cells | in P-lipids | Remarks |
|---|---|---|---|
| Total P-lipids | 4.2 | | |
| Sulfolipids | 0.01 | | |
| Steroids | n.d.[a] | | |
| Lipoaminoacid: (o-ornithine ester of phosphatidyl glycerol) | | 46.5 | Reported in various bacteria including *Rhodopseudomonas palustris* |
| Phosphatidyl choline | | 26.5 | Found in *Agrobacterium, R. palustris*, etc |
| Phosphatidyl glycerol | | 9.7 | |
| bis-Phosphatidic acid | | 6.7 | |
| Phosphatidic acid | | 1.8 | |
| Phosphatidyl ethanolamine | | 4.5 | Unusually low for bacteria |
| Lysophosphatidyl glycerol-o-ornithine ester | | 3.2 | |
| Phosphatidyl-N-methyl ethanolamine | | n.d. | Compare to *Hyphomicrobium* |
| Phosphatidyl-N,N'-dimethyl ethanolamine | | n.d. | Compare to *Hyphomicrobium* |
| Cardiolipin | | n.d. | Present in other photosynthetic bacteria |
| N,N-ornithine amide of an unidentified fatty acid | | 0.95 | |

[a] n.d. = not detected.

The motility of *Rhodomicrobium* buds still deserves attention. Peritrichous flagellation has been observed, but some isolates of the author were monotrichously flagellated. A strain isolated from Lake Bolshoi Kichier produced heat resistant, angular "spores" (78). Hyphal outgrowth occurred at one to four sites. Sometimes spores arranged in chains resembled conidia. Mature cells contained large amounts of PHB, but spores were free of this storage compound. Other sporulating strains have been isolated subsequently (61). N. Pfennig (personal communication) found better "spore" formation with trace element solution SL4 added (193). Heat resistance of angular, nonmotile spores could not be shown conclusively and thus it was suggested that the term *spore* be replaced by *cyst* (61). Also, cyst formation seemed to be triggered by nutrient exhaustion or by cell age, but not by the types of N or C source present.

### *Ancalomicrobium*

Budding bacteria with long and tapering cellular appendages (prosthecae) were isolated by Staley (241). The cell body consisted mainly of the arms and was irregularly shaped. The peculiar mechanism of multiplication was studied with slide cultures. Buds grew from the central part of the cell (*Ancalomicrobium adetum*) or from the tip of a prostheca.

Similar organisms observed previously were interpreted as involution forms (229). Those found and described by Henrici & Johnson (96) even contained gas vesicles as were later observed in *A. adetum.* Starfish-shaped, similar bacteria from effluent water of an Uppsala sewage plant were enriched for by adding 1% cellulose powder to a mineral salts medium (122). However, these forms multiplied by a fission process. Ancalomicrobia with terminal buds were seen in *Hyphomicrobium* enrichments (108). Originally these organisms were thought to be saprophytic mycoplasmas. Using the method of "thermal adhesion" and electron microscopy, Nikitin (178) observed ancalomicrobia in soil suspensions. They also grew on electron microscope grids submerged in water of a forest pond (115).

Only two strains of *Ancalomicrobium* have been isolated: one was obtained by a percolation procedure (*A. adetum* did not attach to glass surfaces), and the second culture originated from a pulp mill oxidation pond (241, 245). An enrichment procedure has been described as follows: 10 mg Difco peptone were added to 100 ml sample in a sterile beaker. After covering with foil, the beaker was incubated for 3–5 weeks at 20–25°C. Then the growth was streaked onto mineral agar containing vitamins and 0.01% peptone (241, 266).

*A. adetum* is Gram-negative and has 2–8 tapering appendages with a basal width of 0.25 μm and a length of up to 3.0 μm (241); it contains gas vesicles, some of which are in the prosthecae. Occasionally an appendage is bifurcated. Growth occurs between 6 and 39°C and between pH 6.3 and 7.5. The type strain is catalase-positive, and facultatively anaerobic. Growth occurs in a medium containing $NH_4^+$, glucose, Casamino Acids, vitamins, and minerals. Glucose is fermented. Casein is not used as a sole source of carbon; $NO_3^-$ is not a suitable N source. A large variety of sugars or sugar alcohols, as well as succinate or fumarate are suitable carbon sources. Starch, methanol, ethanol, formate, propionate, or butyrate are not utilized. Pantothenic acid is required for growth.

## *Ancalochloris*

The use of morphology and replication processes as taxonomic criteria can be expected to result in the finding of physiologically different "morphological counterparts" of "unusual" bacteria. This was the case with *Hyphomicrobium* and *Rhodomicrobium,* and it greatly stimulated comparative research. Likewise, *Ancalochloris,* a photosynthetic, green counterpart to *Ancalomicrobium* was recently discovered (81). *Ancalochloris perfilievii* is the only species in this new genus; pure cultures were not isolated. The organism is apparently widely distributed in pond or lake water. Blooms occurred in hypolimnic layers of karst lakes in the Mari ASSR where there was an $H_2S$ concentration of 50 to 60 mg/1, an $rH_2$ of 9–10, and a pH of 6.8–7.0 (139). *A. perfilievii* occurred also in Pluss See, Germany (September), and Wintergreen Lake, Michigan (August), where it was a common inhabitant of the hypolimnion (J. Overbeck, personal communication; Hirsch, unpublished observations). Enrichment cultures for *Pelodictyon* spp. also yielded *Ancalochloris* (81). Pfennig's medium (193) was used; it contains 330 mg/l $Na_2S \cdot 9H_2O$, 20 mg/l $B_{12}$, Pfennig's vitamin mixture, and 400 mg/l ammonium acetate. Incubation was at 18–20°C and at low light intensity. The cells have one to six tapered prosthecae, approximately 0.7 μm wide at the base. Some appendages are branched and one is often considerably larger than the others. They contain *Chlorobium* vesicles and gas vesicles. The cells have a slime capsule and are aggregated; peripheral individuals have longer prosthecae. Multiplication is initiated by budding. A smaller daughter cell is separated from the parent by constriction. Sulfur is not deposited; the organisms are not motile.

## *Prosthecomicrobium*

The cell surface of these Gram-negative rods is normally occupied by tapering, cellular appendages (241). Two species (three strains) of *Prosthecomicrobium pneumaticum* and *Prosthecomicrobium enhydrum* were both first isolated from the same (Davis, California) Putah creek water as was *Ancalomicrobium.* However, contrary to the latter, prosthecomicrobia have shorter and more numerous prosthecae, are aerobic, and appear to reproduce by a fission process rather than by budding. But, the mode of daughter cell formation was not at all clear: several micrographs were suggestive of budding or at least uneven division. The rationale for treating *Prosthecomicrobium* in this review lies in the fact that the appendages must be produced by a budding-type process.

Prosthecomicrobia are widely distributed. They were found in soil suspensions (178, 180) or water samples (179). *Prosthecomicrobium* spp. grew on Formvar®-coated grids submerged for five days in a polluted Michigan river (106). Their seasonal and spatial distribution in this river was followed by Staley (243). They also were reported to exist in acid-bog or peat water (224, 270). The author observed a bloom of prosthecomicrobia under the ice of a small Michigan forest pond. "Ooze-dwelling" prosthecomicrobia have been detected with slit peloscopes and electron microscopy (140). They even occur in cattle rumen (252).

A total of 15 strains has been isolated to date; the type cultures are *P. pneumaticum* ATCC 23633 and *P. enhydrum* ATCC 23634 (245). Contrary to the latter, *P. pneumaticum* has longer prosthecae, usually contains gas vesicles, utilizes more carbon sources, and is motile. It requires vitamins $B_{12}$, thiamin, and biotin, while *P. enhydrum* only requires thiamin. The DNA base composition of *P. pneumaticum* strains was generally higher than that of *P. enhydrum.* Staley (241) showed a *P. pneumaticum* cell with seven short prosthecae ($<1$ μm) and one long appendage ($> 2$ μm) which had the appearance of a nontapering hypha. Thin sections clearly demonstrated the presence, in tapering prosthecae, of a cytoplasmic membrane, cytoplasm, and cell wall. The carbon utilization pattern of three prosthecomicrobia is similar to that of *A. adetum.* But, *P. enhydrum* is less active on alcohols and sugar alcohols.

### *Prosthecochloris*

These photosynthetic counterparts to prosthecomicrobia were found by Gorlenko (77). Two strains isolated came from mud from a brakish water pond mud ($E_h =$ $-160$ mV, 5% NaCl; strain Sk-413) or from a similar location ($E_h = -185$ mV, 1.5% NaCl; strain S-405). Enrichment cultures using mud cores contained 1 g/l of $Na_2S \cdot 9H_2O$ and of $Na_2S_2O_3$. The pH was adjusted to 7.0–7.3, and vitamin $B_{12}$ (10 μg/l) was added. *Prosthecochloris aestuarii* cells are nonmotile, spherical (0.5–0.7 μm), and have about 20 tapering prosthecae up to 0.17 μm wide and 1.7 μm long. A capsule is formed, and clusters of slime strands appear on appendages of older cells. After constrictive division, the cells often do not separate but form chains which could be branched. Prosthecae of strain S-405 are generally very short. Anaerobic growth in the light occurs on mineral media with $Na_2S$ or thiosulfate as the hydrogen donors; $S^0$ is then deposited intracellularly. Growth also occurs in liquid media when supplemented with Na-acetate (lg/l) and when kept illuminated at 50 foot candles and at 30°C. Bacterioviridine was found in spectra of both strains. *Chlorobium*-type vesicles are attached along the inner surface of all prosthecae (82). Two additional strains recently isolated from marine sediments (158) are reported to utilize pyruvate (0.05%) and acetate for growth. One of these strains grows best with 3% NaCl (range 1–6%), while the other tolerates a range of 0.5–10.0%.

Apparently, *Prosthecochloris* has been overlooked by many investigators. Staley (243) found these in a polluted Michigan river, and the author has seen them frequently in Michigan marl lakes or ponds. Mixed aggregates of *Prosthecochloris* and *Clathrochloris* spp. in 3–6 m hypolimnic layers of Wintergreen Lake (Michigan) comprised the majority of the bacterial population during summer months (61). The presence of *Prosthecochloris,* in acid-bog water habitats has also been reported (224, 225).

### *Star-Shaped Bacteria*

There are flat bacteria which resemble the Star of David in that their six (5–8) tapering prosthecae lie all in one plane (Figure 4.3). Such organisms have been observed by several investigators (178, 180, 241) in soil suspensions or creek water. Hirsch (unpublished observations) found star-shaped bacteria in rapidly flowing forest brook water, which was rich in humic substances, in a polluted Michigan river, in a marl lake (11 m), and in a small forest pond. Most individuals were six-pronged, but some stars had 5, 7, or even 8 prosthecae. Multiplication was initiated by an increase in cell length (so as to separate three appendages from the other three), followed by constriction, and septation. The two daughter cells appeared to be morphologically equal; each "regenerated" the prosthecae of the missing cell half. Star-shaped bacteria often contain a small, light refractile granule. Laboratory enrichments contained such organisms for up to 11 months.

Pure cultures have not been obtained as yet. A certain morphological resemblance exists between these stars-shaped bacteria and a Precambrian microfossil, *Kakabekia umbellata.* Although nearly twice as large, this fossil had 5–7 prosthecae and can be likened to a flat wheel with a central string attached to it (23). Growth of a *Kakabekia*-like "organism" was obtained in enrichment cultures for ammonia-tolerant organisms which were inoculated with heavily urinated soil from Wales and kept under an atmosphere of 39% $N_2$, 10% $O_2$, 25% $CH_4$, and 25% $NH_3$ (232). The maximum cell number obtained was small. In glucose-peptone-ammonia broth, the yield was 300 cells/ml. Additional soil samples from Alaska and Iceland also yielded *Kakabekia*-like, star-shaped "organisms" (233).

## *Planctomyces*

These stalked bacteria originally described as planctonic fungi (73) have the appearance of a drumstick. The spherical cell of *Planctomyces bekefii* has a thin, straight stalk and initiates multiplication by budding process type 1 (Figure 1). Usually several cells aggregate to form planctonic rosettes. In lake water, *P. bekefii* stalks are usually covered with iron deposits. An identical organism, *Blastocaulis sphaerica,* was described as a bacterium (96). Hirsch reviewed properties of both organisms, pointed to their identity, and confirmed the bacterial nature (104).

At present four species are recognized (117). *P. bekefii* Gimesi 1924 has spherical cells (1.4–1.7 μm) and stalks up to 10 μm long. *Planctomyces condensatus* Skuja 1964 is smaller (0.7–1.7 μm) and sometimes has short, "gel-like stalklets". The cells are often grouped around a central material containing iron (237). *Planctomyces kljasmensis* (Razumov) Hirsch 1972 has spherical to oblong cells (0.3–0.5 μm or larger) and a slender stalk which may also be encrusted with iron oxides. The cells are attached with their long axis perpendicular to the stalk axis. *Planctomyces gracilis* Hortobagyi 1965 is small (0.3–0.6 μm) and spherical; the crescent stalks (0.3–0.4 μm thick) may be up to 11 μm long. Two other species, *Planctomyces ferrimorula* Wawrik 1956 and *Planctomyces guttaeformis* Hortobagyi 1965 have been excluded from this genus because they lack stalks. *P. bekefii* stalks investigated recently, consist of a straight bundle of parallel fibers, which may have been excreted (89; P. Hirsch and D. E. Caldwell, unpublished observations). None of these organisms has been cultured or studied physiologically; their occurrence in nature appears to be sporadic but frequent (137).

*Planctomyces* spp. are reported to occur as planktonic organisms in late summer or fall in eutrophic freshwater lakes (116, 137, 183, 188, 221). They have been found in fish ponds (123), acid-bog water (224), brackish water (102, 116), aquarium water (116), marine sediments (116), and forest brook sediments (286). Kristiansen (137) related *P. bekefii* occurrence in ten Danish lakes and ponds to pH, conductivity, and temperature measurements and concluded that this species preferred eutrophic or polluted localities. Many *Planctomyces* spp. from oligotrophic environments could have been other, new species with piriforme cells which have already been observed and shown long ago (96; Figures 4.1 and 4.2).

*P. bekefii* carries up to 25 rigid, filamentous appendages at the distal cell pole (137, 183). Budding occurs sequentially from the cell pole opposite to the stalk. Rows of two or three attached, immature buds indicate premature budding (87, 123). Motility of buds has not been described, but Hirsch (unpublished observations) observed monotrichously flagellated swarmers of a piriform *Planctomyces* sp. The rigid pili described above were formed before the buds produced a stalk. Micrographs of piliated, coccal bacteria resembling young *Planctomyces* cells have been published (180, 183, 241).

## *Pasteuria*

These pear-shaped bacteria are attached to *Daphnia* spp. with their narrow cell pole. They were thought to multiply by longitudinal fission and form endospores (160). The latter process has been interpreted as budding (96), when budding forms similar to *Pasteuria* were found attached to glass slides immerged in lake water. Zavarzin (286) questioned this similarity to *Pasteuria* and placed such organisms in his newly created genus *Blastobacter* which also accommodated bacteria attaching with their wider cell pole. Re-evaluation of this problem became possible when *Daphnia* material from Lake Erie could be studied recently (105). These *Daphnia* specimens indeed had budding, aggregated, pear-shaped bacteria attached to them, and thus part of the original life cycle description could be verified. Longitudinally cleaved structures observed in the same material were interpreted as crystals. It was proposed, therefore, to abandon endospore formation and longitudinal division as claimed by Metchnikoff, but to otherwise retain the original description (107). Isolation of two *Pasteuria* strains was reported recently (244). One of these (ATCC 27377) has been proposed as the neotype strain of *Pasteuria ramosa*. The micrographs published by Staley compare favorably with original drawings of Metchnikoff, as well as with those micrographs presented by others (96, 105). It is just unfortunate that the specific epithet "*ramosa*" does not apply to such recent organisms. For this review, *P. ramosa* is defined as the neotype culture (244).

*Pasteuria* spp. have been found in seawater (116), aquarium water, and in freshwater lakes (Hirsch, unpublished observations). The organisms attach easily to glass slides brought into the neuston zone or into the epilimnion down to 7 m deep. Enrichments were obtained by transferring exposed slides into sterilized lake water without any further additions and by incubating them at room temperature. Staley (244) added a trace of peptone to a water sample and *Pasteuria* cells appeared in large numbers after two to four weeks and persisted throughout another month. Colonies on dilute peptone-yeast extract-glucose medium grew slowly and were light yellow. The cells of both new isolates were pear-shaped to ovoid, 0.5–3.0 × 1–5 μm, and attached to surfaces with their narrower cell pole. Aggregates of two to six cells were common, but a holdfast could not be detected. Motile cells attached and detached randomly, but mature cells became permanently attached.

The bud on the distal (unattached) pole was monotrichously flagellated and motile. This pole also carried fimbriae. In thin sections the DNA was located near the pointed cell pole; the wall structure resembled that of Gram-negative bacteria, but the organisms stained Gram-positively.

Growth occurred on a peptone and yeast extract medium with a number of sugars and carbohydrates. Organic acids, amino-acids, or lower alcohols were not utilized. Glucose was utilized oxidatively. No vitamins were required. The strictly aerobic organism was oxidase- and catalase-positive.

A thermophilic form morphologically identical to *P. ramosa* was found at 60°C in hot springs of Tiberias, Israel (131). The cells were reported to be Gram-variable and to aggregate to form free-floating groups or chains. Motile cells were monotrichously flagellated. This thermophilic organism grew well at 50°C in autoclaved spring water or seawater with 0.005% yeast extract and was inhibited by concentrations higher than 0.02%. No growth occurred at 30°C. The aerobic organisms tolerated 1–6% total salt concentration. Growth on solid agar media was not obtained with more than 0.2% purified agar; a pH of 6.2–9.5 was tolerated.

*P. guttaeformis,* of similar shape but with longer cells, may also belong to this group. Originally described as a sporulating fungus, it was found in fall plankton of Hungarian fish ponds (123). The slender, drop-shaped cells ("arms") were 1.0–1.6 X 2.8–4.7 μm in size. They aggregated to form three- to seven-membered rosettes. Similar bacteria were found by the author in neuston of Michigan marl or soft water lakes or in an acid-bog water lake.

### *Blastobacter*

In his review of budding bacteria, Zavarzin (286) proposed the genus, *Blastobacter,* to accommodate nonparasitic *Pasteuria*-like organisms. The type species, *Blastobacter henricii,* had "slightly curved, wedge- or rod-shaped cells grouped into rosettes in the center of which was usually a glistening corpuscle." Multiplication occurred by small, single buds (0.3 μm) appearing on the distal mother cell pole. From the description it is evident that the generative, budding pole was rounded and the tapering end attached to other cells. This is of some importance since Namsaraev & Zavarzin (172) suggested that a pure culture recently isolated from the same location with methane in the atmosphere was probably a *Blastobacter.* However, this new strain (1442) was later identified as *Methylosinus trichosporium* (173, 277, 280). The micrographs of it show rosettes of tapering cells attached with the wider, rounded pole and budding with the pointed, distal end (172). *Blastobacter* buds were nonmotile; however, the buds of strain 1442 showed motility. Constrictive division during the exponential growth phase was a characteristic of *M. trichosporium* (280), while budding was the sole mode of replication in *Blastobacter* (286). Therefore, it remains possible that there indeed exist two different types of organisms, and in this review the genus *Blastobacter* will be retained as in Bergey's Manual, eighth edition (118). The organisms drawn by Henrici & Johnson (96) and claimed to be *Blastobac-*

*ter* spp. (286) were indeed attached with their narrow poles, as could be seen on original micrographs prepared by A. T. Henrici and provided by E. McCoy.

Massive growth of *B. henricii* was observed in cylinders filled with iron water from a forest brook to which shreds of filter paper had been added. Multiplication occurred in a zone containing reduced iron and with a pH of 6.2 (286). Bacteria of the *Blastobacter* type populated Formvar-coated electron microscope grids submerged 10–20 cm deep into a small Michigan forest pond during late summer. These rod-shaped organisms were encapsulated, showed successive, multiple budding, and attached with polarly excreted mucilage (Hirsch, unpublished observations). *Blastobacter* was also found in acid-bog water habitats (224).

## *Methylosinus*

Among more than 100 isolates of Gram-negative, methane-oxidizing bacteria were forms with curved, rod-shaped cells which produced "exospores" (277). They formed rosettes by excreting a polysaccharide holdfast from the flagellated pole. During the exponential growth phase, multiplication proceeded by constrictive division. During later growth phases many of the cells became drop-shaped (*M. trichosporium*) or vibrio-shaped (*Methylosinus sporium*) and budded off one "exospore" from the distal, now pointed, cell pole. The mother cells then disintegrated. The bud spores were resistant to heat (85°C/15 min), ultrasonication (10 min), and desiccation (18 months, without $CH_4$) (280). Aged spores became refractile, acid-fast, and spore-stain positive; they did not respire measurably with or without $CH_4$. The spore fine structure was similar to that of other bacterial endospores. However, the spores did not contain dipicolinic acid. Germination lasted longer (7–15 days) in older spores.

Vegetative cells had paired membranes along the cell periphery or running throughout the cell. Exospores of *M. trichosporium* were heavily encapsulated while those of *M. sporium* were not. Growth occurred only with $CH_4$; in *M. sporium* growth with $CH_4$ was enhanced by the addition of 0.1% malate, acetate, or succinate. There was no growth with methanol (0.1%). Both species were strictly aerobic, catalase- and oxidase-positive, and $CH_4$ oxidation was inhibited by nutrient agar or yeast extract agar. Likewise, addition of methanol, ethanol, or ethane was inhibitory to $CH_4$ oxidation; and methanol inhibited ethanol oxidation.

$CH_4$ oxidation was also inhibited (competitively?) by $NH_4^+$ at concentrations equal to or greater than 0.05%. Small amounts of ammonia were tolerated and oxidized to $NO_2^-$. The optimal generation time was 5–6 hr when grown at a pH of 6.6–6.8 and at 30–37°C. Strain PG of *M. trichosporium* reduced acetylene.

*M. trichosporium* was also found in soils near natural gas leaks (1). One culture (IG) formed one to three exospores per cell and grew also on methanol, but not with ethanol, methylamine, glucose, casamino acids, or yeast extract. $NaNO_3$ (0.2%) or casamino acids (0.2%) were suitable N sources; yeast extract (0.05%) was stimulating. $NH_4^+$ salts allowed only initial growth since nitrite was produced at inhibitory concentrations. Attempts to grow the organisms without combined nitrogen were repeatedly successful. However, acetylene reduction could not be detected.

The presence, in cell-free extracts of these methylobacteria, of all enzymes of the tricarboxylic acid cycle, was verified (51). In other methylobacteria, $\alpha$-ketoglutarate dehydrogenase was missing. Additionally the two subgroups of *Methylosinus* had a NADH oxidase of flavoprotein type.

## *Naumanniella*

These rod-shaped bacteria are surrounded by a delicate, regular capsule ("torus"), onto which iron compounds can be deposited to render it golden yellow (290). The cells then resemble diatoms. Two of six species, *Naumaniella pygmaea* Beger 1949 and *Naumaniella polymorpha* Te 1969, multiply by budding. Cells of the former measure 1.0 X 2.0 $\mu$m, the torus included. *N. polymorpha* has ellipsoidal to coccoid cells (0.7–1.0 X 1.0–2.0 $\mu$m) and produces motile buds which are free from metal oxides. Colonies on Mn-carbonate or Mn-acetate agar are minute and swarm on the surface. Iron compounds are not oxidized.

*Naumanniella* has been grown on or in agar media covered with an organo-mineral complex of humic substances or on Beijerinck's medium with manganese carbonate; the colonies were dark brown (91). The life cycle was rather complex. At first ellipsoidal cells (1–2 $\mu$m long) became granular in appearance. The capsule thinned and ruptured at one or several sites to form coccal buds; the mother cells disintegrated. Eventually the growth consisted mainly of light refractile, encapsulated cocci which increasingly became impregnated with manganese hydroxide. Now the cells resembled *Siderocapsa* spp. Finally, after an increase in length, the cells acquired the ellipsoidal shape described above (91).

*Naumanniella* was found on the surface of mountain rocks, in soils, and in the upper horizons of rice soils (231). For capillary microscopy of *Naumanniella,* the pedoscope inner walls were coated with an agar medium containing organo-mineral complexes of humic acids. Brook water (pH= 6.25, Eh= 600 mV, 6.1 mg/1 Fe, and 0.13 mg/1 Mn) was reported to contain 12.4 X $10^3$ cells/ml of *Naumanniella* (58).

## *Budding Cocci and Siderococcus*

Most budding cocci from aquatic habitats have not been cultured as yet. *Siderococcus* spp. have spherical cells (0.2–0.5 $\mu$m), occur singly or in small, motile colonies of 6–15 cells, and aggregate, as do kernels of corn on a cob. Capsules are lacking. Before budding the cells become pear shaped (290). Older colonies may be covered with iron oxides but the cells remain free of deposition. Microzones of *Siderococcus* growth can be found in mud horizons with low $pO_2$ and neutral pH (191). *Siderococcus limoniticus* Dorff 1934 grows poorly on synthetic media; iron deposits usually contain only $Fe_2O_3$ (190). Published micrographs (141, 289) do not allow a clear morphological description of this organism. *Planctomyces ferrimorula* has been described as an agglomeration of spherical, budding bacteria (0.5–1.5 $\mu$m) which are arranged around a dark, HC1-soluble, central body of 1–8 $\mu$m size (275). But this cannot be a *Planctomyces,* since it entirely lacks stalks. The aggregates can be regularly found in iron-containing spring water, in acid-bog lakes, or in *Sphagnum* squeezings. Budding of the delicate cocci can create immense masses in laboratory-stored samples (Hirsch, unpublished observations). The organisms are aerobic.

Somewhat similar forms live symbiotically with flagellates or amoebae in swamp water habitats (258).

Masses of larger, budding cocci (1.3–1.6 μm) grow in the hypolimnion of Michigan marl lakes or German village ponds (Hirsch, unpublished observations). Multiple, premature budding resulted in rows of up to four cells of decreasing size. The presence of such organisms was paralleled by substantial formation of methane. No isolation attempts have been made.

Oval-shaped, budding bacteria (0.4 X 0.6–1.1 μm) can be found in direct smears of human feces (83). Densities of 8 X $10^9$/g wet wt have been observed. Anaerobic bacteria of such morphology and size grew on peptone-yeast extract media under $CO_2$. Maltose and some other sugars, but not glucose, supported growth; there was no acid production. The organisms were not motile.

## *Seliberia*

Cells of *Seliberia stellata* are rod shaped and tightly spirally twisted, with a size of 0.5–0.7 X 1–12 μm (13). They form rosettes where individual cells are held together by an excreted holdfast (178). Multiplication is by transverse fission or by budding from the end or side of one of the cell poles; round or ovoid "generative" cells can be wider than the twisted rods (10). *Seliberia* cells can be transparent and slightly inflated at the attaching end (9, 190). Subpolarly, monotrichously flagellated cells are formed by transverse fission. In this respect, *Seliberia* spp. cannot be considered to be "only" budding as defined above. The generative cells (buds) can germinate into one to several rods and form a new rosette (14). The organisms are chemo-organotrophic and facultatively anaerobic and they grow best at 24–25°C on media containing organomineral complexes of fulvic acids with sesquioxides. Growth also occurs on soil extract agar, water agar, very dilute broth, etc. When grown with humic complexes or on Fe-$NH_4^+$-citrate agar, ferric hydroxide is slowly excreted and gradually stains the colonies yellow. Twisting of the cell bodies is greatly enhanced, as is their length, when they are grown on humic complexes.

An isolate from tundra soil was more prolific than *Seliberia stellata;* the buds formed clusters around the mother cell pole (9). Multiple, successive budding resulted in the formation of rows of buds similar to those of *Planctomyces* spp.

*S. stellata* is common in soils or aquatic habitats. An original micrograph made by A. T. Henrici (but unpublished) shows *Seliberia* cells from Lake Alexander which attached to a submerged glass slide. *Seliberia*-like bacteria have been found in forest pond water, laboratory distilled water, Michigan marl lakes (epilimnion), and polluted rivers. Electron microscopic observation revealed their twisted cell bodies, one inflated pole, and one single, polarly attached flagellum (Hirsch, unpublished observations). They were also seen in water samples of Lakes Beloje and Chernoje near Moscow (179). A twisted, rod-shaped bacterium with a short, polar stalk similar to *Caulobacter* spp. has been found in soil (178). Another new species, *Seliberia carboxydohydrogena,* grew in a CO-$O_2$-$CO_2$ (7:2:1) or $H_2$-$O_2$-$CO_2$ atmosphere but did not develop on agar media (219). The twisted, rod-shaped cells (0.3 X 0.6–1.2 μm) were often bent (289). Growth under CO-$O_2$ (8:2) was markedly slower than under $H_2$-$O_2$-$CO_2$ (75:15:10) but this *Seliberia* also grew in an atmosphere of water gas (220). With hydrogen, cell yields of 3 g/l were obtained and poly-$\beta$-hydroxybutyrate was accumulated. Autotrophic assimilation of $CO_2$ with either CO or $H_2$ as the energy source was investigated (181). In a CO-$O_2$ atmosphere the growth rate and total yield of *S. carboxydohydrogena* were considerably lower than under the $H_2$-$O_2$-$CO_2$. The activity of ribulose-1,5-diphosphate carboxylase was alike in CO- or $H_2$-grown cells. A phosphoribulokinase activity could not be detected in extracts. In liquid media ribose, succinate, malate, acetate, pyruvate, or tartrate were used. Cytochromes of the *b, c,* and *a* types were found.

### *Mycococcus and Nocardioform Organisms*

In an attempt to differentiate nonacidfast, Gram-positive bacteria with budding and resting stages from *Mycobacterium* spp., Krasil'nikov (135) created the genus *Mycococcus.* The cells were coccal (0.2–1.0 μm) and occasionally grew out to short, branched rods. They were nonmotile, and multiplied either by ordinary fission (constrictive) or by budding. Buds appeared as tiny protuberances of the mother cell and separated only after growing up to the mature cell size. Tetrads or chains of cocci were common; older cultures contained refractile resting stages. These, as well as the buds, germinated by swelling and outgrowth of one to four germ tubes which subsequently became vegetative cells. Colonies on solid media were round, usually smooth and of pastelike consistency.

Mycococci grew well on ordinary media, utilizing proteins, amino acids, $NH_4^+$ or $NO_3^-$ as N sources and sugars, starch, acetate, citrate, fats, paraffin or other compounds as C sources. Six species (*Mycococcus ruber, Mycococcus capsulatus, Mycococcus citreus, Mycococcus albus, Mycococcus luteus,* and *Mycococcus flavus*) were recognized—together with a number of subspecies—in the seventh edition of *Bergey's Manual of Determinative Bacteriology.* Unfortunately, confusion arose from the observation (135) that *Mycococcus* spp. could give rise to "races or mutants resembling mycobacteria." No studies were made on possible revertants to the mycococcal stage. Confusion was deepened by successful attempts to produce *Mycococcus* forms from previously known pure cultures of *Mycobacterium tuberculosis* and other, atypical mycobacteria (49).

Evidence supporting the validity of a *Mycococcus* genus came from recent work on isolates obtained from lichens of high-mountain habitats (53, 209). Fifteen strains generally had the characteristics given by Krasil'nikov; resting cells and budding were observed. All isolates utilized glucose, galactose, glycerol, and mannitol; some grew on acetate, citrate, lactose, or maltose. The acid, short-chain carotenoid pigments of this latter group were identical to those of *M. ruber.* The fine structure and morphology of some strains were investigated together with additional isolates (53). Single cocci ranged in size from 0.5–3.5 μm; giant forms were coenobia formed by multiple, irregular, and uneven septation similar to that of *Geodermatophilus* spp. This was thus quite different from mycobacteria. Some cells were angular and compressed, an indication of their formation inside a mother cell. On wort agar the cells increased about fivefold in size before they formed visible septa. After release into the medium, angular cells assumed normal shape and divided by fission. W. Vishniac (personal communication) discovered such bacteria in Antarctic soils.

They grew under low humidity conditions and showed the same irregular, uneven septation.

Immunochemically, *Mycococcus* spp. are related to *Actinomycetales.* Cytoplasm of mycococci was closely related to 7 cytoplasm serogroups of nocardiae, to 4 serogroups of scotochromogenic mycobacteria, and to *Dermatophilus* (142). Fatty acids of 11 *Mycococcus* strains obtained from lichens were high in numbers of branched-chain acids; myristic acid (14:0) was the main component in 4 strains (199). Amino acid and sugar composition studies of these 11 strains confirmed their close relationships to each other (200). Oligonitrophily of *M. albus* and protein yields on various nitrogen sources were investigated by Maltseva (151). *M. albus* grew best with $KNO_3$.

Budding also occurred in *Pseudonocardia* spp. Recent findings indicate that *Pseudonocardia spinosa* shows acropetal hyphal budding and production of "blastospores" (97).

## *Geodermatophilus and Blastococcus*

Some desert soil actinomycetes resemble *Dermatophilus* spp. in that their hyphae septate transversely as well as longitudinally (149). During the life cycle of such organisms cubical cells germinate into filaments with occasional branching. Compressed coccal cells arise by transverse and longitudinal septation. Rigid spheroidal cells develop a small pore through which the protoplasm emerges and grows out to become a zoospore (149). Initially motile "spores" were thought to have a certain resemblance to *Bdellovibrio* cells entering their hosts. Larger, budding individuals also resembled, with their buds still attached, *Hyphomicrobium* spp. Abundant growth of these actinomycetes occurs at 26°C on media containing yeast extract, starch, sucrose, and malt extract. The organisms do not hydrolyze casein, are not $\beta$-hemolytic, but reduce $NO_3^-$ (some strains). The following carbohydrates are utilized (mostly with acid formation): L-arabinose, D-levulose, D-xylose, D-galactose, D-glucose, sucrose, glycerol, D-mannitol, and inositol (some strains).

Actually, similar actinomycetes were known from Mount Everest soils: their morphogenesis was found to be controlled by an unidentified factor contained in tryptose (Difco) (125, 126). These organisms were identified as *Geodermatophilus* spp. A study of their fine structure indicated the following life cycle: 1. spherical forms multiply by multiple, irregular, and asymmetrical septation and binary fission; the daughter cells remain attached, thus composing a growing aggregate ("C form"). 2. Upon reaching maximal size the aggregate divides into equal fractions, which 3. could grow up and divide again (C cycle). Transfer to a medium containing vitamin-free Casamino acids, glucose, trace minerals, and vitamins resulted in the formation of small, hyphal buds on C-form cocci. At the tip of such a stalk-like structure a motile bud (swarmer, R-form) develops and detaches after completion of a septum, leaving the stalk on the mother aggregate.

Repeated budding was not observed. R-form swarmers have one to four polar flagella. Their cell walls have an outer, adhesive layer and lack a "cementing" layer found on C forms. Large mesosomes observed were thought to function in budding.

Multiplication of R-form swarmers is exclusively by budding ("R cycle"). Buds develop polarly or subpolarly on a short, slender tube and strongly resemble hyphomicrobia. Conversion of R-form swarmers to C-form aggregates is preceded by loss of motility, and formation of several irregular septa.

At the same time when this peculiar life cycle was published, *Blastococcus aggregatus,* a similar organism, was isolated from the Baltic Sea (4). Close resemblance of this form to *Mycococcus* spp. and to animal pathogens of a new genus, *Polysepta,* was pointed out (253). Morphologically, swarmers of the aquatic form also bear close resemblance to *Hyphomicrobium* swarmers. Other stages are comparable to *Geodermatophilus* spp. *Blastococcus* cells are not acid fast and have a generation time of approximately 2 hr when grown at 20°C in a peptone-yeast extract medium. They grow aerobically or microaerophilically with a temperature optimum of 25°C and a maximum of 40°C; there is only slow development at 3°C. *Blastococcus* is halotolerant and grows up to a maximum concentration of 5% NaCl. There is no growth on (1%) glucose, acetate, citrate, methanol, ethylamine, petrol ether, phenol, or paraffin, but weak growth was observed with 1% ethanol. There is no acid or gas formation on the variety of sugars tested; the Voges-Proskauer reaction is negative. Chitin, alginate, starch, and cellulose are not hydrolyzed; gelatin is not liquified. $NH_4^+$ or peptone can serve as nitrogen sources. *Blastococcus* is catalase-positive and does not nitrify or oxidize thiosulfate. Its pigment was identified as a carotenoid.

### *Bacterial Protoplasts and L Forms*

It has often been claimed that budding initiates the process of protoplast or L-form replication (138). However, in cells lacking rigid walls this process should be more accurately called a pinching-off mechanism followed by constriction. Chlamydial cells such as psittacosis agents, meningopneumonitis agents, etc go through stages in their life cycle which lack rigid walls (159). In the presence of penicillin, "large cells" apparently multiply by budding (86). A detailed study is needed to compare true budding of cell wall-carrying bacteria with this mode of replication of protoplasts.

### *Mycoplasma, Acholeplasma, and Thermoplasma*

The initiation of mycoplasma multiplication by budding has been observed frequently. The buds are pinched off and separated by constriction; they often are minute in size and hence considered to be "elementary reproductive units" (251). Many published micrographs allow this conclusion; the replicative stages have been reviewed (207). A sterol-requiring *Mycoplasma* sp. (strain Y) has cell forms remarkably similar to those of hyphomicrobia when grown with oleate plus palmitate, elaidate, or elaidate plus palmitate (212). A variant of a *Mycoplasma* from goats showed an "axial fiber" with terminal "base plate" or knob and also resembled hyphomicrobia to a surprising extent (192). *Mycoplasma*-like organisms found in soil suspensions had the beaded-rosary appearance of *Rhodomicrobium* cell chains (247). However, budding of at least some mycoplasmas was questioned in a recent review (155). Confusion arises here from the poor differentiation between formation of a protoplast bud with a special mode of obtaining a constant, rigid shape—as compared to the separation process of the nucleated daughter cell, which leads to multiplication. The proper way of expressing the situation would be: " . . . cell separation and multiplication are preceded by the formation of bud-shaped protuberances. . . ."

In an attempt to compare *Gallionella* stalk fibers to filaments of an organism resembling a *Mycoplasma,* Balashova (19) inoculated an ultrafiltered *Gallionella* enrichment culture into a medium for *Acholeplasma laidlawii.* This medium was five times diluted and contained agar, yeast extract (0.005%), and DNA (0.005%). Feeble growth of small colonies was obtained under an atmosphere of low $pO_2$. When horse serum (0.01%) was added, filamentous structures similar to those in *Gallionella* ribbons appeared to grow. Such structures were not found in controls. It was concluded that *Gallionella* was similar, in these enrichment cultures, to mycoplasmas. Upon reinoculation of the *Mycoplasma* culture into *Gallionella* mineral medium, growth of *Gallionella*-like structures was obtained. It cannot be excluded, however, that this may have been due to a transfer of remnants of the original inoculum. Along this line of experimentation are also two recent studies of *A. laidlawii* devoted to the demonstration, in this organism, of filaments and of ferrous iron oxidation (20, 22). A significant ability for iron oxidation could be correlated with the period of active growth; oxidized iron was deposited onto budding *A. laidlawii* cells. The addition of catalase to the medium arrested iron oxidation. On this basis it was concluded that the oxidation process is a secondary effect of *A. laidlawii* metabolic activities and that mycoplasmas can take part in iron oxidation under natural conditions. An acidophilic and thermophilic representative of the mycoplasmas has been isolated from a coal-refuse pile which had undergone self-heating (50). A temperature of 56°C and a pH (1:1 mixture in water) of 1.96 were measured in the organisms' habitat. Enrichment was achieved by adding approximately 0.5 g of black refuse to 5 ml of a mineral salts medium containing 0.1% Difco yeast extract and 1% glucose and with a pH of 2–3; incubation was at 55°C. Three strains were isolated of which ATCC 25905 was named *Thermoplasma acidophila.* Its base ratio (25 Mol % G + C) falls into the range of other mycoplasmas.

Several additional strains came from hot springs. *Thermoplasma* cells are pleomorphic spheres (0.3–2.0 μm) which can enlarge up to 10 μm in diameter (36). Filamentous forms were detected in young cultures. Budding of these organisms is evident from micrographs published (36). Cell walls can not be detected in ultrathin sections; the membrane outer layer contains 20 nm particles. Rapid lysis was produced by sodium lauryl sulfate. Insensitivity to vancomycin (5 mg/ml) and ristocetin also indicates the absence of cell wall synthesis.

Growth is optimal at 55–59°C (doubling time 4 hr); no growth occurs at 37 or 65°C. The tolerable pH range of strain 122-1 B2 was reported to be 0.96–3.0, with an optimum of about 2. Yeast extract is utilized at concentrations below 0.5%. A variety of sugars tested does not stimulate growth; these included glucose which had been present in the initial enrichment medium. The organisms are aerobic; they are neither autotrophic nor can they oxidize sulfur (36).

*Thermoplasma* membranes do not lyse in 30 min when cells are washed in distilled water or up to 1.0 M of NaCl (30). Storage in triple distilled water for 36 hr did not affect cell membrane stability either. Concentrations of detergents needed to obtain lysis were found to be eight times higher than for other mycoplasmas. Lysozyme, trypsin or pronase, primary alcohols, or digitonin did not affect *Thermoplasma* spp. Heat resistance (30 min, up to 100°C) was much more pronounced than that of bacterial protoplasts. The pH range of cell stability was 1–7; above pH 8 lysis occurred. The amino acid composition of *Thermoplasma* membrane proteins is similar to that of other mycoplasmal membranes, but the numbers of free amino and carboxyl groups is less than half of those in *Acholeplasma* (239). This was offered as an explanation for *Thermoplasma* acidophily. Serological cross reaction patterns of 38 strains indicated 5 affinity groups; all strains react to some degree with the type strain (35). Immunofluorescence could thus be used successfully for in situ detection and identification of *T. acidophila* in coal-refuse piles.

## *Metallogenium*

Bacteria of this genus were first postulated by Perfil'ev (189) as causing biogenic ore formation. *Metallogenium invisum* was named "invisum" because "its existence was not confirmed at that time." Later the use of capillary microscopy allowed the study of microbial metal oxide deposition and a real bacterium, *Metallogenium personatum,* was found and described (190). Pure cultures of a *Metallogenium* were not obtained until much later by Dubinina (57). It is not clear, however, which species was investigated. Some of the studies were carried out on "organisms free of fungi"; from this remark it can be assumed that the object was *Metallogenium symbioticum,* the second species described (291). Considerable attention has been paid to these unusual and little-understood bacteria. Doubts expressed about their real existence were understandable, since they cannot be seen easily. D. R. Gabe and G. A. Zavarzin have supplied the author with authentical growth of *M. personatum* and *M. symbioticum.* The latter organism's reproductive cocci were demonstrated alive and germinated to the "trichospherical" stage. Moreover, Hirsch (unpublished observations) succeeded in growing *M. personatum* in Perfil'ev capillaries visually controlled in the laboratory. Growth of *Metallogenium* on electron microscope grids submerged in natural water gave additional confirmation of the presence and nature of this organism (57).

There can be no doubt, therefore, that there exist true bacteria with the properties ascribed to *Metallogenium* spp. Much of the confusion over forms may have arisen from the rapid encasement of the true cell body by manganese deposits. However, *Metallogenium* does not need to oxidize and deposit manganese (57). A UV mutant of *Metallogenium* was obtained which was incapable of manganese oxidation and deposition, but still grew well (289). Such organisms closely resemble mycoplasmas with beaded filaments ("arais") radiating from a common center, the initial reproductive cell. Observations on naturally growing *Metallogenium* showed that the degree of encrustation varies with the environment; excellent growth without deposition occurs in ponds or lakes (Hirsch, unpublished observations). The *Metallogenium* life cycle begins with coccoid, often light refractile elementary bodies ("reproductive cells"), 0.5–1.5 μm in diameter, which either reproduce by direct budding or "germinate" to form one to five flexible, and occasionally branched filaments, 0.02–0.25 μm in diameter ("arais"). The microcolony now has the "trichospherical" appearance, i.e. that of a star with a central sphere. The arais produce terminal or subterminal coccoid buds which may separate or remain attached. In the latter case, germination results in satellite colony formation at the filament tip. Motility of the coccoid bodies has been claimed (190, 191), but neither flagella nor direct motion were observed. Rapid encrustation with manganese oxides proceeds basipetally and soon causes the individual filaments to join to a dense mass ("zoogloeal stage"). Occasionally, cocci with only one to three filaments point in one direction (e.g. when attached to glass surfaces). Heavy manganese deposition then results in "clavate forms." The main propagation forms are coccoid elementary bodies which can be produced in such numbers that the medium becomes turbid. Apart from terminal or lateral budding, these minute cocci may be formed endogenously (57).

These morphological similarities with mycoplasmas have caused recent authors to place *Metallogenium* among the *Mycoplasmatales* (19, 56). Organisms resembling *Metallogenium* spp. have been described under the name of *Leptothrix echinata* Beger 1935 as "an iron bacterium storing predominantly manganese" (28, 236). *Metallogenium* spp. may be geologically very old organisms. *Eoastrion simplex* and *Eoastrion bifurcatum* described as fossil organisms from Precambrian gunflint chert (23, 46) showed great resemblance to metallogenia. The two living species presently recognized, *M. personatum* and *M. symbioticum*, both deposit manganese oxides but not iron compounds. They are differentiated on the basis of symbiotic growth by the latter and by the tapering filament structure of the former (291). Recently an iron-oxidizing and -requiring, acid-tolerant *Metallogenium* has been isolated from streams (272, 273). The organisms tolerate a pH from 3.5–6.8 (optimum 4.1), are insensitive to penicillin (up to 331 IU/ml), but are inhibited by chloramphenicol (0.005 mg/ml). Growth was obtained on FeS medium used to culture *Gallionella ferruginea*, or on the isolation medium with 1–10% horse serum. Growth on this medium was stimulated by the addition of up to 40 mg/l of ferrous iron. Serum could be replaced by ferrous iron. The base ratio of 72 Mol % G + C was much above the mycoplasma range (273). Little information is available on the physiology of symbiotic metallogenia. Fungi for *M. symbioticum* isolated from soils were identified as *Coniothyrium, Mycogone, Fusarium, Alternaria*, and *Cephalosporium* spp. Free-living forms resembling *Metallogenium* spp. have been found in ooze (141), or in lakes (55, 59, 79, 80, 139, 183). In many cases growth of the *Metallogenium* was confined to a narrow zone characterized by a low $pO_2$ of approximately 0.5 mg/l (79).

## *Caulococcus and Kusnezovia*

Both organisms have been found only rarely (191). Their life cycle is still not well understood since pure cultures have not been obtained as yet (291). *Caulococcus* cells are coccoid, 0.5 μm, and connected by filaments (hyphae?) about 0.1 μm thick. The filaments can be dichotomously branched at the colony edge. Young cells (buds?) are motile but flagellation has not been observed. Manganese precipitation heavily encrusts the colonies and causes these to appear brownish-black. About 10–20% Fe has been found in the deposits. These observations indicate a certain relationship to *Pedomicrobium podsolicum. Kusnezovia* is still more difficult to understand. The basic cells and filamentous units bear a certain resemblance to pedomicrobia. However, the shape of *Kusnezovia* microcolonies is quite different from anything described so far for the pedomicrobia: "lily-of-the-valley leaves", "goblets with toothed margins", etc can hardly be interpreted with our present state of microbiological knowledge. The organisms seem to exist, however, and one therefore has to await further, experimental data. While investigating samples of swamp ore and freshwater lakes with electron microscopic techniques, organisms and structures were discovered which could be compared to stages of *Kusnezovia,* but no attempts were made to cultivate these organisms from such samples (58). Similarly, *Caulococcus*-like forms have been observed in ooze (140).

## GENOMES OF BUDDING BACTERIA

### *Base Ratios and DNA Homology Studies*

The ranges of DNA base compositions of some budding bacteria are shown in Table 4. Most of these are above 60 Mol % G + C, the exceptions being *Prosthecochloris* and *Thermoplasma.* The marked GC differences of the two genera of prosthecate bacteria is noteworthy. *Thermoplasma* as a representative of the mycoplasmas can be expected to have a low GC content. DNA base sequence homology studies of hyphal, budding bacteria and a few related forms revealed the presence of distinct and little-related groups among a collection of hyphomicrobia. There was a high intragroup homology within these groups (164). The grouping agreed well with that obtained from studying base ratios (153). There was essentially zero homology between *Hyphomicrobium* DNA and that of two *Hyphomonas* strains. The type culture of *Hyphomicrobium neptunium* also showed little or no relation to the hyphomicrobia. However, *H. neptunium* DNA did reassociate to 28 and 40% with the two *Hyphomonas* strains. This confirmed previous physiological and fine structural observations (Hirsch, unpublished observations). *H. neptunium* will have to be transferred to the genus *Hyphomonas.* The DNA relationship between hyphomicrobia and *Rhodomicrobium vannielii, Prosthecomicrobium enhydrum, Prosthecomicrobium pneumaticum,* or *Ancalomicrobium adetum* is essentially zero.

### *The Nuclear Apparatus and Genome Size*

*Hyphomicrobium* sp. B-522 was studied by light and electron microscopy as well as tracer techniques (166). In ultrathin sections, nucleoids had often polyphosphate granules associated with one end of the DNA whorls, an observation that has been made already previously (48). Specific DNA staining of first generation cells with Giemsa and DNA labeling with tritiated thymidine or adenine over up to two doublings of culture turbidity as well as sectioning, showed nucleoids only in mother cells and older buds but not normally in hyphae or very young buds. This confirmed earlier findings in *Hyphomicrobium* sp. (286) and in *R. vannielii* (171).

**Table 4** Base ratios (mol % G+C) of DNA's of budding bacteria as determined by the CsCl buoyant density method

| Organism | No. strains tested | Base ratio (Range) | References |
|---|---|---|---|
| *Hyphomicrobium* spp. | 67 | 59.2–66.8 | 153; 234 |
| *Hyphomicrobium neptunium* | 1 | 61.7 | 153 |
| *Hyphomonas polymorpha* | 2 | 60.2, 61.2 | 153 |
| *Rhodomicrobium* spp. | 8 | 61.8–63.8 | 154; 234 |
| *Ancalomicrobium adetum* | 2 | 70.4, 71.4 | 245 |
| *Prosthecomicrobium enhydrum* | 11 | 66.1–68.9 | 245 |
| *Prosthecomicrobium pneumaticum* | 3 | 69.4–70.4 | 245 |
| *Prosthecochloris aestuarii* | 2 | 50.0, 56.4 | 154 |
| *Rhodopseudomonas palustris* | 8 | 64.8–66.3 | 154 |
| *Rhodopseudomonas viridis* | 18 | 66.3–71.4 | 154 |
| *Rhodopseudomonas acidophila* | 8 | 62.2–66.8 | 154 |
| *Nitrobacter* spp. | 6 | 60.2–61.7 | 274 |
| *Pasteuria ramosa* (neotype) | 1 | 57.1 | 244 |
| *Sulfolobus acidocaldarius* | 5 | 60.0–68.0 | 36 |
| *Thermoplasma acidophila* | 4 | 24.0–29.0 | 36 |
| *Metallogenium* sp. | 1 | 72.0–73.0 | 273 |

Previous reports of nuclear material presence at hyphal tips may have been due to investigation of older cells (101, 112). DNA, found very rarely in hyphal sections of young cells, occupies less space than does the mother cell nucleoid but is not really denser in structure. Giemsa-stained *Hyphomicrobium* B-522 has round nuclear bodies as compared to the bar-shaped nucleoids of hyphomicrobia or *R. vannielii* studied previously (171, 286). Those hyphomicrobia possessing two to three nucleoids are either mother cells with young buds or very old cells of irregular shape (166). The average number of Giemsa-stained nucleoids per swarmer cell was found to be 1.03; this value remains constant for the first 5 hr (= one third of the generation time) and reached 1.5 after 10 hr. By DNA reassociation experiments and comparison with reassociation rates of *E. coli* DNA, the genome size was determined to be $4.7 \times 10^6$ nucleotide pairs. Assuming an average molecular weight of 600 per nucleotide pair, the molecular weight of the B-522 genome could be calculated to be $3.1 \times 10^9$. With tracer techniques the total amount of DNA per cell was determined to be $5.57 \times 10^{-15}$ g. Using the equation:

$$\text{No. DNA molecules per cell} = \frac{(\text{g DNA/cell}) \times (\text{Avogadro's No.})}{\text{mol wt of DNA}}$$

it was calculated that an average cell of *Hyphomicrobium* B-522 had 1.08 DNA molecules, a figure which compares favorably to that of 1.03 found by Giemsa-staining. Thus a limited amount of DNA replication must have occurred in the swarmers during maturation. Radiolabeling experiments also showed that one half of the original DNA was transferred to the daughter cell at each generation. This agrees with the semiconservative DNA replication. However, only 43% of the stable swarmer RNA came from the mother cell, indicating there was some RNA synthesis by the bud nucleoid. Only little mixing could have occurred with the pre-existing mother cell RNA while the bud was still attached. UV sensitivity of synchronized B-522 swarmer populations was also investigated (166). Populations grown either for 1 hr or for 11 hr gave the same response. Since 63% of the 11 hr cell population had buds which were probably already nucleated (i.e. contained two nucleoids) a greater sensitivity to UV could be expected for the less developed, uninucleated 1 hr cells. However, both populations were alike. This could indicate a limited but existent means of communication between the mother cell and bud nucleoid. The first DNA transfer from the site of synthesis (the mother cell) to the bud was assumed to proceed rapidly in *Hyphomicrobium* B-522. DNA was not detected on its way to the bud except for a very few cases. Experiments with better synchronized swarmer populations are needed to clarify this point.

The nucleoid of the new *Pasteuria* isolate is preferentially located near the attached cell pole (244). A significance of this location for morphogenetic processes can be assumed. Information on the timing of bud nucleation in *Pasteuria* is still lacking. Another interesting phenomenon is the multiple septation process of the budding actinomycetes, *Geodermatophilus* (149), *Blastococcus* (4), or *Mycococcus* (53). One wonders if there exists a controlled mechanism of DNA synthesis and distribution to ensure the enclosure of exactly one nucleoid per cell. The nuclear apparatus of *R. vannielii* has been studied by Giemsa-staining of agar slide cultures (171) or by thin sectioning (34, 48, 257). One to several nucleoids were found and early appearance of DNA in very young buds was reported (171).

### *Pure Culture Storage and Genetic Stability*

Optimal preservation conditions for pure cultures of budding bacteria have not been reported as yet. Hyphomicrobia growing with C1 compounds and not lysing easily can be stored for several months at 5°C without subculturing. Strains forming surface pellicles survive up to two years in their mineral salts media even when sealed in test tubes (Hirsch, unpublished observations). Preservation in sterile, glycerol-containing buffer (205), as suggested by R. Brubacker (personal communication), gave good results. Well-grown cells were washed off from a slant by using sterile phosphate buffer (pH 7.0, 0.15 M); 1 ml of this suspension was added to 4 ml of sterile, concentrated glycerol in a screw cap tube. Rapid mixing and immediate cooling to about –25°C produced a viscous suspension which could be subcultured directly by streaking onto solid media. Once warmed up the glycerol suspension lost viability rapidly unless it was immediately cooled down again to –20°C. Lyophilization of hyphomicrobia in skim milk has also been successful. Agar shake cultures of rhodomicrobia were stored refrigerated for up to two years (P. Hirsch and S. F.

Conti, unpublished observations). Hyphomicrobia and *Hyphomonas* spp. with a tendency to lyse had to be stored in peptone-containing liquid media; frequent subculturing was mandatory. Genetic recombination events as a result of heterokaryosis could occur in hyphal, budding bacteria at a higher rate than in other bacteria. Cell arrangements and cell forms suggestive of conjugation have been observed (48). Zavarzin (286) postulated a genetic exchange by his hyphomicrobia during rosette formation. Bacteriophages specific for hyphomicrobia have been obtained but were easily lost during subsequent purification steps (P. Hirsch, M. Macpherson, and H. Boltes, unpublished observations). A *Hyphomicrobium* phage "Hy $\phi$ 30" was found to adsorb only to the tips of growing stalks or to young buds prior to flagellation (72). Motile, mature swarmers were immune to phage infection. Visible phage formation occurred mainly in buds and hyphae but not in mother cells. Obviously, phage attachment and assembly was confined to growing portions of the cell.

## MORPHOGENESIS AND LIFE CYCLES

### *Definitions and General Remarks*

Morphogenesis can be defined in two ways: 1. the processes leading to forms and stages of an individual cell's life cycle, and 2. processes leading to the formation of any kind of specific cell type or shape. Both aspects have interested microbiologists working with budding bacteria.

The first stage in a morphogenesis study would be the investigation of an organism's "normal" life cycle. But how do we define what is normal? Laboratory cultures may contain forms or cell sizes which are not detected in nature. Conversely, the appearance of pure cultures when transferred into the natural habitat is often not known. For answering such questions growth chambers sealed by membrane filters or dialysis membranes were inoculated with pure cultures and brought into the natural habitat (106). Another method consisted of direct, water immersion microscopy of organisms growing in the undisturbed habitat (242). Observation of bacteria attached to glass slides (96) or use of glass capillaries (190) were further useful techniques. Seminatural conditions were obtained by employing two-dimensional, agar diffusion gradient techniques (39–41). In the latter case considerable differences in cell size and shape of *Rhodomicrobium* have been detected (40). Because of the different budding mechanisms and obvious group relationships, morphogenesis will have to be discussed groupwise. A recent review has pointed to several interesting aspects (222).

### *Pleomorphy and Development of Hyphal Bacteria*

The first growing stages of all members of this group are similar. Swarmers of *Hyphomicrobium, Hyphomonas, Pedomicrobium,* or *Rhodomicrobium* produce initially one polar hypha and bud from the hyphal tip (6, 108, 111, 171, 202, 264). Lateral outgrowth of the first hypha occurs in *Pedomicrobium* spp. Multiple formation of hyphae has not been reported; direct microscopy of agar slide cultures showed that additional polar hyphae form later, usually as a result of changing environmental conditions (Hirsch, unpublished observations). Intercalary buds have been observed only in *Rhodomicrobium* and *Pedomicrobium* spp. (116). A great variability exists with respect to cell shape and size, hyphal number and length, and site of origin or branching. This pleomorphy has been related to differences in growth conditions (40, 101, 113, 133). Zavarzin (286) and others found significantly less branching of hyphomicrobia grown on methanol. The type and concentration of C or N source determines size and hyphal branching, even the hyphal diameter, of *Hyphomicrobium* and *Pedomicrobium* spp. (102, 108, 264). Acetate or formamide stimulates branching. Lowering the phosphate concentration in the medium increases hyphal length up to 300-fold (P. Hirsch and M. Macpherson, unpublished observations). In *Pedomicrobium* T37 the "*Hyphomicrobium* facies" morphology was observed with cells grown on mineral medium 337 (108) with methanol (125 mM) as the carbon source. Some cells exhibit extensive cellular lobing (26) or produce multiple and lateral hyphae when cultivated with methylamine (100 mM).

Rhodomicrobia react to environmental changes in a similar way. Fast growth results in slender, spindle-shaped cells with little-branched hyphae, while slow growth gives nearly spherical cells (40). High light intensity has been shown to suppress the formation of thylakoids in rhodomicrobia (257). In prosthecomicrobia, the appendage length also depends on environmental factors. Staley (241) presented a micrograph of a *Prosthecomicrobium* cell which lacked prosthecae on one cell pole.

## *Cell Polarity*

A distinct polarity of structure and physiology exists in hyphal bacteria. Swarmers of rosette-forming hyphomicrobia had their DNA and poly-β-hydroxybutyrate (PHB) granule located at the distal cell pole (133, 286), while hyphal outgrowth occurred from the pole formerly attached to the mother cell (133); a hold-fast was secreted from the distal pole only (48). Similar polarity was observed in *Hyphomicrobium neptunium,* while *Hyphomicrobium* B-522 usually produced the first hypha at the distal cell pole (Hirsch, unpublished observations).

## *Life Cycles*

Budding bacteria are easily studied in slide cultures (25, 112, 133, 161, 171, 195, 241, 244, 278). Since most information has been gathered on methanol- or methylamin-grown *Hyphomicrobium* B-522, this organism's life cycle will be described in greater detail. The availability of swarmer populations with a fair degree of synchrony made it possible to follow the sequential events of the first generation in greater detail (113, 165). A newly liberated swarmer cell is usually smaller than the mature mother cell (165). It contains approximately 1.03 DNA molecules and the nucleoid shows multiple membrane attachment sites (166). The distal (blunt) pole caries a PHB storage granule while the proximal, formerly attached cell pole has some bag-like membrane invaginations (113). During the swarmer maturation time, which lasted approximately 28–34% of the first generation life cycle, the swarmer becomes immotile, grows in length up to 1⅓ of its birth size, and then shortens and widens to reach the final, mature size of a mother cell, its size then normally remains constant. Preliminary experiments indicate that cessation of mother cell wall growth is connected with the initiation of hyphal wall growth. Treatment of maturing swarmer cells with platinum salts (214) resulted in continuous elongation of swarmer cells similar to filament formation of *Escherichia coli* (P. Hirsch and H. E. Jones, unpublished observations).

Hyphal growth is exponential and initially occurs at the basis (112). During this time, DNA is continuously synthesized in the mother cell (166). At the moment of cessation of hyphal growth, a terminal bud arises by asymmetrical, subpolar wall growth, as revealed by primuline fluorescence surface staining. Similar observations have been reported for rhodomicrobia (171). Omission of phosphate at this time results in continuing growth of the hypha without bud formation. L. R. Berger (personal communication) observed the same effect in rhodomicrobia.

After the bud reaches a size slightly larger in volume than that of a mature genome, it becomes rapidly nucleated (166). The genome arrives in the bud with stable mother cell RNA (43% of the level measured at birth time). Ultrathin sections show polyribosomes pushed forward by the arriving genome. The bud immediately commences DNA and RNA synthesis (166), and soon formation of a septum is observed (Figure 3.4). A small PHB storage granule appears at this stage at the distal cell pole. Flagellar growth also begins at this time, but some cells have flagellar stubs already before bud nucleation. Vigorous movements in spurts then result in bud liberation. The average mother generation time is 14.25 hr in agar slide cultures (112) and 14.5 hr in liquid, shaken cultures (165). Of this period, 28–39% is used for hyphal growth and 33–38% for bud formation and detachment.

After giving birth to the first swarmer cell, the mother cell hypha recommences growth. However, primuline staining indicates apical growth rather than at the basis, as during the first generation. The new increment of stalk length is approximately one half to one third of the previous one; each consecutive daughter cell formation is followed by less hyphal growth than in the preceeding one until a finite hyphal length is reached which is constant for a given set of growth conditions (108, 165). Up to eight daughter cells are produced during the active period of mother cell reproduction (133, 161). Still favorable growth conditions at this time result in formation of a new budding hypha from the other cell pole. Again older cells have side branches capable of bud formation. Most individual cells observed reproduce actively only at one hyphal tip at a time (Hirsch, unpublished observations).

The shorter intervals of hyphal growth during the formation of second and subsequent daughter cells result in shorter cell-doubling times during these "daughter generations." Shorter hyphal growing times during constant rates of DNA, RNA, or protein synthesis may also have been responsible for larger periods of bud growth and hence greater length of subsequent daughter cells (113). Shorter doubling times of hyphal (older) parent cells have already been observed in *H. neptunium* (276).

There may well exist fundamental differences between strains or species, as rosette-forming hyphomicrobia appear to have DNA in young buds from the first moment on (286). More work with synchronous populations is necessary. The degree of synchrony reported for *Hyphomicrobium* B-522 was only "fair"; although the swarmer population obtained was free of hyphae, it still showed considerable size variation. It probably consisted of first- and later-born swarmers, as well as those at various stages of maturation.

Hyphal and bud growth appear to be mutually exclusive processes. A requirement of hyphal growth before bud formation has been postulated (166), and cessation of budding after the final hyphal length has been reached indicates this requirement. It was suggested that this growth requirement was connected with the mechanism of DNA transport to the bud (166). Another explanation was a requirement for a minimal distance between the mother nucleoid and that of the mature but not yet separated bud cell. A "*Hyphomicrobium,*" isolated from manganese deposits, lacked hyphae entirely and still multiplied by budding (25).

In *Hyphomicrobium neptunium,* nalidixic acid specifically and immediately inhibited DNA synthesis and budding, but RNA synthesis remained initially nearly unaffected (276). Inhibited cells produced abnormally long hyphae but did not bud. It was concluded that, in this organism, bud formation was coupled to chromosome replication.

An interesting phenomenon is the fairly constant but different diameter of mother cells and hyphae. In hyphomicrobia the hyphal diameter is approximately one fourth that of the mother cell. Conditions resulting in smaller (thinner) mother cells also lessened the hyphal diameter (108). One wonders if differences in cell wall structure could be responsible for this. A related problem is the relatively constant size of *Geodermatophilus* or *Blastococcus* swarmer cells (4, 126, 149).

Hyphal formation may be a necessary growth process in the developmental cycle of hyphomicrobia, but prosthecae of *Ancalomicrobium* or *Prosthecomicrobium* do not appear to have such a function but rather represent just an increase in cell surface (241).

Morphogenesis of *Metallogenium* has not yet been investigated. Some "hot" questions must be asked, however. What is the real nature of the arais? Do they contain cytoplasm and the two membrane layers of a normal cell? How do arais branch? How does enough DNA (one genome) travel through these very thin tubes to nucleate the growing, coccoid reproductive cells? This is a wide-open and rewarding field for research.

## ECOLOGICAL OBSERVATIONS AND INTERPRETATIONS

### *Natural Habitats*

Budding bacteria inhabit many extreme locations and often show great resistance to stress conditions occurring in their habitat. They do not appear to be parasitic, with perhaps the exception of *Hyphomonas* and *Pasteuria* spp. Budding is rare among photosynthetic *Chromatiaceae* and *Chlorobiaceae.* It seems as if budding is a characteristic of bacteria which live in habitats that undergo frequent and sudden changes. The tendency to attach to surfaces and the frequent formation of rosettes or other aggregates can be seen in the same light. Aggregation or attachment are particularly advantageous in habitats poor in nutrients (292) or with a changing nutrient supply. Rosette formation in hyphomicrobia has been studied by Zavarzin (286). Newly born swarmers attached themselves to the common holdfast soon after their release from the mother hypha. Rosettes of *Seliberia* were supposed to arise by budding of individual cells (14).

### *Parasites of Budding Bacteria*

Only few natural parasites of budding bacteria are known so far. Phage Hy$\phi$30 has been studied with respect to its attachment sites (72). *Hyphomicrobium* enrichments or stock cultures were easily overgrown and lysed by psychrophilic fungi. Ectoparasitic soil bacteria introduced with membrane-filtered soil extract (0.45 $\mu$m pore width) were found to "lyse" *Hyphomicrobium* cells and leave "ghosts" which still retained the original shape and size. Such ectoparasites did not invade the host cells, and their clearing action was slow as compared to that of *Bdellovibrio* spp. (Hirsch, unpublished observations). Eleven pure cultures of similar ectoparasites were obtained from brackish water sewage mud with *Hyphomicrobium* spp. or *Pseudomonas fluorescens* cells as the bait (284). Both host genera were attacked by all of the isolates. Nine strains resembled *Pseudomonas* spp. and two were tentatively identified as *Xanthomonas* sp. The parasites were only motile when grown with living host cells in liquid media. Attack was initiated by specific attachment to the host cell surface; there was no attachment to *Hyphomicrobium* hyphae.

### *Some Ecological Consequences of Budding*

One could argue for the case where an attached, budding organism suffers from encasement by various substances and survives only because of the formation of buds (262). However, the opposite could be true: only an organism capable of budding can afford to have the main cell body encrusted with mucilage, humic substances, or metal oxides and still survive and reproduce by means of its often motile buds. In some cases budding may have to be envisioned as a consequence of permanent attachment of the parent cell; the smaller bud then represents the mobile, propagative stage of this organism. Since there seem to exist different modes of budding (Table 1, Figure 1) the ecological implications of this may be quite variable.

### *Budding Bacteria as Indicators for Environmental Quality*

Among the morphologically nondescript coccal, rod- or spiral-shaped bacteria the budding forms stand out through their recognizable buds. This could make them useful as indicators for environmental conditions, provided their presence or morphology could be specifically related to known growth conditions. Such organisms would only be useful if the whole range of their morphological variability and if their physiological peculiarities were known. For all we know, there might be the possibility of using hyphomicrobia for this purpose (102). The distribution of prosthecate bacteria along a polluted stream has been studied successfully with this approach (243). Perhaps the other budding forms can be employed similarly once we know more about them.

## SUMMING UP AND CONCLUSIONS

Several different mechanisms of bud formation can be demonstrated. Likewise, budding bacteria represent morphologically, physiologically, and ecologically different and distinct groups within which closer relations can be recognized. Budding-type mechanisms of cell wall growth may therefore have evolved for different reasons. It seems to be impossible to find some unifying properties or consequences for all the groups of budding organisms.

Why do some organisms bud and others do not? Why does budding only rarely (if at all) occur together with "normal" wall growth and fission? Attempts to relate budding to a specific cell wall composition or structure would still be premature. The presence, in budding bacteria, of otherwise rarely found fatty acids or phospholipids may point in this direction (17, 74, 185, 186). A unifying hypothesis might be the assumption that some microbial cells could retain, during all of their lifetime, a capability for rearranging their cell wall structure and/or composition to reinitiate growth processes, while others (the budding forms) lay down a wall or hull which soon becomes permanent and fixed. Such forms, then, could only reproduce by breaking locally the most recently formed wall part, thus bulging out with the cytoplasm and initiating localized wall growth. This hypothesis could be modified by assuming the presence of fundamentally different wall structures in budding bacteria, or by postulating, in such organisms, the production of very different enzymatic and lytic events.

Once evolved, bud-forming bacteria may survive better in the attached state, i.e. in a relatively quiet environment where their fragile, partially naked daughter cells are less likely to be mechanically damaged. It is difficult to decide whether budding is a primitive property retained from the ancestral, wall-free stage, or whether it has been adopted later as a response to environmental conditions.

Asking a number of questions pertaining to morphogenesis might now be quite rewarding. Preformation of a bud until it is large enough to accept the genome requires intricate and well-coordinated enzymatic activities at specific sites. What triggers bud growth during the DNA replication cycle, and what determines the site of bud or hyphal formation? What stops bud growth when it has reached the proper diameter and length? Cell wall synthesis at some wall growing sites must be discontinuous.

Hyphal branching in some of the budding bacteria brings additional problems. If the genome is produced in the mother cell, how does the "traveling genome" recognize the proper hyphal branch that leads to the bud to be nucleated? The branching point fine structure needs to be investigated.

Still unanswered is the intriguing question of DNA translocation from the mother cell into the bud. What force drives the genome mechanically? Cytoplasmic streaming has been suggested as one possibility (166), but other models must be formulated and discussed.

Much can be learned from a study of these "unusual" organisms; "unusual" should here be understood as "exceptional to the rule." These exceptions, the unusual bacteria, may well hold explanations to secrets that cannot even be visualized from studying the well-known, "usual" organisms. As knowledge of "odd bugs" increases, these become less odd, and they may be easier to handle, too!

ACKNOWLEDGMENTS

This review could not have been completed without the active help of many scientific friends from several countries who supplied information, experiences, and organisms. I thank my wife, Mrs. A. M. Hirsch, for bearing with me during this time and for helping with the manuscript. The technical assistance of Mrs. A. Gräter, Miss A. Ingram, Miss E. Prehn, and several others is also gratefully acknowledged. A travel grant from the Board of Trustees, Bergey's Manual of Determinative Bacteriology, and several travel grants from the Deutsche Forschungsgemeinschaft provided the basis for much of the information contained in this review.

*Literature Cited*

1. Adamse, A. D., Hoeks, J., DeBont, J. A. M., van Kessel, J. F. 1972. *Arch. Mikrobiol.* 83:32–51
2. Adler, H. I., Fisher, W. D., Cohen, A., Hardigree, A. A. 1967. *Proc. Nat. Acad. Sci. USA* 57:321–26
3. Adler, H. I., Hardigree, A. A. 1964. *J. Bacteriol.* 87:1240–42
4. Ahrens, R., Moll, G. 1970. *Arch. Mikrobiol.* 70:243–65
5. Anagnostidis, K., Rathsack-Künzenbach, R. 1967. *Schweiz. Z. Hydrol.* 29:191–98
6. Aristovskaya, T. V. 1961. *Dokl. Acad. Nauk SSSR* (Engl. transl.) 136:111–14
7. Aristovskaya, T. V. 1963. *Microbiology USSR* 32:564–68
8. Aristovskaya, T. V. 1963. *Potchvoved. Akad. Nauk SSSR* 1, 30–42
9. Aristovskaya, T. V. 1964. *Microbiology USSR* 33:929–34
10. Aristovskaya, T. V. 1974. *Bergey's Manual of Determinative Bacteriology.* Baltimore: Williams & Wilkins. 8th ed. In press
11. Aristovskaya, T. V., Hirsch, P. See Ref. 10
12. Aristovskaya, T. V., Parinkina, O. M. 1961. *Potchvoved. Akad. Nauk SSSR* 1, 20–28
13. Aristovskaya, T. V., Parinkina, O. M. 1963. *Isvestiya Akad. Nauk SSSR Ser. Biol.* 1:49–53
14. Aristovskaya, T. V., Zavarzin, G. A. 1971. *Soil Biochem.* 2:385–408
15. Attwood, M. M., Harder, W. 1972. *Antonie van Leeuwenhoek J. Microbiol. Serol.* 38:369–78
16. Ibid 1973. 39:357
17. Auran, T. B., Schmidt, E. L. 1972. *J. Bacteriol.* 109:450–51
18. Balashova, V. V. 1967. *Microbiology USSR* 36:879–81
19. Balashova, V. V. 1969. *Dokl. Acad. Nauk SSSR* (Engl. transl.) 184:82–86
20. Balashova, V. V. 1972. *Microbiology USSR* 41:173–75
21. Balashova, V. V., Chernie, N. E. 1970. *Microbiology USSR* 39:298–302
22. Balashova, V. V., Zavarzin, G. A. 1972. *Microbiology USSR* 41:808–10
23. Barghoorn, E. S., Tyler, S. A. 1965. *Science* 147:563–77
24. Bauld, J., Marshall, K. C. 1971. *Antonie van Leeuwenhoek J. Microbiol. Serol.* 37:401–7
25. Bauld, J., Tyler, P. A. 1971. *Antonie van Leeuwenhoek J. Microbiol. Serol.* 37:417–24
26. Bauld, J., Tyler, P. A., Marshall, K. C. 1971. *Antonie van Leeuwenhoek J. Microbiol. Serol.* 37:408–16
27. Bavendamm, W. 1924. *Die farblosen und roten Schwefelbakterien des Süss- und Salzwassers,* 93–94. Jena: Fischer
28. Beger, H. 1935. *Zentralbl. Bakteriol. Abt. II.* 92:401–6
29. Bellion, E., Hersh, L. B. 1972. *Arch. Biochem. Biophys.* 153:368–74
30. Belly, R. T., Brock, T. D. 1972. *J. Gen. Microbiol.* 73:465–69
31. *Bergey's Manual of Determinative Bacteriology* 1974. Baltimore: Williams & Wilkins. 8th ed. In press
32. Biebl, H., Drews, G. 1969. *Zentralbl. Bakteriol. Abt. II.* 123:425–52
33. Bisset, K. A. 1961. *J. Gen. Microbiol.* 24:427–31
34. Boatman, E. S., Douglas, H. C. 1961. *J. Biophys. Biochem. Cytol.* 11:469–83
35. Bohlool, B. B., Brock, T. D. 1973. *Am. Soc. Microbiol.* (Abstr.), p. 6

36. Brock, T. D., Brock, K. M., Belly, R. T., Weiss, R. L. 1972. *Arch. Mikrobiol.* 84:54–68
37. Brown, J. P., Edwards, M. R. 1971. *Can. J. Microbiol.* 17:609–16
38. Buhagiar, R. W. M., Barnett, J. A. 1973. *J. Gen. Microbiol.* 77:71–78
39. Caldwell, D. E., Hirsch, P. 1971. *Bacteriol. Proc.* G–175
40. Caldwell, D. E., Hirsch, P. 1973. *Can. J. Microbiol.* 19:53–8
41. Caldwell, D. E., Lai, S. H., Tiedje, J. M. 1973. *Bull. Ecol. Res. Comm. Stockholm* 17:151–58
42. Carbonell, L. M. 1967. *J. Bacteriol.* 94:213–23
43. Carr, N. G., Exell, G. 1965. *Biochem. J.* 96:688–92
44. Chapman, V. J. 1962. *The Algae.* London: MacMillan
45. Cholodny, N. 1926. *Pflanzenforschung* 4:1–160
46. Cloud, P. E. Jr. 1965. *Science* 148:27–35
47. Conti, S. F., Benedict, C. R. 1962. *J. Bacteriol.* 83:929–30
48. Conti, S. F., Hirsch, P. 1965. *J. Bacteriol.* 89:503–12
49. Czillag, A. 1964. *J. Gen. Microbiol.* 34:341–52
50. Darland, G., Brock, T. D., Samsonoff, W., Conti, S. F. 1970. *Science* 170: 1416–18
51. Davey, J. F., Whittenbury, R., Wilkinson, J. F. 1972. *Arch. Mikrobiol.* 87:359–66
52. Devidé, Z. 1952. *Schweiz. Z. Hydrol.* 16:446–55
53. Dobrovol'skaya, T. G., Sokolov, A. A. 1972. *Microbiology USSR* 41:287–91
54. Doman, N. G., Vasil'eva, Z. A., Romanova, A. K., Zavarzin, G. A. 1965. *Microbiology USSR* 34:1–7
55. Drabkova, V. G., Stravinskaya, E. A. 1969. *Microbiology USSR* 38:304–9
56. Dubinina, G. A. 1969. *Dokl. Akad. Nauk SSSR* 184:1429–36
57. Dubinina, G. A. 1970. *Z. Allg. Mikrobiol.* 10:309–20
58. Dubinina, G. A., Derjugina, Z. 1972. *Arch. Hydrobiol.* 71:90–102
59. Dubinina, G. A., Gorlenko, Y. M., Suleimanov, Y. I. 1973. *Microbiology USSR* 42:919–24
60. Duchow, E., Douglas, H. C. 1949. *J. Bacteriol.* 58:409–16
61. Duong, T. 1972. *Nitrogen fixation and productivity in a eutrophic hard-water lake: in-situ and laboratory studies.* Ph.D. Thesis, Mich. State Univ., 241 pp.
62. Eady, R. R., Jarman, T. R., Large, P. J. 1971. *Biochem. J.* 125:449–59
63. Eady, R. R., Large, P. J. 1971. *Biochem. J.* 123:757–71
64. Ehrlich, H. L. 1963. *J. Bacteriol.* 86:350–52
65. Fell, J. W. 1966. *Antonie van Leeuwenhoek J. Microbiol. Serol.* 32:99–104
66. Geitler, L. 1936. *Handb. Pflanzenanalyse II. Abt.* VI:53–55
67. Geitler, L. 1954. *Oesterr. Bot. Z.* 101:304–14
68. Geitler, L. 1955. *Arch. Mikrobiol.* 22:324–34
69. Ibid 1963. 46:238–42
70. Ibid 1965. 51:399–400
71. Geitler, L. 1966. *Oesterr. Bot. Z.* 113:459–64
72. Gerenczer, V. F., Voelz, H. 1971. *Am. Soc. Microbiol.* (Abstr.), p. 207
73. Gimesi, N. 1924. *Kiadja a Magyar Ciszterci Budapest Rend,* 1–8
74. Goldfine, H., Hagen, P. O. 1968, *J. Bacteriol.* 95:367–75
75. Golubić, S. 1967. *Arch. Hydrobiol* (Suppl.) 33:172–205
76. Gordon, M. A., Edwards, M. R., Ghiorse, W., Brown, J. P. 1969. *Bacteriol. Proc.,* pp. 111–112
77. Gorlenko, V. M. 1968. *Dokl. Acad. Nauk SSSR* (Engl. transl.) 179:195–97
78. Gorlenko, V. M. 1969. *Microbiology USSR* 38:106–11
79. Gorlenko, V. M., Kusnezov, S. J. 1971. *Microbiology USSR* 40:651–52
80. Gorlenko, V. M., Kusnezov, S. J. 1972. *Arch. Hydrobiol.* 70:1–13
81. Gorlenko, V. M., Lebedeva, E. V. 1971. *Microbiology USSR* 40:1035–39
82. Gorlenko, V. M., Zhilina, T. N. 1968. *Microbiology USSR* 37:892–97
83. Gossling, J. 1972. *Am. Soc. Microbiol.* (Abstr.), p. 81
84. Grove, S. N., Oujezdsky, K. B., Szaniszlo, P. J. 1973. *J. Bacteriol.* 115:323–29
85. Guillard, R. R., Watson, S. W. 1962. *Oceanus* 8:22–23
86. Gumpert, J., Schuhmann, E., Taubeneck, U. 1971. *Z. Allg. Mikrobiol.* 11:283–300
87. Guseva, K. A. 1956. *Tr. Biol. Sta. Borok Acad. Nauk SSSR* 2:24–31
88. Hagen, P. O., Goldfine, H. 1966. *Science* 151:1543–44
89. Haidu, L. 1971. *Hung. Conf. Electronmicroscopy, 7th.* (Abstr.)
90. Ha-mung, T. 1967. *Microbiology USSR* 36:276–81
91. Ibid 1968. 37:621–24
92. Hanert, H. 1968. *Arch. Mikrobiol.* 60:348–68

93. Harder, W., Attwood, M. M., Quayle, J. R. 1973. *J. Gen. Microbiol.* 78:155–63
94. Hazen, W., Steenis, P. J. 1970. *Antonie van Leeuwenhoek J. Microbiol. Serol.* 36:67–72
95. Henrici, A. T. 1932. *J. Bacteriol.* 25:277–88
96. Henrici, A. T., Johnson, D. E. 1935. *J. Bacteriol.* 30:61–93
97. Hensen, A., Schäfer, D. 1971. *Int. J. Syst. Bacteriol.* 21:29–34
98. Hersh, L. B., Bellion, E. 1972. *Biochem. Biophys. Res. Comm.* 48:712–19
99. Hirsch, P. 1965. *Bacteriol. Proc.*, p. 108
100. Hirsch, P. 1968. *Arch. Mikrobiol.* 60:201–16
101. Hirsch, P. 1968. *Microbiology USSR* 37:953–55
102. Hirsch, P. 1968. *Mitt. Int. Ver. Limnol.* 14:52–63
103. Hirsch, P. 1972. *Am. Soc. Microbiol.* (Abstr.), p. 33
104. Hirsch, P. 1972. *Int. J. Syst. Bacteriol.* 22:107–11
105. Ibid 112–16
106. Hirsch, P. 1972. *Z. Allg. Mikrobiol.* 12:203–18
107. Hirsch, P. See Ref. 10
108. Hirsch, P., Conti, S. F. 1964. *Arch. Mikrobiol.* 48:339–57
109. Ibid 48:358–67
110. Hirsch, P., Conti, S. F. 1964. *Bacteriol. Proc.*, p. 28
111. Hirsch, P., Conti, S. F. 1965. *Zentralbl. Bakteriol. Abt. I* (Suppl.) 1:100–10
112. Hirsch, P., Jones, H. E. 1968. *Bacteriol. Proc.*, pp. 44–45
113. Hirsch, P., Moore, R. L. 1973. *Proc. Int. Congr. Bacteriol. 1st, Jerusalem,* (Abstr.), p. 81
114. Hirsch, P., Morita, S., Conti, S. F. 1963. *Bacteriol. Proc.*, p. 97
115. Hirsch, P., Pankratz, H. S. 1970. *Z. Allg. Mikrobiol.* 10:589–605
116. Hirsch, P., Rheinheimer, G. 1968. *Arch. Mikrobiol.* 62:289–306
117. Hirsch, P., Skuja, H. See Ref. 10
118. Hirsch, P., Zavarzin, G. A. See Ref. 10
119. Hoare, D. S., Gibson, J. 1964. *Biochem. J.* 91:546–59
120. Hoare, D. S., Hoare, S. L. 1969. *J. Bacteriol.* 100:1124–25
121. Hoffmann, B. 1967. *Zentralbl. Bakteriol. Abt I.* 205:77–78
122. Hofsten, B. V., Berg, B., Beskow, S. 1971. *Arch. Mikrobiol.* 79:69–79
123. Hortobágyi, T. 1965. *Bot. Közlem.* 52:111–19
124. Imšenecki, A. 1934. *Arch. Mikrobiol.* 5:451–76
125. Ishiguro, E. E., Fletcher, D. W. 1966. *Bacteriol. Proc.* G 48
126. Ishiguro, E. E., Wolfe, R. S. 1970. *J. Bacteriol.* 104:566–80
127. Jensen, A., Aasmundrud, O., Eimhjellen, K. E. 1964. *Biochem. Biophys. Acta* 88:466–79
128. Johnson, R. M., Weisrock, W. P. 1969. *Int. J. Syst. Bacteriol.* 19:295–307
129. Jones, H. E., Hirsch, P. 1968. *J. Bacteriol.* 96:1037–41
130. Kaffka, A. 1960. *Stoffwechselphysiologische Untersuchungen an Hyphomicrobium vulgare Stutzer et Hartleb.* Doctoral thesis, Univ. Hamburg, 60 pp.
131. Kahan, D. 1961. *Nature* 192:1212–13
132. Kelly, D. P. 1971. *Ann. Rev. Microbiol.* 25:177–210
133. Kingma-Boltjes, T. Y. 1936. *Arch. Mikrobiol.* 7:188–205
134. Korte, I., Engel, H. 1955. *Arch. Mikrobiol.* 21:248–54
135. Krasil'nikov, N. A. 1938. *Microbiology USSR* 7:335–52
136. Kriss, A. E. 1963. *Marine Microbiology, Deep Sea.* Edinburgh: Oliver & Boyd. (Engl. transl.)
137. Kristiansen, J. 1971. *Bot. Tidsskr.* 66: 293–302
138. Kusaka, J. 1967. *J. Bacteriol.* 94: 884–88
139. Kusnezov, S. J., Gorlenko, V. M. 1973. *Arch. Hydrobiol.* 71:475–86
140. Kutuzova, R. S. 1972. *Microbiology USSR* 41:765–68
141. Kutuzova, R. S., Gabe, D. R., Kravkina, J. M. 1972. *Microbiology USSR* 41:973–77
142. Kwapinski, J. B. G., Cheng, A. F. B., Alcasid, A., Dowler, J. 1971. *Can. J. Microbiol.* 17:1537–44
143. Large, P. J., Boulton, C. A., Crabbe, M. J. C. 1972. *Biochem. J.* 128:137–38
144. Large, P. J., Peel, D., Quayle, J. R. 1961. *Biochem J.* 81:470–80
145. Leifson, E. 1964. *Antonie van Leeuwenhoek J. Microbiol. Serol.* 30:249–56
146. Leifson, E., Cosenza, B., Murchelano, R., Cleverdon, R. C. 1964. *J. Bacteriol.* 87:652–66
147. Lieske, H. 1911. *Jahrb. Wiss. Bot.* 49:91–99
148. Lindstrom, E. S., Lewis, S. M., Pinsky, M. J. 1951. *J. Bacteriol.* 61:481–87
149. Luedemann, G. M. 1968. *J. Bacteriol.* 96:1848–58
150. Luedemann, G. M., Casmer, C. J. 1973. *Int. J. Syst. Bacteriol.* 23:243–55
151. Mal'tseva, N. N. 1971. *Microbiology USSR* 40:180–83
152. Maclean, F. J., Forrest, H. S., Hoare, D. S. 1966. *Arch. Biochem. Biophys.* 117:54–58

153. Mandel, M., Hirsch, P., Conti, S. F. 1972. *Arch. Mikrobiol.* 81:289–94
154. Mandel, H., Leadbetter, E. R., Pfennig, N., Trüper, H. H. 1971. *Int. J. Syst. Bacteriol.* 21:222–30
155. Maniloff, J., Morowitz, H. J. 1972. *Bacteriol. Rev.* 36:263–90
156. Mardanyan, S. S., Balashova, V. V. 1971. *Microbiology USSR* 40:104–6
157. Marshall, K. C., Stout, R., Mitchell, R. 1971. *Can. J. Microbiol.* 17:1413–16
158. Matheron, R., Baulaigue, R. 1972. *Arch. Mikrobiol.* 86:291–304
159. Matsumoto, A., Manire, G. P. 1970. *J. Bacteriol.* 101:278–85
160. Metchnikoff, M. E. 1888. *Ann. Inst. Pasteur* 2:165–70
161. Mevius, W. Jr. 1953. *Arch. Mikrobiol.* 19:1–29
162. Millar, W. N. 1973. *Int. J. Syst. Bacteriol.* 23:142–50
163. Moll, G., Ahrens, R., Rheinheimer, G. 1967. *Kiel. Meeresforsch.* 23:137–47
164. Moore, R. L., Hirsch, P. 1972. *J. Bacteriol.* 110:256–61
165. Ibid 116:418–23
166. Ibid 116:1447–55
167. Morita, S., Conti, S. F. 1962. *Plant Physiol.* 37:xxxii
168. Morita, S., Conti, S. F. 1963. *Arch. Biochem. Biophys.* 100:302–7
169. Morita, S., Conti, S. F. 1963. *Bacterial Photosynthesis,* 327–31. Yellow Springs, Ohio: Antioch Press
170. Morita, S., Olson, J. M., Conti, S. F. 1965. *Arch. Biochem. Biophys.* 104: 346–53
171. Murray, R. G. E., Douglas, H. C. 1950. *J. Bacteriol.* 59:157–67
172. Namsaraev, B. B., Zavarzin, G. A. 1972. *Microbiology USSR* 41:887–92
173. Namsaraev, B. B. 1973. *Microbiology USSR* 42:741–45
174. Naumann, E. 1921. *Kgl. Sv. Wetensk. Akad. Handl.* 62:1–10
175. Näveke, R. 1957. *Arch. Mikrobiol.* 27:375–99
176. Näveke, R., Engel, H. 1955. *Arch. Mikrobiol.* 21:371–75
177. Netrusov, A. I., Verkhoturov, V. N., Kirikova, N. N., Kondrat'eva, E. N. 1971. *Microbiology USSR* 40:168–73
178. Nikitin, D. J. 1973. *Bull. Ecol. Res. Comm. (Stockholm)* 17:85–92
179. Nikitin, D. J., Kusnezov, S. J. 1967. *Microbiology USSR* 36:934–41
180. Nikitin, D. J., Vasil'eva, L. V., Lokhmacheva, P. A. 1966. *New and Unusual Forms of Soil Microorganisms.* Moscow: Isdat. Nauka. 70 pp. In Russian
181. Nozhevnikova, A. N., Savel'eva, N. D. 1972. *Microbiology USSR* 41:837–43
182. Oka, T., Udagawa, K., Kinoshita, S. 1968. *J. Bacteriol.* 96:1760–67
183. Olah, J., Hajdu, L., Elekes, K. 1972. *Ann. Biol. Tihany* 39:123–29
184. Paerl, H. W. 1973. *Science* 180:496–98
185. Park, C. E., Berger, L. R. 1967. *J. Bacteriol.* 93:221–29
186. Ibid 230–36
187. Patel, R. N., Mandy, W. J., Hoare, D. S. 1973. *J. Bacteriol.* 113:937–45
188. Pavoni, M. 1963. *Schweiz. Z. Hydrol.* 25:219–341
189. Perfil'ev, B. V. 1937. *Proc. Int. Geol. Congr., 18th, ONTI NKTP, USSR* (Abstr.)
190. Perfil'ev, B. V., Gabe, D. R. 1969. *Capillary Methods of Investigating Micro-organisms.* Edinburgh: Oliver & Boyd. 627 pp. In English
191. Perfil'ev, B. V. et al 1965. *Applied Capillary Microscopy. The Role of Microorganisms in the Formation of Iron-Manganese Deposits.* (Engl. transl.) New York: Consultants Bureau. 122 pp.
192. Peterson, J. E., Rodwell, A. W., Rodwell, E. S. 1973. *J. Bacteriol.* 115: 411–25
193. Pfennig, N. 1965. *Zentralbl. Bakteriol. Abt. I, Suppl.* 1:179–89
194. Pfennig, N. 1967. *Ann. Rev. Microbiol.* 21:285–324
195. Pfennig, N. 1969. *J. Bacteriol.* 99: 597–602
196. Pfennig, N. 1970. *J. Gen. Microbiol.* 70:ii–iii
197. Pfennig, N., Cohen-Bazire, G. 1967. *Arch. Mikrobiol.* 59:226–36
198. Pfennig, N. Trüper, H. G. 1971. *Int. J. Syst. Bacteriol.* 21:19–24
199. Pinevich, T. G., Aseeva, J. V. 1972. *Microbiology USSR* 41:460–63
200. Ibid 42:40–44
201. Poindexter, J. S. 1964. *Bacteriol. Rev.* 28:231–95
202. Pongratz, E. 1957. *Schweiz. Z. Pathol. Bakteriol.* 20:593–608
203. Pontefract, R. D., Thatcher, F. S. 1965. *Can. J. Microbiol.* 11:271–75
204. Potthoff, H. 1924. *Zentralbl. Bakteriol. Abt. II* 61:249–55
205. Quadling, C. 1960. *Can. J. Microbiol.* 6:475–77
206. Quadri, S. M. H., Hoare, D. S., Hoare, S. L. 1972. *Am. Soc. Microbiol.* (Abstr.), p. 164
207. Razin, S. 1969. *Ann. Rev. Microbiol.* 23:317–56
208. Reeve, J. N., Mendelson, N. H., Coyne, S. J., Hallock, L. L., Cole, R. M. 1973. *J. Bacteriol.* 114:860–73

209. Reshetova, I. S., Sokolov, A. A., Kirillova, N. F. 1971. *Microbiology USSR* 40:1029–34
210. Ribbons, D. W., Harrison, J. E., Wadzinski, A. M. 1970. *Ann. Rev. Microbiol.* 24:135–58
211. Roberts, D. S. 1961. *Aust. J. Exp. Biol.* 39:463–76
212. Rodwell, A. W., Peterson, J. E. 1971. *J. Gen. Microbiol.* 68:173–86
213. Rohrer, E. 1952. *Schweiz. Z. Hydrol.* 16:348–57
214. Rosenberg, B., Renshaw, E., Van Camp, L., Hartwick, J., Drobnik, J. 1967. *J. Bacteriol.* 93:716–21
215. Ryvarden, L., Jensen, S. L. 1964. *Acta Chem. Scand.* 18:643–54
216. Salem, A. R., Hacking, A. J., Quayle, J. R. 1973. *J. Gen. Microbiol.* 77:xii
217. Salem, A. R., Large, P. J., Quayle, J. R. 1972. *Biochem. J.* 128:1203–11
218. Sandhu, G. R., Carr, N. G. 1970. *Arch. Mikrobiol.* 70:340–47
219. Sanzhieva, E. U., Zavarzin, G. A. 1971. *Dokl. Akad. Nauk SSSR* 196:956–59
220. Savel'eva, N. D., Nozhevnikova, A. N. 1972. *Microbiology USSR* 41:719–23
221. Schegg, E. 1971. *Schweiz. Z. Hydrol.* 33:425–532
222. Schmidt, J. M. 1971. *Ann. Rev. Microbiol.* 25:93–110
223. Schmidt, K. 1971. *Arch. Mikrobiol.* 77:231–38
224. Schulz, E. 1972. *Ungewöhnliche Mikroorganismen in sauren Moorgewässern.* MS thesis. Univ. Kiel. 94 pp.
225. Schulz, E., Hirsch, P. 1973. *Am. Soc. Microbiol.* (Abstr.), p. 60
226. Schweisfurth, R. 1972. *GWF-Wasser/Abwasser* 113:562–72
227. Schweisfurth, R., Hehn, G. V. 1972. *Zentralbl. Bakteriol. Abt. I. Orig. A.* 220:357–61
228. Sentandreu, R., Northcote, D. H. 1969. *J. Gen. Microbiol.* 55:393–98
229. Sewerin, S. A. 1897. *Zentralbl. Bakteriol.* 3:504–17
230. Shah, R. G., Bhat, J. V. 1968. *Curr. Sci.* 37:571–73
231. Shchapova, L. N. 1971. *Microbiology USSR* 40:613–16
232. Siegel, S. M., Siegel, B. Z. 1968. *Am. J. Bot.* 55:684–87
233. Siegel, B. Z., Siegel, S. M. 1970. *Proc. Nat. Acad. Sci. USA* 67:1005–10
234. Silver, M., Friedman, S., Guay, R., Couture, J., Tanguay, R. 1971. *J. Bacteriol.* 107:368–70
235. Skuja, H. 1926. *Acta Hort. Bot. Univ. Latv. Riga* 1:1–5
236. Skuja, H. 1956. *Nova Acta Reg. Soc. Sci. Upsaliensis Ser. IV* 16:1–404
237. Ibid 1964. 18:16
238. Smillie, R. M., Fuller, R. C. 1960. *Biochem. Biophys. Res. Comm.* 3:368–72
239. Smith, P. F., Langworthy, T. A., Mayberry, W. R., Hougland, A. E. 1973. *J. Bacteriol.* 116:1019–28
240. Sperl, G. T., Hoare, D. S. 1971. *J. Bacteriol.* 108:733–36
241. Staley, J. T. 1968. *J. Bacteriol.* 95:1921–42
242. Staley, J. T. 1969. *Bacteriol. Proc.*, pp. 25–26
243. Staley, J. T. 1971. *Appl. Microbiol.* 22:496–502
244. Staley, J. T. 1973. *Can. J. Microbiol.* 19:609–14
245. Staley, J. T., Mandel, M. 1973. *Int. J. Syst. Bacteriol.* 23:271–73
246. Starr, M. P., Skerman, V. B. D. 1965. *Ann. Rev. Microbiol.* 19:407–54
247. Stefanov, S. B., Nikitin, D. J. 1965. *Microbiology USSR* 34:261–64
248. Stevenson, J. L. 1969. *Can. J. Microbiol.* 15:707–11
249. Stutzer, A., Hartleb, R. 1898. *Mitt. Landwirt. Inst. Univ. Breslau* 1:75–100
250. Suessenguth, K. 1927. *Zentralbl. Bakteriol. Abt. II* 69:327–39
251. Tanaka, T., Woods, D. A. 1970. *J. Gen. Microbiol.* 63:281–87
252. Tarakanov, B. V. 1971. *Microbiology USSR* 40:294–99
253. Thompson, R. E. M., Bisset, K. A. 1957. *Nature* 179:590–91
254. Thyagarajan, T. R., Conti, S. F., Naylor, H. B. 1962. *J. Bacteriol.* 83:381–94
255. Tkacz, J. S., Lampen, J. O. 1972. *J. Gen. Microbiol.* 72:243–47
256. Trentini, W. C. 1967. *J. Bacteriol.* 94:1260–61
257. Trentini, W. C., Starr, M. P. 1967. *J. Bacteriol.* 93:1699–1704
258. Tschermak-Woess, E. 1950. *Oesterr. Bot. Z.* 97:188–206
259. Tyler, P. A. 1967. *Microbial deposition of manganese in fresh water distribution systems.* Ph.D. Thesis. Univ. Tasmania, Hobart
260. Tyler, P. A. 1970. *Antonie van Leeuwenhoek J. Microbiol. Serol.* 36:567–78
261. Tyler, P. A., Marshall, K. C. 1967. *Antonie van Leeuwenhoek J. Microbiol. Serol.* 33:171–83
262. Tyler, P. A., Marshall, K. C. 1967. *Arch. Mikrobiol.* 56:344–83
263. Tyler, P. A., Marshall, K. C. 1967. *J. Am. Water Works Assoc.* 59:1043–48
264. Tyler, P. A., Marshall, K. C. 1967. *J. Bacteriol.* 93:1132–36
265. Uhlken, A. 1959. *Untersuchungen über die Begeisselung von Hyphomicrobium*

*vulgare Stutzer et Hartleb.* MS Thesis. Univ. Hamburg
266. Van Ert, M., Staley, J. T. 1971. *J. Bacteriol.* 108:236–40
267. Van Iterson, W. 1958. *Verh. Kon. Ned. Akad. Wetensch. Afd. Natuurkunde* 52:1–185
268. Van Veen, W. L. 1973. *Antonie van Leeuwenhoek J. Microbiol. Serol.* 39:657–62
269. Vela, G. R., Rosenthal, R. S. 1972. *J. Bacteriol.* 111:260–66
270. Volarovich, M. P., Terent'ev, A. A. 1970. *Microbiology USSR* 39:416–21
271. Volk, W. A., Pennington, D. 1950. *J. Bacteriol.* 59:169
272. Walsh, F., Mitchell, R. 1972. *J. Gen. Microbiol.* 72:369–76
273. Walsh, F., Mitchell, R. 1973. *Arch. Mikrobiol.* 90:19–25
274. Watson, S. W., Mandel, M. 1971. *J. Bacteriol.* 107:563–69
275. Wawrik, U. 1956. *Oesterr. Bot. Z.* 103:191–99
276. Weiner, R. M., Blackman, M. A. 1973. *J. Bacteriol.* 116:1398–1404
277. Whittenbury, R., Davies, S. L., Davey, J. F. 1970. *J. Gen. Microbiol.* 61:219–26
278. Whittenbury, R., McLee, A. G. 1967. *Arch. Mikrobiol.* 59:324–34
279. Whittenbury, R., Nicoll, J. M. 1971. *J. Gen. Microbiol.* 66:123–26
280. Whittenbury, R., Phillips, K. C., Wilkinson, J. F. 1970. *J. Gen. Microbiol.* 61:205–18
281. Wilkinson, T. G., Hamer, G. 1972. *J. Appl. Bacteriol.* 35:577–88
282. Wilkinson, T. G., Harrison, D. E. F. 1973. *J. Appl. Bacteriol.* 36:309–13
283. Wood, B. V. B., Nichols, B. W., James, A. T. 1965. *Biochem. Biophys. Acta* 106:261–73
284. Wood, O. L., Hirsch, P. 1966. *Bacteriol. Proc.*, pp. 25–26
285. Woodfolk, C. A., Whiteley, H. R. 1962. *J. Bacteriol.* 84:647–58
286. Zavarzin, G. A. 1960. *Microbiology USSR* 29:38–42
287. Ibid 1961. 30:774–91
288. Zavarzin, G. A. 1968. In: *The Ecology of Soil Bacteria,* 612–35. Liverpool: Univ. Press
289. Zavarzin, G. A. 1972. *Lithotrophic Microorganisms.* Moscow: Isdat. Nauka. 323 pp. In Russian
290. Zavarzin, G. A. See Ref. 10
291. Zavarzin, G. A., Hirsch, P. See Ref. 10
292. Zobell, C. E. 1943. *J. Bacteriol.* 46:39–56

# MODELS OF GENETIC RECOMBINATION[1]

❖1645

*Rollin D. Hotchkiss*[2]
The Rockefeller University, New York, N.Y. 10021

CONTENTS

PURPOSES AND PROBLEMS OF A RECOMBINATION MODEL .................... 447
FUNDAMENTAL STRUCTURAL PROCESSES OF RECOMBINATION ............... 449
INITIATION OF RECOMBINATION EVENTS ....................................... 452
SITES AND PRINCIPLES GOVERNING EARLY EVENTS .......................... 454
THE RESOLUTION OF INTERCONNECTED HELICES ............................. 458
GENE CONVERSION AND THE DYNAMICS OF RECOMBINATION ............... 461
SUMMARY—A RECOMBINATION OF RECOMBINATION MODELS ................ 465

It will be my intention to compare established and recently proposed models for genetic recombination, with special attention to the separate component principles they contain and the function of these principles in the various models. As increasing attention has been paid to realistic details of DNA structure and enzymology, recombination models have become molecular ones, sufficiently detailed that such a comparison may be useful to enable us to view experimental results in this area in a variety of different lights.

There is no conceptual distinction separating the ideas concerning DNA recombination in microorganisms and those concerning genetic recombination in general. Recombination in higher organisms principally occurs during meiotic events highly organized through evolution and therefore relatively refractory to experimental intervention. In these forms the reproductive cycles are often long, large postmeiotic populations may be cumbersome to deal with, and the genetic fine structure can

[1]This review is primarily a study of recombination models rather than of data on genetic recombination. Recent helpful reviews of the facts of recombination include some covering biochemical and molecular biological work (21, 91, 116), several with a broad genetic coverage (31, 32, 49, 115), and others on special topics such as molecular symmetry (99), bacteriophage (78), and bacterial transformation (55).

[2]The reviewer gained experience and insight on this topic through work supported by Grant BO-6696 from the National Science Foundation, and Grant AI-03170 from the National Institutes of Health.

hardly ever be defined by a large number of markers (a few nucleotides apart, as in some microorganisms), so with them the geneticist is not often deeply concerned about deviations from expectations for a simple classical crossover model. Nevertheless, wherever maps are sufficiently detailed, or recombination modifiers are known, evidence can be found that classical chromosomal recombinations may not be reciprocal at the level of their finest detail. This can be most clearly seen in the Ascomycetes—which are microorganisms and also eukaryotes—with which single ascospore isolation permits a degree of intervention in late steps of the meiotic process and gives direct insight into the structure of the primary postmeiotic chromatids. As first realized by Mitchell (76) and amply confirmed in later work [e.g. reviewed by Whitehouse (115) and Fogel & Mortimer (36)], "aberrant asci" showing gene conversions reveal that for limited segments of parental chromosomes, recombination may often be nonreciprocal, i.e. parental alleles (or closely linked pairs of alleles), entering in equal proportions are recovered from tetrads in 3:1 rather than normal 2:2 ratios.

Such gene conversion has long been recognized to be frequently (31, 32, 49, 115), or in almost precisely one half of the cases (34), associated with reciprocal recombination of nearby (outside) markers. So it is clear that many conversions are accompaniments of DNA strand exchanges. One question of interest is how to look upon those conversions in which flanking markers remain in parental configuration. They may be classically referred to as "conversion without recombination," but this apparently conservative definition implies something that is really by no means actually known—that this group of conversions does not involve strands of DNA molecules in recombination-like events, or potential recombinations. Since models of recombination must nowadays be concerned with DNA structure and actual events, we shall speak here of exchanges of DNA segments as recombination, regardless of whether or not the segments are identified by known genetic markers.

The reviewer has argued (56–58) and others have implied (2, 60, 86, 93) that it is indeed likely that "molecular conversion"—recovery of copies of a DNA segment representing one of two parental molecules in disproportionate excess—may be a characteristic of the detailed molecular events occurring at the boundary of all or virtually all normal recombinations. However, conversion is only properly defined when primary products are analyzed from an exchange event in which the normal expectation is fully understood, as for example when individual ascospores are all recovered, grown, and analyzed. Where the mating is between populations, the deviations from expectation produced by conversion-like events would appear in another form: as map distortions, nonadditivity of the map intervals, high negative interference, nonreciprocality, etc, of just the types which are prevalent in fine genetic analysis of microorganisms. In general, these distortions, like conversions, are all manifestations that some particular subclass of recombinants occurs more often or less often than expected (upon some other basis) within a chosen population or subpopulation.

For this reason attention will be paid in this review to the sophisticated question of conversion, treating it as a part of molecular models for genetic recombination, even though for most microorganisms conversions are probably hidden and brought to our attention as various deviations from expectancy in recombination. A few comments will first be made about the nature and function of the models in general.

## PURPOSES AND PROBLEMS OF A RECOMBINATION MODEL

I take a model to be a mechanistic description of a plausible series of events which can in their aggregate be supposed to account for observed features of a complex process. We speak of it as a model, rather than an hypothesis, when it represents one of many possible sets of choices in a multifactorial situation, and is not readily tested in its entirety by experiment. Models are sometimes merely a framework summarizing known results, but preferably they are intended to describe a reality and to be tested for prediction of reality. Ideally, a model should account for as large a number and variety of observations as possible. But it is here that the model builder meets his greatest difficulty: the more degrees of freedom and permissiveness that enter into his scheme, the less forceful are its predictions, and the less satisfactorily can it be tested experimentally. On the other hand, as more restrictions are specified in the component steps of the model, it becomes effectively more testable, but also very likely narrower in applicability.

In the specific case of recombination models, we are presently being made aware of a rapidly growing variety of biochemical and physical specifications about DNA and the enzymes acting upon it. We have also been presented with a large accumulation of genetic data, which by reason of the wide variety of organisms, conventions, bases of reference, modes of calculation, assumptions of opportunities for recombination, etc, may seem to be more disparate than they really are. My view is that at this particular stage we should resist the temptation to devise many special hypotheses and should embrace first the larger task of seeking unifying principles instead. The unifying principles will always have their value (and therefore in one sense acquire lasting reality among our working concepts), even if later they have to be broken down to some degree as they reveal their limitations.

Nevertheless, there are serious specific arguments for multiple recombination mechanisms rather than a unifying one. First of all, available systems show substantial differences: phage-phage recombinations may involve approximately equivalent genomes interacting during a race between exponential replication and segregation into a capsule, while the various donor chromosome fragments introduced in bacterial mating, transformation and transduction, or present in added or resident virus, episome or merozygote, all must have to react on somewhat uneven terms with relatively intact host chromosomes. The products will naturally appear somewhat different in these different systems. Thus, virus-virus recombination often results in rejoining of double-stranded components from two parental molecules (3, 4, 71, 72, 108), and so may transduction (26), while transformation (9, 11, 25, 38, 45, 83, 88) appears to lead to insertion of single strand segments of donor DNA. Viral and episomal interaction with chromosomes can be reciprocal both when all (13, 27) or only part (73) of the episome is inserted into the prophage site; in the former case, the homology must be limited, except near the insertion point.

Donor chromosome fragments in bacterial mating appear to be at least partly replicated while undergoing recombination (20). The possibility of DNA synthesis and repair of donor-transforming DNA before incorporation is suggested by indications that both strands of heteroduplex DNA sometimes contribute information (94) to the one strand believed to be integrated in recipient bacteria, and that mixed clones may be induced by such DNA (104). These last observations suggest an *early* repair of at least part of the donor DNA. On the other hand, the effect of low efficiency markers upon integration of their DNA region in transformation (30, 65) led to the postulate (30) that sometimes there is DNA heteroduplex-repair *after* a donor-recipient intermediate has been established, and a consequent early duplication and homozygotization of the incoming donor marker (30, 69, 107). These last findings demonstrated a different treatment of low- rather than high-efficiency markers in transformation of normal pneumococcal strains; a somewhat similar differential efficiency of incorporation of specific alleles has been found in transduction (23).

It was found that transduction generally introduces larger DNA regions than does transformation (24) and therefore it is more sensitive to species differences in homology. On this basis, the mechanisms of transformation and transduction were concluded to be different. A detailed investigation of recombination-deficient *Escherichia coli* has led to the proposal of different pathways of recombination. In brief, it is found that mutants selected for such deficiency and identified to be of the *rec*B or *rec*C type (defective in an ATP-dependent exonuclease) are still able to undergo recombination at a lowered ($10^{-2}$) frequency (70). This low rate is further reduced by other mutations of different site and nature (e.g. *rec*F) (51). A further suppressor mutation (*sbc*B) which restores recombination to the exonuclease-deficient *rec*B$^-$ and *rec*C$^-$ types, brings in yet another deficiency, in Exonuclease I (64)! Yet it cannot offset the *rec*F$^-$ block, which it might be expected to do were the latter affecting the same events as the *rec*BC. These results and others are interpreted with reference to a scheme in which there are multiple pathways leading to recombination (17, 18). The emphasis upon pathways (series of unknown but discrete steps in a defined sequence) is fortunate and admirable, insofar as it draws us away from an excessive concentration upon exotic recombination intermediates to a more dynamic view.

The phage λ of *E. coli* is also subject to a number of mutable genes affecting recombination [its own *Int* for integration and *Red* for vegetative recombination (27, 41), as well as the *rec* systems of the host]. Nevertheless, in all these cases just mentioned, the argument for different pathways of recombination depends upon our assumptions about what is implied in the mutations at specific sites. These might or might not lead to reduction of activity, leakiness or absence of an enzyme, to production of co-factors, an inhibitor, or a competing system, or to diversion of its substrate to another system. For a substrate such as DNA (with one or two giant molecules per cell) the simple pathway-related concept of accumulation of unused substrate may be inappropriate. The enzyme—or inhibitor—may have to act in a particular way at a very special time which may be difficult to fathom or measure by the in vitro tests we can make upon cell extracts. Therefore, our arguments for different pathways cannot at present be very firm ones. Furthermore, it can also be said that both the recombinations occurring in bacterial mating and in transformation are helped by the *sbc*B mutation (18, 84) and reduced by the *rec*F mutation mentioned (17, 51). Deficiency of an ATP-dependent exonuclease in Pneumococcus (109), and in *Bacillus subtilis* (90), also modifies transformation.

It is possible, then, that these mutable systems are only different sources of individual enzymes and modifiers acting within essentially a single pathway. That is, the chain of events leading to recombination may have certain parallel branches, but these may be of the same character—differing principally in the source of the catalysts and their effective rates. I shall suggest in what follows that in several of the detailed models for recombination there is opportunity, and in the experimental work some evidence, for the view that different relative rates of formation and conversion of DNA intermediates can act competitively within a single pathway to produce recombinants and convertants in substantially different patterns.

## FUNDAMENTAL STRUCTURAL PROCESSES OF RECOMBINATION

The fundamental idea that genes normally linked would on occasion separate in proportion to some kind of distance between them of course required breakage of that linkage. Homologous chromosomes, as carriers of the genes, seemed at meiosis to give X-figures or chiasmata appropriate for gene crossing-over. Furthermore, breakage with later rejoining of chromosomes could be observed after irradiation. The already mentioned evidence that early recombinants often contain actual segments of rearranged parental DNA, has virtually eliminated consideration of the copy-choice mechanism in which these arrangements were derived from alternation of templates during replication.

With the proposal of the double helical structure of DNA the problem of how to imagine breakage and rejoining in precise register became much easier, and now is a matter of the stepwise opening and closing of at least four single strands of two parental helices. Recombination models now began, notably exemplified in those of Whitehouse (111, 112) and Holliday (48), to provide register and exact fit between heterologous double strands by having one strand from each helix interact with the neighbor. In this way, through concerted opening and closing of regions of complementary pairing, the continuity is established in a hybrid strand before it is surrendered in the parental strands. The modern recombination models differ mainly in the postulated sequences of such steps, and in the corollary specifications which make these steps less arbitrary and more realistic.

Accordingly, the metabolism of DNA most relevant to recombination is that involving linear whole segments of DNA or chromosome arms. Since the enzymologist acquires his knowledge from the side of monomer exchanges, it has been necessary to devise means of labeling segments as well as monomers in DNA strands. For this, heavy atoms are useful since excess density due to heavy atom substitution reflects the fate of segments, not single residues. But it should not be forgotten that the classical gene, analyzed at the level of fine structure, is an excellent tool for doubly or multiply labeling just such packets of DNA; what the heavy atoms show us is that these packets generally maintain their integrity.

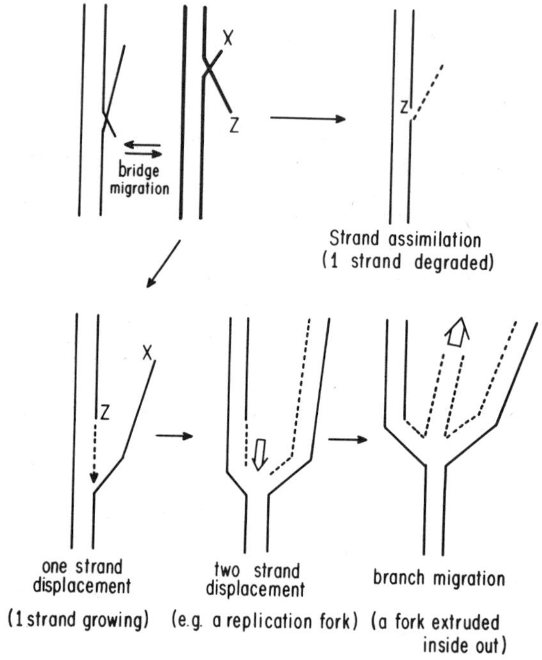


*Figure 1* Various postulated conversions of strands in a DNA helix bearing an overlap in one strand.

The strand overlap (region X to Z in upper left) can migrate, be eliminated through removal of overhanging ends by exonucleases, or a hanging strand with 3'-end can be assimilated through degradation of a previously paired 5'-end by a possibly unique type of exonuclease induced by λ-phage (14). In these cases (upper half of the figure) strands are displaced by previously existing strands; changes of partners are probably catalyzed by DNA-binding proteins like the gene-32 protein of T4 phage (1), of which several examples are known in other systems.

Newly synthesized strands are also believed to displace others from paired relationship (bottom half of figure). This can happen either by extension of one strand, 3'-wards by DNA polymerase or by growth of two strands in a replication process. The one-strand displacement shown (lower left) could take an alternate form, with displacement arising from growth of a copy along the right-hand limb, X. This would be distinguishable from the one portrayed, in terms of the identity of the limb X or of the origin or attachment of the growing or attacking strand in another helix.

All of the figures given here can be construed also as representing bridged pairs of double helices: in the latter cases the branches X and Z would be continued and become corresponding strands of a neighboring homologous helix. Such pairs are typical intermediates of various recombination models, postulated to undergo the conversions indicated here as steps in those models. These conversions can be supposed to proceed efficiently by conservation of base-pairing energy, or through the driving force of energy needed for polynucleotide synthesis.

Branch migration is here adapted as a diversion of an interrupted replication fork, pulled inside out as shown for a hybrid pair by Broker & Lehman (12). If the central pair is drawn downwards instead, the same figure becomes simply a cross-bridged pair of helices as described above, and the branch migration becomes another version of the bridge migration shown.

Let us then consider some of the principal metabolic processes of strand transfer in DNA (see Figure 1). As pictured, it is supposed that single strand branches can change position in several ways, e.g. by replacing a degraded strand or by trading their former pairing relationship with either a preexisting strand or a strand being extended by new synthesis. These basic conversions can generally be expected to occur also in the two-helix cases in which the branches (X and Z in Figure 1) are imagined to continue as cross-bridges into another double helix. The conversions in this form will be applied at numerous points in various recombination models to be discussed in the next section.

For specific illustration, let us observe the relation of some of these structures to the important cross-bridged intermediate of the Holliday model (shown in Figure 2 and to be discussed later). This intermediate is equivalent to the mirror-image double of the simple branched helix (Figure 1, upper left), with both branches continuing to become partners in another helix. Again, by interrupting further extension at a replication fork (Figure 1, lower right), untwisting the already replicated regions, and removing the newly synthesized strands as a pair (conservative segregation of the replica), one obtains the same structure undergoing a branch migration similar to that postulated by Broker & Lehman (12). The extruded pair is for better comparison pictured as stripped backward through the fork as indicated by these authors. If one pulls the same pair downward, the configuration easily converts to the symmetrical, bridged helix figure already mentioned. In the next section we shall superimpose upon these structural similarities the genetic similarities and differences that arise when the strands are genetically marked and different assumptions are made about their origins. As I have adapted the branch migration here, it would extract a partial replica from replicating DNA, as for example when replication was interrupted or inhibited. Very likely by virtue of the Okazaki effect (85) the partial replicas would have staggered ends with a single-stranded overhang. In passing we may note that these could participate in two-strand displacement and joining exchanges in other helices.

One other important structural relationship of strands in bridged DNA helices was clearly set forth by Sigal & Alberts (97), who pointed out the easy steric equilibrium between bridged and nonbridged strands. Using letters simply to denote continuity of strands, we can represent thus a bridge formed by switching of strands B and C:

```
AAAAAAAAAAAAAAAAAAAAAAAAAAA
BBBBBB     CBBBBBBBBBBBBBBBBBBBB
       B C
        X
       C B
CCCCCC     BCCCCCCCCCCCCCCCCCCCC
DDDDDDDDDDDDDDDDDDDDDDDDDDD
```

By rotating the two right ends about the central bridge made up of the two biparental strands BB—CC and CC—BB, we obtain an isomer in which the bridge now contains the other two, the uniparental strands AA—AA and DD—DD:

```
BBBBBBBBBCCCCCCCCCCCCCCCCCCCC
AAAAAA      DDDDDDDDDDDDDDDDDD
          A  D
           X
          D  A
DDDDDD      AAAAAAAAAAAAAAAAA
CCCCCCCCCCBBBBBBBBBBBBBBBBBBB
```

In our nonhelical version we have also accommodated the left ends (pairs AB and CD) to show better the bridge; in a true helix, this accommodation is automatic (but it makes the isomerization more difficult to visualize).

To anticipate somewhat the genetic applications of this inversion, if we now imagine that the bridge would be recognized as a misfit and subject to DNA repair nicking, and in the meantime it had undergone a bridge (or branch) migration toward the right, the products of nicking the two sets would be, respectively:

```
AAAAAAAAAAAAAAAAAAAAAAAAAA
BBBBBBBBBCCCCCCCCBBBBBBBBBBB

BBBBBBBBBCCCCCCCCCCCCCCCCCCCC
AAAAAAAAAAAAAAAAAAADDDDDDDD
```

and

```
CCCCCCCCCCBBBBBBBBCCCCCCCCCCCC
DDDDDDDDDDDDDDDDDDDDDDDDDDD

DDDDDDDDDDDDDDDDDDDAAAAAAAA
CCCCCCCCCCBBBBBBBBBBBBBBBBBBBB
```

It is easily seen that this is an attractive and plausible system for obtaining either of two kinds of partner-switch, a double switch in two of the strands, or a general exchange of former partners, with a region of biparental overlap in between. This strand equivalence for resolution had figured implicitly in several recombination models (12, 29, 48, 49, 56, 99), and more explicitly so since the publications mentioned (50, 91, 92, 97).

## INITIATION OF RECOMBINATION EVENTS

As already mentioned, at least four strand openings and closings will ordinarily be necessary if four strands are to give a single crossover (between two pairs) or a double crossover (between two strands). Although endonuclease and ligase are often mentioned in connection with opening and joining of strands, the breaks are usually unexplained; meaning that little attempt is made to describe in terms of ascertained properties of known enzymes, how a particular strand comes to be opened in a particular region (at an appropriate time) to move the sequence of events irresistibly in the postulated manner and not in some other. Indeed, it is difficult to provide proposed strand modifications and displacements with a plausible drive requiring them to go in one direction always, or more often in one direction than another.

In these respects, all recombination models tend to be soft, to contain many degrees of freedom, and to not be restrictive enough to be predictive. Refuge is characteristically taken in the assumption of random occurrence of particular events whenever multiple choices are deemed to be present, even though at the level of fine structure the choices may not be by any means equivalent. The reviewer has expressed the view (52, 53, 56) that randomness is a counsel of ignorance, and biochemical events commonly turn out to be random only within a narrow class so structurally specific that the probability function eventually turns out to be a "stuffed and mounted Michaelis constant" (54). There are evidences of recombination hot-spots (22–24, 78, 79), of genes controlling such sites (16, 44), selective repair (11, 29, 30, 42, 62, 65, 100), site-specific recombination factors (16, 27, 41), and site-specific restriction endonucleases (74). These points cannot yet be interpreted adequately. We may suppose that in recombination pathways, preceding steps change the interacting DNA structures in such ways that probabilities for succeeding steps are greatly altered or indeed specifically determined in time and location. We are searching then for realistic models, which use ascertained properties of enzymes and cofactors in a compelling sequence of postulated events—and offer explanations that are not only sufficient, but necessary, or at least highly plausible, for obtaining the several phenomena of recombination.

We will be able to explore the sufficiencies and nature of a number of recombination models by relating them to the framework already erected. It will be important to continue to distinguish clearly between the material of DNA strands, and the genetic markers which they may or may not bear in different cases.

As is illustrated in Figure 2, precursors for many proposed models are differentiated by what is assumed to accompany or follow the first strand break. In many cases the first break is assumed to be closely accompanied by at least a second one, in particular relation to the first. One group of models would have the second strand break occur in the homologous strand at or about the same level as the first. If the second break is precisely at the same level, no DNA trimming or synthesis is needed for rejoining homologs and the pattern is that of the original Holliday model (48). There is now a willingness by other authorities and by the originator himself (50), to allow some flexibility in this model, so that breaks can be near each other and fitted by some synthesis and trimming.

A principal other start is made by postulating a nearby break in the antiparallel or complementary strand of the neighboring helix (Figure 2, II). This is a beginning for such models as those of Whitehouse (111–114), Boon & Zinder (10), or Broker & Lehman (12). The multiple choices of synchronous and nonsynchronous breaks in parallel or nonparallel strands tabulated without preference by Sigal & Alberts (97) lead to the same possibilities contained in Figure 2.

These initial sequences tended, with some exceptions, to lead to symmetrical intermediates for which asymmetric or fluctuating later steps, such as repair processes, had to be superimposed in order to account for the often nonreciprocal, asymmetric, even polarized, results of recombination. If there is a trend noticeable in recent postulates, it is toward initial steps in which one parent acts as a donor, the other as recipient, these steps leading to asymmetric intermediates (6, 10, 38,

56, 58, 65, 86, 92, 101, 102), which even when resolved by processes essentially symmetric or random can lead to asymmetry in the products. In this way the generalized models are coming closer to the ones devised for the clearly asymmetric donor-receptor systems such as transformation, transduction, and bacterial mating.

Asymmetric intermediates have usually been postulated as arising from an initial process in which only one of the four strands takes part (Figure 2, I). In so doing, it can alter the structure and ensure that the second and later steps are not merely equal and opposite balancing ones, as are the postulated second breakages mentioned above. A different asymmetric start is achieved in the model of Boon & Zinder (10) by an assumed set of three initial strand breaks.

## SITES AND PRINCIPLES GOVERNING EARLY EVENTS

Detailed steps of several recently proposed recombination models are presented in the accompanying figures and tables. This will permit discussion to center upon a more general and comparative treatment of the models, as well as of some others omitted from the tables for economy.

The doubly bridged hybrid helix or "Holliday structure" already mentioned constitutes an important stage in many models. The models presented in Table 1 all lead to it by specific modification of the original postulates, while those to be

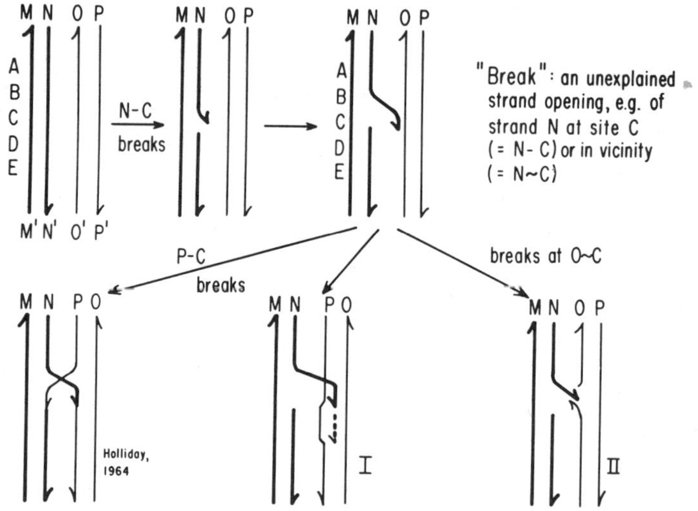


*Figure 2* Steps following an initial DNA strand breakage, leading to various postulated recombination models.

Symbols are those used in Figure 1. The first strand breakage may be taken as adventitious, the other ones as assumed for various models. Notice exchange of strand pair O and P to simplify the nonhelical diagrams. See Table 1 and text for discussion of the Holliday structure, lower left.

discussed separately may come to it indirectly. For general recombination, Holliday postulated a precise site determining the initial co-parallel strand breaks (48), possibly an intergenic base sequence (the recombinator) recognized by a specific endonuclease (49). For the special case of λ prophage insertion, Cross & Lieb (19) pictured a host chromosome as not suffering breakage until the circular phage has already synapsed with it; after an opening, probably achieved by site-specific endonucleases in λ [*Int* system (27, 41)] and other phages (68, 98), a reciprocal recombination ensues (13).

**Table 1** Models with co-parallel strands initially active: description of detailed steps (in reference to Figure 2, Holliday pattern, N–C broken)

Holliday model (48)

1. Co-parallel break at P–C, position identical to N–C.
2. Crossed joining of N–C with P′–C, and P–C with N′–C, making hybrid DNA.
3. Resolution by two further breaks, either:
   a. Breaks at M–D and O–D, with rejoining of M–D with O′–D and O–D with M′–D (flanking marker recombination), or
   b. Breaks again in strands N and P at level D, with rejoining of N back to N′ and P back to P′ (internal segments CD exchanged).
4. Random repair of the heteroduplex DC regions—if asymmetric—leads to conversions there; it should also sometimes lead to reciprocal conversions; flanking markers are outside of heteroduplex regions.

Cross & Lieb model (19) (For chromosome and episome)

1. Parental helices cross-pair in loops before breaking.
2. Breaks at corresponding pairs and site as in Holliday model; similar further breaks and closure, giving provirus incorporation.

Fogel-Hurst model (33)

1. Strands broken at site of mutant difference in the two helices, N–C and P–C and rejoin making two heteroduplexes.
2. Same two strands tend to break and cross back (other pair can do so), but bridge can migrate toward end of cistron, where only the opposite pair can break and cross, giving outside marker recombination; polarity can be the result of preferential movement of bridge.

Emerson model (29) (Detailed specification of the Holliday model)

1. Strand ends formed on newly synthesized strands at ends of replicons as synthesis stops before meiosis (consider a replicon ending at C and strands N and P as new copies of two nonsister strands M and O).
2. Co-parallel ends, probably of either chemical polarity, form hybrid DNA; limitation to these pairs prevents sister-hybrid formation, limits multiple chromatid exchange in one region (replicon).
3. Sister chromatids exchange only by detachment at replicon junctions.
4. Repair and resolution as in Holliday model; conversions by mismatch repair; resolution by synchronous breaks in one or other pair of parallel strands.
5. Occasionally hybrid DNA forms in only one chromatid (cf. Stadler-Towe).

One advantage of a defined point of initiation is that it can offer a basis for the observation that conversion frequency often shifts in a polarized way in relation to certain sites. These considerations in part had led Whitehouse successively to propose breakages (in antiparallel strands) to be exactly opposite (111), at sites near gene termini (112), at one particular end (113), at the operator region (114), or at the ends of replicons (116). Hastings suggests that the termini at which newly replicated strands cease replication until meiotic prophase are the sites of strand exchange. Since they would be antiparallel, they would be differently restricted in reacting with certain other chromatids, depending upon whether parallel or antiparallel exchange is assumed (47). Barring sister chromatid exchange, the pattern of results would suggest that both types must occur. Emerson (Table 1) (29), assuming for the same new strands the Holliday type of interaction, also at ends of replicons, rationalizes all observations by proposing a moderate amount of sister chromatid exchange (by swivel at the ends of replicons) to equilibrate the potential multiple chromatid involvements. Kitani & Olive accounted for the imbalance of recombination and nonrecombination of outside markers by attributing the former to the Whitehouse sequence, and the latter to the Holliday pattern, of strand exchanges (62). Sobell, from considerations of molecular symmetry, proposes the initial sites to open between self-complementary regions in the intergene DNA (99). Fogel & Hurst postulated that hybrid DNA bridges are formed at breaks initiated by mismatch between whole helices where mutant/wild sites are in synapse (33).

Pritchard had suggested that at effective pairing regions there are multiple close synapses and exchanges (89); it has been suggested that these are fixed regions (81) and polytene (102). Multiple switches were also adduced for phage recombinations to explain high negative interference (28); such distortions were also attributed to a requirement or propensity for double crossover insertions at the molecular level (5, 52, 53, 110). The detail of events at these regions was not, however, specified by these workers. Later emphasis on multiple co-correction of heteroduplex regions has removed some of the need for multiple pairings.

As indicated above, recombination results required the assumption of asymmetric resolution processes, unless the intermediates themselves were asymmetric. Stadler & Towe (101) proposed that recombination in *Ascobolus* strains include, besides bilateral Holliday exchanges (taken to be reciprocal), some unilateral ones accounting for the nonreciprocal events. This possibility is also considered as a variant in models by others (29, 50, 62, 114, 116); it would give rise to one recombinant and one parental product, a feature also of the Boon & Zinder model (10).

Asymmetric intermediates, reflecting one parent as donor, are almost inevitable for bacterial transformation by fragmented DNA, and the finding of single strand insertion (see above) led to postulates of ends (38, 40) or middles (9, 43, 65) of single- (30, 43, 65) or double-stranded (9, 38, 83) donor DNA interacting with intact recipient helices. The efficiency with which donor DNA markers are integrated once they are intracellular can be very high (37, 66, 67, 82, 105)—even if there is some repair of incoming marker (30, 42, 69, 107). Thus it seems that if heterologous DNAs confront each other they sometimes readily interact. We may ask: what is different in transformation, transduction or conjugational merozygotes from the situation in heterozygotic diploid cells that makes the former highly susceptible to recombination?

One possibility is the presence of DNA ends or discontinuities. There are signs that recombination is stimulated at ends or gaps of DNA. In phage heterozygotes there is an excess of recombination at the ends of overlapping DNA (22, 79), and defective phages which accumulate gaps or nicks show increased recombination (7, 8, 63), or formation of joint molecules (4) or branches (12). Recombination is also increased by the presence of unfilled gaps in donor chromosomes (59), or by opening of a circular episome (87). Various workers have thought it likely that single strand ends or gaps engage in recombinations (6, 12, 39, 95, 106) somewhat akin to transformations (35, 86, 96).

With some of these principles in mind, Paszewski (86) and the reviewer (56–58) have proposed two rather similar models for recombination (Figure 3, Table 2). Both start with a single strand broken in one helix and invading another helix, being there extended by synthesis along the heterologous template. The reviewer sees this strand displacement as a 3'-ward extension by polymerase, likely to build sufficient competition eventually to stimulate nicking by repair enzymes in the co-parallel strand. This is supposed to liberate another 3'-end and trigger an equivalent return attack farther along the original helix in the 3'-direction, producing a Holliday bridged pair. Paszewski has the same initial invasion bring about instead a capture of a segment of the template strand (a Whitehouse complementary bridge appears for a time). The resolution outlined involves a return of template, as well as its copy upon the wandering strand, back to the original helix as a double crossover, polarities not being specified. The other parental helix is reconstituted intact. But the models are rather similar; both lead to a conversion, at a site and in a direction determined by the original strand break, and its extent determined by the amount of extra copying which occurred at the borderline of a recombinational breakage-and-joining. The models become in all likelihood even more similar if one attempts to picture the alternative ways of resolving the intermediates of Paszewski—only hinted at by him—so as to obtain a recombination of flanking markers.

A model recently proposed by Radding & Meselson (92) takes an analogous direction with some significant differences. Again, a nicked single strand invades another helix, but the 5'-end is the invading end; it is progressively displaced from its complement by extension of the 3'-side of the nick along the complement. The wandering 5'-end is assimilated (cf. Figure 1) into the recipient helix through a more or less coordinated exonucleolytic degradation of the homolog after in some way nicking it (and becoming at some time linked to it). This single bridge migrates (3'-ward for the strand involved) along the helices a distance, depending upon the amount of new synthesis; as it does so a redundant copy of the donor helix region is laid down. This conversional synthesis terminates at some time by joining of the growing end with the degrading end of the homolog, forming now the familiar Holliday double bridge. The last process is probably facilitated by the rotational shift (97), already discussed, which would bring the two unsealed termini into approximate orientation in a continuous helix.

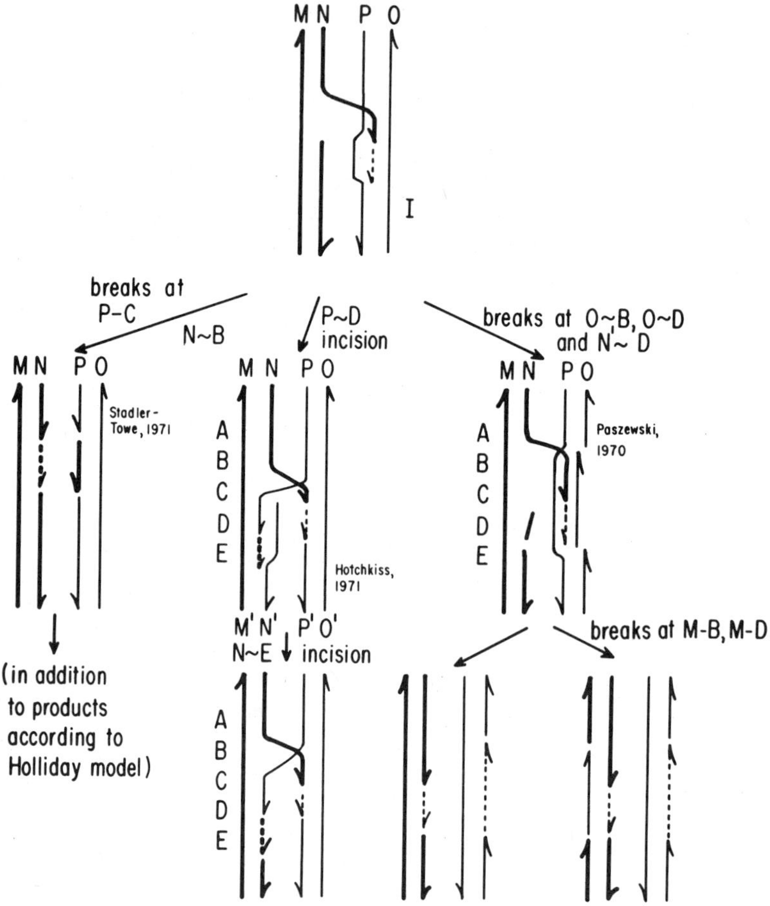


*Figure 3* Steps postulated in models depending upon an initial single bridge between parental helices, leading to asymmetric intermediates.

Symbols relate to Figures 1 and 2, also to Table 1. The unpairing and pairing of single strands with different templates is imagined to be assisted by proteins resembling the gene 32 protein [(1); see legend, Figure 1].

## THE RESOLUTION OF INTERCONNECTED HELICES

The Holliday cross-bridged helical intermediate, or half-chiasma, occurs in all recombination models, even those still to be discussed in which antiparallel strands are those first involved. It may take a form with one bridging strand (10, 38, 56, 86, 101) or more often two (12, 19, 33, 48–50, 56, 92, 97, 111), or may call for a pair of double bridges sometimes (50) or always (77, 99, 112). In some cases the bridges seemingly implied (71, 72) or actually pictured (10, 56, 102) are a succession

**Table 2** Models with one strand initially active: description of detailed steps (in reference to Figure 3 derived from pattern I, Figure 2; strand N broken at C only)

Paszewski model (86)

1. Strand end N–C pairs with complement O in other helix and is extended as copy of O to N–D (P remains intact).
2. Complement O breaks at or near O–B and O–D; strand end N′ is degraded from C to N′–D.
3. Strand N with extension CD as copy of O, returns to rejoin N′–D (double crossover giving conversion in region CD).
4. Broken complement O–BD returns with N–D; it may or may not be inserted into M–BD thus completing or not completing correction of O–CD in MN. (Paszewski implies there could be other resolutions; presumably other strands break to recombine flanking markers?)

Hotchkiss model (56)

1. Strand end N–C pairs with complement O in other helix and if a 3′-end, is extended as copy of O to N–D (O remains intact).
2. Growing N displaces P, causes incision at P–D, joins P′–D.
3. New 3′-end P–D pairs with M and copies it to E, displacing N′ along DE, causing incision at N′–E, joins N′–E; result is a Holliday structure, however, one hybrid bridge joins homolog farther 3′-wards than the other.
4. Strand N carries an extra copy of O (conversion) in its extension CD; but strand P creates no conversion as its extension DE regenerates N′–DE which is degraded.
5. Equilibration of the helices with some lateral migration of the bridges produces Holliday structure structurally symmetrical and genetically asymmetrical; random repair nicking of one of four strands near bridge releases another 3′-end which attacks as before and releases its homolog as a 3′-end, etc; if original pair involved, return is a double crossover in these two strands; if other pair involved, resolution is to a crossover reciprocal for flanking markers.
6. With either resolution, gene conversion heteroduplex has been made at the boundary of crossover junctions, over a distance determined by polymerase versus incision rates (57, 58).

Radding-Meselson model (Aviemore model) (92) (Not drawn here; refer to structure I, Figures 1 and 2, in which end N–C must be taken as a 5′-end)

1. Strand end N–C pairs with O and somehow ruptures and joins P′ at C.
2. Synthesis extends broken N′–C towards B and displaces location of bridge 3′-wards (upwards) towards B and A; N is assimilated to pairing with O at CBA by simultaneous degradation of P over CB toward A; the coupled growth of end N′–C and degradation of P–C leaves three copies of MN and one of OP (conversion) along CBA.
3. Helix swivel isomerization (97) about bridge juxtaposes growing end N′–CB and degrading end P–BC; if these are joined the structure becomes a fixed Holliday pair in the "symmetric mode" and conversion ceases.
4. Bridge migration occurs either before or after sealing; point of migration determines location, and isomerization the orientation of point at which double clipping of bridge occurs; the former determines length of heteroduplex regions and the latter whether flanking markers are exchanged outside the overlap.

**Table 2** (continued)

| Stadler-Towe model (101) (As supplement to the Holliday model) |
|---|
| 1. Co-parallel break at P–C as in Holliday model but end P–C not active and becomes degraded to B. |
| 2. Crossed joining of N–C with P′–C; no synthesis implied. |
| 3. N breaks at B, leaves segment BC paired with O–BC and end N–B returns to N; segment BC is resynthesized in original form and intact N is reestablished; conversion is at BC in P. (Authors suppose the alternative Holliday mechanism with P–C also crossing over is always resolved to give flanking marker recombination.) |

of single ones. The reason for this common form is of course that the most plausible way to connect two DNA double helices at their middles is by crossing of two parallel chain segments, other pairing merely leading to this eventually. But the different authors do not all propose to resolve this complex in the same way.

The mobility of this bridge seems not to have been recognized at first, although it can travel by simple coupled rotation of the helices (75, 97). Fogel & Hurst were perhaps earliest to propose migration (terminalization, partial or complete) (33), and Hotchkiss proposed a lateral migration and equilibrium (56) of such a bridge. Broker & Lehman described, and to some degree demonstrated in micrographs (12), migration of branches which they picture as formed in two configurations from adventitious strand breakages. They appeared not to notice that the form pictured in Figure 1 is a doubled back isomer of the Holliday bridged pair, but mentioned this for their other configuration. With their publication and that of Sigal & Alberts (97) several authors have recognized that such migration would create or extend heteroduplex regions (50, 92, 97, 99) and lead to conversion, or sites for conversion.

The more obvious lateral mobility of single bridges had of course been invoked whenever such bridges were the principal structure (10, 38, 65, 86, 101) or a specific first stage (56, 92) in the interconnection of two helices.

Even without migration, the position of cross links between two helices is imagined to be at some distance—not fixed but up to the magnitude of a gene or more—from the site of the primary breakages. Thus, the length of the hybrid region has always been supposed to vary within populations and more recently to change within the individual recombining pairs.

The resolution of the bridged structure has been described in varied terms, but in essence, the nicking of one pair of parallel strands leads rather simply to two independent helices recombinant for flanking markers, while nicks in the other pair would yield double recombinants in each half of two helices. If nicking does not occur at the same base pair, trimming and synthesis, as well as DNA ligase, would be needed for the rejoining process. In the earlier versions of the models, the opening of parallel strand pairs was simply one of the assumptions (19, 33, 48, 49, 102, 111, 112), even when the strand nicks were preformed (12) and the bridge dissolved when it reached them. More recently the assumption may include a bifunctional nuclease (50, 92, 97) traveling along one strand and breaking the opposite pair (29) or acting with twofold symmetry (99). Others have attributed the opening and separation of strands to the progress of strand replacement by strand synthesis (10, 56, 86, 92,

111). In the reviewer's proposal the unpaired regions at the bridge stimulate repair-incision of one randomly chosen strand, and this in turn displaces and stimulates nicking of its homolog (56). All of these authors have assumed something near equality in the choice of the pair which is opened in resolution of the complex.

With the description of the strand equivalence in crossed helices, it was easy to imagine the cutting of the bridged cross strands—a pair of homologs—in the two alternative isomers of the structure. In each case one pair of strands would remain continuous and the other would newly recombine (see above, pp. 451–52), leading either to recrossing in the previously switched pair of strands, or completing a two-strand recombination of flanking markers, joined by a heteroduplex region. It has already been applied in the latest recombination models (29, 50, 92, 97) as an elegant way of exhibiting the previously assumed equal strand choice.

Before coming to the topic of gene conversion, more should be said about the detailed models involving complementary strand breakage (Figure 4, Table 3). The original model of Whitehouse (111) early provided the in-place anchoring of cross-links in perfect register between two helices. Since the breakages need not be at the same level, overlap and copying lead to a hybrid with a heteroduplex region. But no convincing mechanism was suggested for rejoining the opposite pair before they are severed completely. The modification of Whitehouse & Hastings (112) provided synthesis (strand displacement?) creating the anchoring branches (see Figure 4) in advance of cross-linking so the register of fit could always be maintained. Furthermore, predetermined points of breakage were assumed to explain polarity effects, as described above. The strand displacement in the Boon & Zinder model (10) takes the organized form of a replication fork along one hybrid, and one parental strand. The interruption of the replication and the six successive strand breakages are explained only as possibly induced by previous events or structural requirements. Recent experiments with the f1 phage system for which it was developed (46), indicate that the asymmetric intermediate may be a long heteroduplex instead of the double-stranded one postulated. The branch-migration model (12) (above) has been related closely to the Holliday structure—only here the bridged helices lead in most configurations to the sacrifice of one helix to make the final nonreciprocal recombinant with its zones of heteroduplex DNA.

The double-stranded recombinant molecules formed in λ-phage recombinations (71, 72, 103), with postulated heteroduplex junctions (72, 110) (at least when DNA synthesis is restricted), might be formed from actual fragments released by enzymes (39, 71, 106) or by a complementary bridge joining two parental molecules (111), with discard of the other elements (see Figure 4). There is now evidence that the single strand ends involved in the overlap are 3'-ends (110), which is in agreement with the postulate that these ends, being extensible by synthesis, can penetrate into a neighboring helix (56).

## GENE CONVERSION AND THE DYNAMICS OF RECOMBINATION

The basis for gene conversion is always pictured as an extra DNA copy of one parent; although no longer visualized as a copy-choice mechanism, present-day models generally combine the breakage-fusion and copying mechanisms, as astutely suggested long ago by Pritchard (89). The extra copy may be pictured in two ways, as made before or after hybrid DNA is formed. Thus a heterologous strand, *X*, may be displaced by formation of its duplicate, *X'*, and thereupon invade another helix, displacing a homolog, *x*, which becomes degraded or lost. The result will be three single strand copies of *X* and one of *x*. Or, the strands *X* and *x* might exchange places, forming symmetrical Holliday heteroduplexes, which are then randomly "repaired"—an inclusive term supposed in part to involve resynthesis of the one or the other parental type (48, 112). Some of the reciprocal conversions expected from this scheme are, however, rarely found.

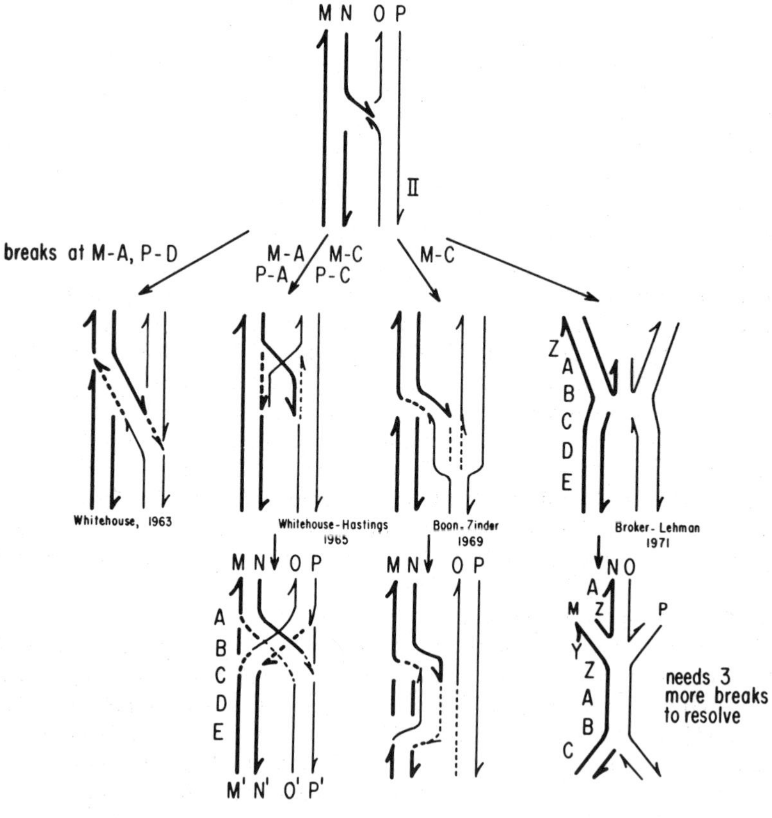


*Figure 4* Steps postulated in models depending upon nicks in antiparallel strands of two parental helices.

Symbols relate to Figures 1 to 3 and to Table 2. The Broker & Lehman proposals (12) include a version starting with nicks in parallel strands; both structures can be rearranged to the Holliday structure (Figure 2), the one shown here by twisting the strand pair NO downwards (see legend, Figure 1).

**Table 3** Models with two antiparallel strands initially active: description of detailed steps (in reference to Figure 4 derived from pattern II, Figure 2; strand N broken at C and O near C)

Whitehouse model (111)

1. Complementary ends N–C and O′–C pair and extend as copies of each other; additional breaks M–A and P–D allow M and N to join O′ and P′.
2. Ends M′–A and P′–D find each other and process repeats, N′O′ joining to complete a crossover; double crossover requires repeat of whole.

Whitehouse-Hastings model (112)

1. Complementary ends N′ and O′ extended along C to B by synthesis on own templates; ends N–C and O–C pair with them and they continue to grow now along heterologous templates toward A.
2. The hybrid pairs cause breaks in strands M and P both at C and A and join them; original broken ends join them at C and growing ends join them at A, completing a full crossover; double crossover requires repeat of whole process.
3. Repair in heteroduplex regions AB; if asymmetric, give conversion; the hybrid regions AB need not be exactly opposite or equal.

Boon-Zinder model (10)

1. Third break at M in B to C; M becomes joined to end O′–C.
2. Complementary ends N–C and O–C extended by synthesis toward D, O–C along its template P and N–C along heterologous template O′–C, displacing the pair O′P′ by a replication fork.
3. Three new breaks occur, in M′ and N′ near E and in fork strand MO′ in same region, allowing recombinant strand M–E and new end N–E to return to M′ and N′ producing double-strand insertion into MN over region CE with short heteroduplexes at junction points C and E.
4. Parental strand O has been reconstituted by the extension, joins O′ as a partly new parental duplex.

Broker-Lehman model (12) (Two strands sacrificed)

1. Complementary ends N–C and O–C pair with each other, move outward and expose gaps in BC; intact strands M and P pair in BC region.
2. As the NO pair are pulled out of the junction, pair MP move together at B, A and beyond; effect is to move branches (pairs) along each other without loss of base pairing, until two additional opposite nicks or gaps in opposite pairs are reached beyond A, and one or more below C, to allow release of branches (alternative form has exonuclease removing the branch strands until nicks are reached).

Sobell model (99) (Special route to bridge and branch models)

1. At intergene sites self-complementary regions allow loops to form; ends of loops expose special sites to complementary nicking and pairing in antiparallel homologs (not shown here); these pull out as branches creating two hybrid pairs; process continues as in the Broker-Lehman pattern or if the ends pulled out find each other two Holliday bridges with fixed distance form and can migrate together.
2. Bridge migration used to explain various genetic effects.

**Table 3** (continued)

Two-strand joining with overlap (By implication in various models)

1. Various results, especially with λ-phage (71, 72, 103, 110), suggest that parental helices may join at an overlap of complementary ends; other fragments not accounted for—perhaps implies Whitehouse type of junction with recovery of only one end of each parent.

Sigal-Alberts model (97)

1. Point out symmetry of structure in double bridge which allows mobility along rotating helices; also equivalence of bridging strands—by simple twist alternate parallel pairs can become the bridging pair.
2. These principles used to specify structural details in Holliday model.

There is additional possibility for asymmetry or nonreciprocality in the conversions if at least part of the DNA copying occurs as a step in the formation of the interhelical bonds. This is explicitly assumed by advocates of the asymmetric routes to the bridge model (56, 86, 92, 102) or half-bridge (10, 101). The advantage is that without repair asymmetric bridges can be split to lead to the 5:3 type of segregation of ascospores, and with simple repair, to 3:1 yields of specific arrays of the markers in the heteroduplex. The most extreme proposal for precopying of parental strands (102) calls for local formation of eight strands, from which four survive after various amounts of crossing. In general, the Whitehouse models offer the same precopying of one parent over a greater distance than the other, to form nonreciprocal heteroduplexes. Again, subsequent repair—random (112) or selective (15, 29, 62)—can be superimposed.

It has become clear from these considerations that several dynamic processes can be supposed to change the apparent patterns and course of recombination: (*a*) a variable amount of synthesis during strand displacement; (*b*) lateral migration or equilibration of a bridge strand, bridge pair, or pair of bridges; (*c*) an impulse for DNA repair which may or may not result in nicking, near sites of imperfect pairing, perhaps including mutant mismatch; (*d*) a variable amount of exonucleolytic degradation at nicks, perhaps competing with (*e*) nick transfer by DNA polymerase (61); and (*f*) a still mysteriously regulated urge to rejoin nicks with help of DNA ligases (possibly at specifically favored sites?).

Those interested in mechanisms have begun to express awareness of a competition between the rates of some of the above processes. In essence, all recombination frequencies in a population can be interpreted as dependent on rates of occurrences of given biochemical events having a low probability per cell. It is in this sense that I would interpret the alternative pathways proposed by Clark (17, 18, 51)—varying extents of a recombination step depending upon greater or lesser participation or inhibition of enzymes diverting or terminating the opportunity for that step. The effect of various phage deficiencies upon recombination can likewise be viewed as playing upon the enzymatic endowment, notably the exonucleases, and more indirectly or by implication, the ligases and polymerases. An interesting indication that host polymerase furthers single crossovers but not double ones in T4 phage has been noted (80).

All of the above factors, (*a*) to (*f*), and all genetically determined enzymes can be subject to physiological influence—one has only to recall the relative infrequency of recombination in mitosis, or at meiosis in male gametogenesis in *Drosophila.* There are such variables as: temperature sensitivity (solicited or innate), availability of substrates, precursors, monomers, ATP energy (or as indicated the various target sites of mismatch), nicks, gaps, 3'- or 5'-hydroxyl, phosphoryl or pyrophosphoryl termini, etc. Only a few concrete suggestions have appeared thus far.

Implicitly, the concept of multiple pairing (28, 89) is an hypothesis of cooperative favoring of reaction rates, so is to some extent that of polarity determining the assumed length of a fixed hybrid region. Various views on the mobility of the cross bridges have been described above, and we shall undoubtedly hear more about this in the future. The resolution of bridged intermediates has been seen as dependent on the probability of preformed nicks (12), or the rate of stimulation of repair (56, 58). Holliday has also proposed that rates of nicking (referred to as excision) in relation to degradation would determine the probability and extent of the repair step in heteroduplex conversion (50).

The reviewer has emphasized the effect of relative rates, particularly that of polymerase 3'-extension of strands to that of repair nicking (57, 58) in affecting the region and pattern of conversion, suggesting a kind of physiological quotient of (polymerase):(incision) average distances that would modify recombination distances and rates. Radding & Meselson in particular (92) have now also stressed the effect of displacement (coordinated synthesis and degradation) to extend a region of conversion, with helix isomerization and sealing by ligase operating to terminate it. In these ways, we can visualize the fluid asymmetric events of recombination being converted to the more classic symmetric intermediates from which the possible recombinational outcomes now become relatively determined. We can expect to see more of this kind of predictivity as our knowledge of the reacting components increases.

## SUMMARY—A RECOMBINATION OF RECOMBINATION MODELS

Recombination is coming to be seen as a template-switching process, reminiscent of copy-choice, but one in which preformed whole blocks or segments of DNA rather than monomers are laid down along the heterologous complementary strand. The process probably begins at ends of single strands, which form a bridge structure of one or two parallel strands joining and twisted into the two parental helices. After some lateral migration these bridges can be cut to release helices with either new or old arrays of outside markers. Template copying which precedes strand integration, and any which follows excision (repair copying) in heteroduplex regions, produce disproportionate recovery (conversion) of parental markers in the region of crossover. Different patterns of recombination probably result from different relative enzymatic rates of DNA strand extension, degradation, repair, and joining in different genetic and physiological systems.

*Literature Cited*


1. Alberts, B. M., Frey, L. 1970. *Nature* 227:1313–18
2. Amati, P., Meselson, M. 1965. *Genetics* 51:369–79
3. Anraku, N., Tomizawa, J. 1965. *J. Mol. Biol.* 11:501–8
4. Anraku, N., Anraku, Y., Lehman, I. R. 1969. *J. Mol. Biol.* 46:481–92
5. Baker, R., Tessman, I. 1967. *Proc. Nat. Acad. Sci. USA* 58:1438–45
6. Benbow, R. M., Zuccarelli, A. J., Sinsheimer, R. L. 1974. *J. Mol. Biol.* In press
7. Berger, H., Warren, A. J., Fry, K. E. 1969. *J. Virol.* 3:171–75
8. Bernstein, H. 1968. *Cold Spring Harbor Symp. Quant. Biol.* 33:325–31
9. Bodmer, W. F. 1966. *J. Gen. Physiol.* 49:233–58
10. Boon, T., Zinder, N. D. 1971. *J. Mol. Biol.* 58:133–51
11. Bresler, S. E., Kreneva, R. A., Kushev, V. V. 1971. *Mol. Gen. Genet.* 113:204–13
12. Broker, T. R., Lehman, I. R. 1971. *J. Mol. Biol.* 60:131–49
13. Campbell, A. M. 1962. *Advan. Genet.* 11:101–45
14. Cassuto, E., Radding, C. M. 1971. *Nature New Biol.* 229:13–16; Ibid 230:128
15. Catcheside, D. G. 1968. *Replication and Recombination of Genetic Material,* ed. W. J. Peacock, R. D. Brock, 216–26. Canberra: Australian Acad. Sci.
16. Catcheside, D. G., Austin, B. 1971. *Aust. J. Biol. Sci.* 24:107–15
17. Clark, A. J. 1971. *Ann. Rev. Microbiol.* 25:437–64
18. Clark, A. J. 1973. *Ann. Rev. Genet.* 7:67–86
19. Cross, R. A., Lieb, M. 1967. *Genetics* 57:549–60
20. Curtiss, R. III, 1968. *Genetics* 58:9–54
21. Davern, C. I. 1971. *Progress in Nucleic Acid Research and Molecular Biology,* ed. J. N. Davidson, W. E. Cohn, 229–58, New York: Academic
22. Doermann, A. H., Parma, D. H. 1967. *J. Cell. Physiol.* (Suppl. 1) 70:147–64
23. Drapeau, G. R., Brammar, W. J., Yanofsky, C. 1968. *J. Mol. Biol.* 35:357–67
24. Dubnau, D., Davidoff-Abelson, R., Smith, I. 1969. *J. Mol. Biol.* 45:155–79
25. Dubnau, D., Davidoff-Abelson, R. 1971. *J. Mol. Biol.* 56:209–21
26. Ebel-Tsipis, J., Fox, M. S., Botstein, D. 1972. *J. Mol. Biol.* 71:449–69
27. Echols, H., Gingery, R., Moore, L. 1968. *J. Mol. Biol.* 34:251–60
28. Edgar, R. S., Steinberg, C. M. 1958. *Virology* 6:115–28
29. Emerson, S. Unpublished observations
30. Ephrussi-Taylor, H., Gray, T. 1966. *J. Gen. Physiol.* No. 6 (Suppl.) 49:211–31
31. Fincham, J. R. S. 1970. *Ann. Rev. Genet.* 4:347–72
32. Fincham, J. R. S., Day, P. R. 1971. *Fungal Genetics,* Vol. 4. Oxford: Blackwell. 3rd ed.
33. Fogel, S., Hurst, D. D. 1967. *Genetics* 57:455–81
34. Fogel, S., Hurst, D. D., Mortimer, R. K. 1971. *Stadler Symp.* 1 and 2:89–110
35. Fogel, S., Mortimer, R. K. 1969. *Proc. Nat. Acad. Sci. USA* 62:96–103
36. Fogel, S., Mortimer, R. K. 1971. *Ann. Rev. Genet.* 5:219–36
37. Fox, M. S. 1957. *Biochim. Biophys. Acta* 26:83–85
38. Fox, M. S. 1966. *J. Gen. Physiol.* 49:183–96
39. Friedman, E. A., Smith, H. O. 1973. *Nature New Biol.* 241:54–58
40. Gábor, M., Hotchkiss, R. D. 1966. *Proc. Nat. Acad. Sci. USA* 56:1441–48
41. Gottesman, M. E., Yarmolinsky, M. B. 1968. *J. Mol. Biol.* 31:487–505
42. Gray, T. C., Ephrussi-Taylor, H. 1967. *Genetics* 57:125–53
43. Guild, W. R., Cato, A. Jr., Lacks, S. 1968. *Cold Spring Harbor Symp. Quant. Biol.* 33:643–45
44. Gutz, H. 1971. *Genetics* 69:317–37
45. Harris, W. J., Barr, G. C. 1971. *Mol. Gen. Genet.* 113:331–44
46. Hartman, N., Zinder, N. D. 1974. *J. Mol. Biol.* In press
47. Hastings, P. J. 1973. *Genet. Res.* 20:253–56
48. Holliday, R. 1964. *Genet. Res.* 5:282–304
49. Holliday, R. 1968. *Replication and Recombination of Genetic Material,* ed. W. J. Peacock, R. D. Brock, 157–74. Canberra: Australian Acad. Sci.
50. Holliday, R. 1974. *Genetics.* In press
51. Horii, Z-I., Clark, A. J. 1973. *J. Mol. Biol.* 80:327–44
52. Hotchkiss, R. D. 1958. *Symp. Soc. Exp. Biol.* 13:49–59
53. Hotchkiss, R. D., Evans, A. H. 1958. *Cold Spring Harbor Symp. Quant. Biol.* 23:85–97
54. Hotchkiss, R. D. 1968. *Cold Spring Harbor Symp. Quant. Biol.* 33:857–70
55. Hotchkiss, R. D., Gábor, M. 1970. *Ann. Rev. Genet.* 4:193–224
56. Hotchkiss, R. D. 1971. *Advan. Genet.* 16:325–48

57. Hotchkiss, R. D. 1973. *Stadler Symp.* 5:145–60
58. Hotchkiss, R. D. 1974. *Genetics.* In press
59. Howard-Flanders, P., Rupp, W. D., Wilkins, B. M. 1968. *Replication and Recombination of Genetic Material,* ed. W. J. Peacock, R. D. Brock, 142–51. Canberra: Australian Acad. Sci.
60. Hurst, D. D., Fogel, S., Mortimer, R. K. 1972. *Proc. Nat. Acad. Sci. USA* 69:101–5
61. Kelly, R. B., Cozzarelli, N. R., Deutscher, M. P., Lehman, I. R., Kornberg, A. 1970. *J. Biol. Chem.* 245:39–45
62. Kitani, Y., Olive, L. S. 1967. *Genetics* 57:767–82; Ibid 1969. 62:23–66
63. Kozinski, A. W., Kozinski, P. B., James, R. 1967. *J. Virol.* 1:758–70
64. Kushner, S. R., Nagaishi, H., Templin, A., Clark, A. J. 1971. *Proc. Nat. Acad. Sci. USA* 68:824–27
65. Lacks, S. 1966. *Genetics* 53:207–35
66. Lacks, S., Greenberg, B., Carlson, K. 1967. *J. Mol. Biol.* 29:327–47
67. Lerman, L. S., Tolmach, L. J. 1967. *Biochim. Biophys. Acta* 26:68–82
68. Lindahl, G. 1969. *Virology* 39:861–66
69. Louarn, J. M., Sicard, A. M. 1968. *Biochem. Biophys. Res. Commun.* 30: 683–89
70. Low, B. 1968. *Proc. Nat. Acad. Sci. USA* 60:160–67
71. Meselson, M., Weigle, J. J. 1961. *Proc. Nat. Acad. Sci. USA* 47:857–68
72. Meselson, M. 1964. *J. Mol. Biol.* 9:734–45
73. Meselson, M. 1968. *Replication and Recombination of Genetic Material,* ed. W. J. Peacock, R. D. Brock, 152–56. Canberra: Australian Acad. Sci.
74. Meselson, M., Yuan, R., Heywood, J. 1972. *Ann. Rev. Biochem.* 41:447–66
75. Meselson, M. 1972. *J. Mol. Biol.* 71:795–98
76. Mitchell, M. B. 1955. *Proc. Nat. Acad. Sci. USA* 41:215–20
77. Mosevitsky, M. 1971. *Sov. Sci. Rev.* March:104–8
78. Mosig, G. 1970. *Advan. Genet.* 15:1–53
79. Mosig, G., Ehring, R., Schliewen, W., Bock, S. 1971. *Mol. Gen. Genet.* 113:51–91
80. Mosig, G., Freeman, P., Tarpley, J. 1973. *Symp. Genet. Recombination,* Roche Inst. Mol. Biol., Abstr.
81. Murray, N. E. 1961. *Genetics* 46:886
82. Notani, N. K. 1971. *J. Mol. Biol.* 59:223–26
83. Notani, N. K., Goodgal, S. H. 1966. *J. Gen. Physiol.* 49:197–209
84. Oishi, M., Cosloy, S. D. 1972. *Biochem. Biophys. Res. Commun.* 49:1568–72
85. Okazaki, R., Okazaki, T., Sakabe, K., Sugimoto, K., Sugino, A. 1968. *Proc. Nat. Acad. Sci. USA* 59:598–605
86. Paszewski, A. 1970. *Genet. Res.* 15:55–64
87. Pittard, J., Adelberg, E. A. 1964. *Genetics* 49:995–1007
88. Piechowska, M., Fox, M. S. 1971. *J. Bacteriol.* 108:680–89
89. Pritchard, R. H. 1960. *Symp. Soc. Gen. Microbiol.* 10:155–80
90. Prozorov, A. A., Kalinina, N. A., Naumov, L. S., Chestukhin, A. V., Shemyakin, M. F. 1972. *Genetika* 8:142–48
91. Radding, C. M. 1973. *Ann. Rev. Genetics* 7:87–111
92. Radding, C. M., Meselson, M. Unpublished observations
93. Rizet, G., Rossignol, J. L. 1966. *C. R. Acad. Sci.* 262:1250–53
94. Roger, M. 1972. *Proc. Nat. Acad. Sci. USA* 69:466–70
95. Sadowski, P., Ginsberg, B., Yudelevich, A., Feiner, L., Hurwitz, J. 1968. *Cold Spring Harbor Symp. Quant. Biol.* 33:165–77
96. Sermonti, G., Carere, A. 1968. *Mol. Gen. Genet.* 103:141–49
97. Sigal, N., Alberts, B. 1972. *J. Mol. Biol.* 71:789–93
98. Smith, H. O., Levine, M. 1967. *Virology* 31:207–16
99. Sobell, H. M. 1973. *Advan. Genet.* 17:411–90
100. Spatz, H. C., Trautner, T. A. 1970. *Mol. Gen. Genet.* 109:84–106
101. Stadler, D. R., Towe, A. M. 1971. *Genetics* 68:401–13
102. Stahl, F. W. 1969. *Genetics* Suppl. 61:1–13
103. Stahl, F. W., McMilin, K. D., Stahl, M. M., Nozu, Y. 1972. *Proc. Nat. Acad. Sci. USA* 69:3598–3601
104. Strauss, N. 1966. *Genetics* 66:583—93
105. Stuy, J. H. 1965. *J. Mol. Biol.* 13:554–70
106. Thomas, C. A. 1966. *Progr. Nucl. Acid Res. Mol. Biol.* 5:315–37
107. Tiraby, J. -G., Fox, M. S. 1973. *Proc. Nat. Acad. Sci. USA* 70:3541–45
108. Tomizawa, J., Anraku, N. 1964. *J. Mol. Biol.* 8:516–40
109. Vovis, G. F., Buttin, G. 1970. *Biochim. Biophys. Acta* 224:42–54
110. White, R. L., Fox, M. S. 1974. *Proc. Nat. Acad. Sci. USA* 71:1544–48
111. Whitehouse, H. L. K. 1963. *Nature* 199:1034–40
112. Whitehouse, H. L. K., Hastings, P. J. 1965. *Genet. Res.* 6:27–92

113. Whitehouse H. L. K. 1966. *Nature* 211:708–13
114. Ibid 1967. 215:1352–59
115. Whitehouse, H. L. K. 1969. *Towards an Understanding of the Mechanism of Heredity,* 317. New York: St. Martins. 2nd ed.
116. Whitehouse, H. L. K. 1970. *Biol. Rev.* 45:265–315

# OTHER REVIEWS OF MICROBIOLOGICAL INTEREST

From the *Annual Review of Biochemistry,* Volume 43 (1974):

Boos, W. *Bacterial Transport*
Braun, V., Hantke, K. *Biochemistry of Bacterial Cell Envelopes*
Gooday, G. W. *Fungal Sex Hormones*

From the *Annual Review of Entomology,* Volume 20 (1975):

David, W. A. L. *The Status of Viruses Pathogenic to Insects and Mites*

From the *Annual Review of Genetics,* Volume 8 (1974):

Catcheside, D. R. *Fungal Genetics*
Eckhart, W. *Genetics of DNA Tumor Viruses*
Gotts, J. S., Benson, C. E. *Biochemical Genetics of Bacteria*
Halpern, Y. S. *Genetics of Amino Acid Transport in Bacteria*
Temin, H. M. *Origin of RNA Viruses*

From the *Annual Review of Medicine,* Volume 25 (1974):

Barker, W. H. Jr., Gangarosa, E. J. *Food Poisoning Due to Vibrio parahaemolyticus*
Brummer, D. L. *Preventive Therapy of Tuberculosis*
Luby, J. P., Johnson, M. T., Jones, S. R. *Antiviral Chemotherapy*

From the *Annual Review of Pharmacology,* Volume 14 (1974):

Thrupp, L. D. *Newer Cephalosporins and "Expanded-Spectrum" Penicillins*
Tilles, J. G. *Antiviral Agents*

From the *Annual Review of Phytopathology,* Volume 12 (1974):

Brown, M. E. *Seed and Root Bacterization*
Hamilton, R. I. *Replication of Plant Viruses*
Hayward, A. C. *Latent Infections of Bacteria*
Mirocha, C. J., Christensen, C. M. *Fungus Metabolites Toxic to Animals*
Patil, S. S. *Toxins Produced by Phytopathogenic Bacteria*
Schroth, M. N., Hildebrand, D. C., Thomson, S. V., Moller, W. J. *Epidemiology of Fire Blight*
Schuster, M. L., Coyne, D. P. *Survival Mechanisms of Phytopathogenic Bacteria*
Verhoeff, K. *Latent Infections by Fungi*

# AUTHOR INDEX


A

Aaronson, S. A., 242, 259
Aasmundrud, O., 414
Abbonenc, E., 197
Aboud, M., 358, 365
Abramova, V. M., 127
Acheson, E. D., 247
Acheson, N. H., 327, 328
Achtman, M., 266
Ackermann, H. W., 271
Adair, F. W., 92
Adamova, N. P., 47
Adams, C. A., 96
Adams, D. H., 30, 37, 243, 258
Adams, J. M., 247
Adams, J. N., 271
Adams, M. H., 268, 276
Adamse, A. D., 400, 421
Adelberg, E. A., 225, 457
Adhya, S., 361, 362
Adler, H. I., 395
Adler, S., 189, 190, 192, 195, 200, 204, 211
Adolf, A. C., 147
Agabian, N., 354
Agabian-Keshishian, N., 355, 357
Ahmadjian, V., 63
Ahmed, A., 252, 255
Ahmed, S. I., 73
Ahrens, R., 395, 426, 432, 436
Akagi, J. M., 94
Akazawa, T., 168
Akiba, T., 268, 273, 280
Akiyama, H. J., 195, 207, 208
Albert, A. A., 238, 258
Alberts, B., 451-53, 457-61, 464
Alberts, B. M., 450, 458
Albrecht, R. M., 140, 142
Alcasid, A., 425
Alden, R. A., 48
Aldrich, H. C., 140, 142
Aleem, M. I. H., 85, 86, 88-90, 96-98
Alekseev, A. N., 198
Alekseyeva, O. G., 131, 134
Aleman, C., 207
Alexander, D. J., 340
Alexander, H. E., 220
Alexander, M., 86
Alexander, S. P., 357
Alfes, H., 109
Alger, N., 195
Aliev, E. I., 207, 211
Allen, M. M., 172
Allen, R. D., 375
Allen, T. C., 314
Allison, A. C., 253-55, 337, 338
Allsopp, A., 176
Alper, T., 37, 258
Alpers, M., 37, 232, 238, 245, 250-52, 259, 260
Altenbern, R. A., 224
Alvares Fuertes, G., 200
Amati, P., 446
Ames, B. N., 227, 356
Ames, E., 289
Amesz, J., 45, 55
Amici, A., 303
Amin, F. M., 196
Amin, P. W., 316
Amini, H., 197
Aminuddin, M., 96
Amrhein, N., 353
Anagnostidis, K., 395
Anagnostopoulos, C., 225
Anderson, A. D., 249
Anderson, J. H., 86-88
Anderson, M. L., 151, 152
Anderson, P. S. Jr., 274
Anderson, T. F., 276
Anderson, W. B., 356, 358, 360, 361
Angelopoulos, E., 207
Anger, H. S., 257
Anraku, N., 447-57
Anraku, Y., 156, 447, 450-53, 457, 460-65
Antipov, V. V., 123-25
Apirion, D., 358
Appley, C. A., 65
Appleyard, G., 344
Arai, S., 307
Arber, W., 267, 271, 275
ARDEN, S. B., 265-99; 269
Arditti, R., 356, 357, 361
Arfin, S., 225
Aristovskaya, T. V., 394, 400, 408, 410, 423, 433, 437
Armedilla, A. L., 316
Arnheim, N., 278
Arnold, W., 43
Arnon, D. I., 54
Aronson, J. N., 172
Aronson, N. N., 104
Asbell, M. A., 87, 89
Aseeva, J. V., 425
Ashcroft, E., 225
Asher, D. M., 232, 238, 240, 257
Asher, Y., 343
Asheshov, E. H., 270
Ashford, R. W., 195, 197-99, 211, 212
Ashworth, J. M., 140, 141, 144, 145, 147, 150, 153, 154, 157, 160
Åström, K. E., 237, 240, 252
Asuyama, H., 302, 311, 312, 316, 317
Atanasoff, D., 303, 314
Atherton, J. G., 312
Atkinson, D. E., 365
Atkinson, P. H., 331
Atlas, D., 76
Attwood, M. M., 400, 403, 405, 407
August, J. T., 35
Auran, T. B., 404, 438
Austin, B., 453
Avakyan, A. A., 197, 207, 211
Avery, O. T., 284
Avigad, G., 168, 170
Azar, H. A., 207
Azevedo, M., 201
Azuma, I., 104, 109

B

Babcock, G. E., 106
Babczinski, P., 114
Babos, P., 35
Bächi, T., 336
Bacon, D. F., 73
Baddiley, J., 115
Badman, W. S., 140, 142
Baess, I., 279
Bagdian, G., 271
Bagnall, B. G., 274
Bagnall, R. H., 24, 25
Bahr, G. F., 372, 377, 385, 387
Bailey, R. B., 341, 342
Baker, E. E., 277
Baker, F. D., 126, 127
Baker, R., 456
Balashova, V. V., 396, 427, 429
Balassa, R., 220
Balban, E. J., 124
Bales, H., 53
Balish, E., 104
Ball, E. M., 113
Ball, F. L., 66, 180, 182
Ballio, A., 227
Ballou, C. E., 105, 106, 180
Baltscheffsky, M., 54, 55

Bandiera, M., 223
Bandyopadhyay, A. K., 71
Banerjee, A. K., 35
Banttari, E. E., 314, 315
Barbanti-Brodano, G., 257, 259
Barber, L. C., 178
Bardzhadze, B. G., 190
BARER, R., 371-89; 374, 375, 382, 385
Barghoorn, E. S., 418, 429
Barker, S. A., 107
Barkley, D. S., 140
BARKSDALE, L., 265-99; 174, 268, 269, 272, 274, 277-80, 283, 285-88
Barksdale, W. L., 268, 285
Barlow, A. J. E., 105
Barnet, Y. M., 271
Barnett, J. A., 392, 396, 397
Barnley, G. R., 193
Baron, L. S., 220, 271
Baron, S., 194
Barondes, S. H., 142
Barr, A. R., 318
Barr, G. C., 447
Barr, R. M., 114
Barrell, B. G., 35
Barrett, J., 85
Barsky, E. L., 45, 55
Bartholomä, K. P., 127
Bartnicki-Garcia, S., 104, 114, 115
Barton, R. W., 227
Bartsch, R. G., 45-49, 52, 54
Barzilai, N., 282
Basarab, O., 107
Baseman, J. B., 289
Bates, J. H., 269
Bates, S. B., 332
Batty, I., 383
Baublis, J. V., 233, 254
Bauer, H., 331
Bauer, K., 72
Bauer, S., 114, 115
Bauerle, R. H., 226
Baulaigue, R., 417
Bauld, J., 409, 410, 434, 436
Baumberg, S., 225
Baumunk, C. N., 75
Bavendamm, W., 410
Baxter, L., 145, 148
Beale, W. L., 35
Beam, R. E., 269
Beard, J. W., 334
Bearden, L., 73
Bearn, A. G., 251
Beaujean, R., 127
Beck, J. S., 210
Beck, J. V., 90
Becker, G. E., 89, 90
Becker, Y., 343
Beckwith, J. R., 278, 355-57, 359, 361, 364
Beeman, D. K., 357
Beeston, B. E. P., 381
Beger, H., 429
Behforouz, N., 211
Behme, R. J., 184
Behrens, N. H., 114
Beischer, D. E., 123
Bell, E. J., 196, 208
Bell, T. M., 247
Bellanti, J., 253
Bellion, E., 406, 407
Belly, R. T., 305, 397, 427, 428, 431
Belova, E. M., 192, 194, 196-98, 205
Belser, W. L., 220, 226
Benbow, R. M., 453, 457
Bender, M. A., 128
Benedict, C. R., 414
Benevolenskiy, V. N., 127
Beng, H., 142
Bengson, M. H., 131-33
Benjamin, W., 36
Bennett, G., 337
Bennett, J. H., 250
Ben Osman, F., 191, 192
Ben-Porat, T., 343
Ben Rachid, M. S., 191
Benson, C. E., 355, 356
Benson, C. L., 126, 127
Benson, L., 242
Berberich, M. A., 227
Beretta, M., 220
Berezesky, I. K., 327, 328
Berg, B., 415
Berger, H., 457
Berger, L. R., 404, 413, 414, 438
Bergere, J. L., 176
Berkowitz, D., 356
Bernhard, W., 333
Bernhardt, S. A., 67
Bernlohr, R. W., 354, 364, 365
Bernstein, H., 457
Bernstein, R. L., 281
Berry, C. A., 130-32, 134
Bertani, G., 224, 268, 272, 274, 275
Bertani, L. E., 268, 271, 272, 274, 275
Berthet, J., 353
Beskow, S., 415
Bessman, S. P., 69
Beteta, P., 112, 113, 115
Betti, M., 220
Beulke, I., 276
Bhaskaran, K., 220
Bhat, J. V., 400
Bhattacharjee, S. S., 105
Bhattacharya, A. K., 256
Biagi, F. F., 200, 201
Bianchi, L., 208
Biberfeld, G., 248
Bidwell, R. G. S., 61, 140, 154
Biebl, H., 412
Bieglmayer, C., 68
Biely, P., 114
Bigger, C. H., 112
Bignami, M., 226
Bilezikian, J. P., 358
Billen, D., 75
Bingel, K. F., 270
Birch-Andersen, A., 308
Bird, J., 315, 317, 318
Bird, R. G., 207
Birdwell, C. R., 327, 329
Birnbaum, G., 248
Bishop, C. T., 107-9
Bishop, J. M., 36
Bishop, R., 105
Bisset, K. A., 396, 426
Bizzini, B., 287, 289
Black, F. T., 308
Black, L. M., 318
Black, S. H., 172
Blackman, M. A., 435, 436
Blaedel, W. J., 80
Blair, J. E., 270
Blanco, E., 203
Blank, F., 107-9
Blasi, F., 227
Blasingame, D. J., 307, 309
Blaylock, B. A., 90
Bless, J. W., 97
Block, R., 357
Blomstrand, I., 225
Blough, H. A., 338, 340
Blouse, L. E., 220
Blum, E., 37
Blum, J. J., 68, 69
Blumberg, S., 76
Boatman, E. S., 304, 312, 432
Bock, E., 96, 168, 170, 182
Bock, S., 453, 457
Bodley, J. W., 358
Bodmer, W. F., 447, 456
Boedtker, H., 28, 29
Boer, P., 113
Boguslaski, R. C., 80
Bohlool, B., 428
Boice, L. B., 268, 275
Boiteux, A., 70, 71
Bollon, A. P., 74
Bolognesi, D. P., 334
Bolton, E. T., 74
Bolton, J. R., 50
Bonar, R. A., 334
Bonciu, O., 270
Bongers, L., 97
Bonhoeffer, F., 71
Bonicke, R., 269
Bonissol, C., 306, 318
Bonner, J., 145, 147, 148, 153, 160
Bonner, J. T., 140, 147
Bonventre, P. F., 289

Booher, Z. K., 285
Boon, T., 453, 454, 456, 458, 460, 461, 463, 464
Bordjoski, A., 190
Borek, E., 272
Borges, M., 313, 316
Borisova, O. K., 131-33
Bos, L., 303
Bose, H. R., 328
Bossie, A., 195
Bossie-Agavriloaiei, A., 194
Bostrom, R. C., 372, 387
Botsford, J. L., 362
Botstein, D., 447
Bott, K., 276
Böttger, B., 72
Bouanchaud, D. H., 266
Boulter, E. A., 344
Boulton, C. A., 407
Bouteille, M., 240
Bové, J.-M., 306-9, 311, 313, 318
Bowen, C. C., 168, 172, 180, 184
Bowen, T. J., 93, 94
Bower, R. J., 293
Bowers, E., 115
Bowman, C. G., 289
Bowyer, J. W., 312
Boyd, J. S. K., 282, 284
Boyde, A., 381
Boyer, H., 224
Bradley, D. E., 313
Brammar, W. J., 448, 453
Bramwell, E. C., 255
Braná, H., 364
Brandige, M. A., 328
Brandt, W. E., 327, 328
Brault, J. W., 375
Braun, A. C., 353
Bravard, L. J., 157
Bray, D., 282
Bray, M. A., 197-99, 211, 212
BRAY, R. S., 189-217; 190, 195, 197-201, 203, 204, 207, 211, 212
Braymer, H. D., 112
Brčák, J., 307, 314, 316
Bredt, W., 308
Breedlove, J. R., 387
Brehmeyer, B. A., 355, 356
Breitman, T. R., 356
Bremer, H., 74
Brenner, M., 149
Brenner, S., 265, 268
Bresler, S. E., 447, 453
Bretthauser, R. K., 115
Brickman, E., 355, 364
Brock, K. M., 397, 427, 431
Brock, T. D., 115, 305, 397, 427, 428, 431
Brody, J. A., 247, 249, 258
Broker, T. R., 450-53, 457, 458, 460-63, 465
Bronson, M. J., 279
Brooks, G. C., 72
Brotherston, J. G., 243
Broun, G., 77
Brown, A. C., 386
Brown, D. D., 144, 146
Brown, D. H., 66, 180, 182
Brown, D. T., 327-29
Brown, E. G., 353
Brown, G. W. Jr., 176, 178
Brown, J. H., 270
Brown, J. P., 392, 396, 397
Brown, P., 37, 247
Brown, R., 289
Brown, R. M., 184
Brownell, G. H., 220
Bruce, M., 69
Bruner, D. W., 273, 280
Bryant, C., 192, 210
Bryceson, A. D. M., 199, 204, 211, 212
Bublitz, C., 158
Buchanan, B. B., 47, 54
Bücker, H., 127, 129, 132
Buckland, B., 180
Buettner, M. J., 363
Buhagiar, R. W. M., 396
Buhl, R., 376
Bulow, P., 270
Bune, R. P., 253
Bunina, T. L., 249
Bunkenburg, J., 54
Bunting, M. I., 220
Burge, B. W., 327, 328, 330
Burger, D., 245
Burger, M., 67, 358, 365
Burger, M. M., 66
Burnet, F. M., 274
Burnett, J. H., 104
Burrous, J. W., 268, 272, 273, 280, 281, 285
Burrows, T. W., 220
Burtner, C., 94
Busch, H., 36
Busch, W., 72
Butcher, R. W., 355, 366
Butler, M. A., 226
Butler, P. J., 94
Butler, R. D., 176
Buttin, G., 449
Buzzi, S., 288
Byington, D. P., 237, 252, 257

C

Cabib, E., 114, 115, 160
Caccam, J. F., 114
Cadilhac, B., 303
Calavan, E. C., 306, 307, 316
Caldwell, D. E., 403, 412, 433, 434
Caldwell, W. J., 383
Caliguiri, L. A., 336, 337, 339, 342
Callewaert, A., 247
Callis, J. B., 54, 55
Calvin, M., 43
Camerlynck, P., 197
Campbell, A. M., 447, 455
Campbell, A. M. G., 247
Campbell, J. J. R., 73
Campbell, L. L., 167
Campbell, P. N., 69
Campo-Aasen, I., 207
Cannela, C., 94
Cantacuzene, J., 270
Cantor, H. M., 249
Cantwell, G. E., 129
Caplan, S. R., 77, 80
Carbonell, L. M., 104, 105, 392, 396
Carchman, R., 148
Cardiff, R. D., 327, 328
Carere, A., 226, 227, 457
Carlson, K., 456
Carlton, B. C., 225, 226
Carne, H. R., 274
Carosi, G., 207, 208
Carr, M., 270
Carr, N. G., 169, 182, 413
Carreira, L. B., 75
Carrere, L., 275
Carter, R. L., 198, 212
Casciano, S., 223
Case, G. D., 45-48, 51-56
Casman, E. P., 270
Casmer, C. J., 394
Caspary, E. A., 243
Casper, Von R., 303
Caspersson, T. O., 381
Cassuto, E., 450
Castaigne, P., 247
Castorph, H., 73
Catcheside, D. G., 453, 464
Catena, A., 226
Cater, M. S., 226
Cathala, F., 37, 247
Cato, A. Jr., 456
Cavalcanti, U., 207
Cavallini, D., 94
Cawley, T. N., 105
Ceccarini, C., 148, 153-55, 160
Chabbert, Y. A., 266
Chadli, A., 191
Chagas, E., 199
Chain, E. B., 172
Chaing, C., 97
Chaki, F., 115
Chakrabarty, A. M., 222, 224, 226
Chakraborty, J., 195
Chakravorty, M., 356
Chambers, D. A., 359
Chance, B., 46-49, 54
Chandler, J. A., 384

Chandler, R. L., 243
Chaney, T. H., 44, 45, 48-50
Chang, C., 156
Chang, P. L. Y., 104, 112
Chang, W., 271
Chang, Y. Y., 157
Chao, F., 178
Chao, L., 168
Chapman, A. G., 365
Chapman, D. J., 171
Chapman, V. J., 397
Charles, A. M., 91, 93, 94
Chassay, C. E., 129
Chassy, B. M., 157
Chater, K. F., 222, 225
Chattaway, F. W., 105
Chatterjee, A. K., 220, 224
Chatterjee, T., 210
Chen, B., 361, 362
Chen, C., 229
Chen, G. S., 355
Chen, K., 249
Chen, M.-h., 314, 315
Chen, T.-A., 308-10
Cheng, A. F. B., 425
Chenulu, V. V., 307
Chepelev, S. A., 127
Cherepova, N., 208
Chernie, N. E., 396
Chernyshov, M. I., 190
Chestukhin, A. V., 449
Cheung, W. Y., 364
Chiang, M. H., 364
Chittenden, G. J. F., 115
Cho, K. Y., 184
Chojnacki, T., 114
Cholodny, N., 396
Choppin, P. W., 242, 253, 336, 339, 340, 344
Chopra, H., 240, 260
Chou, S. M., 237
Christensen, H. A., 203
Christensen, J. R., 272, 275
Chukhlovin, B. A., 131, 132
Chung, D. W., 289-91
Chytil, F., 364
Ciegler, A., 104
Ciongoli, A. K., 247
Clark, A. J., 448, 449, 464
Clark, C. M., 220
Clark, D. G., 80
Clark, M. A., 148
Clark, M. C., 27, 33
Clark, V. L., 354, 364, 365
Clarke, M. C., 37, 245, 258, 259
Clarke, P. H., 225
Clark-Walker, G. D., 176
Clayton, B. J., 42
Clayton, M. L., 44, 47
Clayton, R. K., 42-44, 50-53, 55
Clecner, B., 270
Cleland, S. V., 143, 154
Clements, I., 176
Cleverdon, R. C., 395
Cloud, P. E. Jr., 429
Clutterbuck, P. W., 110
Clyde, W. A. Jr., 315
Coats, J. H., 222
Cobb, J. M., 133
Cobet, A. B., 133
Coe, E. L., 143, 154
Coelho, M. de V., 196, 198, 206
Coetzee, J. N., 220, 224, 279
Cogdell, R. J., 52, 54
Cohen, A., 395
Cohen, G. H., 331
Cohen, G. N., 73
Cohen, W. S., 46
Cohen-Bazire, G., 172, 184, 393, 394
Colby, C., 36
Colby, E. D., 260
Cole, G. A., 243, 254
Cole, H. A., 289-91, 293
Cole, J. S., 97, 98
Cole, R. M., 306, 308, 309, 313, 383, 395
Coleman, R., 67, 70, 71
Collier, R. J., 289-93
Collins, J. F., 289
Colvin, H. J., 112
Compans, R. W., 327-30, 333, 334, 336-40, 342, 344
Comtois, R. D., 270
Conde, F., 358
Conic, V., 190
Connelly, J. L., 49, 50
Conners, J. N., 98
Connett, R. J., 68
Conti, S. F., 176, 180, 182, 184, 305, 395, 397, 400, 402-5, 407-9, 412-15, 427, 430-36, 438
Converse, R. H., 316
Convit, J., 191, 207
Cooper, F. P., 108
Cooper, G. N., 271
Cooper, T. G., 73
Cooperband, S. R., 293
Cordy, D. R., 260
Corey, R. R., 220
Cori, C. F., 61
Corina, D. L., 105
Cosenza, B., 395
Cosloy, S. D., 449
Cosslett, V. E., 381
Cost, K., 50
Costa, A. S., 303
Costilow, R. N., 172
Coston, M. B., 153
Cote, J. R., 269
Cotter, D. A., 140-42, 154, 155, 163
Cotton, R. G. H., 73
Coura, J. R., 201
Courington, D., 334
Courmes, E., 199
Cousin, M.-T., 303, 312, 316
Couture, J., 431
Coward, J. E., 240
Cowie, D. B., 68, 74
Cowles, P. B., 274
Cowshall, S., 247
Coyne, L., 44, 45
Coyne, S. J., 395
Cozzarelli, N. R., 464
Crabbe, M. J. C., 407
Craig, A. S., 168
Cramer, W. A., 52
Cramp, W. A., 37, 258
Crandall, M. A., 115
Crane, F. L., 53
Crane, R. K., 69
Crawford, I. P., 225, 226
Creaser, E. H., 73
Creemers, J., 207
Crespi, H., 44
Crispeels, C., 289
Crofts, A. R., 52, 54, 55
Cross, P. M., 380
Cross, R. A., 455, 458, 460
Cruden, D. L., 184
Cruickshank, C. N. D., 107, 109
Cruickshank, J. G., 242
Cuadros, C. V., 247, 253
Cunin, R., 225
Curtiss, R. III, 220, 266, 448
Cusanovich, M. A., 45-47, 52, 53
Cuzin, F., 265, 268
Czarnecky, D., 307
Czillag, A., 424

D

Dabbagh, M. A., 190
da Costa, O. R., 201
Da Cruz, F. S., 210
Dahl, R., 356, 358
Dahlberg, D., 152, 159
Dales, S., 339, 343-45
D'Alesandro, P. A., 207, 208
Damsker, B., 269
Danesco, P., 191
Danielli, J. F., 372
Daniels, M. J., 306-8, 314, 315
Dankert, M., 281, 282
Darland, G., 305, 427
Darling, H. M., 35
Darlington, R. W., 342
Darnell, J. E., 327-29
Darpoux, H., 303
Das Gupta, N. N., 195
Datta, A. G., 210
Davern, C. I., 445
Davey, J. F., 421, 422
David, A., 328-31
David, H. L., 269

David, R. E., 312, 318
Davidoff-Abelson, R., 448, 453
Davidson, J. T., 93
Davies, A. J. S., 198, 212
Davies, H. G., 374, 385
Davies, R., 104, 112
Davies, S. L., 421
Davis, R. E., 303, 306-10, 316, 317
Davis, R. H., 67
Dawes, E. A., 178
Dawson, A. M., 257
Day, P. R., 445, 446
Dayan, A. D., 248, 254
Dayan, J., 73
Deacon, T. E., 93
de Alencar, J. E., 199
Deane, L. M., 199
DeBellis, R. H., 36
De Boer, G. F., 240
de Boer, W. E., 179, 184
DeBont, J. A. M., 400, 421
De Borms, S. T., 285
Decker, G. L., 168, 176, 180
de Crombrugghe, B., 356, 359, 360
Dedet, J. P., 191, 192, 205
Dedonder, R., 172, 174
Deeb, S. S., 267, 271
Deering, R. A., 147
De Jimenez, G., 210
De Jong, R. N., 240, 251
Dekker, C. A., 176
de Klerk, H., 45, 53
Delafield, F. P., 174
DeLamerens, S., 253
Delarue, J., 240
Delbruck, M., 267, 276
del Camo, F. F., 358
Delisle, G., 68
Delk, A. S., 176
Demerec, M., 224, 225, 277
Demerec, Z. E., 225
Demis, C., 69
De Monge, E., 203, 210
DeMoss, J. A., 68, 72
DeMoss, R. D., 226, 362
den Dooren de Jong, L. E., 276
Dendy, P. R., 288
Dengler, K., 140
Dennis, E. S., 224
Deracheva, T. I., 197
Derjugina, Z., 422, 430
Dernuet, S., 269
de Serres, F. J., 128
DeSimone, J. A., 80
Des Neves, V. M., 190, 205
Dessel, B. H., 237
Detels, R., 258
DeToma, F. J., 146
Detroy, R. W., 104
Deutscher, M. P., 71, 464
Devauchelle, G., 314
DeVault, D., 46-48, 52
de Vellis, J., 147
Devidé, Z., 396
deWaart, J., 269
Diamond, J. M., 62
Dickerson, R. E., 48
Dickinson, A. G., 243
DIENER, T. O., 23-39; 23-35, 37, 243, 258
Dierksheide, W. C., 171
Dietlein, L. F., 134
Dietschy, J. M., 62
Dietzman, D., 232
Dijkstra, J., 312, 313
Dimler, R. J., 106
Dimmock, N. J., 336
Dimond, R. L., 149
Dimroth, P., 71, 72
Din, G. A., 90, 91
Dincoulesco, M., 194, 195
Dinius, L. L., 288, 289, 292
Dirkx, J., 289
Disney, R. H. L., 200, 201
Dittmar, W., 72
Dixon, F. J., 242, 254
Dobardzic, R., 269, 270
Dobrogosz, W. J., 355, 357
Dobrovol'skaya, T. G., 424, 432
Doermann, A. H., 453, 457
Doi, R. H., 174
Doi, Y., 302, 311, 312, 316
Dollahan, N. R., 205
Dolmatova, A. V., 191
Dolphin, D., 45
Doman, N. G., 405
Donawa, A. L., 97
Doolittle, W. F., 286
Dorner, F., 115
Dottin, R. P., 356
Doudoroff, M., 178, 179
Douglas, H. C., 394, 407, 410, 412, 430-35
Dowding, J. E., 222, 225
Dowell, C. E., 220
Dowler, J., 425
Doy, C. H., 72, 184
Doyle, D., 105
Drabkova, V. G., 429
Drapeau, G. R., 448, 453
Dratz, E. A., 44, 45
Drazin, R., 289, 292
Dressler, D., 265
Drew, E. A., 63, 64
Drewes, L. R., 107, 110, 111, 114
Drews, G., 53, 66, 412
Drobnik, J., 435
Drost-Hansen, W., 62
Drozdova, V. I., 132
Druyan, M. E., 44, 45
Druzhinin, Yu. P., 127
Dubinina, G. A., 422, 428-30
Dubnau, D., 224, 448, 453
Dubois, R. J., 343
Dubois-Dalcq, M., 247
Dubos, R., 65
Dubrovin, V. N., 47
Dubrovsky, Y. A., 197, 198
Duchow, E., 394, 407, 410, 412
Duc-Nguyen, H., 336, 344
Duesberg, P. H., 36
Duffy, P., 258
Dugan, P. R., 91
Dumonde, D C., 198, 204, 211, 212
Duncan, C. L., 174
Duncan, D., 140, 141
Duncan, J. L., 288
Dunlop, W. F., 178
Duong, T., 412, 413, 415, 417
Dupont, G., 306
Dupouy, G., 379, 381, 386
Durr, I. F., 354
Durwald, H., 276
Dus, K., 47-50
Dussoix, D., 267, 271, 275
Duthoit, J.-L., 317, 318
Dutton, P. L., 46-52, 54, 55
Duval-Iflah, Y., 270
Duysens, L. N. M., 43, 45, 55
Dvorak, H. F., 156
Dzhumaev, M. D., 211

E

Eady, R. R., 407
Eanes, E. D., 179
Easterbrook, K. B., 343
Eaton, M., 285
Ebel-Tsipis, J., 447
Eberhard, A., 356
Eberhardt, U., 97
Ebersold, W. T , 125, 126
Ebrey, T. G., 44
Echols, H., 268, 447, 448, 453, 455
Eckroade, R. J., 237
Eddy, A. A., 105
Edgar, R. S., 457, 465
Edmond, C. J., 260
Edwards, G. A., 105
Edwards, M. R., 172, 392, 396, 397
Edwards, P. R., 271, 273, 280
Egan, A. F., 226
Eggerer, H., 72
Ehrenfeld, R. K., 316
Ehring, R., 356, 453, 457
Ehrlich, H. L., 400
Ehrman, L., 318
Eigener, U., 168, 170
Eimhjellen, K. E., 414
Eisen, H., 356
Eisenberg, R., 148

Eisenmann, C., 203
Eiserling, F. A., 125, 126
Ejercito, P. M., 342
Eklund, C. M., 256, 257
Eklund, M. W., 269
Elbein, A. D., 168
El Dadah, A. H., 250
Eldan, M., 69
Eliseev, L. N., 197, 198
Ellar, D., 178
Ellingson, J. S., 147
Ellis, D. S., 207
Ellis, W. L., 122, 127, 132-34
Elorza, M. V., 114
Elseviers, D., 225
Emerson, S., 452, 453, 455, 456, 460, 461, 464
Emerson, S. U., 330
Emeruwa, A. C., 178
Emmer, M., 359, 360
Enge, W., 127
Engel, H., 405
Engel, W. K., 251
Engelhardt, D. L., 31
Enger, M. D., 71
Englesberg, E., 356
Ephrussi-Taylor, H., 448, 453, 456
Epstein, W., 361
Epurean, E., 195
Ercoli, N., 210
Erdos, G. W., 140, 148
Erickson, R. H., 86, 87, 89
Erickson, R. J., 266
Ericson, M. C., 72
Erlandson, R. A., 341, 342
Eron, L., 357
Escobar, M. R., 271
Essenfeld-Yahr, E., 201, 202
Esudie, A., 199
Etges, F. J., 196
Etievant, M., 271
Evangelista, I., 240
Evans, A. H., 453, 457
Evans, D. M. D., 372, 377, 387
Evans, E. L., 172
Evans, M. C. W., 54
Eveleigh, D. E., 106
Every, D., 140
Every, M., 157
Exell, G., 413
Expert, D., 270
Eylar, E. H., 114

F

Facius, R., 127
Faghih, M., 197, 198
Fair, D. S., 210
Faivre-Amiot, A., 316
Falaki, N., 190
Falcone, A. B., 86, 88
Falcone, G., 104, 105
Falken, D., 341, 342
Falkenberg, P., 180
Falkow, S., 220, 224
Fall, L., 365
Fano, U., 277
Fargie, B., 221, 224, 225
Faris, A. A., 237
Farkaš, V., 114, 115
Farkas, W., 93
Farmer, F., 243
Farrell, C. A., 146
Fauré-Fremiet, E., 179
Fauvan, P., 199
Favero, M. S., 122
Federici, G., 94
Feher, G., 43, 44, 50-52, 55
Feiner, L., 457
Feinstone, M., 259
Feldhege, A., 176
Felix, J., 66
Fell, J. W., 396
Felton, R., 45
Fenner, F., 253, 327, 330, 333, 336, 339, 341
Fennessey, P., 281
Feorino, P. M., 248
Ferber, E., 158
Ferber, R. A., 258
Ference, M., 227
Ferguson, H. M., 223
Ferguson, J. K., 122, 131, 132
Fernow, K. H., 35
Ferreira, O. A., 202
Field, E. J., 232, 243, 245, 247
Fields, N. D., 122
Filer, T. H., 316
Filner, P., 353
Filosa, M. F., 140, 157, 158, 160
Filshie, B. K., 327
Finazzi Agrò, A., 94
Fincham, J. R. S., 445, 446
Finnerty, W. R., 184
Fiorillo, P., 193
Firtel, R. A., 145-48, 153, 160
Fischer, H., 158
Fishetti, V. A., 270
Fisher, E., 94
Fisher, W. D., 395
Fitz-James, P. C., 184
Flatgaard, J. E., 72
Flawia, M. M., 158
Fleischhauer, P., 248
Fleischman, D. E., 55
Fleissner, E., 333
Fleming, H., 51-53
Fleming, P. C., 248
Fletcher, D. W., 425
Floch, H., 202
Flory, B., 210
Fobes, W. S., 115
Fogel, S., 446, 455, 457, 458, 460
Folkes, B. F., 68
Foner, A., 192, 195-97
Forattini, O. P., 201, 202
Forget, B. G., 35
Formal, S. B., 220, 271
Forrest, H. S., 414
Foster, B. G., 130
Foster, F., 269
Fowler, C. F., 42, 44-47, 49, 184
Fox, C. H., 64
Fox, L., 130-32
Fox, M. S., 447, 448, 453, 456, 458, 460, 461, 464
Fraenkel, D. G., 355
Fraga de Azevedo, J., 190, 205
Fraiha, H., 202
Fraker, P. J., 42
Francis, A. E., 220
Francis, D., 147, 148
Francki, R. I. B., 35
Francon, M., 374, 375
Franke, J., 147, 151-53
Franklin, B. A., 129
Franklin, N. C., 271
Franklin, R. M., 31
Fraser, D., 276
Frederick, R. J., 316, 317
Freed, J. J., 381
Freeman, N. K., 338
Freeman, P., 464
Freeman, V. J., 269, 284
Freer, S. T., 48
Fregly, A. R., 123
Freitag, J. H., 316
French, W. J., 318
Frenkel, A. W., 45, 53
Frenster, J. H., 36
Freundlich, G., 225
Freundt, E. A., 304, 308
Frey, L., 450, 458
Fridland, A., 75
Fridovich, I., 93
Frieben, W. R., 174
Friedberg, I., 168, 170
Frieden, C., 71
Friedman, D. L., 75
Friedman, E. A., 457, 461
Friedman, R. M., 36, 327, 328
Friedman, S., 431
Friend, E. J., 224
Fritz, I. B., 68
Frobisher, M., 270
Frommhagen, L. H., 338
Frothingham, T. E., 195
Fry, K. E., 457
FUCCILLO, D. A., 231-64; 232, 233, 245, 257
Fuchila, J., 157
Fudl-allah, A. E. A., 306
Fujino, T., 178
Fujitani, H., 36
Fuller, N. A., 271
Fuller, R. C., 42, 44, 47,

53, 182, 184, 413

G

Gabe, D. R., 422, 423, 428, 429, 433
Gábor, M., 226, 445, 456
Gaertner, F. H., 72
Gage, L. P., 144
Gahmberg, C. G., 330
Gajdusek, D. C., 37, 232, 238, 240, 243, 245, 249-52, 255-60
Galbraith, J. C., 147
Gall, L. S., 132
Gallo, M., 355
Gamboa, E., 250
GANDER, J. E., 103-19; 107, 110-13, 115
Gandu, J. E., 259
Gantt, E., 171, 172, 176, 180, 182
Garcia, A. F., 50
Garcia, J. H., 253
Gardashian, A. M., 249
Gardener, P. J., 207
Gardines, A. C., 245
Gardner, I. C., 176
Gardner, M. B., 249
Gardner, M. W., 303
Garmise, L., 277, 278, 285, 288
Garnham, P. C. C., 192, 205, 207
Garon, C., 343, 344
Garren, L. D., 157
Garrick-Silversmith, L., 226
Garrod, D., 144, 153, 160
Gasanzade, G. B., 197, 211
Gasca, E. F., 200
Gascón, S., 111-15
Gatner, E. M. S., 176
Gatts, J. D., 131, 132
Gavard, R., 176
Gazdar, C., 364
Geitler, L., 395, 402
Gelbart, S. M., 220, 269
Gelberg, A. B., 69
Gelderblom, H., 334
Gellert, H., 249
Gellhorn, A., 36
George, R. P., 140-42, 157
Gerenczer, V. F., 433, 437
Gerhard, W., 336
Gerisch, G., 142, 143, 157, 158
Gerna, G., 208
Gerson, K. L., 253, 255
Gestrelius, S., 77-79
Gettner, S., 211
Gezelius, K., 140, 153, 156
Gherna, R. L., 179
Ghiorse, W., 392, 397
Ghosh, D. K., 210
Ghosh, S. K., 303, 307
Giammanco, G., 271
Giannattasio, M., 353
Giannotti, J., 303, 307, 314, 317, 318
Gibbons, J. L., 248
Gibbons, N. E., 385
Gibbons, R. A., 243, 258
Gibbs, C. J., 37
Gibbs, C. J. Jr., 232, 238, 240, 243, 245, 249-52, 255-60
Gibson, F., 73, 226
Gibson, J., 414
Gibson, K., 289
Gielow, L., 356
Giesbrecht, P., 66
Gilbert, W., 265, 361
Gilboa-Garber, N., 356
Gilden, D. H., 243, 254
Giles, N. H., 72
Gill, D. M., 281-83, 285-92
Gill, G. N., 157
Gill, P., 313
Gillaspie, A. G. Jr., 312, 318
Gillette, M. U., 157, 158
Gillissen, G., 220
Gimesi, N., 396, 418
Gingery, R., 447, 448, 453, 455
Gingras, G., 43, 44
Ginsberg, B., 457
Ginsberg, H. S., 132
Ginsburg, A., 71
Giovagnoli, C., 94
Girard, R., 271
Gislason, G., 251
Githens, S., 140, 154
Gladstone, R. M., 248
Glansdorff, N., 225
Glaser, L., 66
Glaser, P., 208
Glasgow, J. E., 115
Glatron, M. F., 172
Glazunova, Z. I., 198
Gleiberman, S. E., 192, 194, 196
Goebel, W. F., 277
Goheen, A. C., 318
Goldberg, N. D., 358
Goldberger, R. F., 226, 227
Goldfine, H., 403, 404, 438
Goldman, R., 77, 78
Goldschmidt, E. P., 226
Goldstein, D. J., 382
Goldstein, G., 330
Goldstein, L., 76
Goldthwaite, C., 224
Goldzimer, E., 269
Golubić, S., 395
Golvan, Y. J., 190-92
Gomersall, M., 313
Gomez-Nunez, J. C., 201, 202
Gonatas, N. K., 240
Gonzales, H. A., 201
Good, R. A., 259
Goodgal, S. H., 447, 456
Goor, R. S., 289, 291
Gordon, J., 358
Gordon, M. A., 392, 397
Gorham, J. R., 252
Gorin, F. A., 69
Gorin, P. A. J., 104-6
Gorini, L., 74
Gorlenko, V. M., 414-17, 429
Gossling, J., 423
Gots, J. S., 355, 356, 364
Gots, R. E., 69
Gottesman, M. E., 356, 358, 361, 362, 448, 453, 455
Gould, G. W., 167
Gould, H. J., 172
Gourlay, R. N., 308, 313
Gourret, J.-P., 312
Goust, J. M., 253, 255
Gouterman, M., 54, 55
Govindjee, 45
Govindjee, R., 45, 54
Graf, J., 68
Graf, T., 334
Granados, R. R., 303, 308-10, 312, 314, 316, 318
Grancini, P., 303
Granett, A. L., 312
Grappel, S. F., 108
Graveson, G. S., 248
Gray, B. H., 42, 44, 171, 172, 184
Gray, T. C., 448, 453, 456
Graziani, M. T., 94
Greany, R., 285, 286, 291, 292
Green, R. H., 122
Greenawalt, J. W., 168, 176, 180
Greenberg, B., 456
Greenblatt, C. L., 208, 211
Greene, A., 226
Greengard, P., 359
Gregg, J. H., 140, 142, 144, 156
Gregoriades, A., 333, 336
Gregory, K. F., 293
Griebel, R. J., 178
Griffith, F., 220
Griffith, J. S., 258
Griffiths, A. H., 255
Grigoryev, Yu. G., 127, 132
Grimley, P. M., 327, 328
Grimsson, H., 240
Grodzicker, T., 356, 357, 361
Groman, N. B., 269, 285, 287, 288
Grootsen, C., 269
Gros, F., 35
Grose, C., 248
Grove, S. N., 392, 397
Grover, W. D., 253
Groves, T., 122
Gryder, J. W., 89, 90
Guay, R., 431

Guazzi, G. C., 240
Gudnadottir, M., 240, 253
Gugliemi, S., 193
Guild, W. R., 456
Guillard, R. R., 400
Guirges, S. Y., 212
Gumpert, J., 426
Gunderman, J. R., 248
Gunders, A. E., 197, 212
Gundersen, W. B., 269
Gunsalus, C. F., 226
Gunsalus, I. C., 222, 224, 226, 355
Guseva, K. A., 419
Gustafson, G. L., 142-45, 148-53, 159, 160, 162
Gutman, A., 284
Gutz, H., 453
Guynn, R. W., 69
György, E., 330

H

Hacking, A. J., 406
Hadden, C. T., 75
Haddock, J. W., 115
Hadlow, W. J., 256, 257
Hadsell, R. M., 42
Hageage, G. J. Jr., 179
Hagen, P. O., 403, 404, 438
Haidu, L., 418
Haig, D. A., 37, 245, 258, 259
Haight, R. D., 195, 207
Hajdu, L., 418, 419, 429
Halff, L., 204
Hall, B. D., 267, 271
Hall, C. A., 224
Hall, H. E., 122
Hall, R. L., 50
Hall, T. A., 383
Hallock, L. L., 395
Halsey, Y., 50, 52-54
Halvorson, H. O., 167
Hamamoto, S. T., 140-42, 163
Hamano, S., 271
Hamer, G., 403, 405
Hames, B. D., 144
Hamilton, I. R., 354, 359, 364
Hamilton, P. B., 355, 357
Hamilton, R., 257
Hamon, C., 312
Hampel, A., 71
Hampton, R. O., 303
Ha-mung, T., 408, 410, 422
Handler, P., 93
Hanert, H., 396, 410
Hanissian, A. S., 253
Hansen, H. J. M., 70
Hanson, R. P., 37, 245
Hanson, R. S., 167
Hanson, W. L., 193
Hapel, A. J., 344
Happold, F. C., 93, 94
Hara, F., 168
Harder, W., 400, 403, 405, 407
Hardigree, A. A., 395
Hargunding, H. C., 251
Hariharasubramanian, V., 26
Harize, M., 269
Harold, F. M., 168, 170
Harold, R. J., 223
Harper, A. A., 286, 289, 291, 292
Harrington, M. G., 105
Harris, H., 288
Harris, P., 289
Harris, W. J., 447
Harrison, D. E. F., 405
Harrison, J. E., 406
Harrison, S., 336
Harrison, S. C., 328, 329
Hart, B. A., 72
Harter, D. H., 36, 240, 242, 253, 344
Hartleb, R., 392, 394, 399, 402
Hartman, N., 461
Hartman, P. E., 226, 227
Hartsough, G. R., 245
Hartwick, J., 435
Harwood, J., 355, 356
Haselkorn, R., 42, 44, 365
Hashimoto, I., 193
Hasin, M., 306
Haslam, R. H. A., 253, 255
Hastings, J. W., 365
Hastings, P. J., 449, 453, 456, 458, 460-64
Hathaway, G., 276
Hauser, R. E., 338
Hausmann, R., 276
Hawirko, R. Z., 178
Haworth, W. N., 110, 111
Hawtrey, A. O., 279
Hayaishi, O., 289-91, 356, 358, 363
Hayes, W., 265
Hayflick, L., 307
Hazen, W., 400
Healey, F. P., 170
Hearle, J. W. S., 380
Heden, C. G., 381
Hegeman, G. D., 225
Hehn, G. V., 408
Heimpel, A. M., 129
Heine, J. W., 330, 337, 342
Heinrich, G., 182
Heisch, R. B., 193
Helgadottir, H., 240
Heller, M., 343
Hellerqvist, C. G., 271
Hemenway, C. L., 122, 127, 128
Hemmes, D. E., 140, 143, 155, 156
Hemming, F. W., 114
Hempfling, W. P., 93, 98, 357
Hendee, E. D., 288, 289
Henney, M. R., 132-34
Henning, U., 72
Henrici, A. T., 392, 400, 402, 415, 418-20, 433
Henriksen, S. D., 220, 269
Henriksson, E., 64
Hensen, A., 425
Hensley, D. E., 106
Henson, J. B., 252
Heppel, L. A., 66, 74, 156
Heptinstall, J., 178
Herbert, B. N., 172
Heremans, J. F., 247
Herman, R., 194, 201, 203-5
Hermier, J., 176
Herndon, R. M., 237, 247, 253, 256, 257
Herriot, R. G., 276
Hersh, L. B., 406, 407
Hershey, A. D., 265, 267, 268, 272, 274, 275
Hertig, M., 203, 208
Hess, B., 70, 71
Hesse, J. E., 361
Heumann, W., 220
Heyneman, D., 193, 194, 205
Heywood, J., 453
Hierholzer, J. C., 113
Higashi, N., 327, 328
Higgins, H., 210
Hill, D. J., 63, 64
Hill, J. E., 90
Hind, G., 45
Hindle, E., 191, 192
Hinze, G., 184
Hirano, A., 249
Hirao, F., 109
Hirata, M., 363
Hirota, Y., 266
Hirs, C. H. W., 171
Hirsch, A., 355, 357
HIRSCH, P., 391-444; 392, 395, 400, 402-5, 407-10, 412, 414-20, 428-38
Hirschberg, E., 148
Hiruki, C., 312, 313
Hirumi, H., 303, 310-15, 318
Hoagland, G. L., 343
Hoar, D. I., 356
Hoare, D. S., 178, 180, 182, 400, 405, 412-14
Hoare, S. L., 413
Hoeks, J., 400, 421
Hoeniger, J. F. M., 176
Hoff, A. J., 44, 55
Hoffmann, B., 396
Hoffmann-Berling, H., 276
Hofman, T., 86
Hofschneider, P. H., 276
Hofsten, B. V., 415
Hogness, D. S., 267
Hohl, H. R., 140-42, 147, 155-57, 163

Hohn, B., 276
Hojiro, O., 207
Holborow, E. J., 383
Holbrook, T. W., 194
Holcomb, W G., 372, 387
Holden, J. H., 107
Holden, M., 341
Holland, J. J., 336
Holliday, R., 445, 446, 449, 452, 453, 455, 456, 458, 460-62
Holloway, B. W., 220-22, 224, 225, 271
Holme, T., 271
Holmes, F. O., 318
Holmes, K. V., 339, 340
Holmes, M. R., 105
Holmes, R. K., 277, 279, 285, 286
Holowczak, J. A., 344
Holt, A. S., 43
Holt, S. C., 167, 182, 184
Homma, M., 339
Hong, J.-S., 356
Honig, G. R., 147
Honigberg, B. M., 194
Honjo, T., 289-91
Hoogstraal, H., 193, 194, 205
Hooks, J. J., 240, 260
Hooper, A. B., 86, 88, 168, 170
Hopkins, D. L., 318
Hopwood, D. A., 220, 222-25
Horecker, B. L., 355
Horibata, K., 285, 288
Horii, Z.-I., 448, 449, 464
Horio, T., 45, 48, 49
Hornabrook, R. W., 238
Horne, R. W., 105, 303
Horneck, G., 127, 129
Horta-Barbosa, L., 232, 233, 245, 247, 252-54, 256, 257
Hortobágyi, T., 419, 420
Horvath, J., 303
Hotchin, J., 122, 126-28, 242, 243
HOTCHKISS, R. D., 445-68; 266, 445, 446, 452-54, 456-61, 464, 465
Houdart, R., 240
Hough, J. S., 113
Hougland, A. E., 428
Houwink, A. L., 179, 184
How, M. J., 109
Howard, A., 91, 98
Howard-Flanders, P., 457
Howe, C., 327, 329
Howell, L. G., 93
Howells, R. E., 207
Hranisavljevic-Jakovljevic, M., 107, 108
Huang, A. S., 330
Huberman, A., 364
Hübscher, G., 70
Huebner, R. J., 259
Huhtanen, D. P., 316
Huiskamp, W. J., 43
Hull, R., 303
Hultin, H. O., 154
Hulyalkar, R. K., 109
Hummeler, K., 332
Hung, P. P., 333
Hunsley, D., 104
Hunter, D. E., 35
Hunter, G. D., 37, 243, 257, 258
Hunter, H. S., 327-29
Huotari, F. I., 112
Hurst, A., 167
Hurst, D. D., 446, 455, 457, 458, 460
Hurwitz, J., 457
Hutchinson, M. A., 226
Hutchinson, M. P., 198, 199, 211, 212

I

Ichihashi, Y., 343, 344
Ide, M., 354, 364, 365
Iglewski, B. H., 286
Igwegbe, E. C. K., 306, 316
Iida, H., 269
Iida, T., 302
Iida, T. T., 316, 317
Iijima, T., 272
Ikeda, H., 266, 268, 275
Ikeda, T., 140, 143
Ikeda, Y., 224
Ilardi, A., 193
Imagawa, D. T., 247
Imai, K., 92, 95
Imaya, M., 115
Imhoff, J. G., 289
Immken, L., 358
Imšenecki, A., 395
Ingram, L. O., 180, 182
Inoue, K., 269
Inoue, T., 184
Inouye, M., 278
Ionesco, H., 269
Irwin, W. E., 115
Isaacson, R. A., 44, 55
Isayev, L. M., 191, 196
Iseki, S., 268, 271, 280
Ishaque, M., 97
Isherwood, J. E., 129
Ishiguro, E. E., 425, 436
Ishihara, H., 287
Ishiie, T., 302, 316
Ishijima, T., 306, 309, 310
Iskierko, J., 289
Islam, M. F., 113
Itabashi, H. H., 233, 240, 251
Ito, J., 226, 276
Ittelson, T. R., 291
Ivanova, S. P., 131, 132
Iwasaki, Y., 247
Iyer, S. S., 220

J

Jabbour, J. T., 253
Jackson, A. O., 35
Jackson, J. B., 48-50, 52, 54, 55
Jackson, J. J., 114
Jackson, J. L. W., 270
Jacob, F., 225, 227, 265, 268, 279
Jacobson, A., 145, 147
Jacobson, J. W., 72
Jacobson, M. K., 75
Jacoby, G. A., 225
Jacquet, M., 358
Jadin, J. M., 207
James, A. T., 337, 338, 404, 414
James, R., 457
Jamieson, J. D., 337
Janeček, J., 365
Janicek, L., 381
Janik, A., 220
Janovy, J., 205, 208, 209
Jarman, T. R., 407
Jastorff, B., 157
Jawad, J., 190
Jeanes, A., 106
Jehli, J., 140, 142
Jenkins, D. W., 123, 124, 128
Jennings, D. H., 69
Jennings, P. A., 221
Jensen, A., 414
Jensen, D. D, 306
Jensen, R. A., 226
Jensen, S. L., 414
Jensen, T. E., 168, 170, 178, 180, 184
Jentoft, N. H., 110, 112
Jessen, O., 270
Joffe, J. S., 91
Johansson, A. C., 76
Johnson, D. E., 392, 402, 415, 418-20, 433
Johnson, E. J., 98
Johnson, E. M., 156
Johnson, H. M., 376
Johnson, J. L., 176
Johnson, K. P., 232, 237, 252, 257, 260
Johnson, M., 335
Johnson, P. H., 122
Johnson, R., 251, 257
Johnson, R. M., 395
Johnson, R. T., 232, 237, 249, 256, 257, 260
Johnson, S. J., 287
Joklik, W. K., 343
Jolchine, G., 44
Jollick, J. D., 270
Jones, D., 219
Jones, E. P., 341
Jones, G. H., 106
Jones, H. E., 403, 404, 431, 434, 435
Jones, L. M., 279

Jones, M. E., 67, 71
Jones, O. T. G., 49, 50, 54
Jones, T. H., 149, 150, 153, 154, 160
Jones, W. D. Jr., 269
Jordan, E., 267
Jost, M., 168
Joy, R. T., 386
Joyce, G., 243
Juhasz, S. E., 220, 269
Jung, P., 114
Juni, E., 220
Jurtshuk, P., 176

K

Kääriäinen, L., 330
Kackell, Y. M., 247
Kaempfer, R. O. R., 358
Kaerner, H. C., 276
Kaffka, A., 405
Kafka, J. A., 142
Kahan, D., 420
Kaiser, A. D., 267
Kakuno, T., 48, 49
Kalckar, H. M., 267
Kalinina, N. A., 449
Kallai, O. B., 48
Kalyakin, V. N., 197, 198
Kamen, M. D., 45-49, 52-54, 179
Kamen, R., 33
Kanagisawa, K., 148
Kandel, J., 289-92
Kanegasaki, S., 280, 281
Kanehisa, T., 36
Kanei, C., 285-87
Kanetsuna, F., 104, 105
Kang, C. Y., 330
Kano, Y., 36
Kaper, J. M., 30, 31
Kapikian, A. F., 259
Kaplan, A. S., 288, 343
Kaplan, G. S., 249
Kaplan, H. S., 272
Kaplan, J. G., 67
Kaplan, S., 42
Kapul'tsevich, Yu. G., 127
Karakhodzhaeva, S., 211
Karlin, A., 77
Karnovsky, M. L., 140, 154
Kartha, K. K., 312
Kashiwagi, K., 268, 271
Kasuga, T., 356
Katagiri, H., 95
Katchalski, E., 76-78
Kates, M., 337, 338
Katkin, S. G., 249
Kato, I., 289, 290
Katz, D., 114
Katz, E., 355
Katz, F. E., 142
Katz, J., 80
Katz, J. J., 44, 45
Katz, M., 245, 256, 257
Kauffmann, F., 280
Kaushik, B. D., 220
Kawakami, M., 276
Kawata, T., 184
Kawerse, T., 248
Ke, B., 44, 45, 48-50
Kedem, O., 77
Keister, D. L., 54
Kelker, N., 285
Kellenberger, G., 267
Keller, E. C. Jr., 125, 126
Keller, J. M., 281, 341, 342
Kellerman, G. M., 335
Kelley, J. M., 330
Kellina, O. I., 197, 198
Kelly, B., 224
Kelly, D. P., 85, 96, 392
Kelly, L., 194
Kelly, R. B., 464
Kemmerer, W. W., 134
Kemmerer, W. W. Jr., 122
Kempner, E. S., 70
Kennedy, R. C., 256, 257
Kennedy, R. S., 184
Kennel, S. J., 46-48, 54
Kenny, F. T., 158
Kenny, G. E., 304
Kenyon, A. J., 259
Kepes, A., 358
Kepes, J. H., 253
Kerdel-Vegas, F., 201, 202
Kernaghan, R. P., 318
Kessler, G., 105, 107
Ketchum, P. A., 89, 90
Kettunen, M. L., 330
Khandelwal, R. L., 354, 359, 364
Khondkarian, O. A., 249
Kida, S., 267, 271
Kidby, D. K., 104, 112
Kidwell, W. R., 75
Kiefer, G., 372, 374, 382, 385
Kieff, E. D., 342
Kiehn, E. O., 336
Kiesow, L., 89, 90, 96, 98
Kiesow, L. A., 89, 97
Kihara, T., 46-49, 51
Kiley, M. P., 331
Kilham, L., 260
KILLICK, K. A., 139-66; 140, 142, 155, 161
Kim, K., 288
Kim, K. S., 174, 287
Kimball, P. C., 32, 36
Kimberlin, R. H., 257
Kimura, H., 109
Kimura, M., 315, 318
King, G. J., 174
King, M. T., 53
Kingma-Boltjes, T. Y., 392, 399, 400, 402, 403, 434, 435
Kinoshita, S., 396
Kirikova, N. N., 405, 420
Kirillova, N. F., 424
Kirkpatrick, C. H., 253
Kirkpatrick, H. C., 318
Kirkwood, S., 112
Kissel, T. R., 80
Kitajima, E. W., 303
Kitani, Y., 453, 456, 464
Kitchen, F. D., 251
Kiyakawa, T., 314, 315
Kjeldgaard, A., 272
Klein, A., 71
Klein, D. T., 220
Klein, M., 314-17, 320
Klein, R. M., 220
Kleinhempel, H., 303, 307, 316, 317
Kleinschmidt, A. K., 30
Klemme, J.-H., 54
Klenk, H. D., 336, 339, 340
Kleppe, K., 113
Kline, B. W., 180, 182
Klingenberg, M., 53
Kloos, W. E., 226
Knaff, D. B., 47
Knight, C. A., 32, 36, 338
Knippers, R., 276
Knittel, M. D., 122
Knull, H. R., 111
Kobayashi, Y., 171
Koch, A. L., 80
Koch, G. L. E., 73
Kocourek, J., 105, 106
Kodairo, K., 248
Kodama, A., 92
Kodicek, E., 338
Köhler, A., 75
Köhler, W., 75
Koj, A., 94
Kojima, K., 168
Kojima-Buddenhagen, E. S., 140, 143, 155, 156
Kok, B., 45
Koller, T., 30-32
Kollmann, A., 316
Komarova, L. V., 197, 198
Kondo, E., 266, 267, 271
Kondo, M., 178
Kondo, S., 128
Kondrat'eva, E. N., 405, 420
Kong, W. Y., 151-53
Konijn, T. M., 140, 366
Kononenko, A. A., 45, 47
Konstantinova, I. V., 121, 132, 134, 135
Kopac, M. J., 73
Kopacka, B., 268, 272
Koprowski, H., 245, 247, 256, 257
Korczynski, M. S., 91
Korinek, J., 146
Korn, E. D., 105, 208
Kornberg, A., 74
Korner, H. K., 176
Korogodin, V. I., 127
Korte, I., 405
Koshelev, B. A., 197, 207, 211

Kotani, S., 178
Kourilsky, P., 35
Kovach, J. S., 226, 227
Kowalski, M., 220
Kozak, L. P., 115
Kozevnikov, P. V., 197
Kozinski, A. W., 457
Kozinski, P. B., 457
Kozlov, V. A., 125
Krakow, J. S., 360
Kralik, O., 314, 316
Krampitz, H. E., 194
Krantz, M. J., 180
Krasil'nikov, N. A., 424
Krass, C. J., 303
Krassner, S. M., 209, 210
Kraut, J., 48
Kravkina, J. M., 422, 429
Krebs, H. A., 69
Kreneva, R. A., 447, 453
Krishnapillai, V., 221
Kriss, A. E., 400
Kristiansen, J., 418, 419
Kropp, K., 122
Krug, W., 374, 375
Kryukova, A. P., 190
Kuchler, R. J., 288
Kühl, L., 26
Kühn, L., 73
Kuhrt, M., 176
Kunisawa, R., 184
Kuntz, I. D., 43
Kuo, J. F., 359
Kuo, S.-C., 113, 114
Kurahashi, K., 267, 282
Kurban, A. K., 207
KURENT, J. E., 231-64
Kurland, C. G., 167
Kurland, L. T., 248, 249
Kurnick, J. T., 289
Kurtzke, J. F., 247
Kusai, A., 47
Kusaka, J., 426
Kushev, V. V., 447, 453
Kushner, S. R., 448
Kusnezov, S. J., 416, 423, 429
Kutuzova, R. S., 408, 410, 416, 422, 429, 430
Kuwano, M., 358
Kwapinski, J. B. G., 425
Kwasniak, J., 157
Kwok, S. C., 87-89, 91

L

LaBelle, J. W., 220
Lacks, S., 448, 453, 454, 456, 460
Lafferty, R. M., 97
Lafleche, D., 306, 318
Lai, S. H., 433
Laine, R., 330
Lainez, N. H., 200
Lainson, R., 192, 195, 198-203, 205
Laishley, E. J., 176
Lalavsky, S. M., 248
Lamb, W. L., 131
Lambert, R., 180
Lampen, J. O., 104, 106, 111-14, 397
Lampert, P. W., 238, 256, 257
Lampidis, T., 274, 285
Lamy, L. H., 194
Lanas, C., 210
Landau, B. R., 69
Landman, O., 276
Landsberger, F. R., 336, 338-40
Lang, D., 31
Lang, D. R., 66
Lang, N. J., 168, 170, 171
Langworthy, T. A., 428
Lanotte, G., 192
Lapis, E., 110, 111
Large, P. J., 405-7
La Riviere, J. W. M., 179, 184
Lariviere, M., 197
Lark, K. B., 75
Larsen, A. E., 252
Lascelles, J., 94
Latarjet, R., 37
Laterre, E. C., 247
Latyshev, N. I., 190
Laudelout, H., 89, 90, 96, 97, 180
Laurent, T. C., 80
Laveran, A., 192
Lavin, G. I., 343
Lavorel, J., 45
Lavrova, M. Y., 197
Layton, D. C., 249
Lawson, D. E. M., 338, 340
Lawson, R. H., 24, 25, 27
Lawton, W. D., 220, 271
Lazaroff, N., 91
Leadbetter, E. R., 167, 182, 184, 431
Leader, R. W., 252
Lebedev, K. A., 131, 134, 135
Lebedeva, E. V., 416
Leblond, C. P., 337
Lecadet, M. M., 172, 174
Leclant, F., 303, 307
Lederberg, E. M., 267, 275
Lederberg, J., 220, 267, 275, 284
Lederberg, S., 267, 271, 275
Lederman, M., 359
Lee, C.-S., 316
Lee, K. C., 142
Lee, S. G., 72
Lee, Y. C., 105
Lees, H., 86, 88-91, 98
Lefort-Tran, M., 172
Lehmann, W., 303, 307, 316, 317
Lehtimaki, E., 195
Leidy, G., 220
Leifson, E., 395, 402
Leigh, J. S., 47, 49-52, 54
Leloir, L. F., 114, 160
Lemberg, R., 85
Le Minor, L., 268, 271
Le Minor, S., 271
Lemma, A., 194
Lenard, J., 336, 338-40
Lennarz, W. J., 114
Lennox, E. S., 220, 288
Lerer, R. J., 248
Lerman, L. S., 456
Lester, R. L., 53
Letters, R., 105
Leuchars, E., 198, 212
Leuchtenberger, C., 382
Levander, O. A., 36
Levin, J. G., 327, 328
Levin, Y., 76
Levine, H. B., 133
Levine, M., 268, 272, 275, 279, 454
Levine, S. A., 249
Levinthal, M., 222, 227
LEVINTHAL, M(ARK), 219-30; 222, 227
Levy, J. A., 271, 275
Lewandowski, L. J., 32, 36
Lewis, D. H., 63, 64
Lewis, D. J., 191
Lewis, M., 240, 260
Lewis, M. J., 114
Lewis, S. M., 413
L'Hospital, M., 306
Li, K., 277, 278
Liang, T., 68
Liddel, G. U., 142, 143
Lidin-Janson, G., 248
Lieb, M., 268, 272, 455, 458, 460
Lieberherr, M., 156
Lieske, H., 396
Liggins, G. L., 226
Lightfoot, H. N., 286
Liivak, M., 269
Lima, G., 307
Limberk, J., 307, 316
Lin, F. H., 242, 259
Lin, M. C., 353
Lin, S.-C., 316
Lindberg, A. A., 271
Lindberg, B., 271
Lindeman, J., 336
Lindstrom, E. S., 413
Ling, K. C., 303
Linger, R., 203
Lingrel, J. B., 144, 146
Lins, Z. C., 199
Lipman, M. P., 343
Lipmann, F., 72, 78, 364
Lippman, E., 114
Lipschultz, C. A., 171, 172
Liras, P., 114
Lis, J. T., 356, 362

Lisbonne, M., 275
Lischer, H. W., 253
Litchfield, W. J., 47-50
Liu, L. J., 317, 318
Liu, P. V., 271
Lizko, N. N., 131-33
Lloyd, K. O., 106, 107
Lloyd-Davies, K. A., 70
Loach, P. A., 42, 43, 50, 52
Lockard, R. E., 144, 146
Lodish, H. F., 145-48
Loening, U. E., 27
Loescher, J. H., 168, 172
Lokhmacheva, P. A., 416, 417, 419
Lomakka, G., 385
Lombardo, G., 307
London, J., 95
Long, B. H., 143
Longlands, M., 147
Loomis, W. F. Jr., 142, 146-49, 153, 156
Lopes, D. A., 44, 52
Lopez, C., 259
Lorenz, P. R., 122, 126-28
Lösche, W., 75
Losick, R., 282
Louarn, J. M., 448, 456
Loutit, J. S., 220-22
Low, B., 448
Lowe, S. K., 318
Lucas, J. J., 114
Luckey, T. D., 131-35
Lüderitz, O., 143, 271, 280, 283
Lue, P. F., 67
Luedemann, G. M., 394, 425, 432, 436
Lukasev, E. P., 47
Lukin, A. A., 123, 125, 127
Lund, P., 69
Lundgren, D. G., 66, 91, 93, 94, 98, 176, 178, 180, 182
Lupasco, G., 194, 195
Luria, S. E., 268, 271-73, 275, 280-82, 285
Lwoff, A., 268, 272, 276, 284
Lynen, F., 71
Lyon, L., 269
Lyric, R. M., 93-95, 98
Lysenko, A. J., 195

M

Maas, W., 285
Maas, W. K., 225
MacAlister, T. J., 176
Macchia, V., 353
Machado, J. O. L., 211
MacKenzie, A. P., 140, 142
Mackey, B. M., 176
Maclean, F. J., 414
MacLeod, C. M., 284
MacLeod, R. A., 66
MacLeod, R. M., 93
Macnab, R., 74
Maddox, I. S., 113
Maeba, P., 355
Maeda, Y., 140, 142
Magasanik, B., 354, 356-58
Mahadevan, P. R., 104, 111
Maier, S., 179
Maillet, P.-L., 312
Maistrello, I., 288
Mäkelä, P. H., 221, 224, 280
Makino, T., 282
Makman, R. S., 354, 363
Malamud, N., 249
Malchow, D., 143, 157
Malkin, R., 47
Malkinson, A. M., 157
Malmgren, B., 381
Mal'tseva, N. N., 425
Mancall, E. L., 237, 240, 252
Mancilla, R., 210
Mandel, H., 431
Mandel, M., 395, 408, 415, 417, 430, 431
Mandels, M., 113
Mandelstam, J., 147
Mandy, W. J., 405
Mangum, J. H., 90
Maniloff, J., 313, 426
Manire, G. P., 426
Mankiewicz, E., 269
Mankowski, Z. T., 115
Manly, K. F., 267, 271
Manson-Bahr, P. E. C., 193, 205, 212
Mansour, N. S., 194
MARAMOROSCH, K., 301-24; 303-18, 320
Marcaud, L., 35
Marchoux, G., 303, 307, 310, 317, 318
Marcovich, H., 272
Mardanyan, S. S., 306
Mardon, D., 104
Margolin, P., 226
Margolis, G., 260
Marinus, M. G., 222
Marion, P. L., 334
Markusen, A. M., 128
Marmur, J., 224
Maroc, J., 53
Marques da Cunha, A., 199
Marrou, J., 310
Marrs, B., 220
Marsh, R. F., 37, 238, 245, 258
Marshall, K. C., 400, 408-10, 433, 434, 436, 437
Marshall, R., 143, 150, 160, 161
Martin, J., 240
Martin, L. C., 379
Martin, R. G., 227
Martinez, A. J., 237
Martinez, A. L., 316
Martinez Ruiz, J. L., 200
Martins, M. M., 313, 316
Maruashvili, G. M., 190
Marucci, A. A., 245
Marunoucki, T., 98
Marvin, D. A., 276
Marzluf, G. A., 112
Masland, W. S., 257
Mason, J. A., 122
Masselin, S., 240
Massey, G. M., 274
Mata, A. D., 200
Matchett, W. H., 68, 72
Matheron, R., 417
Mathewson, J. H., 47, 48
Matney, T. S., 226
Matorin, D. N., 47
Matsuda, M., 285-87
Matsui, C., 314, 315
Matsui, S., 271
Matsumoto, A., 327, 328, 426
Matsumoto, S., 343, 344
Matsumoto, T., 268, 271
Matsumura, T., 327
Matsushiro, A., 267, 271
Matsuyama, T., 280
Mattiasson, B., 77-79
Mattoni, R. H. T., 125, 126
Maurer, R., 226
Mauzerall, D. C., 44, 51
Maximesco, P., 269
Maxwell, E. S., 289, 291
May, W. W., 240, 251
Mayall, B. H., 372, 387
Mayberry, W. R., 428
Mayer, R. J., 70
Mayer, R. M., 115
Maze, R., 276
Mazzotta, M. Y., 98
McAlpine, J. C., 207
McBeath, J. H., 310
McBrien, D. C. H., 74
McCarty, G., 284
McCloy, E., 270, 279, 284
McClure, F. T., 68
McConnell, E., 194, 203, 206
McCoy, J. R., 194
McCoy, R. E., 316
McCray, J. A., 46, 47, 49, 51, 54
McCrea, J. F., 343
McDaniel, L. E., 106
McDuff, C. R., 279
McElroy, J. D., 44, 50, 51, 55
McFadden, B. A., 178
McFall, E., 356
McGeoch, D., 360
McIntosh, A. H., 307-9, 311
McKie, M., 274
McLaren, A. D., 77
McLee, A. G., 434
McLellan, W. L., 106

McMahon, P. C., 220
McMilin, K. D., 461, 464
McMillan, B., 205
McMurrough, I., 115
McQuillan, N. K., 195, 207, 208
McSharry, J. J., 330, 332
Meachum, Z. D., 112
Medina, H., 204
Meikle, V. N. H., 243
Meinke, W., 276
Melo, A., 66
Memmer, R., 285
Mendelsohn, M. L., 372, 387
Mendelson, N. H., 395
Mendershausen, P. B., 105
Mercer, E. H., 140, 184
Merek, E. L., 122
Merker, H.-J., 67
Merrick, J. M., 178
Merritt, H. H., 250
Meselson, M., 446, 447, 452-54, 457-61, 464, 465
Mesghali, A., 196, 197, 205
Mesnil, F., 192
Metchnikoff, M. E., 419
Metzenberg, R. L., 112
Mevius, W. Jr., 399, 400, 402, 405, 434, 435
Meyer, T. E., 47, 48
Meyers, M., 227
Meynell, G. G., 266, 275
Michel, A., 289
Michel, M. F., 269
Mikhaylovskiy, G. P., 131
Milhaud, G., 176
Mill, P. J., 115
Millar, W. N., 395
Miller, H. C., 195
Miller, H. G., 248
Miller, I. R., 128
Miller, J. H., 70, 357
Miller, J. H. M., 285
Miller, J. M., 245
Miller, M. M., 171
Miller, P. A., 286
Miller, R. E., 356
Mills, D. A., 201
Millson, G. C., 37
Minagawa, T., 253
Minson, A. C., 73
Minter, D. M., 193
Minton, N. J., 54
Mitchell, F. J., 122, 127
Mitchell, J. L., 131
Mitchell, M., 168
Mitchell, M. B., 446
Mitchell, P., 54, 97
Mitchell, R., 396, 400, 429, 431
Mitchell, R. H., 70
Mitchell, W. M., 146
Mitruka, B. M., 172
Mitsuhashi, S., 266, 267, 271
Miura-Santo, L. Y., 140-42, 155, 163
Miyake, T., 224
Miyazaki, T., 111
Mizrahi, L., 356
Mizutani, A., 67
Mizutani, S., 334, 344
Moehring, J. M., 288
Moehring, T. J., 288
Moll, G., 395, 426, 432, 436
Mollenhauer, H. H., 318
Mollenstedt, G., 376
Molnar, D. M., 271
Monard, D., 364, 365
Monier, C., 289
Monjan, A. A., 243, 254
Monnerville, A., 199
Monod, J., 225, 354, 356
Montagnier, L., 36
Montgomery, P. O'B., 372, 377, 382
Montiglio, B., 195
Montilio, B., 197
Montillo, B., 211
Moog, F., 156
Moolten, F. L., 293
Moon, H. M., 289
Moor, H., 112
Moore, D. H., 337
Moore, L., 447, 448, 453, 455
Moore, R. L., 400, 403, 408, 410, 430-36, 438
Mora, P. T., 335
Morales, M. C., 200
Moreau, J. P., 316
Moreno, R. E., 104
Morgan, C., 240, 327, 328, 336, 337, 341, 342
Mori, T., 92, 98
Moriarty, D. J. W., 92, 95, 97
Morita, S., 45, 46, 404, 413
Morowitz, H. J., 312, 426
Morris, B. C., 220
Morris, J. G., 176, 178
Morris, J. H., 107
Morris, T. J., 28-30, 34
Morse, D. E., 285
Morse, D. S., 48, 55
Morse, I. U., 269, 284
Morse, M. L., 220, 267, 356, 358
Mortensen, J. A., 318
Mortimer, R. K., 446, 457
Morvan, C., 307
Mosbach, E. H., 343-45
MOSBACH, K., 61-83; 64, 65, 76-79
Moscovic, E. A., 207
Moses, V., 61, 73, 74
Mosevitsky, M., 458
Mosig, G., 445, 453, 457, 464
Moskovskij, S. D., 198
Moskowitz, E., 44, 52
Moss, B., 343, 344
Moss, L. H., 342
Most, H., 195
Mould, D. L., 257
Moulias, R. L., 253, 255
Mountcastle, W. E., 339
Mowbray, J., 74
Moyer, J. E., 131
Muel, B., 37
Mueller, J. H., 287
Mueller, K., 74
Mühlethaler, K., 336
Mühlpfordt, H., 194
Mukherjee, A. M., 195, 211
Mulder, D. M., 249
Müller, D., 247
Müller, E., 157
Müller, H. J., 303
Müller, H. M., 303, 307
Müller-Hill, B., 361
Mumford, F., 203
Munday, K. A., 105
Munder, P. G., 158
Muniz, J., 204
Murata, N., 46
Murayama, D., 316
Murchelano, R., 395
Murphy, J. R., 285
Murray, N. E., 456
Murray, R. G. E., 179, 180, 430-35

N

Nadim, A., 196-98, 205
Nadler, K. D., 47
Nadzhafov, A. Y., 197, 211
Naficy, A., 205
Nagaishi, H., 448
Nagatomo, Y., 327, 328
Nagele, B., 157
Naggan, L., 197
Nahmias, A. J., 341
Nairn, R. C., 383
Naito, Y., 156
Nakagawa, T., 268, 273, 280
Nakanishi, S., 361, 362
Nakata, H. M., 178
Nakazawa, T., 356, 358
Namsaraev, B. B., 410, 420
Naquira, C., 210
Narayan, O., 237, 251, 256, 257
Nariani, T. K., 316
Narong, H. K., 247
Nason, A., 86-91, 96
Nasser, D. S., 226
Nasu, S., 302
Nathanson, N., 243, 250, 254
Natoli, D., 271
Naumann, E., 408
Naumov, L. S., 449

Näveke, R., 405
Naylor, H. B., 397
Nealson, K. H., 356
Neeman, Z., 306
Nefedov, Yu. G., 131, 132, 134, 135
Nelson, T. E., 112
Neronov, V. M., 197, 198
Nery-Guimarães, F., 201
Nesom, M. G., 142, 144
Nester, E., 226
Netrusov, A. I., 405, 420
Neumann, N. P., 111
Newell, P. C., 140, 147, 152
Newton, R. P., 353
Ngo, E., 48
Nicholas, D. J. D., 85-89, 92, 95-98
Nichols, B. W., 404, 414
Nickerson, A. W., 140
Nickerson, W. J., 104, 105, 107
Nicoli, R. M., 192
Nicoll, J. M., 410
Nicolle, C., 192
Nicolle, P., 271
Nicolson, G. L., 179, 349
Nielsen, L. D., 364
Niemeyer, R., 168, 170
Nii, S., 341, 342
Nikaido, H., 280, 283
Nikitin, D. J., 400, 415-17, 419, 423, 426
Nikoforova, E. N., 131
Nishikawa, K., 48, 49
Nishimura, M., 49, 53-55
Nishizuka, Y., 289-91
Nissley, S. P., 356, 358, 361
Nöel, H., 44
Nomarski, G., 375
Nomura, M., 167
Nora, D. M., 316
Nordin, J. H., 113
Norris, F. H., 248
Norris, J. R., 44, 45, 172, 174
Northcote, D. H., 105, 396
Notani, N. K., 447, 456
Nouri, L., 190
Novick, R. P., 221
Nozaki, M., 54
Nozhevnikova, A. N., 424
Nozu, Y., 461, 464
Nu, G. V., 198
Nugent, N. A., 42, 44, 47, 184
Nurse, P., 68
Ny, G., 197, 198
Nyland, G., 316, 318

O

Oaks, A., 61, 140, 154
Oatley, C. W., 380
Obara, T., 334
Öberg, B., 33
O'Brien, M. J., 34
O'Day, D. H., 140, 154
Odds, F. C., 105, 113
O'Dea, R. F., 358
Officer, J. E., 249
Ogg, J. E., 271
Ogul, E., 248
Ohe, K., 35
Ohuchi, M., 339
Oishi, M., 449
Oka, T., 396
Okabayashi, T., 354, 365
Okabe, K., 53
Okamoto, K., 267, 271
Okamura, M. Y., 43, 44, 50, 52
Okazaki, H., 247
Okazaki, R., 451
Okazaki, T., 451
O'Kelley, J. C., 89, 90, 96
Okuzumi, M., 95
Olah, J., 418, 419, 429
Oldstone, M. B. A., 242, 254
Olive, L. S., 453, 456, 464
Oliveira, B. S. Jr., 307
Olson, J. M., 41-48, 413
Omar, A., 196
Ono, H., 148
Oprisan, A., 269
Ordal, E. J., 176
Orlob, G. B., 127, 128
Orpin, C. G., 168
Ortigoza, R. O., 168, 170
Orton, W. L., 104, 113
Osborn, M. J., 280
Osburn, B. I., 260
Osler, T., 303
Osnos, M., 148
Ossowski, L., 335
Ostroumov, P. B., 131, 132
O'Sullivan, A., 224
Otero, R. B., 220
Otsuji, N., 272
Otsuka, K., 307
Ott, K. J., 193
Oujezdsky, K. B., 392, 397
Oxborrow, G. S., 122
Oyama, V. I., 122
Ozeki, H., 266

P

Packchanian, A., 194
Packer, L., 77
Padawer, J., 375
Padgett, B. L., 237, 238, 258
Padgett, G. A., 252
Padilla, H. C., 200
Paerl, H. W., 400
Paigen, K., 354
Palade, G. E., 337
Palamarczyk, G., 114
Paliwal, Y. C., 312
Pallas, P., 191
Pálsson, P. A., 240, 247, 251, 253, 256, 257
Pampiglione, G., 255
Pan, I. C., 245
Pankratz, H. S., 180, 184, 395, 415
Pannbacker, R. G., 148, 157
Pappenheimer, A. M. Jr., 268, 285-87, 289-92
Paraense, L. W., 204
Parfenov, G. P., 123, 125, 127
Parinkina, O. M., 408, 410, 423
Park, C. E., 404, 413, 414, 438
Park, W. H., 274, 285
Parker, C. W., 293
Parker, J. A., 247, 253
Parkes, J. H., 48
Parma, D. H., 453, 457
Parry, H. B., 251
Parson, E. I., 287
PARSON, W. W., 41-59; 43-56
Parsons, D. F., 376
Pastan, I., 354, 356-62, 364
Paszewski, A., 446, 454, 457-60, 464
Pate, J. L., 176, 178
Patel, R. N., 405
Patrick, J. M., 357
Pattee, P. A., 226
Pattison, I. H., 243, 247
Pattoli, D. G. B., 202
Patton, S., 329, 334, 343
Paul, R. J., 66
Pavlasová, E., 67
Pavoni, M., 418
Paxton, J., 336, 338, 339
Payne, F. E., 233, 254
Payne, J. I., 385
Pazur, J. H., 104, 111, 113
Pearce, L. E., 220, 222
Pearse, A. G. E., 373
Pearson, M. L., 356
Peat, S., 105
Pecht, M., 76
Peck, H. D. Jr., 85, 90, 91, 93, 94, 96-98
Peel, D., 405, 406
Peeters, T., 96
Pelc, S., 257
Pemberton, J. H., 221, 222, 224
Penman, S., 36
Penney, J. B., 237, 256, 257
Pennington, D., 414
Pepper, R. E., 172
Pereira, A., 307
Perfil'ev, B. V., 400, 422,

423, 428, 429, 433
Périer, O., 257
Perlin, A. S., 105
Perlman, E., 277
Perlman, R. L., 354, 356-61, 364
Perry, M. B., 108, 109
Péry, R., 287
Peterkofsky, A., 364
Peters, G. A., 44
Peterson, E. A., 316
Peterson, J. A., 167
Peterson, J. E., 174, 402, 426
Peterson, L. C., 35
Peterson, W. D., 383
Petriščeva, P. A., 197, 198
Petrishcheva, P., 190, 191, 197
Petrov, R. V., 131, 132, 134, 135
Petrovic, Z., 190
Petru, E., 307
Petursson, G., 253
Pfefferkorn, E. R., 327-29
Pfennig, N., 184, 392-94, 412, 415, 416, 431, 434
Pfister, R. M., 171, 178
Phaff, H. J., 104
Pham, T. D., 207
Phang, J. M., 227
Pheinwald, J. G., 222
Philipson, K. D., 41-44
Phillips, A. W., 104
Phillips, K. C., 420, 421
Philpott, D. E., 178
Philpott, G. W., 293
Piechowska, M., 447
Pifano, C. F., 199
Pignattelli, P., 307
Piller, H., 387
Pinevich, T. G., 425
Pinsky, M. J., 413
Pittard, J., 457
Pittsley, J. E., 106
Plaisted, R. L., 35
Plavsic-Banjac, B., 317, 318
Ploaie, P. G., 303, 307, 314, 317, 318
Plummer, G., 269
Pogell, B. M., 362
Poindexter, J. S., 395
Pollard, E., 70
Pollard, E. C., 168
Pollister, A. W., 372, 382
Polsinelli, M., 220
Pong, S. S., 147, 153
Pongratz, E., 400, 407, 433
Ponirovsky, E. N., 191
Pontefract, R. D., 396
Pontremoli, S., 355
Poorman, A. E., 208
Pop, A., 269
Pope, C. G., 287
Pope, L. M., 176, 178, 180
Popkin, T. J., 306, 308, 309, 313
Popova, L. M., 249
Popovic, D., 191
Porter, D. C., 252
Portier, M. M., 35
Poskanzer, D. C., 249
Poste, G., 339, 340
Postma, P. W., 356
Potorac, E., 269
Potthoff, H., 410
Poul, J., 191
Pouphile, M., 172
Povalishina, T. P., 190
Powers, M., 357
Powls, R., 53
Poysky, F. T., 269
Pramer, D., 87
Prestayko, A. W., 36
Preston, J. F., 110, 111
Preston, K., 372, 387
Preston, P. M., 198, 211, 212
Preuss, A., 276
Prevec, L., 330
Prewitt, J. M. S., 372, 387
Price, B., 46-49, 54
Price, D., 251, 257
Price, W. H., 250
Priess, J., 168
Prince, A. E., 131, 132
Prince, A. M., 259
Prince, R. C., 54
Prineas, J., 247
Pringle, G., 196
Pritchard, R. H., 456, 462, 465
Prival, M. J., 356
Proctor, H. M., 174
Profeta, A., 195
Prokhorov, V. Ya., 131-33
Prozorov, A. A., 449
Prudhomme, R. O., 289
Prusiner, S., 356
Ptashne, M., 275
Puleo, J. R., 122
Purcell, R., 307
Purcell, R. H., 259

Q

Quadling, C., 403, 432
Quadri, S. M. H., 413
Quayle, J. R., 403, 405-7
Queener, S. W., 226
Quenum, C., 197
QUIGLEY, J. P., 325-51; 333-35
Quilici, M., 197
Quiot, J.-B., 310

R

Rabello, E. X., 202
Rabinowitz, M., 147
Racker, E., 158
Radding, C. M., 267, 271, 445, 450, 452, 454, 457-61, 464, 465
Raeburn, S., 289
Rahim, G. A. F., 197, 198, 211
Rahim, G. F., 212
Raistrick, H. K., 110, 111
Rall, T. W., 353
Ramakrishnan, T., 225
Ramirez, J., 55
Ramirez, J. M., 358
Ramkova, N. V., 131
Ranby, B. G., 140
Ranque, P., 197
Rao, P. R., 334
Rao, P. S., 316
Rao, R. N., 275
Raper, K. B., 140, 142, 148, 154, 155
Rapp, F., 233, 252, 257
Rathsack-Künzenbach, R., 395
Ratzkin, B., 225
Raugi, G. J., 68
Raychaudhuri, S. P., 303, 307, 316
Raymer, W. B., 24, 25, 27, 31, 34, 35
Raynaud, M., 287, 289
Razin, S., 306, 426
Read, S. E., 270
Redfearn, E., 53
Redman, W., 220
Reed, D. W., 43-45, 49-52
Reed, L. J., 72
Reed, S. M., 269
Reel, J. R., 158
Rees, M. K., 86-89
Reese, E. T., 113
Reeve, J. N., 395
Reeve, P., 340
Refatti, E., 303
Rehacek, J., 327
Reich, E., 335
Reich, P. R., 35
Reichenbach, H., 176, 184
Reidel, V., 157
Reinert, D. H., 253, 255
Reiness, G., 360
Reiss-Husson, F., 44
Reissig, J. L., 115
Remsen, C. C., 178, 179, 182
Renkonen, O., 330
Renshaw, E., 435
Rensing, U., 35
Renwick, C. C., 243
Reshetova, I. S., 424
Reusch, V. M. Jr., 66
Reuser, A. J. J., 356
Reynolds, O. E., 125
Rezai, H., 211
Reznikoff, W. S., 357
Rheinheimer, G., 395, 400 402, 403, 405, 408, 410, 418, 419, 434
Rhodes, F. A., 250
Ribbons, D. W., 178, 406

Ribier, J., 174
Richards, W. P. C., 260
Richardson, D. H. S., 63-65
Richardson, E. P. Jr., 237, 240, 252
Richmond, M. H., 222
Richter, G., 168, 170
Rick, P. D., 107, 110-12
RICKENBERG, H. V., 353-69; 363-65
Riely, P. E., 131, 132
Rienitz, J., 374, 375
Rietschel-Berst, M., 110, 112, 113
RIFKIN, D. B., 325-51; 333-36
Riggs, A. D., 360
Righelato, R. C., 105
Rigler, R., 373
Rigopoulos, N., 53
Rioux, J. Z., 190-92
Rippon, J. E., 220, 270
Risse, H. J., 69
Ritchie, G. A. F., 86-89
Ritenberg, S. C., 95, 174
Rittenhouse, H. G., 178
Rivero, N., 203
Rivers, T. M., 343
Rizet, G., 446
Roane, J. A., 253
Robards, A. W., 178
Robbins, P. W., 281-83, 335
Robenkranz, H. S., 242
Roberts, D. S., 394
Robertson, J., 313
Robinow, C. F., 172
Robinson, H. L., 333
Robinson, W. S., 333
Robison, G. A., 355, 366
Robson, H. N., 250
Robson, R. L., 178
Robson, R. M., 178
Rode, L. J., 174
Rodriquez, J., 104
Rodwell, A. W., 174, 402, 426
Rodwell, E. S., 174, 426
Roeser, J., 222
Rogatina, L. N., 131
Roger, M., 448
Rogers, H. J., 66
Rogers, N., 245, 252, 260
Rognstad, R., 80
Rogoff, M. H., 174
Rohrer, E., 396
Rohrs, L. C., 193, 205
Roizman, B., 337, 341, 342
Romano, A. H., 104
Romanova, A. K., 405
Romanova, E. A., 127
Romero, E., 208
Romero, J., 35
Romero, M. J., 199
Romig, W. R., 125, 126
Rondanelli, E. G., 207, 208
Roos, R., 232
Rorke, L. B., 257
Roscoe, D. H., 276
Rose, H. M., 242, 327, 328, 336, 341, 423
Rose, J. A., 35
Roseman, S., 114
Rosen, O. M., 354, 355, 357
Rosen, S. D., 142
Rosenbaum, R. A., 249
Rosenberg, B., 435
Rosenberg, M. D., 80
Rosenberg, S., 225
Rosenberger, R. F., 114
Rosenblum, E. D., 220, 270
Rosenblum, E. N., 343, 344
Rosendal, K., 270
Rosenthal, A., 113, 172
Rosenthal, R. S., 396
Roskoski, R. Jr., 72
Rosner, J. L., 356
Rosness, P. A., 140, 150, 153, 155, 159, 160
Ross, A. J., 97
Ross, H., 221
Ross, K. F. A., 374, 375, 385
Ross, R., 189
Rossignol, J. L., 446
Rossomando, E. F., 145, 150, 153, 154, 158
Rost, F. W. D., 373
Roth, C. W., 98
Roth, R., 140, 147, 153-55, 160, 161
Rothblat, G. H., 332
Rothman-Denes, L. B., 361, 365
Rothstein, A., 69
Rott, R., 336
Rottem, S., 306
Rouiller, C., 179
Rountree, P. M., 270
Rousseau, M., 176, 270
Rowe, A. J., 140, 141
Rowe, W. P., 242
Roy, A. B., 85, 95
Rubin, A. B., 47
Rubin, L. B., 47
Rubinow, S. I., 75
Ruch, F., 375
Rudbach, J. A., 111
Rudzinska, M. A., 207, 208, 210
Ruegg, E. F., 312
Ruis, H., 68
Ruiz, C. B., 200
Rupp, W. D., 457
Ruschke, I., 75
Russell, P. K., 327, 328
Russell, W. C., 341
Russi, S., 226, 227
Rutherford, C. L., 140
Ryan, A., 272
Ryvarden, L., 414

S

Saboor, A., 196
Sachs, I. B., 140, 142
Sadler, M. H., 98
Sadowski, P., 457
Saelinger, C. B., 289
Safranski, M. J., 106
Safyanova, V., 190, 191, 197
Safyanova, V. M., 197, 198, 207, 211
Saglio, P., 305, 306, 311, 318
Sagman, D. L., 248
Saito, H., 224, 269
Sakabe, K., 451
Sakaguchi, O., 109, 111
Sakai, T., 268, 280
Sakai, Y., 140
Saksonov, P. P., 125
Salem, A. R., 406
Salemme, F. R., 48
Sallee, V. L., 62
Samagh, B. S., 293
Samso, A., 194
Samsonoff, W., 305, 427
Samuilov, V. D., 45, 55
Sand, G., 225
Sanders, H. K., 89, 90
Sanders, R., 360
Sanderson, K. E., 221, 224
Sandhu, G. R., 169, 413
Sandritter, W., 372, 374, 382, 385
Sänger, H. L., 24, 26-28, 34, 35
Sankaran, L., 362
Sano, M., 36
Santo, L. Y., 174
Sanwal, B. D., 355, 357
Sanyal, A. B., 207
Sanzhieva, E. U., 423
Sargent, D., 140, 142, 143, 150, 160
Sasaki, I., 224
Sassine, J., 307
Sati, M. H., 194
Sato, K., 267, 271
Sauer, K., 41-45
Saunders, J. F., 125
Saunders, R. E., 66, 180, 182
Saunders, V. A., 49, 50, 54
Savel'eva, N. D., 424
Savin, Z., 190
Saxena, J., 97, 98
Sayhoun, N., 354
Sayles, V. B. Jr., 172
Scavizzi, M. R., 266
Schaechter, M., 287
Schaeffer, F. W., 196
Schafer, D., 425
Schegg, E., 418
Scheglova, G. V., 131
Scheid, A., 339
Scher, M., 114

Schiller, E. L., 194
Schimke, R. T., 151
Schito, G. C., 365
Schjeide, O. A., 147
Schlegel, H. G., 97
Schleif, R., 356, 362
Schlesinger, H. R., 327, 328, 332
Schlesinger, M. J., 327, 328
Schlesinger, R. W., 327
Schlesinger, S., 327, 328
Schlessinger, D., 358
Schliewen, W., 453, 457
Schlom, J., 36
Schmidt, E.L., 404, 438
Schmidt, G. L., 45, 179
Schmidt, J. M., 392, 433
Schmidt, K., 414
Schnaitman, C. A., 91, 330, 331
Schnaitman, T. A., 330
Schneider, A. B., 360
Schneider, C. R., 203, 208
Schneider, H., 220, 224
Schneider, I. R., 30, 33, 37
Schnur, L. F., 211
Schockov, N. F., 197
Schoenhoff, R. L., 97
Schrenk, W. J., 285
Schuhmann, E., 426
Schuinke, R. N., 253
Schultz, J., 65
Schulz, E., 400, 416, 417, 419, 421
Schulz, G., 374, 375
Schulze, I. T., 336
Schumacher, G., 247
Schwager, M., 129
Schwartz, D., 345, 359
Schwartz, E. F., 32
Schwartz, J., 341
Schwartz, R. J., 147
Schwarz, H., 157
Schwarz, R. E., 316
Schweisfurth, R., 408, 410
Schweizer, E., 73
Schwenker, V., 43
Scolnick, E., 242, 259
Scott, G. D., 64
Scott, J. R., 272, 275
Scriba, M., 115
Segel, I. H., 355
Sehgal, S. N., 385
Seibert, M., 46, 47, 52
Sekiguchi, M., 272
Sekura, D. L., 42
Sélégny, E., 77
Sell, K. W., 252, 255
Semancik, J. S., 24, 25, 27-30, 33, 34
Sen Gupta, P. C., 193, 195, 207, 208, 211
Sentandreu, R., 105, 114, 396
Septier, A., 378
Sercarz, E. E., 74
Serebryakov, V. A., 198, 211
Sermonti, G., 222, 224, 226, 457
Sery, V., 196
Setlow, P., 354
Seto, J. T., 336
SEVER, J. L., 231-64; 232, 233, 245, 247, 251, 253, 257
Sewell, D. L., 90, 96
Sewerin, S. A., 415
Seyedi-Rashti, M. A., 196, 197, 205
Sfaello, Z., 247
Shaffer, B. M., 140
Shafia, F. M., 90
Shah, K. V., 237
Shah, R. G., 400
Shaham, M., 222
Shapiro, D., 327, 328
Shapiro, J., 168
Shapiro, L., 354, 355, 357
Sharma, K. M., 253
Sharp, P. B., 74
Shaw, D. C., 73
Shaw, J. J., 192, 195, 198-203, 210
Shaw, W. N., 69
Shaw, W. V., 356
Shchapova, L. N., 408, 410, 422
Shearer, G. B., 35
Sheehan, M. C., 330
Shelton, J. B., 97
Shelton, W., 123
Shemyakin, M. F., 449
Sherman, L. A., 46
Shikata, E., 303, 309, 312, 316
Shilov, V., 131, 133
Shilov, V. M., 131-35
Shiner, L. S., 356
Shinkareva, M. M., 130-34
Shipkey, F. H., 341, 342
Shiraki, H., 249
Shishlyaeva-Matova, Z. S., 197, 198
SHIVELY, J. M., 167-87; 66, 168, 176, 180, 182
Shizuta, Y., 356, 358
Shoaf, W. G., 71
Shorenstein, D., 131, 132
Shug, A. L., 86, 88
Shumway, L. K., 178
Shvinka, Y. E., 47
Sicard, A. M., 448, 456
Sicko, L. M., 170, 178
Siegel, A., 35
Siegel, B. Z., 418
Siegel, P. J., 287
Siegel, S. M., 418
Siegelman, H. W., 171
Siegert, R., 341, 342
Siekevitz, P., 336
Sierra, J. M., 114
Sigal, N., 451-53, 457-61, 464
Signer, E. R., 267, 268, 271
Sigurdsson, B., 232, 240, 242
Sikes, S., 226
Sikora, E., 242
Silman, I. H., 77
Silver, M., 91, 94, 431
Silver, S. M., 147
Silverman, M. P., 122
Silverstein, A. M., 251, 257
Silverstein, S. J., 75
Silverstone, A. E., 357
Simmonds, R. C., 129
Simoes Barbosa, F., 201
Simon, M., 358
Simon, R. D., 171
Simonart, P. C., 96
Simonovitch, L., 272, 343, 344
Simons, K., 330
Simpson, D. L., 111, 142
Simpson, J. R., 89
Simpson, L., 208, 210, 211
Simpson, R. W., 338
Sims, A. P., 68
Sims, E. A. H., 69
Singer, J., 356
Singer, R. A., 285-87
Singer, S. J., 349
Singh, M., 72
Singh, R. P., 24, 25, 27, 33
Sinha, R. C., 312, 316
Sinsheimer, R. L., 453, 457
Siracusano, A., 227
Skerman, V. B. D., 184, 392
Skowronski, B. S., 307, 309, 311
Skuja, H., 402, 418, 429
Slater, J. S., 257
Sletten, K., 171
Slodki, M. E., 106
Slooten, L., 44, 50
Smadel, J. E., 343
Smando, R., 355, 357
Smillie, R. M., 53, 413
Smith, A. J., 94, 178, 180
Smith, C. A., 269
Smith, D. B., 128
Smith, D. C., 63, 64
Smith, D. H., 355, 356
Smith, D. R., 27, 28, 30, 33, 34, 37
Smith, F., 112
Smith, F. H., 382, 385
Smith, G., 110
Smith, G. D., 125
Smith, G. R., 356
Smith, H. O., 454, 457, 461
Smith, I., 224, 448, 453
Smith, J. E., 147
Smith, L., 55

Smith, P. F., 428
Smith, P. M., 318
Smith, S. H., 316
Smith, W. R., 47-50
Smith, Z., 178
Sneath, P. H. A., 219
Snyder, R. M., 330, 331
Sobell, H. M., 445, 452, 456, 458, 460, 463
Sofios, M., 133
Sogo, J. M., 30-32
Sokol, F., 330
Sokolov, A. A., 424, 432
Soll, L., 355, 364
Solomon, E. P., 156
Solomon, L. R., 356
Solotorovsky, M., 288
Sols, A., 69
Somerville, H. J., 174
Sommer, A., 114
Sonea, S., 269, 270
Sonenshein, A. L., 271, 276
Southgate, B. A., 193, 198, 205, 212
Spaar, D., 307, 316, 317
Spada-Sermonti, I., 223
Sparrow, J. T., 380
Spatz, H. C., 453
Spear, P. H., 341, 342
Spearman, T. N., 359
Spelsberg, T. C., 146
Spencer, J. F. T., 104-6
Sperl, G. T., 400
Spiegelman, H., 36
Spitz, E., 363
Spizizen, J., 129, 131, 220, 276
Spors, S., 67
Spranson, D. B., 73
Spring, S. B., 341, 342
Sprovieri, G., 207
SRERE, P. A., 61-83; 70, 72, 78
Staack, K., 356
Stacey, M., 110, 111
Stadie, W. C., 69
Stadler, D. R., 454, 456, 458, 460, 464
Stadtman, E. R., 71
Stahl, F. W., 454, 456, 458, 460, 461, 464
Stahl, M. M., 461, 464
Staley, J. T., 400, 415-17, 419, 431, 432, 434, 436, 437
Stamp, J. T., 243
Stanier, R. Y., 184, 225
Stanisich, V. A., 221, 222
Stanton, J. B., 248
Staron, T., 316
Starr, M. P., 184, 220, 224, 392, 414, 432, 434
Staub, A. M., 268, 271, 272, 280, 283
Stauber, L. A., 193, 194
Steele, J. C., 248
Steenis, P. J., 400
Steere, R. L., 306, 309, 310, 316
Stefanov, S. B., 400, 426
Steinberg, C. M., 457, 465
Steindl, D. R. L., 318
Steiner, L. A., 43, 44, 52
Stemer, A., 42
Stern, R., 36
Sterner, G., 248
Sternglanz, R., 278
Sternlicht, E., 114
Stevens, A., 122
Stevenson, J. L., 396
Stewart, C., 72
Stewart, J. M., 210
Stewart, T. S., 105
Steyn-Parve, E. P., 113
Stinebring, W. R., 288
Stockdale, H., 178
Stocker, B. A. D., 268, 272, 280, 285
Stokes, M. I., 254
Stollar, B. D., 32, 33, 36
Stollar, V., 36, 327, 328
Stone, L. B., 242, 259
Story, G. E., 306
Stout, R., 400
Straat, P. A., 90
Straley, S. C., 44, 50
Strangways-Dixon, J., 200, 205
Strannegård, O., 248
Strasdine, G. A., 176, 178
Straub, O. C., 251
Strauss, B., 276
Strauss, J. H., 327, 328
Strauss, N., 288, 289, 448
Strauss, P. R., 211
Stravinskaya, E. A., 429
Strelkova, M. V., 197
Strong, D. M., 252, 255
Studier, F. W., 268, 278
Stulberg, C. S., 383
Stumeyer, D. H., 87
Stutzer, A., 392, 394, 399, 402
Stuy, J. H., 456
Subramanian, K. N., 67
Sueoka, N., 224
Suessenguth, K., 396
Sugimoto, K., 451
Sugimura, T., 53
Sugino, A., 451
Sugiura, M., 302
Sugiyama, H., 176, 178
Suleimanov, Y. I., 429
Summers, D. F., 331
Sumper, M., 71
Sunayama, H., 109
Sussman, M., 143, 145, 147, 148, 150, 152-55, 158, 160, 161
Sussman, R., 147, 148
Sutherland, E. W., 353-55, 363, 366
SUZUKI, I., 85-101; 87, 89-91, 93, 94, 98
Suzuki, M., 109, 111, 115
Suzuki, S., 109, 115
Suzuki, Y., 144, 146
Svensson, S., 271
Svihla, G., 381
Svoboda, A., 114, 115
Swann, P. R., 379, 381
Swanson, R., 48
Swatek, F. E., 133
Swift, J. A., 386
Sybesma, C., 45-50, 54
Sykes, R. B., 222
Szaniszlo, P. J., 392, 397
Szuts, E. Z., 51-53

T

Tabata, K., 327, 328
Tabita, R., 94
Tabor, C. W., 74
Tabor, H., 74
Tagawa, K., 54
Tahama, Y., 316
Taj-Eldin, S., 190
Takagi, A., 176
Takagi, Y., 272
Takahashi, H., 224
Takahashi, I., 276
Takamiya, A., 50, 53
Takamiya, K.-I., 50, 53
Takano, T., 48
Takeda, K., 281
Takemoto, K., 242, 259
Takeuchi, I., 140, 142, 143
Tamm, I., 327, 328
Tamura, T., 178
Tanabe, O., 104
Tanaka, T., 36, 426
Tanguay, R., 431
Taniguchi, S., 49
Tanikawa, K., 207
Tanner, W., 114
Tano, T., 92
Tao, M., 364
Tarakanov, B. V., 416
Tarpley, J., 464
Tatum, E. L., 104, 109, 111, 220, 284
Taub, J., 191
Taubeneck, U., 426
Taylor, A. L., 224
Taylor, B. F., 92, 93
Taylor, C. P. S., 90
TAYLOR, G. R., 121-37; 122, 129-35
Teakle, D. S., 318
Tedro, S. M., 48
Telford, S. R., 201, 203
Telser, A., 147, 153
Temin, H. M., 334, 344
Templin, A., 448
Terenaka, J., 307
Terenaka, M., 302, 311, 312
Trent'ev, A. A , 416
Ter Meulen, V., 247

Terni, M., 342
Terry, G., 340
Terry, K. R., 87, 89, 168, 170
Tessman, I., 456
Thanasophon, S., 249
Thatcher, F. S., 396
Thatcher, V. E., 203
Thein, P., 257, 258
Theodore, O., 190-92, 200
Thirumalachar, M. J., 316
Thiry, L., 257
Thomae, F. W., 121-33
Thomas, C. A., 457, 461
Thomas, D., 77
Thompson, R. E. M., 426
Thomson, J. G., 191
Thormar, H., 232, 240, 242, 245, 259
Thornber, J. P., 41, 42, 44, 46, 47, 51
Thurman, G. B., 252, 255
Thurman, P., 66
Thurston, E. L., 180, 182
Thyagarajan, T. R., 397
Tiedje, J. M., 433
Tiffany, J. M., 338, 340
Tikasingh, E. S., 201
Till, U., 75
Tinelli, R., 268, 272, 280
Ting, R. C., 271
Tiraby, J.-B., 448, 456
Tkacz, J. S., 112, 397
Tobie, E. J., 210
Todaro, G. J., 259
Tolles, W. E., 372, 377
Tolmach, L. J., 456
Tomasz, A., 266
Tomizawa, J., 268, 275, 447
Tonato, M., 36
Tonomura, K., 104
Torjesen, P. A., 171
Torrealba, J. F., 199, 200
Torrealba, J. W., 199-202
Torres, H. N., 158
Toshach, S., 284
Tourtellotte, W. W., 247, 252, 253
Towe, A. M., 454, 456, 458, 460, 464
Trager, W., 207, 208, 210
Trammell, G. T., 387
Traugh, J. A., 289, 290, 293
Trautner, T. A., 453
Trejo, G., 115
Tremonti, L., 212
Trentini, W. C., 412, 414, 432, 434
Trevithick, J. R., 104, 112
Trinci, A. P. J., 105
Tronson, D. A., 87, 89
Trotter, C. D., 224
Trotter, M. D., 107
Truby, C. P., 122
Trudinger, P. A., 85, 93-95
Trujillo Ortiz, D., 191
Trüper, H. G., 179, 412
Trüper, H. H., 431
Tschermak-Woess, E., 423
Tsubura, E., 109
Tully, J. G., 306, 308, 309, 313
Tumblatt, J., 328, 329
Tung, K. K., 113
Turnbill, C., 178
Turpin, A., 287, 289
Turvey, J. R., 105
Twarog, R., 220, 226
Twohy, D. W., 195
Tyeryar, F. J. Jr., 220
Tyler, P. A., 400, 408-10, 433, 434, 437
Tyler, S. A., 418, 429
Tyrell, D. A. J., 337, 338

U

Uchida, T., 281-83, 285-87, 289, 291, 292
Udagawa, K., 396
Ueda, M., 176
Uetake, H., 268, 272, 273, 280-82, 285
Uhlken, A., 402
Uhr, J. W., 337
Ulane, R., 115
Ullman, A., 354, 356
Ulloa, G., 201, 202
Ulrich, M., 191
Ulrychova, M., 307, 316
Umbarger, H. E., 222, 227
Unkeless, J. C., 156, 335
Unwin, P. N. T., 376
Uphaus, R. A., 44
Urano, T., 248
Urban, P. F., 53
Urm, E., 285
Utermohlen, V., 247
Utkina, T. G., 130-34

V

Vaes, G., 156
Vago, C., 303, 307, 314, 317, 318
Vakili, N. G., 315
Valentine, R. C., 356
Valois, F. W., 87, 89
van Baalen, C., 184
van Bogaert, L., 240
Van Camp, L., 435
Van de Meere, J. C. C., 140
Van de Putte, P., 220
Vanderhaeghen, J. J., 257
van der Hart, J. M., 43
van der Vijver, J. C. M., 269
Van Droogenbroeck, R., 96
Van Ert, M., 415
van Es-Boon, M., 269
Van Gool, A., 89, 90, 96, 180
Van Iterson, W., 176, 396
van Kessel, J. F., 400, 421
Van Rijn, H. J. M., 113
Van Veen, W. L., 400, 410
Van Vuuren, S. P., 316
van Zanten, E. N., 176
Varma, A., 307
Varmus, H. E., 356
Vashkov, V. I., 131
Vasil'eva, L. N., 416, 417, 419
Vasil'eva, Z. A., 405
Veech, R. L., 69
Vela, G. R., 396
Veles, L. R., 204
Venediktov, P. S., 47
Venetianer, P., 227
Venkataraman, G. S., 220
Verkhoturov, V. N., 405, 420
Vernon, L. P., 48, 50, 53, 90
Vernon, M. L., 240
Vestal, J. R., 93, 94
Vianna, G., 202
Villanueva, J. R., 114
Vincent, J. M., 271
Virtanen, A. J., 65
Vishniac, W. V., 98
Viswanath, S. M., 316
Vivian, A., 222, 223, 225
Voelz, H., 168, 170, 184, 433, 437
Voelz, U., 168, 170
Vogel, H. J., 73, 74
Vogel, O., 72
Vogel, R. H., 73
Vogel, T., 227
Vogen, L. K., 140
Vogt, P. K., 334
Volarovich, M. P., 416
Volk, W. A., 414
Volkova, A. P., 134
Voller, A., 192, 210
Volz, P. A., 130
von Brand, T., 208, 210
von der Rest, M., 44
von Stedingk, L.-V., 54, 55
Vos, J. J., 43
Vovis, G. F., 449
Vredenberg, W. J., 45, 55
Vreven, J., 156

W

Wadzinski, A. M., 406
Waechter, C. J., 114
Wagner, R. R., 330-32
Waite, M. R. F., 327-29
Wake, R. G., 224
Wakimoto, T., 302
Waksman, S. A., 91
Walker, D. A., 54
Walker, D. L., 237, 238, 258
Walker, P. D., 167, 383
Walker, P. M. B., 381
Walkup, R., 180, 182

Wallace, D. C., 312
Wallace, E. G., 208
Wallace, W., 85, 96
Walsby, A. E., 179, 180
Walsh, F., 396, 429, 431
Walsh, J., 275
Walsh, R. S., 220
Walter, H., 71
Walther, G., 72
Walton, B. C., 212
Walton, G. M., 365
Wang, R. J., 356, 358
Wang, R. T., 43
Wang, W. S., 178, 180
Ward, A. J., 269
Ward, C., 159
Ward, R. D., 202
Warnes, G. M., 96
Warren, A. J., 457
Washington, A. C., 153, 160
Washington, O., 271
Watanabe, I., 247
Waterbury, J. B., 180, 182
Waterworth, H. E., 30, 31
Watson, D. H., 341
Watson, P. R., 106
Watson, S. W., 87, 89, 179, 180, 182, 400, 431
Wawrik, U., 422
Wear, D. J., 233, 252, 257
Weathers, L. G., 24, 25, 27-30, 33, 34
Weavers, B., 384
Webber, B. B., 128
Weeks, G., 144, 145, 150, 157
Wegman, J., 226
Weid, G. L., 372, 375, 377, 381-83, 387
Weigle, J. J., 267, 447, 458, 461, 464
Weimberg, R., 104, 113
Weinberg, E. D., 355
Weinberg, R. A., 36
Weiner, L. P., 237, 245, 256, 257
Weiner, R. M., 435, 436
Weinstein, C. B., 338
Weisrock, W. P., 395
Weiss, P., 62
Weiss, R. L., 67
Weissman, S. M., 35
Wells, H. J., 332
Werkman, C. H., 91
Werner, E. R., 272, 275
Werner, R., 75
West, S. S., 373, 375, 383
Westerhouse, S., 110
Westphal, O., 280, 283
Wetekam, W., 356
Wetzel, B. K., 208
Wheeler, H. O., 134
Wheelis, M. L., 225
Whitaker, J. N., 251
Whitcomb, R. F., 303, 306-11, 316, 317
White, A., 269
White, D. O., 253
White, G. J., 143
White, H. H., 253
White, M. R., 112
White, R. L., 456, 461, 464
Whitehouse, H. L. K., 445, 446, 449, 453, 456, 458, 460-64
Whiteley, H. R., 413
Whitney, P. A., 73
Whitt, D. D., 225, 226
Whittenbury, R., 410, 420-22, 434
Wickus, G. G., 335
Widnell, C. C., 156
Wiemken, A., 68
Wiener, E., 140, 154
Wiesenfeld, S. L., 251
Wiggins, P. M., 62
Wijers, D. J. B., 193, 203
Wildman, R. B., 168, 172, 180
Wildy, P., 341
Wilhelms, H., 143
Wilkins, B. M., 457
Wilkins, J. R., 131-33
Wilkinson, J. F., 168, 170, 184, 420-22
Wilkinson, T. G., 403, 405
Williams, A. W., 274, 285
Williams, D. M., 44, 47
Williams, L. G., 67
Williams, L. S., 222, 227
Williams, P., 200, 206
Williamson, D. H., 69, 105
Williamson, D. L., 318
Williamson, K. I., 168
Wilson, D. F., 90
Wilson, F. A., 62
Wilson, G. S., 288
Wilson, J. B., 279
Wiman, M., 224
Windsor, I. M., 318
Winfree, A. T., 62
Wingard, L. B. Jr., 80
Winkler, K. C., 268, 269
Winn, M. M., 193
Wise, E. M. Jr., 357
Withnall, M. T., 109
Wittels, B., 68
Wittes, R. E., 75
Wittig, B., 257
Woese, C., 227
Wolanski, B. S., 309, 314-16, 320
Wolfe, R. S., 425, 436
Wolk, C. P., 168, 170-72, 180, 184
Wollenhaupt, H., 129
Wollman, E. L., 267, 271
Wolstencroft, R. A., 204, 212
Wonde, T., 194
Wong, A. M., 48, 55
Wood, H. N., 353
Wood, O. L., 437
Wood, S. R., 107
Wood, V. B. V., 404, 414
Wood, W. A., 355
Woodfolk, C. A., 413
Woods, D. A., 426
Wooley, B. C., 122, 130, 131
Woolley, D., 146
Worley, J. F., 303, 306, 309, 310, 312, 318
Wraight, C. A., 44, 50, 51, 54
Wrathall, C. R., 109
Wrenn, R. T., 129
Wright, A., 280-82
WRIGHT, B. E., 139-66; 140, 142-45, 147-54, 156, 159-62
Wright, E. M., 62
Wright, H. M., 220
Wright, J. H., 195, 196
Wu, C. C., 191
Wykoff, D. E., 193

X

Xuong, N. H., 48

Y

Yaari, A., 212
Yabrov, A. A., 288
Yabuno, K., 142
Yadomae, T., 111
Yakimov, V. L., 197
Yamada, M., 253
Yamada, T., 148
Yamamoto, T., 176
Yamamura, Y., 104, 109
Yamanaka, T., 47
Yamazaki, S., 331
Yanagisawa, K. O., 148
Yang, H., 285
Yanofsky, C., 226, 448, 453
Yarmolinsky, M. B., 448, 453, 455
Yates, D. W., 49, 50
Yates, M. G., 90, 91
Yau, H. F., 44, 50, 51
Yeh, J., 233
Yen, A., 75
Yen, J. H., 318
Yike, N. J., 54
Yoeli, M., 195
Yokota, K., 109, 111
Yokota, T., 355, 356, 358, 364
Yolton, D. P., 174
Yoneda, M., 285-87
Yora, K., 302, 311, 312, 316
Yoshida, T., 86
Yoshikawa, H., 224
Yoshimoto, A., 354
Young, C., 176
Young, H. L., 178

Yount, V., 53
Yousten, A. A., 167, 174
Yuan, R., 453
Yudelevich, A., 457
Yusupov, K. A., 198

Z

Zabriskie, J. B., 247, 270
Zahn, R. K., 30
Zagury, D., 337
Zaikin, A. M., 62
Zaitlin, M., 26, 34
Zajic, J. E., 85
Zakut, V., 356
Zaloguyev, S. N., 130-35
Zalokar, M., 68
Zanen, J., 289
Zankel, K. L., 52
Zasukhin, D., 190, 191, 197
Zavarzin, G. A., 392, 402, 405, 408, 410, 419-23, 427-31, 433-35, 437
Zeegers, B. J. H., 269
Zeh, R. M., 375
Zeitler, E., 385
Zeledón, R., 203, 210
Zeman, W., 233, 245
Zeyen, R. J., 314, 315
Zhabotinsky, A. M., 62
Zhilina, T. N., 417
Zhukov-Verezhnikov, N. N., 123-26
Ziegler, L., 221
Zigas, V., 238
Zil'ber, L. A., 249
Zimmerman, H. M., 249
Zinder, N. D., 220, 272, 275, 285, 453, 454, 456, 458, 460, 461, 463, 464
Zipser, D., 278
Zlotnik, I., 243, 257
Zobell, C. E., 436
Zolotukhin, N. V., 97
Zubay, G., 285, 356, 359, 360
Zuccarelli, A. J., 453, 457
Zuckerman, A., 211
Zuckerman, A. J., 37
Zu Rhein, G. M., 237, 238, 245, 252, 255, 258
Zvyagintseva, T. V., 197, 198
Zwartouw, H. T., 343

# SUBJECT INDEX

A

Acetylcholine esterase
  membrane effect on, 77
Acholeplasma
  characteristics of, 305, 308
  iron oxidation by, 427
  viruses of, 313
Acholeplasma laidlawii, 308, 313
Achromatium
  division in, 395
Acid phosphatases
  of yeasts, 113
Actinomycin D
  and differentiation, 147, 148
Acyl carrier protein, 72
Adenosine-phosphosulfate reductase
  and adenylate kinase, 98
  in sulfite oxidation, 98
Adenoviruses
  replication of, 35
Adenylate kinase
  and APS reductase, 98
Adenyl cyclase
  and chemotaxis, 158
  in Dicytostelium, 157
  membrane associated, 158
  mutants in, 364
  in prokaryotes
    discovery of, 363, 364
    in E. coli, 364
  regulation of, 363-65
ADP-ribosylation, 289-91
Aerobacter aerogenes
  in space flight, 124
Aeromonas proteolytica
  UV sensitivity of, 130
Alcaligenes faecalis
  cyclic AMP in, 354
Alcohol dehydrogenase, 413
Aleutian disease, 252, 259
Alkaline phosphatase
  and membranes, 126
Amine dehydrogenase, 407
Aminoacyl-tRNA synthetases
  as enzyme complex, 71
Ammonia oxidation
  cell-free, 87
  in Nitrosocystis, 87
  in Nitrosomonas
    cytochromes in, 86-88
    efficiency of, 96
    fractionation of, 87
    inhibitors of, 89
    reactions of, 86, 88
    stoichiometry of, 87
    substrate for, 89
  reviews of, 85
Amphotericin B, 210
Amylomalatase
  membrane bound, 67
Amyotrophic lateral sclerosis
  occurrence of, 248, 249
  poliovirus in, 246, 249
  transmission of, 249
Anabaena cylindrica
  cyanophycin granules of, 171
Anacystis nidulans
  cyclic AMP in, 353
Ancalochloris
  morphology of, 416
Ancalomicrobium
  budding in, 393, 415
  enrichment of, 415
  morphology of, 393, 415
Anthranilate synthetase, 226
Antimycin A, 50
Arboviruses
  composition of, 327
  maturation of, 327, 328
  membranes of
    and budding sites, 328
    components of, 328, 329
    origin of, 327
  nucleocapsids of, 327, 328
  proteins of, 327
  Semliki Forest Virus, 330
  Sindbis virus
    lipids of, 329
    membranes of, 328
  see also specific viruses
Arenoviruses
  electron microscopy of, 242
  and slow virus diseases, 232, 242
Arginine biosynthesis

and compartmentation, 67
Arthrobacter
cyclic AMP in, 354
Ascomycetes
recombination in, 446
Aspergillosis, 109
Aspergillus fumigatus
and aspergillosis, 109
peptidogalactomannan of, 109
Aspergillus niger
amylases of, 113
Aster-yellows disease
agent of
degeneration of, 313
intracellular growth of, 312, 313
morphology of, 311, 312, 319
and viruses, 313, 314
antibiotic effect, 316, 317
and sterility, 317
Asticcacaulis excentricus
cell division in, 395
ATPase
in avian myeloblastosis virus, 334
Avian myeloblastosis virus
enzymes of, 334
Azobacter vinelandii
budding in, 396
protein synthesis, 356

B

Bacillus cereus
bacteriophage W of, 279
lysogeny in, 276
membrane bound enzymes of, 66
poly-β-hydroxybutyrate granules of, 178
Bacillus licheniformis
adenyl cyclase of, 364
cyclic AMP in, 354
cyclic GMP in, 354
membrane bound enzymes of, 66
Bacillus megatherium
cyclic AMP in, 354
induction of, 272
phage conversions in, 269
Bacillus subtilis
crystal formation in, 174, 175
DNA synthesis in, 75
linkage map of, 224
lysogeny in, 276
miniature cells of, 395
protein inclusions of, 184
transformation in, 449
UV sensitivity of, 129
viability of
and HZE particles, 127
in space, 122, 126, 127
Bacillus thuringiensis
parasporal inclusions of, 172-74
sporulation of, 174
toxin production of, 129
UV sensitivity of, 129
Bacteriochlorophyll
degradation of, 42
and P870, 44
protein complex of
in Chlorobacteriaceae, 42
in Chlorobium, 41
in Chromatium, 42
interactions in, 42
protein of, 41-43
in Rhodopseudomonas, 42
Bacteriophage β
genetic markers of, 286
lysogeny in
curing of, 285
induction of, 272-74
and virulence, 279
map of, 285, 286
and toxin formation
and genome state, 287
in vitro, 285, 286
iron effect, 287
and lysogeny, 285
virulent, 285
Bacteriophage CEβ, 269
Bacteriophage D3, 271
Bacteriophage D29, 269
Bacteriophage ε15
in phage conversions
action in, 282, 283
endorhamnosidase in, 281
and O-factors, 280-83
and receptor sites, 273, 281, 282, 284
Bacteriophage ε34
receptor sites for, 282, 283
susceptibility to, 273, 281
Bacteriophage fd, 276
Bacteriophage fr, 276
Bacteriophage λ
induction of
as model system, 124-26
in space flight, 124-26
in lysogeny
curing of, 267, 275
definition of, 268
and E. coli properties, 267, 271
induction of, 124-26, 272, 274
prophage insertion in, 455
and recombination, 448, 455, 461
repressor of, 275
virulence in, 279
Bacteriophage M13, 276
Bacteriophage P1
effects of, 271, 275
induction of, 272, 275
Bacteriophage P2
in E. coli, 271
and induction, 272, 274
Bacteriophage P22
antigen 1 in, 285
and O-antigen, 272, 275
virulent, 279
Bacteriophage persistence
lysogeny in
characterization of, 272
and curing, 274, 275
definition of, 268, 272
and induction, 272, 274
stability of, 272, 274, 275
modes of, 265
and phage conversions
nature of, 266
and prophage state, 272
summary of, 268-71
pseudolysogeny in
and bacterial modification, 276
and endolysin action, 278
and mutant accumulation, 279
and receptor availability, 277
and receptor destruction, 278, 279
and spores, 276
terminology in, 266-68
Bacteriophage φ, 269, 270
Bacteriophage Qβ
low molecular weight RNA of, 35
Bacteriophage T1
viability of
models for, 127, 128
in space, 122, 126-28
Bacteriophage T2, 276
Bacteriophage T3, 276
Bacteriophage T7
lysis by, 276
in Shigella, 278, 279
UV sensitivity of, 129
Bacteriophage V, 271
Bacteriophage W, 279
Bacteriophage 1pt, 269
Bacteriopheophytin
formation of, 42
and P870, 44
Blastobacter
characteristics of, 420, 421
and Methylosinus, 420
Blastococcus
and Mycococcus, 426
Blue-green algae
budding in, 395
carboxysomes in, 180
crystalline inclusions in, 176
gas vacuoles in, 179, 180
lipid deposits in, 184
phycobilisomes of
appearance of, 172, 173
function of, 171

proteins of, 171
polyglucoside granules of, 168, 169
polyhydroxybutyrate in, 178
ribulose-1, 5-diphosphate carboxylase of, 182
Bosch yaws, 202
Bovine rhinotracheitis virus
in space, 127
Brevibacterium
ammoniagenes, 396
liquefaciens
adenyl cyclase of, 363, 364
cyclic AMP in, 354
Budding
in Ancalochloris, 416
in Ancalomicrobium, 393, 415
and cell division, 395
cell wall changes in, 396
of cocci, 422, 423
and culture preservation, 432, 433
definition of, 392, 393, 397
and DNA homology, 430
ecological consequences, 437
and environmental quality, 437
in fungi, 396, 397
and habitat, 436-38
hyphal, 410
in Hyphomicrobium
and branching, 393, 394
and hyphal growth, 436
liberation of, 435
and life cycle, 401, 435
and morphogenesis, 433
observation of, 392
in Hyphomonas, 393, 407, 408, 433
of L-forms, 426
and life cycle, 401, 434, 435
in Metallogenium, 429
in Methylosinus, 421
and morphogenesis
in hyphal bacteria, 433, 434
methods of study, 433
in Mycococcus, 393, 424
in Mycoplasma, 426
in Naumanniella, 422
and parasites, 437
in Pasteuria, 393, 419, 420
in Pedomicrobium, 393, 394, 408, 433
in Planctomyces, 393, 418, 419
in Prosthecomicrobium, 393, 416
reviews of, 392
in Rhodomicrobium
and branching, 394
form of, 393, 433
and motility, 415
in Siderococcus, 422
in Thermoplasma, 427
types of
for branching, 393, 394
morphological, 397-99
for multiplication, 393-95
and sporulation, 394, 395
in yeasts, 396, 397

C

Candida albicans
in space flight, 132-34
Candida utilis
compartmentation in, 68
Canine hepatitis virus
in space, 127
Carbamyl phosphate synthetase, 67
Carboxysomes
appearance of, 180, 181
composition of, 182
function of, 182
Carotenoids
determination of, 10
and electron transfer, 55
energy transfer in, 43
Catabolite gene activator protein
action of, 360, 361
discovery of, 359
distribution of, 360
gene for, 360
and transcription, 360, 361
Caulobacter crescentus
CAP in, 360
cyclic AMP in, 354
differentiation of, 355, 357
Caulococcus, 429, 430
Cellulase, 155
Cell walls
electron microscopy of, 105
enzymes of
amylases, 113
functions of, 115
galactofuranosidase, 112, 113
invertase, 111, 112
mycodextranase, 113
of fungi
components of, 104
glycoproteins of, 104-11
layers of, 104
glycoproteins of
in Aspergillus, 109, 110
in dermatophytes, 107-9
functions of, 115
in Neurospora, 109
in Penicillium, 110, 111
in yeast, 105-7
and morphology, 104, 105
of rickettsia-like organisms, 318
Chemotaxis
and adenyl cyclase, 158
and cyclic AMP, 140, 156
Chitin
biosynthesis of, 114, 115
in cell walls
of dermatophytes, 107
of Neurospora, 104
and chitin synthetase, 114, 115
Chlamydomonas reinhardii
cyclic AMP in, 353
Chlorobacteriaceae
bacteriochlorophyll complex of, 42
Chlorobium limicola
bacteriochlorophyll complex of, 41, 184
cytochromes of, 47
P870 of, 44
Chlorobium thiosulfatophilum
bacteriochlorophyll a complex of, 184
cytochromes of, 47
thiosulfate oxidation in, 47
Chlorobium vesicles
appearance of, 182-84
chlorophyll in, 182, 184
Chloroplasts, 62
Chloropseudomonas ethylica
bacteriochlorophyll complex of, 41
Chromatium vinosum
bacteriochlorophyll complex of, 42
cytochromes of, 46, 48, 54
electron transfer in, 51, 54
P870 of, 44
Chrysanthemum stunt disease
agent of
molecular weight of, 27
as RNA, 24, 25
see also Viroids
Circular dichroism
of P870, 44
Citrus exocortis disease
agent of
isolation of, 29
molecular weight of, 27, 28
radiation sensitivity of, 30
as RNA, 24, 25
electron microscopy in, 25
see also Viroids
Citrus-stubborn disease
agent of, 304, 307
and corn stunt, 311
Cladosporium werneckii

peptidophosphogalactomannan
of, 106, 107
Clostridium
botulinum
phage conversions in, 269
poly-β-hydroxybutyrate granules in, 178
polyglucoside granules of, 176
butyricum
growth in space, 123, 124
cochlearium
parasporal crystals in, 174, 175
pasteurianum
polyglucoside granules in, 176, 177
pectinovorum
cell division in, 395
perfringens
parasporal crystals in, 174, 175
Clover club leaf disease, 318
Clover phyllody disease, 316
Compartmentation
of acetyl CoA, 68, 69
and amino acid pools, 67, 68
in carbohydrate metabolism, 68
within compartments, 69
and differentiation, 61, 154
and enzyme complexes
advantages of, 71
and cell dimensions, 70
as compartment form, 62
in histidine synthesis, 73
isolatable, 71, 72
and metabolite pools, 74, 75
within mitochondria, 70, 71
multifunctional enzymes as, 73
putative, 74, 75
reviews of, 71
and enzyme regulation, 140, 154
forms of, 62
glycolytic, 69, 70
glyoxalate shunt, 68
and membrane binding, 66, 67, 77
and metabolic pools
of acetyl CoA, 68, 69
of amino acids, 67, 68, 74
of carbamyl phosphate, 67
of nucleotides, 74, 75
in prokaryotes, 74
in microenvironment
and enzyme activity, 77
and hydrophobicity, 76, 77
kinetic advantages, 78, 79
matrix effects, 76, 77, 79, 80
and multi-step systems, 77, 78
nature of, 62, 75, 76
and Nernst diffusion layer, 80
and pH, 79
and multifunctional enzymes, 73
need for, 69, 70
and nitrogen fixation, 65
organelles in
chloroplasts, 62
endoplasmic reticulum, 67, 69
in eukaryotes, 67-70
lysosomes, 62, 66
mesosomes, 66
microsomes, 68
mitochondria, 62, 67-71, 79
nuclei, 62, 67, 69
and periplasmic space, 62, 66
peroxisomes, 62, 68
in prokaryotes, 66, 67
vacuoles, 62, 67, 68
in pyrimidine synthesis, 67
and regulation, 61
reviews of, 61
symbiotic
as functional entity, 65
lichens in, 62-65
nodular bacteria, 65
transport in, 63-65
Concanavalin A
and Dictyostelium, 157, 158
Corn stunt disease
agent of, 304, 308, 309
electron microscopy in, 309
microscopy of, 309, 310
serology of, 310, 311
and viruses, 314
Corynebacterium diphtheriae
curing of, 274
and diphtheria toxin
action of, 288-92
and iron, 287
and permeability, 287
and phage induction, 269, 284, 285
production of, 269, 284
synthesis of, 285-87
viral function of, 285
phage conversions in, 269, 277
phage resistant, 274
toxinogenic, 277, 284
Corynebacterium equi
cyclic AMP in, 354
Creutzfeldt-Jakob disease
agents of, 232, 239
clinical features of, 238, 240
cytopathic effects of, 232
genetic factors in, 251
as viroid disease, 37
and viruses, 240
Cryptococcus neoformans, 397
Cutaneous leishmaniasis
causes of, 195, 197-204
nature of, 196
Cyanobacteria
budding in, 395
Cyanophycin granules
appearance of, 169-71
function of, 171
Cyclic AMP
and adenyl cyclase, 363, 364
in algae, 353
assay for, 354, 363
in bacteria
and adenyl cyclase, 363, 364
and CAP, 359-62
and catabolite repression, 354-62
concentration of, 362, 363
discovery of, 354
and eukaryotes, 365, 366
morphogenetic effects, 355
and protein kinase, 359
and protein synthesis, 354-56
binding proteins for, 157
and cAMP phosphodiesterase, 364, 365
and CAP
action of, 360, 361
and β-galactosidase synthesis, 359, 361
isolation of, 359
sensitivity to, 362
and transcription, 361
and catabolite repression
and CAP, 359-62
and protein synthesis, 354, 355
and transcription, 357, 358
and translation, 358
and chemotaxis, 140, 156, 357
concentration of, 157
in differentiation, 156-58
discovery of, 353
and G-factor, 358
in plants, 353
pools of, 362, 363
and protein kinase, 359
and protein synthesis
and catabolite repression, 354-57

and nonessential functions, 355
and transcription, 357
and translation, 358
release of, 365
and transcription, 146, 357, 358
and translation, 358
Cyclic AMP phosphodiesterase
and concanavalin A, 157, 158
in Dictyostelium, 157
of E. coli, 364, 365
in regulation, 365
Cyclic GMP
assay of, 354
in prokaryotes, 354
Cytochrome b557.5, 49
Cytochrome c
from Nitrobacter, 89
and sulfite oxidase, 93
Cytochrome c2
and P870, 48, 49
structure of, 48
Cytochrome c552
in Chromatium, 46
photooxidation of, 46, 47
Cytochrome c555
in Chromatium, 46, 54
photooxidation of, 46, 47
Cytochrome c', 47, 49
Cytochrome c reductase
and iron oxidation, 90
and nitrite oxidation, 89
Cytochrome o
in Nitrosomonas, 86
Cytochrome oxidase
and ammonia oxidation, 86-88
in Nitrosomonas, 86, 87
Cytochrome P450
in Nitrosomonas, 86
Cytochrome P460
in ammonia oxidation, 86, 88
in Nitrosomonas, 86
Cytochromes
of hydroxylamine oxidase, 86
in Hyphomicrobium, 404, 405
in nitrite oxidase, 89, 90
in photosynthesis, 45-50
review of, 85
in Rhodomicrobium, 413
see also specific cytochromes

D

DDT
analysis of, 20
and human health, 18
in salmon, 17
Debaryomyces
and Mycoderma, 6
Deoxyribonuclease, 24
Depsides, 64, 65
Depsidones, 65
Depsones, 65
Dermal leishmaniasis
causes of, 192
Dermatophilus dermatonomus
budding in, 394, 395
Dermatophytes
allergenic agents of, 107
galactomannans of, 107, 108
glucans of, 108, 109
Desulfovibrio desulfuricans
sulfite oxidation in, 93
Dibenzofurans, 65
Dictyostelium discoideum
adenyl cyclase of, 157
agglutination of, 157
aggregation of, 156
and concanavalin A, 157, 158
cyclic AMP effect, 366
cyclic AMP phosphodiesterase of, 157
differentiation of
and actinomycin D, 147, 148
and adenyl cyclase, 158
alkaline phosphatase in, 156
biochemical, 143-62
cellulase in, 155
and compartmentation, 154
and composition, 143
and cyclic AMP, 156-58
definition of, 139, 140
and enzyme concentration, 151-53
and enzyme stability, 154
and glycogen phosphorylase, 159, 160
and glycogen synthetase, 159
initiation of, 140
membranes in, 142, 156, 158
and metabolite flux, 150, 151
morphological changes in, 140-43
in mutants, 148-50
and nucleic acids, 145-50
prespore vacuole in, 141, 142
saccharide interconversions in, 143-45
and starvation, 142
trehalase in, 154, 155
and trehalose phosphate synthetase, 160-62
ultrastructural, 140-43
variables in, 144, 145
glycogen phosphorylase of, 159, 160
life cycle of, 140
membranes of
and adenyl cyclase, 158
and alkaline phosphatase, 156
in differentiation, 142
mitochondria of, 141
mRNA of, 145
mutants of
developmental, 148-50
in morphogenesis, 149
in recombination, 148
Diethylstilbesterol
intake of, 21
Differentiation
compartmentation in, 61
definition of, 139, 140
in Dictyostelium
and actinomycin D, 147, 148
alkaline phosphatase in, 156
biochemical, 143-62
cellulase in, 155
and compartmentation, 154
and composition, 143
and cyclic AMP, 156-58
drug effects, 147, 148
and enzyme concentration, 151-53, 162
and enzyme stability, 154
and glycogen phosphorylase, 159, 160
and glycogen synthetase, 159
initiation of, 140
membranes in, 142
and metabolite flux, 150, 151
morphological changes in, 140-43
in mutants, 148-50
and nucleic acids, 145-50
prespore vacuole in, 142
saccharide interconversions in, 143-45
and starvation, 142
trehalase in, 154, 155
trehalose phosphate synthetase, 160-62
UDP glucose pyrophosphorylase in, 151, 152
ultrastructural, 140-43
variables in, 144, 145
electron microscopy of, 140
Diffuse cutaneous leishmaniasis, 198-201
Diphtheria toxin
action of
in ADP ribosylation, 289-91
and interferon, 288
and protein synthesis, 288-93
sensitivity to, 288
and translocase, 289-91
altered, 286

fragment A of, 289-93
fragment B of, 289, 291-93
and iron, 287
model of, 290, 292
production of, 269, 285
synthesis of, 285-87
and toxoid, 292
and viral function, 285
DNA
ligase
in recombination, 460
polymerase
as multifunctional enzyme, 73, 74
repair
and recombination, 448
synthesis
compartmentation of, 75
in enzyme complex, 71
and scrapie, 257, 259
Drosophila
and yeasts, 10, 11

E

EB virus
in Guillain-Barré syndrome, 248
in infectious mononucleosis, 248
Ectothiorhodospira shaposhnikovii, 47
Electron microscopy
of arboviruses, 327
of arenoviruses, 242
of carboxysomes, 180, 181
of cell walls, 105
of chlorobium vesicles, 182-84
and citrus exocortis viroid, 25
in citrus-stubborn disease, 307
in corn stunt disease, 309
of cyanophycin granules, 169-71
and dehydration, 385, 386
and differentiation, 140
electron microscope microanalyzer in, 384
future developments in, 387, 388
of gas vacuoles, 179-81
in Guillain-Barré syndrome, 248
high voltage
advantages of, 381
of living organisms, 386
resolution of, 381
of Leishmania, 207, 211
in mass measurement, 385
microscopes in, 376, 377
of mollicute-like organisms, 303
of mollicutes, 309
of multiple sclerosis lesions, 247
of mycoplasmas, 302
of parasporal inclusions, 172, 173
of phycobilisomes, 172, 173
of polyglucoside granules, 168, 169, 176-78
of poly-β-hydroxybutyrate granules, 176-78
of polyphosphate granules, 168-70
of potato spindle tuber viroid, 30-32
resolution in
and aberrations, 376, 378
and contrast, 379, 386, 387
in high voltage microscope, 381
in scanning microscope, 379, 380
temporal, 385
of ribulose-1, 5-diphosphate carboxylase, 182, 183
of rickettsia-like organisms, 317
scanning
advantages of, 380, 381
image formation in, 379, 380
of living organisms, 386
resolution of, 379, 380
stereo images in, 381
of sulfur globules, 176, 177, 179
transmission
phase contrast effects in, 376
resolution in, 376
of viroids, 30-32
Electron probe microanalyzer, 383, 384
Endolysin, 278
Endorhamnosidase, 281
Erwinia carotovora
cyclic AMP in, 354
Escherichia coli
adenyl cyclase of, 364
bacteriophage λ of
induction of, 124-26
in space flight, 124, 125
see also Bacteriophage λ; Lysogeny
budding in, 396
cAMP phosphodiesterase in, 364, 365
cell division in, 395
chemotaxis in, 357
citrate lyase of, 72
compartmentation in, 74, 75
cyclic AMP in
and adenyl cyclase, 364
and cAMP phosphodiesterase, 364, 365
and CAP, 359
and catabolite repression, 354-56
concentration of, 363
discovery of, 354
and enzyme activity, 355, 356
and protein synthesis, 354-56
cyclic GMP in, 354
fertility factor in, 221
in free space, 127
histidine operon in, 226
lac operon of
and CAP, 359-61
and cyclic AMP, 355-57, 362
linkage maps of, 224
lysogenic derivatives of
curing of, 267, 275
effects of, 267, 271
induction of, 272, 274, 275
properties of, 267
miniature cells of, 395
polyglucoside granules of, 168, 169
proline biosynthesis in, 73
protein synthesis in, 354-56
recombination-deficient, 448
R-factors of, 222
and space flight, 124, 125
tryptophan synthetase of, 72
virus infected
low molecular weight RNA in, 35
Extraterrestrial life
detection of
and astronaut flora, 130
in lunar material, 122
and viability, 122
and spacecraft sterilization, 126-28
and terrestrial organisms
growth of, 123
viability of, 122, 126, 127

F

Ferrobacillus ferrooxidans
iron oxidation in
and cytochrome c reductase, 90
and nucleic acids, 90, 91
reactions of, 90
and sulfate, 91
sulfur oxidation in, 91, 93, 94
Flavobacterium acidurans
mini-cells of, 395
Flavocytochrome c552, 47

Fluorescence microscopy, 372, 373
Food technology
development of, 2-4
Forest yaws, 202
Formate oxidase, 90
Formate utilization, 405
Fowl plague virus
neuraminidase in, 336
Fruit dehydration
and browning, 8

G

Galactofuranosidase, 112, 113
Galactomannans, 107, 108
β-Galactosidase
synthesis of
and CAP, 359, 361
cyclic AMP effect, 354-56, 361
Gallionella
buds in, 396
and mycoplasmas, 427
Gas vacuoles
appearance of, 179-81
function of, 180
membrane of, 180
Gene arrangements
and genetic regulation, 225
in histidine operon, 226, 227
and operons, 225
and regulons, 225
and tryptophan synthesis, 226
Gene conversions
in Ascomycetes, 446
asymmetry in, 464
basis for, 461, 462
and molecular conversions, 446
and reciprocal recombination, 446
Gene transfer
by conjugation
definition of, 219
distribution of, 220
fertility factor in, 221, 222
mechanism of, 220, 221
plasmids in, 221-23
and surface structure, 222
mechanisms for, 219
by transduction
definition of, 219, 220
distribution of, 220
by transformation
definition of, 219, 220
distribution of, 220
Geodermatophilus
morphogenesis of, 425
Glomerulonephritis, 243
Glutathione
in sulfur oxidation, 91, 92, 94
Glyceraldehyde phosphate dehydrogenase, 413
Glycogen phosphorylase, 159, 160
Glycogen synthetase
in Dictyostelium, 159
forms of, 159
Glyco-invertase
in Neurospora, 112
in Saccharomyces, 111-13
synthesis of, 113
Glycolysis
compartmentation of, 74
Glycoproteins
biosynthesis of
cycloheximide effect, 114
glycosyl intermediates in, 114, 115
invertase, 113, 114
in Penicillium, 114, 115
of dermatophytes, 107-9
extracellular, 104-11
function of, 115
galactomannans, 107, 108
glycoenzymes
amylases, 113
galactofuranosidase, 112, 113
invertase, 111, 112
phosphatases, 113
proteases, 113
in membranes, 345, 346
mural, 104-11
phosphomannans, 105, 106
of pox viruses, 343, 344
release of, 104
of vaccinia virus, 343, 344
of yeasts, 105-7
Glyoxalate shunt
and compartmentation, 68
Glyoxisomes
and glyoxalate shunt, 68
Gramicidin S
biosynthesis of, 72
Guillain-Barré syndrome
mycoplasma pneumoniae in, 246, 248
virus role in, 246, 248
Gyrophoric acid
biosynthesis of, 64
catabolism of, 64, 65

H

Halobacterium halobium
gas vacuoles in, 180
striated organelles of, 184
Hanseniaspora
and Drosophila, 11
Hepatitis
as viroid disease, 37
Herpes virus
composition of, 341
infection by
and cell membranes, 342
and viral proteins, 342, 343
lipids of, 343
maturation of, 341
membranes of
lipids of, 343
proteins of, 341, 342
sources of, 341
morphology of, 341
proteins of, 341, 342
Hexachlorobenzene
environmental effect, 19, 20
Hexokinase, 69
Histidine operon
control of, 226, 227
gene arrangement in, 226, 227
gene clusters in, 226
tRNA in, 226, 227
Hodgkin's disease
and progressive multifocal leukoencephalopathy, 237
Hydrogenase, 413
Hydrogenomonas
energy coupling in, 97
Hydrogenomonas eutropha
in space, 127
Hydrogen oxidation
by Hydrogenomonas, 97
and oxidative phosphorylation, 97
reviews of, 85, 97
Hydroxylamine-cytochrome c reductase
and hydroxylamine oxidation, 86, 88
Hydroxylamine oxidase
cytochromes of, 86
and nitrite reductase, 86
Hyphomicrobium
budding in
for cell branching, 393
and cell cycle, 435
and hyphal growth, 436
liberation, 435
and morphogenesis, 433
observation of, 392
characteristics of, 399, 400
composition of, 404
cytochromes of, 404, 405
DNA in, 402, 430, 431, 434
enrichment of, 400
fine structure of, 402, 403
formate utilization by, 405
genome size in, 431
growth of, 403-7
and Hyphomicrobium indicum, 395
life cycle of
budding in, 401, 435, 436
stages in, 401, 434, 435
light effect, 403, 404

methanol utilization by, 405, 406
morphology of, 402
occurrence of, 400, 402
and pedomicrobia, 400
preservation of, 403
RNA synthesis in, 432, 435, 436
Hyphomonas
budding in, 393, 407, 408, 433
HZE particles, 127

I

Inclusion bodies
groups of, 167
lipid deposits, 184
membrane enclosed
carboxysomes, 180-82
chlorobium, 182-84
gas vacuoles, 179-81
polyglucoside, 176-78
poly-β-hydroxybutyrate granules, 176-78
ribulose-1, 5-diphosphate carboxylase in, 182
sulfur globules, 176, 177, 179
nonmembrane enclosed
appearance of, 168, 169
cyanophycin granules, 170, 171
parasporal inclusions, 172-76
phycobilisomes, 171, 172
polyglucoside granules, 168, 169
polyphosphate, 168-70
Infantile visceral leishmaniasis
causes of, 190
symptoms of, 191
Infectious mononucleosis
and EB virus, 248
Influenza virus
composition of, 336
infection by, 336, 337
membranes of
lipids of, 338
origin of, 337, 338
protein in, 336, 338
proteins of
glycosylation of, 337
in membranes, 336
M protein, 336, 337
synthesis of, 336, 337
in space, 127
stability of, 336
Interferon
and diphtheria toxin, 288
Invertase
biosynthesis of, 113, 114
glycosylation of, 111, 112
in Saccharomyces, 111-13
synthesis of, 113
Iron oxidation
in Ferrobacillus
cytochrome c reductase in, 90
and nucleic acids, 90, 91
reactions of, 90
and sulfate, 91
reviews of, 85
in Thiobacillus, 90

J

JC virus, 237

K

Kakabekia umbellata, 418
Kala azar
causes of, 190, 192
distribution of, 190
symptoms of, 191
Kinetoplasts
in Leishmania, 208, 209
Klebsiella aerogenes
CAP in, 360
citrate lyase of, 72
protein synthesis in, 356
Kloeckera
and Drosophila, 11
Kuru
agents of, 232, 239
and cannibalism, 238
clinical features, 238
cytopathic effects of, 232
genetic factors in, 250, 251
as viroid disease, 37
Kusnezovia, 429, 430

L

Lac operon
and CAP, 359-61
transcription of
and cyclic AMP, 355-57, 362
and lac promoter, 361
Lactobacillus plantarum
cyclic AMP in, 354
Leghemoglobin
in nitrogen fixation, 65
Leishmania
aethiopica, 198, 199
biochemistry of
drug action in, 210
glucose metabolism in, 210
and temperature, 208-10
and transformation, 208-10
braziliensis braziliensis, 202
braziliensis guyanensis, 202, 203
braziliensis panamensis, 203, 204
chagasi
behavior of, 200
distribution of, 199
reservoirs of, 199
taxonomy of, 200
vectors of, 199
and cutaneous leishmaniasis, 195-204
donovani
behavior of, 193-95
distribution of, 192, 193
hosts for, 193-95
reservoirs of, 193
taxonomy of, 195
vectors of, 193
enriettii, 204
fine structure of
diagram of, 209
kinetoplast DNA in, 208, 209
microscopy in, 206, 207
microtubules in, 207, 209
mitochondria in, 207, 209
in rosettes, 207
hertigi, 204, 205
immunology of
and identification, 211
and immunity to, 212
and leishmaniasis, 211
and infantile visceral leishmaniasis, 190-92, 199
infantum
behavior of, 191, 192
distribution of, 190
hosts for, 190-92
isolation of, 192
reservoirs of, 190, 191
taxonomy of, 192
vectors of, 191
in lizards, 205
major
distribution of, 197
taxonomy of, 198
vectors of, 197
mexicana amazonensis, 201, 202
mexicana mexicana, 200, 201
new-world species of, 199-205
old-world species of, 190-99
peruviana, 204
review of, 189
transmission of, 205, 206
tropica
behavior of, 196
distribution of, 195, 196
taxonomy of, 196, 197
vectors of, 196
and visceral leishmaniasis, 190-92, 199
L-forms
budding in, 426
Lichens
and compartmentation
metabolism in, 63-65
symbiosis in, 62-64

transport in, 63-65
compounds formed in, 65
as functional entity, 65
separation of, 65
transport in
of carbohydrates, 63, 64
mechanism of, 65
of nitrogen, 64
of vitamins, 64
Linkage maps
in Bacilli, 224
in Enterobacteriaceae, 224
and genetic relatedness, 223
Lipopolysaccharide
in fungi, 104
Lodderomyces
in food spoilage, 11
Luminescence microscopy, 372
Lymphocytic choriomeningitis
and arenoviruses, 232, 242
pathology of, 242
Lysogeny
in Bacillus cereus, 276
characterization of, 272
curing of, 274, 275
definition of, 268, 272
and diphtheria toxin formation, 274, 285
and induction, 272, 274
molecular basis, 272, 274
in Proteus, 279
in Salmonella, 275, 282, 285
in Salmonella citri virus, 313
and spores, 276
stability of, 272, 274, 275
Lysomes
and compartmentation, 62, 66
and mesosomes, 66
and periplasmic space, 66

M

Maedi, 240
Malate lyase
in hyphomicrobium, 406, 407
Mannans
biosynthesis of, 114
of yeasts
antisera to, 106
phosphomannans, 105, 106
and species, 105
Mastigocladus, 394
Measles virus
in multiple sclerosis, 246, 247
and slow virus diseases, 232, 233, 246
and subacute sclerosing panencephalitis, 232-36
Membranes
and acetyl choline esterase, 77
of arboviruses
and budding sites, 328
lipids in, 328, 329
origin of, 327
proteins of, 327, 328
in Dictyostelium
adenyl cyclase in, 158
and alkaline phosphate, 156
and differentiation, 142
in electron transfer, 55
enzymes bound to
and compartmentation, 66, 67
and function, 66, 67
of gas vacuoles, 180
of herpes virus
lipids of, 343
proteins of, 341, 342
source, 341
of inclusion granules, 176
inclusions within
carboxysomes, 180, 181
chlorobium vesicles, 182-84
gas vacuoles, 179, 180
polyglucoside granules, 176-78
poly-β-hydroxybutyrate granules, 176-78
sulfur globules, 179
of influenza virus
lipids of, 338
origin of, 338
proteins of, 336, 338
of mollicute-like organisms, 312, 319, 320
of Mollicutes, 311
of Mycoplasmatales, 304
of myxoviruses
lipids of, 337, 338
origin of, 336, 337
proteins of, 336-38
of paramyxoviruses
and cell fusion, 339, 340
lipids of, 339, 340
proteins of, 340
of pox viruses
and cell membranes, 344
development of, 344, 345
lipids of, 345
of rhabdoviruses
lipids of, 330, 332
origin of, 330
proteins in, 331, 332
synthesis of, 331
of RNA tumor viruses
enzymes of, 334
lipids of, 334, 335
origin of, 333
proteins of, 333, 334
and transformation, 335
of Spiroplasma, 306
and virus envelopes
biogenesis of, 326
as derivatives, 325, 326
glycoproteins in, 345
lipids of, 326
as models, 345
Mesosomes
and lysosomes, 66
nature of, 66
and periplasmic space, 66
Metallogenium
budding of, 429
as contaminant, 396
encrustation of, 428, 429
growth of, 428, 429
and Mycoplasmas, 429
Methanol utilization, 405, 406
Methylosinus
alcohol dehydrogenase of, 405
and Blastobacter, 420
budding in, 421
characteristics of, 421, 422
Micrococcus flavus
cyclic AMP in, 354
Micrococcus lysodeikticus
cyclic AMP in, 354
polyphosphate granules of, 170
Micromonospora chalcea
sporulation in, 394
Microscopy
absorption, 372, 373
chemical resolution in
for DNA, 382
electron probe microanalyzer in, 383, 384
and fluorescence, 382, 383
limits of, 382
and luminescence, 383
and mass, 384, 385
quantitation in, 381, 382
contrast in, 386, 387
in corn stunt disease, 309, 310
electron
see Electron microscopy
fluorescence, 372, 373, 382, 383
history of, 371
luminescence, 372, 373, 383
microscopes in
and auxiliary equipment, 377
electron, 376, 377
optical, 372-75
optical
absorption, 372, 373
fluorescence, 372, 373
future improvements in, 387

luminescence, 372, 373
and microspectrophotometry, 372
polarizing, 375
refraction, 373-75
staining in, 372
phase contrast, 373-76, 385
phosphorescence, 372
refraction in
dark ground illumination in, 373
methods in, 373
phase contrast, 373-75
resolution in
chemical, 381-85
and contrast, 377, 378, 386, 387
and depth, 379-81
spatial, 378, 379
temporal, 385, 386
in transmission electron microscopy, 376
stereo images in, 381
temporal resolution in, 385
X-ray, 376
Microspectrophotometry, 372, 381
Microsporum
allergenic agents of, 107
Microtubules
in Leishmania, 207, 209
Mitochondria
and compartmentation
of acetyl CoA, 68
enzyme complexes in, 70, 71
and glycolysis, 69
of Krebs cycle, 68, 79
of ornithine transcarbamylase, 67
in Dictyostelium, 141
in Leishmania, 207, 209
and prespore vacuoles, 142
Mitomycin C
and induction, 272
Mollicute-like organisms
antibiotic effects, 316, 317, 320
in aster-yellows disease
degeneration of, 313
intracellular growth of, 312, 313
morphology of, 311, 312, 319
and viruses, 313, 314
in corn stunt disease
isolation of, 308, 309
microscopy of, 309, 310
serology of, 310, 311
definition of, 303
dual infection with, 314, 315
fragility of, 312
intracellular growth of, 312, 313
membranes of, 312, 319, 320
mycoplasma, 302, 303
serology of, 310, 311
spiroplasma as
bacteriophage in, 306
and citrus-stubborn disease, 304, 311
cultivation of, 306, 307
distinguishing characteristics of, 306
and insect vectors, 307, 308
and sterility, 317
tetracycline effect, 303
transmission of, 315
vectors of, 303, 312
viruses of, 313-15
as virus vectors, 314
Mollicutes
as disease agents
in plants, 302, 303
and viruses, 302
electron microscopy of, 309
and L-forms, 304
membranes of, 312
and mollicute-like organisms
in aster-yellows disease, 311, 312
intracellular growth of, 312, 313
morphology of, 311, 312
requirements of, 305
taxonomy of, 304, 305
viruses in, 313, 314
Mucocutaneous leishmaniasis, 202
Multiple sclerosis
infectious basis of, 246, 247
and measles virus, 246, 247
pathogenicity of, 247
and visna virus, 242
Mycobacterium smegmatis
phage conversions in, 269
Mycococcus
budding in, 393, 424
fatty acids of, 425
morphology of, 424, 425
taxonomy of, 426
Mycoderma
and Debaromyces, 6
and film-forming yeasts, 6
Mycodextranase, 113
Mycoplasma gallisepticum, 308
Mycoplasma pneumoniae
in Guillain-Barré syndrome, 246, 248
Mycoplasmas
budding in, 426
and Gallionella, 427
growth requirements of, 305
membranes of, 304
Metallogenium as, 429
and mollicute-like organisms, 302, 303
paracrystalline fiber in, 174, 175
in plant diseases
as agents of, 302
and PLT agents, 302
tetracycline effects, 302
taxonomy of, 304, 305
Mycorrhiza
and compartmentation, 65
Myxoviruses
assembly of
at cell surfaces, 336
and protein synthesis, 336, 337
composition of, 336
membranes of
lipids of, 337, 338
origin of, 336, 337
protein in, 336-38
organization of, 336

N

Naumanniella
budding in, 422
life cycle of, 422
Neurospora
and arginine biosynthesis, 67
aromatic amino acid synthesis in, 72
carbamyl phosphate in, 67
pyrimidine biosynthesis in, 67
trifunctional enzyme of, 73
Neurospora crassa
cell walls of
glycoprotein of, 109
invertase of, 112
layers of, 104
and ionizing radiation, 128
in space, 128
Newcastle disease virus, 340
Nitrate reductase
and nitrite oxidase, 90
of Thiobacillus denitrificans, 96
Nitrite oxidase
cytochrome c reductase in, 89
cytochromes in, 89, 90
formate oxidase in, 90
and nitrate reductase, 90
substrate for, 89
Nitrite oxidation
in Nitrobacter
cytochromes in, 89, 90
efficiency of, 96
of nitrite oxidase, 89
reviews of, 85
Nitrite reductase

and hydroxylamine oxidase, 86
and nitroxyl oxidase, 88
Nitrobacter
budding in, 393, 397
nitrite oxidation in
cytochromes in, 89, 90
efficiency of, 96
and nitrite oxidase, 89
oxidative phosphorylation in, 96
Nitrogen fixation
and compartmentation, 65
leghemoglobin in, 65
Nitrosocystis oceanus
ammonia oxidation in, 87
Nitrosolobus
budding in, 393, 397
Nitrosomonas
ammonia oxidation in
and cytochrome oxidase, 86, 87
cytochromes in, 86-88
efficiency of, 96
fractionation of, 87
inhibitors of, 89
reactions of, 86, 88
Nitroxyl oxidase, 90
Nocardia erythropolis, 354
Nutrition
and prunes, 4, 5

O

O-factors
and phage conversion, 280-83
Oncorna viruses
see RNA tumor viruses
Ornithine transcarbamylase, 67
Oxidative phosphorylation
and hydrogen oxidation, 97
and inorganic compound oxidation, 96
measurement of, 96
nitrite effect, 96
and thiosulfate oxidation, 97

P

P870
circular dichroism of, 44
components of, 44
and cytochromes, 45, 48, 49
electron acceptor for, 50
immunology of, 44
model of, 45
nature of, 43
oxidation of, 43
proteins of, 44
purification of, 43
spectra of, 43
Panthetheine, 72
Papovaviruses
and oncogenicity, 238
in progressive multifocal leukoencephalopathy, 232, 236, 237
and slow virus diseases, 232, 236, 237
Paracoccidioides brasiliensis
dimorphism in, 104, 105
Paracoccioides brasiliensis, 396
Paramyxoviruses
composition of, 339
lipids of
and cell fusion, 339, 340
and host lipids, 340
membranes of
and cell fusion, 339, 340
lipids of, 339, 340
proteins of, 340
proteins of
organization of, 339
synthesis of, 339
and virus envelope, 340
Parasporal inclusions
in algae, 176
in Bacillus thuringiensis, 172-74
in clostridia, 174, 175
polypeptides of, 172
and sporulation, 174
Parkinson's disease
etiology of, 250
influenza virus in, 246, 250
Pasteuria
budding in, 393, 419, 420
characteristics of, 419, 420
nucleoid of, 432
thermophilic, 420
Pedomicrobium
budding in, 393, 394, 408, 433
characteristics of, 408
morphology of, 409, 410
occurrence of, 408, 410
Pelodictyon clathratiforme
budding in, 393
Peltigera polydactyla
transport in, 63
Penicillium charlesii
cell walls of, 110, 111
galactofuranosidase of, 112, 113
peptidophosphogalactomannan synthesis in, 114
polysaccharides of, 110
Penicillium chrysogenum
cell wall of, 105
Penicillium roqueforti
viability of
models of, 128
in space, 122, 126-28
Peptidoglycans, 104
Peptidophosphogalactomannans, 106, 107
Peptido-polysaccharides
biosynthesis of, 113-15
of cell walls
in Aspergillus, 109, 110
in dermatophytes, 107-9
in Neurospora, 109
in Penicillium, 110, 111
in yeast, 105-7
Periplasmic space
and compartmentation, 62, 66
enzymes in, 66
Peroxisomes, 62, 68
Phage
see Bacteriophage
Phialophora dermatitidis
bud formation in, 397
Phosphofructokinase, 105
Phosphomannans, 105, 106
Phosphorescence microscopy, 372
Photophosphorylation
chemiosmotic theory of, 54, 55
Photoredoxin, 50
Photosynthesis
antenna in, 41
bacterial
bacteriochlorophyll in, 41-43
cytochromes in, 45-50
electron acceptors in, 50-53
P870 in, 43-45
and reduced pyridine nucleotides, 54
bacteriochlorophyll in
and carotenoids, 43
as complex, 41-43
interactions of, 42, 43
cytochromes in
and action spectra, 46
in bacteria, 45-50
electron flow in, 49
nature of, 45-49
and P870, 45, 48, 49
electron acceptors in
nonheme iron as, 50-52
photoredoxin as, 50
primary, 50-52
and proton uptake, 54
secondary, 51-53
ubiquinone as, 50, 52, 53
energy transfer in
and action spectra, 46
in antenna, 42
and cytochromes, 46-50
free energy change in, 53, 54
and geometry, 47
and P870, 43-45
and photophosphorylation, 54, 55
P870 in

components of, 44
and cytochromes, 45-49
electron acceptors for, 50-53
model of, 45
nature of, 43
oxidation of, 43
proteins of, 44
purification of, 43
and photophosphorylation, 54, 55
ubiquinone in, 44, 50, 53
Phycobilisomes
appearance of, 172, 173
biliproteins of, 171
Planctomyces
budding in, 393, 418, 419
occurrence of, 418, 419
Plasmids
and gene transfer, 221-23
in Pseudomonas, 221, 222
in Streptomyces coelicolor, 223
and viruses, 266
Poliovirus
in amyotrophic lateral sclerosis, 246, 249
in space, 127
Poly(A)
in Dictyostelium mRNA, 145
Polyacrylamide gel electrophoresis
of RNA
and secondary structure, 27-29
of viroids, 27
Polychlorinated biphenyls
analysis of, 20
and DDT, 20
Polyglucoside granules
membrane enclosed
appearance of, 176-78
occurrence of, 176
nonmembrane enclosed
appearance of, 168, 169
polymers of, 168
Poly-β-hydroxybutyrate granules
appearance of, 176-78
function of, 178
Polyhydroxybutyrate synthetase, 178
Polyoxin D, 114
Polyphosphate granules
appearance of, 169, 170
formation of, 170
function of, 170
polyphosphate in, 168-70
Polyphosphate kinase, 170
Polysaccharides
biosynthesis of, 113-15
of cell walls
in Aspergillus, 109, 110
chitin-glucan, 104
in dermatophytes, 107-9
glucan-mannan, 104
mannans, 105, 106
in Neurospora, 109
in Penicillum, 110, 111
and taxonomy, 104
in yeasts, 105-7
Potato spindle tuber disease
agent of, 24
virions in, 25
Potato spindle tuber viroid
aggregation of, 28
as double-stranded RNA, 24, 30-33
electron microscopy of, 30-32
electrophoresis of, 27
isolation of, 29
localization of, 26
molecular weight of, 26-31
nuclease sensitivity of, 24, 26
pathogenesis of, 34, 35
radiation sensitivity of, 30
replication of, 33, 34
sedimentation of, 24, 26
thermal denaturation of, 30
and virions, 25
Pox viruses
composition of, 343
glycoproteins of, 343-45
hemagglutinin of, 344
membranes of
and cell membranes, 344
development of, 344, 345
lipids of, 345
release of, 345
Prodigiosin, 357
Progressive multifocal leukoencephalopathy
clinical features, 237, 257
and demyelination, 237, 252, 257
immune deficiency in, 252, 255
and malignancy, 237, 238, 252, 259
and papovaviruses, 232, 236, 237
Prosthecochloris, 417
Prosthecomicrobium
budding in, 393, 416
occurrence of, 416
star-shaped, 393
Protein kinase
and cyclic AMP, 359
Protein synthesis
cyclic AMP effect, 354-56
and diphtheria toxin, 288-93
translocase in, 289-91
and virus assembly, 336, 337
Proteus mirabilis
CAP in, 360
genetic map of, 224
lysogeny in, 279
Prunes
laxative principle, 5
nutritive value, 4, 5
Pseudomonas
aeruginosa
linkage map of, 224
phage conversions in, 271
protein synthesis in, 356
in space, 132
conjugation in, 221
gene arrangements in, 225
plasmids in, 221, 222
saccharophila
hydrogen oxidation in, 97
Pulvic acid, 65
Pyrimidine biosynthesis
and compartmentation, 67
Pyrophosphatase, 98
Pyruvate dehydrogenase, 72

R

Rabies virus
lipids of, 332, 333
Raphidosomes, 176
Rauschler leukemia virus
lipids of, 335
Recombination
in Ascomycetes, 446
and DNA repair, 448
helix resolution in, 458, 460, 461
in higher organisms, 445, 446
hot-spots in, 453
initiation of
and asymmetric intermediates, 453, 454
defined point of, 455, 456
strand opening in, 452
mechanism of
copy-choice, 449
and DNA ends, 457-59
and heavy atom labels, 449
initiation of, 452-56
multiple, 447, 448
physiological influence on, 465
rate competition in, 464
strand transfer in, 450, 451
in transduction, 447
in transformation, 447
in viruses, 447
models of
asymmetric, 454, 456
and bridge mobility, 460
cross-bridged intermediate in, 451, 452

and DNA ends, 457-59
first strand break in, 453
and gene conversion, 461, 464
helix resolution in, 458, 460, 461
Holliday, 449, 451, 453-55
purposes of, 447
randomness in, 453
register in, 449
and strand exchange, 451, 452, 454-56
symmetrical intermediates in, 453
unilateral exchange in, 456
nonreciprocal, 446
replication in, 448
in viruses, 447
Regulation
of adenyl cyclase, 363-65
and CAP, 359-62
compartmentation in, 61
of cyclic AMP, 362-65
of cyclic AMP levels, 157
and cyclic AMP phosphodiesterase, 365
in differentiation
of alkaline phosphatase, 156
of cellulase, 155
and compartmentation, 140, 154
and enzyme concentration, 151-53, 162
of glycogen phosphorylase, 159, 160
of glycogen synthetase, 159
and metabolite flux, 150, 151
of threonine deaminase, 158, 159
of trehalase, 154, 155
of trehalose phosphate synthetase, 160-62
and turnover, 151, 152, 162
of UDP-glucosepyrophosphorylase, 151, 152
microenvironmental effects, 77
of protein synthesis
and CAP, 359-62
and cyclic AMP, 354
and transcription, 357-62
of pyruvate dehydrogenase, 72
of transcription, 357-62
Replicons, 268
Restriction endonucleases, 453
Reverse transcriptase
in visna virus, 242, 259
R-factors, 222
Rhabdoviruses
composition of, 330
dimensions of, 330
lipids of, 332
membranes of
components of, 330-32
formation of, 331
origin of, 330
proteins of, 330, 331
rabies, 332, 333
and T particles, 330
vesicular stomatitis virus, 329-32
Rhizobium trifolii, 271
Rhodanese
as sulfur transferase, 94
in thiosulfate oxidation, 94
Rhodomicrobium
budding in, 393, 394, 410, 433
enzymes of, 413
growth of, 412-14
isolation of, 412
lipids of, 414
and spirillum, 396
Rhodopseudomonas
budding in, 393, 397
gelatinosa, 47
spheroides
bacteriochlorophyll complex of, 42
cytochromes of, 48
P870 of, 43, 44
viridis
cytochromes of, 47
electron transfer in, 51
Rhodospirillum rubrum
bacteriochlorophyll in, 42
carotenoid-protein complex in, 43
cytochromes of, 46, 48
P870 of, 44
Rhodotorula glutinis
bud formation in, 397
Ribonuclease
and potato spindle tuber viroid, 24, 26
Ribulose-1, 5-diphosphate carboxylase
in blue-green algae, 182
electron microscopy of, 182, 183
in inclusion bodies, 66, 182
microenvironmental effects on, 79
in Thiobacillus, 66
Rice yellow dwarf disease
agent of, 302
Rickettsia-like organisms
cell wall of, 318
definition of, 304
localization of, 318, 319
and plant diseases, 317
RNA polymerase
in development, 146
RNA tumor viruses
classification of, 333
core of, 333
membranes of
enzymes of, 334
lipids of, 334, 335
origin of, 333
proteins of, 333, 334
and transformation, 335
Rous sarcoma virus
assembly of, 333
lipids of, 334, 335
low molecular weight RNA of, 36
Rubredoxin, 52

S

Saccharomyces
carlsbergensis, 113
cell walls of
and culture conditions, 105
glycoproteins of, 105
mannans of, 105, 106
peptido-polysaccharide of, 105-7
cerevesiae
budding in, 396, 397
histidine biosynthesis in, 73
nitrogen metabolism in, 73
UV sensitivity of, 130
glycoprotein synthesis in, 113, 114
invertases of, 111-13
Salmonella
lipopolysaccharide synthesis in, 281
phage conversions in, 271-73
Salmonella anatum
characterization of, 280
O-factors in, 280-83
phage conversion in
and antigenic changes, 273, 280-83
and O-factors, 280-83
and receptors, 273, 281, 282, 284
and Salmonella newington, 280, 284
Salmonella enteritidis, 274
Salmonella newington
bacteriophage in, 284
and Salmonella anatum, 280
Salmonella typhimurium
bacteriophage induction in
in space, 125, 126
CAP in, 360
curing of, 275
gene map of, 221, 224
histidine biosynthesis in, 73

histidine operon of, 226, 227
lysogeny of, 275, 282, 285
phage P22 of
antigen 1 in, 285
and O-antigen, 272, 275
virulent, 279
protein synthesis in
and cyclic AMP, 356
Schilder's disease, 240
Scrapie
agents of, 232, 234, 235, 243, 244, 258
cytopathic effects of, 232, 245, 257, 259
genetic factors in, 251
genome of, 232, 258
infectivity of, 233, 243
radiation inactivation of, 37
as viroid disease, 37, 243, 258
Seliberia
budding in, 423
occurrence of, 423
Semliki Forest Virus, 330
Sendai virus
and cell fusion, 339
lipids of, 340
Serratia marcescens
cAMP phosphodiesterase of, 365
cyclic AMP in, 354
Shigella
dysenteriae
bacteriophage T7 in, 278, 279
phage conversion in, 271
phage receptors on, 277
flexneri
genetic map of, 224
Siderococcus, 422
Sindbis virus
lipids of, 328, 329
maturation of, 327
membranes of, 328
Slow virus diseases
agents of
conventional, 232-38, 240-43
and persistence, 255
unconventional, 232, 234, 235, 238-40, 243-45, 260
amyotrophic lateral sclerosis as, 248, 249
characteristics of, 232
Creutzfeldt-Jakob disease
agents of, 232, 239
clinical features, 238, 240
cytopathic effects of, 232
genetic factors, 251
and viruses, 240
demonstration of, 259, 260
features of
antigenicity in, 255, 256
genetic, 250-52
host-related, 250-54
immunological, 252-54
incubation period, 254
viral persistence in, 254, 255
virus-related, 254-56
Guillain-Barré syndrome as, 248
kuru
agents of, 232, 239
and cannibalism, 238
clinical features, 238
cytopathic effects of, 232
genetic factors, 250, 251
lymphocytic choriomeningitis
and arenoviruses, 232, 242
pathology of, 241, 242
multiple sclerosis as, 246, 247
Parkinson's disease as, 250
pathogenesis of
mechanisms of, 257
and transmissibility, 256-58
presenile dementias as, 250
progressive multifocal encephalopathy
clinical features, 237, 251
and demyelination, 237, 251, 252
immunodeficiency in, 252, 255
and malignancy, 237, 238, 252
and papovaviruses, 232, 236, 237
reviews of, 232
scrapie
agent of, 232, 234, 235, 243, 244, 258
cytopathic effects of, 232, 245, 257
genetic factors in, 251
genome of, 232, 258
infectivity of, 233, 243
as viroid, 243, 258
subacute sclerosing panencephalitis
clinical features, 233, 257
and immune mechanisms, 237, 252, 253
and measles virus, 232-36
pathogenesis of, 233, 237, 257
persistence of, 259
transmissible mink encephalopathy
agents of, 232, 244, 245
cytopathic effects of, 232
pathology of, 245
virus-host interactions in
host-range in, 257
and transmissibility, 256-58
virus replication in, 258, 259
visna
cytopathic effects of, 240
genetic factors in, 251
transmission of, 240
and visna virus, 232, 240-42
Space microbiology
and astronaut flora
and illnesses, 130
and immunocompetence, 131
and life-support system, 132
mycological, 132-34
of potential pathogens, 130, 131
and stress, 132
transfer of, 131, 134
and bacteriophage induction
$\lambda$, 124-26
as model system, 124-26
and mutagenesis, 124, 125
and radiation protection, 125
of Salmonella, 125, 126
and extraterrestrial life, 121, 122
and genetic effects
bacteriophage induction in, 124-26
ionizing radiation in, 128
mutagenesis, 124, 125
and spacecraft sterilization, 126-28
and terrestrial organisms
genetic effects, 124-26, 128
growth of, 123
in high altitude balloons, 123
in orbital flight, 123
organisms tested, 123
and solar UV, 128-30
spacecraft sterilization, 126-28
vacuum effect, 128, 129
Spirilloxanthin, 43
Spirillum serpens, 396
Spiroplasma
citri
antibodies to, 311
characteristics of, 306
and citrus-stubborn disease, 304
cultivation of, 306, 307
insect vectors of, 307, 308
virus of, 306, 313
and citrus-stubborn disease,

304, 311
and corn stunt, 308-11
definition of, 303, 304
membranes of, 306
and spiral forms, 306, 309, 310
taxonomy of, 305
Spores
and lysogeny, 276
surface structure of, 381
Sporulation
of Bacillus thuringiensis, 174
and budding, 394, 395
and parasporal inclusions, 174
Staphylococcus aureus
on astronauts, 131, 134
histidine operon of, 226
linkage map of, 224
phage conversions in, 269, 270
and space flight, 124, 131, 134
Star-shaped bacteria, 393, 417, 418
Streptococcus
pyogenes
phage conversions in, 270
salivarius
adenyl cyclase of, 364
cyclic AMP in, 354
Streptomyces coelicolor
conjugation in, 222, 223
linkage map of, 224
mutagenesis of, 223
Subacute sclerosing panencephalitis
clinical features of, 233, 257
and immune mechanisms, 237, 252, 253
and measles virus, 232-36
pathogenesis of, 233, 237, 257
persistence of, 259
Sugar cane ratoon stunt, 317, 318
Sulfide oxidase, 95
Sulfite:cytochrome c oxidoreductase
purification of, 93
in sulfite oxidation, 91, 93
Sulfite oxidase, 93
Sulfite oxidation
in Thiobacillus, 93-95
Sulfolobus
budding in, 393, 397
Sulfur globules
appearance of, 176, 177, 179
sulfur in, 179
Sulfur oxidation
cell free
fractionation of, 92
glutathione in, 91, 92, 94
sulfite in, 91, 93-95
thiosulfate in, 94
and energy coupling, 97
mechanism of, 91
review of, 85
scheme of, 95
SV-5 virus
and cell fusion, 339
composition of, 340
SV-40 virus
and progressive multifocal encephalopathy, 237
Systemic lupus erythematosis, 243

T

Tay-Sachs disease, 240
Teichoic acid
in fungi, 104
Tetrahymena pyriformis, 68
Thermoplasma
budding of, 427
isolation of, 427
Thiobacillus
denitrificans
nitrate reductase of, 96
sulfite oxidation in, 93
ferrooxidans
iron oxidation in, 90
polyhedral bodies in, 182
neapolitanus
carboxysomes in, 180, 181
organelle in, 66
thiooxidans
sulfur oxidation in, 91
Thiocapsa pfennigii, 47, 48
Thiorhodaceae
sulfur globules in, 179
Thiosulfate oxidation
and glutathione, 94
and oxidative phosphorylation, 97
and pyridine nucleotide reduction, 98
rhodanese in, 94
tetrathionate in, 93-95
Thiovulum majus
inclusions of, 184
Threonine deaminase
in Dictyostelium, 158, 159
regulatory role of, 227
Tobacco mosaic virus
viability of
models for, 128
in space, 122, 126-28
Torulopsidosira
budding in, 395
Torulopsis glabrata, 396
T particles, 330
Transcription
CAP effect, 360, 361
cyclic AMP effect, 357, 358, 361
Transduction
DNA incorporation in, 448
mechanism of, 447
Transformation
in Bacillus subtilis, 449
DNA incorporation in, 448, 456
mechanism of, 447
neoplastic, 335
Transmissible mink encephalopathy
agents of, 232, 244, 245
cytopathic effects of, 232
pathology of, 245
as viroid disease, 37
Transport
in lichens, 63-65
Trehalase, 154, 155
Trehalose phosphate synthetase
in Dictyostelium, 160-62
in differentiation, 160-62
inhibitor of, 161
Trichophyton
allergenic agents of, 107
galactomannan of, 107, 108
trichophytin of, 107
Tristeza virus, 315
Tryptophan
pyrrolase, 151
synthetase
as enzyme complex, 72
Tryptophanase, 356, 358
Tyrocidin, 72

U

Ubiquinone
and P870, 44, 50, 52, 53
as primary electron acceptor, 50
as secondary electron acceptor, 52, 53
UDP-glucose pyrophosphorylase
in Dictyostelium
degradation of, 152
in differentiation, 151, 152
synthesis of, 151
Umbilicaria papulosa, 64
Uta, 204

V

Vaccinia virus
glycoproteins of, 343, 344
hemagglutinin of, 344
in space, 127
Vesicular stomatitis virus

composition of, 330
lipids of, 329, 332
proteins of, 330, 331
sterols in, 332
Vibrio fetus, 271
Viroids
in animals, 37
definition of, 23, 24
diseases caused, 24
electron microscopy of, 30-32
evidence for
as RNA, 24, 25
and virion absence, 25, 26
as free nucleic acid
double-stranded, 24
sedimentation of, 24, 25
localization of, 26
molecular weight of, 26-28
origin of, 35, 36
pathogenesis of, 34, 35
polyacrylamide gel electrophoresis of, 27
purification of, 29
replication of, 33, 34
scrapie as, 243, 258
structure of, 31-33
transmission of, 35
Virolysin, 278
Viruses
in amyotrophic lateral sclerosis, 248, 249
arboviruses
maturation of, 327, 328
membranes of, 327-30
proteins of, 327, 328
arenoviruses
and slow virus diseases, 232, 242
in Creutzfeldt-Jakob disease, 232, 238-40, 251
in Guillain-Barré syndrome, 246, 248
herpes
lipids of, 343
maturation of, 341
proteins of, 341, 342
structure of, 341
influenza, 250
in kuru, 232, 238, 239, 250, 251
in lymphocytic choriomeningitis, 232, 241, 242
measles
in multiple sclerosis, 246, 247
and slow virus diseases, 232, 233, 246
membranes of
biogenesis of, 326, 345, 346
characterization of, 326
as derivatives, 325, 326
glycoproteins in, 345, 346
lipids of, 328, 329, 332, 334, 335, 337-40, 343, 345, 347, 348
morphogenesis of, 345, 346
in multiple sclerosis, 246, 247
myxoviruses
assembly of, 336, 337
composition of, 336
membranes of, 336-38
nucleocapsid proteins of, 346, 347
papovaviruses
oncogenicity of, 238
and slow virus diseases, 232, 236, 237
paramyxoviruses
composition of, 339
lipids of, 339, 340
proteins of, 339, 340
in Parkinson's disease, 250
polio, 246, 249
pox viruses, 343
and presenile dementias, 250
in progressive multifocal leukoencephalopathy, 232, 236-38, 252, 255, 257, 259
rhabdoviruses
composition of, 330
membranes of, 330-32
proteins of, 330, 331
and T particles, 330
RNA tumor viruses
classification of, 333
composition of, 333
membranes of, 333-35
in scrapie, 232-35, 243-45, 251, 255, 257, 258
and slow virus diseases
antigenicity of, 255, 256
characteristics of, 232
incubation period in, 254
pathogenesis of, 256-59
persistence in, 254, 255
replication in, 258, 259
reviews of, 232
see also specific diseases
in subacute sclerosing panencephalitis, 232-37, 252, 253, 257, 259
in transmissible mink encephalopathy, 232, 244, 245
visna
and carcinogenesis, 242
cytopathic effects of, 240
immune response in, 253
and myxoviruses, 241, 242
replication of, 242
reverse transcriptase in, 242
and slow virus diseases, 232, 240-42
see also specific bacteriophages and viruses
Visceral leishmaniasis, 192, 199
Visna virus
clinical features of, 240
and maedi, 240
properties of, 240, 242
and slow virus diseases, 232, 240-42

X

Xanthoria aureola, 63

Y

Yeasts
budding in, 396, 397
and Drosophila, 10, 11
ecology of, 10
film yeasts
and Mycoderma, 6
in pickle-brine tanks, 6
and food spoilage, 3, 8
on food surfaces, 6
taxonomy of, 10, 11
wine yeasts, 7, 8
see also specific yeasts

Z

Zoonotic cutaneous leishmaniasis
cause of, 197
nature of, 197, 198

# CUMULATIVE INDEXES

## CONTRIBUTING AUTHORS VOLUMES 24 -28


A

Achong, B. G., 27:413
Alexander, M., 25:361
Andersson, B., 25:291
Andrewes, A. G., 26:225
Andrewes, C. H., 27:1
Arden, S. B., 28:265
Austen, K. F., 25:309

B

Bachrach, U., 24:109
Barer, R., 28:371
Barksdale, L., 28:265
Bauchop, T., 25:429
Blair, C. D., 24:539
Bonner, J. T., 25:75
Boyer, H. W., 25:153
Bray, R. S., 28:189
Brener, Z., 27:347

C

Cagen, L. M., 24:159
Calendar, R., 24:241
Cameron, D. S., 27:243
Catalano, L. W. Jr., 25:255
Chapman-Andresen, C., 25:27
Chatterjee, A. K., 26:389
Clark, A. J., 25:437
Clasener, H., 26:55
Coetzee, J. N., 26:23
Colby, C., 25:333
Culbertson, C. G., 25:231
Cury, A., 25:49

D

Demain, A. L., 26:369
Diener, T. O., 28:23
Duesberg, P. H., 24:539

E

Enomoto, M., 26:279
Epstein, M. A., 27:413

F

Fahey, J. L., 25:679
Fenner, F., 24:297
Fjerdingstad, E., 25:563
Forrest, H. S., 24:91
Fraenkel, D. G., 27:69
Fraenkel-Conrat, H., 24:463
Friedmann, H. C., 24:159
Fuccillo, D. A., 28:231

G

Gander, J. E., 28:103
Gigli, I., 25:309
Goldstein, S., 27:13
Gottlieb, S. F., 25:111
Grunberg, E., 27:317

H

Haines, T. H., 27:403
Handmaker, S. D., 27:189
Hanson, R. S., 24:53
Harris, R. H., 27:27
Harrison, J. E., 24:135
Haslam, J. M., 26:163
Hausmann, R., 27:51
Hegeman, G. D., 24:429
Helinski, D. R., 27:437
Hellström, I., 24:373
Hellström, K. E., 24:373
Henderson, P. J. F., 25:393
Hirsch, P., 28:391
Horio, T., 24:399
Hotchkiss, R. D., 28:445
Hough, J., 25:583
Howard, R. J., 24:525
Huang, A. S., 27:101
Hutner, S. H., 26:313

I

Ishida, Y., 26:127

K

Kadota, H., 26:127
Kamen, M. D., 24:399
Kelly, D. P., 25:177
Kihlberg, R., 26:427
Killick, K. A., 28:139
Killington, R. A., 26:503
Kleyn, J., 25:583
Korant, B. D., 26:467
Kurent, J. E., 28:231

L

Lester, W., 26:85
Levinthal, M., 28:219
Liaaen-Jensen, S., 26:225
Lindberg, A. A., 27:205
Linnane, A. W., 26:163
Lipps, J. H., 27:471
Lonberg-Holm, K. K., 26:467
Lukins, H. B., 26:163
Lwoff, A., 25:1

M

Mann, D. L., 25:679
Maramorosch, K., 28:301
Mergenhagen, S. E., 24:525
Milstein, C., 24:335
Mitchell, R., 27:27
Morgan, M. J., 25:333
Mosbach, K., 28:61
Mrak, E. M., 28:1
Munro, A. J., 24:335

N

Nagley, P., 26:163
Nakamura, M., 24:359
Nichols, W. W., 24:479
Notkins, A. L., 24:525
Nozawa, Y., 26:249

P

Parson, W. W., 28:41
Pato, M. L., 26:347
Payne, W. J., 24:17
Pestka, S., 25:487
Peterson, J. A., 24:53
Pine, M. J., 26:103
Pirie, N. W., 27:119
Porter, D. D., 25:283
Pringsheim, E. G., 24:1

Q

Quigley, J. P., 28:325

R

Ribbons, D. W., 24:135
Rickenberg, H. V., 28:353
Rifkin, D. B., 28:325
Riva, S., 26:199
Rosenberg, S. L., 24:429

Rosenkranz, H. S., 27:383

S

Sadoff, H. L., 27:133
Saito, M., 26:279
Schaechter, M., 27:261
Schmidt, J. M., 25:93
Schulze, J. A., 24:359
Seidler, R. J., 25:649
Sencer, D. J., 25:465
Sever, J. L., 25:255; 28:231
Shapiro, B. M., 24:501
Shively, J. M., 28:167
Siegel, P. J., 27:261
Silvestri, L. G., 26:199
Soriano, S., 27:155
Sprague, V., 25:211
Srere, P. A., 28:61
Stadtman, E. R., 24:501
Starr, M. P., 25:649; 26:389
Stewart, W. D. P., 27:283
Stott, E. J., 26:503
Sugiyama, T., 26:467
Suzuki, I., 28:85

T

Taylor, D. L., 27:171
Taylor, G. R., 28:121
Taylor, I. E. P., 27:243
Temin, H. M., 25:609
Thompson, G. A. Jr., 26:249
Titsworth, E. H., 27:317
Travassos, L. R. R. G., 25:49

V

Valentine, R. C., 26:139
Van Baalen, C., 24:91
Veldkamp, H., 24:209
Vinopal, R. T., 27:69

W

Wadzinski, A. M., 24:135
Wigzell, H., 25:291
Wilson, P. W., 26:1
Wright, B. E., 28:139

Y

Yoch, D. C., 26:139
Yousten, A. A., 24:53

# CHAPTER TITLES VOLUMES 24-28

| | | |
|---|---|---|
| PREFATORY CHAPTERS | | |
| Contributions Toward the Development of General Microbiology | E. G. Pringsheim | 24:1-16 |
| From Protozoa to Bacteria and Viruses: Fifty Years with Microbes | A. Lwoff | 25:1-26 |
| Training a Microbiologist | P. W. Wilson | 26:1-22 |
| Fifty Years with Viruses | C. H. Andrewes | 27:1-11 |
| A Microbiologist Turned Administrator—How it Happened | E. M. Mrak | 28:1-22 |
| ANIMAL PATHOGENS AND DISEASES | | |
| Clostridium perfringens Food Poisoning | M. Nakamura, J. A. Schulze | 24:359-72 |
| Diseases of Oysters | V. Sprague | 25:211-30 |
| The Pathogenicity of Soil Amebas | C. G. Culbertson | 25:231-54 |
| The Role of Viruses as Causes of Congenital Defects | L. W. Catalano Jr., J. L. Sever | 25:255-82 |
| Stomach Microbiology of Primates | T. Bauchop | 25:429-36 |
| Emerging Diseases of Man and Animals | D. J. Sencer and Staff | 25:465-86 |
| Pathogenicity of the L-Phase of Bacteria | H. Clasener | 26:55-84 |
| Carcinogens Produced by Fungi | M. Enomoto, M. Saito | 26:279-312 |
| The Genus Erwinia: Enterobacteria Pathogenic to Plants and Animals | M. P. Starr, A. K. Chatterjee | 26:389-426 |
| Algal Symbionts of Invertebrates | D. L. Taylor | 27:171-87 |
| Biology of Trypanosoma cruzi | Z. Brener | 27:347-82 |
| Aspects of Microbiology in Cancer Research | H. S. Rosenkranz | 27:383-401 |
| Viroids: The Smallest Known Agents of Infectious Disease | T. O. Diener | 28:23-39 |
| Leishmania | R. S. Bray | 28:189-217 |
| Slow Virus Diseases | D. A. Fuccillo, J. E. Kurent, J. L. Sever | 28:231-64 |

APPLIED MICROBIOLOGY AND ECOLOGY

| | | |
|---|---|---|
| Clostridium perfringens Food Poisoning | M. Nakamura, J. A. Schulze | 24:359-72 |
| Biochemical Ecology of Microorganisms | M. Alexander | 25:361-92 |
| Microbial Criteria of Environment Qualities | E. Fjerdingstad | 25:563-82 |
| Microbiology of Brewing | J. Kleyn, J. Hough | 25:583-608 |
| Training a Microbiologist | P. W. Wilson | 26:1-22 |
| Riboflavin Oversynthesis | A. L. Demain | 26:369-88 |
| The Microbe as a Source of Food | R. Kihlberg | 26:427-66 |
| The Role of Polymers in Microbial Aggregation | R. H. Harris, R. Mitchell | 27:27-50 |
| Algal Symbionts of Invertebrates | D. L. Taylor | 27:171-87 |
| Nitrogen Fixation by Photosynthetic Microorganisms | W. D. P. Stewart | 27:283-316 |
| A Microbiologist Turned Administrator—How it Happened | E. M. Mrak | 28:1-22 |
| Fungal Cell Wall Glycoproteins and Peptido-Polysaccharides | J. E. Gander | 28:103-19 |
| Space Microbiology | G. R. Taylor | 28:121-37 |
| Microscopes, Microscopy, and Microbiology | R. Barer | 28:371-89 |

CHEMOTHERAPY AND CHEMOTHERAPEUTIC AGENTS

| | | |
|---|---|---|
| Rifampin: A Semisynthetic Derivative of Rifamycin—A Prototype for the Future | W. Lester | 26:85-102 |
| Rifamycins: A General View | S. Riva, L. G. Silvestri | 26:199-224 |
| Chemotherapeutic Properties of Heterocyclic Compounds: Monocyclic Compounds with Five-Membered Rings | E. Grunberg, E. H. Titsworth | 27:317-46 |
| Plasmid Determined Resistance to Antibiotics: Molecular Properties of R Factors | D. R. Helinski | 27:437-70 |

DIVERSITY AND SYSTEMATICS

| | | |
|---|---|---|
| Contributions Toward the Development of General Microbiology | E. G. Pringsheim | 24:1-16 |
| Saprophytic Coryneform Bacteria | H. Veldkamp | 24:209-40 |
| From Protozoa to Bacteria and Viruses: Fifty Years with Microbes | A. Lwoff | 25:1-26 |
| Biology of the Large Amoebae | C. Chapman-Andresen | 25:27-48 |
| Thermophilic Enteric Yeasts | L. R. R. G. Travassos, A. Cury | 25:49-74 |
| Aggregation and Differentiation in the Cellular Slime Molds | J. T. Bonner | 25:75-92 |
| Prosthecate Bacteria | J. M. Schmidt | 25:93-110 |
| Stomach Microbiology of Primates | T. Bauchop | 25:429-36 |
| The Bdellovibrios | M. P. Starr, R. J. Seidler | 25:649-78 |
| The Genus Erwinia: Enterobacteria Pathogenic to Plants and Animals | M. P. Starr, A. K. Chatterjee | 26:389-426 |
| Zoosporic Marine Fungi (Thraustochytriaceae and Dermocystidiaceae) | S. Goldstein | 27:13-26 |
| Flexibacteria | S. Soriano | 27:155-70 |
| Algal Symbionts of Invertebrates | D. L. Taylor | 27:171-87 |
| Nitrogen Fixation by Photosynthetic Microorganisms | W. D. P. Stewart | 27:283-316 |
| Biology of Trypanosoma cruzi | Z. Brener | 27:347-82 |
| Test Structure in Foraminifera | J. H. Lipps | 27:471-88 |
| Inclusion Bodies of Prokaryotes | J. M. Shively | 28:167-87 |
| Budding Bacteria | P. Hirsch | 28:391-444 |

GENETICS

| | | |
|---|---|---|
| The Genetics of Animal Viruses | F. Fenner | 24:297-334 |
| The Evolution of Bacterial Enzyme Systems | G. D. Hegeman, S. L. Rosenberg | 24:429-62 |
| DNA Restriction and Modification Mechanisms in Bacteria | H. W. Boyer | 25:153-76 |
| Toward a Metabolic Interpretation of Genetic Recombination of E. coli and its Phages | A. J. Clark | 25:437-64 |
| Mechanism of Cell Transformation by RNA Tumor Viruses | H. M. Temin | 25:609-48 |
| Genetics of the Proteus Group | J. N. Coetzee | 26:23-54 |
| Regulation of Chromosome Replication and the Bacterial Cell Cycle | M. L. Pato | 26:347-68 |
| RNA Virus Gene Expression and its Control | T. Sugiyama, B. D. Korant, K. K. Lonberg-Holm | 26:467-502 |

| | | |
|---|---|---|
| The Genetics of T-Odd Phages | R. Hausmann | 27:51-67 |
| Hybridization of Eukaryotic Cells | S. D. Handmaker | 27:189-204 |
| Plasmid Determined Resistance to Antibiotics: Molecular Properties of R Factors | D. R. Helinski | 27:437-70 |
| Bacterial Genetics Excluding E. coli | M. Levinthal | 28:219-30 |
| Models of Genetic Recombination | R. D. Hotchkiss | 28:445-68 |
| GROWTH AND NUTRITION | | |
| Energy Yields and Growth of Heterotrophs | W. J. Payne | 24:17-52 |
| Microbial Biosynthesis of $B_{12}$-Like Compounds | H. C. Friedmann, L. M. Cagen | 24:159-208 |
| Effect of Hyperbaric Oxygen on Microorganisms | S. F. Gottlieb | 25:111-52 |
| The Biogenesis of Mitochondria in Microorganisms | A. W. Linnane, J. M. Haslam, H. B. Lukins, P. Nagley | 26:163-98 |
| Inorganic Nutrition | S. H. Hutner | 26:313-46 |
| IMMUNOLOGY | | |
| The Genetic Basis of Antibody Specificity | C. Milstein, A. J. Munro | 24:335-58 |
| Immunological Enhancement as Studied by Cell Culture Techniques | K. E. Hellström, I. Hellström | 24:373-98 |
| Effect of Virus Infections on the Function of the Immune System | A. L. Notkins, S. E. Mergenhagen, R. J. Howard | 24:525-38 |
| Destruction of Virus-Infected Cells by Immunological Mechanisms | D. D. Porter | 25:283-90 |
| Isolation of Lymphoid Cells with Active Surface Receptor Sites | H. Wigzell, B. Andersson | 25:291-308 |
| Phylogeny and Function of the Complement System | I. Gigli, K. F. Austen | 25:309-32 |
| Interferon Induction and Action | C. Colby, M. J. Morgan | 25:333-60 |
| Histocompatibility Antigens | D. L. Mann, J. L. Fahey | 26:679-710 |
| METABOLISM, BIOCHEMISTRY, AND REGULATION | | |
| Unique Biochemical Events in Bacterial Sporulation | R. S. Hanson, J. A. Peterson, A. A. Yousten | 24:53-90 |
| Microbiology of Unconjugated Pteridines | H. S. Forrest, C. Van Baalen | 24:91-108 |
| Metabolism and Function of Spermine and Related Polyamines | U. Bachrach | 24:109-34 |
| Metabolism of Single Carbon Compounds | D. W. Ribbons, J. E. Harrison, A. M. Wadzinski | 24:135-58 |
| Microbial Biosynthesis of $B_{12}$-Like Compounds | H. C. Friedmann, L. M. Cagen | 24:159-208 |
| Bacterial Cytochromes: II. Functional Aspects | T. Horio, M. D. Kamen | 24:399-428 |
| The Regulation of Glutamine Synthesis in Microorganisms | B. M. Shapiro, E. R. Stadtman | 24:501-24 |
| Autotrophy: Concepts of Lithotrophic Bacteria and Their Organic Metabolism | D. P. Kelly | 25:177-210 |
| Ion Transport by Energy-Conserving Biological Membranes | P. J. F. Henderson | 25:393-428 |
| Inhibitors of Ribosome Functions | S. Pestka | 25:487-562 |
| Turnover of Intracellular Proteins | M. J. Pine | 26:103-26 |
| Production of Volatile Sulfur Compounds by Microorganisms | H. Kadota, Y. Ishida | 26:127-38 |
| Ferredoxins and Flavodoxins of Bacteria | D. C. Yoch, R. C. Valentine | 26:139-62 |
| Microbial Carotenoids | S. Liaaen-Jensen, A. G. Andrewes | 26:225-48 |
| Lipids of Protozoa: Phospholipids and Neutral Lipids | G. A. Thompson Jr., Y. Nozawa | 26:249-78 |
| Riboflavin Oversynthesis | A. L. Demain | 26:369-88 |
| The Role of Polymers in Microbial Aggregation | R. H. Harris, R. Mitchell | 27:27-50 |
| Carbohydrate Metabolism in Bacteria | D. G. Fraenkel, R. T. Vinopal | 27:69-100 |
| Preparation and Quantitative Analysis of Fungal Cell Walls: Strategy and Tactics | I. E. P. Taylor, D. S. Cameron | 27:243-59 |
| Nitrogen Fixation by Photosynthetic Microorganisms | W. D. P. Stewart | 27:283-316 |
| Halogen- and Sufur-Containing Lipids of | | |

| | | |
|---|---|---|
| Ochromonas | T. H. Haines | 27:403-11 |
| Bacterial Photosynthesis | W. W. Parson | 28:41-59 |
| Metabolic Compartmentation: Symbiotic, Organellar, Multienzymic, and Microenvironmental | P. A. Srere, K. Mosbach | 28:61-83 |
| Mechanisms of Inorganic Oxidation and Energy Coupling | I. Suzuki | 28:85-101 |
| Fungal Cell Wall Glycoproteins and Peptido-Polysaccharides | J. E. Gander | 28:103-19 |
| Regulation of Enzyme Activity During Differentiation in Dictyostelium discoideum | K. A. Killick, B. E. Wright | 28:139-66 |
| Cyclic AMP in Prokaryotes | H. V. Rickenberg | 28:353-69 |
| MORPHOLOGY, ULTRASTRUCTURE, AND DIFFERENTIATION | | |
| Unique Biochemical Events in Bacterial Sporulation | R. S. Hanson, J. A. Peterson, A. A. Yousten | 24:53-90 |
| Aggregation and Differentiation in the Cellular Slime Molds | J. T. Bonner | 25:75-92 |
| "On Being the Right Size" | N. W. Pirie | 27:119-32 |
| Comparative Aspects of Morphogenesis in Three Prokaryotic Genera | H. L. Sadoff | 27:133-53 |
| Preparation and Quantitative Analysis of Fungal Cell Walls: Strategy and Tactics | I. E. P. Taylor, D. S. Cameron | 27:243-59 |
| The Role of the Host Cell Membrane in the Replication and Morphogenesis of Bacteriophages | P. J. Siegel, M. Schaechter | 27:261-82 |
| Test Structure in Foraminifera | J. H. Lipps | 27:471-88 |
| Metabolic Compartmentation: Symbiotic, Organellar, Multienzymic, and Microenvironmental | P. A. Srere, K. Mosbach | 28:61-83 |
| Fungal Cell Wall Glycoproteins and Peptido-Polysaccharides | J. E. Gander | 28:103-19 |
| Regulation of Enzyme Activity During Differentiation in Dictyostelium discoideum | K. A. Killick, B. E. Wright | 28:139-66 |
| Inclusion Bodies of Prokaryotes | J. M. Shively | 28:167-87 |
| Microscopes, Microscopy, and Microbiology | R. Barer | 28:371-89 |
| PLANT PATHOGENS AND DISEASES | | |
| The Genus Erwinia: Enterobacteria Pathogenic to Plants and Animals | M. P. Starr, A. K. Chatterjee | 26:389-426 |
| Mycoplasmas and Rickettsiae in Relation to Plant Diseases | K. Maramorosch | 28:301-24 |
| Viroids: The Smallest Known Agents of Infectious Disease | T. O. Diener | 28:23-39 |
| VIROLOGY | | |
| The Regulation of Phage Development | R. Calendar | 24:241-96 |
| The Genetics of Animal Viruses | F. Fenner | 24:297-334 |
| Reconstitution of Viruses | H. Fraenkel-Conrat | 24:463-78 |
| Virus-Induced Chromosome Abnormalities | W. W. Nichols | 24:479-500 |
| Effect of Virus Infections on the Function of the Immune System | A. L. Notkins, S. E. Mergenhagen, R. J. Howard | 24:525-38 |
| Myxovirus Ribonucleic Acids | C. D. Blair, P. H. Duesberg | 24:539-74 |
| From Protozoa to Bacteria and Viruses: Fifty Years with Microbes | A. Lwoff | 25:1-26 |
| The Role of Viruses as Causes of Congenital Defects | L. W. Catalano Jr., J. L. Sever | 25:255-82 |
| Destruction of Virus-Infected Cells by Immunological Mechanisms | D. D. Porter | 25:283-90 |
| Interferon Induction and Action | C. Colby, M. J. Morgan | 25:333-60 |
| Toward a Metabolic Interpretation of Genetic Recombination of E. coli and its Phages | A. J. Clark | 25:437-64 |
| Mechanism of Cell Transformation by RNA Tumor Viruses | H. M. Temin | 25:609-48 |
| RNA Virus Gene Expression and its Control | T. Sugiyama, B. D. Korant, K. K. Lonberg-Holm | 26:467-502 |
| Rhinoviruses | E. J. Stott, R. A. Killington | 26:503-24 |
| Fifty Years with Viruses | C. H. Andrewes | 27:1-11 |

| | | |
|---|---|---|
| The Genetics of T-Odd Phages | R. Hausmann | 27:51-67 |
| Defective Interfering Viruses | A. S. Huang | 27:101-17 |
| Bacteriophage Receptors | A. A. Lindberg | 27:205-41 |
| The Role of the Host Cell Membrane in the Replication and Morphogenesis of Bacteriophages | P. J. Siegel, M. Schaechter | 27:261-82 |
| The EB Virus | M. A. Epstein, B. G. Achong | 27:413-36 |
| Viroids: The Smallest Known Agents of Infectious Disease | T. O. Diener | 28:23-39 |
| Slow Virus Diseases | D. A. Fuccillo, J. E. Kurent, J. L. Sever | 28:231-64 |
| Persisting Bacteriophage Infections, Lysogeny, and Phage Conversions | L. Barksdale, S. B. Arden | 28:265-99 |
| Virus-Induced Modification of Cellular Membranes Related to Viral Structure | D. B. Rifkin, J. P. Quigley | 28:325-51 |